OXFORD STUDIES IN EUROPEAN LAW

Economic Governance in Europe

Comparative Paradoxes and Constitutional Challenges

OXFORD STUDIES IN EUROPEAN LAW

Series Editors

Paul Craig, Professor of English Law at St John's College, Oxford and
Gráinne de Búrca, Professor of Law at New York University School of Law

The aim of this series is to publish important and original research on EU law. The focus is on scholarly monographs, with a particular emphasis on those which are interdisciplinary in nature. Edited collections of essays will also be included where they are appropriate. The series is wide in scope and aims to cover studies of particular areas of substantive and of institutional law, historical works, theoretical studies, and analyses of current debates, as well as questions of perennial interest such as the relationship between national and EU law and the novel forms of governance emerging in and beyond Europe. The fact that many of the works are interdisciplinary will make the series of interest to all those concerned with the governance and operation of the EU.

OTHER TITLES IN THIS SERIES

Private Regulation and the Internal Market
Sports, Legal Services, and Standard Setting in EU Economic Law
Mislav Mataija

The EU Deep Trade Agenda Law and Policy
Billy A. Melo Araujo

The Human Rights of Migrants and Refugees in European Law
Cathryn Costello

An Ever More Powerful Court? The Political Constraints of Legal Integration in the European Union
Dorte Sindbjerg Martinsen

The Concept of State Aid under EU Law
From internal market to competition and beyond
Juan Jorge Piernas López

Justice in the EU The Emergence of Transnational Solidarity
Floris de Witte

The Euro Area Crisis in Constitutional Perspective
Alicia Hinarejos

The European Fundamental Freedoms
A Contextual Approach
Pedro Caro de Sousa

National Identity in EU Law
Elke Cloots

The Constitutional Foundations of European Contract Law
A Comparative Analysis
Kathleen Gutman

The Criminalization of European Cartel Enforcement
Theoretical, Legal, and Practical Challenges
Peter Whelan

Fundamental Rights in Europe
Challenges and Transformations in Comparative Perspective
Federico Fabbrini

Economic Governance in Europe

Comparative Paradoxes and Constitutional Challenges

FEDERICO FABBRINI

OXFORD
UNIVERSITY PRESS

OXFORD
UNIVERSITY PRESS

Great Clarendon Street, Oxford, OX2 6DP,
United Kingdom

Oxford University Press is a department of the University of Oxford.
It furthers the University's objective of excellence in research, scholarship,
and education by publishing worldwide. Oxford is a registered trade mark of
Oxford University Press in the UK and in certain other countries

First Edition published in 2016

Published in the United States of America by Oxford University Press
198 Madison Avenue, New York, NY 10016, United States of America

British Library Cataloguing in Publication Data
Data available

Library of Congress Control Number: 2015959803

ISBN 978–0–19–874913–4

Series Editors' Preface

The EEC has had to weather significant difficulties since its inception, but most would agree that the financial crisis has been one of the most serious challenges faced by what is now the EU. The crisis generated a plethora of measures. Some were designed to impose tighter budgetary constraints on Member States, thereby reflecting the realization that the original Maastricht settlement for Economic and Monetary Union was predicated on an imbalance between centralized power over monetary policy, and much weaker controls over economic policy, with the quid pro quo being retention of state fiscal responsibility when things went wrong. There were other measures designed to provide aid in order to prevent financial collapse in ailing Member States, culminating in the European Stability Mechanism. Yet other measures were introduced to prevent a recurrence of the crisis, as exemplified by the controls over banking in the form of the Single Supervisory Mechanism and the Single Resolution Mechanism, and also by the close scrutiny and conditionality exercised over those states receiving aid.

It is unsurprising that the crisis generated a significant body of literature from all academic disciplines, including economics, political science and law. Federico Fabbrini's book provides a valuable addition to this discourse. He writes from a legal perspective, but the analysis is informed by insights drawn from the wider literature on economics and political science. The author's primary purpose is to assess how the euro-crisis and the responses thereto have changed the constitutional architecture of economic governance in Europe. This is addressed in terms of three more specific research questions, which relate to the implications of the crisis for the vertical relations of power between the Member States and the EU; the horizontal relations of power between the courts and the political branches of government broadly conceived; and the horizontal relations of power between the Member States themselves.

The analysis is overtly comparative, with the USA being the principal comparator in this respect. It was chosen for a variety of reasons including, inter alia, the fact that it is a pluralist constitutional system, with separation of powers operating at various levels to balance power between the federal government and the states, between the political and the judicial branches, and between the states themselves. The USA has moreover created an economic and monetary union with a single currency, and in doing so has had to face endemic problems in this regard, such as where to strike the balance between centralization and decentralization in budgetary policy.

Federico Fabbrini's book advances three claims, which he frames in terms of paradoxes. He contends, firstly, that the measures adopted to meet the financial crisis have led to significant centralization of power in the vertical relations of power between the states and the EU. This is said to denote the paradox of centralization, in the sense that shift in power from the Member States to the EU in budgetary affairs is greater than that in a fully-fledged federal state like the US. The second paradox is that of judicialization, connoting in this regard the fact that while EMU reforms were based on an intergovernmental strategy in which national executives played a significant role, the reality is that EU courts have a greater role in economic and monetary affairs than do the courts in the US. The third and final paradox is termed the paradox of domination, capturing the fact that while the European Council is based on the premise that each state has one vote, with a premium placed on state equality, this is belied by reality since the more powerful states in the EU dominate to a greater extent than in the US, notwithstanding the fact that the states in the US are not represented in the central executive.

These are important arguments and the author does not shy away from proposing reforms that will alleviate the problems adumbrated above. Thus he suggests that centralization can be mitigated by raising a separate fiscal capacity for EMU, which reduces asymmetric economic shocks but preserves a degree of autonomy for the states in budgetary affairs; he contends that judicialization can be limited by restoring the centrality of the EU legislative process, enhancing the role of supranational democratic institutions in the decision-making process in EMU affairs; and he argues that the balance between the Member States can be achieved through a new system of executive decision-making and legitimation at the supranational level, which is able to control pressures from the largest states.

The book raises issues that will be of value and interest to all those concerned about the future of the EU, its economic governance and constitutional architecture.

Paul Craig and Gráinne de Búrca

Acknowledgments

This book project commenced in Spring 2012 at the University of California Berkeley, it continued at Tilburg Law School, and it concluded at iCourts—the Center of Excellence on International Courts of the Faculty of Law of the University of Copenhagen in Summer 2015. The library of European University Institute in Fiesole, the network of the EU institutions in Brussels, and my family house in Trento provided perfect venues to read, discuss, and write the manuscript. At the same time, I greatly benefited from presenting parts or drafts of this monograph at lectures, seminars, and workshops in several universities, including at Università Bocconi, the Université Libre de Bruxelles, Cambridge University, Harvard Law School, the Hungarian Academy of Sciences, Universiteit Maastricht, Melbourne Law School, NYU Law School, Oxford University, and Princeton University. I also had the opportunity to present sections of this book at the 2014 World Congress of the International Association of Constitutional Law in Oslo and at the 2015 annual meeting of the European Constitutional Law Network in Thessaloniki—as well as the 2013 yearly Conference of the Commission pour l'étude des Communautés européennes/Association d'études européennes, housed by the Assemblée Nationale française in Paris, and at a 2015 Conference of the Deutsch-Italienisches Zentrum für Europäische Exzellenz/Centro italo-tedesco per l'eccellenza europea, in Villa Vigoni on the Lago di Como. Finally, in 2015 I presented some of the themes of this book at a meeting organized at the European Parliament in Brussels by the Legal Service of the European Parliament, with the participation of the Legal Service of the European Commission and the Legal Service of the Council, on "The Law of Economic Policies of the Union."

I am grateful to many friends and colleagues for discussing, commenting, and reviewing several ideas, chapters, or drafts of this book, including Maurice Adams, Fred Aman, Giuliano Amato, Kenneth Armstrong, Augusto Barbera Stefania Baroncelli, Emmanuelle Bribosia, Marta Cartabia, Sabino Cassese, Deirdre Curtin, Alberto de Gregorio Merino, Bruno de Witte, Edouard Dubout, Malcom Feeley, Claudia Foroni, Sylvie Goulard, Kasia Granat, Óli Hannesson, Christoph Herrmann, Alicia Hinarejos, Ernst Hirsch Ballin, Vicki Jackson, András Jakab, Jean-Paul Keppenne, Helle Krunke, Konrad Lachmayer, Kim Lane Scheppele, Joris Larik, Pierre Larouche, Koen Lenaerts, Anita Lope Garcia, Jean-Victor Louis, Mikael Madsen, Miguel Maduro, Beppe Martinico, Jason Mazzone, Paolo Mengozzi, Russ Miller, Enzo Moavero Milanesi, Ulla Neergaard, Kalypso Nicolaïdis, Henrik Palmer Olsen, Lina Papadopoulou, Ingolf Pernice, Laura Puccio, Uwe Puetter, Michel Rosenfeld, Harm Schepel, Pascal Schonard, Elena Simina Tănăsescu, Han Somsen, Adrienne Stone, Kaarlo Tuori, Mark Tushnet, Laura van den Eynde, Arianna Vedaschi, Mila Versteeg, Joseph Weiler, Marlene Wind, and Chiara Zilioli. I am particularly grateful then to Paul Craig and Gráinne de Búrca, for encouraging my work, supporting the publication of this book, and kindly accepting to include it in their series. As usual, the staff at OUP—Alex Flach, Natasha Flemming, Elinor Shields, and their editorial team—deserves a lot of credit for helping me turn a draft manuscript into this book, and I want to specially thank them here.

I finally want to thank also my brother and my parents, Sebastiano, Manuela, and Sergio, who were very close while I worked on this book—albeit being physically far.

I am glad to acknowledge that this book develops previous works of mine on the Euro-crisis and economic governance in Europe. Chapter 1 enlarges and updates an article published as "The Fiscal Compact, the 'Golden Rule' and the Paradox of European Federalism" (2013) 36 Boston College International & Comparative Law Review 1–38. Chapter 2 shortens but updates an article appeared as "The Euro-Crisis and the Courts: Judicial Review and the Political Process in Comparative Perspective" (2014) 32 Berkeley Journal of International Law 64–123. Chapter 3 mostly reproduces my article "States' Equality v States' Power: the Euro-Crisis, Inter-State Relations and the Paradox of Domination" (2015) 17 Cambridge Yearbook of European Legal Studies 3–35. The ideas presented in Chapter 4 then were initially articulated in an abridged form in "From Fiscal Constraints to Fiscal Capacity: The Future of EMU and its Challenges" in Federico Fabbrini et al (eds), *The Constitutionalization of European Budgetary Constraints* (Hart Publishing 2014). Chapter 5 connects arguments I made in "Representation in the European Parliament: Of False Problems and Real Challenges" (2015) 75 Zeitschrift für ausländisches öffentliches Recht und Völkerrecht, and "A Principle in Need of Renewal? The Euro-Crisis and the Principle of Institutional Balance" (2016) 50 Cahiers de droit européen. Finally, Chapter 6 takes its title from "From Executive Federalism to Executive Government: Current Problems and Future Prospects in the Governance of EMU," in Federico Fabbrini et al (eds), *What Form of Government for the European Union and the Eurozone?* (Hart Publishing 2015), but mainly summarizes the content of another article entitled "Austerity, the European Council and the Institutional Future of the European Union" (2015) 22 Indiana Journal of Global Legal Studies 269–334.

A hundred years ago, Europeans were slaughtering each other, from the Dolomites to the fields of Flanders, to the seas of Jutland, in a Great War that sought to redraw the map of Europe by accident and force. This book is dedicated to all those who have worked restlessly to build the Union of Europe through reflection and choice.

Table of contents

PART II. REFLECTION AND CHOICE

"The important question [is] whether societies of men are really capable or not of establishing good government from reflection and choice, or whether they are forever destined to depend for their political constitutions on accident and force"

(Alexander Hamilton, *The Federalist Papers* No. 1, 1787)

Introduction

The New Constitutional Architecture of European Economic Governance

1. Introduction

Since the outburst of the Euro-crisis in 2009, the member states and the institutions of the European Union (EU) have hectically adopted new legal instruments and devised new policy strategies which have profoundly increased the degree of integration in the European Economic and Monetary Union (EMU). Between 2010 and 2014 a new constitutional architecture of economic governance has gradually emerged in the EU. Tighter budgetary constraints have been enacted at national and supranational level; new tools of fiscal stabilization have been created in the EU and international legal order; and a complex decision-making framework has been put in place to coordinate states' economic policies and dictate programs of economic adjustment for countries in fiscal distress. Yet, the overhaul of the European system of economic governance has been heavily influenced by the state of emergency in which the EU and the member states found themselves after the explosion of the Euro-crisis. The legal and institutional responses to the Euro-crisis have been taken in a context of urgency, and with limited reflection on their long-term effects. How has economic governance in Europe changed as a result of the Euro-crisis and the responses to it? How should we evaluate the new EU architecture of economic governance from a constitutionalist perspective? And what steps should be taken to create a more perfect EMU?

The book aims to offer a legal analysis of the new constitutional architecture of European economic governance by examining how the Euro-crisis and the responses to it have changed relations of powers in the EU. In particular, the book seeks to illuminate through the use of the *comparative* method several *paradoxes* in the new EMU constitutional architecture and considers their problematic implications for the long-term sustainability of the EU. At the same time, the book aspires to contribute to the ongoing debate about the future of economic governance in Europe and discusses the *constitutional challenges* that arise along the way toward a deeper and more genuine EMU. While the book underlines problems in the new constitutional architecture of EMU governance, it also proposes possible solutions to address them, advancing targeted legal and institutional reforms aimed at perfecting the governance of economic affairs in Europe. In this Introduction I outline the core themes of the book. Section 2 provides a quick summary of the main legal and institutional developments that have taken place in the EU since the beginning of the Euro-crisis. Section 3 defines the research question of this book and explains its methodology. Section 4 summarizes the core arguments of the book. Section 5 reports its main policy proposals. Section 6, finally, maps the structure of the book.

2. Legal and Institutional Reforms Following the Euro-Crisis

Since the outburst of the Euro-crisis, EU institutions and member states have engaged in a major effort to overhaul the architecture of economic governance of the EMU.[1] Although the causes of the Euro-crisis specifically, and of the global financial crisis more generally, are heavily contested in the economic literature,[2] the main political narrative that prevailed in Europe since 2009 has been that the deterioration of the European economy found its roots in the irresponsible fiscal behavior of several member states. As Miguel Maduro has argued,[3] another plausible narrative of the Euro-crisis could have put the blame on the banking sector, and their irresponsible lending to debtors lacking sufficient creditworthiness. Nevertheless, the EU institutions and the member states unequivocally embraced an interpretation of the crisis as a problem of sovereign debt and reformed the setup of EMU accordingly.[4] Regardless of the real socio-economic roots of the crisis, the EMU constitution architecture has been profoundly changed in specific directions.

[1] According to Art 3 TEU, "[t]he Union shall establish an economic and monetary union whose currency is the euro". Participation in the EMU is an obligation for all EU member states. However, at the moment, two member states have obtained a specific opt-out from the single currency, while seven states do not yet fulfill the technical criteria to become part of the single currency and thus members of the so-called "Eurozone." See European Commission, *Who can Join and When?* available at <http://ec.europa.eu/economy_finance/euro/adoption/who_can_join/index_en.htm> (last accessed July 15, 2015). See generally Pier Carlo Padoan, "EMU as an Evolutionary Process" in David M. Andrews et al (eds), *Governing the World's Money* (Cornell UP 2002), 105 (describing the process of EMU integration and resultant benefits).

[2] Compare generally Carmen M. Reinhart and Kenneth S. Rogoff, *This Time is Different: Eight Centuries of Financial Folly* (Princeton UP 2009) (arguing that higher levels of public debt are responsible for economic contraction), with Paul Krugman, *End This Depression Now!* (Norton 2012) (defending a Keynesian view, which advocates public spending to boost growth and criticizes austerity). In the EU context, then, compare Hans-Werner Sinn, *The Euro Trap* (OUP 2014) with Jean Pisany-Ferry, *The Euro Crisis and Its Aftermath* (OUP 2014).

[3] Miguel Maduro, "A New Governance for the European Union and the Euro: Democracy & Justice," Study commissioned by the European Parliament Constitutional Affairs Committee, September 2012, PE 462.484 (contrasting a narrative of the crisis based on excessive spending by some states with one based on irresponsible lending by some banks).

[4] See e.g., Benjamin Friedman, "The Pathology of Europe's Debt," 61 The New York Review of Books, October 9–22, 2014, 50 and Harold James, *Making the European Monetary Union* (Harvard UP 2012).

The 1992 Maastricht Treaty—while setting up a purely federal framework on monetary affairs,[5] centered on a common currency and the role of the European Central Bank (ECB) to maintain "price stability"[6]—relied, in fiscal affairs, on mild budgetary constraints, economic policy coordination, and unlimited faith in the capacity of the markets to rein-in governmental fiscal mismanagement.[7] The constitutional architecture of EMU that has recently emerged from the responses to the Euro-crisis, on the contrary, is based on three main components. First, the EMU is characterized by tighter budgetary constraints, which subject state fiscal policies to hard domestic limits and pervasive supranational controls. Second, it is endowed with new instruments of financial stabilization, aimed at providing solidarity to countries in economic difficulties and preventing contagious effects from sovereigns' or banks' defaults in the EMU. Third, it provides a clear mandate for economic adjustment, introducing powers for the EU institutions to dictate—and, simultaneously, duties for the member states (especially those which receive financial support) to implement—reforms to their economies as a condition for benefitting from transnational aid. Given the by-now extensive literature on this topic,[8] few words will suffice here to describe the elements of the new EMU constitutional architecture.

First, on the assumption that the root causes of the crisis lay in unsustainable public finances, one of the main reforms adopted by both the member states and the EU institutions since 2009 has been the *introduction of tighter budgetary constraints* aimed at strengthening fiscal discipline and limiting government spending. The objective of ensuring the sustainability of state budgets was already enshrined in the Stability and Growth Pact (SGP) originally enacted in two Council regulations in 1997,[9] and currently attached as Protocol No. 12 to the EU Treaties, which requires member states to maintain their public deficit below the yearly ratio of 3% of GDP and the total public debt below 60% of GDP.[10] The weaknesses of the enforcement mechanisms of the SGP, however, ensured widespread non-compliance by EMU countries with the SGP debt and deficit criteria.[11] In response to the failure of the existing legal mechanism, the EU institutions and the member states adopted a two-pronged legal strategy.

[5] See Barry Eichengreen, *European Monetary Unification: Theory, Practice, Analysis* (OUP 1997).

[6] See Art 127 TFEU.

[7] See Ian Harden, "The Fiscal Constitution of EMU" in Paul Beaumont and Neil Walker (eds), *The Legal Framework of the Single European Currency* (Hart Publishing 1999), 71.

[8] See text accompanying nn 63–70.

[9] See Council Regulation (EC) No. 1466/97 of July 7, 1997 on strengthening of the surveillance of budgetary positions and the surveillance and coordination of economic policies [1997] OJ L209/1; Council Regulation (EC) No. 1467/97 of July 7, 1997 on speeding up and clarifying the implementation of the excessive deficit procedure [1997] OJ L209/6.

[10] See Protocol No. 12 on excessive deficit procedure [2008] OJ C115/279.

[11] See Stefan Collignon, "The End of the Stability and Growth Pact?" (2004) 1 International Economics and Economic Policy 15. See also Case C-27/04 *Commission v. Council* [2004] ECR I-6649, ECLI:EU:C:2004:436 (recognizing wide discretion to the Council whether to impose sanctions under the SGP or held in abeyance the excessive deficit procedure against two member states recommended by the Commission).

On the one hand, several EU legislative acts were enacted to improve the capacity of the EU institutions to supervise and correct budgetary policies of the member states. Pursuant to the so-called "six-pack" of five regulations and one directive of November 2011,[12] the preventive and corrective arms of the SGP were changed, creating new capacities for the European Commission to sanction and fine member states for breaches of the deficit and debt rules, as well as establishing a new "macro-economic imbalance procedure" to alert member states of the destabilizing elements of their economies. At the same time, EU law introduced minimum requirements for the design and operation of state budgetary laws, which will be assessed in the framework of the so-called "European semester" in which member states submit their draft budgets to the Commission for compliance with the broader economic forecasts of the EU.[13] Moreover, pursuant to the so-called "two-pack" of regulations of May 2013,[14] the Commission's power of surveillance over the budgetary policies of the member states was increased even further, with the ability to object to budget bills drafted by national governments and to require further changes before they are tabled for approval in state parliaments.

On the other hand, new rules were introduced in the domestic legislation of member states to secure balanced budget obligations and internal mechanisms of automatic correction. The Euro-Plus Pact, adopted by the European Council in March 2011, encouraged member states to enhance the sustainability of public finances by translating EU fiscal rules into national legislation.[15] But it was especially the Treaty on the Stability, Coordination and Governance of the EMU, the so-called Fiscal Compact, signed by 25 EU heads of state and government in March 2012, which required member states to tighten internal fiscal controls.[16] The Fiscal Compact mandated that signatory parties enact at the state level a balanced budget

[12] See Regulation (EU) No. 1173/2011 of the European Parliament and of the Council of November 16, 2011 on effective enforcement of budgetary surveillance in the euro area [2011] OJ L306/1; Regulation (EU) No. 1174/2011 of the European Parliament and of the Council of November 16, 2011 on enforcement measures to correct excessive macroeconomic imbalances in the euro area [2011] OJ L306/8; Regulation (EU) No. 1175/2011 of the European Parliament and of the Council of November 16, 2011 amending Council Regulation (EC) No. 1466/97 on strengthening of the surveillance of budgetary positions and the surveillance and coordination of economic policies [2011] OJ L306/12; Regulation (EU) No. 1176/2011 of the European Parliament and of the Council of November 16, 2011 on prevention and correction of macroeconomic imbalances [2011] OJ L306/25; Council Regulation (EU) No. 1177/2011 of November 8, 2011 amending Regulation (EC) No. 1467/97 on speeding up and clarifying the implementation of the excessive deficit procedure [2011] OJ L306/33; Council Directive 2011/85/EU of November 8, 2011 on requirements for budgetary frameworks of the member states [2011] OJ L306/41.

[13] See also European Council Conclusions, June 17, 2010, EUCO 13/10, 5.

[14] See Regulation (EU) No. 473/2013 of May 21, 2013 of the European Parliament and the Council on monitoring and assessing draft budgetary plans and ensuring the correction of excessive deficits in euro-area member states [2013] OJ L140/11; Regulation (EU) No. 472/2013 of May 21, 2013 of the European Parliament and the Council on enhanced surveillance of euro-area member states experiencing or threatened with serious difficulties with respect to their financial stability [2013] OJ L140/1.

[15] See European Council Conclusions, March 24/25, 2011, EUCO 10/1/11, Annex 1, para c.

[16] See Treaty on Stability, Coordination and Governance in the Economic and Monetary Union, March 2, 2012, [hereinafter Fiscal Compact], available at <http://www.eurozone.europa.eu/media/304649/st00tscg26_en12.pdf> (last accessed June 1, 2014).

requirement through provisions of binding force and permanent character, preferably constitutional, or otherwise guaranteed to be fully respected throughout the national budgetary process.[17] The Fiscal Compact, moreover, empowered the European Court of Justice (ECJ) to review whether member states duly comply with this obligation.[18] As a result of these pressures, following the German constitutional reform of 2009,[19] most EU member states have amended their domestic constitutions to include a balanced budget requirement, prohibiting structural deficits and the accumulation of excessive debt.[20]

Second, on the understanding that the state or bank defaults in the Eurozone could produce deleterious, contagious effects throughout the EMU, EU institutions and member states have devised *new mechanisms of financial stabilization* for countries or credit institutions in financial distress. These tools represent an entirely new addition to the architecture of the EMU constitution. The original design of the EMU was based on the idea—enshrined in Article 125 Treaty on the Functioning of the EU (TFEU), the so-called "no bail-out clause"[21]—that member states would be solely responsible for the service of their debt and that other EU member states or the ECB would be prohibited from taking up the debt burden of another state.[22] Nevertheless, the eruption of the Euro-crisis and the complex interconnection between sovereigns and banks revealed that it was actually much easier on paper than in reality to let a country of the Eurozone default without this producing a systemic effect on the stability of the Eurozone as a whole.[23] Hence, the EU institutions and the member states endowed themselves with new mechanisms to face this challenge.[24]

The legal response proceeded in several steps. In May 2010, the Council adopted, on the basis of the powers of Article 122(2) TFEU,[25] a regulation establishing a

[17] Art 3(2) Fiscal Compact. [18] Art 8 Fiscal Compact.

[19] Gesetz zur Änderung des Grundgesetz (Artikel 91c, 91d, 104b, 109, 109a, 115, 143d), BGBl. I S. 2248 (Nr. 48), July 29, 2009.

[20] For more on this see Federico Fabbrini et al (eds), *The Constitutionalization of European Budgetary Constraints* (Hart Publishing 2014) (reviewing incorporations of balanced budget rules in the domestic systems of, among others, Germany, France, Italy, Spain, Poland, Slovakia, Hungary, Greece, the Netherlands, and Ireland).

[21] See Art 125 TFEU (stating that "[t]he Union shall not be liable for or assume the commitments of central governments, regional, local or other public authorities, other bodies governed by public law, or public undertakings of any Member State."). See also Art 123 TFEU (stating that "[o]verdraft facilities or any other type of credit facility with the European Central Bank [...] in favour of Union institutions [...or] central governments [...] shall be prohibited, as shall the purchase directly from them by the European Central Bank or national central banks of debt instruments.").

[22] See Jean-Victor Louis, Guest Editorial: "The No-Bailout Clause and Rescue Packages" (2010) 47 Common Market Law Review 971.

[23] See Hannes Hofmeister, "To Bail Out or Not to Bail Out? Legal Aspects of the Greek Crisis" (2011) 13 Cambridge Yearbook of European Legal Studies 113.

[24] See Phoebus Athanassiou, "Of Past Measures and Future Plans for Europe's Exit from the Sovereign Debt Crisis: What is Legally Possible (and What is Not)" (2011) 36 European Law Review 558.

[25] See Art 122(2) TFEU (stating that "[w]here a Member State is in difficulties or is seriously threatened with severe difficulties caused by natural disasters or exceptional occurrences beyond its control, the Council, on a proposal from the Commission, may grant, under certain conditions, Union financial assistance to the Member State concerned.").

European Financial Stabilization Mechanism (EFSM) to grant immediate financial assistance to Greece.[26] Subsequently, through a private company incorporated under Luxembourg law, the heads of state and government of the Eurozone established a European Financial Stability Facility (EFSF),[27] charged to operate beyond the short-term emergency which had prompted the creation of the EFSM and effectively providing support to Ireland, Portugal, and (for a second time) Greece. Finally, with the aim to set up a long-term mechanism to stabilize the Eurozone, and on the assumption that a brand new legal basis was needed in the Treaty to avoid incompatibilities with Article 125 TFEU, the EU member states unanimously secured, through a simplified revision procedure, an amendment to Article 136 TFEU which allowed the establishment of a permanent stability mechanism for the EMU.[28] On this basis, the Eurozone countries created a European Stability Mechanism (ESM) through an international treaty.[29] A first version of the treaty establishing the ESM was concluded in 2011 but was then revised and signed again by the member states of the Eurozone in February 2012. The ESM Treaty entered into force in November 2012, and since then provided new financial support to Spain, Cyprus, and (for a third time) to Greece.

The ESM, in particular, is an international institution, modeled on the International Monetary Fund (IMF),[30] whose purpose is "to mobilise funding and provide stability support under strict conditionality, appropriate to the financial assistance instrument chosen, to the benefit of ESM Members which are experiencing, or are threatened by, severe financing problems, if indispensable to safeguard the financial stability of the euro area as a whole and of its Member States."[31] Eurozone member states contribute to the authorized capital stock of the ESM—totaling €700 billion[32]—pro-quota on the basis of the subscription by their national central banks to the ECB's capital.[33] The ESM can grant financial support to a state in need,[34] provide precautionary financial assistance,[35] directly (since the entry into force of a single EU supervisory mechanism) recapitalize banks,[36] grant loans,[37] and purchase government bonds on the primary and secondary market.[38] Decisions about the ESM are mainly

[26] See Council Regulation (EU) No. 407/2010/EU of May 11, 2010 establishing a European financial stabilization mechanism [2010] OJ L118/1.

[27] See Decisions of the Representatives of the Government of the Euro Area Member States Meeting within the Council of the EU, ECOFIN, May 9, 2010. Doc. No. 9614/10.

[28] See European Council Decision No. 2011/199/EU of March 25, 2011, amending Article 136 TFEU with regard to a stability mechanism for member states whose currency is the euro [2011] OJ L91/1.

[29] See Treaty Establishing the European Stability Mechanism [hereinafter ESM Treaty], February 2, 2012, available at <http://www.european-council.europa.eu/media/582311/05-tesm2.en12.pdf> (last accessed June 1, 2014).

[30] See Giulio Napolitano, "Il Meccanismo Europeo di Stabilità e la nuova frontiera costituzionale dell'Unione" [2012] Giornale di Diritto Amministrativo 461. As an international organization, the ESM also enjoys several privileges, including the immunity of persons (Art 35 ESM Treaty), the inviolability of the premises (Art 32 ESM Treaty), and the privilege of professional secrecy (Art 34 ESM Treaty).

[31] Art 3 ESM Treaty. [32] Art 8 ESM Treaty.

[33] Art 11 and Annex I ESM Treaty. [34] Art 13 ESM Treaty.

[35] Art 14 ESM Treaty. [36] Art 15 ESM Treaty. [37] Art 16 ESM Treaty.

[38] Arts 17 and 18 ESM Treaty.

made by the Board of Governors—consisting of the ministers of finance of the Eurozone member states—on the basis of unanimity rule.[39] Nevertheless, pursuant to Article 4(4), "an emergency voting procedure shall be used where the Commission and the ECB both conclude that a failure to urgently adopt a decision to grant or implement financial assistance [...] would threaten the economic and financial sustainability of the euro area." In this case, a decision requires only a qualified majority of 85% of the votes cast, calculated on the basis of the contributing shares to the ESM capital. Any dispute involving the ESM Treaty can, however, be subject to adjudication before the ECJ,[40] thus contributing to the constitutional anchoring of the ESM to the EU institutional regime.[41]

Associated to the new mechanism of financial stabilization designed to support states in fiscal distress, the EU and its member states have also created a new legal framework for bank supervision and resolution at the supranational level. In order to break the negative loop between banks and sovereign in the Eurozone, and with the aim to strengthen prudential supervision of transnational financial establishments the Council set up, on the basis of Article 127(6) TFEU, a Single Supervisory Mechanism,[42] granting to the ECB the power to supervise—in co-operation with national authorities—the functioning of the banking sector.[43] At the same time, the EU Banking Union was complemented by a Single Deposit Guarantee Scheme,[44] securing harmonized protection of bank account holders throughout the EU in case of bank defaults, and by a Single Resolution Mechanism, creating a back-stop to wind down failing banks.[45] With regard to the latter, the EU institutions adopted a regulation establishing a Single Resolution Fund (SRF),[46] with an ad hoc Board tasked to decide about the resolution of credit institutions, while 26 EU member states opted to conclude, in May 2014, a separate intergovernmental agreement to regulate the transfer of state contributions

[39] Art 4 ESM Treaty. [40] Art 37 ESM Treaty.

[41] Pursuant to Art 44 ESM Treaty, any new state of the EU who adopts the euro as its currency shall become a member of the ESM by ratifying its founding Treaty.

[42] See Art 127(6) TFEU (stating that "[t]he Council, acting by means of regulations in accordance with a special legislative procedure, may unanimously, and after consulting the European Parliament and the European Central Bank, confer specific tasks upon the European Central Bank concerning policies relating to the prudential supervision of credit institutions.").

[43] See Council Regulation (EU) No. 1024/2013 of October 15, 2013 conferring specific tasks on the European Central Bank concerning policies relating to the prudential supervision of credit institutions [2013] OJ L287/63.

[44] See Directive 2014/49/EU of the European Parliament and of the Council of April 16, 2014 on deposit guarantee schemes [2014] OJ L173/149.

[45] See further Federico Fabbrini, "On Banks, Courts and International Law. The Intergovernmental Agreement on the Single Resolution Fund in Context" (2014) 21 Maastricht Journal of European & Comparative Law 444.

[46] See Regulation (EU) No. 806/2014 of the European Parliament and of the Council of July 15, 2014 establishing uniform rules and a uniform procedure for the resolution of credit institutions and certain investment firms in the framework of a Single Resolution Mechanism and a Single Bank Resolution Fund and amending Regulation (EU) No. 1093/2010 of the European Parliament and of the Council [2014] OJ L225/1.

(levied from the national banking sector) into national compartments within the SRF and their progressive mutualization over an eight-year time-span.[47]

Third, a last key innovation in the constitution of EMU emerging from the Euro-crisis is the creation of a *new framework of economic adjustment*, based on the principle of conditionality as the counterweight to increasing financial solidarity. Pursuant to this criterion, EU member states that obtain financial aid to address a situation of quasi-default are not only required to enact tight budgetary constraints (as any other country of the EU),[48] but are also subject to specific economic adjustment programs designed to reform the fundamentals of their economy and address structural weaknesses in their systems in areas as far ranging as the flexibility of the labor market, the effectiveness of tax collection, the size and organization of the public administration, the nature and degree of social entitlements, and the characteristics of the banking sector.[49] The last component of the legal response to the Euro-crisis designed in EU legislation and treaties, therefore, comprises a set of measures whereby the European Commission and the ECB, mostly together with the IMF in what came to be known as the "troika,"[50] are empowered to elaborate country-specific programs of economic adjustments, and member states contractually agree to implement them within their domestic systems under supranational supervision.[51]

Besides Article 5(2) of the Fiscal Compact, which foresees the possibility of adopting an economic partnership program, the ESM Treaty now codifies the general legal template for the negotiation of a program of economic adjustment. Pursuant to Article 13(3), if the ESM Board of Governors decides to grant assistance to a Eurozone member state, it shall entrust the European Commission—in liaison with the ECB and, wherever possible, together with the IMF—with the task of negotiating, with the ESM member concerned, a memorandum of understanding (MoU) detailing the conditionality attached to the financial assistance facility. The content of the MoU shall reflect the severity of the weaknesses to be addressed and the financial assistance instrument chosen. As the MoUs signed by Greece, Portugal, Ireland, Spain, and Cyprus make clear, these instruments constitute a binding road-map that member states receiving financial assistance must respect in order to continue obtaining financial assistance.[52] The MoU shall

[47] See Agreement on the transfer and mutualization of contributions to the Single Resolution Fund [hereinafter SRF Agreement], May 21, 2014 available at: <http://register.consilium.europa.eu/doc/srv?l=EN&f=ST%208457%202014%20INIT> (last accessed May 25, 2014).

[48] See text accompanying nn 15–20.

[49] See Damian Chalmers, "The European Redistributive State and a European Law of Struggle" (2012) 18 European Law Journal 667 (emphasizing the capacity of the EU institutions to dictate to member states policy reforms in a broad range of fields).

[50] See also European Parliament Resolution of March 13, 2014 on the enquiry on the role and operations of the Troika (ECB, Commission, and IMF) with regard to the euro area programme countries, P7_TA(2014)0239 (criticizing the invasive role of the "troika" in the EU member states subject to economic adjustment program).

[51] See Vestert Borger, "How the Debt Crisis Exposes the Development of Solidarity in the Euro Area" (2013) 9 European Constitutional Law Review 7.

[52] See e.g., Greece: Memorandum of Understanding on Specific Economic Policy Conditionality, May 3, 2010 available at <http://www.minfin.gr/content-api/f/binaryChannel/minfin/datastore/a8/52/57/a85257bc11624aa0a2f89a6bebea2219687ce5f0/application/pdf/EU%2BBundle2.pdf> (last accessed June 1, 2014).

be fully consistent with the measures of economic policy coordination provided for in the TFEU, in particular with any act of EU law, including any opinion, warning, recommendation, or decision addressed to the state concerned.[53] At the same time, the "troika" is empowered to constantly monitor progress by the state under an assistance program and demand the adoption of new policies to reach the agreed goals.[54]

Economic adjustment programs are carried out domestically by national governments and legislatures through appropriate legislation. Nevertheless, as Kenneth Armstrong has underlined, for those Eurozone states that have received financial support to stabilize their economies, the degree and manner of the constraint on their policy autonomy is significantly heightened. Indeed, the regular mechanisms of accountability and governance are typically suspended for such states which are subject instead to the discipline imposed via MoU and controls exercised in the context of macroeconomic adjustment programmes.[55] In sum, in the aftermath of the crisis the EU institutions have acquired significant competences to intervene in the field of economic policy, while states receiving financial support have been mandated to implement domestically economic reform programs—which often include a profound restructuring of the welfare state system.[56] In connection with this, the new EMU institutional system has also experienced a rise in importance of the ECB, which has played a crucial role in supporting economic recovery in peripheral Eurozone countries.[57] In particular, after the adoption ad hoc policies of government bonds purchase subject to the implementation of domestic reforms,[58] the ECB devised the Outright Monetary Transaction (OMT) program, which foresees the purchase of states' bonds on the secondary market subject to a state entering into a ESM-led assistance program with related conditionality rules,[59] and launched a vast program of quantitative easing, consisting in the purchase of public and private securities as a way to restore a healthy degree of inflation within the Eurozone.[60]

[53] Art 13(3) ESM Treaty. [54] Art 13(7) ESM Treaty.

[55] Kenneth Armstrong, "The New Governance of EU Fiscal Discipline" (2013) 38 European Law Review 601.

[56] See Klaus Busch et al, "Euro Crisis, Austerity Policy and the European Social Model: How Crisis in Southern Europe Threatens the EU's Social Dimension," Friedrich Ebert Stiftung International Policy Analysis 2013 (discussing the threat that austerity policies produce on the welfare state).

[57] See Thomas Beukers, "The New ECB and Its Relationship with the Eurozone Member States" (2013) 50 Common Market Law Review 1579.

[58] See Decision of the ECB of May 14, 2010 establishing a securities market programme (ECB/2010/5), [2010] OJ L124/8 (inaugurating purchase of government bonds on the secondary market). But see also Letter of the ECB to the Italian Government, August 5, 2011, available at <http://www.corriere.it/economia/11_settembre_29/trichet_draghi_inglese_304a5f1e-ea59-11e0-ac06-4da866778017.shtml?fr=correlati> (last accessed June 1, 2014) (conditioning continuing application of the securities market program in favor of Italy to the implementation of drastic domestic reforms).

[59] See ECB press release, "Technical Features of Outright Monetary Transactions," September 6, 2012 (stating that the ECB can buy government bonds on the secondary market with the aim to safeguard an appropriate monetary policy transmission and the singleness of the monetary policy, conditional to the member state concerned entering into an agreement with the ESM).

[60] See ECB press release, "ECB Announces Expanded Assets Purchase Program," January 22, 2015.

In conclusion, reforms in the area of budgetary constraints, financial stabilization, and economic adjustment, with steps taken toward economic, banking, and fiscal union, have profoundly affected the architecture of European economic governance.

3. The Research Question and the Methodology of the Book

The primary purpose of this book is to assess how the Euro-crisis, and the legal and institutional responses to it, have changed the constitutional architecture of economic governance in Europe. The book adopts a legal perspective, and is not concerned with the economic causes of the Euro-crisis. Rather, the project fits in the scholarly remit of European constitutional law and essentially focuses on structural issues of relations of powers.[61] The book explores how the legal and institutional reforms following the Euro-crisis and summarized in the previous section have changed the allocation of powers in the EU, shifting authority among levels of government, and re-shaping relations between institutions. As such, I wish to answer the following research question: What are the constitutional implications of the Euro-crisis and the responses to it on the *relations of power within the EU*? To achieve this goal, I disarticulate the research question into three sub-questions, considering how the Euro-crisis and the responses to it affected:

1. *vertical relations of power between the member states and the EU*
2. *horizontal relations of power between courts and political branches*
3. *horizontal relations of power between the member states themselves*

Whereas since the outburst of the crisis the new constitutional architecture of economic governance in the EU has grown in bits and pieces, and without a comprehensive design, the aim of this book is to take a step back and to explain how the constitutional structure of the EU looks like today. According to several accounts, the Euro-crisis is still far from being over.[62] Yet, the time seems ripe to analyze the substance of power-relations in the new EMU constitutional architecture. This in turn will set the ground for a critical discussion of how the new EMU regime fares in terms of constitutional principles of balance of powers and how it could be reformed in the future.

[61] See Martin Redish, *The Constitution as Political Structure* (OUP 1995) (discussing the role of a constitution as structuring relations of power) and Miguel Poiares Maduro, "The Importance of Being Called a Constitution: Constitutional Authority and the Authority of Constitutionalism" (2005) 3 International Journal of Constitutional Law 332 (discussing alternative concepts of constitutionalism in the EU, including the idea of separation of powers).

[62] See IMF, *World Economic Outlook*, April 14, 2014, 53 (indicating challenges toward economic recovery in Europe) as well as IMF, *World Economic Outlook*, April 14, 2015 (indicating an improvement in the European economic situations but warning about remaining challenges due to uncertainties in the resolution of the Greek crisis).

To answer the research questions, this project adopts a comparative perspective. While this book focuses on economic governance in Europe, it uses a comparative approach to inform and enlighten our understanding of the constitutional implications of the Euro-crisis and the responses to it. Whereas the issue of the implications of the Euro-crisis and the responses to it has increasingly attracted scholarly attention,[63] the studies dealing with the topic have mainly examined the new constitutional architecture of EMU in isolation.[64] Lawyers, economists and political scientists are dedicating greater attention to the legal reforms and institutional changes brought about by the Euro-crisis.[65] Scholars compared the structure of EMU before and after the crisis,[66] discussed the correlation between the various components of the new EMU architecture,[67] and examined how the new EMU governance functions.[68] Specific courts' decisions dealing with EMU have been the subject of scholarly focus,[69] and attention has been given to the relations between the EU member states and between the EU institutions since the beginning of the crisis.[70]

The ideographic approach which has been followed in analyzing the Euro-crisis and its implications, however, presents relevant methodological limits. Most crucially, a study which focuses exclusively on the EMU and its historical evolution is unable to provide an *external benchmark* by which to measure the nature of the

[63] See Kaarlo Tuori and Klaus Tuori, *The Eurozone Crisis: A Constitutional Analysis* (CUP 2014); and Alicia Hinarejos, *The Euro Area Crisis in Constitutional Perspective* (OUP 2015).

[64] But see Aart Loubert, "Sovereign Debt Threatens the Union: The Genesis of a Federation" (2012) 8 European Constitutional Law Review 442 (recalling the history of the creation of a fiscal union accomplished at the beginning of the American constitutional project by Alexander Hamilton).

[65] See e.g., Paul Craig, "Economic Governance and the Euro Crisis: Constitutional Architecture and Constitutional Implications," in Federico Fabbrini et al (eds), *The Constitutionalization of European Budgetary Constraints* (Hart Publishing 2014), 19 and Edoardo Chiti and Pedro G. Teixeira, "The Constitutional Implications of the European Responses to the Financial and Public Debt Crisis" (2013) 50 Common Market Law Review 683.

[66] See e.g., Martin Heipertz and Amy Verdun, *Ruling Europe: The Politics of the Stability and Growth Pact* (CUP 2011) and Jean-Victor Louis, "L'Union économique et monétaire de Maastricht à la crise" (2012) 19 Revue des Affaires europeennes 57.

[67] See e.g., Koen Lenaerts, "EMU and the EU's Constitutional Framework" (2014) 39 European Law Review 753 and Fabian Amtenbrink, "The Economic and Monetary Union: Constitutional and Institutional Aspects of the Economic Governance within the EU: General Report," in Ulla Neergaard et al (eds), *The Economic and Monetary Union: Constitutional and Institutional Aspects of the Economic Governance within the EU. Proceedings of the XXVI FIDE Congress* (Djøf 2014), 73.

[68] See e.g., Dermot Hodson, *Governing the Euro Area in Good Times and Bad* (OUP 2011) and Uwe Puetter, "New Intergovernmentalism: The European Council and its President," in Federico Fabbrini et al (eds), *What Form of Government or the European Union and the Eurozone?* (Hart Publishing 2015), 253.

[69] See e.g., Bruno De Witte and Thomas Beukers, "The Court of Justice Approves the Creation of the European Stability Mechanisms Outside the EU Legal Order: *Pringle*" (2013) 50 Common Market Law Review 805 and Mattias Wendel, "Judicial Restraint and the Return to Openness: The Decision of the German Federal Constitutional Court on the ESM and the Fiscal Treaty" (2013) 14 German Law Journal 21.

[70] See e.g., Mark Dawson and Floris De Witte, "Constitutional Balance in the EU after the Euro-Crisis" (2013) 76 Modern Law Review 817 and Sergio Fabbrini, "Intergovernmentalism and Its Limits: Assessing the European Union's Answer to the Euro Crisis" (2013) 46 Comparative Political Studies 1003.

developments brought about by the Euro-crisis and the responses to it. In the general constitutional law literature the weakness of single-system studies have been repeatedly emphasized.[71] Because legal science does not have a laboratory in which to test its theses, it is only by resorting to the comparative method that the validity of a legal hypothesis can be verified.[72] In the specific field of European constitutional law, moreover, Robert Schütze has convincingly criticized *sui generis* approaches to questions of EU law and governance,[73] and in another book I have emphasized the added value of using a comparative approach to the study of fundamental rights in Europe.[74]

In this book, therefore, I seek to examine the new EU constitutional architecture of economic governance in light of a comparative benchmark with the aim to unveil the implications of the Euro-crisis and the responses to it on the constitutional fabric of the EU. As I will point out, a comparative outlook reveals several unexpected developments occurring in the EU, shedding new light on the dynamics at play in the European system of economic governance. In particular, the book follows Ran Hirschl's "most similar cases logic of comparison."[75] According to this logic of case selection, the object of study A is compared to another case B, which shares with A similarities on most independent variables. This permits the isolation of the dependent variable—where case A and case B differ—and its specific analysis. The "most similar cases logic of comparison" is particularly appropriate to study the effects that an intervening variable plays in a legal system, and thus seems well suited to assess the effects of the legal and institutional changes produced by the Euro-crisis and the responses to it.[76]

To explore the implications of the Euro-crisis and the responses to it on structures of power in Europe, the book selects as a comparator the United States of America (US). Why is the US chosen here as the most similar comparative case? To begin with, the US is a pluralist constitutional system,[77] characterized by multiple separations of powers aimed at ensuring a balance between the federal government and the states, between the political and the judicial branches, and between the

[71] See generally Maurice Adams and Jacco Bomhoff (eds), *Practice and Theory in Comparative Law* (CUP 2012) and Mark Tushnet, "The Possibilities of Comparative Constitutional Law" (1999) 108 Yale Law Journal 1225.

[72] See Mauro Cappelletti et al, "General Introduction" in Mauro Cappelletti et al (eds), *Integration Through Law: Europe and the American Federal Experience. Volume 1, Book 1* (de Gruyter 1986), 5 (defining the comparative method as the only available laboratory for legal analysis).

[73] Robert Schütze, *From Dual to Cooperative Federalism. The Changing Structure of European Law* (OUP 2009), 59 (stating that by "not providing any external standard, the *sui generis* [approach to EU studies] cannot detect, let alone measure, the European Union's evolution").

[74] Federico Fabbrini, *Fundamental Rights in Europe: Challenges and Transformations in Comparative Perspective* (OUP 2014) (comparing EU and US human rights systems).

[75] See Ran Hirschl, "The Question of Case Selection in Comparative Constitutional Law" (2005) 53 American Journal of Comparative Law 125 (distinguishing between different logics of comparative analysis—the most similar cases logic, the most different cases logic, the prototypical cases logic, and the most difficult cases logic).

[76] See also Vicki Jackson, "Narrative of Federalism: Of Continuities and Comparative Constitutional Experience" (2001) 51 Duke Law Journal 223, 258 (suggesting that comparative law can work as "an illuminating mirror" to better understand one's own system).

[77] See generally Daniel Elazar, *Constitutionalizing Globalization* (Rowman & Littlefield 1998).

states themselves.[78] Like the EU, therefore, the US is a system constitutionally founded on the idea that power should be divided and balanced along multiple vertical and horizontal axes.[79] Moreover, as a system creating an economic and monetary union endowed with a single currency, the US has had to deal with many of the challenges that the EMU is currently facing, for instance, where to strike the balance between centralization and decentralization in budgetary policy,[80] what role to recognize to courts in economic and monetary affairs,[81] and how to ensure an equilibrium between states of asymmetrical size and different economic performances.[82]

Certainly, the existence of multiple separations of powers is not a feature which is exclusive of the US, since it can be found also in systems such as Australia, Brazil, Canada, India, or Switzerland. However, compared to these other regimes, the US also appears more similar to the EU for reasons of economic development[83] and population size.[84] In fact, whether one likes it or not, the US is systematically taken as a model or anti-model in European debates. From Joseph Weiler's idea of the "Sonderweg"[85] to Mario Draghi's reflection on the "more perfect Union"[86] the US is always considered as an example of what Europe should—or should not—become, and thus appears as an inevitable comparative example with which to engage. Last but not least, a final reason prominently pleads in favor of using the US as a comparative benchmark to analyze the constitutional implications of the Euro-crisis and the responses to it in the EU: the US is today typically regarded

[78] See generally Laurence Tribe, *American Constitutional Law. Volume 1* (Foundation Press 1999) and Bruce Ackerman, "The New Separation of Powers" (2000) 113 Harvard Law Review 642.

[79] The most well-known statement of this vision can be found in *The Federalist Papers* No. 51 where James Madison defined the US constitutional architecture as a system in which "the power surrendered by the people is first divided between two distinct governments, and then the portion allotted to each subdivided among distinct and separate departments." See Federalist Paper [1787] (Penguin 1987) 321.

[80] See e.g., Jonathan A. Rodden, *Hamilton's Paradox: The Promise and Peril of Fiscal Discipline* (CUP 2006).

[81] See e.g., Richard Timberlake, *Constitutional Money: A Review of the Supreme Court's Monetary Decisions* (CUP 2013).

[82] See e.g., Peter Conti-Brown and David Skeel (eds), *When States Go Broke: The Origins, Context, and Solutions for the American States in Fiscal Crisis* (CUP 2012).

[83] See e.g., IMF, *World Economic Outlook Database*, access available at <http://www.imf.org/external/pubs/ft/weo/2014/02/weodata/index.aspx> (last accessed January 18, 2015) (reporting that in 2013 the GPD in current prices of the EU amounted to $17,512.109 billion, and that of the US to $16,760.050 billion—while for instance Brazil had a GDP of $2,246.037 billion and India of $1,876.811 billion).

[84] See e.g., *World Bank, World Development Indicators: Population (total)*, access available at <http://databank.worldbank.org/data/views/reports/tableview.aspx#> (last accessed January 18, 2015) (reporting that in 2013 the euro area had a population of 334 million inhabitants, and the US of 316 million—while for instance Australia had a population of 23 million, Canada of 35 million, and Switzerland of 8 million).

[85] See Joseph H.H. Weiler, "Federalism Without Constitutionalism: Europe's *Sonderweg*," in Kalypso Nicolaïdis and Robert Howse (eds), *The Federal Vision: Legitimacy and Levels of Governance in the United States and the European Union* (OUP 2001), 54 (making the case for a Sonderweg, that is, a "special way" in EU integration, compared to the US).

[86] See ECB President Mario Draghi, "Europe's Pursuit of 'A More Perfect Union'," Speech at the Harvard Kennedy School of Government, Cambridge, October 9, 2013 (explaining that the process of European integration follows the same logic stated in the Preamble of the US Constitution, of creating "a more perfect Union.").

in the comparative constitutional law literature as the emblematic case of a political regime with a strong central government,[87] an all-powerful judiciary,[88] and a limited recognition of the states at the federal level.[89] Exploring how the EU now allocates powers vertically and horizontally in the field of economic governance in comparison to the US can therefore provide an enlightening yardstick to appreciate the paradoxical implications of the Euro-crisis and the responses to it on the structural relations of powers in the EU.

4. The Arguments of the Book

The book advances three claims. It answers the research questions posed above arguing that the EMU constitutional system has developed since the beginning of the Euro-crisis in ways which are striking when measured with the comparative benchmark offered by the US case. As I will suggest, each of these developments reflects a paradox, because it reveals an unexpected feature of the new EU constitutional architecture of economic governance.[90] As the book argues, the constitutional architecture of economic governance in Europe is characterized today by:

1. Great centralization of powers in the vertical relations of power between the states and the EU. While EMU reforms were inspired by the desire to preserve states' fiscal sovereignty, in fact, the power shift from the states to the EU in budgetary affairs is greater than that existing in a fully fledged federal state like the US. Paradoxically, the states of the US enjoy greater autonomy than the EU member states vis-à-vis the central government in budgetary affairs. I call this development, the *paradox of centralization*.
2. Major role of the courts vis-à-vis the political branches. While EMU reforms were based on an intergovernmental strategy centered on the role of national executives, in fact, in the EU courts now play a greater role in economic and monetary affairs than the one played by courts even in a system of strong judicial review par excellence like the US. Paradoxically, courts in the US are

[87] See Stanley Elkins and Eric McKitrick, *The Age of Federalism* (OUP 1993) (contrasting the initial experience of the US federation with the ensuing process of centralization) and Susan Low Block and Vicki Jackson, *Federalism* (Prager 2013) (analyzing US federalism in historical perspective).

[88] See Stephen Gardbaum, *The New Commonwealth Model of Constitutionalism* (CUP 2013) 4–6 (contrasting the new Commonwealth model of constitutionalism of, for example, the United Kingdom to the model of judicial supremacy epitomized by the US) and Tom Ginsburg, *Judicial Review in New Democracies: Constitutional Courts in Asian Cases* (CUP 2003) 17 (stating that, despite some obvious idiosyncrasies, "the experience of the U.S. *is* helpful" as a model case when discussing judicial review, and the emergence thereof, in new Asian democracies) (emphasis in original).

[89] See Ernest Young, "Protecting Member State Autonomy in the European Union: Some Cautionary Tales from American Federalism" (2002) 77 NYU Law Review 1612 (discussing limited autonomy of US states compared to EU member states) and Allan Erbsen, "Horizontal Federalism" (2009) 93 Minnesota Law Review 493 (analyzing interstate relations in the US).

[90] See also *Webster's 7th New Collegiate Dictionary* (Merriam Co. 1965) (defining paradox as "1. A tenet contrary to received opinion; 2a. A statement that is seemingly contradictory or oppose to common sense and yet is perhaps true").

less involved than courts in the EU in reviewing measures adopted by the political branches in the economic and monetary domain. I call this development, the *paradox of judicialization.*

3. Domination by some states over others. While the EU's highest decision-making forum (the European Council) is based on the rule "one state, one vote" and the EU is supposed to protect the principle of states' equality more than the US, in fact, the relationship between the EU member states has turned out to be less balanced than that existing in a system like the US where the states are not represented in the central executive. Paradoxically, states in the US remain more equal than in the EU, where states' economic power has trumped long-standing attention for states' equality. I call this development, the *paradox of domination.*

This book builds upon a growing body of scholarly literature on the Euro-crisis and the EMU discussed above. However, it goes beyond the existing scholarship by drawing on comparative analysis to offer a comprehensive picture of the implications that the Euro-crisis and the responses to it have had on structural relations of powers within the European constitutional architecture. Whereas in the public discourse the reforms of EMU inaugurated since the beginning of the Euro-crisis have been described as resisting pulls toward centralization,[91] promoting the centrality of political branches,[92] and ensuring the balance between the states in the European Council,[93] this research provides a reality check to these statements. Resorting to comparative analysis, the book explores the implications of the legal and institutional reforms enacted in the state of financial emergency, and argues that—paradoxically—the new EU constitutional architecture of economic governance has become characterized by greater centralization, greater judicialization, and greater asymmetry between states than what occurs in a fully fledged federal regime with all-powerful judicial review like the US.

At the same time, the book critically evaluates the developments taking place in the new architecture of EMU and assesses them in light of important constitutional imperatives such as the need to ensure a degree of autonomy to the

[91] See e.g., European Commission President Manuel D. Barroso, Speech at the "State of the Union" Conference of the European University Institute, Florence, May 9, 2013 (stating that "'More Europe' does not mean 'more Brussels', in the sense of more centralization. [...] Subsidiarity is indeed an essential democratic concept and should be practiced. [...] And this is precisely what we are doing [in the EMU].").

[92] See French President Nicolas Sarkozy, Speech, Toulon, December 1, 2011 (stating that "L'Europe a besoin de plus de démocratie. [...] La refondation de l'Europe, ce ne pas la marche vers plus de supranationalité. [...] La crise a poussé les Chefs d'Etats et du gouvernments à assumer des responsabilités croissantes parce qu'au fond eux seuls disposaient de la légitimité démocratique qui leu permettai de décider.").

[93] See German Chancellor Angela Merkel, Speech at the Opening Ceremony of the 61st academic year of the College of Europe, Bruges, November 2, 2010 (expressing the view that within the European Council "the Heads of State and Government of the 27 member states and the President of the European Commission lay down jointly [*gemeinsam*] with the President of the European Council guidelines on how the Union should develop.").

budgetary processes of the states, the need to ensure democratic decision-making in EMU affairs, and the need to ensure an equilibrium between states' power and states' equality within the EU institutional system. As the book claims, from a normative perspective the preservation of a balance between levels of governments, between institutions, and between states, is necessary for the long-term sustainability of the EU. In fact, centralization undermines state autonomy, judicialization threatens democratic self-governance, and domination strikes at the heart of the EU post-war anti-hegemonic project. Each of these developments is therefore problematic. As such, the book endeavors to discuss alternative institutional arrangements which, while suitable to govern the complexities of an economic and monetary union, are able to restore a new balance of powers in the EU constitutional architecture of economic governance.

5. The Policy Proposals of the Book

Given the problematic aspects of the developments which have occurred in the European architecture of economic governance as a result of the Euro-crisis and the responses to it, the book also seeks to propose ways to redress the paradoxes of centralization, judicialization, and domination identified through the use of the comparative method. As such, after a primary, analytical, and critical assessment of the implications of the Euro-crisis and the responses to it on the architecture of EMU, the book also engages in a subsequent, normative, and propositive discussion of the possible ways forward to restore a vertical and horizontal constitutional balance in the European architecture of economic governance. By doing so, the book joins the debate about the future of EMU and offers its contribution to it with several policy proposals aimed at improving the constitutional architecture of economic governance in Europe.

The debate on the future of EMU is currently ongoing at the highest policy-making level in Europe. Following an explicit mandate of the European Council, the President of the European Council, jointly with the Presidents of the European Commission, the Eurogroup, and the ECB, delivered in December 2012 a report entitled "Towards a Genuine EMU,"[94] which outlined a road-map of reform for the EMU, including deeper economic, banking, and fiscal union coupled with a new framework of democratic legitimacy and accountability. In addition, in November 2012 the European Commission published a Communication outlining a blueprint for a deep and genuine EMU and opening a debate on future reforms.[95] Furthermore, following the European Parliament (EP) election in May 2014, and the appointment of a new European Commission in October 2014, the heads of state and government of the Eurozone entrusted the President of the European

[94] President of the European Council, Final Report "Towards a Genuine EMU," December 5, 2012.

[95] See European Commission Communication, "A Blueprint for a Deep and Genuine EMU. Launching a European Debate," November 28, 2012, COM(2012)777 final.

Commission, in close cooperation with the Presidents of the European Council, the Eurogroup, and the ECB, with the task to bring forward the work on the future of EMU[96]—an effort which resulted in the publication, in June 2015, of a new report, also signed by the President of the EP, on "Completing Europe's EMU."[97]

At the same time, the EP has repeatedly expressed its desire that constitutional changes be brought back on the agenda of the EU institutions, including by reviving the Convention method to re-discuss the architecture of the EU for a new era.[98] And it has stated that the EU member states shall live up to the obligation enshrined in the Fiscal Compact to bring back the content of that treaty within EU law by 2018 at the latest,[99] using this as a window of opportunity for a broader overhaul of the EU constitutional system.[100] Moreover, several member states' governments have made the case for further reforms in the EU, including a new round of changes to the EU treaties, aimed at achieving a new constitutional settlement in the EU.[101] Last but not least, a growing emphasis has emerged in academia,[102] and the public debate,[103] on the need for institutional reforms in the EU and the Eurozone, aimed at improving the effectiveness and legitimacy of its constitutional architecture of economic governance. Notwithstanding obvious resistances, therefore, pressures seem to be mounting for a new round of legal and constitutional changes in Europe.[104]

This book contributes to the debate about the constitutional future of the European architecture of economic governance by advancing several options for EMU reform. These proposals specifically address the paradoxical, and problematic, dynamics previously identified: centralization, judicialization, and domination. Hence, the book's normative part outlines possible ways to restore a

[96] See Euro Summit Statement, October 24, 2014, para 2.

[97] President of the European Commission, Report "Completing Europe's EMU," June 22, 2015.

[98] See European Parliament Resolution of November 20, 2012 on the report "Towards a Genuine EMU," P7_TA(2012)0430.

[99] See Art 16 Fiscal Compact (requiring the signatory states to incorporate the content of the treaty within the law of the EU by 2018 at the latest). See also now Art 16 SRF Agreement (requiring the signatory states to incorporate the content of the treaty within the law of the EU by 2024 at the latest).

[100] See European Parliament Resolution of February 2, 2012 on the European Council meeting of 30 January 2012, P7_TA(2012)0023, para 7.

[101] See e.g., French President François Hollande, Intervention liminaire de lors de la conférence de presse, Paris, May 16, 2013, 7 (speaking in favor of new steps in the integration process) and German Chancellor Angela Merkel, Speech at the Bundestag, Berlin, December 18, 2013 (indicating the need for Treaty change in the EU). But see also British Prime Minister David Cameron, Speech, London, January 23, 2013 (recognizing the need for treaty changes especially to integrate the Eurozone further).

[102] See e.g., Ingolf Pernice et al, *A Democratic Solution to the Crisis: Reform Steps Towards a Democratically Based Economic and Financial Constitution for Europe* (Nomos 2012); Jean-Claude Piris, *The Future of Europe: Toward a Two Speed EU?* (CUP 2011).

[103] See e.g., Glienicker Group, "Toward a Euro Union," October 17, 2013 and Eiffel Group, "For a Euro Community," February 14, 2014 (demanding new institutional arrangements for the Eurozone).

[104] See also Sergio Fabbrini, *Which European Union? Europe after the Euro-Crisis* (CUP 2015) (outlining alternative perspectives on the EU and proposing a new constitutional settlement) as well as Federico Fabbrini et al (eds), *What Form of Government for the European Union and the Eurozone?* (Hart Publishing 2015) (discussing alternative scenarios for institutional reforms in the EU and the Eurozone).

vertical and horizontal balance in the European constitutional architecture of economic governance. In doing so, the book again seeks to take advantage from comparative law, drawing lessons from the examples of other legal systems, and benefitting from the trials and errors that these have undergone to address problems analogous to those currently facing the EU.[105] Moreover, while, in critically analyzing the implications of the Euro-crisis and the responses to it on the EU constitutional architecture of economic governance, the book uses as a comparative benchmark the US case, in articulating options for future reforms, the book moves beyond a focus on the US only, and also includes references to the legal and institutional experience of other nations, such as Argentina, Australia, Brazil, Canada, France, Germany, India, Indonesia, Israel, Japan, Switzerland, and the United Kingdom.

In particular, from a policy perspective, the book suggests that:

1. The dynamic of centralization can be mitigated by raising a separate fiscal capacity for EMU, which reduces asymmetric economic shocks but preserves a degree of autonomy for the states in budgetary affairs.
2. The dynamic of judicialization can be reverted by restoring the centrality of the EU legislative process, enhancing the role of supranational democratic institutions in the decision-making process in EMU affairs.
3. The balance between the member states can be achieved through a new system of executive decision-making and legitimation at the supranational level which is able to control, rather than suffer, pressures from the largest states.

Needless to say, each of these proposals is controversial and would likely face a number of challenges. The possibility to reform the EU legal and institutional system is constrained by legal obstacles. At the EU level, most visibly, the principle of conferral and the unanimity requirement to change the EU treaties poses an important impediment to a reform of the EMU.[106] At the national level, several hurdles have been raised by legislatures,[107] or courts,[108] in authorizing further steps forward in the process of EU integration. At the same time, the possibility to reform EMU is hampered by political obstacles:[109] in the recent rounds of national

[105] See e.g., Tom Ginsburg (ed), *Comparative Constitutional Design* (CUP 2012).

[106] See e.g., Stephen Weatherill, "The Constitutional Context of (Ever-Wider) Policy-Making," in Erik Jones et al (eds), *The Oxford Handbook of the European Union* (OUP 2012), 570 (discussing the principle of conferral) and Steve Peers, "The Future of EU Treaty Amendments" (2012) 31 Yearbook of European Law 17 (explaining the process of revision of the EU Treaties).

[107] See e.g., Paul Craig, "The European Union Act 2011: Locks, Limits and Legality" (2011) 48 Common Market Law Review 1881 (discussing the limits on further EU treaty change posed in the UK by the EU Act 2011).

[108] See e.g., Sabino Cassese, "L'Unione europea e il guinzaglio tedesco" [2009] Giornale di diritto amministrativo 1003 and Alicia Hinarejos, "The Euro Area Crisis and Constitutional Limits to Fiscal Integration" (2012) 14 Cambridge Yearbook of European Legal Studies 243 (discussing constitutional limits to fiscal integration in the EU posed in Germany by the federal Constitutional Court).

[109] See e.g., Alexander Somek, "What is Political Union?" (2013) 14 German Law Journal 561 (discussing obstacles toward further integration).

and EP elections, voters have increasingly cast their ballots for anti-European parties, expressing their discontent toward a system of governance perceived as remote and unresponsive.[110] These challenges must necessarily be taken into account in any discussion about constitutional change in the EU.

Yet the book does not adopt a naïve stand. It acknowledges the challenges that any prospect of reform would need to address and seeks to explain how and why these can be met. In fact, the book suggests that targeted reforms of the EU constitutional system, increasing the autonomy of the member states and clarifying the separation of powers of the EU executive and legislative branches, may actually go a long way toward addressing the concerns of citizens across the EU. In pragmatic fashion, then, the book underlines what are the potentials of the legal mechanisms currently existing in the armory of the EU legal order, and discusses what would be the advantages for the relevant stakeholders in pursuing a strategy of constitutional revision of the EU treaties along the lines set out above. As such, in discussing each of these alternative scenarios on how to restore a balance of powers in the EMU, the book considers the challenges that would arise along the way and yet emphasizes how reason and choice can lead the EU toward a more satisfactory constitutional settlement for the states, the EU institutions, and the European people themselves.

6. The Structure of the Book

This book is opened by the celebrated citation from Alexander Hamilton's *The Federalist Papers* No. 1, distinguishing constitutional arrangements established out of accident and force from constitutional systems designed on the basis of reflection and choice. This book illuminates beyond conventional wisdom the reality of power-relations in the EMU, critically evaluates this state of affairs in light of constitutionalist balance-of-powers principles and advances new ideas on how to perfect the constitutional architecture of EMU in the near future. As such, the book is structured along a dual logic, inspired by Hamilton's pressing question.

Part I examines how developments that occurred in the EMU after the beginning of the Euro-crisis have changed the constitutional architecture of the EU through *accident and force*. Chapter 1 examines the effects of the Euro-crisis and the responses to it on the vertical relations of power between the states and the EU, and underlines the paradox of centralization, visible in the growth in power of central institutions vis-à-vis the member states which is unparalleled even when

[110] See e.g., Nicole Scicluna, "Politicization without Democratization: How the Eurozone Crisis is Transforming EU Law and Politics" (2014) 12 International Journal of Constitutional Law 545 (discussing the rise of anti-system parties in national elections) and Corinne Deloy and Pascale Joannin, "Les forces de droit sortent victorieuses des elections européenne marquees par une poussée populiste dans plusiers Etats members," Fondation Robert Schuman—Observatoire des Elections en Europe (2014) (discussing the rise in turnout of Euro-skeptic, populist parties in a plurality of EU member states during the May 2014 elections to the EP).

compared with a highly centralized federal system like the US. Chapter 2 explores the effects of the Euro-crisis and the responses to it on the horizontal relations of power between the political branches and the courts and stresses the unprecedented judicialization of economic and monetary affairs that has recently occurred in the EU. Chapter 3, finally, considers the effects of the Euro-crisis and the responses to it on the horizontal relations of power between the member states themselves, and argues that a dynamic of domination of larger, wealthier states over others has increasingly emerged since the eruption of the Euro-crisis, upsetting the original EU institutional balance.

Part II of the book then moves from the critical to the constructive, and discusses how the paradoxes generated by the Euro-crisis and the responses to it could, and should, be addressed by reforming the EU constitutional architecture of economic governance through *reflection and choice*. Chapter 4 focuses on the idea to endow the EMU with a fiscal capacity and considers how this may constitute an alternative way to manage economic interdependencies in the EU and the Eurozone and yet avoid complete centralization of budgetary processes. Here I discuss the challenges toward a meaningful fiscal capacity and take as a case study the recent proposal for a financial transaction tax. Chapter 5 criticizes the use of intergovernmental agreement outside the EU legal order and makes the case in favor of a full legislative involvement in EMU affairs. To this end, I consider how restoring the centrality of the EU legislative process, while reforming the role of the EP and the Council, can ensure democratic control of decision-making in financial affairs, inverting the trend toward judicial aggrandizement in this field. Chapter 6, finally, reflects upon possible institutional solutions to restore a balance between the member states, discussing how an effective and properly legitimated executive government at the EU level may ensure greater equilibrium between states' interests than a regime of executive federalism in which larger states dominate the decision-making process. A brief conclusion ends the book, making the case for future steps toward a more perfect EMU.

PART I

ACCIDENT AND FORCE

1

The Paradox of Centralization

1. Introduction

Complex economic reasons lay at the roots of the Euro-crisis.[1] Yet, following revelations by the Greek government in 2009 that its deficit was higher than previously declared,[2] policy-makers in the European Union (EU) and its member states came to interpret the crisis in Europe as a problem of sovereign insolvency, and sought to respond to it with consequential legal measures.[3] Although the Economic and Monetary Union (EMU) had been characterized by the existence of deficit and debt brakes since the adoption of the Maastricht Treaty in 1992, the lack of clear enforcement mechanisms was blamed for the irresponsible fiscal behavior of some Eurozone member states.[4] In response to the Euro-crisis, therefore, EU institutions and member states rushed to adopt a broad swath of legal measures aimed at strengthening budgetary constraints and imposing clear obligations of fiscal consolidation on the EU member states.[5] The introduction of new budgetary constraints at the national and supranational level reflects the understanding that the existence of a common currency (the euro), coupled with a no-bail-out clause in Article 125 Treaty on the Functioning of the EU (TFEU), requires tighter fiscal constraints in the member states to prevent negative externalities from spilling over across the Eurozone.[6]

[1] See generally Paul De Grauwe, *Economics of Monetary Union* (10th ed. OUP 2014).

[2] See Mark Hallerberg, "Fiscal Federalism Reforms in the European Union and the Greek Crisis" (2012) 12 European Union Politics 127; Gianluigi Tosato, "La riforma costituzionale sull'equilibrio di bilancio alla luce della normativa dell'Unione: l'interazione fra livello europeo e interno" [2014] Rivista di diritto internazionale 5.

[3] See Matthias Ruffert, "The European Debt Crisis and European Union Law" (2011) 48 Common Market Law Review 1777; Christoph Hermann, "Die Bewältigung der Euro-Staatsschulden-Krise an den Grenzen des deutschen und europäischen Währungsverfassungsrechts" [2012] Europäische Zeitschrift für Wirtschaftsrecht 805.

[4] See Martin Heipertz and Amy Verdun, *Ruling Europe: The Politics of the Stability and Growth Pact* (CUP 2011) and Marco Buti and Nicolas Carnot, "The EMU Debt Crisis: Early Lessons and Reforms" (2012) 50 Journal of Common Market Studies 899.

[5] See Frédéric Allemand and Francesco Martucci, "La nouvelle gouvernance économique européene—Partie I" (2012) 46 Cahiers de droit européen 17 and "– Partie II" (2012) 46 Cahiers de droit européen 409 and Corrado Caruso and Marta Morvillo, "Economic Governance and Budgetary Rules in the European Context" [2014] Diritto dell'Unione Europea 699.

[6] See Federico Fabbrini et al (eds), *The Constitutionalization of European Budgetary Constraints* (Hart Publishing 2014).

As mentioned in the Introduction, the efforts by the member states and the EU institutions to strengthen budgetary constraints have advanced along two lines. On the one hand, measures to improve the monitoring of states' fiscal performances have been enacted within the framework of EU law.[7] On the other hand, however, a key element in responding to the Euro-crisis came through an intergovernmental agreement.[8] On March 2, 2012, 25 out of the then 27 member states of the EU[9]—including all the member states of the Eurozone—signed in Brussels the Treaty on the Stability, Coordination, and Governance in the Economic and Monetary Union (TSCG), generally referred to as the Fiscal Compact.[10] This treaty raises a number of new issues in the fields of international law, EU law, and comparative constitutional law. Technically drafted as an international treaty, but functionally connected to the EU legal order, the Fiscal Compact pursues the goal of strengthening member states' budgetary discipline by requiring them to incorporate fiscal rules within their legal system as a way to promoting domestic ownership of these rules in the national budgetary process.[11] In particular, the Fiscal Compact imposes on signatory states an obligation to enact the so-called "golden rule"—a requirement that annual government budgets be balanced—in state constitutions.[12] As this chapter maintains, this requirement, which is unprecedented in the history of European integration, significantly affects the fiscal sovereignty of the member states as well as their relations toward supranational institutions.[13]

The aim of this chapter is to analyze the implications of the Euro-crisis and the responses to it on *the vertical relations of powers between the EU and the member*

[7] See Nicolas De Sadeleer, "The New Architecture of the European Economic Governance: A Leviathan or a Flat-Footed Colossus?" (2012) 19 Maastricht Journal of European & Comparative Law 354 and Herwig Hofmann and Katerina Pantazatou, "The Transformation of the European Economic Constitution," University of Luxembourg Law Working Paper No. 01/2015.

[8] See Paul Craig, "The Stability, Coordination and Governance Treaty: Principle, Politics and Pragmatism" (2012) 37 European Law Review 231 and Anna Kocharov et al, "Another Legal Monster? An EUI Debate on the Fiscal Compact Treaty" European University Institute Department of Law Working Paper No. 9/2012.

[9] The Fiscal Compact was originally signed by all EU member states, except the United Kingdom (UK) and the Czech Republic. See House of Lords European Union Committee, *The Euro Area Crisis*, 2012, HL. 260, 75. Since then, the Czech government has changed course and expressed its commitment to join the Treaty, but the ratification has not yet been completed in Parliament due to the requirement of a 3/5 majority. See Denisa Tomanová, "Le gouvernement tchèque confirme son adhésion au Pact budgétaire européen," *Radio Prague*, March 24, 2014. Instead, Croatia, which became the 28th EU member state on July 1, 2013, has so far not signed the Fiscal Compact.

[10] See Treaty on Stability, Coordination and Governance in the Economic and Monetary Union, March 2, 2012, [hereinafter Fiscal Compact], available at <http://www.eurozone.europa.eu/media/304649/st00tscg26_en12.pdf> (last accessed June 1, 2014).

[11] Pmbl. Fiscal Compact.

[12] Arguably, this provision represents the key legal novelty introduced by the Fiscal Compact. A few months before the adoption of the Fiscal Compact, in fact, EU institutions enacted the so-called "six pack," namely a package of five regulations and one directive aimed at strengthening the surveillance of state budgetary policies. See n 38. See Editorial Comments, "Some Thoughts Concerning the Draft Treaty on a Reinforced Economic Union" (2012) 49 Common Market Law Review 1, 5 n 12.

[13] See also Robert P. Inman and Daniel L. Rubinfeld, "The EMU and Fiscal Policy in the New European Community: An Issue for Economic Federalism" (1994) 14 International Review of Law and Economics 147 (discussing state fiscal policy within EMU).

states. The chapter focuses in particular on the "golden rule" set in the Fiscal Compact, tracing its origin in the constitutional experience of Germany and assessing the institutional challenges that its adoption raised in four other EU member states—France, Italy, Spain, and the Netherlands—and at the EU level. The developments taking place in the EMU are then compared to the experience of the United States (US) in the field of fiscal federalism. The comparative example of the US is used as a benchmark to evaluate the nature of the developments produced by the Euro-crisis and the responses to it on the European system of economic governance. The EU and the US, in fact, appear to share several common structural features. The US established a single federal currency among its federated states through a long and difficult process.[14] Moreover, the central government in the US is barred from bailing out defaulting states, and most US states have budgetary constraints in their constitutions prohibiting governments from running their budget at a deficit.[15] Yet, in the US, the enactment of "golden rules" at the state constitutional level was never required by federal law, but rather emerged in the mid-nineteenth century as an autonomous decision of the states to ensure their access to the financial market.[16] Moreover, specific constitutional doctrines still constrain the powers of the central government vis-à-vis the states,[17] and federal authorities cannot interfere in the states' budgetary processes.

In light of the comparison with the US, the chapter argues that a paradox emerges in the new constitutional architecture of the Eurozone: the Euro-crisis and the legal and institutional responses to it have dramatically shifted powers in the budgetary domain from the member states toward the EU institutions, making budgetary policy in the EMU more centralized than in a federal state like the US. This development is striking. On the one hand, the US is often regarded as a highly centralized federal state, with the federal government playing a dominating role in the governance of the economy that is at odds with the reality in EMU.[18] In fact, since the New Deal in the 1930s, the US federal government has acquired sweeping economic powers, by using its capacity to tax and spend as a powerful lever to manage the national economy.[19] On the other hand, the latest reforms in the EMU were largely driven by the desire to prevent the EU from evolving into

[14] See Kathleen R. McNamara, "State Building, the Territorialisation of Money, and the Creation of the American Single Currency" in David Andrews et al (eds), *Governing the World's Money* (Cornell UP 2002), 128, 138–9.

[15] See James D. Savage, *Balanced Budgets and American Politics* (Cornell UP 1988) 79–80, 117–18.

[16] See Erik Wibbels, "Bailouts, Budget Constraints and Leviathans: Comparative Federalism and Lessons from the Early United States" (2003) 36 Comparative Political Studies 475, 498.

[17] See Vicki Jackson, "Federalism and the Uses and Limits of Law: *Printz* and Principle" (1998) 111 Harvard Law Review 2180.

[18] See Aart Loubert, "Sovereign Debt Threatens the Union: The Genesis of a Federation" (2012) 8 European Constitutional Law Review 442.

[19] This constitutes an important caveat to the argument that is being made here. For a more detailed explanation of how the existence in the US of a strong budgetary power at the federal level qualifies the lack of supervisory powers by the central government vis-à-vis the federated states see further my analysis in the text accompanying nn 242–8.

a fully fledged federal state.[20] Yet, although, in reforming the EMU, state governments have consistently discarded the federal model as being too centralized and centripetal for Europe, they have ended up establishing a regime that is much less respectful of state autonomy than the US federal one in the budgetary domain.

Paradoxically, while the governments of the EU member states reacted to the Euro-crisis by deliberately discarding a federal arrangement for the EMU as disrespectful of state sovereignty, the very sovereignty of the states would have been better off under a federal system like that of the US: in fact under the regime created by the Fiscal Compact and the latest EU legislative reforms the EU has acquired powers of oversight on the budgetary policy of the states which would be inconceivable in the US federal system. Of course, to say that the EU is witnessing more centralization than the US in the budgetary field only emphasizes part of the story: as I will underline, the US central government enjoys a broad authority to tax and spend, and today it manages a major federal budget, which amply compensates for the lack of supervisory powers over the budgetary processes of the federated states. Although throughout the nineteenth century federal spending was modest, since the 1930s central government spending has on average been close to 20% of national GDP.[21] And yet, the fact that in the US the central government never required states to constitutionalize balanced budget rules, and that it would (still today) be unconstitutional for the federal authorities to oversee the budgetary policies of the states, marks a striking difference with the post-crisis system of EMU governance.

As the chapter suggests, however, the development of the EMU toward a highly centralized regime, in which EU institutions wield significant power to police the budgetary policy of the EU member states appears problematic. Although it has been argued that the centralizing dynamic occurring in response to the crisis was an inevitable development, necessary to prevent negative externalities from spilling over from states in fiscal distress toward other countries of the Eurozone, there is a plausible claim to be made that EU member states ought to enjoy a meaningful autonomy in designing their budgetary policy.[22] Decisions about budgets are at the heart of the national democratic process and influence the capacity of the states to shape themselves. After all, even the experience of the US—a federal state, with a powerful central government—points in this direction, recognizing the need for a degree of states' autonomy in the budgetary field and preventing the federal government from directly encroaching into this sphere of self-governance.[23] In the case of the US, of course, the autonomy of the federated states in the field of budgetary policy is compensated by the existence of a broad authority for the

[20] See Pieter-Augustijn Van Malleghem, "(Un)Balanced Budget Rules in Europe and America," in Federico Fabbrini et al (eds), *The Constitutionalization of European Budgetary Constraints* (Hart Publishing 2014), 151.

[21] See further *US Government Spending History from 1900*, available at <http://www.usgovernmentspending.com/spending_brief.php> (last accessed July 30, 2015).

[22] See generally Ken Kollman, *Perils of Centralization: Lessons from Church, State and Corporation* (CUP 2014).

[23] See generally Jonathan A. Rodden, *Hamilton's Paradox: The Promise and Peril of Fiscal Discipline* (CUP 2006).

federal government to tax and spend, independently from the states. Instead, as Alicia Hinarejos has pointed out, by rejecting the US model of fiscal federalism, the EU has drifted toward a "surveillance model" in which the center enjoys no budgetary capacity of its own, but has invasive oversight power on the budgetary policies of the member states.[24] Because this state of affairs threatens the sustainability of EMU, Chapter 4 will consider the potentials of a fiscal capacity for the EU as an alternative to centralized control of states' budgetary policy, and discuss the challenges connected to this option.

This chapter is structured as follows. Section 2 examines the constitutionalization of European budgetary constraints, analyzing in particular the new "golden rule"[25] set at the EU level to maintain fiscal discipline and summarizing its incorporation in a number of selected EU member states. Section 3 considers the institutional implications of the introduction of the "golden rule," both for state political and judicial branches, and for the EU bodies charged with enforcing it, arguing that the constitutionalization of budgetary constraints strengthens the role of EU institutions vis-à-vis the member states. Section 4 then engages in a comparative analysis with the experience of the US, surveying the US model of fiscal federalism and explaining how, in the US, the federal government, while having autonomous fiscal capacity, exercises only limited powers over the budgetary policies of the states. By contrasting the US experience with the current European one, I advance the claim that the EMU has become more centralized than the US in the field of budgetary policy and that this centralization is paradoxical. Section 5, however, critically discusses what are the limits associated with this centralization and suggests that there are plausible arguments why the member states ought to maintain some autonomy in their budgetary process. Section 6, finally, concludes.

2. The Constitutionalization of European Budgetary Constraints

In the efforts to address the Euro-crisis, since 2010 both the EU institutions and the member states enacted a swath of legal measures aimed at strengthening budgetary constraints at all levels of government.[26] This section examines the constitutionalization of budgetary constraints in the framework of EU and international law, and their domestication in the legal system of the member

[24] See generally Alicia Hinarejos, "Fiscal Federalism in the European Union: Evolution and Future Choices for EMU" (2013) 50 Common Market Law Review 1621.

[25] Notice that the term "golden rule" is used in the legal jargon of some countries with different meanings. In Italy, for example, it often refers to the subtraction of investments from the calculus of the national deficit. See Giacinto della Cananea, "Government Deficits and Investments: A European Legal Framework" (2013) 5 Italian Journal of Public Law 103.

[26] See Kaarlo Tuori and Klaus Tuori, *The Eurozone Crisis: A Constitutional Analysis* (CUP 2014) and Paul Craig, "Economic Governance and the Euro Crisis: Constitutional Architecture and Constitutional Implications," in Federico Fabbrini et al (eds), *The Constitutionalization of European Budgetary Constraints* (Hart Publishing 2014), 19.

states. The first sub-section surveys the new EU legal instruments adopted to enhance the oversight of states' compliance with budgetary rules and considers the case of the Fiscal Compact as the most advanced example of the attempt to introduce binding fiscal rules restraining the budgetary policy of the member states. In light of the analysis of the Fiscal Compact's provisions, then, subsequent sub-sections consider the constitutionalization of budgetary constraints in five selected Eurozone member states: Germany, France, Italy, Spain, and the Netherlands.[27] Selection of these countries as case studies is based on both pragmatic and methodological reasons. On one hand, Germany, France, Italy, Spain, and the Netherlands are the biggest states of the Eurozone and alone account for more than 80% of the entire EMU's GDP.[28] Assessing how fiscal constraints are designed in these states is therefore important in any discussion about the future financial stability of the Eurozone. On the other hand, these countries are also endowed with very different institutional settings, with regard to both the framework of government and the system of constitutional review.[29] Spain, Germany, Italy, and the Netherlands have parliamentary systems (although the first two are consolidated bipolar democracies while the last two have fragmented party systems) while France is a semi-presidential regime.[30] Moreover, whereas the Netherlands tout court bans judicial review,[31] the other four selected member states are endowed with specialized Constitutional Courts empowered to review the constitutionality of legislation.[32] Yet, there are important differences in the judicial procedure in force in the four countries. For example, in France, legislation can be reviewed a priori, while in Italy, review is only conducted *ex post*, and generally upon referral of a judge.[33] Alternatively, Spain and Germany allow for

[27] For a comparative examination of the constitutionalization of EU budgetary constraints in the domestic legal systems of other EU member states, see Marek Antoš, "Fiscal Stability Rules in Central European Constitutions", in Federico Fabbrini et al (eds), *The Constitutionalization of European Budgetary Constraints* (Hart Publishing 2014), 205 (reviewing incorporations of balanced budget rules in the domestic systems also of Poland, Slovakia, and Hungary); Lina Papadopoulou, "Can Constitutional Rules, Even if 'Golden', Tame Greek Public Debt?," in Federico Fabbrini et al (eds), *The Constitutionalization of European Budgetary Constraints* (Hart Publishing 2014), 223 (reviewing incorporation of balanced budget rules in Greece); and Roderic O'Gorman, "An Analysis of the Method and Efficacy of Ireland's Incorporation of the Fiscal Compact" in Federico Fabbrini et al (eds), *The Constitutionalization of European Budgetary Constraints* (Hart Publishing 2014), 273 (reviewing incorporation of budget rules in Ireland).

[28] See Eurostat, *Gross Domestic Product at Market Prices*, available at <http://ec.europa.eu/eurostat/tgm/refreshTableAction.do?tab=table&plugin=1&pcode=tec00001&language=en> (last accessed July 18, 2015). In 2013, the aggregate GDP of Germany (€2,809,480.0), France (€2,116,565.0), Italy (€1,609,462.2), Spain (€1,049,181.0), and the Netherlands (€650,857.0) amounted to 83.2% of the Eurozone's GDP (€9,896,715.0).

[29] See Ran Hirschl, "The Question of Case Selection in Comparative Constitutional Law" (2005) 53 American Journal of Comparative Law 125 (explaining "most-different-cases logic of comparison.").

[30] See generally Augusto Barbera and Carlo Fusaro, *Il governo delle democrazie* (Il Mulino 2001).

[31] See Art 120 Const. NI. (prohibiting judicial review). But see also Arts 93–4 Const. NI. (recognizing supremacy of international law over conflicting domestic law).

[32] See Alec Stone Sweet, *Governing with Judges: Constitutional Politics in Europe* (OUP 2000) 40–1, 44–6.

[33] See Federico Fabbrini, "Kelsen in Paris: France's Constitutional Reform and the Introduction of *A Posteriori* Constitutional Review of Legislation" (2008) 9 German Law Journal 1297; Tania Groppi,

direct individual recourse to the Constitutional Court.[34] This variety of institutional settings can, therefore, offer valuable insights to differentiate, in Section 3, the implications that the Fiscal Compact's implementation at the state level may have for political branches and courts.

A. European Union

The objective of ensuring the sustainability of member state budgets was already enshrined in the Stability and Growth Pact (SGP) originally enacted in two Council regulations in 1997,[35] and currently attached as Protocol No. 12 to the TFEU,[36] which requires the member states of the EU to maintain their public deficit below the yearly ratio of 3% of the GDP and the total public debt below 60% of the GDP. The weaknesses of the enforcement mechanisms of the SGP, however, allegedly ensured widespread non-compliance by EU countries with the SGP.[37] To address this situation, in November 2011 the EU institutions enacted a package of five EU regulations and one EU directive—generally referred to as the "six pack"[38]—which profoundly modified the architecture of EU economic governance, enhancing the capacity of EU institutions to prevent and correct member states' deviations from the SGP standards. On the one hand, the "six pack" improved the so-called "preventive arm" of the SGP, strengthening the reporting commitments of member states with respect to their fiscal performance and introducing a new

"The Italian Constitutional Court: Towards a 'Multilevel System' of Constitutional Review?" (2008) 3 Journal of Comparative Law 100, 102–3.

[34] See Victor Ferreres Comella, "The Spanish Constitutional Court: Time for Reforms" (2008) 3 Journal of Comparative Law 22; Donald P. Kommers and Russell A. Miller, "Das Bundesverfassungsgericht: Procedure, Practice and Policy of the German Federal Constitutional Court" (2008) 3 Journal of Comparative Law 194.

[35] See Council Regulation (EC) No. 1466/97 of July 7, 1997 on strengthening of the surveillance of budgetary positions and the surveillance and coordination of economic policies [1997] OJ L209/1; Council Regulation (EC) No. 1467/97 of July 7, 1997 on speeding up and clarifying the implementation of the excessive deficit procedure [1997] OJ L209/6.

[36] See Protocol No. 12 on excessive deficit procedure [2008] OJ C115/279.

[37] See Stefan Collignon, "The End of the Stability and Growth Pact?" (2004) 1 International Economics and Economic Policy 15. See also Case C-27/04 *Commission v. Council* [2004] ECR I-6649 ECLI:EU:C:2004:436 (recognizing wide discretion to the Council on whether to impose sanctions under the SGP or hold in abeyance the excessive deficit procedure against two member states recommended by the Commission).

[38] See Regulation (EU) No. 1173/2011 of the European Parliament and of the Council of November 16, 2011 on effective enforcement of budgetary surveillance in the euro area [2011] OJ L306/1; Regulation (EU) No. 1174/2011 of the European Parliament and of the Council of November 16, 2011 on enforcement measures to correct excessive macroeconomic imbalances in the euro area [2011] OJ L306/8; Regulation (EU) No. 1175/2011 of the European Parliament and of the Council of November 16, 2011 amending Council Regulation (EC) No. 1466/97 on strengthening of the surveillance of budgetary positions and the surveillance and coordination of economic policies [2011] OJ L306/12; Regulation (EU) No. 1176/2011 of the European Parliament and of the Council of November 16, 2011 on prevention and correction of macroeconomic imbalances [2011] OJ L306/25; Council Regulation (EU) No. 1177/2011 of November 8, 2011 amending Council Regulation (EC) No. 1467/97 on speeding up and clarifying the implementation of the excessive deficit procedure [2011] OJ L306/33; Council Directive 2011/85/EU of November 8, 2011 on requirements for budgetary frameworks of the member states [2011] OJ L306/41.

"macro-economic imbalance procedure" run by the EU Commission to alert member states on the destabilizing elements of their economies. On the other hand, the "six pack" overhauled the so-called "corrective arm" of the SGP, empowering the European Commission to sanction member states for breaches of the deficit and debt rules and depriving the Council (the EU body representing the executives of the member states) of most discretion in the application of fines against states subject to the "excessive deficit procedure." Moreover, the "six pack" introduced minimum requirements for the design and operation of state budgetary laws, and gave formal recognition to a new governance framework—the so-called "European semester," informally set up in 2010[39]—in which member states submit their draft budgets to the Commission for evaluation and discussion about their compliance with the broader economic forecasts of the EU.

Following on this line of reform, a second set of EU regulations—generally referred to as the "two-pack"[40]—adopted in May 2013, compelled member states to establish independent national authorities—so-called fiscal councils—entrusted with the task of controlling the quality of the economic forecasts of national governments.[41] Moreover, it required that member states submit their draft budget bills to the European Commission for prior assessment of their compliance with the reinforced SGP.[42] Pursuant to this innovation, that integrates the "European semester," national governments are required to present to the European Commission a draft of their budget bills in September of every year—even before the text is tabled for debate and approval in national Parliaments—and the Commission may demand member states to introduce changes to their budgetary bills within three weeks if these appear to be grossly in deviation of EU standards of budgetary performance.[43] As Roland Bieber has argued "[t]he common denominator of those acts is a *reduction* of Member States' competence in matters of general economic policy and a resulting transfer to the Union."[44]

[39] See European Council Conclusions, June 17, 2010, EUCO 13/10, 5.

[40] See Regulation (EU) No. 473/2013 of May 21, 2013 of the European Parliament and the Council on monitoring and assessing draft budgetary plans and ensuring the correction of excessive deficits in euro-area member states [2013] OJ L140/11; Regulation (EU) No. 472/2013 of May 21, 2013 of the European Parliament and the Council on enhanced surveillance of euro-area member states experiencing or threatened with serious difficulties with respect to their financial stability [2013] OJ L140/1.

[41] See Elena Griglio and Cristina Fasone, "Can Fiscal Councils Enhance the Role of National Parliaments in the European Union? A Comparative Analysis" in Bruno de Witte et al (eds), *The Euro Crisis and the State of European Democracy* (European University Institute Press 2014), 264 (analyzing fiscal councils).

[42] See also Alicia Hinarejos, *The Euro Area Crisis in Constitutional Perspective* (OUP 2015) 32.

[43] See Art 7(2) Regulation (EU) No. 473/2013 (stating that "where, in exceptional cases, after consulting the Member State concerned within one week of submission of the draft budgetary plan, the Commission identifies particularly serious non-compliance with the budgetary policy obligations laid down in the SGP, the Commission shall adopt its opinion within two weeks of submission of the draft budgetary plan. In its opinion, the Commission shall request that a revised draft budgetary plan be submitted as soon as possible and in any event within three weeks of the date of its opinion.").

[44] Roland Bieber, "The Allocation of Economic Policy Competences in the European Union," in Loïc Azoulai (ed), *The Question of Competence in the European Union* (OUP 2015), 86, 92 (emphasis in original).

Besides the reform introduced through EU legislation, another major step toward centralization in EMU, however, has resulted from measures adopted by the member states outside the framework of EU law.[45] Already in March 2011, a plurality of member states acting on the side of the European Council, adopted the Euro Plus Pact, a non-binding declaration which encouraged member states to enhance the sustainability of public finances by translating EU fiscal rules into national legislation.[46] As mentioned above then, most EU member states agreed to sign, in March 2012, a binding international treaty—the Fiscal Compact—which further overhauled the EU architecture of economic governance.[47] The overall objective of the Fiscal Compact, as stated in the preamble, is to reaffirm "the need for governments to maintain sound and sustainable public finances and to prevent a general government deficit [from] becoming excessive [...in order] to safeguard the stability of the euro area as a whole."[48] In particular, in order to ensure fiscal sustainability, the Fiscal Compact requires "the introduction [at the state level] of specific rules, including a 'balanced budget rule' and an automatic mechanism to take corrective action."[49]

The core provision of the Fiscal Compact, Article 3, introduces an obligation for the Contracting Parties to respect the "golden rule" of a balanced budget in every fiscal year.[50] Article 3(1)(a) codifies the general rule by stating that "the budgetary position of the general government of a Contracting Party shall be balanced or in surplus."[51] This rule is further specified by Article 3(1)(b), which states that the rule shall be deemed to be respected if the "annual structural balance of the general government" (to be intended as "the annual cyclically-adjusted balance net of one-off and temporary measures")[52] is "with a lower limit of a structural deficit of 0.5% of [GDP] at market prices."[53] The European Commission is empowered to indicate country-specific objectives to ensure a sustainable convergence path toward this standard.[54] Article 3(1)(c) then introduces an exception to the "golden rule," stating that "the Contracting Parties may temporarily deviate from [the rule] only in exceptional circumstances," defined in Article 3(3)(b) as "an unusual event outside the control of the Contracting Party concerned which has a major impact on the financial position of the general government or to periods of severe economic downturn."[55] Finally, Article 3(1)(e) sets up corrective mechanisms to be automatically triggered "in the event of significant observed deviations from the medium-term objective or the adjustment path towards it."[56]

[45] See Steve Peers, "The Stability Treaty: Permanent Austerity or Gesture Politics?" (2012) 8 European Constitutional Law Review 404 and Javier Garcia Roca and Miguel Martinez Lago, *Estabilidad presupuestaria y consagración del freno constitucional al endeudamiento* (Civitas 2013).

[46] See European Council Conclusions, March 24/25, 2011, EUCO 10/1/11, Annex 1, para c.

[47] See text accompanying nn 8–10.

[48] Pmbl. (third recital) Fiscal Compact.

[49] Ibid.

[50] See Craig (n 8) 231. See also Rita Perez, "Il Trattato di Bruxelles e il Fiscal Compact" [2012] Giornale di diritto amministrativo 469.

[51] Art 3(1)(a) Fiscal Compact.

[52] Art 3(3)(a) Fiscal Compact.

[53] Art 3(1)(b) Fiscal Compact.

[54] Ibid.

[55] Arts 3(1)(c)–(b) Fiscal Compact.

[56] Art 3(1)(e) Fiscal Compact.

The Article 3 "golden rule" is, upon ratification, binding for the signatory parties as an obligation deriving from international law.[57] Nevertheless, the Fiscal Compact goes further than traditional international law and, with a rather unconventional step, requires the Contracting Parties to incorporate the "golden rule" in the domestic legal system with a specific source of law: constitutional law or other supra-legislative sources of law.[58] According to Article 3(2), in fact:

> [t]he rules set out in paragraph 1 shall take effect in the national law of the Contracting Parties at the latest one year after the entry into force of this Treaty through provisions of binding force and permanent character, preferably constitutional, or otherwise guaranteed to be fully respected and adhered to throughout the national budgetary processes. The Contracting Parties shall put in place at national level the correction mechanism referred to in paragraph 1(e) on the basis of common principles to be proposed by the European Commission.[59]

The Fiscal Compact, hence, requires states to enact the "golden rule" in the state constitutions or—where this would be substantially impossible due to difficulties in amending a constitution—in special domestic sources of law that are hierarchically superior to ordinary acts of Parliament and that can work as benchmarks for the constitutional review of budgetary laws.[60]

To ensure that the Contracting Parties comply with the obligation to adopt the "golden rule" at the constitutional—or quasi-constitutional—level in their domestic legal systems, the Fiscal Compact sets up a mechanism of judicial enforcement centered on the EU Court of Justice (ECJ).[61] According to Article 8:

> [t]he European Commission is invited to present in due time to the Contracting Parties a report on the provisions adopted by each of them in compliance with Article 3(2). If the European Commission, after having given the Contracting Party concerned the opportunity to submit its observations, concludes in its report that such Contracting Party has failed to comply with Article 3(2), the matter will be brought to the [ECJ] by one or more Contracting Parties. Where a Contracting Party considers, independently of the Commission's report, that another Contracting Party has failed to comply with Article 3(2), it may also bring the matter to the [ECJ]. In both cases, the judgment of the [ECJ]

[57] Although functionally connected to EU law, the Fiscal Compact does not seem to enjoy the supremacy and direct effect of EU law. See generally Bruno de Witte, "Direct Effect, Supremacy and the Nature of the Legal Order" in Paul Craig and Gráinne de Búrca (eds), *The Evolution of EU Law* (OUP 1999), 177 (explaining the legal status of EU law).

[58] See also Gianni Bonvicini and Flavio Brugnoli (eds), "Il Fiscal Compact," Centro Studi sul Federalismo & Instituto Affari Internazionali, September 2012.

[59] See Art 3(2) Fiscal Compact.

[60] The possibility to incorporate the golden rule through a sub-constitutional, but supra-legislative, domestic source of law is a concession that was made in the latest drafts of the Fiscal Compact. See further Valentin Kreilinger, "The Making of a New Treaty: Six Rounds of Political Bargaining," Notre Europe Policy Brief No. 32/2012.

[61] The possibility of employing the ECJ, an EU institution, in the context of the Fiscal Compact, which is technically an international treaty adopted by 25 EU member states outside the framework of the EU, is supported by Art 273 TFEU, which allows the ECJ to "have jurisdiction in any dispute between Member States which relates to the subject matter of the Treaties if the dispute is submitted to it under a special agreement between the parties."

shall be binding on the parties to the proceedings, which shall take the necessary measures to comply with the judgment within a period to be decided by the [ECJ].[62]

If a party does not comply with the first decision of the ECJ, then a second case can be brought before the ECJ which may impose on the disobedient state "a lump sum or a penalty payment appropriate in the circumstances and that shall not exceed 0.1% of its [GDP]."[63] Moreover, as clarified in the preamble of the Fiscal Compact, the possibility for EMU countries to receive financial assistance under the new European Stability Mechanism (ESM) will be conditional "as soon as the transposition period referred to in Article 3(2) of [the Fiscal Compact] has expired, on compliance with the requirements of that Article."[64]

In conclusion, the legal reforms adopted in the aftermath of the Euro-crisis have established a pervasive legal regime to tighten the budgetary policies of the member states. In particular, the Fiscal Compact has identified the constitutionalization of budgetary constraints as the solution for the sovereign debt crisis faced by the Eurozone.[65] First, the Fiscal Compact provides a very detailed and technical "golden rule," which defines in strict mathematical terms the yearly structural deficit permitted in every member state and specifies conditions for disrespecting the rule, as well as automatic mechanisms to ensure compliance.[66] Second, the Fiscal Compact—breaking with the tradition of ordinary international law, which leaves member states free to choose the domestic means to give effect to the commitments undertaken at the international level—obliges the Contracting Parties to incorporate the "golden rule" in state constitutions or in other sources of law which bind the ordinary budgetary process.[67] Third, the Fiscal Compact sets up an intrusive enforcement mechanism, which authorizes Contracting Parties to bring cases against non-compliant states before the ECJ and empowers the ECJ to sanction disobedient states with substantial financial penalties.[68]

From a purely formalist perspective, one could argue that the EU member states which decided to sign the Fiscal Compact did so out of an autonomous decision: under international law, states freely choose whether to subject themselves to external constraints.[69] Yet, such a reading fails to capture the reality of peer pressure existing in the framework of EMU governance (a feature on which I will return in Chapter 3). The adoption of the Fiscal Compact was strongly promoted by Germany.[70] In fact, as made clear by the preamble of the Fiscal Compact,

[62] Art 8(1) Fiscal Compact. [63] Art 8(2) Fiscal Compact.

[64] Pmbl. (twenty-seventh recital) Fiscal Compact.

[65] See Editorial Comments (n 12) 1–3. [66] See Art 3(1) Fiscal Compact.

[67] See Art 3(2) Fiscal Compact. [68] See Art 8 Fiscal Compact.

[69] See Nikos Skoutaris, "On Sovereign Debt Crisis and Sovereignty: A Constitutional Law Perspective on the Greek Crisis," paper presented at the 20th International Conference of Europeanists on "Crisis and Contingency: States of (In)stability," Amsterdam, June 25, 2013 (on file with author).

[70] See also Leonard Besselink and Jan Herman Reestman, Editorial: "The Fiscal Compact and the European Constitutions: 'Europe Speaking German'" (2012) 8 European Constitutional Law Review 1.

introduction of, and compliance with, the "golden rule" was made a condition to obtain financial assistance under the ESM.[71] As a result of this, for many EU member states the choice whether to conclude the Fiscal Compact was formal at best: given the need, or the expectation to need, financial assistance to face speculations on the international markets, many Eurozone states were effectively compelled to sign the treaty. From this point of view, therefore, the Fiscal Compact reflects a top-down approach to Euro-crisis management. Given the sweeping nature of the Fiscal Compact, it is worth exploring the legal source that has been taken as a model for the "golden rule" of the Fiscal Compact and examine the challenges that its incorporation raised in several key EU member states.[72]

B. Germany

Given the prominent role Germany has played in managing the Eurozone crisis and requiring that EMU states enact tighter budgetary constraints in exchange for greater financial solidarity, it is not a surprise that Article 3 of the Fiscal Compact largely copies the "golden rule" that Germany enacted in its Basic Law in July 2009.[73] In the context of a broader reform of the German federal system, the so-called Föderalismusreform II introduced a number of relevant amendments to the Finanzwesen, the chapter of the Basic Law dedicated to the fiscal relationship between the Bund and the Länder.[74] In particular, the new Article 109 of the Basic Law, besides reaffirming the budgetary autonomy of the Federation and the Länder, and noting their joint responsibility in the maintenance of the budgetary discipline set at the EU level in the SGP, states the general rule that:

> [t]he budgets of the Federation and the Länder shall in principle be balanced without revenue from credits. The Federation and Länder may introduce rules intended to take into account, symmetrically in times of upswing and downswing, the effects of market developments that deviate from normal conditions, as well as exceptions for natural disasters or unusual emergency situations beyond governmental control and substantially harmful to the state's financial capacity. For such exceptional regimes, a corresponding amortisation plan must be adopted.[75]

The content of the "golden rule" is further specified, as far as the German federal government is concerned, in Article 115(2) of the Basic Law, which states

[71] See Pmbl. (twenty-seventh recital) Fiscal Compact.

[72] On the constitutionalization of Euopean budgetary constraints in the five member states examined hereinafter, see also Giacomo Delledonne, "A Legalization of Financial Constitutions in the EU? Reflections on the German, Spanish, Italian and French Experiences" in Federico Fabbini et al (eds), *The Constitutionalization of European Budgetary Constraints* (Hart Publishing 2014), 181 and Michal Diamant and Michiel van Emmerik, "Mandatory Balanced Budget in Dutch Legislation Following Examples Abroad?," in Federico Fabbini et al (eds), *The Constitutionalization of European Budgetary Constraints* (Hart Publishing 2014), 249.

[73] See Gesetz zur Änderung des Grundgesetz (Artikel 91c, 91d, 104b, 109, 109a, 115, 143d), BGBl. I S. 2248 (Nr. 48), July 29, 2009 (Ger.).

[74] See Lars P. Feld and Thushyanthan Baskaran, "Federalism, Budget Deficits and Public Debt: On the Reform of Germany's Fiscal Constitution" (2010) 6 Review of Law and Economics 365, 384–5.

[75] Art 109 Basic L. Ger.

that "[r]evenues and expenditures shall in principle be balanced without revenue from credits," and clarifies that "[t]his principle shall be satisfied when revenue obtained by the borrowing of funds does not exceed 0.35% in relation to the nominal [GDP]."[76] This provision thus sets a more restrictive deficit brake than the 0.5% allowed by Article 3(1)(b) of the Fiscal Compact.[77] The strict "golden rule" is mitigated, however, by the possibility of taking into account symmetrical periods of upswing and downswing "when economic developments deviate from normal conditions," and allowing for minor deviations on the basis of the economic cycle.[78] In addition, the balanced budget requirement is accompanied by an exception clause which largely anticipated the one later enshrined in Article 3(3)(b) of the Fiscal Compact.[79] Thus, "[i]n cases of natural catastrophes or unusual emergency situations beyond governmental control and substantially harmful to the state's financial capacity, these credit limits may be exceeded [...] by a majority" decision of the members of the Bundestag, the lower house of the federal Parliament.[80] "The decision has to be combined with an amortisation plan."[81] The 1949 Basic Law, as amended in 2009, therefore, is endowed with a very comprehensive and technically detailed balanced budget requirement that Germany decided autonomously to enact to ensure compliance with its EMU obligations, and to safeguard the sustainability of public finances.[82]

C. Spain

Even before serving as a model for the Fiscal Compact, the German example was used as a source of inspiration for constitutional reform in Spain.[83] As the interest rates of Spanish sovereign bonds were beginning to skyrocket in the summer of 2011, the incumbent Spanish government rushed through Parliament a constitutional amendment aimed at establishing a balanced budget requirement and

[76] Art 115(2) Basic L. Ger.
[77] Compare Art 115(2) Basic L. Ger. with Art 3 Fiscal Compact.
[78] Art 115(2) Basic L. Ger.
[79] Compare Art 115(2) Basic L. Ger. with Art 3(3)(b) Fiscal Compact.
[80] Art 115(2) Basic L. Ger. [81] Ibid.
[82] See Christian Mayer, "Greift die Neue Schuldenbremse?" (2011) 136 Archiv des öffentlichen Rechts 266. In light of the analysis of the "golden rule" in the Basic Law, and of the direct influence that this provision has played in the drafting of the Fiscal Compact, it is ironic that the German government decided to ratify the Fiscal Compact with a two-thirds parliamentary majority, as if the Fiscal Compact was introducing a new amendment to the Basic Law. See "Testing the Limits: Even Germany Has Constitutional Worries About More European Integration," *The Economist*, March 25, 2012, 31. As has been suggested, the decision to opt for qualified majority voting may be driven by the desire to "impress" the increasingly euro-skeptic German Constitutional Court, which was ultimately empowered to decide whether the Fiscal Compact was compatible with the Basic Law or required a constitutional revision to be ratified. In its decision of September 12, 2012, the German Constitutional Court eventually validated the constitutionality of the Fiscal Compact, and simultaneously upheld the ESM Treaty's compatibility with the Basic Law. See Bundesverfassungsgericht, BVerfG No. 2 BvR 1390/12 et al, judgment (preliminary measures) of September 12, 2012. On this decision, see further Chapter 2.
[83] See Victor Mallet, "Spanish MPs Approve Debt Limit," *The Financial Times*, September 2, 2011.

allegedly reassuring the financial markets.[84] The new Article 135 of the Spanish Constitution—which was approved with bipartisan support in both chambers of the legislature in less than two weeks and entered into force on September 27, 2011[85]—now affirms, in its first two paragraphs, that "[a]ll public administrations will conform their actions to the principle of budgetary stability. The State and the Autonomous Communities shall not incur a structural deficit that exceeds the standard established by the EU."[86] A numerical indication of the maximum structural deficit in relation to the GDP for both the State and the Autonomous Communities is not directly provided by the Spanish Constitution, but will be specified in a ley organica, a special source of law with infra-constitutional but supra-legislative status, which the Congresso de los Diputados approves by an absolute majority.[87] Together with the deficit brake, the reform entrenches in the Spanish Constitution the limits of the SGP on public debt.[88] According to Article 135(3), "the total volume of debt of the public administrations with reference to the GDP shall not exceed the reference value established in the TFEU."[89]

Also in Spain, the "golden rule" of a balanced budget is subject to an exception clause.[90] Article 135(4) states that:

> [t]he limits of the structural deficit and of the volume of public debt can only be exceeded in cases of natural catastrophes, economic recession or situations of extraordinary emergency beyond the control of the State which considerably endanger the financial situation or the economic and social sustainability of the State, to be assessed by the absolute majority of the members of the Chamber of Deputies.[91]

While the Spanish constitutional reform left the task to develop the principles established in new Article 135 of the Spanish Constitution to an organic law,[92] it can be argued that the 2011 amendment largely anticipates the obligations of the Fiscal Compact and may thus be regarded as compatible with the "golden rule" which is therein established.[93] Article 135 of the Spanish Constitution

[84] See generally Enrique Alvarez Conde, "La Reforma de l'Articulo 135 CE" [2011] Revista española de derecho constitucional 159 (analyzing the reforms to Art 135 and its impact on the Spanish Constitution).

[85] Reforma del artículo 135 de la Constitución Española, B.O.E. n. 233, November 27, 2011 (Sp.).

[86] Art 135 Const. Sp. (author's translation) ("Todas las Administraciones Públicas adecuarán sus actuaciones al principio de estabilidad presupuestaria. El Estado y las Comunidades Autónomas no podrán incurrir en un déficit estructural que supere los márgenes establecidos, en su caso, por la Union Europea [...]").

[87] See Arts 81 and 135(2) Const. Sp.

[88] See Art 135 Const. Sp.

[89] Art 135(3) Const. Sp. (author's translation) ("El volumen de deuda pública del conjunto de las Administraciones Públicas en relación con el producto interior bruto del Estado no podrá superar el valor de referencia establecido en el TFUE.").

[90] See ibid.

[91] Art 135(4) Const. Sp. (author's translation) ("Los límites de déficit estructural y de volumen de deuda pública sólo podrán superarse en caso de catástrofes naturales, recesión económica o situaciones de emergencia extraordinaria que escapen al control del Estado y perjudiquen considerablemente la situación financiera o la sostenibilidad económica o social del Estado, apreciadas por la mayoría absoluta de los miembros del Congreso de los Diputados.").

[92] See now Ley orgánica 2/2012, B.O.E. n. 103, April 30, 2012 (Sp.).

[93] Compare Art 135 Const. Sp. with Art 3 Fiscal Compact.

dynamically refers to the deficit and debt limits set up at the EU level, and can thus easily be adapted to the new, stricter requirements imposed by the Fiscal Compact.[94] Moreover, through the enactment of an organic law, the balanced budget rule of the Spanish Constitution can be further specified with technical criteria.[95] Accordingly, it would seem that no additional measures would be needed at the constitutional level for Spain to implement domestically the Fiscal Compact.[96]

D. France

The constitutional situation of Spain contrasts with that of France.[97] France has not amended its 1958 Constitution to establish a balanced budget requirement.[98] A constitutional reform bill was introduced in Parliament by the (center-right) government on March 16, 2011 and approved in the same wording, after several readings, by the Assemblée Nationale and the Sénat on July 13, 2011.[99] To enter into force, however, the constitutional amendment would have required either a vote of approval by the two chambers of Parliament sitting jointly in Congress, or by the electorate in a referendum.[100] Nevertheless, the changes in the government after the election of May 2012 have ended any prospect of constitutional reform.[101] Moreover, it is doubtful whether the proposed constitutional reform would have been fully consistent with the strict requirements of the Fiscal Compact.[102]Arguably,

[94] See also Tribunal Constitucional, judgment no. 134/2011 of July 20, 2011 (holding that the principle of budgetary stability has constitutional foundation).

[95] See Delledonne (n 72) 188.

[96] A different matter concerns the Spanish government's compliance with the new fiscal rules. See recently European Commission Opinion on the draft budgetary plan of Spain, October 12, 2015, C(2015) 6892 final, para 15 (holding that Spain's draft budget for 2016 is at risk of non-compliance with EU deficit rules, and asking the government to take the necessary measures as soon as possible to make the budget plan compliant).

[97] See Delledonne (n 72) 190.

[98] See generally Michel Bouvier et al, "L'introduction de la 'Règle d'Or' budgetaire dans la Constitution" [2011] Constitutions 23 (reporting the opinion of academics and parliamentarians on the constitutional reform bill).

[99] Helene Fouquet, "French Lawmakers Endorse Constitutional Rule on Balanced Budgets," *Bloomberg News*, July 13, 2011.

[100] See Art 89 Const. Fr.

[101] The new French President, François Hollande of the Socialist Party, during the spring 2012 presidential campaign, expressed his intention to renegotiate the Fiscal Compact if elected. See Steven Erlanger and Nicholas Kulish, "French Front-Runner Says He'd Seek to Renegotiate Fiscal Treaty if Elected," *New York Times*, April 26, 2012, A8. Incidentally it may also be noticed that the Fiscal Compact—breaking also on this account with the established tradition in the EU—requires the approval of only 12 states for its entry into force, rather than unanimity. See Art 14(2) Fiscal Compact. The reason for introducing this rule was to avoid the veto of those member states where the ratification or implementation of the Fiscal Compact might have been more troublesome. France, which rejected key European treaties in 1954 and 2005, is certainly one of the countries where the risk of a "no-vote" on the Fiscal Compact could be significant. See Carlos Closa Montero, "Moving Away from Unanimity: Ratification of the Treaty on Stability, Coordination and Governance in the Economic and Monetary Union," Reconstituting Democracy in Europe Working Paper No. 38/2011.

[102] See Projet de loi constitutionelle du 13 juillet 2011 relatif a l'equilibre des finances publiques, Assemblée Nationale, July 13, 2011 (Fr.) available at <http://www.assemblee-nationale.fr/13/ta/ta0722.asp> (last accessed May 30, 2014).

the proposed amendment to the French Constitution would have only introduced a "golden rule lite." According to the proposed new Article 34(20) of the French Constitution, the objective of strengthening budgetary constraints was ensured through the enactment of a new source of law—called lois-cadres d'équilibre des finances publiques, or framework laws on the equilibrium of public finance—which determined "the multi-annual orientations, the norms of evolution and the management rules of the public finances, with the goal to assure the equilibrium of the budget of the public administrations" for at least three years.[103] The framework laws on the equilibrium of public finance were expected to dictate the fiscal standards to be followed in enacting the yearly budgetary law, and—as clarified by the proposed new Article 47(1) of the French Constitution—no budget could be approved in the absence of a framework law applicable to the fiscal year concerned.[104] Furthermore, according to the prospective Article 61(2) of the French Constitution, the French Conseil Constitutionnel would have had to review budgetary laws every year "before their entry into force"[105] for their compatibility with the loi-cadres d'équilibre des finances publiques.[106]

As this summary reveals, significant differences existed between the provisions of the proposed amendment to the French Constitution and the rules of the Fiscal Compact.[107] The French reform did not codify a clear rule to prevent government deficit or impose a yearly balanced budget.[108] By devising a new legal instrument—the framework laws—the constitutional reform bill would have only established a flexible duty for the government to ensure fiscal equilibrium over a three-year span.[109] The indeterminacy of this obligation explains the absence of exception clauses analogous to those in the Fiscal Compact, the German Basic Law, and the Spanish Constitution. Moreover, according to draft Article 46-1 of the French Constitution, the conditions for approval of the framework law had to be set in a loi organique—an organic law to be approved by absolute majority of the National Assembly[110]—thus granting the governing majority wide room to modulate the effects of the budgetary constraints on the basis of other political incentives.[111] All in all, it would seem that the French project of constitutional reform was not in line with the developments which have subsequently occurred in the EU through the enactment of the Fiscal Compact.[112] Be that as it may, however, the new (center-left) French government eventually abandoned the prospect of a constitutional reform to incorporate the Fiscal Compact in domestic

[103] See ibid Art 1, draft amendment of Art 34(20) Const. Fr. (author's translation) ("pour au moins trois années, les orientations pluriannuelles, les normes d'évolution et les règles de gestion des finances publiques, en vue d'assurer l'équilibre des comptes des administrations publiques.").

[104] Ibid Art 5(1), draft amendment of Art 47(1) Const. Fr.

[105] Ibid Art 10(2), draft amendment of Art 61(2) Const. Fr. (author's translation) ("avant leur promulgation.")

[106] Ibid.

[107] See text accompanying nn 48–68.

[108] See Delledonne (n 72) 190.

[109] See Art 1, Projet de loi constitutionelle, draft amendment of Art 34(20) Const. Fr.

[110] See Art 46 Const. Fr.

[111] See Art 4, Projet de loi constitutionelle, draft amendment of Art 46-1 Const. Fr.

[112] See Art 3(2) Fiscal Compact.

law. Instead, it opted for the enactment of a loi organique,[113] as permitted by the Fiscal Compact itself.[114]

E. Italy

Contrary to the high level of politicization that has characterized the proposal to amend the Constitution to introduce tighter budgetary rules in France, the reform of the 1948 Italian Constitution to enshrine the "golden rule" has been notable for the high level of political consensus among parties—an unusual phenomenon in a country which is otherwise characterized by extremely polarized and litigious political elites.[115] The peculiar conditions that led to the creation of the Monti government in November 2011, at the height of the speculative attack against the Italian sovereign bonds, may explain the widespread support that the proposal to introduce the "golden rule" in the Italian Constitution has received from political parties in both chambers of Parliament.[116] The constitutional revision bill to amend the budgetary provisions of the Italian Constitution was originally sponsored by the Berlusconi government.[117] Yet, the Monti government explicitly endorsed the proposal while in office, identifying the amendment as an important commitment Italy had to undertake vis-à-vis its EU partners.[118] This ensured speedy approval both in the Camera dei deputati and in the Senato, which are required to vote twice on the same text at a distance of three months between the first and the second reading,[119] and the Constitutional Revision Act was signed into law on April 20, 2012.[120]

The new Article 81 of the Italian Constitution provides that:

> [t]he State ensures the balance between revenue and expenditures in its budget, considering the upswings and the downswings of the economic cycle. The State can resort to the emission of debt only with the purpose to consider the effects of the economic cycle and,

[113] See now Loi organique no. 2012–1403 du 17 décembre 2012 relative à la programmation et à la gouvernance des finances publiques, J.O.R.F. n°294 du 18 décembre 2012 p. 19816 (Fr.).

[114] Note that the President of the French Republic submitted to the Constitutional Council a request pursuant to Art 54 Const. Fr., to ask prospectively whether the ratification of the Fiscal Compact required a constitutional revision. See Conseil constitutionnel, Décision No. 2012-653DC, judgment of August 9, 2012. In its decision, the Constitutional Court replied that the ratification of the Treaty did not require a constitutional change and that the obligation to incorporate the "golden rule" in French law could be undertaken via the enactment of a loi organique. On this decision, see further Chapter 2.

[115] See Shoaib-ur-Rehman Siddiqui, "Italy approves balanced-budget amendment to constitution," *Business Recorder*, April 18, 2012.

[116] See Michael Schuman, "The Most Important Man in Europe," *Time*, February 20, 2012, 28, 30 (describing the economic conditions that led to the creation of the Monti government).

[117] See Siddiqui (n 115).

[118] See generally Daniele Cabras, "L'introduzione del principio del c.d. pareggio di bilancio: una regola importante per la stabilizzazione della finanza pubblica" [2012] Quaderni Costituzionali 111 (discussing the constitutional reforms in Italy).

[119] See Art 138 Const. It.

[120] See Legge Costituzionale 20 aprile 2012, n. 1, in G. U. del 23 aprile 2012, n. 95 (It.).

upon authorization of the two chambers of Parliament adopted at the absolute majority of its members, in cases of exceptional events.[121]

Article 81 of the Italian Constitution then introduces a new source of law in the Italian legal system, modelled on the Spanish ley organica and the French loi organique, empowering Parliament to adopt, at the absolute majority of its members, a special budgetary statute.[122] The statute is designed to establish "[t]he content of the budgetary laws, the fundamental norms and the criteria to ensure the balance between the revenues and the expenditures of the budget and the sustainability of the debt of all public administrations."[123] The obligation of a balanced budget is then extended, by the new Article 119 of the Italian Constitution, to the Regions, which are required to "ensure respect of the economic and financial constraints deriving from the European Union."[124] Overall, the constitutional amendment of the Constitution strengthens Italy's commitment toward budgetary discipline.[125] Nevertheless, it could be argued that, because of their rather generic formulation, the new constitutional provisions do not entirely incorporate the "golden rule" of the Fiscal Compact.[126] Despite these discrepancies, Parliament fulfilled the requirement of the Fiscal Compact in enacting the special statute required by Article 81 of the Italian Constitution.[127] Yet, at the moment, the effects of this new special statute remain uncertain, and much will also depend on the functioning of the new fiscal council—the Ufficio parlamentare di bilancio—which the law created in execution of the EU mandate.[128]

F. The Netherlands

The incorporation of the Fiscal Compact produced, finally, special challenges in the Netherlands. As Michal Diamant and Michiel van Emmerik have explained,[129] the Dutch constitutional system presents a number of particularities that put it at odds with the other EU member states which were previously analyzed in this chapter. To begin with, the Dutch Constitution can be amended only through a burdensome revision process, which requires the double approval by super-majorities in both houses of Parliament, with an election between each

[121] Art 81 Const. It. (author's translation) ("Lo Stato assicura l'equilibrio tra le entrate e le spese del proprio bilancio, tenendo conto delle fasi avverse e delle fasi favorevoli del ciclo economico. Il ricorso all'indebitamento è consentito solo al fine di considerare gli effetti del ciclo economico e, previa autorizzazione delle Camere adottata a maggioranza assoluta dei rispettivi componenti, al verificarsi di eventi eccezionali.").

[122] See Art 81(6) Const. It.

[123] Ibid (author's translation) ("Il contenuto della legge di bilancio, le norme fondamentali e i criteri volti ad assicurare l'equilibrio tra le entrate e le spese dei bilanci e la sostenibilità del debito del complesso delle pubbliche amministrazioni [...]").

[124] Art 119 Const. It. (author's translation) ("assicurare l'osservanza dei vincoli economici e finanziari derivanti dall'ordinamento dell'Unione europea.").

[125] See Cabras (n 118).

[126] Compare Art 81 Const. It. with Art 3(2) Fiscal Compact.

[127] See Legge 24 dicembre 2012, n. 243 in G. U. del 15 gennaio 2013, n. 12 (It.).

[128] See Giuseppe Pisauro, "Le valutazioni sulla legge di stabilità del Fiscal Council" [2015] Astrid Rassegna 1.

[129] See Diamant and van Emmerik (n 72) 249.

vote.[130] Moreover, the Dutch Constitution is one of the few high laws which still prohibits judicial review of legislation, reflecting a profound distrust on the role of courts in reining in the political process—and simultaneously a remarkable faith in the capacity of parliamentary institutions to curb their excesses.[131] Yet, the Dutch Constitution is also one of the most open toward international law, recognizing the supremacy of international law over conflicting domestic law, and delegating to the judiciary the task to ensure compliance of Dutch legislation with international commitments.[132]

Because of these peculiarities, in early 2013 the Dutch government proposed to give effect to the "golden rule" mandated by the Fiscal Compact through an ordinary piece of legislation—the Wet Houdbare Overheidsfinanciën (Wet HOF)—which was approved by the Lower House of the Dutch Parliament in April 2013 and by the Senate in November 2013, entering into force on December 11, 2013.[133] Article 2 of the Wet HOF codifies the balanced budget rule, stating that the national budgetary policy must be exercised "taking into account i. the MTO [medium term objective] applicable for structural EMU balance; ii. the EU legal standards on the deficit; iii. the EU legal standards for the actual EMU debt."[134] Moreover, the statute introduces an automatic correction mechanism, which will enter into effect if the national budgetary policy is not sufficient to achieve the MTO.[135] Finally, it establishes that local governments are also required to comply with European budgetary rules.[136] Because the Wet HOF is an ordinary act of Parliament approved as a normal budget bill, its legal status seems to be inconsistent with the requirement of the Fiscal Compact.[137] The Wet HOF will not be legally binding on any future Dutch government, which will remain able to replace it with a simple majority. Furthermore, the lack of judicial review in the Netherlands prevents courts from playing any role in enforcing the balance budget rule. In fact, the Netherlands has recently failed, repeatedly, to meet the deficit standards set in the SGP.[138]

Yet, because, as mentioned, in the Dutch legal order duly ratified international treaties have a higher rank than domestic norms,[139] the Netherlands may still find a way to end up in compliance with the Fiscal Compact. Besides proposing new fiscal legislation in the form of the Wet HOF, the Dutch

[130] See Art 137 Const. NI. (regulating the revision process).

[131] See Maurice Adams and Gerhard van der Schyff, "Judicial Review by the Judiciary in the Netherlands: A Matter of Politics, Democracy or Compensating Strategy?" (2006) 66 Zeitschrift für ausländisches öffentliches Recht und Völkerrecht 399.

[132] See Arts 93-4 Const. NI. (granting supremacy to international treaties and mandating compliance with them).

[133] See Wet van 11 december 2013, *Stb.* 2013, 531 (Nl.).

[134] See Art 2(3) Wet HOF (author's translation) ("met inachtneming van: i) de geldende MTO voor het structureel EMU-saldo; ii) de binnen de Europese Unie geldende norm voor het feitelijk EMU-saldo; iii) de binnen de Europese Unie geldende norm voor de feitelijke EMU-schuld.").

[135] See Art 2(4)-(6) Wet HOF.

[136] See Art 3 Wet HOF.

[137] Compare Art 1 Wet HOF with Art 3 Fiscal Compact.

[138] See also Jorick Straatman, "The incorporation of the Fiscal Compact in the legal system of the Netherlands," Tilburg Law School unpublished LLM thesis, 2013.

[139] See also Erika de Wet, "Belgium and the Netherlands," in Alec Stone Sweet & Hellen Keller (eds.), *A Europe of Rights* (OUP 2009), 229.

government also advanced legislation to ratify the Fiscal Compact—and the Staten-Generaal approved the treaty in October 2013.[140] As a duly ratified treaty, the Fiscal Compact now operates as a constraint on the action of the Dutch government—and domestic courts could in theory review compliance with the treaty: although this seems unlikely, and compliance with budget rules will be mainly a question for political competition,[141] the Netherlands has formally met the requirement of domesticating the "golden rule" as a limit on the budgetary policy of the government.[142]

3. Institutional Implications

As the previous section has explained, the introduction of the "golden rule" in the Fiscal Compact was anticipated by the enactment of tight budgetary constraints in Germany[143] and Spain.[144] Similarly, the prospect of the enactment of the Fiscal Compact has worked as a powerful incentive for completing constitutional revision in Italy,[145] enacting quasi-constitutional norms in France,[146] and passing new legislation in the Netherlands.[147] Leaving aside the question whether all these state provisions are fully consistent with the detailed obligations of the Fiscal Compact, an overview of the major economies of the Eurozone reveals a consistent trend toward the constitutionalization of budgetary rules.[148] In light of this, this section discusses the institutional implications of the adoption of the "golden rule" on the internal system of the EU member states—as well as on the relationship between the states and the EU institutions. Sub-section A focuses on the role of state executives and legislatures, analyzes how budgetary constraints affect the relationship between parliaments and cabinets, and suggests that the impact of the "golden rule" is likely to change in light of each state's form of government. Sub-section B focuses on the role of state courts, emphasizes how the introduction of the "golden rule" in state constitutional law will strengthen the role of courts throughout Europe, but hints that this development is bound to raise significant procedural challenges in several EU member states. As sub-section C explains, however, the constitutionalization of fiscal rules combined with the other recent EMU reforms is likely to have profound

[140] See Wet van 23 juni 2013, *Stb.* 2013, 290. *Trb.* 2012, 51 (Nl.).

[141] See Diamant and van Emmerik (n 72) 260.

[142] See also Jan Herman Reestman, "Constitutioneel minimalisme, het Stabiliteitsverdrag in de Nederlands rechtsorde" [2013] Tijdschrift voor Constitutioneel Recht 6, 19–20.

[143] See text accompanying nn 73–82.

[144] See text accompanying nn 83–96.

[145] See text accompanying nn 115–28.

[146] See text accompanying nn 97–114.

[147] See text accompanying nn 129–42.

[148] See also, for a broad confirmation of this conclusion, Antoš (n 27) 205, Papadopoulou (n 27) 223, O'Gorman (n 27) 273, Delledonne (n 72) 181, Diamant and van Emmerik (n 72) 249. Interestingly, in Spring 2015, the new Conservative Government in the UK also expressed its commitment to abide by a balanced budget rule, which is very similar to the one enshrined in the Fiscal Compact. See Chancellor of the Exchequer George Osborne, Speech, London, June 10, 2015 (stating that "in normal times, governments of the left as well as the right should run a budget surplus" and that legislation will be adopted "to entrench this permanent commitment to [budgetary] surplus").

implications on the vertical balance of powers in the EU: both the EU political and judicial institutions, in fact, will find themselves in a stronger position to guide and oversee the budgetary policies of the member states.

A. The role of state executives and legislatures

The existence of a balanced budget requirement in state constitutions (or other supra-legislative sources of laws) places an obligation on the political branches to devise budgetary laws that comply with the fiscal constraints of the state constitution.[149] As such, executives are expected to propose, and parliaments ultimately to approve, annual budget laws which are either at a surplus or on balance (or at worst have a deficit not exceeding that permitted by the Fiscal Compact). Generally speaking, these new legal constraints are likely to have an impact on the budgetary policies of various EU member states, notably in countries like Italy or Spain where political elites have traditionally been less concerned with the sustainability of public finances, and have repeatedly subsidized government spending by raising public debts.[150] Yet, besides the relevant cultural factors, it is likely that the impact of the "golden rule" on the role of the political branches of state governments will vary on the basis of the institutional features of the system of government of each member state.[151] In particular, the adoption of the "golden rule" will affect executives and legislatures and their relationship in different ways depending on the nature of the budgetary process in place in any given state.

In this regard, a crucial factor in explaining the implications of the "golden rule" is the role parliaments currently exercise in the budgetary process.[152] In comparative terms, parliaments can function either as decision-makers—with a sizeable role in designing the substance of the yearly budget—or as oversight bodies—with limited capacity to influence the drafting of the budget, but greater powers in overseeing its implementation.[153] Parliaments generally exercise a more prominent decision-making function in parliamentary systems in which executives do not enjoy political majorities and where the budget is the result of political bargaining between the cabinet and parliamentary leaders.[154] On the contrary, in semi-presidential systems and parliamentary systems in which executives have strong and obedient parliamentary majorities, parliaments largely exercise an *ex post* function in the budgetary process, which focuses on the oversight, mostly by

[149] See Kocharov (n 8) 5.

[150] See Carlo Bastasin, *Saving Europe: How National Politics Nearly Destroyed the Euro* (Brookings Institution Press 2012).

[151] See generally Maurice Duverger, *Institutions politiques et droit constitutionnel* (PUF 1978) and Giovanni Sartori, *Comparative Constitutional Engineering: An Inquiry into Structures, Incentives, and Outcomes* (NYU Press 1994) (comparing forms of government in different institutional regimes).

[152] See generally Ian Lienert, "Who Controls the Budget: The Legislature or the Executive?" International Monetary Fund Working Paper No. 115/2005 (explaining the various roles legislatures and executives play in budget-making).

[153] See ibid 7–8. [154] See ibid 9.

the opposition in parliament, of the execution of the budget by the cabinet.[155] In light of this distinction, it is plausible to maintain that, in the first institutional model, the introduction of a "golden rule" will likely strengthen the position of the executive branch vis-à-vis parliament.[156] In the second institutional context, however, the effects of the "golden rule" are less visible and more difficult to predict.[157] While the existence of balanced budget constraints is not likely to affect the role of the executives, it may provide instruments for parliamentary opposition to make its voice heard.

The EU member states considered in this chapter offer a broad spectrum of institutional settings which help empirically explain the institutional dynamics that the "golden rule" may trigger between executives and legislatures. For instance, in Italy, where the executive enjoys limited constitutional instruments to force Parliament to approve its budget,[158] the new Article 81 of the Italian Constitution may give the government a new means to close the debate on its budget proposal and force Parliament to vote its bill.[159] Similarly, in the fragmented party-system of the Netherlands, constraints set in the Fiscal Compact, albeit incorporated simply through ordinary legislation, may strengthen the role of the executive.[160] In the semi-presidential system created by the 1958 French Constitution, by contrast, the government—which, save during the so-called cohabitation, is under the full leadership of the directly elected President—already enjoys almost total control of the budgetary process.[161] Indeed, according to Article 49(3) of the French Constitution, the government may commit its political responsibility and consider a bill approved by Parliament without even submitting it to a vote.[162] In this context, the "golden rule" is unlikely to strengthen the position of the executive. Yet, it could perhaps give a new opportunity for the opposition in Parliament to control the activity of the executive by challenging a bill before the Conseil Constitutionnel.[163]

[155] See ibid 7–8, 11.

[156] See ibid 11. It goes without saying, at the same time, that the "golden rule" will also reduce the room for maneuvering by the executive, especially by limiting the capacity to spend to obtain political consensus. Ibid 13.

[157] See ibid 11–14.

[158] See Massimo Rubechi, "La sessione di bilancio in Parlamento: Governi in fuga," in Augusto Barbera and Tommaso Giupponi (eds), *La prassi degli organi costituzionali* (Bononia UP 2008), 269, 276–7, 282.

[159] See Art 81 Const. It. See also Nicola Lupo, "Le procedure di bilancio dopo l'ingresso nell'Unione economica e monetaria" [1999] Quaderni Costituzionali 523, 550–1.

[160] But see Arend Lijphart, *Patterns of Democracy* (Yale UP 1999) (emphasizing the consensual nature of decision-making in the Dutch political system).

[161] See Roger Chinaud, "Loi de finances: Quelle marge de manouvre pour le Parlement?" (1993) 64 Pouvoirs 99.

[162] Art 49(3) Const. Fr. (explaining that the legislature may only defy the executive's decision with a no-confidence vote).

[163] See Alec Stone, *The Birth of Judicial Politics in France: The Constitutional Council in Comparative Perspective* (OUP 1992) 120. In fact, as mentioned, the revision bill of the French Constitution aimed at entrenching the "golden rule" would have made the review of budgetary laws by the French Constitutional Council mandatory before the law's entry into force. See text accompanying nn 105–6.

The cases of Germany and Spain, finally, lay somewhere in between the Italian and French extremes. Both countries are parliamentary democracies in which the executives enjoy significant leeway in the budgetary process.[164] Yet, in both systems the government may be dependent on the political support of junior parties, increasing the difficulties it may face in imposing its budget on Parliament.[165] As a consequence, it seems likely that the "golden rule" will have either empowering or constraining effects on these countries' executive branches, depending on specific political factors.

B. The role of state courts

The "golden rule" constitutionalizes an obligation on executives to propose, and legislatures to approve, balanced budget laws yearly. Yet, it also invites courts to operate as guardians of fiscal discipline and comptrollers of the budgetary policies of the political branches: in Germany, Spain, Italy, and France, specialized constitutional courts are tasked to review compliance by the legislatures with the constitution;[166] and in the Netherlands, although courts are banned from reviewing the constitutionality of acts of Parliaments, they are simultaneously empowered to ensure their compliance with international treaties.[167] The increasing empowerment of state courts as a result of developments in EU law is in itself nothing new.[168] Many scholars have emphasized how EU law has consistently enhanced the institutional position of courts vis-à-vis the political branches of EU member states.[169] Nevertheless, whereas EU law has traditionally favored the position of ordinary judges, the introduction of the "golden rule" in the state constitutions benefits the role of constitutional courts more than ordinary courts[170]—except in the Netherlands, where no such court exists.[171] Constitutional courts in centralized systems of judicial review such as Germany, Spain, Italy, and France[172]—and ordinary courts in decentralized systems of conventionality review such as the Netherlands[173]—acquire as a result of the "golden rule" new competences in the fiscal field, including the ability to scrutinize—and strike down—the budgets approved by Parliaments, to ensure compliance with the constitutional and EU budgetary constraints.

164 See Violeta Ruiz Almendral, "Estabilidad Presupuestaria y Reforma Constitucional" (2012) 41 Revista española de derecho europeo 33, 82; Joachim Wehner, "Reconciling Accountability and Fiscal Prudence: A Case Study of the Budgetary Role and Impact of the German Parliament" (2001) 7 Journal of Legislative Studies 57, 59–61.

165 See Lienert (n 152) 14.

166 See Delledonne (n 72) 191.

167 See Diamant and van Emmerik (n 72) 260

168 See Joseph H.H. Weiler, "The Transformation of Europe" (1991) 100 Yale Law Journal 2403, 2420 2.

169 See Monica Claes, *The National Courts Mandate in the European Constitution* (Hart Publishing 2006) 221–2.

170 See Stone Sweet (n 32) 33–5.

171 See Adams and Van der Schyff (n 131) 399.

172 See Dominique Rousseau, *La justice constitutionnelle en Europe* (3rd ed. Montchrestien 1998) 20–4.

173 See Maartje de Visser, *Constitutional Review in Europe: A Comparative Analysis* (Hart Publishing 2014).

As I will point out further in Chapter 2, this development is in itself quite remarkable since, until now, the role of the judiciary in this area of the law has been negligible in almost all the countries considered here.[174] The empowerment of state courts in reviewing governmental budgetary policies, however, raises serious questions as to the judges' capacity to master the technically complex economic variables condensed within the "golden rule;" and makes it difficult to predict the degree of deference that courts may be willing to grant to the political branches.[175] Significant concerns are also raised by the possibility that a court may be asked to rule on the constitutionality of a budgetary law long after the law's enactment.[176] It is hard to imagine the effect of a court ruling which retroactively strikes down a budget many years after its enactment. Having said so, it seems plausible to suggest that the role played by courts in the budgetary field will greatly depend upon the underlying features of the state system of constitutional review. In particular, institutional and procedural factors such as the existence of a specialized constitutional court, the mechanisms by which a court can be activated, and the timing within which a court has to decide a case will be of central importance.[177] Therefore, the "golden rule" will most likely be relevant for courts in systems endowed with broad mechanisms of constitutional review, while it will be more restricted—if not irrelevant—in those systems which lack a constitutional court or in which constitutional courts can only be involved much after the conclusion of the budgetary process.

The five EU member states considered in this chapter offer examples of how the effects of the "golden rule" will likely combine with alternative procedural mechanisms of constitutional review. Hence, for instance, the constitutionalization of budgetary constraints works well in a state like Germany, characterized by a powerful constitutional court which can review acts of Parliament in essentially any form.[178] Under the procedural mechanisms of the German Basic Law, in fact, the Bundesverfassungsgericht could be requested to review the constitutionality of a budget at an early stage, thus ensuring quick oversight on the activity of Parliament.[179] The same considerations seem to apply also for the Spanish Tribunal Constitucional, whose powers are largely based on the German model.[180] In France, the Conseil Constitutionnel has been traditionally entrusted to review

[174] See Delledonne (n 72) 191, citing Fritz Ossenbühl, "Zur Justitiabilität der Finanzverfassungs" in *Einigkeit und Recht und Freiheit: Festschrift für Karl Carsten, Vol. 2 Staatsrecht* (Heymanns 1984), 743.

[175] I am grateful to Elena Simina Tănăsescu for making this point clear to me.

[176] See e.g., Giovanni Bognetti, "Il pareggio di bilancio nella Carta Costituzionale" [2011] Rivista AIC 1.

[177] See Stone Sweet (n 32) 50–2.

[178] See Kommers and Miller (n 34) 194 (describing the Constitutional Court's authority to review acts of Parliament before or after their enactment, upon referral from members of Parliament or ordinary courts, or even on the basis of a direct individual petition).

[179] See e.g., Bundesverfassungsgericht, BVerfG No. 2 BvF 1/04, judgment of July 9, 2007, paras 96, 119 (reviewing the federal budget through a constitutional challenge raised by the opposition). In this case, which was decided before the constitutional revision of 2009, the Court rejected the challenge but clarified that the German Basic Law had to be modified to strengthen the control against unwarranted spending.

[180] See P. Acosta, "National Legal Tradition–Spain" in Sergio Galera (ed), *Judicial Review: A Comparative Analysis Inside the European Legal System* (Council of Europe Publishing 2010), 113, 126.

legislation before its enactment.[181] Hence, the possibility of scrutinizing a budget bill (which, according to the proposed new Article 61 of the French Constitution, would have been a duty)[182] would not have significantly altered its current function. In Italy, on the contrary, the Corte Costituzionale can only review acts of Parliament *a posteriori*, either upon referral of a judge who doubts the constitutionality of a statute she must apply to a pending case or upon a challenge by a Region.[183] Since the recent Italian constitutional reform has not introduced any change in the procedural mechanisms of constitutional review, it is unclear how effectively a case against a budget bill could be brought before the Corte Costituzionale.[184] And in the Netherlands, where no ad hoc constitutional court exists, it seems unlikely that ordinary judges will take advantage of their power to review compliance of national budgets with the Fiscal Compact and EU law.[185]

C. The role of supranational institutions

As the preceding analysis has clarified, the enactment of the "golden rule" in state constitutions is bound to have institutional implications on both the relationships between the political branches and the role of constitutional courts in the member states. The nature of such institutional changes is likely to vary from state to state on the basis of pre-existing factors like the function of parliaments in budgetary procedures, and the mechanisms of judicial review of legislation. What seems instead to be occurring in all member states as a result of the latest EMU legal reforms is a power-shift in favor of supranational institutions.[186] The Fiscal Compact imposes strict budgetary rules on the member states and provides for new enforcement mechanisms, which are likely to empower both the ECJ and the European Commission vis-à-vis the states.[187] Regarding the role of the supranational judiciary, it has already been mentioned that the obligation of the states to incorporate the "golden rule" in domestic law is policed by the ECJ.[188] Because it is empowered to decide whether a state has fulfilled its obligations under Article 3(2) of the Fiscal Compact, the ECJ is vested with the authority to oversee the national constitutional revision processes, and to sanction states whose constitutional amendments are inconsistent with the Fiscal Compact.[189] Although EU precedents show that the ECJ has never hesitated to declare the unlawfulness of

[181] See Fabbrini (n 33) 1302–3. [182] See text accompanying nn 105–6.

[183] See Groppi (n 33) 102–3.

[184] During the debate leading toward the revision of the Italian Constitution, a proposal was made to empower the Court of Auditors to bring a case before the Italian Constitutional Court to challenge budgetary laws that failed to comply with the new Art 81 Const. It. See Bognetti (n 176) 5–6. The proposal was eventually rejected, however, leaving uncertain how the Italian Constitutional Court may review a budgetary law without dangerous delays.

[185] See Diamant and van Emmerik (n 72) 260 (cautioning against the likeliness that ordinary courts in the Netherlands will play any role in the oversight of the government's budgetary policy).

[186] Arguably, however, the shift of power toward the center is more significant for some member states than for others. See further on this Chapter 3.

[187] See text accompanying nn 50–68. [188] See text accompanying nn 61–4.

[189] See Kocharov (n 8) 5.

state constitutional provisions that were incompatible with EU law,[190] the additional power of judicial review that the ECJ now enjoys on the basis of the "golden rule" appears more sweeping, as it directly impacts the *exercise* of the constituent power of a state to amend its constitution.[191]

In addition, although Article 8 of the Fiscal Compact technically only empowers the ECJ to enforce the obligation to *enact* the "golden rule" at the state level, it cannot be overlooked that the ECJ may over time acquire a role in enforcing the obligation of states to *respect* the "golden rule" in the budgetary procedures.[192] As explained in the previous section, state courts will be primarily vested with the duty to review state political branches' compliance with the "golden rule."[193] Yet, budgetary policy and fiscal standards are increasingly regulated by EU law: besides the Fiscal Compact, one must consider the provisions of the EU treaties along with the new comprehensive legislative framework established by the so-called "six-pack" and "two-pack,"[194] which provide detailed indications on how state budgets should look.[195] Taking into account the obligation of state courts to refer preliminary questions to the ECJ on matters of interpretation of EU law,[196] it is conceivable that the ECJ may be asked to rule on the compatibility of a state budget with provisions of EU law.[197] Needless to say, this hypothesis is advanced here in merely speculative terms; it seems likely at the same time, that relevant national variations may shape the state courts' willingness to refer questions concerning state budgetary law to the ECJ.[198] Nevertheless, the prospect of something of this sort happening elucidates the potentially unprecedented transformations that the "golden rule" may generate in the role of the ECJ.[199]

The power shift toward the EU that the Fiscal Compact produces, however, is not exclusively to the advantage of the judiciary.[200] Political institutions like the European Commission will also gain influence from the existence of strict rules binding national authorities in the exercise of their budgetary competences.[201] As underlined in section 2 of this chapter, the Fiscal Compact is part of a set of EU legislative measures which have recently accorded to the Commission a pervasive role in the guidance and oversight of the national budgetary

[190] See e.g., Case C-285/98 *Kreil v. Germany* [2000] ECR I-69, ECLI:EU:C:2000:2, para 32 (holding that the clause of the German Basic Law prohibiting women from serving in the military was incompatible with the principle of equal access to work recognized in secondary EU law).

[191] See Kocharov (n 8) 12.

[192] See ibid 13.

[193] See text accompanying nn 166–85.

[194] See nn 38 and 40.

[195] See Craig (n 26) 22.

[196] See Art 267 TFEU.

[197] I am grateful to Sabino Cassese for making this point clear to me.

[198] See generally Marlene Wind et al, "The Uneven Legal Push for Europe: Questioning Variation when National Courts go to Europe" (2009) 10 European Union Politics 63 (assessing variations across a variety of member states in the number of disputes referred to the ECJ).

[199] I am grateful to Wojciech Sadurski for making this point clear to me.

[200] See Thomas Beukers and Tom Eijsbouts, Editorial: "The Euro Crisis: Storm, Meet Structure" (2011) 7 European Constitutional Law Review 349, 353 and Renaud Dehousse and Laurie Boussaguet, "L'impact de la crise sur la gouvernance européene" (2014) 149 Pouvoirs 7.

[201] See Giulio Napolitano, "L'incerto futuro della nuova governance economica europea" [2012] Quaderni Costituzionali 141, 144 and Michal Bauer and Stefan Becker, "The Unexpected Winner of the Crisis: The European Commission Strenghtened Role in Economic Governance" (2014) 36 Journal of European Integration 213.

procedures.[202] In particular, the so-called "European semester" requires states to submit to the Commission a draft of their budget laws that takes into account the parameters of the economic situation of the country previously prepared by the Commission. The Commission can request changes when it believes that the draft national budget would run afoul of EU economic and fiscal objectives.[203] Budgets are then presented domestically in parliaments, after having received the Commission's approval.[204] Moreover, pursuant to the excessive deficit procedure of Article 126 TFEU, the Commission is empowered to propose to the Council the adoption of measures, including fines, against states that do not comply with the deficit limits of the SGP.[205] For the states that signed the Fiscal Compact, Article 7 enhances the Commission's power in this procedure by committing the states to accept the Commission's proposal, unless a qualified majority in the Council opposes the decision.[206]

In this context, the "golden rule" in the Fiscal Compact provides another instrument of control for the Commission over the states' budgetary procedures, contributing further to the centralization at the EU level of core policy-making functions in the budgetary domain. By relying on the strict and detailed balanced budget rules mandated by the Fiscal Compact, the Commission will be able to exercise a more pervasive *ex ante* scrutiny on the sustainability and appropriateness of the draft budget bills which the governments submit for approval during the European Semester.[207] At the same time, the Commission will gain more effective powers of *ex post* oversight on the budgetary performances of the states, with the possibility—besides naming the states which have not incorporated the "golden rule," and thus opening the way for a case before the ECJ[208]—of adopting semi-automatic sanctions against states with excessive deficits.[209] From this point of view, the Fiscal Compact, with its balanced budget requirement, adds another stone to the path of increasing centralization in the EU constitutional framework, enhancing the role of the EU judicial and political institutions.[210] Nevertheless, it must be critically emphasized that this development does not involve the European Parliament (EP), which is left out of the new architecture of EMU, weakening the legitimacy of the transfer of growing slices of political authority at the EU level.[211] In light of the implications of the Fiscal Compact on the existing vertical balance

[202] See text accompanying nn 38–44.

[203] See Francesco Costamagna, "The Impact of Stronger Economic Policy Co-ordination on the European Social Dimension: Issues of Legitimacy," in Federico Fabbini et al (eds.), *The Constitutionalization of European Budgetary Constraints* (Hart Publishing 2014) 359, 364.

[204] See text accompanying n 43.

[205] See Art 126(11) TFEU.

[206] See Art 7 Fiscal Compact.

[207] See Art 3 Fiscal Compact.

[208] See Art 8 Fiscal Compact.

[209] See Art 7 Fiscal Compact.

[210] See Giovanni Pitruzzella, "Chi governa la finanza pubblica in Europa?" [2012] Quaderni Costituzionali 9, 16; Roland Bieber, "Observer–Policeman–Pilot: On Lacunae of Legitimacy and the Contradictions of Financial Crisis Management in the European Union," European University Institute Department of Law Working Paper No. 16/2011, 3.

[211] See Cristina Fasone, "European Economic Governance and Parliamentary Representation: What Place for the European Parliament?" (2014) 20 European Law Journal 164 and Ingolf Pernice, "Domestic Courts, Constitutional Constraints and European Democracy: What Solution for the

between the states and the EU, it is now worth comparing how the challenges of ensuring state fiscal discipline in an economic and monetary union have been historically addressed in the US federal system.

4. The Paradox of Centralization

As Randall Henning and Martin Kessler have emphasized, the experience of the US in the field of fiscal federalism offers a number of valuable points of comparison to analyze "the dilemmas that Europe faces."[212] From a historical perspective, the US, like the EU, has had to address the challenges of creating a common currency and managing a union in which states have diverging economic interests and performances.[213] Moreover, the US and the EU are endowed with comparable systems of independent central banks—the US Federal Reserve and the European Central Bank (ECB).[214] As the Euro-crisis represented a turning point for EMU, it is therefore helpful to explore the extent to which the legal and institutional responses adopted by the EU to manage shocks in an asymmetric economic union are similar to, or different from, those historically developed in the US.[215]

A comparative analysis reveals the existence of several *similarities*.[216] Since the mid-nineteenth century, the US fiscal architecture has been characterized by two basic structural tenets.[217] First, the federal government has consistently applied a policy of refusing to bail out defaulting states, making the states fully responsible for the service of their debt.[218] Second, the states have incorporated budget constraints in their constitutions to prevent excessive government spending and debt accumulation.[219] These features—which are reflected in the EU context in the bailout prohibition of Article 125 TFEU, and in the "golden rule" mandated by the Fiscal Compact—emerged simultaneously in antebellum America.[220] Shortly after the foundations of the US, the federal government, under the leadership of Secretary of the Treasury Alexander Hamilton, agreed on the federal assumption of the debt incurred by the states during the Revolutionary War.[221] Nevertheless,

Crisis?" in Federico Fabbrini et al (eds), *The Constitutionalization of European Budgetary Constraints* (Hart Publishing 2014), 297, 314.

212 Randall Henning and Martin Kessler, "Fiscal Federalism: US History for Architects of Europe's Fiscal Union," Bruegel Essay and Lecture Series 2012, 6.

213 See McNamara (n 14) 128–9, 132–3.

214 See Lawrence Broz, *The International Origins of the Federal Reserve System* (Cornell UP 1997) and Stefania Baroncelli, *La Banca Centrale Europea: Profile giuridici e istituzionali: un confronto con il modello americano della Federal Reserve* (European Press Academy Publishing 2000) (comparing the ECB and the Federal Reserve).

215 See Robert P. Inman and Daniel L. Rubinfeld, "Fiscal Federalism in Europe: Lessons from the United States Experience" (1992) 36 European Economic Review 654, 659–60 and Jerome W. Sheridan, "The *Déjà Vu* of EMU: Considerations for Europe from Nineteenth Century America" (1996) 30 Journal of Economic Issues 1143, 1143–4.

216 See Sheridan (n 215) 1143. 217 See Rodden (n 23) 71–2. 218 See ibid 7.

219 See ibid 63. 220 See ibid 63–4.

221 Ron Chernow, *Alexander Hamilton* (Penguin 2004) 298–9.

during the 1840s, when a number of states faced financial collapse due to an accumulation of speculative investments in infrastructures and public utilities, the federal government refused to bail out the defaulting states, setting an enduring precedent and creating a strong incentive for each state to ensure sustainable budgetary policies.[222] Notwithstanding pressures from creditors, notably in the United Kingdom, the US federal government—which in antebellum America only had a limited fiscal capacity—left the states alone in bearing the costs of their individual fiscal policy.[223]

Hence, beginning with New York in 1846, states have introduced constitutional provisions limiting public debt and requiring that state budgets be balanced.[224] The trend toward the constitutionalization of budgetary constraints remained steady after the Civil War, and by the end of the nineteenth century most states had adopted "golden rules."[225] A contemporary survey reveals that 35 states currently have constitutional balanced budget requirements, and 14 more have statutory or de facto obligations to ensure a balanced budget—Vermont being the only state with no such constraints whatsoever.[226] The "golden rules" adopted by the US states vary significantly in their technical formulation and procedural effects.[227] While some state constitutions include a clear requirement that the legislature approves (and the governor signs) a budget law which is on balance,[228] other states more flexibly require that the governor submits (and the legislature approves) a budget in which expenditures do not exceed the estimated revenues.[229] In the first case, the "golden rule" works as a strict condition for the approval of legislation, binding the hands of the political branches, while in the second case the rigidity of the "golden rule" can be bypassed by over-optimistically predicting the amount of financial resources that will be available in the fiscal year and increasing the spending accordingly.[230] At the same time, the enforcement of the "golden rule" also

[222] Wibbels (n 16) 490–1, 498.

[223] See also Daniel Kelemen & Terence Teo, "Law, Focal Points and Fiscal Discipline in the United States and the European Union" (2014) 108 American Political Science Review 355.

[224] See Arthur Grinath, III et al, "Debt, Default and Revenue Structure: The American State Debt Crisis in the Early 1840s," National Bureau of Economic Research, Historical Working Paper No. 97/1997, 34–5.

[225] See Henning and Kessler (n 212) 16–17.

[226] See U.S. Government Accountability Office, *Balanced Budget Requirements: State Experiences and Implications for the Federal Government* (1993) 3, available at <http://www.gao.gov/products/AFMD-93-58BR> (last accessed May 30, 2014); National Conference of State Legislatures, *Fiscal Brief: State Balanced Budget Provisions* (2010) 1–13, available at <http://www.ncsl.org/documents/fiscal/StateBalancedBudgetProvisions2010.pdf> (last accessed May 30, 2014).

[227] See Henning and Kessler (n 212) 21.

[228] See e.g., Art IV, Sec. 12(g) Cal. Const. (West, Westlaw through 2012 ballot propositions) ("[T]he Legislature may not send to the Governor for consideration, nor may the Governor sign into law, a budget bill that would appropriate from the General Fund, for that fiscal year, a total amount that . . . exceeds General Fund revenues for that fiscal year.").

[229] See e.g., Art VIII, Sec. 2(a) Ill. Const. (West, Westlaw through Sept. 2012 amendments) ("The Governor shall prepare and submit to the General Assembly . . . a State budget for the ensuing fiscal year. . . . Proposed expenditures shall not exceed funds estimated to be available for the fiscal year as shown in the budget.").

[230] I am grateful to Daniel Rubinfeld for making this point clear to me.

varies significantly among the states.[231] While courts in few states—notably New Jersey, Ohio, and Texas—have played a rather active role in reviewing budget laws to ensure that, despite balanced budget requirements, proper financing is guaranteed to public education as required by the state constitution,[232] attempts in many other states at legal enforcement of balanced budget constraints have been barred under the "political question doctrine."[233]

Beyond these analogies, a comparative assessment also highlights the existence of relevant *differences* between the US federal system and the economic architecture of the EMU.[234] First, while almost all US states have enacted balanced budget requirements in their constitutions, "[i]t is worth emphasizing that this outcome was not the result of a strong central government."[235] Each state opted for the "golden rule" through political debates that were largely autonomous, albeit driven by a common "Jacksonian distrust" for financial institutions.[236] As it has been argued "[t]he federal government was passive during the adoption of these provisions by the states. The federal government certainly did not mandate the adoption of these provisions and it does not appear that it was promoting them either."[237] Here lies a first major difference from the dynamics currently at play in the EU, where the adoption of balanced budget amendments in state constitutions is instead dictated, and policed, top-down.[238] The process that led to the constitutionalization of balanced budget rules in the US states reflected the notion that states were—and ought to be regarded as—fully sovereign fiscal entities.[239] This view, premised on the theory of "dual federalism," arguably no longer appropriately describes the fiscal relationships between the states and the central government in the US, which is now characterized by an overlap of competences.[240] Nevertheless, the budgetary processes of the states continue even today to remain independent, and the federal government has no authority to mandate state compliance with federal budgetary standards.[241]

231 The question whether balanced budget rules are effective has been disputed. See Van Malleghem (n 20) 169 (emphasizing limited capacity of courts to enforce them). But see Daniel Kelemen, "Law, Fiscal Federalism and Austerity" (2015) 22 Indiana Journal of Global Legal Studies 379 (discussing judicial enforcement of balanced budget rules).

232 I am grateful to David Super for making this point clear to me.

233 Under this doctrine, courts refuse to hear disputes which are best left to the political branches of government. See Louis Fisher, *Constitutional Dialogues: Interpretation as Political Process* (Princeton UP 1988) 110–16.

234 See Sheridan (n 215) 1143.

235 Wibbels (n 16) 498.

236 See David A. Super, "Rethinking Fiscal Federalism" (2005) 118 Harvard Law Review 2544, 2606.

237 Henning and Kessler (n 212) 17.

238 See ibid.

239 See Rodden (n 23) 140–1, 145.

240 See generally Edward S. Corwin, "The Passing of Dual Federalism" (1950) 36 Virginia Law Review 1 (discussing the progressive change in the nature of the relationship between the states and the federal government in the US, from a time in which sovereignty was presumptively strictly divided between the states and the federation—each empowered to act in mutually exclusive fields of competence—to a time in which the action of the states and the federal government are understood as overlapping and intertwining).

241 See *New York v. United States*, 505 U.S. 144, 176–77 (1992) (holding that the federal government cannot commandeer a state legislature to regulate according to a scheme set at the federal level). See also *Printz v. United States*, 521 U.S. 898 (1997) (declaring unconstitutional a federal statute

Second, in the US, the fiscal powers of the states have been complemented by the rising role of the federal government.[242] Beginning with the Progressive Era, and then markedly with the New Deal, the federal government has become a prominent actor in the governance of macroeconomic policy and plays a key role in financially supporting the states through grants and monetary transfers for the management of specific programs.[243] As David Super has explained, the federal government's fiscal relationships with state governments today reflect a cooperative model, based on compensation, capacity, and leadership.[244] In addition, because state balanced budget rules essentially force state governments to adopt pro-cyclical policies, the Keynesian task to support the economy in times of downswing is entirely exercised at the federal level.[245] Ultimately, "[t]he New Deal amended [the US's] implicit fiscal constitution by recognizing a new federal responsibility to provide countercyclical assistance."[246] Here lies a second major difference between the US and the EMU: the US government has sweeping instruments to govern the economy—backed by taxing power and the (unlimited) capacity to borrow money[247]—which instead supranational institutions in the EU lack. As a consequence, during the last 80 years, while the US states have managed their autonomous fiscal policies within the limits of their balanced budget constraints, the federal government has simultaneously acquired broad control over the general economic and monetary policy of the US and developed means to soften the implications of a recession.[248]

As the brief comparison underlines, in sum, both the EU and the US have central governments committed to, or bound by, no bail-out policies regarding defaulting states.[249] Moreover, in both systems states are endowed with strict budgetary requirements in their constitutions.[250] Nevertheless, in the US, the federal government plays a macroeconomic role in the economy which finds no

commandeering state police officers to execute a federal mandate). The fact that the federal government cannot directly interfere with the budgetary processes of the states, however, leaves intact the possibility for the federal government to transfer to the states the task of providing several services, thus effectively mandating them to spend their resources on ad hoc programs. See John M. Quigley and Daniel L. Rubinfeld, "Federalism as a Device for Reducing the Budget of the Central Government," in Alan J. Auerbach (ed), *Fiscal Policy: Lessons from Economic Research* (MIT Press 1997), 7, 21 (discussing the expansion of federal mandates and their implications for economic federalism in the US).

[242] See Harry N. Scheiber, "State Law and 'Industrial Policy' in American Development, 1790–1987" (1987) 75 California Law Review 415, 426–8.

[243] See also Ajay Mehrotra, *Making the Modern American Fiscal State: Law, Politics, and the Rise of Progressive Taxation 1877-1929* (CUP 2014).

[244] See Super (n 236) 2571.

[245] See ibid 2592–3.

[246] Ibid at 2575 (footnote omitted).

[247] See generally James V. Saturno and Megan Suzanne Lynch, "A Balanced Budget Constitutional Amendment: Background and Congressional Options," Congressional Research Service, December 20, 2011, R41907 (discussing efforts to constrain federal expenditures).

[248] See Scheiber (n 242) 428–30, 433–4. But see Robert Ward Shaw, "The States, Balanced Budgets and Fundamental Shifts in Federalism" (2004) 82 North Carolina Law Review 1195, 1213–14 (explaining how the revival of federalist ideas in the US, with the shift of important tasks from the federation back to the states, creates new financial difficulties for the states given their balanced budget constraints).

[249] See text accompanying nn 218–23.

[250] See text accompanying nn 224–31.

equivalent in the role currently played by the EU institutions.[251] At the same time, the fiscal sovereignty that the US states enjoy vis-à-vis the federal government contrasts with the direct interference that EU institutions have on the budgetary policy of the member states.[252] In light of this comparison, however, it seems possible to reconsider the main innovations introduced by the Fiscal Compact and the latest legislative reforms at EU level and to illuminate a paradox in the new constitutional architecture of the EMU. The paradox is that, while EU member states have willingly refused to adopt a federal solution for the governance of the EMU on the assumption that this was too restrictive of state sovereignty, they have established a regime which is much less respectful of state fiscal sovereignty than the US one. In the US, in fact, the emergence of the "golden rule" at the state level was not imposed by federal law, and the budgetary processes of the states and the federal government remain fully separated.[253] On the contrary, Eurozone member states are obliged to adopt "golden rules" by the Fiscal Compact and forced to submit their budgetary procedures to pervasive supranational constraints.[254] The latest legal and institutional reforms in the EU architecture of economic governance, therefore, produced the paradoxical situation of making budgetary policy management in the EU supranational system much more centralized than in the US federal one. This is striking considering that in comparative terms the US is typically regarded as the example of a highly centralized federal system.

The emergence and spread of the financial crisis since 2009 in Europe made a number of opinion makers call for a constitutional change in the architecture of the EMU.[255] Many observers pointed specifically at the US federal system as a model for EMU, arguing that the adoption of a federal arrangement in the EU context would improve the efficiency and legitimacy of the EU response to the crisis.[256] Yet, the governments of the EU member states have repeatedly discarded the option of moving the EU in the direction of a federal system, seeing this step as incompatible with the preservation of state sovereignty.[257] This position has been forcefully defended, especially by France and Germany, who played a leading role in crafting the response to the Euro-crisis.[258] For instance, in a public speech in Toulon on December 1, 2011, then French President Sarkozy affirmed that the new architecture of the Eurozone would be designed to safeguard the full

[251] See also Henrik Enderlein et al, "The EU Budget: How Much Scope for Institutional Reform?," ECB Occasional Paper Series No. 27/2005 (contrasting the small EU budget to the large US federal budget).

[252] See Bieber (n 210) 3–5.

[253] See text accompanying nn 234–41.

[254] See text accompanying nn 38–68.

[255] See e.g., "1789 and All That," *The Economist*, February 11, 2012, and Luigi Guiso and Helios Herrera, "Solo l'unione fiscale salverà l'euro" *Il Sole 24 Ore*, February 23, 2012.

[256] See Giuliano Amato, Op-Ed, "Il modello federale per essere più liberi," *Il Sole 24 Ore*, April 29, 2012. See also "European Disunion Done Right," *The Economist*, December 22, 2012, 71.

[257] See further Sergio Fabbrini, "Intergovernmentalism and Its Limits: Assessing the European Union's Answer to the Euro Crisis" (2013) 46 Comparative Political Studies 1003.

[258] See Besselink and Reestman (n 70) 3.

sovereignty of the EU member states.[259] German Chancellor Merkel supported analogous arguments, perhaps under the noxious influence of the jurisprudence of the German Constitutional Court.[260] The option of a federal arrangement for the EMU was discarded as an unacceptable form of "Transfer Union," a system in which virtuous Germany would have to give up its sovereignty to take care of the financial follies of other EU member states.[261]

The position of the member states' governments fits comfortably within a general trend against federalism and constitutionalism in the EU, which, at least since the failure of the European Constitutional Treaty in 2005, seems to have gained the upper hand in European public discourse.[262] Whereas the US federal model loomed large in the minds of EU political elites at the beginning of the twenty-first century—the most prominent example being the speech by German Foreign Minister Fischer at Humboldt Universität in 2000,[263] paving the way to the establishment of a Constitutional Convention on the Future of Europe[264]—a backlash seems to have occurred in the last few years.[265] As Renaud Dehousse has argued, an "anti-federalist" vision has recently prevailed, leading to a system in which state rights and national identity are at the center of the EU integration project.[266] The Fiscal Compact and the latest institutional responses to the economic crisis by EU member states partake of this "sovereign-tist" narrative. As its sponsors underline, these reforms did not create a powerful central government and leave intact the fiscal sovereignty of the member states.[267] Nevertheless, if one scratches the surface of this self-congratulating public narrative, a striking paradox emerges. The Fiscal Compact and the new

[259] See Charles Jaigu, "Nicolas Sarkozy trace les pistes pour sortir de la crise," *Le Figaro*, December 1, 2011, 2.

[260] See further on this Chapter 2.

[261] See Tony Czuzcka, "Merkel Says Euro-Area Fiscal Union Won't Be 'Transfer Union'," *Bloomberg Businessweek*, February 7, 2012.

[262] The federalist vision of Europe, despite becoming minoritarian, has nonetheless remained active. See e.g., Guy Verhofstadt, Op-Ed, "Europe Must Pool Its Debts to Survive," *Wall Street Journal*, April 18, 2012.

[263] See Joschka Fischer, "From Confederacy to Federation," Speech at Humboldt Universität, Berlin, May 12, 2000, transcript available at <http://cadmus.eui.eu/bitstream/handle/1814/17255/ResponsesToJ.FISCHER_2000.pdf> (last accessed June 1, 2014).

[264] See Michel Rosenfield, "The European Convention and Constitution Making in Philadelphia" (2003) 1 International Journal of Constitutional Law 373, 375–8 (comparing the European Constitutional Convention to the US Constitutional Convention) and Jacques Ziller, "The Constitutionalization of the European Union: Comparative Perspectives" (2009) 55 Loyola Law Review 413 (discussing European Constitutional Convention).

[265] See Bruno De Witte, "Saving the Constitution? The Escape Routes and their Legal Feasibility" in Giuliano Amato et al (eds), *Genesis and Destiny of the European Constitution* (Bruylant 2007) 919, 919–38.

[266] Renaud Dehousse, "'We the States': Why the Anti-Federalists Won" in Nicolas Jabko and Craig Parsons (eds), *With US or Against US? European Trends in American Perspective* (OUP 2005), 105, 112–14.

[267] See e.g., European Commission President Manuel D. Barroso, Speech at the "State of the Union" Conference of the European University Institute, Florence, May 9, 2013 (stating that "'More Europe' does not mean 'more Brussels', in the sense of more centralization. [...] Subsidiarity is indeed an essential democratic concept and should be practiced. [...] And this is precisely what we are doing [in the EMU].").

legislative measures adopted within EU law produced in the governance of the EMU a centralization of powers that is significantly greater than that existing in the US.[268]

As previously explained, the Fiscal Compact has introduced a very detailed "golden rule" which member states are required to incorporate within their highest laws under the threat of judicial action before the ECJ. Moreover, on the basis of the "six pack" and the "two pack", the European Commission has been attributed unprecedented power to direct and police the budgetary policies of the EU member states.[269] Nothing similar has ever happened in the US: despite the progressive rise of the federal government in the economic and fiscal realm, the states decided in total independence to adopt balanced budget amendments in their constitutions and are fully autonomous in the management of their budgetary processes.[270] Indeed, in the US, *because of the federal system of government*, it would arguably be impossible for the federal government to mandate to the states the incorporation of specific budgetary rules in the state constitutions and to require state legislatures and governors to submit draft budgets for prior approval in Washington, DC.[271] Yet, this is precisely what happens now in the EMU as a result of legal and institutional measures adopted in response to the Euro-crisis.[272] This development is paradoxical given the commitment of the member states to design a new EMU architecture which would leave the sovereignty of the states wholly intact. As the comparative analysis shows, the legal response to the economic crisis embodied in the Fiscal Compact tips the EU balance of powers in favor of the supranational institutions, significantly reducing the fiscal sovereignty and the budgetary autonomy of the member states. Therefore, while the federal model has repeatedly been considered inadequate for a "Europe of nation-states,"[273] its embrace in the new architecture of EMU governance would paradoxically have been not only more efficient to address the economic crisis, but also more protective of state autonomy and self-governance.

5. Budgetary Process and States' Autonomy

The dynamics of centralization in the vertical relations of power between the member states and the EU institutions following the outburst of the Euro-crisis have been often described as inevitable.[274] The revelations of widespread lack of compliance by the EU member states with the deficit and debt targets set in the SGP,

[268] See also Vlad Constantinesco, "Fédéralisme économique et fédéralisme politique" in Stéphane De la Rosa et al (eds), *L'Union européenne et le fédéralisme économique* (Bruylant 2015), 439.

[269] See Beukers and Ejisbouts (n 200) 353.

[270] See Wibbels (n 16) 498.

[271] See Scheiber (n 242) 438–9.

[272] See text accompanying nn 38–68.

[273] See David P. Calleo, "De Gaulle's Visions for Europe" in Benjamin Rowland (ed), *Charles De Gaulle's Legacy of Ideas* (Lexington Book 2011), 1 (discussing the Gaullist origin of the idea of a "Europe of nation-states").

[274] See Bodo Herzog and Katja Hengstermann, "Restoring Credible Economic Governance to the Eurozone" (2013) 33 Economic Affairs 3.

and the negative externalities that would spill over from countries in fiscal distress toward other member states of the Eurozone, have called for greater control at the central level over the budgetary policy of the EU member states.[275] At the same time, it has been suggested that the constitutionalization of budgetary constraints into the legal system of the EU member states, along the model designed in the Fiscal Compact, contributed to the ownership of budgetary rules by the member states, and strengthened their willingness and ability to abide by them.[276] From a law and economics perspective, therefore, the strengthening of EU budgetary constraints and their domestication in the legal system of the member states—with the ensuing shift of power from the member states toward the EU—was a logical step to address collective action problems emerging in the integrated economy of the EMU and to restore member states commitments toward previously agreed upon fiscal targets.[277]

As Ken Kollman has emphasized, otherwise, federalism-based systems have a tendency to slip toward centralization.[278] Examining the case of the church, corporations and political unions such as the US and the EU, Ken Kollman has underlined how a common trajectory of centralization occurs when, in systems of decentralized governance, the emergence of crises creates the need for executive action at the central level and sub-units assent to this development, on the assumption that they can still remain in control of the decision-making process through representative institutions.[279] As he pointed out, the mechanisms of centralization "can be summarized by five processes that often happen in rough chronological order: assent, representative centralization, partisanship, executive centralization, and lock-in."[280] Seen through this prism of analysis, the developments occurring in the EMU appear largely predictable: after the member states had assented to the SGP, remaining in control of its enforcement through their action in the Council,[281] the Euro-crisis increasingly created the need for more delegation of authority to an independent supranational institution such as the European Commission to effectively enforce these rules.[282] The legislative innovation produced by the "six-pack" and the "two-pack," coupled with the Fiscal Compact, then, produced an entrenchment of the powers of the Commission, bringing to its extreme the centralization of budgetary policy in the EU.[283]

[275] See Waltraud Schelke, "EU Fiscal Governance: Hard Law in the Shadow of Soft Law?" (2007) 13 Columbia Journal of European Law 705.

[276] See Tuori and Tuori (n 26) 109.

[277] See Antoš (n 27) 205. See also generally, John Elster, *Ulysses and the Sirens. Studies in Rationality and Irrationality* (CUP 1979) (discussing the theory of pre-commitment).

[278] Kollman (n 22) 13. [279] Ibid 15. [280] Ibid 8–9.

[281] See text accompanying nn 36 7.

[282] See Buti and Carnot (n 4) 899. See also Peter Lindseth, "Power and Legitimacy in the Eurozone: Can Integration and Democracy be Reconciled?" in Federico Fabbrini et al (eds), *The Constitutionalization of European Budgetary Constraints* (Hart Publishing 2014), 379 (discussing delegation of powers in the EU).

[283] See also Alexandre de Streel, "The Evolution of the EU Economic Governance Since the Treaty of Maastricht: An Unfinished Task" (2013) 20 Maastricht Journal of European & Comparative Law 336.

In fact, the trend toward centralization of budgetary policy in the EU is not over yet. The recent report "Completing Europe's EMU," written by the President of the European Commission, in close cooperation with the Presidents of the European Council, the Eurogroup, the ECB, and the EP proposes new measures increasing the supervisory powers of the EU institutions toward the member states.[284] As mentioned before, the "two pack" required the creation of national fiscal councils, charged to monitor the fiscal performance of the member states—a step which already implied a significant restriction of state sovereignty.[285] Now the Commission President's report proposes to put these fiscal councils into a network, to be coordinated by the Commission, and to create a European Fiscal Board, charged to provide an independent assessment of states' budgetary performance.[286] Moreover, it called for the establishment of another group of national independent authorities subject to EU-coordination—so-called Competitiveness Councils[287]—with the aim to remove from the national political process discussion about structural reform, subjecting to a centralized technocratic control the management of states' economic policy.[288] At the same time, the Finance Minister of Germany has strongly argued in favor of strengthening centralization of powers in EMU even further, by creating a Budget Commissioner empowered to veto national budgets which fail to respect EU deficit and debt rules.[289]

Yet, as much as the development recently occurring in the EMU seems to follow a path recurrent in federated systems, a crucial question is whether the nature of this centralization, and its degree, is wholly warranted. Whereas some form of supranational control over state budgetary policies seems inevitable in the EMU, there is a plausible argument that the EU member states ought to enjoy some degree of autonomy in decisions about taxing and spending. Historically, in Europe the budgetary process has been the battlefield in which national parliaments have affirmed their role as the institutions representing the popular will, against the wish of the monarchies[290]—and decisions about taxing and spending as reflected through the design of the budgetary act are still today at the core of the ability of democratic states to shape policies.[291] In fact, the literature on fiscal federalism has

[284] President of the European Commission, Report, "Completing Europe's EMU," June 22, 2015.

[285] See Charles Wyplosz, "Fiscal Policy: Institutions versus Rules" (2005) 191 National Institute Economic Review 64 (emphasizing the restrictions which fiscal councils would put on parliamentary sovereignty).

[286] President of the European Commission, Report (n 284) 14.

[287] See also President of the Eurogroup Jeroen Dijsselbloem, Letter to the members of the Eurogroup, July 12, 2015, 3 (saying that "a framework of national competitiveness councils should be established, to assess the fiscal and macroeconomic implications of planned and implemented reforms, in resemblance of the network of national fiscal councils").

[288] President of the European Commission, Report (n 284) 8.

[289] See e.g., German Finance Minister Wolfgang Schäuble, "Strategy for a European Recovery", Keynote Speech at the 5th Bruges European Business Conference, March 27, 2014 (speaking in favor of a "European budget commissioner, who would be able to reject national budgets if they don't correspond to the rules we have jointly agreed.").

[290] See Delledonne (n 72) 184. See also Antonio Padoa Schioppa, *Storia del diritto in Europa* (Il Mulino 2007).

[291] See Van Malleghem (n 20) 151. Se also Valerio Onida, *Le leggi di spesa nella Costituzione* (Giuffré 1969).

repeatedly emphasized the advantages which are associated with states' autonomy in the fiscal domain, in terms of experimentation, competition, and choice.[292] As Francesco Costamagna emphasized, moreover, in modern welfare states, budgetary decisions profoundly affect the nature of social entitlements that citizens can obtain from the government, and the existence of budgetary autonomy at the member states level is a pre-condition for a meaningful political competition on government policies.[293]

Acknowledging this point, the report "Towards a Genuine Economic and Monetary Union" delivered on December 5, 2012 by the President of the European Council, in cooperation with the Presidents of the Commission, the ECB and the Eurogroup, underlined that "[d]ecisions on national budgets are at the heart of Member States' parliamentary democracies."[294] In other words, relevant constitutional arguments on the role of the EU member states point in favor of some degree of states' autonomy in the decisions about budget and shed some critical light on the paradox of centralization produced by the latest legal and institutional responses to the Euro-crisis. The requirement that member states submit their budget draft to the EU institutions for supranational validation prior to approval in the national Parliaments, coupled with the obligation to enshrine in higher laws fiscal targets policed by supranational institutions, produced a relevant compression on the ability of the member states to have autonomous deliberations about their budgets.

Most crucially, however, it is unconvincing that such a significant supranational take-over of the budgetary process of the member states could not be avoided through other, less restrictive, solutions—which could ensure a proper functioning of the EMU and yet secure some autonomy to the member states. The example of the US, after all, points precisely to such an alternative option.[295] While the US has had to face the challenges of managing an asymmetrical economic and monetary union—much like the EU—it has not found it necessary to suspend tout court the ability of the member states to decide autonomously on their budgetary policies. In fact, as explained in the previous section, the US states still today remain sovereign in deciding about their domestic taxing and spending, and no federal framework exists to supervise and approve their budgetary laws.[296] Yet, the federal government, thanks to a set of constitutional transformations beginning during the Progressiva Era and the New Deal, has acquired other instruments

[292] See Jonathan Rodden and Susan Rose-Ackerman, "Does Federalism Preserve Markets?" (1997) 83 Virginia Law Review 1521 and Isabel Rodriguez-Tejedo and John J. Wallis, "Fiscal Institutions and Fiscal Crises," in Peter Conti-Brown and David Skeel Jr. (eds), *When States Go Broke: The Origins, Context and Solutions for the American States in Fiscal Crisis* (CUP 2012), 9. See also ceteris paribus, *New State Ice Co. v. Liebmann*, 285 U.S. 262, 311 (1932) (Brandeis J. dissenting, defining as "one of the happy incidents of the federal system [the fact] that a single courageous State may, if its citizens choose, serve as a laboratory; and try novel social and economic experiments without risk to the rest of the country.").

[293] See Costamagna (n 203) 367.

[294] President of the European Council Final Report, "Towards a Genuine EMU," December 5, 2012, 16.

[295] See Hinarejos (n 24) 1261.

[296] See text accompanying n 241.

to govern the US economy—notably a fiscal capacity, supported by autonomous revenue sources, to counteract asymmetric economic shocks occurring in some US states, and prevent contagious effects throughout the US economy.[297] Because such tools have proved valuable to manage the US economy while securing some degree of autonomy to the states, it is worth inquiring whether a similar option may be considered in the EMU as well, as an alternative to the paradox of centralization. Given the growing attention that the proposal for an EMU fiscal capacity has acquired in the EU debates,[298] Chapter 4 will address face-on this possibility and consider what challenges would arise toward this objective.

6. Conclusion

This chapter has analyzed how the Euro-crisis and the responses to it have affected the vertical relations of power between the member states and the EU institutions. The chapter has examined the reforms strengthening EU budgetary constraints and focused especially on the Fiscal Compact and its requirement that signatory states incorporate a "golden rule" in their constitutions. The Fiscal Compact has been hailed as the solution to the sovereign debt crisis. Yet, the obligation for the states to adopt the "golden rule" of the Fiscal Compact is an unprecedented development in the history of European integration. First, the Fiscal Compact designs an extremely detailed balanced budget rule. Second, states are expressly obliged to incorporate the rule in their domestic systems through constitutional law, or other supra-legislative sources of law. Third, the incorporation of the "golden rule" by the states is policed by strong judicial mechanisms, empowering the ECJ to sanction disobedient states with heavy financial penalties. Fourth, incorporation of the "golden rule" is a condition to receive financial aid. The chapter has explained that the model of the Fiscal Compact can be traced in German constitutional law, and has assessed the reforms introducing budgetary constraints in Spain, Italy, France, and the Netherlands. This selected survey has revealed several divergences between the "golden rules" enacted at the state level and in the Fiscal Compact, but has underlined how overall the largest Eurozone member states consistently moved in the direction of strengthening their budgetary commitments.

The chapter has explained that the latest legislative reforms of EMU generally, and the enactment of the "golden rule" specifically, have had profound constitutional implications on the vertical relations of power between the member states and the EU institutions. While the effects of balanced budget requirements on the relationships between states' executives and legislatures, and on the role of state courts, are likely to vary from one state to another on the basis of several pre-existing governmental institutional features or on the system of constitutional

[297] See Henning and Kessler (n 212) 22; Van Malleghem (n 20) 174.

[298] See e.g., European Parliament Resolution of November 20, 2012 on the report "Towards a Genuine EMU," P7_TA(2012)0430.

review, the Fiscal Compact and the other EU legislative reforms systematically enhances the powers of the supranational institutions. On the one hand, the Fiscal Compact entrusts to the ECJ new tasks to scrutinize and enforce budgetary rules within the states. On the other hand, the Fiscal Compact, coupled with other recent innovations in EU law, endows the European Commission—but critically, not the EP—with new pervasive instruments to direct and police the budgetary policies of the states. These developments reveal an increasing centralization in the EU architecture of economic governance that contrasts with the federal experience of the US. Although almost three-fourths of the US states are endowed with "golden rules" in their state constitutions, the federal government never played a role in the adoption of these balanced budget amendments, and is still today barred from interfering with the budgetary processes of the states.

As the chapter has argued, therefore, an unexpected paradox emerges. While national governments in the EU have systematically discarded calls in favor of a federal arrangement for the EMU as being disrespectful of state sovereignty, they have established a regime for economic governance that sacrifices state sovereignty much more than would have been permitted in a federal system. A comparison with the US sheds light on how intentions and outcome diametrically differed in the political responses to the Euro-crisis and reveals how, in the end, the more EU member states attempt to avoid creating a federal architecture for the EU, the more they end up fostering supranational centralization and reducing state autonomy. Yet, this development is problematic, considering the importance that budgetary decisions have in the capacity of the member states to shape themselves. The name Fiscal Compact, by which the TSCG is usually referred, was suggested by ECB President Mario Draghi in a speech before the EP on December 1, 2011.[299] The concept drew inspiration from Hamilton's statement that "the origin of all civil government, justly established, must be a voluntary *compact* between the rulers and the ruled."[300] Hamilton was also one of the major architects of the US system, supporting the adoption of a complete constitutional framework and the creation of an effective federal government for the US with the power to tax and spend. Drawing inspiration from these ideas, Chapter 4 will discuss proposals for a fiscal capacity, and consider how such an instrument would secure the proper functioning of EMU while restoring a degree of state autonomy in budgetary matters.

[299] ECB President Mario Draghi, Introductory statement in front of the European Parliament, Brussels, December 1, 2011.

[300] Alexander Hamilton, "The Farmer Refuted" in John C. Hamilton (ed), *The Works of Alexander Hamilton* (Federal Edition 1850) 37, 44 (emphasis added).

2

The Paradox of Judicialization

1. Introduction

The Euro-crisis prompted the institutions and the member states of the European Union (EU) to enact a large number of legal and institutional reforms. As I explained in the introductory chapter, the political branches at the national and supranational level have acted to strengthen European budgetary constraints—especially with the Fiscal Compact,[1] to endow the EU with new mechanisms of financial stabilization—notably, with the European Stability Mechanism (ESM),[2] and to set up a framework for economic adjustment guiding countries in serious economic difficulties out of the crisis through ad hoc programs of assistance—visible in the recovery programs concluded in the form of Memoranda of Understandings (MoU).[3] Yet, the legal and institutional measures enacted by the political branches of government to respond to the crisis have increasingly fallen prey to the scrutiny of courts, both at the national and at the supranational level—generating a rich case-law which provides insight on the evolving role of the judiciary in the Economic and Monetary Union (EMU).

The purpose of this chapter is to analyze the constitutional implications of the Euro-crisis and the responses to it on *the horizontal relations of powers between the courts and the political branches of government.* To this end, this chapter analyzes a plurality of rulings by national and supranational courts reviewing the legality of various aspects of the new legal architecture of the EMU put in place in the aftermath of the Euro-crisis. In particular, it considers decisions by high courts in Estonia, France, Germany, Ireland, and Portugal, as well as by the EU Court of Justice (ECJ), and seeks to map judicial reactions to the transformations of the constitutional architecture of the EMU. The developments taking place in the

[1] See Treaty on Stability, Coordination and Governance in the Economic and Monetary Union, March 2, 2012, [hereinafter Fiscal Compact], available at <http://www.eurozone.europa.eu/media/304649/st00tscg26_en12.pdf> (last accessed May 31, 2014).

[2] See Treaty Establishing the European Stability Mechanism [hereinafter ESM Treaty], February 2, 2012, available at <http://www.european-council.europa.eu/media/582311/05-tesm2.en12.pdf> (last accessed May 31, 2014).

[3] See e.g., Greece: Memorandum of Understanding on Specific Economic Policy Conditionality, May 3, 2010 available at <http://www.minfin.gr/content-api/f/binaryChannel/minfin/datastore/a8/52/57/a85257bc11624aa0a2f89a6bebea2219687ce5f0/application/pdf/EU%2BBundle2.pdf> (last accessed May 31, 2014).

EMU are then compared to the experience of the United States (US) by considering the role of the US judiciary in reviewing economic and monetary policy measures adopted by political branches of government. The comparative example of the US is used as a benchmark to evaluate the nature of the developments brought about by the Euro-crisis and the responses to it. The US is characterized by a strong system of judicial review, which in the comparative literature is often regarded as the paradigmatic case of a model of "judicial supremacy."[4] Moreover, in the US system of fiscal federalism, courts have often been asked to adjudicate questions concerning the legality of economic policies of the federal government.[5] Yet, at least since the New Deal in the 1930s, US courts have adopted a deferential position in the economic field, on the understanding that the political process is better placed than the judicial process in answering fundamental budgetary, monetary, and economic questions.[6]

In light of the comparison with the US, the chapter argues that a paradox emerges in the new constitutional architecture of EMU: the Euro-crisis and the legal and institutional responses to it have dramatically increased the powers of the judiciary vis-à-vis the political branches, making economic and monetary affairs in Europe more judicialized than even in a hyper-judicialized system like the US.[7] As the chapter underlines, a trend of increasing judicial involvement in the EMU domain has emerged throughout Europe, and particulary in some EU member states. Considering the limited role that courts traditionally played in EMU, this represents an unprecedented development. While courts have largely upheld the measures under review, validating the reforms of the EMU introduced by the EU institutions and member states, over time, they have also expressed their discomfort with specific aspects of the new EMU rules, especially those on financial stabilization and economic adjustment—and in some recent cases have even introduced important conditions on the validity of the measures under review or struck them down tout court. As the chapter argues, this trend of judicial empowerment in EMU is paradoxical. On the one hand, the US is generally identified as the example par excellence of a strong system of judicial review. On the other hand, the latest reforms in the architecture of EMU were largely driven by an intergovernmental logic—and the central premise of this is the idea that national governments, rather than courts, will be in charge.[8]

[4] See Mark Tushnet, *Weak Courts, Strong Rights: Judicial Review and Social Welfare Rights in Compartive Constitutional Law* (Princeton UP 2008) 21 (stating that "[t]he modern articulation of strong form judicial review is provided [by] the US Supreme Court [which] described the federal courts as 'supreme in the exposition of the law of the Constitution' and inferred from that a duty of the legislature to follow the Court's interpretation").

[5] See David Super, "Rethinking Fiscal Federalism" (2005)118 Harvard Law Review 2544.

[6] See Jeff Shesol, *Supreme Power: Franklin Roosevelt vs. the Supreme Court* (Norton 2010).

[7] On the notion of judicialization see notably Martin Shapiro and Alec Stone Sweet, *On Law, Politics and Judicialization* (OUP 2002) 71 (defining judicialization as the process of mutation of the role of the judicial power with its growing capacity to shape strategic behavior of political actors).

[8] Following the seminal work of Joseph H.H. Weiler, "The Transformation of Europe" (1990) 100 Yale Law Journal 2403, 2423–4, I consider as intergovernmental a system of decision-making in which (1) the political impetus for a policy; (2) the technical elaboration of policies and norms;

As the chapter maintains, the "intergovernmental method" of governance followed in response to the Euro-crisis is instead the main cause of the high degree of judicial intervention in EMU affairs. In reforming the EMU, the EU member states have largely operated along an intergovernmental logic, which put at the center the powers of the member states acting in the European Council and their freedom to resort to international agreements outside the EU legal order. One of the central tenets of intergovernmentalism in EU governance is that the executive branches will dominate decision-making, to the detriment of legislatures and courts. Yet, the outcome of an intergovernmental management of the Euro-crisis has resulted, in reality, in an increasing involvement of the courts, in a way that would have been impossible had the member states acted through the "Community method."[9] As this chapter highlights, in fact, courts were asked to rule on EMU issues because the political branches reformed repeatedly the EMU architecture through international agreements, which—contrary to EU law—are amenable to domestic judicial review. At the same time, the review of EMU-related international treaties has emboldened some national courts to extend their oversight also to measures adopted by EU institutions, including by the European Central Bank (ECB), in the framework of EU law.

As the chapter suggests, however, the developments in the EMU in the direction of greater judicialization of economic and monetary affairs should be seen with skepticism. While, of course, major differences exist between the EU and the US—notably the fact that the political process is more imperfect in the EU, precisely because of the more intergovernmental modes of decision-making in the economic domain—the chapter maintains that there are still compelling constitutional arguments for why courts also in Europe should defer to the political branches in the area of EMU. Because considerations of expertise, voice, and rights,[10] plead in favor of letting the political process take the lead in economic and monetary affairs, this chapter critically evaluates the current trend of increasing judicial involvement in the EMU. At the same time, the chapter emphasizes the limits of the current system of democratic decision-making and points toward the need to improve the legitimacy of the EU political process—as acknowledged by key institutional actors as well.[11] As this chapter seeks to make clear, criticizing judicial interferences in EMU affairs and stressing the legitimacy of the ordinary EU law-making procedure in no way implies idealizing it. On the contrary, the legitimacy of the EU political process urgently needs to be improved. However,

(3) the formulation of a formal proposal; (4) the adoption of the proposal; and (5) the execution of the adopted proposal, is firmly in the hand of the member states.

[9] See Renaud Dehousse, "The Community Method at Sixty", in Renaud Dehousse (ed), *The Community Method* (Palgrave MacMillan 2011), 3 (defining the "Community method" as the default process by which law-making is accomplished in the EU, which involves the power of the Commission to propose legislation, the power of the Council—and now, in most of the cases the EP—to approve it, and the power of the ECJ to review it).

[10] See Daniel Halberstam, "Constitutional Heterarchy: the Centrality of Conflict in the European Union and the United States" in Jeffrey Dunoff and Joel Trachtman (eds) *Ruling the World* (CUP 2009), 326.

[11] See President of the European Council, Report "Towards a Genuine EMU," June 25, 2012.

this should be achieved through greater democratization, rather than greater judicialization—a point to which I will return in Chapter 5, where I will discuss specific proposals to this end.

This chapter is structured as follows. Section 2 analyzes courts' decisions dealing with several aspects of the new EMU architecture and describes the legal reasoning and substantive outcomes of cases delivered by high courts in Estonia, France, Germany, Ireland, and Portugal, as well as by the ECJ. Section 3 compares the decisions of courts, outlines the rising trend of judicial involvement and indicates its institutional consequences. Section 4 then contrasts the current developments in the EMU with the experience of US courts in the area of economic governance, argues that since the beginning of the Euro-crisis the European judiciary has acquired unprecedented powers vis-à-vis the political branches in the economic domain, and explains that this is the result of the intergovernmental strategy that was followed in response to the Euro-crisis, with the use of international treaties outside EU law. Section 5, however, critically discusses the paradox of judicialization in light of constitutional arguments about expertise, voice, and rights—underlying the comparative advantages of the political process over the courts in EMU affairs and yet emphasizing the need for further institutional reforms in the EU decision-making process through greater democratization. Finally, Section 6 concludes.

2. The Euro-Crisis and the Courts

Since the beginning of the Euro-crisis, courts have been asked to resolve challenges on the legality of various measures adopted by the political branches in the areas of budgetary constraints, financial stabilization, and economic adjustment. Courts interact with the new EMU rules in at least two circumstances. On the one hand, judicial bodies are often required to approve *ex ante* the adoption of legal instruments that contain new EMU obligations. In several state jurisdictions, the ratification of international treaties such as the Fiscal Compact or the ESM, is subject to prior judicial review by national high courts.[12] On the other hand, judicial bodies are vested with powers *ex post*, that is, after the establishment of new EMU rules. In almost all EU member states courts can review legislation and generally control whether action by public authorities conforms to constitutional rules.[13] At the same time supranational courts can be asked whether measures enacted in EMU are consistent with EU primary law.[14] Moreover, since the introduction of constitutional balanced budget

[12] See e.g., Art 54 Const. Fr. (stating that if the French Conseil Constitutionnel declares a provisions of an international treaty incompatible with the Constitution, ratification can only be undertaken after amending the Constitution itself).

[13] See e.g., Donald P. Kommers and Russell A. Miller, "Das Bundesverfassungsgericht: Procedure, Practice and Policy of the German Federal Constitutional Court" (2008) 3 Journal of Compartive Law 194 (discussing judicial review in Germany); Federico Fabbrini, "Kelsen in Paris: France's Constitutional Reform and the Introduction of *A Posteriori* Constitutional Review of Legislation" (2008) 9 German Law Journal 1297 (discussing judicial review in France).

[14] See e.g., Art 267 TFEU (stating that the ECJ shall have the power to give preliminary rulings concerning the validity and interpretation of acts adopted by the EU institutions).

obligations, courts can be asked to review whether national governments have complied with new budgetary constraints.[15]

In what follows I will attempt to map early decisions by European courts dealing with the new fiscal constitution of the EMU. To this end, I examine rulings by high courts in Estonia, France, Germany, Ireland, Portugal, and the EU. Besides several pragmatic factors,[16] the following methodological considerations justify selecting these six case studies as test cases to examine the role of courts in the Euro-crisis.[17] In particular, the five member states chosen provide a comprehensive picture of the plurality of political, economic, and legal conditions characterizing the EU. In political terms, France and Germany are founding members of the EU, while Portugal and Ireland joined in the enlargements of the 1970s and 1980s and Estonia is a new member since 2004.[18] In economic terms, France and Germany (the two biggest economies of the Eurozone) are net contributors to the EU financial stabilization regime,[19] as is Estonia (which has, however, a tiny economy), while Portugal and Ireland are two states which fell under financial assistance programs. In legal terms, finally, France and Germany are jurisdictions with ad hoc centralized constitutional courts empowered to exercise judicial review of legislation,[20] as is (partially) Portugal,[21] whereas Ireland and Estonia endow their ordinary Supreme Courts with special powers of review.[22] By taking into account judicial deliberations in jurisdictions that differ politically, economically, and legally, this chapter seeks to provide a comprehensive picture of how courts reacted to the new EMU rules. As such, this section follows a "most-different-cases

[15] See e.g., Art 8 Fiscal Compact (empowering the ECJ to police the obligation of signatory states to incorporate the "golden rule" in their domestic legal system). See further on this Chapter 1.

[16] High courts in these six legal systems were among the first to rule on issues related to the Euro-crisis and for each of these rulings, full-text decisions were publicly available in an original language, or official translation, that I could read.

[17] For additional cases dealing with legal measures adopted in response to the Euro-crisis see e.g., Verfassungsgerichtshof, No. SV 2/12, judgment of April 3, 2013 (Austrian Constitutional Court declaring the constitutionality of the ESM Treaty); Trybunał Konstytucyjny, case K 11/13 and K 12/13, judgment of March 28, 2013 (Polish Constitutional Court rejecting challenges to the Fiscal Compact); Rechtbank s'-Gravenhage, case no. 419556/KG ZA 12-523, judgment of June 1, 2012 (Dutch District Court of the Hague rejecting challenge to the ESM Treaty).

[18] See *Key Dates in the History of European Integration*, available at <http://europa.eu/abc/12lessons/key_dates/> (last accessed May 10, 2013).

[19] See Annex I ESM Treaty (indicating that Germany contributes to the ESM capital with a share of 27% and France with a share of 20%) and Annex II (indicating that Germany contributes to the ESM capital with €190 billion and France with €142 billion).

[20] See Alec Stone Sweet, *Governing with Judges: Constitutional Politics in Europe* (OUP 2000) 40–1.

[21] See Antonio Cortes and Teresa Violante, "Concrete Control of Constitutionality in Portugal: A Means Toward Effective Protection of Fundamental Rights" (2011) 29 Penn. State International Law Review 759 (explaining how under the Portuguese Constitution both ordinary courts and the constitutional court can review legislation, albeit in different situations and with different effects attached to their rulings).

[22] See Anneli Albi, *EU Enlargment and the Constitutions of Central and Eastern Europe* (CUP 2005) (discussing constitutional regimes of Eastern Europe, including the Baltic states); Seamus O'Tuama, "Judicial Review Under the Irish Constitution: More American Than Commonwealth" (2008) 12 Electronic Journal of Compartive Law 1 (explaining the Irish system of judicial review).

logic of comparison,"[23] whereby cases that differ under a plurality of variables are compared to emphasize the common determinant of an independent variable. In this case, the point I will seek to stress is the following: regardless of the political context of the jurisdiction in which they operate, of the economic conditions, and of the peculiarities of its system of judicial review, courts have become increasingly involved in adjudicating budgetary, economic, and monetary questions. By exploring a plurality of rulings delivered by courts since the outbreak of the Euro-crisis, therefore, this section lays the foundation for a critical discussion—to be carried out in the next section—on the role of the judiciary and of the political process in the fiscal domain.

A. Estonia

One of the first challenge against the new architecture of the EMU took place before the Riigikohus, the Supreme Court of Estonia. In a request submitted on February 2, 2012 (before the ratification of the ESM Treaty), the Chancellor of Justice had asked the Court to rule whether the ESM Treaty, and notably its Article 4(4), was in violation of the Estonian Constitution. The contested provision introduces, by way of derogation to the ordinary decision-making rule adopted in the ESM governing bodies (which requires unanimity), the possibility to resort to an emergency voting procedure[24]:

> [W]here the Commission and the ECB both conclude that a failure to urgently adopt a decision to grant or implement financial assistance [...] would threaten to a significant extent the economic and financial sustainability of the euro area [t]he adoption of a decision by mutual agreement by the Board of Governors [...] requires a qualified majority of 85% of the votes cast.

In his request, the Chancellor of Justice, noticing that Estonia's contribution to the capital of the ESM (despite amounting to almost 8.5% of the domestic GDP) was only 0.186%, underlined how the Estonian vote was not decisive under the procedure and therefore raised the question whether Article 4(4) ESM Treaty was compatible with the principle of parliamentary democracy protected by the Estonian Constitution. In a very articulated decision of July 12, 2012, the majority of the nineteen-judge Supreme Court dismissed the request of the Chancellor of Justice, holding that the clause of the ESM Treaty was compatible with the Estonian Constitution.[25]

The Supreme Court began its opinion by summarizing the main provisions of the ESM Treaty, including its relation with EU law,[26] and declared the request of

[23] See Ran Hirschl, "The Question of Case Selection in Comparative Constitutional Law" (2005) 53 American Journal of Compartive Law 125.

[24] See Art 4(4) ESM Treaty.

[25] Riigikohus, Case 3-4-1-6-12, judgment *en banc* of July 12, 2012 (English translation provided by the Court).

[26] Ibid paras 94–107.

the Chancellor of Justice admissible.[27] The Court then outlined the "principles of the Constitution which it deem[ed] the most relevant in the adjudication of this case."[28] First, the Court identified the principle of sovereignty, as protected by Article 1(1) of the Estonian Constitution, but clarified that this provision had to be interpreted in "the present day context"[29] and therefore rejected the idea that sovereignty ought to be regarded as absolute. Second, the Court recalled the principle of a democratic state and clarified that this meant "that the general principles of law that are recognized in the European legal space are valid in Estonia."[30] Third, the Court drew from the previous two principles, "the principle of reservation by Parliament"[31] and underlined how, according to the Estonian Constitution, it was the prerogative of Parliament to pass the national budget. Moreover, the Court remarked that "the budgetary powers [...] are one of the core competences of the [Parliament]"[32] and concluded that the "financial competence of the [Parliament] is closely related to the state's financial sovereignty and the principles of a democratic state subject to the rule of law [...]."[33]

In light of this framework, the Supreme Court examined whether Article 4(4) ESM Treaty conflicted with the Estonian constitutional principles. In this regard, the Court found that the above-mentioned clause "interfere[d] with the financial competence of the [Estonian Parliament]."[34] Because "[d]ecisions are taken under Article 4(4) of the Treaty by a qualified majority of 85% [...] Estonia may not affect the decisions of the ESM."[35] Therefore, by ratifying the Treaty, and contributing to the ESM capital with a substantial share of domestic financial resources, the Estonian Parliament's possibility to make new future political choices on those resources was restricted because the decision could be adopted without the need of Estonia's agreement. As the court held:

> The composition of the [Estonian Parliament] which passes a law giving rise to the state's long-term financial obligations does not thereby restrict only its own possibilities for exercising financial competence within the same year's state budget, but also restricts the budgetary political choices of next compositions of the [Estonian Parliament].[36]

According to the Court, this contrasted "with the principle of a democratic state subject to the rule of law and of the state's financial sovereignty since indirectly the people's right of discretion is restricted."[37]

Nevertheless, having identified an interference by Article 4(4) ESM Treaty with the Constitution, the Supreme Court moved on to assess whether this interference could be regarded as justified on the basis of the proportionality test. The Court explored the purpose of Article 4(4) and underlined how this clause introduced, by way of derogation, a voting procedure to be used only when the Commission and the ECB agree that action is needed to preserve the stability of the euro area. As such "Article 4(4) of the Treaty seeks to ensure the achievement of the goals of the ESM in an emergency."[38] According to the Court, "the economic and financial

[27] Ibid paras 108–21.
[28] Ibid para 126.
[29] Ibid para 128.
[30] Ibid para 131.
[31] Ibid para 133.
[32] Ibid para 136.
[33] Ibid para 140.
[34] Ibid para 149.
[35] Ibid para 150.
[36] Ibid para 151.
[37] Ibid para 153.
[38] Ibid para 162.

sustainability of the euro area is contained in the constitutional values of Estonia as of the time Estonia become a euro area Member State."[39] Moreover, because "Estonia is a part of the euro area and therefore economically and financially integrated with the other euro area Member States,"[40] the Court held that "a threat to the economic and financial sustainability of the euro area is also a threat to the economic and financial sustainability of Estonia."[41] In the view of the Court, therefore, very pragmatic reasons weighed in favor of justifying the provisions of the ESM Treaty:

> Estonia's economy and finance are closely related to the rest of the euro area and if there are economic and financial problems in the euro area, then it inevitably affects Estonia – export and import of goods and services, state budget, and thereby also social and other fields. Problems in the euro area harm also Estonia's competitiveness and reliability. The ESM as a financial assistance system may help to ensure that the euro area as a whole as well as a part of it, Estonia, would be economically and financially competitive. It is necessary to guarantee people's income, quality of life and social security. In a situation where the rest of the euro area would be in difficulties it is not probable that Estonia would be financially or economically successful, including in the field of people's income, quality of life and social security.[42]

At the same time, according to the Court, economic stability and success were clearly instrumental to the preservation of a supreme constitutional value, namely the protection of fundamental rights. As the Court remarked, "[e]xtensive and consistent guarantee of fundamental rights is extremely complicated, if not impossible, without a stable economic environment."[43] From this point of view: "The common purpose of the euro area Member States to counter threats endangering the economy and financial stability, including by way of efficient decision-making in an emergency, coincides with the [constitutional] purpose of Estonia [...], to guarantee rights and freedoms."[44] According to the Court, therefore:

> [b]y disregarding the common purpose of the euro area Member States or the measure planned for the achievement thereof, Estonia cannot follow its objectives arising from the Constitution. Consequently, the purpose of safeguarding the efficiency of the ESM also in case the states are unable to take a unanimous decision to eliminate a threat to the economic and financial sustainability of the euro area, including of Estonia, is legitimate.[45]

These strong arguments of justification for Article 4(4) ESM Treaty fundamentally determined the result of the Court's proportionality analysis. The Estonian Supreme Court held that the contested provision was suitable to achieve the objective of the Treaty,[46] and was necessary to that end, since there were no alternative less restrictive means.[47] As a matter of fact, "because Estonia's contribution to the ESM is 0.186% [in] essence, the seriousness of the interference for Estonia would decrease only if unanimous decisions would be provided for in Article 4(4) of the

[39] Ibid para 163. [40] Ibid para 164. [41] Ibid para 165. [42] Ibid para 165.
[43] Ibid para 166. [44] Ibid para 168. [45] Ibid. [46] Ibid paras 177–80.
[47] Ibid paras 181–5.

Treaty."[48] This option, however, would contrast with the very logic of that provision. Hence in weighing, on the one hand, the purpose of the treaty—namely "the financial stability of the euro area, including of Estonia"[49]—with, on the other hand the principles of the Constitution—namely "the preservation of Estonia's right to decide on its public funds"[50]—the Supreme Court concluded that Article 4(4) did not disproportionately interfere with the Estonian Constitution.[51] The Court underlined how Article 4(4) was an emergency procedure.[52] It stressed that financial assistance under Article 4(4) required strict conditionality.[53] And it recalled how the Fiscal Compact subjected the possibility of obtaining aid under the ESM only to countries that had incorporated a "golden rule" in their Constitution.[54] Finally, the Court emphasized that:

> Estonia's interests are advanced by cooperation with various international organizations and other states. This is the way to carry out the foreign and security policy which is at the final stage aimed at guaranteeing the preservation of the Estonian people, the Estonian language and the Estonian culture through the ages provided for in the preamble to the Estonian Constitution. International cooperation ensures that Estonia has in the international environment better chances of surviving and achieving its objectives.[55]

The Court hence concluded that the ESM Treaty did not violate the Estonian Constitution.[56]

The decision of the Court, nevertheless, prompted five dissenting opinions, including one supporting the substantive outcome of the case but arguing that the Court should have declared the case inadmissible.[57] In a short and poignant dissent, Judge Ilvest rejected the idea that sovereignty was reshaped by globalization, criticized the lack of unanimity under Article 4(4), and concluded that it should have been only up to the Estonian people via referendum to decide whether to ratify the ESM Treaty.[58] Equally, six other judges criticized the majority opinion in a joint concurrence, which notably rejected the use of proportionality analysis used to support the constitutionality of Article 4(4).[59] In their dissent, the six judges emphasized how the Court should have: "assessed whether the contested emergency procedure which leaves the state of Estonia out of the decision-making outweighs the sovereignty of the state of Estonia, including the

[48] Ibid para 184. [49] Ibid para 188. [50] Ibid. [51] Ibid para 202.
[52] Ibid para 192. [53] Ibid para 193. [54] Ibid para 194. [55] Ibid para 201.

[56] Although the issue was, strictly speaking, beyond the reference raised by the Chancellor of Justice, the Supreme Court devoted a last paragraph of its opinion to comment upon the relationship between the EU legal order and the Constitution of Estonia. Even if the ESM was technically neither primary nor secondary law of the EU, the Court expressed its view that the Treaty substantially "concerne[d] EU law and thereby Estonia's membership of the [EU]." Ibid para 221. In this light, the Court clarified that while the constitutional referendum allowing Estonia to accede the EU "allowe[d] Estonia to be part of the changing [EU] [...] [However, i]f it becomes evident that the new founding treaty of the [EU] or the amendment to a founding treaty of the [EU] gives rise to a more extensive delegation of the competence of Estonia to the [EU] and a more extensive interference with the Constitution, it is necessary to seek the approval of the holder of supreme power, i.e. the people, and presumably amend the Constitution once again." Ibid para 223.

[57] Ibid (Kõve, J. dissenting). [58] Ibid (Ilvest, J. dissenting).

[59] Ibid (Jõks, Järvesaar, Kergandberg, Kivi, Kull, and Laarmaa, Js. dissenting).

financial competence of the [Estonian Parliament] and the principle of a state subject to the rule of law which are one of the most substantial principles" and made it clear that in their view the answer to that question ought to be negative.[60] Moreover, while the dissenters acknowledged that "participation in international cooperation is without a doubt an argument in favor of accession to the ESM Treaty," they voiced their worry that Estonia would never be able to enjoy the benefits of participation in the ESM, since, given the sheer size of its economy, a financial crisis in Estonia would not amount to a threat to the euro area as a whole.[61]

In a fourth dissenting opinion, Judge Tampuu criticized the decision of the Court, arguing that the proportionality test is suitable for constitutional review "where the matter of an interference with a person's fundamental rights is being adjudicated."[62] In the present case, on the contrary, the question was whether the Estonian Parliament could "waive part of its budgetary powers to the ESM."[63] According to Judge Tampuu, the answer ought to be in the negative, because the popular referendum by which Estonia had joined the EU did not authorize the transfer "of budgetary powers to the [EU]"[64] with the result that ratification of Article 4(4) ESM Treaty could only be permitted through a constitutional amendment. Particularly critical of the majority opinion, finally, was the dissent by Judge Luik. In his view, the Estonian Constitution introduced an absolute prohibition on the alienation of sovereignty, which ought to be read in light of the history of Soviet occupation of the country.[65] Moreover, according to Judge Luik, the ESM Treaty created a situation in which only wealthy countries of the euro area would benefit—running afoul of the principle of solidarity. As he remarked, "as of the adoption of the euro the consumer prices have constantly risen in Estonia. [Moreover] Estonia is without a doubt one of the poorest countries in the euro area."[66] Yet, with the ESM Treaty "Estonia undertakes to guarantee with the taxpayer's money the sustainability of the states of the euro area which are many times wealthier than Estonia, including the sustainability of the private sector (banks) of the said states."[67] Hence, Judge Luik rejected the trust of the Court's majority opinion in the "mystical efficiency of the ESM"[68] and conclusively expressed disbelief in the capacity of the ESM to safeguard the prosperity of Estonia.

The decision of the Supreme Court of Estonia on the compatibility of Article 4(4) ESM Treaty with the Constitution of Estonia, if read together with the multiple dissenting opinions, reveals a favorable—but hard-fought—stand vis-à-vis the new architecture of fiscal governance in the EMU. Whereas nine dissenting judges emphasized the limitation to national sovereignty, as well as the potential economic burdens that participation in the ESM would cause to Estonia, a bare majority of ten judges emphasized the social and political advantages that would ensue from Estonian involvement in the ESM and concluded that ratification of the ESM pursued a purpose of constitutional value.[69] In

[60] Ibid para 8. [61] Ibid para 12. [62] Ibid (Tampuu, J. dissenting), para 2.
[63] Ibid. [64] Ibid para 3. [65] Ibid (Luik, J. dissenting), paras 5-6.
[66] Ibid para 16. [67] Ibid para 17. [68] Ibid para 19.
[69] But see Carri Ginter and Raul Narits, "The Perspective of a Small Member States to the Democratic Deficiency of the ESM" (2013) 38 Review of Central & Eastern European Law 54.

this regard, the majority opinion sent a message of openness toward the new mechanisms of financial stability being set up at the EU level and indicated that Estonian involvement in this new venture was a necessary condition for the future economic and financial prosperity of the country.[70] Despite the sovereigntist concerns of a large part of the court, in the end, the Riigikohus, as the Supreme Court of one of the smallest member states of the Eurozone, opted for a decision embedding the participation of Estonia in the new European architecture of economic governance and simultaneously reflected the hope that a positive solution to the Euro-crisis would also favor the economic and social development of Estonia.

B. France

The Conseil Constitutionnel, France' Constitutional Council, was asked by the President of the Republic in July 2012 to decide whether the ratification of the Fiscal Compact was compatible with the French Constitution. Pursuant to Article 54 of the 1958 French Constitution, the Constitutional Council can be asked to decide (upon referral of the President, the Prime Minister, the President of each of the two chambers of Parliament or sixty deputies or sixty senators) whether the ratification of an international treaty "contains a clause contrary to the Constitution," in which case ratification of the treaty must be preceded by a constitutional amendment.[71] In its short decision of August 9, 2012, the Constitutional Council ruled that the Fiscal Compact did not require a constitutional change, hence validating French accession to the treaty.[72]

The Constitutional Council began its decision by outlining the frame of reference it would use in its review. The Council recalled that Article 3 of the 1789 Declaration of the Rights of Man and Citizen proclaimed that "the principle of all sovereignty resides essentially in the nation" and that Article 3 of the 1958 Constitution declares that "national sovereignty belongs to the people."[73] At the same time, it emphasized that the preamble to the 1946 Constitution clarified that France "conforms to the rules of public international law" and "under conditions of reciprocity [...] consents to limitations of sovereignty necessary to the organization and defense of peace."[74] Furthermore, it remarked that subsequent constitutional amendments to the 1958 Constitution had "enshrined the existence of a legal order [of the EU] integrated to the domestic legal order and distinct from

[70] See Cesare Pinelli, "Le Corti europee," in Giuliano Amato and Roberto Gualtieri (eds), *Prove di Europa unita: Le istituzioni europee di fronte alla crisi* (Passigli 2013), 325.

[71] See Art 54 Const. Fr.

[72] Conseil constitutionnel, Décision No. 2012-653DC, jugment of August 9, 2012.

[73] Art 3 Const. Fr.

[74] Pmbl. Const. Fr. of 1946. Notice that the French Constitutional Court has recognized that the preamble of the French Constitution of 1946 constitutes part of the constitutional principles on the basis of which it carries out its review. See on this Alec Stone Sweet, *The Birth of Judicial Politics in France* (OUP 1992).

the international legal order."[75] According to the Council, these constitutional provisions "while confirming the position of the Constitution at the summit of the domestic legal order, [...] allowed France to participate in the creation and development of a permanent European organization, endowed with legal personality and vested with decision-making powers by the transfer of competences accorded by the member States."[76] While the Council recognized that the Fiscal Compact was not technically part of EU law, it clarified that its review would not extend to those "clauses of the treaty which replicated obligations already subscribed by France, notably those included in the Treaty on the Functioning of the EU (TFEU)."[77]

On the merits of the case, the Council chose to focus its attention on Article 3 of the Fiscal Compact, neutralizing potential incompatibilities between this clause and the French Constitution. To begin with, the Council stated that the requirement of Article 3 to strengthen the domestic budgetary constraints did not add any novel obligation for France:

> France is already required to respect the rules of Article 126 TFEU, relating to the containment of excessive States deficits, as well as Protocol n° 12, annexed to the [Treaties], on the procedure concerning the excessive deficits [and] these rules include a standard of reference set at 3% for the ratio between the foreseen or effective public deficit and the gross domestic product at market prices.[78]

Moreover, the Council indicated that the "six-pack" had tightened the deficit brake under EU law.[79] As a result, according to the Council, the provisions of the Fiscal Compact simply reaffirmed and reinforced "the provisions putting in place the obligations of the member States of the [EU] to coordinate their economic policies pursuant to Articles 120 to 126 TFEU."[80] From which it followed "that, no more than the previous budgetary obligations, the duty to respect these new rules does not challenge the essential conditions for the exercise of national sovereignty."[81]

[75] Conseil constitutionnel, Décision No. 2012-653DC (n 72) para 8 (author's translation) ("consacré l'existence d'un ordre juridique de [l'UE] intégré à l'ordre juridique interne et distinct de l'ordre juridique international.").

[76] Ibid para 9 (author's translation) ("confirmant la place de la Constitution au sommet de l'ordre juridique interne, ces dispositions constitutionnelles permettent à la France de participer à la création et au développement d'une organisation européenne permanente, dotée de la personnalité juridique et investie de pouvoirs de décision para l'effet de transferts de compétences consentis par les États membres.").

[77] Ibid para 11 (author's translation) ("stipulations du traité qui reprennent des engagements antérieurement souscrits para la France").

[78] Ibid para 15 (author's translation) ("[L]a France est d'ores et déjà tenue de respecter les exigences résultant de l'article 126 du [TFUE], relatif à la lutte contre les déficits excessifs des États, ainsi que du protocole n° 12, annexé aux [TUE], sur la procédure concernant les déficits excessifs [et] ces exigences incluent une valeur de référence fixée à 3% pour le rapport entre le déficit public prévu ou effectif et le produit intérieur brut aux prix du marché.").

[79] Ibid.

[80] Ibid para 16 (author's translation) ("en les renforçant les dispositions mettant en oeuvre l'engagement des États membres de l'[UE] de coordonner leurs politiques économiques en application des articles 120 à 126 du [TFUE].").

[81] Ibid para 16 (author's translation) ("que, pas plus que les engagements antérieurs de discipline budgétaire, celui de respecter ces nouvelles règles ne porte atteinte aux conditions essentielles d'exercice de la souveraineté nationale.").

Secondly, the Council rejected a possible incompatibility between Article 3(2) of the Fiscal Compact, demanding the incorporation of the "golden rule" at the domestic level, and the French Constitution.[82] As the Council clarified, after the ratification of the Fiscal Compact "France will be, pursuant to the rule *pacta sunt servanda*, bound by these obligations"[83] with the result that "it belongs to the various State institutions to ensure, in the framework of their respective competences, the application of the treaty."[84] Nevertheless, on the specific duty to incorporate the "golden rule," the Constitutional Council underlined how Article 3(2) of the Fiscal Compact introduced

> an alternative on the basis of which the contracting States commit to give effect to the rule enshrined in Article 3(1) in their national legal order, either 'through provisions of binding force and permanent character, preferably constitutional,' or through provisions 'otherwise guaranteed to be fully respected and adhered to throughout the national budgetary processes.'[85]

If the French government was following the first option, "choosing to incorporate the rules enshrined in Article 3(1) through provisions of binding force and permanent character, the authorization to ratify the treaty ought to be preceded by a revision of the Constitution."[86] On the other hand, if it was following the second, no constitutional revision was needed.[87]

As the Constitutional Council made clear, the French legal order included a legal source, the loi organique, which allowed the faithful incorporation of the "golden rule" without demanding a constitutional revision. Article 34(22) of the French Constitution made possible the adoption "of an organic law [...] to set up the framework for the program laws relating to the multiannual orientation of public finances."[88] According to the Council these provisions could serve as the benchmark to assess the constitutionality of the budgetary laws adopted by Parliament. In fact, the Constitutional Council reaffirmed its duty under Article 61 of the French Constitution "to review the conformity with the Constitution of the program laws on the multiannual orientation of public finances, of the budget

[82] Ibid. See further on this Chapter 1.

[83] Conseil constitutionnel, Décision No. 2012-653DC (n 72) para 18 (author's translation) ("la France sera, en application de la règle « *pacta sunt servanda* », liée para ces stipulations").

[84] Ibid para 18 (author's translation) ("il appartiendra aux divers organes de l'État de veiller dans le cadre de leurs compétences respectives à l'application de ce traité.").

[85] Ibid para 19 (author's translation) ("une alternative selon laquelle les États contractants s'engagent à ce que les règles énoncées au paragraphe 1 de l'article 3 prennent effet dans leur droit national, soit 'au moyen de dispositions contraignantes et permanentes, de préférence constitutionnelles', soit au moyen de dispositions 'dont le plein respect et la stricte observance tout au long des processus budgétaires nationaux sont garantis de quelque autre façon'.").

[86] Ibid para 21 (author's translation) ("fai[sant] le choix de faire prendre effet aux règles énoncées au paragraphe 1 de l'article 3 au moyen de dispositions contraignantes et permanentes, l'autorisation de ratifier le traité devra être précédée d'une révision de la Constitution.").

[87] Ibid para 28.

[88] Ibid para 24 (author's translation) ("des dispositions de nature organique [...] pour fixer le cadre des lois de programmation relatives aux orientations pluriannuelles des finances publiques").

laws and the laws for the financing of social security."[89] Moreover, it signaled its commitment to exercise this task carefully, including "by taking into account the advice of independent institutions"[90]—whose creation was also demanded by the Fiscal Compact.

Having concluded that the incorporation of Article 3(2) could be accomplished simply with an organic law, the Constitutional Council indicated that Article 8 of the Fiscal Compact, which empowers the ECJ to review the incorporation of Article 3(2) and to sanction disobedient states, raised no constitutional problem either.[91] According to the Council,

> taking into account that Article 3(2) does not require a constitutional revision, the provisions of Article 8 do not have the effect of empowering the [ECJ] to assess, in this context, the conformity of the Constitution with the obligations of this treaty. [...] As a result, if France decides to give effect to the rules of Article 3(1) of the treaty with the modalities foreseen by the second branch of the alternative of the first sentence of Article 3(2), then Article 8 does not challenge the essential conditions for the exercise of national sovereignty.[92]

With this réserve d'interprétation, the Council then briefly surveyed the other provisions of the Fiscal Compact, and found that none of them included "new binding provisions which add upon the provisions included in the [EU] Treaties."[93] As a result, it concluded that the Fiscal Compact "does not include any clause contrary to the Constitution."[94]

The decision of the Constitutional Council with respect to the Fiscal Compact validated the entry into force of a central feature of the new fiscal constitution of the EMU. By interpreting the obligation of Article 3(2) as requiring simply the adoption of a loi organique, rather than a constitutional amendment, the Council largely eased the task for the French government in adopting the domestic legal instruments necessary as a follow-up to the Fiscal Compact.[95] At the same time, the Constitutional Council took the opportunity to reaffirm its position as the institution charged to review the constitutionality of budgetary laws approved by

[89] Ibid para 27 (author's translation) ("de contrôler la conformité à la Constitution des lois de programmation relatives aux orientations pluriannuelles des finances publiques, des lois de finances et des lois de financement de la sécurité sociale").

[90] Ibid para 27 (author's translation) ("en prenant en compte l'avis des institutions indépendantes").

[91] Ibid. See further on this Chapter 1.

[92] Conseil constitutionnel, Décision No. 2012-653DC (n 72) para 30 (author's translation) ("[c]onsidérant que, le paragraphe 2 de l'article 3 n'imposant pas qu'il soit procédé à une révision de la Constitution, les stipulations de l'article 8 n'ont pas pour effet d'habiliter la [CJUE] à apprécier, dans ce cadre, la conformité de dispositions de la Constitution aux stipulations du présent traité. [...] [P]ar suite, si la France décide de faire prendre effet aux règles énoncées au paragraphe 1 de l'article 3 du traité selon les modalités fixées à la seconde branche de l'alternative de la première phrase du paragraphe 2 de l'article 3, l'article 8 ne porte pas atteinte aux conditions essentielles d'exercice de la souveraineté nationale.").

[93] Ibid para 35 (author's translation) ("contient de clause nouvelle contraignante qui s'ajouterait aux clauses contenues dans les traités relatifs à [l'UE].").

[94] Ibid para 36 (author's translation) ("ne comporte pas de clause contraire à la Constitution.").

[95] See David Jolly and Jack Ewing, "France's Highest Court Clears E.U. Fiscal Treaty," *The International Herald Tribune*, August 11–12, 2012, 9.

The French Parliament. Moreover, it attempted to reduce the powers of the ECJ under Article 8 of the Fiscal Compact through a restrictive reserve of interpretation of that treaty. Whether this réserve d'interprétation with regard to the powers of the ECJ has any bite is doubtful. Pursuant to Article 8 of the Fiscal Compact, the ECJ would still be required to verify whether the loi organique adopted by France is compatible with the principles of Article 3(2).[96] Nevertheless, by clarifying that the Fiscal Compact demanded a scrutiny of compatibility of ordinary budgetary legislation with the "golden rule" and by indicating its commitment to exercise this scrutiny attentively, the Conseil Constitutionnel seized the opportunity offered by the new European fiscal architecture and readily welcomed these institutional changes to expand its domestic powers of review.

C. Germany

Among the European courts, the most active one in reviewing legal measures adopted in the framework of the new EMU architecture has been the Bundesverfassungsgericht, the Constitutional Court of Germany.[97] To begin with, on September 7, 2011, the Constitutional Court delivered a judgment on the compatibility with the German Basic Law of the first rescue package adopted to aid Greece.[98] The case concerned the legislation adopted by the German Parliament to implement the European Financial Stability Facility (EFSF) and to allow the payment of an emergency loan for the financial assistance of Greece.[99] Through individual complaints (Verfassungsbeschwerde), a number of citizens had challenged the constitutionality of these domestic measures as a violation of the right of the German Parliament to make decisions about the budget, and therefore as an interference with the right to vote protected as inviolable by the German Basic Law.[100] The Second Senate of the Constitutional Court declared the case admissible but rejected the constitutional complaints, holding that the two pieces of legislation under review did not violate the Parliament's budgetary autonomy.[101] The Court, however, affirmed that any large amount of financial aid had to be approved by Parliament as the locus of democratic legitimacy, and thus required an

[96] See Art 8 Fiscal Compact.

[97] See Frédéric Lamaître, "L'Europe à l'épreuve des tribunaux", *Le Monde*, October 2, 2012 (interviewing the President of the German Constitutional Court, Andreas Vosskuhle, who emphasizes how the German Court had a special responsibility). See also Heriber Prantl, "Karl Lamers rügt Verfassungsrichter", *Suddeutsche Zeitung*, September 1–2, 2012, 5 (interviewing the CDU spokesman on foreign affairs in the Bundestag, Karl Lamer who criticizes the interference by the German Constitutional Court in European affairs).

[98] BVerfG, Case No. 2 BvR 987/10, judgment of September 7, 2011 (upholding the EFSF and the Euro-rescue package).

[99] For a commentary on the decision see Sebastian Recker, "Casenote—Euro Rescue Package Case: The German Federal Constitutional Court Protects the Principle of Parliamentary Budget" (2011) 12 German Law Journal 2071.

[100] See Art 38 Basic L. Ger. (endowing every person who has reached the age of 18 with the right to vote for the Bundestag).

[101] BVerfG, Case No. 2 BvR 987/10 (n 98) paras 94 and 119.

interpretation of the legislation as imposing prior involvement of the Parliament on every decision by the federal Government to accord financial guarantees under the EFSF.[102]

Moreover, the Constitutional Court was also at the center of public attention in 2012 when it was asked to review the constitutionality of the ESM Treaty and the Fiscal Compact. This case, which had originated from an inter-institutional proceeding (Organstreit) brought by the parliamentary group Die Linke and by five individual constitutional complaints, sought to obtain a temporary injunction preventing the German federal President from signing the Fiscal Compact, the ratification of the amendment to Article 136(3) TFEU, and the ESM Treaty. While from the procedural point of view the case only required a decision on preliminary measures (pending decision on the merits), the Constitutional Court carried out a summary review of the complaints, de facto undertaking a substantive control of the legal measures pending before it.[103] In its judgment of September 12, 2012, the Constitutional Court rejected the request for temporary injunction, holding that the Fiscal Compact, the amendment to the Article 136(3) TFEU, and the ESM Treaty were compatible with the German Basic Law, although in the case of the latter, the Court indicated two conditions that Germany had to clarify with a declaration under international law.[104]

The Court, after describing in detail the facts leading to the adoption of the ESM Treaty and of the Fiscal Compact,[105] their content,[106] as well as the legislation adopted by the German Parliament to implement them at the domestic level,[107] outlined the constitutional principles that it would consider in its review. Here, by building on its previous decisions on EU integration,[108] the Court stated that the right to elect the Bundestag, Germany's lower house of Parliament, enshrined in Article 38(1) of the German Basic Law is "a right equivalent to a fundamental

[102] The decision opened a stream of litigation before the Constitutional Court on the precise role of the Parliament vis-à-vis the Government on issues related to the responses to the Euro-crisis. See BVerfG, Case No. 2 BvE 8/11, judgment of 28 February, 2012 (holding that legislation allowing a special nine-member committee of the Bundestag to authorize, in cases of emergency, the government to act in the management of the EFSF violated the right of the Parliament, as a whole, to be involved in decisions relating to the EFSF); BVerfG, Case No. 2 BvE 4/11, judgment of June 19, 2012 (holding that the Government had violated the right of the Parliament to be fully and comprehensively informed about the negotiation undertaken at the EU level for the adoption of the Euro-plus Pact and of the ESM Treaty). See Susanne Schmidt, "A Sense of *Déjà Vu*? The FCC's Preliminary European Stability Mechanism Verdict" (2013) 14 German Law Journal 1, 10–11.

[103] See text accompanying nn 147–9.

[104] BVerfG, Case No. 2 BvR 1390/12 et al, judgment (preliminary measures) of September 12, 2012 (English translation *partially* provided by the court. Please note that, unless otherwise indicated, the citations below are all drawn from the English translation of the judgment. Please also note that, because the decision is not entirely translated into English, the numbering of the paragraphs in the German and the English versions of the judgment do not correspond. When the text cites the decision in German, the footnote will cite explicitly to the German version with the corresponding number referring to the German version of the judgment).

[105] Ibid paras 2–10. [106] Ibid paras 11–107. [107] Ibid paras 108–45.

[108] See Erich Vranes, "German Constitutional Foundations of, and Limitations to, EU Integration: A Systematic Analysis" (2013) 14 German Law Journal 74.

right, guarantees the citizens' self-determination and guarantees free and equal participation in the state authority exercised in Germany."[109] As such, in the Court's view, Article 38(1) renders justiciable the principle of democracy of Article 20 of the Basic Law, which is "protected by Article 79(3) of the Basic Law as the identity of the constitution even against interference by the constitution-amending legislature."[110] Furthermore, the Court clarified that "[t]here is a violation of Article 38(1) of the Basic Law in particular if the German Bundestag relinquishes its parliamentary budget responsibility with the effect that it or a future Bundestag can no longer exercise the right to decide on the budget on its own responsibility."[111] According to the Constitutional Court, in fact, "[t]he decision on public revenue and public expenditure is a fundamental part of the ability of a constitutional state to democratically shape itself."[112]

As a corollary to this, the Court made five additional statements which developed notions already advanced in its decision of September 7, 2011. First, it held that "[a]s representatives of the people, the elected Members of the German Bundestag must retain control of fundamental budgetary decisions even in a system of intergovernmental governing."[113] Second, it noticed that the "Bundestag may not deliver itself up to any mechanisms with financial effect which [...] may result in incalculable burdens with budget significance without prior mandatory consent."[114] Third, it emphasized the need for the "budget legislature [to] make[] its decisions on revenue and expenditure free of other-directedness on the part of the bodies and of other Member States of the European Union [so as to] remain[] permanently 'the master of its decisions.'"[115] Fourth, it repeated that the "Bundestag must individually approve every large-scale federal aid measure on the international or [EU] level made in solidarity resulting in expenditure."[116] And finally, it underlined that the Bundestag ought to be able to have access to the information needed to exercise its budgetary competence.[117] Nevertheless, the Constitutional Court acknowledged that the Bundestag enjoyed "latitude" in deciding what budgetary commitments to undertake vis-à-vis the EU partners,[118] and—after emphasizing how the EU treaties' provisions on EMU had established a "stability community,"[119] aimed at protecting the Bundestag's overall budget responsibility—it stated that "[i]t is for the legislature to decide how possible weaknesses of the monetary union are to be counteracted by amending [EU] law."[120]

In light of this framework of reference, the Constitutional Court held that the legislation implementing the ESM Treaty "essentially [took] account of the requirements of Article 38(1), Article 20(1) and (2) in conjunction with Article 79(3) of the Basic Law."[121] Nevertheless, since certain interpretations of the provisions of the ESM Treaty might violate the Bundestag's overall budgetary responsibility, the Court required that this "be effectively precluded by

[109] BVerfG, Case No. 2 BvR 1390/12 et al (n 104) para 192. [110] Ibid.
[111] Ibid para 194. [112] Ibid. [113] Ibid para 195. [114] Ibid para 196.
[115] Ibid para 197. [116] Ibid para 198. [117] Ibid para 199.
[118] Ibid para 201. [119] Ibid para 203. [120] Ibid para 206.
[121] Ibid para 208.

declarations under international law made upon ratification of the Treaty."[122] One set of provisions of the ESM to be clarified was that on revised increased capital calls.[123] Although Article 8 ESM Treaty "bindingly limit[ed]" Germany's budgetary commitments to €190 billion,[124] the Court indicated that the Basic Law prohibited any increase beyond that amount "without the ratification of the Bundestag."[125] As such, the Court demanded that the German government, at the act of ratification of the ESM Treaty and "to remove [...] doubts,"[126] declare that the "provisions of this Treaty [...], may only be interpreted or applied in such a way that no higher payment obligations are established for [...] Germany."[127]

Another set of provisions of the ESM to be clarified was the inviolability of documents, and the professional secrecy of the legal representatives of the ESM.[128] While these provisions admitted "an interpretation which makes sufficient parliamentary monitoring of the [ESM] by the German Bundestag possible,"[129] the Court held that, since the Treaty made no "exception in favor of the national parliaments,"[130] a specific declaration ought to secure this possibility. According to the Court, the secrecy of the ESM only intended to "prevent a flow of information to unauthorized third parties,"[131] but could not be opposed vis-à-vis "the parliaments of the Member States, including the Bundestag."[132] The duty to keep the national parliaments, as holders of budgetary authority, fully informed about the ESM, was also all the more important for the following reason: "due to the form chosen for the treaty—that of an international treaty complementing the integration programme of the European Union [...]—no monitoring by the European Parliament is possible."[133] For this reason, the Court required the German government, at the act of the ratification of the ESM Treaty, to make a declaration interpreting the Treaty in a way "which guarantees that with regard to their decisions, [both chambers of the German Parliament] will receive the information which they need to be able to develop an informed opinion."[134]

The Constitutional Court, instead, held that Article 4(8) ESM Treaty, which suspends voting rights for states that failed to meet their obligations to pay the ESM, was not incompatible with the German Basic Law.[135] Moreover, it held that the Bundestag was free to decide to contribute up to €190 billion to the ESM capital. According to the Court:

> The Bundestag and the Federal Government stated in detail that the risks involved with making available the German shares in the [ESM] were manageable, while without the granting of financial facilities by the [ESM] the entire economic and social system was under the threat of unforeseeable, serious consequences. Even though these assumptions are

[122] Ibid para 209.
[123] See Art 9(2) and (3) in conjunction with Art 25(2) ESM Treaty.
[124] BVerfG, Case No. 2 BvR 1390/12 et al (n 104) para 212.
[125] Ibid para 222.
[126] Ibid para 220.
[127] Ibid para 222.
[128] See Arts 32(5), 34, and 35(1) ESM Treaty.
[129] BVerfG, Case No. 2 BvR 1390/12 et al (n 104) para 223.
[130] Ibid para 225.
[131] Ibid para 226.
[132] Ibid.
[133] Ibid.
[134] Ibid para 228.
[135] Ibid paras 230–9.

the subjects of great controversy among economic experts, they are at any rate not evidently erroneous. Therefore the Federal Constitutional Court may not replace the legislature's assessment by its own.[136]

Finally, the Court rejected the complaint raised against other provisions of the ESM Treaty for alleged violation of the prohibition of monetary financing, postponing the decision whether the action of the ECB could represent a circumvention of Article 123 TFEU.[137] Here, the Court held that "[t]he ban on monetary financing as an important element for safeguarding the constitutional requirements of the precept of democracy under [EU] law [...] [wa]s not affected by the Treaty establishing the [ESM]."[138] Nevertheless, citing the ECJ[139] in support of the statement that "[a]s an internal agreement between [EU] Member States, the Treaty establishing the [ESM] must at any rate be interpreted in conformity with [EU] law,"[140] it stressed that the ESM could not bypass the prohibition of monetary financing by the ECB enshrined in the EU treaties.[141]

Unsurprisingly, then, the German Constitutional Court in its decision of September 12, 2012, also gave its approval to the ratification of the Fiscal Compact. As I argued in Chapter 1, in fact, the main provisions of the Fiscal Compact were modeled on the balanced budget rules introduced in the German Basic Law with the Föderalismus reform of 2009.[142] The Bundesverfassungsgericht, therefore, acknowledged that Article 3(2) of the Fiscal Compact was almost identical to the existing requirements of the Basic Law,[143] and simultaneously underlined how the other provisions of the Fiscal Compact replicated requirements already existing under EU law.[144] Moreover, cross-referencing the decision of the French Constitutional Council on the matter, the German Constitutional Court excluded that the Fiscal Compact empowered EU institutions to take action that had a direct effect on national budgetary legislation.[145]

Although the preliminary judgment of 12 September 2012 had largely anticipated the final decision,[146] on March 18, 2014, the German Constitutional Court delivered its conclusive ruling on the constitutionality of the Fiscal Compact and the ESM, confirming the gist of its previous decision.[147] However, with regard to

[136] Ibid para 240.

[137] See Art 123 TFEU (stating that "[o]verdraft facilities or any other type of credit facility with the European Central Bank [...] in favour of Union institutions [... or] central governments [...] shall be prohibited, as shall the purchase directly from them by the European Central Bank or national central banks of debt instruments.").

[138] BVerfG, Case No. 2 BvR 1390/12 et al (n 104) para 245.

[139] Case C-235/87 *Matteucci* [1988] ECR I-5899, ECLI:EU:C:1988:460.

[140] BVerfG, Case No. 2 BvR 1390/12 et al (n 104) para 245.

[141] See text accompanying nn 150 66.

[142] See Gesetz zur Änderung des Grundgesetz (Artikel 91c, 91d, 104b, 109, 109a, 115, 143d), BGBl. I S. 2248 (Nr. 48), July 29, 2009 (Ger.).

[143] BVerfG, Case No. 2 BvR 1390/12 et al (n 104) para 301 [German version of the judgment].

[144] Ibid para 303 [German version of the judgment].

[145] Ibid para 311 [German version of the judgment].

[146] See text accompanying n 103.

[147] BVerfG, Case No. 2 BvR 1390/12 et al, judgment (final) of March 18, 2014.

the ESM the Constitutional Court added a new requirement for its validity within the German legal system, asking the Bundestag to adopt specific legislation to ensure the prompt payment of the German shares to the ESM and thus prevent a loss of voting rights for Germany within the ESM decision-making bodies.[148] At the same time the Bundesverfassungsgericht remarked the importance of a continuing German right to veto within the Governing Board of the ESM even in case of future enlargement of the Eurozone (with consequential accession of new member states to the ESM), stating that:

> Germany's veto position, which is required under constitutional law, will also be maintained under changing circumstances. Pursuant to Art. 44 ESM Treaty, accession to the [ESM] requires a unanimous decision by the Board of Governors [...]. This enables, and if necessary requires, the Federal Government to make its approval of an application for membership contingent on an amendment of [the voting rights system within the ESM] in order to safeguard the Bundestag's overall budgetary responsibility.[149]

Whereas the final judgment on the ESM brought to a close two years of wrangling on the main mechanism established to ensure the financial stability of the Eurozone, the Constitutional Court took another step which produced shock waves throughout the EU.[150] Separating the issue from the ESM case,[151] the Constitutional Court decided on February 7, 2014 to send a preliminary reference to the ECJ in a related case dealing with the legality of the Outright Monetary Transaction (OMT) program of the ECB.[152] This case concerned the compatibility with the prohibition of monetary financing enshrined in Article 123 TFEU of the new program launched by the ECB in September 2012,[153] which allowed the purchase of state bonds on the secondary market to ensure the effective transmission of monetary policy to the real economy, and on the condition that the concerned state entered an ESM-led program of financial assistance.[154] The German Constitutional Court's reference to the ECJ—the first in the history of the Bundesverfassungsgericht—made headlines, and has been praised for the recognition by the German Constitutional Court that the legality of the OMT, being a question of EU law, ought to be adjudicated by the ECJ.[155] However, the nature of the reference (framed as an indictment of the ECB), and the legal basis on which the Court came to adjudicate the case revealed how much the Court has

148 Ibid para 200.

149 Ibid para 193. See further on this Chapter 3.

150 See Niels Petersen, "Karlsruhe Not Only Barks, But Finally Bites—Some Remarks on the OMT Decision of the German Constitutional Court" (2014) 15 German Law Journal 321.

151 BVerfG, Case No. 2 BvR 1390/12 partially separated as Case No. 2 BvR 2728/13 et al.

152 BVerfG, Case No. 2 BvR 2728/13 et al, order of February 7, 2014.

153 See ECB press release, "Technical Features of Outright Monetary Transaction", September 6, 2012.

154 See Stefania Baroncelli, "The Independence of the ECB after the Economic Crisis," in Federico Fabbrini et al (eds), *The Constitutionalization of European Budgetary Constraints* (Hart Publishing 2014), 125. See also Marijn van der Sluis, "Maastricht Revisited," in Federico Fabbrini et al (eds), *The Constitutionalization of European Budgetary Constraints* (Hart Publishing 2014), 105.

155 See e.g., Udo di Fabio, "Karlsruhe Makes a Referral" (2014) 15 German Law Journal 107 and Alexander Thiele, "Friendly or Unfriendly Act? The 'Historic' Referral of the Constitutional Court to the ECJ Regarding the ECB's OMT Program" (2014) 15 German Law Journal 241.

overstepped its boundaries and colonized with its case-law the field of European economic governance.[156]

By a majority of six to two, in fact, the German Constitutional Court effectively ruled that the OMT *is* in violation of the EU treaties.[157] The Court only submitted the case to the ECJ out of comity toward the authoritative interpreter of EU law—de facto asking it to confirm its assessment that the OMT cannot withstand scrutiny.[158] The Court emphasized that only one interpretation of the OMT decision could be regarded as consistent with the EU treaties.[159] Yet—as it had been emphasized—this interpretation would render the OMT measure largely useless.[160] Moreover, to anticipate possible objections by the ECJ, the German Constitutional Court concluded its assessment making it clear that, in case the decision of the ECJ did not satisfy it,[161] it would still reserve to itself the power to declare OMT in violation of German constitutional identity[162] —a core of national sovereignty that cannot be infringed even by EU norms.[163] The decision of the majority, however, was strongly criticized in two forceful dissenting opinions by Judge Lübbe-Wolff and Judge Gerhardt.[164] As the first dissenter made clear, in her view the Court was overstepping its boundaries in the case, adjudicating on the basis of the right to vote provision of the German Basic Law a case that had nothing to do with it, and that should have been rejected as inadmissible on procedural grounds.[165] As emphasized by the second dissenter, otherwise, the OMT case concerned a technical question which should have been left to the political process to decide.[166]

In sum, through its decisions dealing with the Euro-crisis, the Bundesverfassungsgericht has come to play a central role in EMU governance.[167] First, although the Court has, perhaps under the pressure of the events, avoided (so far) declaring any measures subject to its review as in violation of the German Basic

[156] See Franz Mayer, "Rebels without a Cause? A Critical Analysis of the German Constitutional Court's OMT Reference" (2014) 15 German Law Journal 111 and Jürgen Bast, "Don't Act Beyond Your Powers: The Perils and Pitfalls of the German Constitutional Court's *Ultra Vires* Review" (2014) 15 German Law Journal 167.

[157] BVerfG, Case No. 2 BvR 2728/13 et al (n 152) para 55.

[158] Ibid.

[159] Ibid para 100.

[160] See Francesco Giavazzi et al, "The wisdom of Karlsruhe: The OMT Court case should be dismissed," *Voyeux.Org*, June 12, 2013 (explaining that limited bond purchases cannot achieve the objective of the transmission of monetary policy).

[161] See text accompanying nn 242–85.

[162] BVerfG, Case No. 2 BvR 2728/13 et al (n 152) paras 102–3.

[163] See Mattias Wendel, "Exceeding Judicial Competence in the Name of Democracy: The German Federal Constitutional Court's OMT Reference" (2014) 10 European Constitutional Law Review 263.

[164] See BVerfG, Case No. 2 BvR 2728/13 et al (n 152) (Lübbe-Wolff, J. dissenting, and Gerhardt, J. dissenting).

[165] See ibid. (Lübbe-Wolff, J. dissenting), para 1 (arguing that the Court "exceed[ed its] judicial competence" and should have rejected the case as inadmissible).

[166] See ibid. (Gerhard, J. dissenting), para 15 (arguing that "the Federal Government and the Bundestag must have a margin of appreciation and discretion, which the citizens need to accept.").

[167] Jan Herman Reestman and Tom Eijsbouts, Editorial: "Watching Karlsruhe/Karlsruhe Watchers" (2012) 8 European Constitutional Law Review 367.

Law, its judgments have expressed a strong skepticism toward the most recent developments occurring in EMU.[168] In fact, in the case of the ESM Treaty, it explicitly required the German government to accompany its ratification with two declarations under international law clarifying that nothing in the Treaty could be interpreted as increasing the share of Germany to the ESM capital without the approval of the Bundestag or as depriving the Bundestag of the right to obtain all information about the internal functioning of the ESM[169]—a requirement later integrated with the obligation also to adopt specific legislation to ensure the payment of the German shares to the ESM.[170] Second, although the Court has proclaimed that the political branches have discretion in devising strategies to address the crisis,[171] and it has formally acted to strengthen the role of the Bundestag as the authority vested with the constitutionally reserved function to make fundamental decisions on budgetary issues, in reality it has made perfectly clear that ultimately it will be up to *itself* to decide about the legality of whatever legal measure is adopted to address the Euro-crisis.[172] Last but not least, although the Court has referred its first preliminary reference procedure to the ECJ, exploiting the official mechanism for judicial cooperation in the EU, it has taken a stand in the case which—in light of the subsequent decision of the ECJ[173]—raises worries about the sustainability of the Eurozone, and the survival of the EU as a Union of equal states.[174]

D. Ireland

The legality of the ESM Treaty was also at the heart of a constitutional challenge in Ireland. On April 13, 2012, Mr. Pringle, a member of the Irish Parliament, commenced an action before the High Court of Ireland against the ratification of the ESM Treaty, arguing that this was in violation of the Irish Constitution as well as EU law. In particular, Mr. Pringle complained that Ireland's participation in the ESM involved a delegation of sovereignty and a transfer of powers in violation of the Irish Constitution, that the obligations stemming from the ESM Treaty were in contravention of EU law and, moreover, that Decision 2011/199/EU of the European Council—modifying through a simplified revision procedure Article 136 TFEU to allow the Eurozone member states to establish a stability mechanism—was adopted unlawfully and was inconsistent with provisions of the

168 See also Dagmar Schiek, "The German Constitutional Court's Ruling on Outright Monetary Transactions (OMT)—Another Step towards National Closure?" (2014) 15 German Law Journal 329.

169 See Karsten Schneider, "Yes, But...One More Thing: Karlsruhe's Ruling on the European Stability Mechanism" (2013) 14 German Law Journal 54.

170 BVerfG, Case No. 2 BvR 1390/12 et al (n 147) para 200.

171 See Mattias Wendel, "Judicial Restraint and the Return to Openness: The Decision of the German Federal Constitutional Court on the ESM and the Fiscal Treaty of 12 September 2012" (2013) 14 German Law Journal 21, 32.

172 See Matthias Goldmann, "Adjudicating Economics? Central Bank Independence and the Appropriate Standard of Judicial Review" (2014) 15 German Law Journal 265.

173 See text accompanying nn 242–85.

174 See further Federico Fabbrini, "After the OMT Case: The Supremacy of EU Law as the Guarantee of the Equality between the Member States" (2015) 16 German Law Journal 1003.

treaties and with the general principles of EU law. For these reasons, Mr. Pringle sought an injunction restraining the Irish government from ratifying the ESM Treaty. The High Court heard the case and, in a judgment of July 17, 2012, dismissed the appellant's claim under all headings.[175]

After analyzing in detail the provisions of the ESM Treaty and the constitutionally entrenched principles of the TFEU, the High Court declared itself "satisfied that the plaintiff's claim that the ESM Treaty is incompatible with [EU] law has not been established."[176] At the same time, the High Court rejected the petitioner's claim with regard to a breach of the Irish Constitution. First, the Court excluded that the ESM affected a limitation of Irish sovereignty, arguing that the "participation of the State in the ESM Treaty [made] its consent [...] necessary in all cases (with the exception of the application of Article 4(4)) where significant decisions must be made."[177] Second, the Court denied that the ratification of the ESM determined a transfer of budgetary powers from the legislature to the executive emphasizing how the "limit on payments by the State to the ESM [...] cannot be exceeded without the approval of [the Irish Parliament]."[178] Third, the Court held that, because the ESM Treaty was not incompatible with EU law, "an amendment of the Constitution approved of by the people in a referendum [wa]s not necessary before [Ireland could] ratif[y]" the Treaty.[179] The Court then considered the legality of the European Council decision modifying Article 136 TFEU and found it "'completely valid' in accordance with [EU] law."[180] As such, citing *Foto-Frost*,[181] the Court discarded the plaintiff's request for a preliminary reference.

Mr. Pringle appealed the decision to the Irish Supreme Court, which on July 31, 2012, delivered its judgment.[182] In its ruling, the Supreme Court summarily upheld the decision of the High Court, rejecting the sovereignty claim of Mr. Pringle and his request for an injunction preventing the ratification of the ESM Treaty.[183] At the same time, the Supreme Court decided to stay proceedings and submit a reference to the ECJ on the question of the compatibility of the ESM Treaty and of European Council Decision 2011/199/EU with the EU treaties.[184] In particular, the Supreme Court asked the ECJ whether European Council Decision 2011/199/EU was valid having regard to the use of simplified revision procedure and the content of the amendment. Moreover, it asked the ECJ whether, in light of the provisions of the EU treaties regulating the EMU and the general principles of EU law, a member state like Ireland was entitled to enter into and ratify an international agreement such as the ESM Treaty. Finally, it asked the ECJ to clarify whether the ratification of the ESM Treaty was subject to the entry into force of the amendment of Article 136 TFEU introduced by Decision 2011/199/EU. Taking into account that "the ESM Treaty Members, including

[175] *Pringle v. The Gov't of Ireland* [2012] IEHC 296. [176] Ibid para 90.
[177] Ibid para 128. [178] Ibid para 133. [179] Ibid para 140.
[180] Ibid para 163.
[181] Case 314/85 *Foto-Frost* [1987] ECR I-4199, ECLI:EU:C:1987:452.
[182] *Pringle v. The Gov't of Ireland* [2012] IESC 47. [183] Ibid (ruling).
[184] Ibid (preliminary reference).

Ireland, and the Member States of the European Union all have pressing interest in Ireland's timely ratification of the ESM Treaty and that the stability of the euro area would be seriously damaged by delayed ratification" and noticing that the ESM Treaty is "of the utmost importance for other Members of the ESM, and, in particular, the Members who are in need of financial assistance," the Supreme Court asked the ECJ to submit its reference to the accelerated procedure, in order to solve as soon as possible a "matter [...] of exceptional urgency."[185]

The position of the Irish judiciary, as emerging both from the decision of the High Court and that of the Supreme Court, reveals the interconnections between domestic and EU questions relating to the legality of the ESM Treaty.[186] While the High Court held that no need arose for a preliminary reference to the ECJ, because the ESM was fully valid, it systematically analyzed the provisions of the ESM Treaty and of the EU treaties also in light of the case-law of the ECJ, and rejected any form of incompatibility with the Irish Constitution or with EU law. The Supreme Court, instead, reflecting more concerns about the legality of the ESM, decided to make direct recourse to the preliminary reference procedure, thus exploiting the institutional machinery specifically designed under EU law to ensure the dialogue between state courts and the ECJ, to demand the opinion of the ECJ in the resolution of a legal matter affecting the entire Eurozone.[187] The Supreme Court's decision, thus, settled the constitutional question surrounding the ESM Treaty and simultaneously offered to the ECJ the opportunity to be involved in the debate about the legality of the ESM.[188]

E. Portugal

While neither the new budgetary rules nor the legal framework of financial stabilization were at issue in Portugal, the Tribunal Constitucional, the Constitutional Tribunal of Portugal, delivered several decisions dealing with the legality of measures adopted in response to the Euro-crisis. In the framework of the Program of Financial and Economic Assistance that Portugal negotiated with the European Commission, the ECB and the International Monetary Fund (IMF) to obtain financial aid,[189] the Portuguese government enacted a series of domestic budgetary measures, aimed at reducing state deficit and improving the economic outlook of the country, which were subject to review by the Constitutional Tribunal. While these measures were technically national, they were in reality enacted by Portugal

[185] Ibid.

[186] See Jonathan Tomkin, "Contradiction, Circumvention and Conceptual Gymnastics: The Impact of the Adoption of the ESM Treaty on the State of European Democracy" (2013) 14 German Law Journal 170.

[187] On the use of preliminary references by Irish courts see Elaine Fahey, *Practice and Procedure in Preliminary References to Europe: 30 Years of Article 236 EC Caselaw from the Irish Courts* (Firstlaw 2007).

[188] See text accompanying nn 212–41.

[189] See Portugal: Memorandum of Understanding on Specific Economic Policy Conditionality, May 3, 2011, available at <http://economico.sapo.pt/public/uploads/memorandotroika_04-05-2011.pdf> (last accessed May 10, 2013).

upon demand of the EU and international institutions, and reflected the policy strategy (embedded in the principle of conditionality of the mechanisms of financial assistance such as the ESM) of adjusting the economic outlook of the country pursuant to the action plan agreed upon in the MoU. In its decisions, however, the Constitutional Tribunal expressed its increasing discontent for the effects that these domestic measures would produce on principles enshrined in the Portuguese Constitution, such as equality and the protection of social rights.

On July 5, 2012,[190] the Constitutional Tribunal, upon referral of the parliamentary opposition, ruled on the constitutionality of a provision adopted in the budget law for 2012, suspending payment of the thirteenth and fourteenth monthly salary for public sector employees.[191] The Constitutional Tribunal acknowledged that the measure under scrutiny was adopted under exceptional circumstances, in the framework of the MoU signed with the European Commission, the ECB, and the IMF[192] "as a condition for the obtainment of the loans accorded by the EU and the IMF."[193] Nevertheless, it reviewed the measure for its compatibility with the principle of equality, which required that the government treat "similar situations alike and different situations differently, subject to the principle of proportionality."[194] Because the reduction of the monthly salaries only affected the employees of the public sector, leaving untouched those of the private sector, the Tribunal found that the provisions of the budget law failed to comply with the principle of proportionality. As the Tribunal stated:

> The need to adopt measures to address in an effective manner the crisis, cannot be the basis to exempt the legislature from respecting fundamental rights and the principles of the Rule of Law, notably the principles of equality and proportionality. The Constitution is certainly not blind to the economic and financial reality and especially to a situation that may be considered of great difficulty. But it possesses a specific normative force that prevents economic and financial objectives from prevailing, without limits, on the principles such as equality, which the Constitution defends and must accomplish.[195]

Yet, having found the measure under scrutiny unconstitutional, the majority of the Constitutional Tribunal decided to suspend the effect of its ruling for 2012. Pursuant to Article 282(4) of the Portuguese Constitution, in fact, the Tribunal

190 Tribunal Constitucional, Acórdão N° 353/2012, judgment of July 5, 2012.

191 Lei do Orçamento de Estado, n° 64-B/2011 (Pt.) (budget law for 2012).

192 Tribunal Constitucional, Acórdão N° 353/2012 (n 190) para 2.

193 Ibid para 3 (author's translation) ("os quais condicionam a concretização dos empréstimos faseados acordados com a União Europeia e com o Fundo Monetário Internacional.").

194 Ibid para 5 (author's translation) ("tratem por igual as situações substancialmente iguais e que, a situações substancialmente desiguais se dê tratamento desigual, mas proporcionado.").

195 Ibid para 6 (author's translation) ("A referida situação e as necessidades de eficácia das medidas adoptadas paraa lhe fazer face, não podem servir de fundamento para dispensar o legislador da sujeição aos direitos fundamentais e aos princípios estruturantes do Estado de Direito, nomeadamente a parâmetros como o princípio da igualdade proporcional. A Constituição não pode certamente ficar alheia à realidade económica e financeira e em especial à verificação de uma situação que se possa considerar como sendo de grave dificuldade. Mas ela possui uma específica autonomia normativa que impede que os objetivos económicos ou financeiros prevaleçam, sem quaisquer limites, sobre parâmetros como o da igualdade, que a Constituição defende e deve fazer cumprir.").

can delay the effects of its decisions[196]—a possibility that came in handy under the circumstances, given "the exceptional public interest" of the Portuguese state, the current context of grave emergency, and the need to continue to keep open access to external financial aid.[197]

The Constitutional Tribunal, however, did not accommodate the arguments of the government in subsequent rulings. Upon referral of the President of the Republic and by the opposition party, the Constitutional Tribunal delivered a decision on April 5, 2013, which declared, this time with immediate effect, the unconstitutionality of several provisions of the budget law for 2013.[198] Much like the budget law of 2012, the budget law of 2013—which had been agreed upon by the Portuguese government with the European Commission, ECB, and IMF—included provisions aimed at containing government deficit by, among other things, a reduction of the stipends and a suspension of the thirteenth and fourteenth monthly salary of public employees.[199] While the Constitutional Tribunal upheld a plurality of measures adopted in the budget law as falling within the discretionary powers of the government, by drawing on its previous decision of July 2012, it subjected the measure affecting the salary of public employees to a proportionality review aimed at verifying their consistency with the principle of equality. In fact, the Tribunal noticed that, "also for the year 2013 public sector workers will be asked to bear an additional effort [in salary reduction] which is not asked to [...] private sector workers in the same economic conditions."[200] Since the previous case had made clear that this situation did not comply with the principle of proportionality, the Tribunal simply restated its conclusion from 2012, holding that the measure under review "failed to comply with the principle of equality as demanding a proportional sharing of the burden of the public charges."[201] In the same case, the Tribunal also reviewed a provision of the budget law aimed at limiting workers' disease and unemployment benefits and struck it down as violating the minimal protection of social right enshrined in the Constitution.[202]

Moreover, on August 29, 2013, the Constitutional Tribunal struck another blow to the economic adjustment measures carried out by the Portuguese government in the framework of the MoU, by declaring unconstitutional a statute introducing

[196] See Art 282(4) Const. Pt. (stating that "[w]hen required for the purposes of legal certainty, reasons of fairness or an exceptionally important public interest, the grounds for which shall be given, the Constitutional Court may rule that the scope of the effects of the unconstitutionality or illegality shall be [...] restricted").

[197] Tribunal Constitucional, Acórdão N° 353/2012 (n 190) para 6 (author's translation). ("un objetivo de excecional interesse publico").

[198] Tribunal Constitucional, Acórdão N° 187/2013, judgment of April 5, 2013.

[199] Lei do Orçamento de Estado n° 66-B/2012 (Pt.) (budget law for 2013).

[200] Tribunal Constitucional, Acórdão N° 187/2013 (n 198) para 40 (author's translation) ("para o ano de 2013, continuará a exigir-se de quem recebe remunerações salariais de entidades públicas um esforço adicional que não é exigido aos [...] titulares de rendimentos idênticos provenientes do trabalho, no âmbito do setor privado.").

[201] Ibid para 45 (author's translation) ("desrespeita o princípio da igualdade proporcional e da justa repartição dos encargos públicos").

[202] Ibid para 95.

the mobility of public workers for violations of the principle of proportionality and legitimate expectations.[203] On December 19, 2013 then, the Constitutional Tribunal once more blocked parts of the budget law adopted by Parliament for the following fiscal year—and implementing the demands of the "troika" of foreign lenders—holding that the reduction of the pensions of public sector workers infringed the principle of legitimate expectations and was therefore unconstitutional.[204] And so it did again on May 31, 2014, setting aside key parts of the budget bill for that fiscal year.[205]

The decisions of the Portuguese Constitutional Tribunal, therefore, signaled the growing unease of the supreme judicial body for the measures that were enacted nationally, but requested by the EU and international institutions to address the Euro-crisis and re-establish the financial standing of the country. While in its first decision the Tribunal Constitucional aptly made use of the powers it enjoys under the Portuguese Constitution to suspend the effect of its ruling of unconstitutionality, de facto giving a one-off free pass to the legislation adopted by the government, in subsequent decisions the Tribunal did not refrain from declaring several provisions of the budgetary law to be in violation of the Constitution and therefore immediately void. By interpreting in an activist manner the principle of equality and the guarantees of the protection of social rights of the state Constitution, the Constitutional Tribunal placed heavy limits on the capacity of the national executive and legislature to implement measures agreed upon with the pool of European and international lenders to restore the financial stability of the country.[206] With its case-law, therefore, the Tribunal signaled that the future of at least one of the central features of the legal responses to the Euro-crisis, that concerning the economic adjustment measures that debtor countries shall adopt as a condition to obtain financial support, may be standing on shaky grounds.

F. European Union

Since the beginning of the Euro-crisis the ECJ was presented with several opportunities to rule on key aspects of the new EMU architecture. As Alicia Hinarejos has pointed out, the ECJ was called to act in at least three different areas: first, reviewing certain general developments or reforms altering the structure of EMU; second, reviewing the legality of rescue packages and the conditionality imposed on receiving member states; and third, reviewing regulatory or legislative measures pushing for greater financial integration against the opposition of a single member state.[207] So far the ECJ has avoided dealing with the second category of cases,

[203] Pt. Const. Ct., Acórdão N° 474/2013, judgment of August 29, 2013.
[204] Pt. Const. Ct., Acórdão N° 862/2013, judgment of December 19, 2013.
[205] Pt. Const. Ct., Acórdão N° 413/2014, judgment of May 31, 2014.
[206] See Gonçalo de Almeida Ribeiro, "Judicial Activism Against Austerity in Portugal" (2013) International Journal of Constitutional Law Blog (criticizing the case law of the Constitutional Tribunal from the point of view of Portugese constitutional law).
[207] Alicia Hinarejos, *The Euro Area Crisis in Constitutional Perspective* (OUP 2015) 122.

declaring all of them inadmissible.[208] The ECJ, instead, has delivered relevant rulings in the third area, notably by allowing member states to use enhanced cooperation to introduce a Financial Transaction Tax[209]—and I will come back to this in Chapter 4. Arguably, however, the decisions of the ECJ with the most profound implications on the European system of economic governance have occurred in the first area—in particular as a result of preliminary references by the Irish Supreme Court,[210] and the German Bundesverfassungsgericht.[211]

In *Pringle*, delivered on November 27, 2012, the ECJ—acting as a Full Court—answered the preliminary reference of the Irish Supreme Court,[212] addressing separately the three questions raised by the referring court. First, whether Decision 2011/199/EU was valid with regard to the use of the simplified revision procedure pursuant to Article 48(6) Treaty on European Union (TEU) and, in particular, whether the proposed amendment to Article 136 TFEU involved an increase in the competences conferred on the EU in the treaties or a violation of the treaties and general principles of EU law. Second, whether a member state of the EU was authorized to ratify the ESM Treaty, having regard to treaty provisions relating to the EU exclusive competence, those relating to economic policy, those concerning the role of the institutions, as well as the principles of sincere cooperation and of effective judicial protection. And third, whether the ratification of the ESM Treaty could be undertaken before the entry into force of Decision 2011/199/EU. The ECJ responded in the affirmative to all three questions.

To respond to the first question, the ECJ started with a clarification of its jurisdiction. Rejecting the position of several states' governments, the ECJ held it was competent to examine the validity of European Council Decision 2011/199/EU. On the one hand, the ECJ recalled how the decision was an act of an institution, and thus fell within its purview under Article 267 TFEU. On the other, the ECJ noted that, because Article 48(6) TEU set a number of conditions on the use of the simplified revision procedure to amend the treaties, it fell "to the Court, as the institution which, under the first subparagraph of Article 19(1) TEU, is to ensure that the law is observed in the interpretation and application of the Treaties, to examine the validity of a decision of the European Council based on Article 48(6)

[208] See e.g., Case C-434/11 *Corpul Național al Polițiștilor*, order of May 10, 2012, ECLI:EU:C:2011:830; Case C-128/12 *Sindacato de Bancários do Norte*, order of March 7, 2013, ECLI:EU:C:2013:149; Case C-665/13 *Sindicato Nacional dos Profissionais de Seguros*, order of October 21, 2014, ECLI:EU:C:2014:2327. For a critical reading of these cases see further Catherine Barnard, "The Charter, the Court—and the Crisis," University of Cambridge Faculty of Law Research Paper No. 18/2013. But see also *Da Silva Carvalho Rico v. Portugal* [ECHR] App. No. 13341/14, judgment of September 24, 2015 (European Court of Human Rights declaring a challenge against austerity measures inadmissible under the European Convention on Human Rights).

[209] Case C-209/13 *United Kingdom v. Council*, judgment of April 30, 2014, ECLI:EU:C:2014:283. But see also Case C-270/12 *United Kingdom v. Parliament and Council*, judgment of January 22, 2014, ECLI:EU:C:2014:18 (ruling that the delegation of power to the European Securities Market Authority to regulate short selling was legal). See on this Takis Tridimas, "Financial Supervision and Agency Power: Reflection on ESMA," in Niamh Nic Shuibhne and Laurence W. Gormley (eds), *From Single Market to Economic Union* (OUP 2012), 55.

[210] See text accompanying n 184.

[211] See text accompanying n 152.

[212] Case C-370/12 *Pringle v. Ireland*, judgment of November 27, 2012, ECLI:EU:C:2012:756.

TEU."[213] In particular, the ECJ indicated that its task was to verify: "[F]irst, that the procedural rules laid down in Article 48(6) TEU were followed and, secondly, that the amendments decided upon concern only Part Three of the FEU Treaty, which implies that they do not entail any amendment of provisions of another part of the Treaties [...], and that they do not increase the competences of the Union."[214]

Having firmly established its jurisdiction to review the legality of treaty amendments, the ECJ moved to consider the substance of the challenge on Decision 2011/199/EU.[215] Here, the ECJ separately examined whether the amendment of the TFEU envisaged by Decision 2011/199/EU solely concerned provisions of Part Three of the TFEU and whether it increased the competences conferred on the EU in the treaties. On the former, the ECJ remarked that Decision 2011/199/EU formally introduced a change to Article 136 TFEU, which is a provision of Part III of the TFEU.[216] However, the ECJ also examined whether the Decision substantially affected other parts of the TFEU, notably the monetary policy indicated by Article 3(1)(c) TFEU as an area of exclusive competence of the EU. According to the ECJ the objectives pursued (and the instruments foreseen) by the stability mechanism envisaged by Decision 2011/199/EU served "to complement the new regulatory framework for strengthened economic governance of the Union"[217] and therefore fell "within the area of economic policy."[218] Otherwise, the ECJ underlined how the provisions of the treaties "d[id] not confer any specific power on the Union to establish a stability mechanism of the kind envisaged by Decision 2011/199."[219] As a result, the "Member States whose currency is the euro are entitled to conclude an agreement between themselves for the establishment of a stability mechanism of the kind envisaged by Article 1 of Decision 2011/199."[220] In addition, on the question of whether the decision increased the competences conferred on the Union, the ECJ stated that the new Article 136(3) TFEU simply "confirm[ed] that Member States have the power to establish a stability mechanism and is further intended to ensure, by providing that the granting of any financial assistance under that mechanism will be made subject to strict conditionality, that the mechanism will operate in a way that will comply with [EU] law."[221] Hence, the ECJ concluded that Decision 2011/199/EU was lawfully adopted in compliance with the simplified revision procedure.[222]

To respond to the second question raised by the Irish Supreme Court, the ECJ examined one-by-one a multiplicity of substantive provisions of the EU treaties indicated by the referring court, in order to assess whether any of them precluded an EU member state from ratifying the ESM Treaty. According to the ECJ, none

[213] Ibid para 35. [214] Ibid para 36.

[215] The ECJ also preliminarily discarded the procedural argument raised by the Irish government that the case was inadmissible, because the applicant should have directly challenged Decision 2011/199/EU with an action under Art 263 TFEU. As the ECJ argued, in fact, "it [wa]s not evident that the applicant in the main proceedings had beyond doubt standing to bring an action for the annulment of Decision 2011/199 under Article 263 TFEU": Ibid para 42.

[216] Ibid para 46. [217] Ibid para 58 (citing the "six-pack"). [218] Ibid para 60.

[219] Ibid para 64. [220] Ibid para 68. [221] Ibid para 72. [222] Ibid para 76.

of these provisions produced such an effect. First, the ECJ restated that the ESM was not incompatible with Articles 3(1)(c) and 127 TFEU regulating the EU monetary policy, including its primary objective of price stability, since "[e]ven if the activities of the ESM might influence the rate of inflation, such an influence would constitute only the indirect consequence of the economic policy measures adopted."[223] Second, the ECJ discarded the argument that the ESM conflicted with Article 3(2) TFEU, which gives to the EU exclusive jurisdiction in concluding international agreements in the fields in which it has exclusive internal powers, holding that—since no "provision of the [...] Treaties confer[red] a specific power on the Union to establish a permanent stability mechanism such as the ESM [...] the Member States [we]re entitled [...] to act in this area."[224] Third, the ECJ held that the ESM was not incompatible with treaty provisions on economic policy—Articles 2(3), 119, 120, 121, and 126 TFEU. The ECJ reiterated that "the Member States have the power to conclude between themselves an agreement for the establishment of a stability mechanism such as the ESM Treaty provided that the commitments undertaken [...] are consistent with [EU] law"[225] and noted that, because "the ESM is not concerned with the coordination of the economic policies of the Member States, but rather constitutes a financing mechanism"[226] no problem of compatibility arose.

Most importantly, however, the ECJ rejected the argument that the ESM violated Articles 122, 123, and 125 TFEU, which concern the well-known rules of solidarity assistance, prohibition of monetary financing, and prohibition of bail-out.[227] On Article 122, the ECJ held that since that clause did "not constitute an appropriate legal basis for any financial assistance from the Union to Member States who are experiencing, or are threatened by, severe financing problems, the establishment of a stability mechanism such as the ESM does not encroach on the powers which that provision confers on the Council."[228] On Article 123, the ECJ underlined how this clause was textually phrased to prohibit the ECB and other central banks from directly purchasing governments' bonds, so that "[t]he grant of financial assistance by one Member State or by a group of Member States to another Member State [was] not covered by that prohibition."[229] On Article 125, then, the ECJ stated that this clause was "not intended to prohibit either the Union or the Member States from granting any form of financial assistance whatever to another Member State."[230] This reading was supported by both a systematic interpretation of the Treaty—given that among others Article 122 TFEU *did* provide for forms of assistance—and by an historical analysis of the original intent of the treaty drafters. According to the ECJ, from the preparatory work of the Maastricht Treaty it emerged that "[t]he prohibition

[223] Ibid para 97. [224] Ibid para 105. [225] Ibid para 109.
[226] Ibid para 110.
[227] See Art 125 TFEU (stating that "[t]he Union shall not be liable for or assume the commitments of central governments, regional, local or other public authorities, other bodies governed by public law, or public undertakings of any Member State.").
[228] *Pringle* (n 212) para 116. [229] Ibid para 125. [230] Ibid para 130.

laid down in Article 125 TFEU [was designed to] ensure[] that the Member States remain subject to the logic of the market when they enter into debt."[231] Hence, Article 125 TFEU only prohibited those grants of financial assistance "as a result of which the incentive of the recipient Member State to conduct a sound budgetary policy [would] diminish[]."[232] This was not, however, the case of the ESM. In fact, on the basis of the ESM Treaty,

> stability support may be granted to ESM Members which are experiencing or are threatened by severe financing problems only when such support is indispensable to safeguard the financial stability of the euro area as a whole and of its Member States and the grant of that support is subject to strict conditionality appropriate to the financial assistance instrument chosen.[233]

The ESM did not act as a guarantor of the debts of the recipient member state,[234] and no other state would be liable for the commitments of an ESM state facing default.[235] In light of this, the ECJ concluded that Article 125 TFEU was no obstacle to the adoption of the ESM Treaty.

The ECJ also briefly set aside the concern that the ESM Treaty was incompatible with the principle of sincere cooperation set out in Article 4(3) TEU.[236] It ruled that the attribution by the ESM Treaty of specific tasks to some EU institutions (the ECB, the Commission, and the ECJ) did not violate Article 13 TEU, stressing that its case-law, or specific provisions of the Treaty such as Article 273 TFEU, entitled the member states, "in areas which do not fall under the exclusive competence of the Union, to entrust tasks to the institutions, outside the framework of the Union, [...] provided that those tasks do not alter the essential character of the powers conferred on those institutions by the EU and FEU Treaties."[237] Last but not least, the ECJ denied that the ESM Treaty ran afoul of the general principle of judicial protection enshrined in the EU Charter of Fundamental Rights. In fact, in the view of the ECJ, the Charter is addressed "to the Member States only when they are implementing Union law."[238] Yet, in establishing the ESM, the member states were not implementing EU law, and, as a result, they were not subject to the scope of application of the Charter.[239] On the third question raised by the Irish Supreme Court, then, the ECJ briefly answered that Ireland was entitled to conclude and ratify the ESM Treaty before the entry into force of the amendment of Article 136 TFEU. Because Decision 2011/199/EU simply confirmed the existence of a power possessed by the member states and did "not confer any new power on the[m]"[240] according to the ECJ the right of a member state to sign and ratify that Treaty was not conditional on the entry into force of Decision 2011/199/EU.[241]

In *Gauweiler*, delivered on June 16, 2015, the Grand Chamber of the ECJ, instead, answered the preliminary reference of the German Bundesverfassungsgericht,[242]

[231] Ibid para 135. [232] Ibid para 136. [233] Ibid para 142.
[234] Ibid para 138. [235] Ibid para 146. [236] Ibid para 152.
[237] Ibid para 158. [238] Ibid para 179. [239] Ibid para 180.
[240] Ibid para 184. [241] Ibid para 185.
[242] Case C-62/14 *Gauweiler*, judgment of June 16, 2015, ECLI:EU:C:2015:400.

ruling on the validity of the OMT program launched by the ECB and the interpretation of the treaty provisions dealing with the conduct of monetary policy and the prohibition of monetary financing. In its judgment, the ECJ unequivocally backed the legality of OMT, rejecting the view that the ECB had acted ultra vires. As a preliminary matter, the ECJ set aside the procedural argument raised by an intervening party, according to which the ECJ should not have answered the case since the German Constitutional Court in its preliminary reference did not accept as binding and definitive the interpretation to be provided by the ECJ: rather, the ECJ observed "that, according to [its] settled case-law [...] Article 267 TFEU establishes a procedure for direct cooperation between the Court and the courts of the Member States,"[243] and it strongly reaffirmed the principle that "a judgment in which the [ECJ] gives a preliminary ruling is binding on the national court, as regards the interpretation or the validity of the acts of the EU institutions in question, for the purposes of the decision to be given in the main proceedings."[244] Equally, the ECJ set aside the view that the case ought to be declared inadmissible since the OMT had never been put into operation, holding that "questions concerning EU law enjoy a presumption of relevance."[245] And it also discarded the claim that the challenge against the ECB ought to have been brought through a direct action of annulment,[246] rather than through a preliminary reference procedure, stating that "it [found] sufficient [that] the national court [wa]s seised of a genuine dispute in which the question of the validity of such an act is raised on indirect grounds."[247]

On the substance of the case, the ECJ separately addressed the questions first, whether the OMT program exceeded the powers of the ECB in the field of monetary policy, as defined by primary law; and second, whether the action of the ECB violated the prohibition of monetary financing, enshrined in primary law. With regard to the former, the ECJ underlined as a starting point that "Article 3(1)(c) TFEU states that the Union is to have exclusive competence in th[e] area [of monetary policy] for the Member States whose currency is the euro"[248] and that, under the treaties, "the ECB and the central banks of the Member States whose currency is the euro, which constitute the Eurosystem, are to conduct the monetary policy of the Union."[249] As the ECJ pointed out, also with reference to its previous case-law,[250] the ECB "is to be independent when carrying out its task,"[251] but, "[i]n accordance with the principle of conferral of powers set out in Article 5(2) TEU, the [ECB] must act within the limits of the powers conferred upon it by primary law."[252] In light of this, the ECJ engaged in an analysis of the limits between economic and monetary policy,

243 Ibid para 15. 244 Ibid para 16. 245 Ibid para 25.

246 See Case T-492/12 *von Storch v. ECB*, order of December 10, 2013 ECLI:EU:T:2013:702 (EU General Court declaring inadmissible action for annulment against decision of the ECB) now appealed as Case C-64/14 P *von Storch v. ECB*, pending ECLI:EU:C:2015:300.

247 *Gauweiler* (n 242) para 29. 248 Ibid para 35. 249 Ibid para 36.

250 See Case C-11/00 *Commission v. ECB* [2003] ECR I-7147, ECLI:EU:C:2003:395.

251 *Gauweiler* (n 242) para 40. 252 Ibid para 41.

holding that "in order to determine whether a measure falls within the area of monetary policy"[253] it was necessary to assess the objectives of the measures and the instrument used.[254]

According to the ECJ, the OMT program certainly fell within the scope of the ECB monetary policy. First, as regards the objectives, the program aimed "to safeguard both 'an appropriate monetary policy transmission and the singleness of the monetary policy'"[255]—and the fact that OMT "might also be capable of contributing to the stability of the euro area, which is a matter of economic policy [...] does not call that assessment into question."[256] Second, as regard the instrument used, the program "entail outright monetary transactions on secondary sovereign bond markets"[257]—but the ECB Statute granted to the ECB such a power,[258] and the "fact that the implementation of such a programme is made conditional upon full compliance with EFSF or ESM macroeconomic adjustment programmes does not alter that conclusion."[259] As the ECJ pointed out, in fact, while OMT may "to some extent, further the economic policy objectives" of economic adjustment programs:[260] "such indirect effects do not mean that such a programme must be treated as equivalent to an economic policy measure, since it is apparent from Articles 119(2) TFEU, 127(1) TFEU and 282(2) TFEU that, without prejudice to the objective of price stability, the ESCB is to support the general economic policies in the Union."[261]

Moreover, the ECJ ruled that the OMT program complied with the principle of proportionality. Following the Advocate General's advice,[262] the ECJ acknowledged that, because the ECB is tasked "to make choices of a technical nature and to undertake forecasts and complex assessments, it must be allowed, in that context, a broad discretion."[263] Nevertheless, the ECJ also stated that "where an EU institution enjoys broad discretion, a review of compliance with certain procedural guarantees is of fundamental importance."[264] Those guarantees include the obligation for the ESCB to examine carefully and impartially all the relevant elements of the situation in question, and to give an adequate statement of the reasons for its decisions.[265] Yet, the ECJ concluded that the OMT program passed the suitability and the necessity tests which are the core of proportionality analysis. As regards, in the first place, the appropriateness of the OMT program, it held that "it does not appear that that analysis of the economic situation of the euro area [made by the ECB when launching the OMT program] is vitiated by a manifest error of assessment."[266] In fact:

> given that questions of monetary policy are usually of a controversial nature and in view of the ESCB's broad discretion, nothing more can be required of the ESCB apart from that it use its

[253] Ibid para 46. [254] Ibid. [255] Ibid para 47. [256] Ibid para 51.
[257] Ibid para 53. [258] Ibid para 54. [259] Ibid para 57. [260] Ibid para 58.
[261] Ibid para 59.
[262] Case C-62/14 *Gauweiler*, Opinion of AG Cruz Villalón of January 14, 2015, ECLI:EU:C:2015:400, para 111.
[263] *Gauweiler* (n 242) para 68. [264] Ibid para 69. [265] Ibid.
[266] Ibid para 74.

economic expertise and the necessary technical means at its disposal to carry out that analysis with all care and accuracy.[267]

As regards, in the second place, the necessity of the OMT program, the ECJ ruled the action of the ECB did "not go manifestly beyond what is necessary to achieve [its] objectives."[268] As the ECJ pointed out, after its announcement the OMT program had never been implemented;[269] its activation is subject to the precondition that a member state concludes an ESM-led program of economic adjustment;[270] and "the commitments which the ECB is liable to enter into when such a programme is implemented are, in fact, circumscribed and limited."[271] At the same time, in the ECJ's view, the ECB "was fully entitled to take the view that a selective bond-buying programme may prove necessary in order to rectify that disruption [of the monetary policy transmission system],"[272] rendering unstainable the argument that OMT was disproportionate.

Having ruled that the ECB had not exceeded the powers conferred to it by the treaties, the ECJ subsequently considered whether OMT violated the prohibition of monetary financing of Article 123 TFEU.[273] In this regard, while the ECJ emphasized that Article 18(1) of the ECB Statute permits the ECB to operate in the financial markets,[274] it stated that the ECB "does not have authority to purchase government bonds on secondary markets under conditions which would, in practice, mean that its action has an effect equivalent to that of a direct purchase of government bonds from the public authorities and bodies of the Member States, thereby undermining the effectiveness of the prohibition in Article 123(1) TFEU."[275] However, as it had done in the *Pringle* case,[276] the ECJ engaged in a historically-informed interpretation of the treaties and it concluded that from the preparatory work of the Maastricht Treaty it emerged that the prohibition laid down in "Article 123 TFEU [was designed to] encourage the Member States to follow a sound budgetary policy."[277] Given the logic of Article 123 TFEU, the ECJ found that the features of the OMT "exclude the possibility of that programme being considered of such a kind as to lessen the impetus of the Member States to follow a sound budgetary policy."[278] First, as the ECJ pointed out, the OMT program "provides for the purchase of government bonds only in so far as is necessary for safeguarding the monetary policy transmission mechanism and the singleness of monetary policy"[279]—and "the Member States cannot, in determining their budgetary policy, rely on the certainty that the ESCB will at a future point purchase their government bonds on secondary markets."[280] Second, the OMT program "is accompanied by a series of guarantees that are intended to limit its impact on the impetus to follow a sound budgetary policy."[281] Finally, "the fact that the purchase of government bonds is conditional upon full compliance with

[267] Ibid para 75. [268] Ibid para 81. [269] Ibid para 84. [270] Ibid para 86.
[271] Ibid para 87. [272] Ibid para 89. [273] Ibid para 94. [274] Ibid para 96.
[275] Ibid para 97. [276] See text accompanying n 231.
[277] *Gauweiler* (n 242) para 100. [278] Ibid para 111. [279] Ibid para 112.
[280] Ibid para 113. [281] Ibid para 115.

the structural adjustment programmes to which the Member States concerned are subject precludes the possibility of a programme, such as that announced in the press release, acting as an incentive to those States to dispense with fiscal consolidation."[282]

As a last observation, then, the ECJ addressed the risk of the potential of losses to which the ECB would be exposed as a result of the OMT program—thus tackling an issue which had been of major concern for the Bundesverfassungsgericht, this being the argument on the basis of which the German Constitutional Court had admitted the challenge against the OMT in the first place.[283] As the ECJ remarked, "a central bank, such as the ECB, is obliged to take decisions which, like open market operations, inevitably expose it to a risk of losses and [...] Article 33 of the Protocol on the ESCB and the ECB duly provides for the way in which the losses of the ECB must be allocated, without specifically delimiting the risks which the Bank may take in order to achieve the objectives of monetary policy."[284] Otherwise, the ECB had emphasized that so far the OMT had costed nothing, while preventing potential major losses which would have occurred had the Eurozone broke up—a development that could not be excluded before the OMT program was announced. Hence, the ECJ concluded "that Articles 119 TFEU, 123(1) TFEU and 127(1) and (2) TFEU and Articles 17 to 24 of the Protocol on the ESCB and the ECB must be interpreted as permitting the ESCB to adopt a programme for the purchase of government bonds on secondary markets, such as the [OMT program]."[285]

In conclusion, as a result of the references of national high courts, the ECJ in *Pringle* and *Gauweiler* delivered major judgments on key components of the new architecture of EMU. In *Pringle* the ECJ set aside any doubt about the compatibility of the ESM Treaty with EU primary law, thus giving its blessing to a Treaty which had already entered into force;[286] and in *Gauweiler*, the ECJ set aside any doubt about the compatibility of the ECB OMT with EU primary law, thus giving its blessing to a program which ironically had never been implemented. In both cases, the ECJ engaged in a historically informed interpretation of the treaties, distinguishing between economic and monetary policy, and neutralized questions about the validity of the measures pending before it.[287] In both decisions, the ECJ revealed a favorable stand vis-à-vis measures designed to improve the resilience of the Eurozone[288]—even when reviewing a Treaty such as the ESM which was developed outside the framework of the EU law. Overall, therefore, the judgments of the ECJ followed the previous practice of the ECJ

[282] Ibid para 120. [283] See text accompanying nn 100–2.

[284] *Gauweiler* (n 242) para 125. [285] Ibid 127.

[286] The ESM Treaty had entered into force on September 27, 2012, after the German deposit of the instrument of ratification.

[287] Pieter-Augustijn Van Malleghem, "*Pringle*: A Paradigm Shift in the European Union's Monetary Constitution" (2013) 14 German Law Journal 141.

[288] See Paul Craig, "*Pringle*: Legal Reasoning, Text, Purpose and Teleology" (2013) 20 Maastricht Journal of European & Compartive Law 3.

in the field,[289] ensuring to the political branches a wide margin to maneuver in EMU, and minimizing the legal obstacles at the EU level toward a satisfactory solution of the Euro-crisis.[290] Yet, they also opened new challenges—notably in connection to the question whether the German Constitutional Court will refuse to abide to the ECJ ruling when reconsidering the legality of the OMT policy of the ECB.[291]

3. Institutional Implications

The previous section analyzed decisions by courts at both the national and supranational level reviewing the legality of various components of the new EMU constitutional architecture. Building on that detailed analysis of the case-law, this section compares the rulings by high courts in Estonia, France, Germany, Ireland, Portugal, and the EU and discusses their institutional implications on the horizontal balance of powers between the political and the judicial branches. Needless to say, a comparison of judicial decisions dealing with aspects of the new architecture of the EMU should be undertaken with some caveats: the nature of the specific measure under review and the scope of the scrutiny carried out by courts differed from one jurisdiction to another, and reflects differences in procedural powers, modes of legal reasoning, and conceptions of the role of the judiciary in a constitutional system.[292] Yet, an overview of judicial decisions in systems that are as varied as Estonia, France, Germany, Ireland, Portugal, and the EU can provide important insights on how, regardless of the many differences between the various case studies, courts have so far reacted similarly to the reforms of the EMU by expanding significantly their powers to review, and possibly void, measures adopted by the political branches in the economic and monetary domain.

Based on the data analyzed in the previous section, in fact, it is possible to identify a consistent trend of judicial involvement in EMU matters across Europe.[293]

[289] See e.g., Case C-27/04 *Commission v. Council* [2004] ECR I-6649, ECLI:EU:C:2004:436 (recognizing wide discretion to the Council whether to impose sanctions under the SGP or held in abeyance the excessive deficit procedure against two member states recommended by the Commission).

[290] See also Bruno de Witte and Thomas Beukers, "The Court of Justice approves the creation of the European Stability Mechanism outside the EU legal order: *Pringle*" (2013) 50 Common Market Law Review 805.

[291] See further Federico Fabbrini (ed), Special issue: "The European Court of Justice, the European Central Bank, and the Supremacy of EU Law" (2016) 23 Maastricht Journal of European & Comparative Law.

[292] See e.g., Jan Komarek, "Judicial Lawmaking and Precedent in the Supreme Courts: The European Court of Justice Compared to the US Supreme Court and the French *Court de Cassation*" (2009) 11 Cambridge Yearbooks of European Legal Studies 399 (comparing reasoning based on precedents); Jacco Bomhoff, "Balancing, the Global and the Local: Judicial Balancing as a Problematic Topic in Compartive (Constitutional) Law" (2008) 31 Hastings International and Compartive Law Review 555 (discussing differences in the way in which courts use the technique of judicial balancing).

[293] See also Fabrizio Galimberti, "Se anche il potere giudiziario critica il rigore", *Il Sole 24 Ore*, April 7, 2013, 10 (discussing the implications of the rulings by the Portuguese Constitutional Court) and Charles Secondat et al, "The German Constitutional Court's decision about the European Central Bank's OMT mechanism: A masterpiece of judicial arrogance," Egmont Royal Institute for

At first glance, it is noticeable how often courts have been called to rule on the legality of EMU measures. This represents a major break from the past. Certainly, in terms of the effects of the decisions, national and supranational courts have, by and large, validated the new legal measures adopted in response to the Euro-crisis. Courts have given their green light to the enactment and entry into force of legal measures aimed at strengthening budgetary discipline, introducing new mechanisms of financial stabilization, prescribing strict programs of economic adjustment, and enhancing the transmission mechanisms of the ECB monetary policy. With the exception of the latest decisions of the Portuguese Constitutional Court and the German Constitutional Court,[294] the rulings analyzed above have validated the legal measure under review. A cursory assessment of the role of courts in the framework of the new EMU constitution might therefore suggest that the judiciary has deferred to the political branches, upheld their action, and provided them with leeway in devising responses to the Euro-crisis.

Nevertheless, if we include a qualitative analysis of the courts' reasoning, it is evident that judicial support for the new constitutional architecture of the EMU has been much less enthusiastic. This emerges not only from decisions such as those of the German Constitutional Court or the Portuguese Constitutional Tribunal, which placed explicit limits on the validity of the measures under review, or by the preliminary reference of the Irish Supreme Court, which suggested worries about the legality of the ESM Treaty. It also emerges from the case-law of the Estonian Supreme Court and the French Constitutional Council, which appeared, overall, to embrace a Europarechtsfreundliche approach.[295] In fact, while the decision of the Estonian Supreme Court is certainly one of the more open toward the constitutional reforms undertaken in the EU in response to the Euro-crisis, the judgment was delivered by a divided court, with nine judges out of 19 fundamentally objecting to the wisdom of the decision, and one judge (casting the decisive ballot for the majority) suggesting that the case ought to have been dismissed on procedural grounds. Similarly, the French Constitutional Council, while largely upholding the Fiscal Compact, added several réserves d'interprétation which potentially restrict the scope of the EMU reform.

Specifically, two main features seem to emerge from a qualitative analysis of courts' decisions in EMU. First, judicial institutions have generally been supportive of new EMU measures introducing tighter budgetary constraints, but have expressed more discomfort toward measures of financial stabilization and economic

International Relations European Policy Brief No. 30/2014 (criticizing intervention of the German Constitutional Court in the OMT case).

[294] See text accompanying nn 296–9.

[295] The notion of *Europarechtsfreundlichkeit*—literally meaning: "friendship toward European law" —finds its origin in German constitutional law. On this see Jacques Ziller, "Zur Europarechtsfreundlichkeit des deutschen Bundesverfassungsgerichtes. Eine ausländische Bewertung des Urteils des Bundesverfassungsgerichtes zur Ratifikation des Vertrages von Lissabon" (2010) 65 Zeitschrift für öffentliches Recht 157 (discussing the notion of openness toward EU law in the judgment of the German Constitutional Court relating to the ratification of the Lisbon Treaty).

adjustment. Hence, while neither the French Conseil Constitutionnel nor the German Bundesverfassungsgericht raised fundamental objections to the ratification of the Fiscal Compact, the latter put important caveats on the ESM Treaty—which recalled analogous skepticism in the dissenting opinions of the Estonian Supreme Court and in the preliminary reference of the Irish Supreme Court to the ECJ. At the same time, of course, the Portuguese Constitutional Court repeatedly underlined the problematic aspects of the budgetary legislation adopted to implement domestically the economic adjustment program agreed to by Portugal and the "troika."

Second, while courts have overall backed the responses to the crisis devised by the EU member states and institutions, over the years courts have also revealed a greater unwillingness to defer to the political branches. This evolution in judicial approach appears in the case-law of the German Constitutional Court:[296] in its September 2011 decision, the Court validated, albeit with its customary lecturing tone, the Bundestag's approval of the German guarantees to the EFSF without putting any specific condition on this. But in September 2012 it demanded ratification of the ESM Treaty to be accompanied by two binding declarations under international law, clarifying for the avoidance of any doubt, the maximum limit of the German contribution to the ESM fund and the enduring right of the Bundestag to access documents handled by the ESM institutions, despite the duty to protect confidential information by ESM bodies. Furthermore, in March 2013, the Court added an additional condition to the validity of the ESM—namely a domestic act ensuring the timely payment of German quotas to the ESM—while simultaneously referring a case to the ECJ on the alleged incompatibility of the OMT decision with the prohibition of monetary financing enshrined in the EU treaties, with the threat that it would not respect the judgment of the ECJ if this did not meet its expectations.

The case of the Portuguese Tribunal Constitucional also exemplifies this judicial shift: as the length of the Euro-crisis, and arguably the harshness of the measures of economic adjustment adopted to tackle it grew, the Constitutional Tribunal became more impatient toward the action of the political branches. In its first ruling from July 2012 (soon after Portugal had entered into a program of financial assistance with the EU and the IMF), the Court resorted to procedural powers it enjoys under the Portuguese Constitution to suspend the effect of a decision of unconstitutionality of a budget law for violation of the principles of equality and proportionality. Nine months later, in April 2013, however, the Court did not refrain from annulling another identical measure. And in August 2013, December 2013, and May 2014, the Court struck a few other blows to the economic policy of the Portuguese government, leaving it in the very difficult situation of having to find new revenue sources for its budget.[297] These decisions signaled that the

[296] See further Bruce Ackerman and Miguel Maduro, "Broken Bond" *Foreign Policy*, September 17, 2012 and Sabino Cassese, "L'Unione europea e il guinzaglio tedesco" [2009] Giornale di diritto amministrativo 1003 (explaining limitations placed by the Bundesverfassungsgericht towards European integration).

[297] See also ECOFIN Presidency Statement, June 12, 2014 (taking note of the decision by the Portuguese Government to forgo the last disbursement tranche from the EFSM in light of the May 2014 ruling of the Portuguese Constitutional Court striking down a domestic budgetary act implementing the adjustment program).

emergency conditions that had justified restrictions of constitutional principles could not be extended forever and shed some pessimistic light on the willingness of courts—in Portugal but perhaps also elsewhere[298]—to uphold those parts of the new EMU constitution which requires the adoption of tough measures of economic adjustment for countries under financial assistance.[299]

A number of economic and institutional reasons may explain these two dynamics. On one side, it is plausible that courts face fewer incentives to oppose budgetary constraints (such as those dictated by the Fiscal Compact) that demand only negative action by their governments in the future. In contrast, they adopt a heightened scrutiny vis-à-vis either measures of financial stabilization (like the ESM), which require positive action by the states in the form of financial contributions, or measures of economic adjustment (as those agreed under the MoUs), which require immediate implementation.[300] At the same time, while courts may actually benefit from the introduction of budgetary rules, by seeing their institutional position vis-à-vis the political branches strengthened,[301] they can perceive a threat from the adoption of measures of economic adjustment or financial stabilization which restrict fundamental social rights, either because of the austerity measures to be adopted in the implementation of an economic adjustment program, or because of the reduced capacity of the state budget to provide social protections due to the contributions to a stability fund.[302] Since a core function of courts in constitutional regimes is to protect rights, taking this task seriously even in the face of economic emergencies may be perceived by courts as a necessity to consolidate their position in the constitutional system.[303]

On the other side, the increased uneasiness of courts vis-à-vis several aspects of the new fiscal constitution of the EMU may be the result of economic and institutional factors. While in the aftermath of an economic emergency courts may trust policy-makers to have better knowledge of how to handle the crisis and therefore be more willing to let them take decisions, over time courts raise

[298] See e.g., Symvoulio tis Epikrateias, 2192/2014 judgment of January 17, 2014 (Greek Council of State striking down a freeze on the salary of public employees introduced in fulfillment of the conditions required by international creditors as in violation of the Greek Constitution); Corte Costituzionale, sentenza n° 70/2015 judgment of March 10, 2015 (Italian Constitutional Court declaring a two-year freeze on the indexization of high-income pensions imposed by the Monti government to be in violation of the Italian Constitution); Ustavno sodišče, U-I-146/12-35, judgment of November 14, 2013 (Slovenian Constitutional Court striking down parts of the Fiscal Balance Act for violating principle of gender equality).

[299] See "Euro Wobbles. Portugal's Constitutional Court Creates New Problem for the Euro" *The Economist*, April 13, 2013 (discussing the decision of the Portuguese Constitutional Court in context).

[300] See also Kaarlo Tuori and Klaus Tuori, *The Eurozone Crisis: A Constitutional Analysis* (CUP 2014) (underlying greater ease in the integration of budgetary rules, compared to the integration of other fiscal policies which have redistributive effects).

[301] See further on this Chapter 1.

[302] See Riigikohus, Case 3-4-1-6-12 (n 25) paras 165–6 (emphasizing the importance of a well-functioning economy for the protection of fundamental rights); Tribunal Constitucional, Acórdão N° 187/2013 (n 198) paras 92–5 (discussing restrictions on pre-existing minimum protections of social rights).

[303] See also Silvana Sciarra (ed), *Labour Law in the Courts* (Hart Publishing 2001).

the threshold of legality that political branches must respect in order for their action to pass judicial muster.[304] Because the Euro-crisis, and the attempts to address it, have lasted for multiple years now, courts may become less concerned with the economic risk that their decisions could produce, and therefore become more vocal in expressing their discontent to the policy strategies followed by the EU institutions or member states. At the same time, courts may be more willing to intervene and sanction alleged illegalities in the measures adopted to reform the EMU legal architecture as they perceive the political process—that is, the set of procedures by which representative institutions adopt decisions—to be malfunctioning.[305]

Be that as it may, the previous analysis underlines a recurrent pattern: regardless of the political, economic, or legal characteristic of the cases considered, courts have acquired an extensive and pervasive influence in the field of economic and monetary policy across the EU—although most notably in some member states. This state of affairs is also reflected in the great preoccupation with which policy-makers and financial markets alike have awaited most of the judgments considered above.[306] In some cases, for example in Estonia or France, the rulings of national high courts were technically not essential for the entry into force of the measure under review, but, rather, affected the capacity of the state to become a party to the challenged treaty.[307] In others, however, the decisions of courts such as the Bundesverfassungsgericht have kept all the relevant stakeholders waiting with bated breath, by threatening to invalidate a whole scheme of regulation adopted to respond to the Euro-crisis. And they have directly influenced the way in which policy-makers have managed new challenges emerging in the EMU.[308] In conclusion, a trend of rising judicial involvement in fiscal affairs seems to emerge throughout Europe, with relevant implications on the horizontal balance of powers between courts and political branches. Yet, to appreciate the profound nature

[304] See ceteris paribus, Federico Fabbrini, "The Role of the Judiciary in Times of Emergency: Judicial Review of Counter-Terrorism Measures in the United States Supreme Court and the European Court of Justice" (2009) 28 Oxford Yearbook of European Law 664 (explaining how courts are more deferent to the political branches in the aftermath of a national security emergency, but that they become more demanding in their scrutiny as time goes by).

[305] See text accompanying nn 368–73.

[306] See e.g., "European Economics Strategy: Concerns about the German Constitutional Court," Morgan Stanley report, August 30, 2012 (emphasizing major financial risks if the German Constitutional Court strikes down the ESM Treaty); Alexander Koch, "A Guide for the German Constitutional Court Hearing on the OMT," Unicredit Research Paper, June 5, 2013 (discussing financial challenges that may result from the German Constitutional Court decision about OMT).

[307] Art 14(2) Fiscal Compact required the ratification of only 12 member states of the Eurozone for its entry into force, while Art 48 ESM Treaty required ratification by a number of states whose initial subscription to the capital of the ESM amounted to no less than 90% of the ESM capital. As a result, ratification of the Fiscal Compact by France or of the ESM Treaty by Estonia was not a *conditio sine qua non* for the entry into force of these two agreements. For a discussion on the lack of unanimous ratification in the entry into force of the Fiscal Compact see Carlos Closa Montero, "Moving Away from Unanimity: Ratification of the Treaty on Stability, Coordination and Governance in the Economic and Monetary Union" Reconstructing Democracy in Europe Working Paper No. 38/2011.

[308] See text accompanying nn 347–50.

of such a development, one needs to contrast the experience of the EMU with an external benchmark.

4. The Paradox of Judicialization

A comparison with the example of the US provides the best evidence to appreciate how paradoxical the degree of judicial involvement in the EMU has become. The US is generally credited as having one of the strongest systems of judicial review world-wide.[309] Both state and federal courts routinely review executive and legislative measures adopted by the political branches, directly influencing policy at all levels of governments.[310] Moreover, in the US federal system the adoption of economic policies at the federal level has historically been subject to judicial challenges, and courts in multiple occasions have been asked to review measures adopted by the political branches—from the constitutionality of a national bank,[311] to the scope of Congress power to regulate commerce, raise taxes, and print money.[312] These features present similarities with the European situation. Yet, if one considers the experience of the US, it is remarkable to notice how small a role the judiciary has played over the last 80 years in the field of economic and monetary policy. While rules of standing have almost entirely foreclosed judicial review of monetary policy, since the New Deal a central tenet of both state and federal courts has been to defer widely to the political branches in matters dealing with the economy, the budget, and fiscal rules.[313] As famously signaled by the US Supreme Court in the *Carolene Products* case,[314] courts are to adopt a more exacting scrutiny in matters dealing with individual rights, where the political process is unable to internalize the interests of insular minorities, while giving legislative determinations in matters of economic affairs broad deference.[315]

The retreat of courts from the arena of economic governance was the result of a long fought battle by the political branches against judicial overreaching.[316]

309 See Tushnet (n 4) 21 as well as Stephen Gardbaum, *The New Commonwealth Model of Constitutionalism* (CUP 2013) 4–6 (contrasting the new Commonwealth model of constitutionalism of, for example, the United Kingdom to the model of judicial supremacy epitomized by the US) and Tom Ginsburg, *Judicial Review in New Democracies: Constitutional Courts in Asian Cases* (CUP 2003) 17 (stating that, despite some obvious idiosyncrasies, "the experience of the U.S. *is* helpful" when discussing judicial review, and the emergence thereof, in new Asian democracies) (emphasis in original).

310 See Vicki Jackson and Judith Resnik (eds), *Federal Courts* (Foundation Press 2010) and David O'Brien, *Storm Center: The Supreme Court and American Politics* (9th ed. Norton 2014).

311 See *McCulloch v. Maryland*, 17 U.S. 316 (1819) (upholding the constitutionality of Congress decision to incorporate the second Bank of the United States on the basis of the Constitution's Necessary and Proper Clause).

312 See generally Richard Timberlake, *Constitutional Money: A Review of the Supreme Court's Monetary Decisions* (CUP 2013).

313 See Pieter-Augustijn Van Malleghem, "(Un)Balanced Budget Rules in Europe and America," in Federico Fabbrini et al (eds), *The Constitutionalization of European Budgetary Constraints* (Hart Publishing 2014), 151.

314 *United States v. Carolene Products*, 304 U.S. 144 (1938).

315 See Bruce Ackerman, *We the People. Volume 1: Foundations* (Harvard UP 1991).

316 See Shesol (n 6).

From the late 1800s until after the Great Depression, courts had systematically hampered the capacity of the state and federal governments to manage the economy and to adopt adequate policy responses to the crisis of 1929, by interpreting the US Constitution as embracing a specific economic theory.[317] Most famously, in *Lochner*,[318] the US Supreme Court read the Due Process Clause of the Fifth and Fourteenth Amendments to the US Constitution as enshrining a substantive commitment to free market and free contract, and thus largely imposed a laissez-faire reading of the Constitution that prevented the US government from taking action in the economic and social sphere.[319] However, as is well known, the New Deal Revolution (and the threat to change the composition of the US Supreme Court) eventually prompted the judiciary to change course and validate the transformation of the US institutional and economic constitution.[320] Since then, it has been customary for US courts to back off from reviewing legislation that has economic implications on the assumption that the "[C]onstitution is not intended to embody a particular economic theory."[321]

An explicit declaration of judicial retreat from the adjudication of economic questions, which are better left to the judgment of the political branches of government, can be found in the 1942 decision of *Wickard v. Filburn*.[322] In this case the Supreme Court upheld a federal regulation on agricultural production stating that economic affairs

> are wisely left under our system to resolution by the Congress under its more flexible and responsible legislative process. Such conflicts rarely lend themselves to judicial determinations. And with the wisdom, workability and fairness of the plan of regulation we have nothing to do.[323]

This tradition of judicial restraint has largely survived until today. Arguably, this was confirmed in the recent US Supreme Court decisions dealing with the single most important piece of federal economic legislation in decades: the Affordable Care Act.[324] In *National Federation of Independence Business v. Sebelius*,[325] a case which was not exempted from criticism,[326] the Supreme Court ultimately upheld the law as an exercise of the federal government's taxing power under the US Constitution

[317] For further references on the New Deal constitutional conflict see Federico Fabbrini, "Europe in Need of a New Deal: On Federalism, Free Markets and the Right to Strike" (2012) 43 Georgetown Journal of International Law 1175, 1215–17.

[318] *Lochner v. New York*, 198 U.S. 45 (1905) (striking down a New York statute limiting the hours of work in bakeries). For a thorough historical examination of *Lochner*, see Sidney Tarrow, "*Lochner v. New York*: A Political Analysis" (1964) 5 Labour History 277.

[319] See generally Cass Sunstein, "*Lochner's* Legacy" (1987) 87 Columbia Law Review 873.

[320] See Bruce Ackerman, *We the People. Volume 2: Transformations* (Harvard UP 1998).

[321] *Lochner* (n 318) at 75 (Holmes J. dissenting).

[322] *Wickard v. Filburn*, 317 U.S. 111 (1942).

[323] Ibid at 129 (footnotes omitted).

[324] Patient Protection and Affordable Care Act, P.L. 111–148 (2010) (US).

[325] *National Federation of Independent Business (NFIB) v. Sebelius*, 567 U.S. __ (2012).

[326] See e.g., Ronald Kahn, "The Commerce Clause and Executive Power: Exploring Nascent Individual Rights in *National Federation of Independent Business v. Sebelius*" (2013) 73 Maryland Law Review 133 (discussing the implication of the decision of a five-justice majority to find the Affordable Care Act inconsistent with the Constitution's Commerce Clause).

and made clear that its task was "not [to] consider whether the Act embodies sound policies. That judgment is entrusted to the Nation's elected leaders."[327] And in *King v. Burwell*,[328] the Supreme Court set aside another challenge to the statute, clearly affirming that "[i]n a democracy, the power to make the law rests with those chosen by the people. Our role is more confined—'to say what the law is.' That is easier in some cases than in others. But in every case we must respect the role of the Legislature, and take care not to undo what it has done."[329]

This brief comparison sheds light on a paradox. The contemporary degree of involvement of courts in EMU affairs (with the latest judicial rulings in Germany and Portugal restricting severely, or striking down tout court, legal measures adopted in the economic and monetary domain) is far greater than what one finds even in a country with strong courts par excellence like the US. Indeed, judicial review of monetary policy action of a central bank appears striking even by US standards—suggesting that European courts have become more involved than their American brethren in economic and monetary affairs. How can we make sense of this trend of judicial empowerment across Europe? The main explanation for this trend lies, in my view, in the overall strategy pursued by the EU member states in responding to the Euro-crisis. While a number of reforms to the architecture of EMU have been carried out within the framework of EU law, the member states have repeatedly decided to act outside the EU legal order, tightening budgetary constraints, establishing new mechanisms of financial stability, and setting up a framework for economic adjustment for countries in fiscal troubles *through international agreements*.[330] This strategy is consistent with an intergovernmental model for the management of the Euro-crisis,[331] which has stressed the centrality of national governments in the European Council and their freedom to act through agreements outside EU law, rather than the centrality of the EU institutional machinery and the potentials of EU law to address the crisis.[332]

Yet, responding to the Euro-crisis through an intergovernmental approach has come with a high price in terms of judicialization.[333] In most cases examined above, national courts have been called to review EMU-related agreements on the basis of their constitutional power to review a priori international treaties.[334]

[327] *NFIB* (n 325) at 2 (Opinion of Roberts C.J.) [of the slip opinion].

[328] *King v. Burwell*, 576 U.S. __ (2015).

[329] Ibid at 21 (Opinion of Roberts, C.J.) [of the slip opinion] citing *Marbury v. Madison*, 1 Cranch 137, 177 (1803).

[330] See also René Simts, From the Board: "Constitutionl Reflections and Crisis Ruminations" (2014) 41 Legal Issues of Economic Integration 315.

[331] See Jean-Paul Keppenne, "Institutional Report" in Ulla Neergaard et al (eds), *The Economic and Monetary Union: Constitutional and Institutional Aspects of the Economic Governance within the EU. Proceedings of the XXVI FIDE Congress* (Djøf 2014), 179.

[332] See French President Nicolas Sarkozy, Speech, Toulon, December 1, 2011 (stating that "L'Europe a besoin de plus de démocratie. [...] La refondation de l'Europe, ce ne pas la marche vers plus de supranationalité. [...] La crise a poussé les Chefs d'Etats et du gouvernments à assumer des responsabilités croissantes parce qu'au fond eux seuls disposaient de la légitimité démocratique qui leu permettai de décider.").

[333] See Shapiro and Stone Sweet (n 7) 71.

[334] See text accompanying n 12.

State courts have been asked on multiple occasions to adjudicate international agreements such as the Fiscal Compact, and the ESM, or the European Council Decision amending Article 136(3) TFEU. At the same time, state courts have been asked to review domestic policies implementing measures of economic adjustment agreed through international agreements—witness the Portuguese Constitutional Tribunal's repeated review of budgetary laws. Of course, technically these measures were domestic bills adopted by the Portuguese legislature. Yet, it does not go unnoticed that their content largely reflected what the Portuguese government and the "troika" had agreed to in the MoU. But a MoU is nothing more than a contractual agreement, under public international law, between a debtor state and its international lenders to obtain financial assistance in exchange for economic reforms.[335] In this situation, the shift "from legislation to contract"[336] also implied that the relevant domestic court found itself empowered to review the national measure implementing the MoU in a way which would have been unlikely had the measure under review been grounded in EU law stricto sensu.

As is has been pointed out, resort by the member states to international agreements outside the EU legal order is in itself nothing new.[337] However, it is argued here a contrario that, if legal measures to respond to the Euro-crisis had been adopted through ordinary EU legislation, they would have been untouchable by national courts, save by raising a preliminary reference to the ECJ. In fact, it is a core principle of EU law that national courts cannot review the legality of EU laws: national courts can refer a preliminary question to the ECJ, but only the ECJ can declare an EU act void.[338] As a result of this, legislation adopted in the EU legal framework, such as the "six-pack" and "two-pack" and the European Financial Stability Mechanism (EFSM), has entirely escaped judicial review.[339] Instead, by using intergovernmental agreement, member states have opened the floodgate to national judicial review. Moreover, the recurrent review of international law measures has in some cases emboldened courts to extend their oversight to real EU measures as well—most dramatically through the judicial review of action by the ECB.[340] As several scholars have underlined, EU law potentially offered room for

[335] See Lina Papadopoulou, "Can Constitutional Rules, Even if 'Golden', Tame Greek Public Debt?," in Federico Fabbrini et al (eds), *The Constitutionalization of European Budgetary Constraints* (Hart Publishing 2014), 230.

[336] See Paul Craig, "Economic Governance and the Euro Crisis: Constitutional Architecture and Constitutional Implications" in Federico Fabbrini et al (eds), *The Constitutionalization of European Budgetary Constraints* (Hart Publishing 2014), 19, 29.

[337] See Bruno De Witte, "European Stability Mechanism and Treaty on stability, coordination and governance: role of the EU institutions and consistency with EU legal order," in "Challenges of Multi-Tier Governance in the European Union," Study commissioned by the European Parliament Constitutional Affairs Committee, March 2013, PE 474.438, 78 (underlying how resort to international treaties adopted outside the EU legal order proper has a long pedigree in the history of EU integration). See further on this Chapter 5.

[338] *Foto-Frost* (n 181).

[339] For a description of these measures see the Introductory chapter.

[340] This is particularly the case for Germany where the initial challenges against action by the ECB were advanced in the context of challenges against the ESM—and later separated. See n 151.

the adoption of crisis measures *as EU legislation*—if needed through enhanced cooperation.[341] In Chapter 5 I will dwell further on how each of the measures enacted outside EU law could be repatriated within the EU treaties, and I will also raise questions about the freedom of the member states to act outside the framework of EU law at will. For now, however, it suffices to emphasize that the use of intergovernmental treaties by the member states has empowered courts to an unprecedented degree.[342]

In conclusion, the choice by the EU member states to respond to the Euro-crisis through a strategy of intergovernmental governance, and with systematic recourse to international agreements outside the EU legal order, has resulted in increasing judicial involvement in EMU affairs. In the context of the new constitutional architecture of the EMU, courts have found ample leeway to become involved in the adjudication of measures adopted so far to tackle the Euro-crisis. The limits of intergovernmentalism in managing the Euro-crisis effectively and legitimately have been emphasized repeatedly.[343] This chapter joins this chorus but from another perspective, underlining how an intergovernmental approach to the Euro-crisis also generated growing judicialization. The degree of judicial involvement taking place in the new EMU institutional architecture is paradoxical. One of the central tenets of intergovernmentalism in EU governance is that the executive branches (acting within the European Council) will dominate decision-making to the detriment of legislatures and courts.[344] Yet, intentions and outcomes here diametrically differed: intergovernmentalism paradoxically produced greater involvement of courts than what would have happened had the member states acted through the "Community method." As the comparison with the US makes clear, in fact, the degree of judicialization characterizing the EMU today outpaces also that of the US—the example par excellence of a system endowed with powerful courts.

[341] See e.g., Angelos Dimopoulos, "The Use of International Law as a Tool for Enhancing Governance in the Eurozone and its Impact on EU Institutional Integrity" in Federico Fabbrini et al (eds), *The Constitutionalization of European Budgetary Constraints* (Hart Publishing 2014), 41 and Michael Schwarz, "A Memorandum of Misunderstanding—The Doomed Road of the European Stability Mechanism and a Possible Way Out: Enhanced Cooperation" (2014) 51 Common Market Law Review 389.

[342] See further Federico Fabbrini, "On Banks, Courts and International Law. The Intergovernmental Agreement on the Single Resolution Fund in Context" (2014) 21 Maastricht Journal of European & Compartive Law 444, examining the latest example of an intergovernmental treaty—the Agreement on the transfer and mutualization of contributions to the Single Resolution Fund, May 21, 2014 available at <http://register.consilium.europa.eu/doc/srv?l=EN&f=ST%208457%202014%20INIT> (last accessed May 25, 2014)—and discussing the judicialization it produces.

[343] See from various perspectives Jürgen Habermas, *The Crisis of the European Union* (Polity 2012), and Mario Monti and Sylvie Goulard, *De la démocratie en Europe. Voir plus loin* (Flammarion 2013) as well the European Parliament President Martin Schultz, "Fiscal Union without Parliamentary Control is Unacceptable," Speech, Brussels, January 30, 2012 (criticizing the management of the Euro-crisis and saying that EMU cannot be legitimate without parliamentary control).

[344] See e.g., Ben Crum, "Saving the Euro at the Cost of Democracy?" (2013) 51 Journal of Common Market Studies 614 and Deirdre Curtin, "Challenging Executive Dominance in European Democracy" (2014) 77 Modern Law Review 1.

5. Judicial Review and the Political Process

Having identified a trend of increasing judicial involvement in fiscal affairs, and explained it in light of the turn toward intergovernmentalism, how should we evaluate this state of affairs? Although part of the European scholarship has welcomed the growing role of the judiciary in the context of the Euro-crisis,[345] it is my argument that the paradox of judicialization in the EMU should be approached with skepticism.[346] One could emphasize the *practical* concerns that this involvement may place on future reforms of the EMU at a time when the EU institutions and member states move on to debate new instruments to address the Euro-crisis.[347] In fact, while the Bundesverfassungsgericht is awaited to deliver its ruling on the follow-up of the *Gauweiler* case,[348] new legal challenges are already pending against other crucial measures adopted in response to the Euro-crisis—including Banking Union[349] and the program of quantitative easing of the ECB.[350] But the real point is that strong *constitutional* arguments plead in favor of letting the political branches, rather than the courts, take fundamental decisions in the fiscal arena. As Daniel Halberstam has explained, in separation-of-powers systems three main considerations should guide the allocation of competences among alternative institutions: expertise, voice, and rights.[351] The first consideration asks which actor has the better claim of knowledge or instrumental capacity to make a decision in a given field. The second asks which actor has the better claim of representing the relevant political will. And the third asks which actor is better placed to protect

[345] For a more favorable discussion on the role of courts in the context of the Euro-crisis see Elaine Fahey and Samo Bardutzky, "Who got to Adjudicate the EU Financial Crisis and Why?" in Federico Fabbrini et al (eds), *The Constitutionalization of European Budgetary Constraints* (Hart Publishing 2014), 341 and Michelle Everson and Christian Joerges, "Who is the Guardian of Constitutionalism in Europe after the Financial Crisis?," LSE 'Europe in Question' Discussion Paper Series No. 63/2013. The literature defending an expansive role of the judiciary usually emphasizes the deliberative nature of the judicial process. See generally on this Christopher Zurn, *Deliberative Democracy and the Institutions of Judicial Review* (CUP 2007).

[346] Needless to say, the debate about judicial review, and the role of courts, is arguably the most controversial in the field of compartive constitutional law. For a sample of this just compare Jeremy Waldron, "The Core of the Case Against Judicial Review" (2006) 115 Yale Law Journal 1346 with Richard Fallon Jr., "The Core of an Uneasy Case For Judicial Review" (2008) 121 Harvard Law Review 1693. This chapter does not engage with this broader debate—but certainly does not challenge the importance of judicial review either. In fact, see Federico Fabbrini, *Fundamental Rights in Europe* (OUP 2014) (recognizing the importance of judicial review to protect human rights). Rather, in the present work I challenge judicial interference in the field of economic governance, for the reasons that will be articulated below.

[347] See Alicia Hinarejos, "The Euro Area Crisis and Constitutional Limits to Fiscal Integration" (2012) 14 Cambridge Yearbook of European Legal Studies 243 (discussing constitutional limits to fiscal integration in the EU posed in Germany by the federal Constitutional Court).

[348] See BVerfGE Case No. 2 BvR 1390/12 et al, pending.

[349] See BVerfGE Case No. 2 BvR 1685/14 pending (challenge against the measures adopted to establish a Banking Union).

[350] See ALFA, Press release, "ALFA klagt in Karlsruhe gegen Billionen-Ankaufprogramm der EZB", September 4, 2015.

[351] Halberstam (n 10) 327.

rights. In the fiscal domain, the first and second considerations (expertise and voice) strongly plead in favor of letting the political branches, rather than the courts, make decisions. At the same time, the third consideration (rights) does not play a fundamental enough role in the economic domain so as to change the balance of institutional capacities in favor of greater judicial involvement.

First, political institutions and other political bodies are endowed with greater expertise than courts in the fiscal domain.[352] By expertise, I mean the professional knowledge to understand economic phenomena and to take informed decisions on them and the institutional capacity to administer effectively measures which achieve the desired results. Governments, parliaments, but also central banks at the national level, and the Commission, the Council, the European Parliament (EP), and the ECB at the supranational level, have the resources and institutional capacity to undertake this activity. Unlike courts—which are generalist institutions, with knowledge mainly in the legal field—these institutions work under the support of ad hoc research units, staffed with economists, statisticians, and social scientists, which monitor fiscal phenomena, and—through impact assessments and scientific evidence—can predict the effects of specific fiscal policies. Moreover, unlike courts—which are by definition reactive institutions, since they can only respond to legal challenges[353]—they can adopt proactive approaches, aimed at anticipating specific phenomena and creating incentives or disincentives toward virtuous economic results. Finally, unlike courts—which are generally ill equipped with instruments to take decision in the policy field—they can resort to a broad swath of policy and legal measures to achieve their goals.

Second, while intergovernmental decision-making in the EU has produced a democratic deficit, which has in fact been magnified by the Euro-crisis,[354] it still appears that political branches enjoy greater voice—meaning the capacity to represent the political will of the people—than courts.[355] Indeed, signs of inter-institutional conflict and democratic contestation have revealed some capacity of the EU regime to respond to popular and democratic pressures in the economic domain. A good example of this dynamic is reflected in the recent

352 See Neil Komesar, *Imperfect Alternatives: Choosing Institutions in Law, Economics and Public Policy* (Chicago UP 1994) (advising a comparative institutional analysis to identify which institution—the courts, the political process, or the market—is better placed to take decision in a given domain) and Miguel Poiares Maduro, "Courts and Pluralism: Essay on a Theory of Judicial Adjudication in the Context of Legal and Constitutional Pluralism" in Jeffrey Dunoff and Joel Trachtman (eds), *Ruling the World* (CUP 2009), 356, 372 (discussing the institutional capacity of courts vis-à-vis that of other institutions).

353 See Mauro Cappelletti, *Il controllo giudiziario di costituzionalita delle leggi nel diritto comparato* (Giuffré 1972) 9 (emphasizing the fact that a legal challenge is the necessary condition for courts' activity, and that conversely: *ubi non est actio, ibi non est jurisdictio*).

354 See further on this Chapters 3, 5, and 6.

355 See Peter Lindseth, "Of the People: Democracy, the Euro-zone and Lincoln's Threshold Criterion" (2012) 22 Berlin Journal 4 (emphasizing how, despite the Euro-crisis, the EU features pretty well in terms of input legitimacy and output legitimacy, while still being deficient in *demos*-legitimacy); Wojciech Sadurski "Democratic Legitimacy of the European Union: A Diagnosis and Some Modest Proposals" (2013) 32 Polish Yearbooks of International Law 9 (emphasizing mechanisms of direct and indirect democratic legitimacy in the EU).

decision by the (EP) to reject the multi-annual financial framework agreed upon by the European Council which reduced the EU budget for the first time ever.[356] With this act, in fact, the EP outlined a political vision alternative to that defended by a majority of member states in the European Council, politicizing fundamental decisions on fiscal issues.[357] Albeit very imperfectly, the EU political process provides a venue for legitimate decision-making that courts can hardly replace.

Third, while of course major weaknesses characterize the EU political process and ought to be addressed in the next institutional reforms of the EMU, it is unclear to what extent the democratic deficit of the EU political process would be cured by greater oversight by institutions like courts, which by definition are non-democratic.[358] As it is well known, the counter-majoritarian nature of courts is a valuable asset especially in the protection of fundamental rights, which are claims that individuals must invoke against majority rule.[359] As argued by many legal scholars, a crucial constitutional task of courts is to check and review action by the political branches in order to secure the rights of those individuals whose interests the political process is unable to internalize.[360] In these situations, thanks to their greater capacity to protect rights, courts can correct the distortions produced by the political process and its bias against insular minorities. In the EMU domain, however, there seems to be no evidence that the political process is biased by structural failures and by the tendency to systematically underrepresent specific interests. In other words, regardless of the content of the legal measures falling under the review of European courts, it seems that in the area of EMU governance the political process is generally able to internalize the interests of the affected stakeholders and to ensure that no group of citizens has its voice systematically discarded in the policy-making process.

In conclusion, judicial involvement in the EMU domain raises a number of constitutional concerns. The political branches and other technical institutions have greater expertise and instrumental capacity than courts to make decisions in EMU matters. At the same time, in this context, the political process is better able to represent the voice of the people and does not seem to be subject to a structural bias against insular minorities, which would justify greater oversight by courts on rights-protecting grounds. The OMT case of the Bundesverfassungsgericht epitomizes this state of affairs.[361]

[356] See European Council Conclusions, EUCO 37/13, February 8, 2013 (deciding the size of the future EU budget) and European Parliament Resolution of March 13, 2013 on the European Council conclusions concerning the Multiannual Financial Framework, P7_TA(2013)0078 para 1 (rejecting the agreement of the European Council).

[357] See Beda Romano, "Strasburgo boccia il budget", *Il Sole 24 Ore*, March 14, 2013, 13 (discussing the political implications of the vote by the EP to reject the budget deal agreed by the European Council, as an example of the opposition between austerity vs. growth politics).

[358] See also text accompanying nn 321–3.

[359] On the counter-majoritarian nature of courts see especially Alexander Bickel, *The Least Dangerous Branch: The Supreme Court and the Bar of Politics* (Yale UP 1986).

[360] See John Hart Ely, *Democracy and Distrust: A Theory of Judicial Review* (Harvard UP 1980); Jesse Choper, *Judicial Review and the National Political Process* (Chicago UP 1980).

[361] See text accompanying nn 150–66.

First, it seems unquestionable that political branches and technical institutions such as the ECB have greater expertise than courts in deciding how to secure the transmission of monetary policy.[362] Second, although the Court seeks to justify its intervention on democracy enhancing terms, it is clear that the decision thwarts the will of the people as expressed through its representatives.[363] Third, given the remote connection between OMT and the right to vote provision of the German Basic Law which is considered as the justification for adjudicating the case, it is uncertain whose rights are actually being violated by the measures adopted by the ECB.[364] Given the comparative advantage of the political process over the judicial process in economic and monetary affairs, it is submitted that courts should play a restrained role and hold their fire for other fields where instead their action is needed to correct the deficiencies of the political process on rights protecting grounds.[365] This is the legacy of the *Carolene Products* case in the US,[366] but its rationale applies well in the EU context too.[367]

Granted, while in the US courts can defer to a reasonably well functioning political process to take decisions in the economic domain, in the EU the capacity and legitimacy of political institutions is much more questionable. In the US, policy-making decisions are taken by a federal government composed of a directly elected legislature and a President who is responsible to the people at periodic elections.[368] In the EU, on the contrary, economic policy is mainly decided through

[362] See also *Gauweiler*, Opinion of AG Cruz Villalón (n 262) para 111 (stating that courts should exercise deference when reviewing "a highly technical terrain in which it is necessary to have an expertise and experience.").

[363] See BVerfG, Case No. 2 BvR 2728/13 et al (n 152) (Gerhardt, J. dissenting), paras 21, 23 (holding that "[t]he citizens can influence the way and objectives of the political process through petitions, the political parties and Members of Parliament" and emphasizing how the fact that none of the German institutions had responded to the OMT policy of the ECB "does not indicate a democratic deficit, but is an expression of its majority decision for a certain policy when handling the sovereign debt crisis in the euro currency area").

[364] See ibid (Lübbe-Wolff, J. dissenting), para 18 (arguing that the recognition that acts of the EU can be challenged on the basis of Art 38(1) Basic L. Ger. "departs from earlier case-law, just recently corroborated, according to which parliamentary or governmental inaction is contestable in constitutional complaint proceedings only if the complainant can rely on an explicit constitutional mandate"). See also Wendel (n 171) 21 (criticizing extensive reading of the conditions for admissibility in Verfassungsbeschwerde based on Art 38 Basic L. Ger.).

[365] Of course, legal challenges against many features of the new constitutional architecture of the EMU were clothed in rights terms—witness the petitioners before the Bundesverfassungsgericht in the ESM case who claimed that the ESM restricted their right to vote. However, it has been emphasized how, in fact, the Constitutional Court has been skewing its procedural rules in order to adjudicate as fundamental-rights-questions issues which instead concern the structure of powers or the governance of the economy. See Wendel (n 171) 24; Mayer (156) 111.

[366] See *Carolene Products* (n 314) 152 fn 4. For a comment on the most famous footnote in US constitutional history see also Bruce Ackerman, "Beyond the *Carolene Products*" (1985) 98 Harvard Law Review 713.

[367] See ceteris paribu, Joined Cases C-402/05 P and C-415/05 P *Yassin A Kadi and Al Barakaat International Foundation v. EU Council and Commission* ,opinion of AG Maduro of January 16, 2008, ECLI:EU:C:2008:11, para 45 (stating that courts ought to get involved when "the political process is liable to become overly responsive to immediate popular concern, leading the authorities to allay the anxiety of the many at the expense of the rights of the few.").

[368] See generally Louis Fisher, *American Constitutional Law. Volume 1: Constitutional Structures, Separated Powers and Federalism* (Carolina Academic Press 2005).

intergovernmental decision-making,[369] and is thus centered on the role of the European Council (the body representing state governments) to the detriment of the EP (representing EU citizens).[370] In fact, as I mentioned previously, the main explanation for the high degree of judicial involvement in the fiscal domain lies paradoxically in the intergovernmental strategy pursued by the EU member states to respond to the Euro-crisis, based on the European Council and international agreements, rather than on the "Community method" and EU law.[371] As I shall argue in Chapters 5 and 6, this situation should be changed. However, as much as the EU political process is urgently in need of reform, it is unclear to what extent its deficiencies could be cured by greater judicial fiat. An intergovernmental system of governance suffers from major legitimacy gaps. Since considerations of expertise, voice, and rights indicate that the political process ought to maintain the lead in the fiscal and economic field, reforms should be adopted in order to increase the legitimacy of the EU political process and its capacity to provide a well-functioning arena for democratic decision-making and contestation.[372] Given the growing attention that this issue has acquired in the EU debates,[373] Chapter 5 will address face-on the potentials of a new democratic regime of decision-making in economic affairs and consider what challenges would arise toward this objective.

6. Conclusion

This chapter has analyzed the role that courts have come to play in the context of the new EMU architecture with the aim to examine the constitutional implications of the Euro-crisis and the responses to it on the horizontal relations of powers between the courts and the political branches. In every area in which the EU institutions and member states have adopted EMU reforms—from the strengthening of budgetary constraints, to the introduction of new mechanisms of financial stability and the setting up a framework of economic adjustments for countries in fiscal troubles—legal challenges have been raised, and courts have been asked to intervene. This chapter, in particular, has focused on decisions by high courts in Estonia, France, Germany, Ireland, Portugal, and the EU. National and supranational courts adjudicated issues as varied as the legality of the constitutional changes brought about by the Fiscal Compact, the constitutionality of the ESM Treaty, the admissibility of a simplified amendment process to the TFEU, the

[369] See Uwe Puetter, *The European Council and the Council: New Intergovernmentalism and Institutional Change* (OUP 2014).

[370] See further on this Chapter 3.

[371] See text accompanying nn 330–43.

[372] See also Edoardo Chiti, "Le istituzioni europee, la crisi e la trasformazione costituzionale dell'Unione" [2012] Giornale di diritto amministrativo 783. But see also Antoine Vauchez, *Démocratiser l'Europe* (Seuil 2014) (arguing in favor of the democratization of technical institutions such as the ECB and the ECJ).

[373] See European Parliament Resolution of November 20, 2012 on the report "Towards a Genuine EMU," P7_TA(2012)0430 para 1 (calling for the renewal of the governance of the EMU within the institutional framework of the EU).

validity of action by the ECB, and the validity of major wage cuts enacted through budgetary legislation implementing domestically the adjustment programs agreed upon in the MoUs.

As the chapter has emphasized, courts throughout the EU have come to play an unprecedented role in EMU governance. By and large courts validated the measures under review, permitting the reforms of EMU to go forward. Nevertheless, a qualitative analysis of legal reasoning and judicial rulings has also revealed that courts have grown increasingly dissatisfied with features of the new EMU legal architecture, especially measures of financial stability and economic adjustment, and in some recent cases have ended up placing important conditions on the validity of the measures under review, or struck them down tout court. As the chapter has argued, the main explanation for this development lies in the intergovernmental strategy followed by the EU member states to respond to the Euro-crisis, with the repeated recourse to international agreements adopted outside the EU legal order, and amenable to domestic judicial review. Paradoxically, intergovernmentalism has created room for judicialization. Had the member states made more use of the "Community method" and the ample possibility offered by EU law to enact measures to address the Euro-crisis, the space for judicial interference—and the threat that came with it—would have been largely reduced. The paradoxical degree of involvement of national and supranational judiciaries in EMU affairs becomes all the more visible when compared with the role courts play in the US. Although the US is endowed with one of the most powerful and pervasive systems of judicial review world-wide, since at least the 1930s courts have widely deferred to the political branches in the economic and monetary domain, on the understanding that the political process is better placed than the judicial one to answer fundamental budgetary, monetary, and economic questions.

As this chapter claimed, however, also in the EMU strong constitutional arguments relating to expertise, voice, and rights plead in favor of courts maintaining, or reverting to, a deferent approach vis-à-vis the political branches in the economic and monetary arena—and suggest that the paradox of judicialization should be looked at with skeptical eyes. But make no mistake: criticizing judicial interferences in the fiscal domain and stressing the advantages of the ordinary EU law-making process does not imply idealizing it; quite the contrary. As I have repeatedly noted, the EU political process is urgently in need of reform. Several proposals are currently being debated to improve the legitimacy and accountability of the EU decision-making regime[374]—and I will come back to these in Part II of this book. Yet, for the purpose of this chapter, the limits of a dynamic of judicialization ought to be stressed. Courts play a crucial function in any constitutional regime, especially in protecting the rights of those individuals who cannot adequately defend themselves through the political process. As Tocqueville noticed almost 200 years ago, "[t]here is hardly a political question in the United States

[374] See e.g., President of the European Council Report (n 11) and Commission Communication, "A Blueprint for a Deep and Genuine EMU. Launching a European Debate", COM(2012)777 final.

which does not sooner or later turn into a judicial one."[375] But the judicial function has limits. In economic and monetary affairs, the political process is better placed than courts to take decisions. Also in the EMU, it should be given room to decide on how best to respond to the Euro-crisis. The goal therefore is to achieve a more democratic regime for decision-making in the highly integrated EMU—a challenge that will be discussed in Chapter 5.

[375] See Alexis de Tocqueville, *Democracy in America*, ed J.P. Mayer & trans G. Lawrence [1835–40] (Doubleday & Co. 1969) 270.

3

The Paradox of Domination

1. Introduction

The Euro-crisis and the responses to it have profoundly influenced the constitutional architecture of the European Economic and Monetary Union (EMU). On the one hand, as I explained in Chapter 1, they have affected the vertical relations of power between the member states and the European Union (EU), producing steady centralization. On the other hand, as I indicated in Chapter 2, they have changed the relationship between the political branches and the courts, increasing the involvement of the latter in economic and monetary affairs. Yet, the Euro-crisis and the legal and political responses to it have produced relevant constitutional implications on the horizontal relations of powers between the member states as well. As a Union of states and citizens, the EU has been historically designed to ensure a balance between state equality and state power. Since the start, the process of European integration involved the aggregation of pre-existing states with asymmetrical features—due to profound differences in the size of population, economic conditions, and military might. The architects of the EU, therefore, sought to strike a compromise between the demands of the smaller states to be represented *qua* states, and the pressure of the bigger states to see their power adequately reflected into the institutional setup. Since the foundation of the EU project, this compromise has been mirrored in a complex institutional architecture, in which no state, or group of citizens, could dominate over the others. Notwithstanding subsequent institutional transformations, the existence of a constitutional balance between the member states has been a crucial factor for the enduring stability and legitimacy of the process of European integration.

The aim of this chapter is to examine how the Euro-crisis and the political and legal responses to it have affected *the horizontal relations of powers between the states.*[1] As the chapter argues, developments in the practice of the EU institutions, as well as changes in the applicable legal framework—notably in high salience

[1] Note that this chapter does not examine the changing relationship between states which are part of the Eurozone and states which are outside it. On this issue see Jean-Claude Piris, *The Future of Europe: Towards a Two-Speed EU?* (CUP 2011). Equally, the chapter does not focus on the inter-state implications of the use of enhanced cooperation. On this issue see Federico Fabbrini, "Enhanced Cooperation Under Scrutiny: Revisiting the Law and Practice of Multi-Speed Integration in Light of the First Involvement of the EU Judiciary" (2013) 40 Legal Issues of European Integration 197.

areas of EMU such as economic adjustment, financial stabilization, and banking resolution—have upset the horizontal balance of powers between the member states, and entrenched the domination of some of them over others. In particular, the increasing intergovernmentalization of the decision-making process, with the rise of the European Council as the forum for high politics and the growing resort to international agreements outside the EU legal framework to implement policy decisions, have diluted the checks and balances which existed in the EU constitutional architecture to ensure fair relations between the member states and prevent the problem of domination. In the aftermath of the Euro-crisis, the EU seems characterized by a significant shift of power from smaller and economically weaker member states toward larger, more prosperous ones—today especially Germany.

As the chapter maintains, the constitutional transformations that have been unleashed by the Euro-crisis and the responses to it are paradoxical. The project of European integration was launched after two bloody European civil wars to ensure that no state could impose its will over the others. The euro was created in the 1990s also as a political guarantee that a unified Germany, as the biggest state of the EU, would not be captured by new hegemonic pulls. Historically, the EU institutional architecture has attempted to ensure a compromise between states' equality and states' power through a combination of supranational and intergovernmental mechanisms.[2] In fact, more than any other federalism-based arrangement world-wide, the EU has given centrality to the idea of state equality—including through intergovernmental features aimed at ensuring to every state an equal seat at the negotiating table. Yet, the Euro-crisis has faulted the idea that an intergovernmental system can be a wall defending the equality of the states, and rather revealed how, on its own, intergovernmentalism opens the door toward the domination of the more powerful states over the others. As a brief comparison with the United States (US) makes clear, a federal system endowed with mechanisms of governance and institutions independent from direct state control is better able to secure states' equality and prevent horizontal imbalances. Ultimately, instead, in the world of intergovernmental politics incarnated by the European Council, the larger and richer states will wield more power than the smaller and poorer ones.

Nevertheless, the paradox of domination strikes at the heart of the anti-hegemonic values on which the EU is founded. Because a balance between the member states is essential to the legitimacy and stability of the process of European integration, the chapter criticizes the developments which have recently occurred and seeks to reflect upon possible options for reform. As the chapter claims, the emergency triggered by the Euro-crisis has taken the EU institutions and member states into a problematic institutional direction, and a new constitutional settlement restoring a fair equilibrium between the member states appears necessary. To this end, the chapter considers the recent efforts to transform the EU into a parliamentary system of government,

[2] See Simone Bunse and Kalypso Nicolaïdis, "Large versus Small States: Anti-Hegemony and the Politics of Shared Leadership," in Erik Jones et al (eds), *The Oxford Handbook of the European Union* (OUP 2012), 249.

but warns that this development would not overcome the current imbalances between the states. Ironically, in a parliamentary system the larger member states would continue to withhold disproportionate influence over the policy-making process, at the expenses of the needs and claims of smaller member states. Because of the sheer size of national delegations in the European Parliament (EP), more populous member states would enjoy an unbalanced majority. As an alternative, therefore, the chapter points to a new constitutional system of separation of powers for the EU, in which the democratization of the EU institutions is achieved through a separation of the legislative and executive branches, and the creation of a European presidency able to withstand the pressures of the biggest and more powerful member states—an idea I will develop further in Chapter 6.

This chapter is structured as follows. Section 2 summarizes, from a historical perspective, the EU institutional balance between states' equality and states' power and explains how the Euro-crisis and its aftermath have increasingly undermined it. In particular, here I examine the institutional rise of the European Council, and the consolidation of a directoire within it, as evidence of the growing power of some states over others in the EU intergovernmental framework. Section 3 analyzes the legal regime established in the context of economic adjustment, financial stabilization, and banking resolution and underlines how, in each of these cases, legal reforms accomplished through international agreements outside EU law have entrenched inequalities between the states based on power, size, and economic performance, without introducing compensating mechanisms. Section 4 critically evaluates these developments and, in light of a brief comparison with the US, argues that—paradoxically—a federal system would have been more protective of state equality than an intergovernmental one. Section 5 considers the proposal to parliamentarize the EU but cautions that this may have the unwanted effect of maintaining an imbalance between the states. Section 6, finally, summarizes and concludes, suggesting that only a new system of separated institutions sharing power can offer an alternative to the status quo.

2. States' Equality vs. States' Power

State power is a key—albeit not the only—determinant of international relations.[3] Although state power comes in different forms, a general correlation can be detected between the territorial dimension of a country, the size of its population, and its economic, political, and military strength:[4] ceteris paribus, larger

[3] See Robert Keohane, *International Institutions and State Power* (Westview Press 1989).

[4] The correlation between the size of a member state's population and its territorial dimension are particularly remarkable in the EU. Hence, for example, in the Eurozone, Germany is the first member state in terms of population size (82 million) and the third member state in terms of territorial dimension (356,854 km²); France is the second member state in terms of population size (64.3 million) and the first member state in terms of territorial dimension (550,000 km²), and Italy is the third member state in terms of population size (60 million) and the fourth in terms of territorial dimension (301,263 km²). For the data see *EU Member Countries*, available at <http://europa.eu/about-eu/countries/member-countries/>

states are likely to be more powerful than smaller states. As a project of reconciliation between warring nations, the construction of the EU was driven by an anti-hegemonic logic: while the EU acknowledged the role of the larger states, it sought to reassure the smaller states that their voice also counted. Since the foundation of the process of European integration maintaining a balance between state power and state equality has been regarded as a necessary condition to the stability and the legitimacy of the EU integration project.[5] To achieve this end, the EU political actors developed a practice of governance based on consensus, rather than coercion.[6] Moreover, the EU institutional architects created a complex institutional system in which the request of the smaller member states to be represented *qua* states was reconciled with the claim of larger member states to be represented on the basis of their size—notably, in light of their population.[7] As sub-section A points out, while the EU institutional architecture has been re-adapted over time, the aim to balance state equality with state power has continued to be one of its defining features. As sub-section B emphasizes, however, the Euro-crisis has represented a watershed as far as the relationship between the states is concerned.

A. Continuity

The Treaty of Rome of 1957 designed an original constitutional compromise. On the one hand, the Rome Treaty weighed the number of votes in the Council of Ministers (in which the executives of the member states were represented), and the number of seats in the Parliamentary Assembly (in which delegates of national parliaments were assembled) on the basis of the population of the states, albeit along a logic of degressive proportionality. This resulted in the bigger states having more votes (through their ministers) in the Council,[8] and more seats (through their parliamentarians) in the Assembly,[9] than the smaller member states, although less votes and seats than would have been the case on the basis of a purely proportional calculation. On the other hand, however, the Rome Treaty established the

(last accessed January 18, 2015). In fact, factors about geography and population are also directly connected with the economic size of a member state, that is, in 2013, Germany had the first highest GDP (equal to \$3,635.959 billion at current prices), France the second highest (\$2,807.306 billion), and Italy the third highest GDP in the Eurozone (\$2,071.955 billion). For the data see International Monetary Fund, *World Economic Outlook Database*, available at <http://www.imf.org/external/pubs/ft/weo/2014/02/weodata/index.aspx> (last accessed January 18, 2015). Among the EU member states who are not part of the Eurozone, the United Kingdom (UK) stands out as a state with a large population (63.4 million inhabitants), a relatively vast territory (248,527.8 km^2) and one of the highest GDP (equal in 2013 to \$2,523.216 billion at current prices). See generally Alberto Alesina and Enrico Spolaore, *The Size of Nations* (MIT Press 2003) (discussing optimal size of nations).

5 See Walter Van Gerven, *The European Union: A Polity of States and People* (Hart Publishing 2005).

6 See Arend Lijphart, *Patterns of Democracy* (Yale UP 1999) 42 (defining the EU as an example of consociational democracy due to the consensus-based nature of decision-making).

7 See Sergio Fabbrini, *Compound Democracies* (OUP 2007) (defining the EU as an example of compound democracy due to the constitutionalization of a complex institutional architecture for decision-making).

8 Art 148 EEC Treaty.

9 Art 138 EEC Treaty.

principle that the Council would be presided by every member state for six months on a rotating basis[10]—hence preventing any one state from taking permanent control of this institution. Moreover, it created new independent supranational institutions like the Commission, or the Court of Justice (ECJ)—in itself an attempt to prevent power-grabs by the larger states—and established that each of them would be composed of at least one national for every member state.[11] The independence of the Commission, and its composition, together with the rotating presidency of the Council and the principle of degressive proportionality in the weighing of votes in the Council and apportionment of seats in the Assembly, signaled the commitment of the founding states toward the principle of state equality.

By combining intergovernmental with supranational features into a new system of governance, the compromise struck in the Rome Treaty is remnant of analogous efforts to balance the needs of larger vs smaller units of government in other experiments of federation building. As Paul Magnette and Kalypso Nicolaïdis argued, "all federal bargains to some extent rest on adopting different principle of representation for different institutions."[12] In the case of the EU, otherwise, the need to embed inter-states relations into an institutional web that would prevent any of them from dominating the others was rooted in the historical awareness of centuries of hegemonic practice. Unsurprisingly, therefore, while the original compromise struck by the Rome Treaty was re-adapted over time, the aim to secure a constitutional balance between state power and state equality remained a guiding logic of subsequent EU institutional revisions.[13] During the 1970s, the introduction of direct election to the EP[14]—in which states would be represented on the basis of their population, albeit subject to an apportionment of seats that over-represented the smaller states—was balanced by the institutionalization of the European Council[15]—in which every state would enjoy a seat, regardless of its size. Similarly, then, the Maastricht Treaty of 1992, in creating the European Central Bank (ECB) in the road toward EMU, devised a new, federal-like compromise between the member states adopting the euro as their currency.[16]

Given the importance of the ECB—especially in devising responses to the Euro-crisis in the course of the last few years[17]—it is useful to underline how the rules on its composition, and its decision-making process, sought to replicate in

[10] Art 146 EEC Treaty. [11] Art 157 EEC Treaty.

[12] Paul Magnette and Kalypso Nicolaïdis, "Large and Small Member States in the European Union: Reinventing the Balance," Notre Europe Research Paper No. 25/2003, 30.

[13] See also Luuk Van Middelar, *The Passage to Europe* (Yale UP 2013).

[14] See Act concerning the election of the representatives of the European Parliament by direct universal suffrage, annexed to Decision 76/787/EEC, [1976] OJ L278/5 (introducing direct elections to the EP).

[15] See Final Communiqué of the Paris Summit, 9–10 December 1974 (establishing the European Council).

[16] Compare Martin Selmayr and Chiara Zilioli, *The Law of the European Central Bank* (Hart Publishing 2001) and Stefania Baroncelli, *La Banca Centrale Europea: Profili giuridici e istituzionali: Un confronto con il modello americano della Federal Reserve* (European Press Academy Publishing 2000).

[17] See Thomas Beukers, "The New ECB and Its Relationship with the Eurozone Member States" (2013) 50 Common Market Law Review 1579.

the context of EMU the delicate balance between large vs small states existing in the governance of the EU. From the structural point of view, although Eurozone member states contribute to the ECB capital pro-quota, based on a combination of their GDP and population,[18] every state, regardless of its size or economic power, is represented in the Governing Council, the main ECB decision-making body, by the governor of its central bank.[19] At the same time, the Governing Council is complemented by six additional members of the Executive Board,[20] to be selected taking into account a number of factors[21]—and the convention has been that the larger member states have always had at least one of their nationals among the members of the Executive Board.[22] Nevertheless, as far as decision-making is concerned, the ECB decides by majority voting, with every member of the Governing Council having one vote.[23] Moreover, in anticipation of the expansion of the number of members of the Governing Council as a result of the enlargement of the Eurozone, the ECB Statute empowered the ECB to enact a rule that, once the number of governors of the national central banks sitting in the Governing Council would be higher than 18, a rotation mechanism would apply whereby every month voting rights are suspended for the governor of the central bank of one of the five biggest states (Germany, France, Italy, Spain, and the Netherlands), and for the governors of the central banks of three of the smaller ones.[24] With the accession of Lithuania to the Eurozone from January 1, 2015 this scenario has become the reality, with the result that, once every five months, even the governor of the central banks of the largest Eurozone member state (Germany) has his right to vote in the Governing Council temporarily suspended.[25]

The process of enlargement of the EU complicated the effort to maintain an equilibrium between the states.[26] Whereas the Community of Six featured three large states (West Germany, France, and Italy) with roughly the same population, and three smaller states (the Benelux) with similar economic power, the entrance into the Union of 22 new members has significantly increased the number of small- and medium-size states, while the reunification of Germany has created a member

[18] See Art 29(1) ECB Statute, [2010] OJ C83/235.

[19] See Art 10 ECB Statute.

[20] See Art 11 ECB Statute.

[21] See also Tommaso Padoa Schioppa, *The Euro and its Central Bank: Getting United after the Union* (MIT Press 2004).

[22] See also "Lorenzo Bini Smaghi démissionne du directoire de la BCE," *Le Monde* November 10, 2011 (reporting how after the appointment of Mario Draghi, an Italian, to the Presidency of the ECB to replace Jean-Claude Trichet, a Frenchman, the French President Nicolas Sarkozy demanded the resignation of Lorenzo Bini Smaghi, another Italian who was at the time member of the Executive Committee, in order to create space for a new French member to be appointed within the Executive Board).

[23] See Art 10(2) ECB Statute.

[24] See Art 10(2) ECB Statute and Decision of the ECB of March 19, 2009 amending the Rules of Procedure of the ECB (ECB/2009/5) [2009] OJ L100/10.

[25] See Sébastien Richard, "L'entrée de la Lituanie dans la zone euro et ses consequences pour la Banque central européenne," Fondation Schuman Policy Paper No. 338/2014 (explaining how the new voting mechanisms in the ECB took off from January 1, 2015).

[26] See Magnette and Nicolaïdis (n 12) 8.

state unrivalled in terms of size of its population and economic might.[27] From the late 1990s, this new reality resulted in increasing debate about how to redesign the EU institutional architecture to give due weight to the claims of the smaller member states to be represented *qua* states and the ever-more assertive demands of the larger states to see their comparatively greater power reflected into the institutional setup.[28] The Amsterdam Treaty of 1997 and the Nice Treaty of 2001 did not introduce any major institutional change, due to inter-state disagreement. In fact, as it has been claimed, "the rift between small and big states may—in part—be to blame for the ratification crisis of the Constitutional [Treaty in 2005]."[29]

In the end, however, the Treaty of Lisbon of 2009 confirmed the EU constitutional compromise.[30] On the one hand, after a long negotiation for the weighing of votes or the apportionment of seats, the Lisbon Treaty continued to allocate the seats in the EP along the principle of degressive proportionality, which privileges more populous states, although to a lesser degree than what they would be entitled on purely proportional terms.[31] And it introduced prospectively a principle of double-majority in the Council, setting as a threshold for the adoption of legal measures a vote by 55% of the states, representing at least 65% of the EU population.[32] On the other hand, the Lisbon Treaty maintained the rotating Presidency of the Council—allowing every state to chair the Council for six months.[33] In addition, after the difficulties in the ratification of the Lisbon Treaty faced by Ireland,[34] the European Council decided to maintain the rule that every member state was entitled to appoint a member of the Commission—despite questions about the functionality of a college with 27 plus members.[35]

At the same time, the Lisbon Treaty—which rescued most of the institutional innovations included in the Treaty establishing a European Constitution of 2005—also introduced an important institutional change.[36] The Lisbon Treaty formally recognized for the first time the European Council (the institution grouping the heads of state and government of the EU member states, plus the

[27] See Bela Plechanovová, "The Treaty of Nice and the Distribution of Votes in the Council—Voting Power Consequences for the EU after the Oncoming Enlargement" (2003) 7 European Integration Online Papers.

[28] See Magnette and Nicolaïdis (n 12) 8 (discussing the so-called "Lilliput Syndrome" whereby larger EU member states felt constrained by smaller states).

[29] Bunse and Nicolaïdis (n 2) 250.

[30] See also Paul Craig, *The Treaty of Lisbon: Law, Politics and Treaty Reform* (OUP 2010).

[31] See Art 14(2) TEU. [32] See Art 16(4) TEU. [33] See Art 16(9) TEU.

[34] See Gráinne De Búrca, "If at First you Don't Succeed: Vote, Vote Again: Analyzing the 'Second Referendum' Phenomenon in EU Treaty Change" (2010) 33 Fordham International Law Journal 1472 (explaining rejection of the Lisbon Treaty in the first Irish referendum and measures paving the way toward a second, successful, referendum).

[35] See Art 17(5) TEU (stating that, from November 1, 2014, the Commission shall consist of a number of members corresponding to two thirds of the number of member states, unless the European Council, acting unanimously, decides otherwise). But see now European Council Decision, October 2, 2012, EUCO 176/12 (deciding, in light of the concern of the Irish people with respect to the Lisbon Treaty reflected in the rejection of the Treaty in a first referendum, that the Commission will continue to include one national for every member state).

[36] See Editorial Comments, "An ever mighty European Council—Some recent institutional developments" (2009) 46 Common Market Law Review 1383.

President of the Commission) as an institution of the EU—an institution, moreover, now entrusted with the task to "provide the Union with the necessary impetus for its development and [to] define the general political directions and priorities thereof."[37] At the same time, the Lisbon Treaty created the post of the permanent President of the European Council.[38] Pursuant to Article 15(5) Treaty on European Union (TEU), the President is to be elected by qualified majority by the other members of the European Council for a period of two and a half years, renewable once, and shall not hold a national office simultaneously. During the debates of the Convention on the Future of Europe of 2002–3, the proposal to create a permanent presidency had been one of the most controversial ones. Initially advanced by Convention President Valéry Giscard d'Estaing and supported by the largest member states, the proposal to establish a permanent President of the EU railed opposition from all the smaller states, which saw in this a fundamental challenge to the fragile compromise between state power and state equality crafted since the beginning of the EU integration process.[39]

Ultimately, the institution of the presidency made its way into the Constitutional Treaty, and later the Lisbon Treaty, but with a few correctives. At the request of the smaller states, the President was entitled to head the European Council—and not the EU as such—and was empowered to act more as a chairman of that institution—rather than as an executive leader.[40] As indicated in Article 15(6) TEU:

> The President of the European Council: (a) shall chair it and drive forward its work; (b) shall ensure the preparation and continuity of the work of the European Council in cooperation with the President of the Commission, and on the basis of the work of the General Affairs Council; (c) shall endeavour to facilitate cohesion and consensus within the European Council; (d) shall present a report to the European Parliament after each of the meetings of the European Council.

Moreover, the Treaty enshrined the rule that the European Council would decide by consensus, save when explicitly otherwise provided,[41] with the aim to avoid the risks of centralizing too much power into one person. And the presidency of the European Council did not affect the system of rotating presidency of the Council.[42] As it were, in November 2009,[43] plausibly to allay the fear of the smaller member states,[44] the position of President of the European Council was first attributed to a Belgian, Mr. Herman Van Rompuy—a former Prime Minister of that country—to whom the mandate was later renovated in March 2012.[45]

[37] Art 15 TEU.

[38] See Ben Crum, "Accountability and Personalisation of the European Council Presidency" (2009) 31 European Integration 685. See also Deirdre Curtin, *Executive Power of the European Union* (OUP 2009).

[39] See Magnette and Nicolaïdis (n 12) 13.

[40] See Paolo Ponzano, "Les institutions de l'Union" in Giuliano Amato et al (eds), *Genesis and Destiny of the European Constitution* (Bruylant 2007), 439, 467 (explaining that the Convention sought to limit the powers of the President).

[41] See Art 15(4) TEU. [42] See Art 16(9) TEU.

[43] European Council press release, November 19, 2009.

[44] See Bunse and Nicolaïdis (n 2) 265.

[45] European Council press release, March 1, 2012, EUCO 37/12.

B. Change

According to the account of people involved in the negotiations, the Lisbon Treaty was not intended to alter the original EU institutional balance.[46] The viability of the new institutional architecture designed by the Lisbon Treaty, however, was soon tested by the Euro-crisis, which erupted almost at the time in which the Lisbon Treaty was entering into force. The Euro-crisis and the need to respond to it profoundly challenged the EU constitutional settlement.[47] In particular, as a growing body of literature in law and political science has underlined, the European Council emerged as the leading institution in managing and coordinating policy responses to the crisis.[48] Although the European Council had historically played an important role at previous moments of crisis in the EU,[49] in the aftermath of the Euro-crisis the European Council quickly became what Uwe Puetter has defined as new center of EU politics, "regularly deciding concrete policy issues in core domains of EU policymaking such as economic governance."[50] In fact, although Article 15(3) TEU foresaw that the European Council would meet at least twice a year, in reality the European Council congressed as often as once a month, reflecting how intergovernmental decision-making became in practice "the predominant strategy in day-to-day crisis management."[51]

Moreover, despite the rising importance of the European Council in the management of the Euro-crisis, a new intergovernmental forum was created to debate the key issues concerning specifically the Eurozone: the Euro Summit.[52] Although the ministers of finance of the Eurozone member states had been meeting in the Eurogroup since 1997,[53] and the Lisbon Treaty had explicitly recognized this informal gathering,[54] in October 2008 then French President Sarkozy took the initiative to group the heads of state and government of the Eurozone member states to discuss at the highest level matters related to EMU—and in October 2011 the leaders of the Eurozone states adopted a statement giving a first structure to the Euro Summit.[55] This statement advanced ten measures to improve the governance

[46] See Jean-Claude Piris, *The Lisbon Treaty: A Legal and Political Analysis* (CUP 2010) 237 (explaining that the Treaty avoided making "any single institution as politically too powerful.")

[47] See Augustín José Menéndez, "The Existential Crisis of the European Union" (2013) 14 German Law Journal 453.

[48] See e.g., Sergio Fabbrini, "Intergovernmentalism and Its Limits: Assessing the European Union's Answer to the Euro Crisis" (2013) 46 Comparative Political Studies 1003; Deirdre Curtin, "Challenging Executive Dominance in European Democracy" (2014) 77 Modern Law Review 1.

[49] See Frederic Eggermont, *The Changing Role of the European Council in the Institutional Framework of the European Union* (Intersentia 2012).

[50] Uwe Puetter, "The European Council—the New Center of EU Politics," Swedish Institute for European Policy Studies, Policy Analysis No. 16/2013, 2.

[51] Dieter Smeets and Marco Zimmerman, "Did the EU Summits Succeed in Convincing the Markets during the Recent Crisis?" (2013) 51 Journal of Common Market Studies 1158.

[52] See Christian Calliess, "The Governance Framework of the Eurozone and the Need for Treaty Reform," in Federico Fabbrini et al (eds), *What Form of Government for the European Union and the Eurozone?* (Hart Publishing 2015), 37.

[53] See European Council Conclusions, December 12–13, 1997.

[54] See Protocol No. 14 on the Eurogroup [2010] OJ C83/283.

[55] See Euro Summit Statement, October 26, 2011.

of the Euro area, including the decision to hold regular Euro Summit meetings at least twice a year, to establish a post of permanent Euro Summit President and to coordinate the work of the Euro Summit with that of the Eurogroup, acting at a lower level.[56] The legal nature of this statement was not clarified, and although part of its content was replicated in the European Council conclusions of October 2011,[57] it was uncertain whether it could be considered an international agreement concluded by the Eurozone member states.

Be that as it may, the Euro Summit was given an official legal recognition, albeit outside the framework of EU law, in the Fiscal Compact.[58] Pursuant to Article 12(1) Fiscal Compact, "[t]he Heads of State or Government of the Contracting Parties whose currency is the euro shall meet informally in Euro Summit meetings, together with the President of the European Commission." The President of the ECB shall be invited to take part in such meetings,[59] while the President of the EP may be invited to be heard.[60] Moreover, the Fiscal Compact created the post of President of the Euro Summit, modeled out of that of President of the European Council, to "ensure the preparation and continuity of Euro Summit meetings."[61] And it required that, in order to provide a platform for coordinating action among the governments of the Eurozone member states,

> Euro Summit meetings shall take place when necessary, and at least twice a year, to discuss questions relating to the specific responsibilities which the Contracting Parties whose currency is the euro share with regard to the single currency, other issues concerning the governance of the euro area and the rules that apply to it, and strategic orientations for the conduct of economic policies to increase convergence in the euro area.[62]

The rise of the European Council and the creation of the Euro Summit produced important changes to the EU institutional system.[63] The Euro-crisis marked a clear shift of powers in the EU system of governance toward national chief executives congressed in these intergovernmental institutions.[64] As Sergio Fabbrini has argued: "The extremely complex system of economic governance set up during the euro crisis [...] has been largely motivated and defined on the basis of the intergovernmental logic and decided through and within the intergovernmental institutional framework."[65]

[56] See also Uwe Puetter, *The Eurogroup* (Manchester UP 2006) (explaining the role of Eurogroup in EMU governance).

[57] European Council Conclusions, October 23, 2011, EUCO 52/11, 5.

[58] See Treaty on Stability, Coordination and Governance in the Economic and Monetary Union, March 2, 2012, [hereinafter Fiscal Compact], available at <http://www.eurozone.europa.eu/media/304649/st00tscg26_en12.pdf> (last accessed May 10, 2014).

[59] Art 12(1) Fiscal Compact.

[60] Art 12(5) Fiscal Compact.

[61] Art 12(4) Fiscal Compact.

[62] Art 12(2) Fiscal Compact.

[63] For a comprehensive analysis of the relationship between the European Council and the other EU institutions see also Uwe Puetter, *The European Council and the Council: New Intergovernmentalism and Institutional Change* (OUP 2014).

[64] See Alicia Hinarejos, *The Euro Area Crisis in Constitutional Perspective* (OUP 2015) ch 6 and Pierre Bocquillon and Mathias Dobbels, "An Elephant on the 13th Floor of the Berlaymont? European Council and Commission Relations in Legislative Agenda Setting" (2014) Journal of European Public Policy 20.

[65] See S Fabbrini (n 48) 1004.

Energized by the emergency posed by the Euro-crisis, the EU heads of state and governments congressed in the European Council and the Euro Summit took the lead in managing the EMU, marginalizing the role of the EP,[66] and directly setting the agenda of the other EU institutions: in fact, while the European Commission retained, and gained, important implementing powers—for instance in the surveillance of member states' budgetary policy, as emphasized in Chapter 1—it mostly lost its role of engine of EU policy-making, mainly turning instead into an executor of the choices made, and the tasks assigned to it, by the European Council.[67]

The shift in power toward an intergovernmental institution such as the European Council, in the absence of adequate counter-balances inherent in the involvement of supranational institutions such as the Commission and the EP, resulted in a profound redefinition of the relations of power between the member states. As Jonas Tallberg has explained, bargaining in the European Council is the result of several sources of power: states' sources of power, institutional sources of power, and personal sources of power.[68] Although, formally speaking, all heads of state or government enjoy equal status in the European Council—every state having one representative which can authoritatively speak for its country—in reality "differences between large and small Member States" shape power relations in the European Council.[69] In particular, aggregate states' sources of power play the most fundamental role in explaining negotiation in the European Council, with the result that large member states can dominate the process, although institutional and individual dimensions of powers can operate to mitigate this trend. Writing before the entry into force of the Lisbon Treaty, Jonas Tallberg thus concluded that "the European Council offers more limited institutional protection to small- and medium-sized Member States. The formal equality of the Member States, as expressed in the principle of unanimity [or consensus], is largely a procedural fiction, that helps to legitimize the outcomes of European Council bargaining."[70]

The experience of the management of the Euro-crisis by the European Council has empirically confirmed this analysis. As underlined both in scholarly research,[71] and public debate,[72] Germany and France, the two biggest states of the EU and the Eurozone, have acquired from 2010 to 2012 a predominant role in the

[66] See Cristina Fasone, "European Economic Governance and Parliamentary Representation: What Place for the European Parliament?" (2014) 20 European Law Journal 164.

[67] See European Parliament Research Service, "European Council Conclusions: A Rolling Check-List of Commitments to Date," Study, October 7, 2014, PE 536.359 (reporting lists of actions the European Council required other EU institutions to take).

[68] Jonas Tallberg, "Bargaining Power in the European Council" (2008) 46 Journal of Common Market Studies 685.

[69] Ibid 687. [70] Ibid 703.

[71] See e.g., Mark Dawson and Floris de Witte, "Constitutional Balance in the EU after the Euro-crisis" (2013) 76 Modern Law Review 817 and Georgios Maris and Pantelis Sklias, "Intergovernmentalism and the New Framework of EMU Governance," in Federico Fabbrini et al (eds), *What Form of Government for the European Union and the Eurozone?* (Hart Publishing 2015), 57.

[72] See Philippe Legrain, Op-Ed, "Eurozone Fiscal Colonialism," *The New York Times*, April 21, 2014 (arguing that management of the Euro-crisis has created a "quasi-colonial relationship" between EU member states); Stuart Jeffries, "Is Germany Too Powerful for Europe?," *The Guardian*, March 31, 2013.

decision-making process, reflected in the practice—proper of a directoire—of holding bilateral meetings before the European Council, resulting in decisions that would be later ratified by the European Council as a whole.[73] In 2012, attempts were made to expand this exclusive summitry system to include Italy and Spain, the third and fourth biggest economies of the Eurozone.[74] However, the recurrent political instability of Italy and the serious economic difficulties of Spain have hampered this attempt. In fact, because of the increasing economic problems of France too, the original directoire between France and Germany has been step-by-step replaced by a new equilibrium, in which Germany—the most populous and most prosperous member state of the EU and the Eurozone—has taken over as the hegemonic player in the European Council as far as economic policy is concerned.[75] Despite the existence of a President of the European Council, its weak political legitimation and its lack of significant powers have prevented the emergence of a meaningful counter-balance within the institution itself—with the result that Germany was largely able to shape the economic agenda of the European Council, and thus of the EU.[76]

According to Jürgen Habermas, "Germany's demographic and economic dominance within the Union, and especially within the Eurozone, has led it to take on a leadership role that is in part urged upon it but mainly inspires fear, and which is now using [...] in its own national interest."[77] Two examples suffice to emphasize the point. On the one hand, by interpreting the Euro-crisis as mainly a problem of excessive public spending and government debts, Germany strongly pushed for the adoption of the Fiscal Compact[78]—which, as explained in Chapter 1, was modeled on the "golden rule" introduced in the German Basic Law in 2009. On the other hand, Germany consistently promoted the adoption of national economic policies based on fiscal consolidation and budget cuts, hailing this strategy as the only solution to overcome the Euro-crisis.[79] Moreover—notwithstanding the growing discontent against these policies in a plurality of member states, as revealed by attempts by center-left governments in France and Italy, as well as recently in Greece, to re-focus the EU economic debate away from austerity toward growth[80]—Germany succeeded in cementing its

[73] See e.g., Declaration by France and Germany at Deauville Summit, October 18, 2010 (requiring that budgetary surveillance and economic policy coordination procedures should be strengthened and accelerated) and European Council Conclusions, October 28–9, 2010, EUCO 25/1/10 (endorsing reform to strengthen budgetary constraints and enhance economic governance).

[74] See e.g., Conference of press by Germany, France, Italy, and Spain at Rome Summit, June 22, 2012 (agreeing to adopt measures in favor of growth) and European Council Conclusions, June 28–9, 2012, EUCO 76/12 (endorsing a compact for growth and jobs).

[75] William Paterson, "The Reluctant Hegemon? Germany Moves Center Stage in the European Union" (2011) 49 Journal of Common Market Studies 57.

[76] See also "A Teutonic Union," *The Economist*, September 13, 2014.

[77] Jürgen Habermas, "Democracy in Europe: Why the Development of the EU into a Transnational Democracy is Necessary and How is it Possible" (2015) 21 European Law Journal 546, 549.

[78] See Leonard Besselink and Jan Herman Reestman, Editorial: "The Fiscal Compact and the European Constitutions: 'Europe Speaking German'" (2012) 8 European Constitutional Law Review 1.

[79] See Armin Schäfer and Wolfgang Streeck (eds), *Politics in the Age of Austerity* (Polity Press 2013).

[80] See further on this Federico Fabbrini, "Austerity, the European Council and the Institutional Future of the EU" (2015) 22 Indiana Journal of Global Legal Studies 269, 278–84.

policy preferences.[81] Of course, some qualifications are necessary. On the one hand, not *all* German economic preferences have been incorporated into EU economic policy.[82] On the other hand, several German policy preferences were also shared by other member states—with for instance countries such as Finland strongly supporting fiscal consolidation. Yet, the ways in which Germany led the decision-making process were perceived as problematic even in this state, due to the increasing marginalization of the national democratic arena.[83] Be that as it may, Germany's self-conception as the hegemonic player in the EU arguably reached its apex in the summer of 2015 when the German government outlined a plan to expel from the Eurozone a sister member state which was unwilling or unable to respect EMU rules.[84]

In conclusion, "although the tension between large and small countries have always been part of EU politics—a trait shared with all federal experiences"[85]—the developments occurring since the eruption of the Euro-crisis have deeply affected the constitutional balance between the member states. The institutional system originally designed by the Rome Treaty, and maintained by subsequent treaty revisions up to the Lisbon Treaty, sought to reconcile the principle of states' equality with the reality of states' size and power. To this end, it created a system of checks and balances in which multiple institutions, each inspired by a different logic of representation, had to share power. Nevertheless, in the aftermath of the Euro-crisis, the European Council—which the Lisbon Treaty had recognized as an official EU institution and endowed with a permanent President—emerged as the ultimate decision-making authority in the EU, and a new intergovernmental body, the Euro Summit, was created to deal with Eurozone matters. The role of

[81] See also Andrew Glencross, *The Politics of European Integration* (Wiley 2014) 305 (stating that "in a new departure for integration, it was one country in particular that set the agenda. Germany, the economic powerhouse of the Eurozone and the biggest contributor to bailout packages, played a central role in determining that indebted countries would need to implement austerity.").

[82] For instance, Germany strongly supported the idea of "contractual arrangements", which aimed to bind EU member states in fragile economic conditions to a detailed program of structural reforms in exchange for financial assistance by wealthier member states—and the European Commission followed up on it. See Commission Communication, "The Introduction of Convergence and Competitiveness Instrument," March 20, 2013, COM(2013)165 final. But opposition by virtually every other EU member state made the proposal moot. See Government of the Netherlands news release, "Contractual Arrangements with EU Member States Not Binding, Says Rutte," December 20, 2013, available at <http://www.government.nl/news/2013/12/20/contractual-arrangements-with-eu-member-states-not-binding-says-rutte.html> (last accessed August 7, 2014) (reporting opinion of Dutch Prime Minister Mark Rutte against binding contractual arrangements imposed by the EU).

[83] See Päivi Leino and Janne Salminen, "The Euro Crisis and its Constitutional Consequences for Finland: Is There Room for National Politics in EU Decision-Making?" (2013) 9 European Constitutional Law Review 51 (detailing Finland's skeptical response to recent EMU developments, especially concerning democratic decision-making).

[84] See the leaked document by the German Ministry of Finance, "Comments on the latest Greek proposal," July 10, 2015 (proposing that Greece should be excluded for five years from the Eurozone). This event was strongly criticized by the former German Minister of Foreign Affairs Joschka Fischer, "The Return of the Ugly German," *Project Syndacate*, July 23, 2015 (arguing that with this act Germany "announced its desire to transform the Eurozone from a European project into a kind of sphere of influence. [...] Greece could either exit [...] or accept a program that effectively makes it a European protectorate.").

[85] Magnette and Nicolaïdis (n 12) 40.

the European Council finds its roots in the design of EMU, with the decision taken at the time of the Maastricht Treaty to integrate new areas of core state sovereignty without delegating new competences to supranational authorities.[86] Yet, the rise of the European Council (and the Euro Summit) in the aftermath of the Euro-crisis significantly altered the EU institutional equilibrium, challenging the balance between state power and state equality which had characterized the EU constitutional settlement.[87]

In a context of intergovernmental governance, and in the absence of strong, legitimated institutional counter-weights, the European Council (and the Euro Summit) unleashed a dynamic of increasing domination by larger states. Notwithstanding the formality of consensus decision-making, the practice of governance since the eruption of the Euro-crisis strikingly revealed how the heads of state and government of the larger member states came to play a leading role in setting the agenda and the direction of the EU. Given the reality of the Eurozone, otherwise, state size was complemented by economic might as a threshold criterion governing inter-state relations of powers within the European Council (and Euro Summit). In this situation Germany—the largest member state of the EU, and its economic power house—inevitably became a hegemonic player in the decision-making process, to the detriment of the other member states. In the aftermath of the Euro-crisis, therefore, the trajectory of inter-institutional change epitomized by the aggrandizement of the European Council opened the door to a dynamic of inter-state domination, which challenged the constitutional balance between the member states historically at the basis of the stability and legitimacy of the process of European integration.

3. Institutional Implications

While changes in the institutional processes, with the rise of the European Council, the creation of the Euro Summit, and the shift toward intergovernmental modes of governance, have upset the constitutional balance between the member states and opened the door toward dynamics of domination of the bigger states over the others, changes in the law have ratified the increasing inequality between the member states. The analysis of legal measures adopted in the field of economic adjustment, financial stabilization, and banking resolution sheds light on this trend.[88] As I have argued in the previous chapters, largely as a result of the intergovernmental mode of decision-making centered on the European Council (and the Euro Summit),

[86] See Uwe Puetter, "Europe's Deliberative Intergovernmentalism: The Role of the Council and the European Council in EU Economic Governance" (2012) 19 Journal of European Public Policy 161.

[87] See Hauke Brunkhorst, "Collective Bonapartism—Democracy in the European Crisis" (2014) 15 German Law Journal 1177.

[88] See generally Kaarlo Tuori and Klaus Tuori, *The Eurozone Crisis: A Constitutional Analysis* (CUP 2014) ch 4 and Kenneth Armstrong, "The New Governance of EU Fiscal Discipline" (2013) 38 European Law Review 601.

during the Euro-crisis member states have increasingly felt free to step outside the legal framework of the EU, and reform the architecture of EMU through international agreements. These agreements negotiated under the rules of international law have crystallized the reality of power asymmetries between the member states. This has emerged in two directions. On the one hand, a first set of legal measures have increased the powers that supranational authorities enjoy vis-à-vis *several* states only, while leaving untouched the powers retained by other states. On the other hand, a second set of legal measures has introduced for the first time in the text of the law the explicit recognition that larger, more prosperous states enjoy more power and rights than smaller, poorer ones.

A. Difference in treatment

The establishment of a new framework of economic adjustment for member states in fiscal distress provides the most emblematic evidence of the first trend—namely the emergence of a difference in the way in which supranational authorities treat the member states, based on factors such as fiscal performance and size of the economy. As I have explained in Chapter 1, the Euro-crisis and the responses to it have produced an unprecedented centralization of power, shifting authority in the economic and budgetary field from the member states to the EU institutions. However, the process of centralization has been uneven: Five member states—Greece, Ireland, Portugal, Spain, and Cyprus—facing peculiar challenges in the fiscal or banking sector, entered into special programs of economic adjustment with the EU institutions. These programs—which were agreed upon through Memoranda of Understandings (MoUs), technically international agreements between the member state and the European Commission, on behalf of the pool of international lenders[89]—provided for the award of financial assistance on the condition that the concerned country implemented abroad set of economic and social reforms.[90] Hence, the signature on an MoU empowered supranational institutions—and notably the so-called "troika:" the European Commission, the ECB, and the International Monetary Fund (IMF)—to dictate economic policies in the countries under adjustment program in a way which they were not entitled to do vis-à-vis the other member states.[91]

[89] See Michael Ioannidis, "EU Financial Assistance Conditionality after 'Two Pack'" (2014) 74 Zeitschrift für ausländisches öffentliches Recht und Völkerrecht 61.

[90] The application of conditionality exposed a rift between creditor and debitor member states. Some creditor member states introduced requirements of collaterals as a condition for the award of financial assistance. See e.g., Korkein hallinto-oikeus [KHO] 2013:90, judgment of May 14, 2013 (Supreme Administrative Court of Finland ordering the publication of the deal between the Finnish Ministry of Finance and the Greek counterpart to obtain collateral as a condition to grant financial aid to Greece). Conversely, some debitor member states were asked as a condition for assistance to impose haircuts on bank depositors. See e.g., Anotato Dikastirio, *Christodoulou v. Central Bank of Cyprus*, Case No 551/2013, judgment of June 7, 2013 (Supreme Court of Cyprus reviewing the legality of bail-in measures imposed on uninsured bank depositors).

[91] See also European Parliament Resolution of March 13, 2014 on the enquiry on the role and operations of the Troika (ECB, Commission and IMF) with regard to the euro area programme countries, P7_TA(2014)0239 (criticizing the invasive role of the "troika" in the EU member states subject to economic adjustment program).

As Lina Papadopoulou emphasized with regard to Greece, the MoU contained "measures concerning fiscal, tax, social and social security policies, such as reform of the pension schemes including pension and salary cuts, bold tax increases, including housing taxes, loosening of labour law protections, as well as deep structural reforms towards a more competitive economy and fiscal sustainability with the aim of regaining the confidence of the markets."[92] For all practical purposes, this resulted in a complete take-over by the "troika" of the economic and budgetary policy of that country—in a way which did not find correspondence with the powers exercised by supranational institutions vis-à-vis other member states.[93] It is questionable whether the size of Greece, besides its peculiar economic challenges, played any role in the elaboration of such a pervasive MoU. Yet, as a comparison between the (first) MoU signed by Greece[94] and that signed by Spain[95] makes clear, the latter member state, albeit facing a major banking crisis and skyrocketing percentages of unemployment, was able to get away with a much lighter set of supranational conditions attaching to its financial assistance program for banks—arguably also because Spain is, after all, the fourth biggest member state of the Eurozone and a much more prominent player in the European Council.[96]

B. Difference in power

The second trend—namely the recognition of an explicit difference in the power enjoyed by states under new institutions designed to tackle the Euro-crisis—is instead epitomized by the Treaty establishing the European Stability Mechanism (ESM).[97] Adopted by the Eurozone member states in February 2012 to endow the EMU with a permanent stability mechanism to assist those countries facing

[92] Lina Papadopoulou, "Can Constitutional Rules, Even if 'Golden', Tame Greek Public Debt?," in Federico Fabbrini et al (eds), *The Constitutionalization of European Budgetary Constraints* (Hart Publishing 2014) 223, 230.

[93] See generally also Damian Chalmers, "The European Redistributive State and a European Law of Struggle" (2012) 18 European Law Journal 667 (emphasizing capacity of the EU institutions to dictate to member states policy reforms in a broad range of fields) and Klaus Busch et al, "Euro Crisis, Austerity Policy and the European Social Model: How Crisis in Southern Europe Threatens the EU's Social Dimension," Friedrich Ebert Stiftung International Policy Analysis 2013 (discussing the threat that austerity policies required by the "troika" produce on the welfare state).

[94] Greece—Memorandum of Understanding on Specific Economic Policy Conditionality, May 3, 2010, available at <http://www.minfin.gr/content-api/f/binaryChannel/minfin/datastore/a8/52/57/a85257bc11624aa0a2f89a6bebea2219687ce5f0/application/pdf/EU%2BBundle2.pdf> (last accessed June 1, 2014).

[95] Spain—Memorandum of Understanding on Financial-Sector Policy Conditionality, July 20, 2012, available at <http://ec.europa.eu/economy_finance/eu_borrower/mou/2012-07-20-spain-mou_en.pdf> (last accessed June 1, 2014).

[96] See De Witte and Dawson (n 71) 839. See also IMF, *World Economic Outlook Database*, available at <http://www.imf.org/external/pubs/ft/weo/2014/02/weodata/index.aspx> (last accessed November 7, 2014) (reporting that in 2012 Spain had a GDP at current prices of €1,029.279 billion, while Greece had one of €193.347 billion).

[97] See Treaty Establishing the European Stability Mechanism [hereinafter ESM Treaty], February 2, 2012, available at <http://www.european-council.europa.eu/media/582311/05-tesm2.en12.pdf> (last accessed May 10, 2014).

fiscal difficulties, the ESM replaced previous rescue funds and established a financial firewall with a capital stock of €700 billion.[98] Eurozone member states contribute to the capital of the ESM pro-quota, on the basis of the subscription by their national central banks to the capital of the ECB. Because of the ways in which the ESM is designed—with state contributions being the source of ESM funding—bigger and richer member states transfer more money to the ESM capital.[99] As a result, states such as Germany, France, and Italy, contribute a larger share of the ESM capital. As indicated in Annex I to the ESM Treaty, in fact, Germany's, France's, and Italy's contributions to the ESM capital amounts to respectively 27%, 20%, and 17%—while, say, the contributions of tiny member states like Malta, Estonia, and Luxembourg correspond to only 0.07%, 0.18%, and 0.25% of the ESM capital.[100] However, the ESM Treaty matches the asymmetry in financial contribution with an asymmetry in power—granting to the larger and more prosperous member states more power of decision-making vis-à-vis the smaller and less rich ones.[101]

To begin with, Article 48 ESM Treaty codified the rule that the Treaty "shall enter into force on the date when instruments of ratification, approval or acceptance have been deposited by signatories whose initial subscription represent no less than 90% of the total subscriptions set forth in Annex II." This provision effectively granted to the four largest member states of the Eurozone—Germany, France, Italy, and Spain—a veto right on the ability of the ESM to start operating, since each of them hold a quota in the ESM capital of more than 10%. The idea to overcome the requirement of the unanimous consent of all the signatory parties as a condition for the entry into force of an EU-related treaty is in itself a major departure from the principle of state equality. As Carlos Closa has explained with regard to the Fiscal Compact, which also introduced a requirement of the approval by a majority of Eurozone member states to enter into force,[102] the abandonment of unanimity breaks the possibility for outlier states to hold-out reforms for idiosyncratic reasons.[103] Yet, it is clear that in the context of the ESM, the requirement that entry into force be conditional on the ratification of states representing at least 90% of the ESM capital stock de facto rendered insignificant the ratification of the other then 13 smaller member states of the Eurozone, whose aggregate contribution to the ESM capital stock amounted, in any case, to less than 10%.

Yet, while the rules on the entry into force of the ESM Treaty already entrenched the disproportionate power of the larger states, it is the governance system of the ESM that underlines more clearly how the delicate balance between states existing in the EU institutional system has been abandoned here in favor of bigger states'

[98] See Art 8 ESM Treaty. [99] See Annex I ESM Treaty. [100] Ibid.

[101] See also Giulio Napolitano, "Il Meccanismo Europeo di Stabilità e la nuova frontiera costituzionale dell'Unione" [2012] Giornale di Diritto Amministrativo 461.

[102] Art 14 Fiscal Compact.

[103] Carlos Closa Montero, "Moving Away from Unanimity: Ratification of the Treaty on Stability, Coordination and Governance in the Economic and Monetary Union" Reconstructing Democracy in Europe Working Paper No. 38/2011.

domination.[104] While the default rule is that decisions within the ESM must be adopted by unanimity, the most important decision-making procedure designed by the Treaty—the decision whether to grant financial assistance to countries facing an emergency financial shortfall[105]—grants a special power to the larger member states. Pursuant to Article 4(3) ESM Treaty decisions by the Board of Governors of the ESM (the body grouping the ministers of finance of the ESM parties)[106] and the Board of Directors (the body grouping representatives of the ESM parties at a non-ministerial level)[107] shall be adopted by unanimity. However,

> By way of derogation from paragraph 3, an emergency voting procedure shall be used where the Commission and the ECB both conclude that a failure to urgently adopt a decision to grant or implement financial assistance [...] would threaten the economic and financial sustainability of the euro area. The adoption of a decision [...] under that emergency procedure requires a qualified majority of 85% of the votes cast.[108]

But votes are equal to the number of shares allocated in the authorized capital stock.[109] So, as a result, decisions may be adopted even without the agreement of all the member states: yet, Germany, France, and Italy are endowed with a veto right, because no emergency decision can be taken against their will (since each of them has a share of more than 15% of the ESM capital).[110]

Moreover, Article 5(7) ESM Treaty provides that a qualified majority of 80% of the votes/shares in the ESM capital is enough for the Board of Governors to adopt decisions as far reaching as the appointment of the ESM Managing Director and the termination of its office, the adoption of by-laws for the ESM, the approval of the annual account of the ESM, and the resolution of a dispute on the interpretation of the Treaty[111]—rendering Germany and France hegemonic parties in the management of the permanent stability fund for the Eurozone. Commenting on

[104] See Carri Ginter and Raul Narits, "The Perspective of a Small State to the Democratic Deficiency of the ESM" (2013) 38 Review of Central & East European Law 54.

[105] This is the most important decision-making procedure because it is the one to be adopted whenever a member state is facing financial shortfalls which risk undermining the stability of the Eurozone. Preventing this scenario is precisely the statutory aim of the ESM. See also Christian Calliess, "From Fiscal Compact to Fiscal Union? New Rules for the Eurozone" (2012) 14 Cambridge Yearbook of European Legal Studies 101, 115 (stating that "there is a danger that the emergency voting, which should rather be an exception, turns into the standard procedure.")

[106] See Art 5 ESM Treaty. [107] See Art 6 ESM Treaty. [108] Art 4(4) ESM Treaty.

[109] Art 4(7) ESM Treaty.

[110] Significantly, in authorizing the ratification of the ESM Treaty by the German Parliament, the German Constitutional Court was explicit in requiring that Germany takes steps to ensure that its veto power be maintained in case new member states access the ESM, and thus that the German percentage of control over the system does not decrease. See BVerfG, Case No. 2 BvR 1390/12 et al, judgment (final) of March 18, 2014, para 193 (stating that "Germany's veto position, which is required under constitutional law, will also be maintained under changing circumstances. Pursuant to Art. 44 ESM Treaty, accession to the European Stability Mechanism requires a unanimous decision by the Board of Governors [...]. This enables, and if necessary requires, the Federal Government to make its approval of an application for membership contingent on an amendment of [the voting rights system within the ESM] in order to safeguard the Bundestag's overall budgetary responsibility."). On this decision see further Chapter 2.

[111] See Art 5(7)(m) in conjunction with Art 37(2) ESM Treaty.

the functioning of the ESM from the perspective of a small member state such as Estonia,[112] Carri Ginter and Raul Naritis noticed the "evident redistribution in the balance of power within the Member States to the detriment of the smaller Member States"[113] and, while rejecting the view that each member state ought to have a right of veto as impractical, and inconsistent with the experience of EU integration, they underlined how alternative options could have been considered for the ESM. In fact, as they argued: "within the decision-making mechanisms of the ESM, small member states have not just lost their 'right of veto' but, also, have relinquished a significant portion of the weight of their votes compared to those existing within the EU. In turn, the significance of the vote of the large Member States has increased. [...] The current decision-making mechanisms of the EU vividly demonstrate that there are valid alternatives that allow a much gentler infringement."[114] The example of the ECB, which was discussed above, comes to mind here.[115]

As it were, the same logic underpinning the ESM has now made its way into the legal framework of the Banking Union—a major legislative overhaul of the rules governing the supervision, resolution, and deposit insurance of systemic banks across the EU.[116] In particular, the second pillar of the Banking Union, on the resolution of failing banks, has resulted in rules akin to those applying in the context of the ESM.[117] As a starter, although the establishment of a Single Resolution Mechanism (SRM) was designed through an EU regulation,[118] the member states of the Eurozone decided to conclude an international agreement regulating the transfer and mutualization of contributions to the Single Resolution Fund (SRF) outside EU law.[119] In fact, even though there was no need, from a legal point of view, to adopt an international agreement to regulate the SRF, the German government strongly pushed for it and had its way.[120] In its final version of May 2014, the agreement codified an ESM-style rule on the entry into force, requiring

[112] The ESM Treaty provisions which rendered Estonia's participation to the ESM effectively irrelevant were challenged before the Estonian Supreme Court. See Riigikohus, Case 3-4-1-6-12, judgment *en banc* of July 12, 2012. In its decision, however, the Court rejected the challenge upholding the constitutionality of the ESM Treaty. On this decision see further Chapter 2.

[113] Ginter and Narits (n 104) 63. [114] Ibid 65.

[115] See text accompanying nn 18–25.

[116] See Gianni Lo Schiavo, "The Single Supervisory Mechanism: The New Top-Down Cooperative Supervisory Governance," in Federico Fabbrini et al (eds), *What Form of Government for the European Union and the Eurozone?* (Hart Publishing 2015), 111.

[117] See Federico Fabbrini, "On Banks, Courts and International Law. The Intergovernmental Agreement on the Single Resolution Fund in Context" (2014) 21 Maastricht Journal of European & Comparative Law 444.

[118] See Regulation (EU) No. 806/2014 of the European Parliament and of the Council of July 15, 2014 establishing uniform rules and a uniform procedure for the resolution of credit institutions and certain investment firms in the framework of a Single Resolution Mechanism and a Single Bank Resolution Fund and amending Regulation (EU) No. 1093/2010 of the European Parliament and of the Council, [2014] OJ L225/1.

[119] See Agreement on the transfer and mutualisation of contributions to the Single Resolution Fund, May 21, 2014 [hereinafter SRF Agreement] available at <http://register.consilium.europa.eu/doc/srv?l=EN&f=ST%208457%202014%20INIT> (last accessed May 25, 2014).

[120] See Fabbrini (n 117) 452.

approval "[b]y signatories participating in the Single Supervisory Mechanism and in the Single Resolution Mechanism that represent no less than 90% of the aggregate of the weighted votes of all Member States participating in the Single Supervisory Mechanism and in the Single Resolution Mechanism, as determined by Protocol (No 36) on transitional provisions annexed to the TEU and the TFEU."[121] Whereas the ESM Treaty weighted the member states' votes in light of their financial contributions, the SRF agreement refers to the Protocol No. 36 provisions on the weighing of votes in the Council, which is broadly based on member states' population (corrected by the principle of degressive proportionality).[122] Nevertheless, the effect of the rule is, once again, to codify a privileged position for larger states as opposed to smaller ones. As a mathematical calculation shows, in fact, by requiring 90% of the weighted votes of the Eurozone member states in Council, the SRF rule grants to the four larger Eurozone member states—Germany, France, Italy, and Spain—a veto on the decision whether the SRF can enter into force.[123]

Moreover, in the functioning of the SRF, the agreement foresaw that national contributions to the SRF—which the member states would collect as levies from the banking sector—would constitute separate national compartments of the SRF, to be mutualized only through a step-by-step process.[124] As a result of this, funding for the resolution of credit institutions must initially be derived from the national compartment of the member state in which the resolution is taking place.[125] Those member states which do not enjoy sufficient resources to wind down a failing bank may ask for assistance and draw on the compartments of other member states which have not yet been mutualized.[126] Yet, when this is the case, Article 7(4) of the SRF Agreement has introduced the power for those states to object to the transfer if:

> (a) it might require the financial means from the national compartment that corresponds to it to finance a resolution operation in the near term or if the temporary transfer would jeopardise the conduct of an ongoing resolution action within its territory; (b) the temporary transfer would take more than the 25% of its part [...]; (c) it considers that the Contracting Party whose compartment benefits from the temporary transfer is not providing guarantees of refunding from national sources [...].

This rule effectively vests in the wealthier states—and ultimately in Germany, as currently the most prosperous one in financial terms—the real decision-making power relating to the SRF.

[121] Art 11(2) SRF Agreement.

[122] See Art 3 Protocol No. 36 on transitional provisions [2010] OJ C83/323 (provisionally attributing to every member state a number of weighed votes in the Council).

[123] Because the member states participating in the SRM are initially the member states of the Eurozone, the total number of weighed votes of these 19 countries (as of January 1, 2015) is 224, meaning that at least 202 votes must be cast in favor of the SRF for it to enter into force. With 29 votes each, Germany, France, and Italy, and with 27 votes Spain, these four member states hold the key to reaching the critical threshold.

[124] See Art 4 SRF Agreement.

[125] See Art 5 SRF Agreement.

[126] See Art 7 SRF Agreement.

In conclusion, the inequality between the member states that emerged in the intergovernmental practice of the European Council (and the Euro Summit) has spilled over into the international agreements reforming the EMU architecture, which have legally entrenched differences between the states. On the one hand, the measures adopted in the framework of programs of economic adjustment for states under financial assistance have deepened the cleavage between states enjoying full status vis-à-vis the EU authorities, and states subject to a more invasive supranational oversight. At its height, in the case of the MoUs, five Eurozone member states have been required to surrender, albeit to different degrees, their economic, budgetary, financial, and arguably social policies to supranational control—while the other states have maintained more autonomy in these fields. On the other hand, international agreements adopted in the area of financial assistance and banking resolution have introduced a direct discrimination between the member states, by codifying differences in power between larger states and smaller ones—supplemented by considerations of economic strength. Hence, the ESM and the SRM explicitly endow larger and more prosperous member states, and especially Germany, with veto rights on the use of the funds, replacing the traditional balance between states existing in the EU institutional system with a new equilibrium in which financial might sets the rules.

While as a result of these EMU reforms the EU is today engaged in more extensive practices of inter-states redistribution than a decade before, the ways and means through which this has been achieved have challenged the anti-hegemonic logic which had underpinned the process of European integration for over half a century. Even if the EU constitutional balance had been subject to subsequent re-adaptations, the EU institutional system had always sought to secure a compromise between state equality and state power as a condition for the stability and legitimacy of the EU integration project. Recent EMU reforms, instead, gave away with this concern. According to some this was an unavoidable, and wholly justified, development: While limitations of the autonomy of the member states under financial assistance have been described as consistent with the motto that "sovereignty ends when solvency ends," the greater power of larger states has been defended as appropriate given their greater financial contribution to EU rescue funds.[127] However, these views conceal the fact that entrenching the asymmetries of power existing between the states in the European Council, without foreseeing forms of checks and balances, was not an inevitable choice. Other options were available—witness the compromise used in the institutional design of the ECB.[128] Yet, they were not considered. At a high price for the cohesion of the EU.

[127] See further Kenneth Dyson, *States, Debt & Power: "Saints" and "Sinners" in European History & Integration* (OUP 2014).

[128] See text accompanying nn 18–25.

4. The Paradox of Domination

The developments taking place in the institutional practice, and the legal changes to the architecture of EMU, have profoundly affected the horizontal relations of power between the EU member states. The Euro-crisis and the responses to it upset the compromise struck in the original EU constitutional bargain, and maintained through subsequent treaty revisions, between the interest of the larger states to be represented in light of their power, and those of the smaller states to be represented *qua* states. In fact, as explained above, the Euro-crisis and the responses to it produced important inter-institutional changes in the EU, epitomized by the rise of intergovernmental bodies such as the European Council, and the creation of the Euro Summit. In the absence of adequate institutional counter-weights, intergovernmentalism in the EU unleashed a dynamic in which the more populous, more prosperous member states have come to dominate over the others, as evidenced by the design of mechanisms of financial assistance and banking resolution outside EU law. As I would like to suggest, this dynamic of domination is to some extent paradoxical. Concerns over state domination informed by the tragedies of history played a major role at any turn of the process of European integration—from the 1950s, when defeated Germany and Italy were invited to join the Community of the Six on the same grounds as the others states, to the 1990s, when German reunification was consented in exchange for the creation of EMU, binding the destiny of Germany to that of the other European states.[129]

As explained in Section 2, the EU institutional architecture mirrored the anti-hegemonic nature of the European integration project. The EU never embraced the traditional international law concept of the sovereign equality of states, attributing to the larger member states greater representation within several institutions such as the Council and the EP.[130] Of course, as it is well known, despite the formal international law claim of the equality of states,[131] in the reality of international relations power heavily influences the horizontal interactions between the states,[132] and several international organizations established in the aftermath of the Second World War have even constitutionalized the inequality between their members:[133] the United Nations (UN), for instance, gives a privileged status to five states by making them permanent members of the UN Security Council based on military power;[134] and the IMF sets up a voting system in which

[129] See Mark Gilbert, *Surpassing Realism: The Politics of European Integration* (Rowman & Littlefield 2003).

[130] See Pavlos Eleftheriadis, "The Standing of States in the European Union," in Nicholas Tsagourias (ed), *Transnational Constitutionalism* (CUP 2010), 44.

[131] See Art 2 UN Charter (recognizing the sovereign equality of states).

[132] See Stephen Krasner, *Sovereignty: Organized Hypocrisy* (Princeton UP 1999).

[133] See Eric Posner and Alan O. Sykes, "Voting Rules in International Organizations," University of Chicago Law School Public Law and Legal Theory Working Paper No. 458/2014.

[134] See Art 23 UN Charter (recognizing the status of permanent members of the UN Security Council to the US, the UK, France, China, and the Soviet Union, now the Russian Federation).

states count on the basis of their financial contribution to the fund.[135] Yet, as a project to restore peace on the European continent, the EU carefully avoided recognizing any special status to any of its member states. At the same time, contrary to what is the case in a purely nation-state context, the EU recognized that member states do matter, and therefore established appropriate fora in which the representation of states *qua* state could still be secured.

From this point of view, the effort to design in the EU a complex institutional architecture able to embed concerns for states' power into a system respecting states' equality, recalls efforts in other experiences of federation building. The case of the US—the paradigmatic example of a federal system[136]—offers a good illustration. In the US, the opposition between, and the need to reconcile the interests of, the large states and small states was the most difficult problem in the constitution-making process, and was resolved in the Philadelphia Constitutional Convention of 1787 only through a great compromise in which state equality and citizens' equality would be balanced through three different institutions of government.[137] First, the US Constitution created a Senate based on the equal representation of the states—every state having two seats, regardless of size.[138] Second, it established a House of Representatives based on degressive proportional representation of citizens—every state having a number of representatives proportional to its population, yet with every state having at least one representative regardless of size.[139] And third, it invented the Electoral College to elect the President in which every state would enjoy as many votes as the sum of its senators and representatives[140]—thus ensuring that no state could hijack the nomination process of the federal executive due to its size or power.

However, possibly because the process of European integration never vested a purely federal cloth, consistent with the hybrid nature of the EU as an in-between national and international law,[141] the push in favor of the protection of states' equality played a larger role in the design and evolution of the EU institutional arrangement. This resulted in the creation within the EU system of governance of intergovernmental bodies typical of an international organization, rather than of a federal regime—such as the European Council. From a legalistic perspective, intergovernmental institutions provide the best assurance of formal state equality. In each of these bodies, every country has a chair at the negotiating table and can consider itself on a par with the others.[142] Nevertheless, intergovernmental

[135] See Art XII(5) IMF Agreement (granting votes pro-quota).

[136] See Daniel Halberstam, "Federalism: Theory, Policy, Law," in Michel Rosenfeld and Andras Sajó (eds), *The Oxford Handbook of Comparative Constitutional Law* (OUP 2012), 576.

[137] See Gordon Wood, *The Creation of the American Republic: 1776-1787* (Norton 1993) and Jack Rakove, "The Great Compromise: Ideas, Interests and the Politics of Constitution Making" (1987) 44 *William and Mary Quarterly* 424 (discussing the grand bargain struck by the US Constitutional Convention in Philadelphia).

[138] Art I, Sec. 3, cl 1 US Const.

[139] Art I, Sec. 2, cl 3 US Const.

[140] Art II, Sec. 1, cl 2 US Const.

[141] See Robert Schütze, "On 'Federal' Ground: The European Union as an (Inter)national Phenomenon" (2009) 46 Common Market Law Review 1069.

[142] See German Chancellor Angela Merkel, Speech at the Opening Ceremony of the 61st academic year of the College of Europe, Bruges, November 2, 2010 (expressing the view that within the

institutions can be double edged swords: in the context of quasi-diplomatic negotiations between states, power matters, and larger and more resourceful states can more easily have it their way.[143] For this reason, smaller EU member states traditionally defended the so-called "Community method"[144] —the default process by which law-making is accomplished in the EU, which involves the power of the Commission to propose legislation, of the Council and (in most cases) the EP to approve it, and (if needed) the ECJ to review it—as most protective of the horizontal balance between the states.[145]

In the aftermath of the Constitutional crisis of 2005, however, national governments, including in small- and medium-sized EU member states, increasingly embraced the intergovernmental logic.[146] Member states agreed to formally recognize in the Lisbon Treaty the role of the European Council and accepted the creation of a permanent presidency, to be exercised separately from any other institutional mandate at the national level.[147] Because of a fear that the European Council presidency could be cannibalized by larger, more powerful states, the smaller EU member states sought and obtained in the final version of the Lisbon Treaty a number of amendments—largely reducing the powers of the President of the European Council to those of a chairman, and reaffirming the principle that the European Council would operate on a consensual basis.[148] The irony, however, is that these innovations played *against* the interests of the smaller member states, rather than in their favor. Ultimately, in the absence of a powerful and strongly legitimated President of the European Council, no counter-balance was available within that institution to check the power of the larger member states.

European Council "the Heads of State and Government of the 27 member states and the President of the European Commission lay down jointly [gemeinsam] with the President of the European Council guidelines on how the Union should develop.").

[143] This dynamic has also emerged in another intergovernmental context: that of the Eurogroup—which brings together the finance ministers of the Eurozone member states, under the chairmanship of a semi-permanent presidency. See text accompanying nn 53–4. The former President of the Eurogroup, Jean-Claude Juncker, famously decided to step down from the job complaining that it was impossible for him to make decisions because of the way Germany and France were running the show. See Brian Parkin, "Juncker Says Ceding Euro Job Due to Franco-German Interference," *Bloomberg News*, April 30, 2012 (reporting Mr. Juncker as stating that Germany and France acted in the Eurogroup "as if they are the only members of the group").

[144] See Renaud Dehousse, "The Community Method at Sixty," in Renaud Dehousse (ed), *The Community Method* (Palgrave MacMillan 2011), 3. See also René Repasi, "Gemeinschaftsmethode Sticht Unionsmethode," *Arbeit Wirschaft*, Feburary 7, 2014 (contrasting the "Community method" and the new, so-called "Union method").

[145] See e.g., Magnette and Nicolaïdis (n 12) 19, citing Prise de position des Premiers et des Ministres des Affaires étrangères du Benelux à la Convention, January 21, 2003 (affirming opposition of the Benelux countries against the Franco-German proposal of a permanent President of the European Council).

[146] See Renaud Dehousse, "'We the States': Why the Anti-Federalists Won" in Nicolas Jabko and Craig Parsons (eds), *With US or Against US? European Trends in American Perspective* (OUP 2005), 105.

[147] See also Paul Craig, "The Financial Crisis, the EU Institutional Order and Constitutional Responsibility," in Federico Fabbrini et al (eds), *What Form of Government for the European Union and the Eurozone?* (Hart Publishing 2015), 17 (emphasizing responsibility of the member states for the current EU institutional setup).

[148] See text accompanying nn 36–45.

In the negotiating room of Justus Lipsius, the building hosting the meetings of the European Council, the more populous and more prosperous member states emerged as the dominating forces, disrupting the delicate equilibrium between the states that had been created over a half a century plus of European integration.

Which leads me to the paradox I would like to emphasize. Although intergovernmentalism has been partially justified also as an institutional arrangement which guarantees the equality of the member states—since every state has a seat at the negotiating table—in fact this mode of governance turned on its head, opening the door for the domination of the larger states over the others. As in the international arena, also in the EU, intergovernmental politics allowed the mighty states to stake their claims. On the contrary, federal compacts that embed the corporate representation of the states in a broader institutional framework can provide a better defense against the self-aggrandizement of the larger states, even in cases where the asymmetry between the states (in power, size, and population) is extreme. Hence, going back to the comparative example used in this book, although the US sees the coexistence of a state like California, of 38 million inhabitants, and a GDP that would make it the seventh world economic power,[149] together with Wyoming, of just 350,000 people and a tiny economy,[150] the former has never been able to dominate the US policy-making process at the expenses of the latter, or seen its strength directly codified in greater constitutional power. As Allan Erbsen put it, in the US federal system "state/state interactions are between entities on an equal plane of constitutional status, and are thus 'horizontal'."[151]

Needless to say, US history is ripe with inter-state confrontations—not least a Civil War—and over the course of its continuous transformations the US constitutional system has at times authorized differences in treatment between the states. Yet, these have only been tolerated on a temporary basis. Notably, the post-Civil War constitutional amendments empowered the federal Congress to enforce due process, equal protection, and voting rights principles on the states[152]—and during the Second Reconstruction the US Congress introduced special rules that subjected Southern states with a history of racial discrimination to enhanced federal oversight, for instance by requiring them to obtain federal approval before enacting their electoral laws.[153] In June 2013, however, in a

[149] See Center for the Continuing Study of California Economy, *California Poised to Move Up in World Economy Ranking 2013*, July 2013, available at <http://www.ccsce.com/PDF/Numbers-July-2013-CA-Economy-Rankings-2012.pdf> (last accessed June 1, 2014) (reporting ranking of California economy in global perspective).

[150] For the data see United States Census Bureau, *Apportionment Population* (2010), available at <http://www.census.gov/population/apportionment/files/Apportionment%20Population%202010.pdf> (last accessed June 1, 2014) and United States Department of Commerce Bureau of Economic Analysis, *Gross Domestic Product by States* (2013), available at <http://www.bea.gov/newsreleases/regional/gdp_state/gsp_newsrelease.htm> (last accessed June 1, 2013).

[151] Allan Erbsen, "Horizontal Federalism" (2009) 93 Minnesota Law Review 493, 501.

[152] See William Nelson, *The Fourteenth Amendment: From Political Principle to Judicial Doctrine* (Harvard UP 1988) and Steven Calabresi and Nicholas Stabile, "On Section 5 of the Fourteenth Amendment" (2009) Pennsylvania Journal of Constitutional Law 1431.

[153] See Richard Valelly, *The Two Reconstructions* (Chicago UP 2004) and Bruce Ackerman, *We the People: Volume 3. The Civil Rights Revolution* (Harvard UP 2014).

controversial decision, *Shelby County v. Holder*,[154] the US Supreme Court struck down this requirement—authorized in the 2006 renewal of the 1965 Voting Rights Act[155]—holding that the application of these rules only vis-à-vis some states, and not others, constituted a "dramatic departure from the principle that all States enjoy equal sovereignty."[156] In other words, the US Supreme Court found that the oversight powers that the federal government enjoyed vis-à-vis several (Southern) states was incompatible with the principle of states' equality. Whereas this decision can be faulted for failing to grasp the seriousness of the threat of disenfranchisement today (and the consequential importance of federal oversight in this field),[157] its defense of the principle of states' equality appears striking when compared with the reality of domination increasingly underpinning the EMU—from the MoUs to the ESM.[158]

In conclusion, the intergovernmental turn impressed by the Euro-crisis generated a paradox of domination in the EU, in which the more populous and more prosperous member states took on a hegemonic role.[159] As a comparison with the US has pointed out, furthermore, such development is inconsistent with a federal logic—which is premised on a maintaining a balance between the states.[160] The measures adopted since 2009 have been taken under the pressure of an exploding crisis. Yet, these developments have opened a deep wound in the fabric of the EU. In fact, the erosion of the constitutional balance between the member states has also contributed to shake at its roots the legitimacy and the stability of the EU—as evident by the rise of extreme, anti-system parties at both the latest national and European elections.[161] By disregarding the problem of a balance between state power and state equality the legal and institutional constellations emerged in the aftermath of the Euro-crisis weakened one of the most essential conditions for the sustainability of the EU.[162] In a Union of states and citizens like the EU, even smaller and poorer member states (and their citizens) must feel they have a voice in the decision-making process. When some states or groups of citizens have the perception that they cannot influence the decision-making process—that is, when they feel their voice does not count—then exit becomes a realistic scenario.[163]

154 *Shelby County v. Holder*, 570 U.S. __ (2013).

155 Voting Rights Act Reauthorization and Amendments Act of 2006, Pub. L. No. 109–246 (US).

156 *Shelby County* (n 154) at 1 [of the slip opinion].

157 See Federico Fabbrini, *Fundamental Rights in Europe: Challenges and Transformations in Comparative Perspective* (OUP 2014) 262. See also critically, John Paul Stevens, "The Court and the Right to Vote: A Dissent," 60 New York Review of Books, August 15–September 25, 2013, 37, 38.

158 See text accompanying nn 88–128.

159 See Paterson (n 75) 57.

160 See further Daniel Elazar, *Exploring Federalism* (Alabama UP 1987).

161 See Nicole Scicluna, "Politicization without Democratization: How the Eurozone Crisis is Transforming EU Law and Politics" (2014) 12 International Journal of Constitutional Law 545 and Ben Crum, "Saving the Euro at the Cost of Democracy?" (2013) 51 Journal of Common Market Studies 614.

162 See Dawson and De Witte (n 71) 817.

163 See Albert Hirschman, *Exit, Voice and Loyalty* (Harvard UP 1970) (developing a framework to explain behaviors in firms, organizations, and states based on notions of exit, voice, and loyalty).

The unraveling of a balance between state equality and state power in the aftermath of the Euro-crisis constitutes in my view one of the greatest challenges to the future of the EU. Because of the tragic history of Europe no member state of the EU, no matter how populous, how prosperous, and how righteous, can afford to play a hegemonic role today. In a Union of states and citizens, the existence of a horizontal balance between the member states is a condition for endurance. As Paul Magnette and Kalypso Nicolaïdis put it: in the EU "legitimacy largely depends on the trust of all constitutive parts: if some states felt that they are considered as minor elements by the larger states, their confidence would be low and the overall level of legitimacy of the EU would be undermined."[164] In fact, although the EU institutional system has been subject to re-adaptations over time, securing a balance between state power and state equality has been the basis for the stability and the legitimacy of the EU integration process for over 50 years. The paradox of domination therefore strikes at the heart of the anti-hegemonic nature of the EU and urgently calls for institutional solutions which are able to restore a sound equilibrium between state equality and state power in the EU system of governance.

5. Anti-Hegemony and the Perils of Parliamentarization

While the Euro-crisis has had profound implications on the EU constitutional order, another recent constitutional development in the EU which requires particular attention is the attempt to transform the EU institutional system into a form of parliamentary government. As it is well known, in view of the May 2014 EP elections, EU political groups decided to bring forward lead candidates for the post of President of the European Commission, with a commitment that the candidate of the party winning a parliamentary majority would be elected President of the Commission.[165] In making this gamble, the EU political groups were relying on the new Article 17(7) TEU—a provision not yet in force at the time of the 2009 EP elections—according to which,

> Taking into account the elections to the European Parliament and after having held the appropriate consultations, the European Council, acting by a qualified majority, shall propose to the European Parliament a candidate for President of the Commission. This candidate shall be elected by the European Parliament by a majority of its component members.

Following this procedure, and notwithstanding many resistances,[166] Mr. Jean-Claude Juncker, the top candidate of the European People's Party (EPP)—which came in as the party with a relative majority of 29.4% of seats in the EP after the May

[164] Magnette and Nicolaïdis (n 12) 31.

[165] See European Parliament Resolution of November 22, 2012 on the elections to the European Parliament in 2014, P7_TA(2012)0462, para 1.

[166] See also Daniel Kelemen and Anand Menon, "Fight Club: When the EU's Campaign Season Ends, The Real Political Battles Will Begin," *Foreign Affairs*, May 18, 2014.

2014 elections[167]—was eventually nominated European Commission President by the European Council in June 2014,[168] and confirmed by a vote of the EP plenary in July 2014.[169]

The idea to politicize the elections of the EP by linking them to the selection of the President of the European Commission has been welcomed in European circles as a way to mobilize political participation in the European public space. From this perspective, granting to European voters the possibility to influence (indirectly) the choice of the President of the European Commission would increase EU citizens' interest in EU affairs, and overcome the alleged democratic deficit of the EU.[170] At the same time, the efforts to link the elections of the EP to the selection of the European Commission have been explained with a view to transform the EU into a fully fledged parliamentary regime, in which the relationship between the Parliament and the Commission would constitute the fulcrum of the EU system of government.[171] As it has been suggested, the attribution to the President of the European Commission of a clear electoral mandate, and the creation of a political relationship of power and accountability between the Commission and the EP, would endow the Commission with the institutional capital needed to function as the government of the EU.[172] And by making the relationship between the EP and the Commission the center of the EU system of governance, the process would revert the intergovernmental slide emerged during the Euro-crisis, and shift back powers from the European Council to the Community institutions.[173]

Much debate has occurred on the efforts to parliamentarize the EU. While some have questioned the opportunity of politicizing the selection of the European Commission,[174] or even challenged its legality,[175] others have raised concern on how the process effectively unfolded in the aftermath of the May 2014 EP

[167] See European Parliament, *Result of the 2014 European Elections*, available at <http://www.europarl.europa.eu/elections2014-results/en/election-results-2014.html> (last accessed August 7, 2014).

[168] European Council Conclusions, June 27, 2014, EUCO 79/14, para 25 (proposing the election of Jean-Claude Juncker with 26 heads of state and government in favor, and two against).

[169] European Parliament press release, "Parliament Elects Jean-Claude Juncker as Commission President," July 15, 2014 (reporting vote to elect Jean-Claude Juncker as Commission President with 422 votes in favor, 250 against and 47 abstained).

[170] See Joseph H.H. Weiler, Editorial: "European Parliament Elections 2014: Europe's Fateful Choices" (2013) 24 European Journal of International Law 747.

[171] See Simon Hix, *What's Wrong with the European Union and How to Fix it?* (Polity Press 2008) 162.

[172] See Miguel Maduro, "A New Governance for the European Union and the Euro: Democracy and Justice," Study commissioned by the European Parliament Constitutional Affairs Committee, September 2012, PE 462.484.

[173] See Mattias Kumm, "What Kind of a Constitutional Crisis is Europe in and What Should be Done About it?," Wissenschaftszentrum Berlin für Sozialforschung (WZB) Discussion Paper No. 801/2013, 18.

[174] See Alexander Somek, "What is Political Union?" (2013) 14 German Law Journal 561.

[175] See Anna Kocharov, "In the Image of State: Constitutional Complexities of Engineering a European Democracy," in Federico Fabbrini et al (eds), *What Form of Government for the European Union and the Eurozone?* (Hart Publishing 2015), 233.

elections, but raised hope that the process may improve over time.[176] In fact, it is not even certain whether the process followed after the May 2014 EP elections will be replicated in the future[177]—although it would seem difficult for the European Council to revert it.[178] In this chapter, I am not interested in taking a position on the question whether the politicization of the European Commission via the elections of the EP can fill the democratic disconnect afflicting the EU today. Rather, I would like to advance a skeptical view on the efforts to transform the EU into a parliamentary form of government *from the perspective of the balance of power between the EU member states*. Is the attempt to transform the EU into a parliamentary regime a positive development in restoring an equilibrium between states' equality and states' power in the EU? In my view, the answer to this question must be in the negative. Regardless of the impact of the politicization of the Commission on EU democracy, the evolution toward a parliamentary regime is unable to restore a meaningful balance between the member states and address the problem of domination. In fact, a parliamentary regime along the lines advocated above is liable to *deepen* the cleavage between larger and smaller states, entrenching, albeit in a different form, the asymmetry that characterizes the EU member states.

To appreciate this point one must recall the significant differences in size which exist between the EU member states. At one extreme, Germany and France total respectively 80 and 64.3 million inhabitants, while at the opposite, Malta and Luxembourg have a population of just 419,000 and 542,000.[179] As I explained in Section 2, the apportionment of the seats between the member states in the EP reflects these profound differences in states' sizes, by attributing to the larger member states more seats than to the smaller member states, albeit subject to the principle of degressive proportionality, which over-represents the smaller states. Pursuant to Article 14(2) TEU no member state can have more than 96 seats in the 751-seat EP, and no member states can have less than six. In its decision on the constitutionality of the Lisbon Treaty, the German Bundesverfassungsgericht criticized this apportionment of seats between the member states as inconsistent with the democratic principle of "one head, one vote," since a member of the EP elected in Germany would represent roughly 12 times more citizens than a EU parliamentarian elected in Malta.[180] However, besides the fact that the decision has been faulted for demonstrating a bad understanding about how electoral representation

[176] See Carlino Antpöhler, "Enhancing European Democracy in Times of Crisis? The Proposal to Politicise the Election of the European Commission's President," in Federico Fabbrini et al (eds), *What Form of Government for the European Union and the Eurozone?* (Hart Publishing 2015), 217.

[177] See European Council Conclusions, June 27, 2014, EUCO 79/14, para 27 (stating, to address the concerns of the UK, that "the European Council will consider the process for the appointment of the President of the European Commission for the future, respecting the European Treaties.").

[178] See Daniel Kelemen, "Towards a New Constitutional Architecture in the EU?" in Federico Fabbrini et al (eds), *What Form of Government for the European Union and the Eurozone?* (Hart Publishing 2015), 197.

[179] For the data see Eurostat, *European Population by Countries* (2013), available at <http://epp.eurostat.ec.europa.eu/tgm/table.do?tab=table&init=1&language=en&pcode=tps00001&plugin=1> (last accessed June 1, 2014).

[180] BVerfG 123, 267 (2009) paras 284–5. On this decision see further Chapter 5.

works in non-centralized systems of government, including in Germany,[181] the German Constitutional Court essentially failed to acknowledge a simple mathematical evidence: 96 is more than six!

Taking this simple fact into account is crucial when discussing the prospect of parliamentarization of the EU. In a parliamentary system of government—even one corrected in light of the principle of degressive proportionality—*larger states count more than smaller states*. While small states may still be overrepresented, their weight is too little to influence the political dynamics of a parliamentary regime. In fact, 56% of the members of the EP (MEPs) are elected in just six states: Germany, France, the UK, Italy, Poland, and Spain.[182] Hence, in the abstract, a majority of 376 seats in the EP could be comfortably achieved just with the seats of these six biggest member states—their seats exceeding the number of seats apportioned to the other 22 member states all together. Of course, Article 10 TEU states that the EP represents EU citizens, and no longer "the peoples of the States brought together in the Community."[183] For many years, the EP has endeavored to structure itself along party lines, rather than national lines.[184] Furthermore, one of the aspirations and expectations behind the call for parliamentarization is that states' differences of MEPs will become irrelevant and that European citizens will only cast their vote in light of political affiliations—recreating at the EU level a distinction between the Left and the Right.[185]

Nevertheless, states' differences still play a major role in the EP. Legally speaking, MEPs are elected in state constituencies, and voters cast their ballots on the basis of national party lists.[186] Politically speaking, then, despite the existence of European political parties, national considerations still influence MEPs' voting behavior within the EP.[187] MEPs regularly coordinate their actions with fellow national ministers in the Council through state ambassadors in Brussels.[188] And national considerations still determine EP elections, as candidates run on national platforms—and voters conceive themselves as voting for national parties.[189] In

[181] See Christoph Schönberger, "Lisbon in Karlsruhe: Maastricht's Epigones at Sea" (2009) 10 German Law Journal 1201 (holding that the standard of democratic legitimacy set by the German Constitutional Court "is unable to account for federal states, including Germany.").

[182] Calculations are based on the data on the apportionment of seats for the EP elections of May 2014 available at <http://www.europarl.europa.eu/news/en/news-room/content/20130308STO06280/html/How-many-MEPs-will-each-country-get-after-European-Parliament-elections-in-2014> (last accessed April 17, 2014).

[183] Art 189 TEC.

[184] See e.g., Simon Hix and Bjørn Højland, *The Political System of the European Union* (3rd ed. Palgrave MacMillan 2011).

[185] See Nereo Peñalver Garcia and Julian Priestley, *The Making of a European President* (Palgrave MacMillan 2015).

[186] See Council Decision of June 25 and September 23, 2002, amending the Act concerning the election of the representatives of the European Parliament by direct universal suffrage 2002/772/EC, Euratom [2002] OJ L283/1.

[187] See Andrea Gratteri, "Parlamento e Commissione: Il difficile equilibrio fra rappresentanza e governabilità nell'Unione Europea" [2014] La Comunità Internazionale 237.

[188] See Stephanie Novak, "Le grand retour des Etats" (2014) 149 Pouvoirs 19, 23.

[189] See David Schleicher, "What if Europe Held an Election and No One Cared?" (2011) 52 Harvard International Law Journal 110.

fact, notwithstanding the efforts by European political parties to overcome the national electoral focus and create a transnational political competition by advancing lead candidates for the position of Commission President, this has remained true even in the May 2014 elections. The most striking evidence of this was offered by the lead candidate for the position of President of the European Commission of the European Socialist Party (S&D): while being one of the strongest promotors of the initiative to have main European party candidates compete across the EU, Mr. Martin Schultz did not hesitate to campaign in Germany by explicitly playing the card of his nationality with voters.[190]

In a Union of states and citizens like the EU, in other words, the state dimension matters even in an institution such as the EP.[191] Unsurprisingly, the strongest endorsements to transform the EU in a parliamentary system have come from the larger states, not from the smallest ones.[192] It is quite significant that the candidates for the post of President of the European Commission brought forward by the main political parties competing in the 2014 European elections were mostly coming from large member states. As mentioned, the S&D advanced as a candidate a German, Mr. Martin Schultz; the European Green Party proposed a ticket made by a German and a Frenchman, Mrs. Ska Keller and Mr. Michel Bové; and, while it is true that the candidate of the EPP, Mr. Jean-Claude Juncker, comes from tiny Luxembourg, it did not go unnoticed to observers that he was chosen mainly because of his ability to speak German (and French) and thus campaign directly in the largest member state(s).[193] In fact, the whole process of promoting a competition between lead candidates for the position of President of the Commission was largely a German initiative: as it has been emphasized, "[s]omewhat tellingly, and indicating a certain unwillingness to embrace the concept in other Member States, the candidates have become known under their German name *Sptizenkandidaten* throughout the EU."[194]

Equally, it is not surprising that, after the May 2014 EP elections, the chairmanship of 19 out of 22 committees that compose the EP have been assigned to MEPs elected in the six largest member states. As the EP reported, five chairmanships of the parliamentary committees have been attributed to MEPs elected in Germany, four to MEPs elected in Poland, three to MEPs elected in Italy, three to MEPs elected in the UK, two to MEPs elected in France, and two to MEPs elected in Spain—while the three remaining committees will be chaired by an

190 Martin Schulz promoted his campaign in Germany with electoral posters stating "Nur wenn Sie Martin Schulz und SPD whälen kann ein Deutscher Präsident der EU-Kommission werden [Only if you vote for Martin Schulz and the SPD you can have a German President of the EU Commission]," available at <http://www.huffingtonpost.de/2014/05/23/spd-anzeige-nur-deutscher_n_5378496.html> (last accessed June 1, 2014).

191 See also Stefano Bartolini, *Restructuring Europe* (OUP 2005).

192 See Kumm (n 173) (showing support for the parliamentarization strategy in Germany).

193 See Beda Romano, "E' Juncker il candidato PPE alla Commissione Europea," *Il Sole 24 Ore*, March 8, 2014.

194 See Editorial Comments, "After the European Elections: Parliamentary Games and Gambles" (2014) 51 Common Market Law Review 1047, 1048.

MEP elected in Bulgaria, an MEP elected in Sweden, and an MEP elected in the Czech Republic.[195] Moreover, the whips of the three largest parliamentary groups come from three large states. Mr. Manfred Weber, who is the whip of EPP, is German; Mr. Gianni Pittella, who leads the S&D, is Italian, and Mr. Syed Kamall, of the European Conservative and Reformists, is British. In the end, in light of the preoccupation raised by the German Bundesverfassungsgericht that the principle of degressive proportionality may undermine Germany's representation within the EP, it is worth emphasizing that the President of the EP, Mr. Martin Schultz, is German—and also the Secretary General of the EP, Mr. Klaus Welle, is German.

Let me be very clear on this point: in itself there is nothing wrong with the fact that many Germans (or for that matter, Italians or Poles) play important roles in the EP. This is a normal consequence of population size. In the US, for instance, it is fairly common that in the House of Representatives delegates elected in California or Texas—the two largest states—occupy many leadership positions.[196] But precisely the example of the US helps me make the point. In the US system of government, the House of Representatives is *just one* of the institutions governing the nation. While in the House of Representatives it is fairly normal that (representatives from) larger states have a greater say than smaller ones, this advantage is counter-balanced by the existence of the Senate (in which states have equal representation) and of the President (which must be elected through a process in which the support of smaller member states is also necessary). This is what makes the proposal to make the EP the center of the EU institutional system problematic from the point of view of the balance between the EU member states. The asymmetry in population between the EU member states—and therefore the different degree of influence they can exercise within the EP—raises serious concerns about the suitability of a parliamentary system of government to provide an acceptable constitutional framework on which to ground the functioning of the EU. Certainly, in a parliamentary regime, states would count on the basis of their population, rather than their economic might, which is clearly more acceptable in democratic terms.[197] But, to put it bluntly: what would be the interest for smaller member states to be part of a Union in which decisions are taken via a game they can hardly influence?

Section 4 emphasized how the success of a federal bargain lies in its capacity to balance the demands of the smaller states to be represented *qua* states and the requests of the larger states to see their power reflected into the institutional setup.

[195] See European Parliament press release, "Members Elect Chairs and Vice-chairs of Parliamentary Committees," July 8, 2014.

[196] See Derek Willis, "In New Congress, House Committees Will Carry a Strong Texas Accent," *The New York Times*, December 26, 2014 (reporting how, in the 114th Congress, from 2015–16, representatives elected in Texas, which is the second largest US state, will assume the leadership of six out of 21 Committees in the House of Representatives, and indicating that, among others, representatives from California, the largest US state, held five committees, and the speakership, in the 111th Congress, from 2009–10).

[197] See text accompanying nn 88–128.

Contrary to the traditional international law claim of the sovereign equality of states, the EU must recognize to larger states a particular weight. Yet, contrary to a conventional nation state, the EU must also secure that in some form all member states have the same status. Hence, the complex institutional system designed since the Rome Treaty, in which multiple checks and balances made sure that no group of states, or citizens, could systematically dominate over the others in the decision-making process. It is from this concept of institutional design that any new effort to revise the architecture of EU, and restore a healthy horizontal balance between the member states in the aftermath of the Euro-crisis, must start. Whereas a transition toward a parliamentary regime would vest governmental function in a single institution, in which the power of size ultimately prevails, a Union of states and citizens characterized by significant asymmetries such as the EU can only prosper in an institutional regime in which separated institutions, each reflecting different logics of representation, share the power.[198] Only a system of separation of powers can make sure that the interests of all parties to the federal compact are taken into account, through the requirement of multiple majorities.

While the rise of the European Council, and the creation of the Euro Summit produced a dynamic of inter-state domination, because in an intergovernmental setting larger states have been able to exploit their relative power to the detriment of smaller states, a transition to a parliamentary system would also entrench the domination of larger states over smaller ones—although for very different reasons. Given the profound asymmetries that characterize the member states, the EU cannot afford to be governed by a single institution—be it a congress of heads of state or government, or a parliamentary assembly giving its confidence to the executive. If the EU is to live up to the anti-hegemonic logic which has inspired its foundation, and guided its transformations through several rounds of treaty reforms, its system of government must be constituted on multiple institutions, each reflecting a different logic of representation, sharing power. Although the EP ought to have a crucial role in checking and balancing the European Council, the resolution of the inter-state imbalances emerged in the aftermath of the Euro-crisis does not come through a parliamentarization of the EU. In Chapter 6 I will return to this point and discuss in depth ideas originally advanced at the time of the Constitutional Convention[199] to strengthen the authority and legitimacy of the President of the European Council as a way to tame the power of the bigger member states within that institution—as well as the challenges that arise along that road.

[198] See also Sergio Fabbrini, *Which European Union? Europe after the Euro Crisis* (CUP 2015) (making the case in favor of a new constitutional settlement in the EU based on separation of powers).

[199] See e.g., Greek minister of Foreign Affairs Georgios Papandreou, contribution to the debate of the European Convention, amendment No. 43 in Convention Secretariat, Summary sheet of proposals for amendments, May 9, 2003, CONV 709/03 (suggesting the direct election of the President of the European Council and explaining that this would "contribute to the substantial equality of the Member States.").

6. Conclusion

This chapter has analyzed the constitutional implications of the Euro-crisis and the responses to it on the horizontal relations of powers between the EU member states. As the chapter explained, the EU institutional system had been characterized since its founding by the attempt to strike a balance between state power and state equality. Subsequent treaty revisions, up to the Lisbon Treaty, updated, but maintained this balance through a complex institutional architecture. However, since the beginning of the Euro-crisis the European Council has emerged as the leading institution in devising the strategy to reform the EMU, outside any check and balance from other bodies. Moreover, a new institution, the Euro Summit, has been created to allow decision-making by heads of state and governments of the Eurozone states only. Yet, within these intergovernmental institutions, the bigger member states—and today especially Germany—have found limited restraints on the exercise of their political and economic power, and have been able to take over the decision-making process in a way which has upset the original balance between large and small member states in the EU constitutional architecture. The institutional implications of the domination by larger states have been reflected in the legal measures adopted in the area of economic adjustment, financial stabilization, and banking resolution. For the first time, supranational rules have introduced in the field of EMU different treatments for the EU member states, and entrenched different powers for them, mainly on the basis of their economic might.

As the chapter has argued in light of a brief comparison with the US federal system, the developments occurring in the EU constitutional system are paradoxical. Not only was the EU established as an anti-hegemonic project, but its institutional system traditionally gave more weight to states' equality than a fully fledged federal system. Yet, in the US, despite the strong asymmetries in economic might and size of the population between the states, a balance has been maintained between the states through a complex system of separated institutions sharing power. In the EU, instead, the rise of intergovernmental modes of decision-making premised on the idea of "one state, one vote" have opened the door toward the domination of larger, richer states over their smaller, economically weaker sisters. As the chapter suggested, the paradox of domination constitutes a serious problem for the stability and legitimacy of the EU. Yet, the proposal to solve this situation by pushing the EU toward a parliamentary system of government would be unable to restore a horizontal balance of power between the member states. In Chapter 6, therefore, I will reflect upon how constitution amenders in the EU could build on the idea of separation of powers to design a new institutional settlement which is able to prevent the worrisome picture depicted by Thucydides, according to whom "the strong do what they can and the weak suffer what they must."[200]

[200] Thucydides, *The Peloponnesian War*, ed T.E. Wick (Modern Library 1982) 351.

PART II
REFLECTION AND CHOICE

4

From Fiscal Constraints to Fiscal Capacity

1. Introduction

Since the outburst of the Euro-crisis, the dominant strategy pursued by the member states and the institutions of the European Union (EU) to address the fiscal emergency threatening the foundations of the Economic and Monetary Union (EMU) has been to strengthen the constraints governing budgetary policies. As I explained in Chapter 1, during the last three years the *Leitmotif* in the reforms of the constitutional architecture of EMU has been the introduction of greater fiscal discipline, combined with new mechanisms of financial stabilization and a revised framework for economic coordination and adjustment. To this end, tighter budgetary rules, new independent institutions charged to review fiscal policy, and automatic mechanisms of fiscal corrections have been set up at the EU level. At the same time, EU member states have been requested to change their legal systems and constitutionalize European budgetary constraints with the aim to increase ownership and effectiveness of EU fiscal rules. As Chapter 1 also underlined, by and large, member states across the EU have incorporated supranational budgetary constraints in their domestic systems, harmonizing their supreme laws to the principles of sound fiscal policy and balanced budget. Whereas the early rules of the Stability and Growth Pact had allegedly been largely ineffectual, the recent reforms of EMU have significantly strengthened budgetary constraints and fiscal discipline at the national and supranational level.

However, as the EU institutions and member states continued in their efforts to reform the EU constitutional architecture of economic governance in the direction of a deeper and more genuine EMU, a proposal which has attracted increasing attention has been the establishment of a fiscal capacity—that is, a central budget, possibly funded through new own resources, by which to assuage asymmetric shocks and carry out counter-cyclical policies no longer possible at the national level due to the budgetary constraints. As Miguel Maduro has argued in a report commissioned by the European Parliament (EP) Constitutional Affairs Committee (AFCO), "[w]hatever our view on the benefits and costs of constitutionalizing fiscal discipline, there are two things that are clear in the current EU context: such discipline is a necessity, if not to reestablish market trust, surely to reestablish trust between the Member States; but such discipline is also insufficient to address the current crisis."[1] As an alternative therefore he proposed an increased EU budget supported by real EU revenue sources, finalized to address the economic emergency of the Eurozone, ensure its future stability, and foster its democratic legitimacy.[2] With different emphases, similar proposals have also made their way in the report "Towards a Genuine EMU," written by the President of the European Council, in cooperation with the Presidents of the European Commission, the Eurogroup, and the European Central Bank (ECB),[3] as well as in other official documents aimed at shaping the debate about the future of EMU.[4]

The purpose of this chapter is to examine from a legal viewpoint the recent proposals in favor of a fiscal capacity for the EMU and to discuss the constitutional challenges that the establishment of this tool raise. As the chapter maintains, the proposals to introduce a fiscal capacity can not only complement the process of constitutionalization of budgetary constraints, it can actually correct its excesses. As I explained in Chapter 1, the Euro-crisis and the responses to it have shifted toward supranational authorities an unprecedented amount of power of oversight on national budgetary policy. While such developments have been justified with the aim to secure the functioning of EMU, they have sacrificed to an excessive degree the autonomy of the member states in the budgetary field. As I claimed in Chapter 1, this development is thus paradoxical in comparative perspective and problematic in constitutional terms. A fiscal capacity, instead, would endow the EU with the tools to manage the economic challenges of EMU, and yet create space for the states to regain meaningful autonomy in their budgetary processes. In fact, a fiscal capacity would make centralization of national budgetary policies unnecessary. With a fiscal capacity, the EU would be able to handle the slumps of the business cycle, managing shocks which are created by interdependences and spillovers within the EMU without the need for a full take-over of states' budgetary policy.

As the chapter explains, a number of different options have been advanced so far by–policy-makers on how to endow the EMU with a fiscal capacity. However, I argue that the establishment of a viable fiscal capacity would have to face at least three constitutional challenges. I label these: the challenge of asymmetry, the challenge of unanimity, and the challenge of representation. In a nutshell, the challenge of asymmetry is generated by the differences in size, wealth, and economic performances among member states. And the challenge of unanimity is triggered by the treaty requirements that decisions in the area of taxation be taken by unanimous vote in the Council. And the challenge of representation is born out of the current lack of powers of the EP—the only EU institution representing directly the EU citizens—in tax policy. In order to achieve its aim, the establishment of a fiscal capacity needs to address these three constitutional challenges. As

[1] Miguel Maduro, "A New Governance for the European Union and the Euro: Democracy and Justice," Study commissioned by the European Parliament Constitutional Affairs Committee, September 2012, PE 462.484, 16.

[2] Ibid 19.

[3] President of the European Council, Final Report "Towards a Genuine EMU," December 5, 2012.

[4] See European Commission Communication, "A Blueprint for a Deep and Genuine EMU: Launching a European Debate," November 28, 2012, COM(2012)777 final.

I will claim, in fact, each of these challenges may be fatal to the achievement of the purposes that animates this new project of EMU reform. No fiscal capacity can endure if it falls prey of the trap of asymmetry in which wealthier states transfer money to poorer member states. Equally, no fiscal capacity can be effectively established if own resources for the EMU—that is, EU taxes replacing inter-state transfers—are subject to unanimity rule for their approval. Finally, no fiscal capacity can be legitimated unless the EP—as the body directly representing European citizens—is endowed with at least a co-equal status to the Council—the body representing the member states and responsive to their interests—in the field of taxation.

As the chapter suggests, a number of legal options are available—in the framework of the current EU treaties—if not to solve, at least to minimize, the burden that the above-mentioned challenges place on the creation of a successful fiscal capacity for the EMU. The challenge of asymmetry can be addressed by replacing state contributions to the EU budget with new, real EU own resources, levied autonomously by the Union and directly connected to the wealth it generates. The challenge of unanimity in the adoption of tax measures at the EU level can be sidestepped by greater resort to enhanced cooperation. And the challenge of representation may be bypassed through the "*passerelle* clauses" that allow the EP to be involved on a par with the Council even in fields which would be subject to special law-making procedures at the exclusive discretion of the Council. None of this solution may be optimal. In the end, more substantive amendments to the constitutional foundations of the EU may be needed to ensure the success of a fiscal capacity, and should be considered if the EU engages in a broader overhaul of its constitutional setup, as I will also posit in Chapters 5 and 6. However, beginning a discussion of what the potentials of EU law are in this context is a due diligence before engaging in the grand project of treaty revision.

By discussing the idea of a fiscal capacity in the EU as a possible alternative to the dynamic of centralization described in Chapter 1, this chapter seeks to contribute to the ongoing debate toward a more perfect EMU. This chapter considers how to improve EMU by focusing on the EU's authority to tax and spend. Chapters 5 and 6 will continue the debate by focusing instead on the institutional reforms that would be needed to underpin a newly created fiscal capacity. In my view, the proposals in favor of a fiscal capacity should be seen as a welcome step toward more effective and legitimate self-government in the EU and the Eurozone. Yet, this is no easy go. While the establishment of a fiscal capacity ultimately lies in the political will of the European citizens and member states, exploring the constitutional challenges facing fiscal capacity will shed light on the risks and opportunities that surround the future of EMU. The chapter is structured as follows. Section 2 maps the proposals in favor of creating a fiscal capacity and summarizes the state of the debate in the field. Sections 3, 4, and 5, analyze separately the challenges of asymmetry, unanimity, and representation, and discuss how each of these could—and ought to—be addressed in designing an EMU fiscal capacity. Section 6, finally, concludes.

2. Raising an EU Fiscal Capacity

The proposals to endow the EMU with a fiscal capacity are recent.[5] The October 2010 report of the taskforce chaired by the President of the European Council, "Strengthening Economic Governance in Europe," which served as the basis for most of the reforms in the architecture of the EMU adopted to respond to the Euro-crisis, did not contain any hint about this idea.[6] In fact, the first time the term fiscal capacity is used in an EU official document is in the interim report "Towards a Genuine EMU," written by the President of the European Council, in collaboration with the Presidents of the European Commission, the Eurogroup, and the ECB, and published in October 2012.[7] Although already in its June 2012 inaugural report[8] the President of the European Council had suggested that "[a] fully fledged fiscal union would imply the development of a stronger capacity at the European level, capable to manage economic interdependences, and ultimately the development at the euro area level of a fiscal body, such as a [T]reasury office,"[9] it is in the October 2012 report that one finds the first articulate presentation of the idea of fiscal capacity and its form. In its discussion about the next pillars of EMU reform—a banking union, a fiscal union, an economic union, and a new framework for democracy, legitimacy, and accountability—the report stated that "strengthening [fiscal] discipline is [...] not sufficient" and suggested that "[i]n the longer term, there is a need to [...] go beyond the current steps to strengthen economic governance to develop a fiscal capacity for the EMU."[10]

According to the European Council President's interim report, a fiscal capacity would pursue functions which are not covered by the EU budget, the so-called multi-annual financial framework (MFF). In particular, "one of the functions of such a new fiscal capacity could be to facilitate adjustments to country-specific shocks by providing for some degree of absorption at the central level."[11] At the same time, "[a]nother important function of such a fiscal capacity would be to facilitate structural reforms that improve competitiveness and growth."[12] These ideas were later developed by the President of the European Council in the December 2012 final report,[13] where the establishment of a fiscal capacity was clearly linked to the creation of a "shock-absorption function" to improve the resilience of EMU.[14] As the European

[5] But see of course Jacques Delors, *Report on Economic and Monetary Union in the European Communities* (Publication Office of the EC 1989) 89 (already emphasizing the importance of shock-absorption mechanisms in the budgetary systems of all existing federal regimes worldwide).

[6] See Task Force to the European Council Report, "Strengthening Economic Governance in the EU," October 21, 2010 (identifying five pillars for reform, namely: 1. greater fiscal discipline, 2. broader economic surveillance, 3. deeper economic coordination via the European Semester, 4. more robust framework for crisis management, and 5. stronger institutions for more effective economic governance).

[7] President of the European Council, Interim Report "Towards a Genuine EMU," October 12, 2012.

[8] President of the European Council, Report "Towards a Genuine EMU," June 25, 2012.

[9] Ibid 5. [10] President of the European Council Interim Report (n 7) 4.

[11] Ibid 5. [12] Ibid. [13] President of the European Council Final Report (n 3).

[14] Ibid 5.

Council President's final report clarified, the economic rationale of this instrument lay in the reduction of the impact of country-specific shock and in the prevention of contagious effects across the currency union.[15] Because of its "insurance-type" nature, at the same time, the report suggested alternative macro- or micro-economic approaches to raise a fiscal capacity,[16] and emphasized that its design would still have to avoid "the risk of moral hazard inherent in any insurance system."[17]

In the vision outlined in the European Council President's final report, therefore, the fiscal capacity of the EMU would largely operate as what in the American jargon is called a "rainy day fund"—that is, like a savings fund to which member states contribute in times of economic upswing and from which they would be able to draw in times of economic downswing, to cushion the effects of a recession.[18] In fact, although the final report leaves open the possibility that the fiscal capacity may be funded by own financial resources, including a capacity to borrow via the establishment of an EU Treasury,[19] the acknowledgment that "the financial implications for national budget would depend on the [fiscal capacity's] precise design and parameters"[20] suggests that state contributions would be, at least in the short term, the main source of its funding. In terms of timing, moreover, the European Council President's final report suggested the possibility to achieve a fiscal capacity in stages. In a first phase, "limited, temporary, flexible and targeted financial incentives"[21] would be developed to support structural reforms in those member states in fiscal difficulties that are willing to enter into contractual arrangements with the EU institutions, while in the long run a more stable instrument to provide "fiscal solidarity [...] over economic cycles" would have to be put in place.[22]

Analogous ideas for the establishment of a fiscal capacity were also advanced by the European Commission. The November 2012 blueprint "For a Deep and Genuine EMU,"[23] in fact, endorsed the idea of a fiscal capacity to underpin structural reforms at the national level and provide a stabilization tool at Eurozone level to support adjustment to asymmetric shocks. Moreover, the Commission also suggested distinguishing between the short term and the long term. in the former, "the economic governance framework should be strengthened further by creating a 'convergence and competitiveness instrument' [(CCI)] within the EU budget—but separate from the MFF—to support the timely implementation of structural reforms, on the condition that 'contractual arrangements' are concluded between Member States and the Commission."[24] In the medium-long term instead a real fiscal capacity

[15] Ibid 10.

[16] Ibid 11 (distinguishing between a macro-economic approach, which looks at contribution to, and disbursement from, the fiscal capacity in light of fluctuations in the economic cycle; and a micro-economic approach, focused instead on specific public functions such as unemployment insurance).

[17] Ibid 10.

[18] On the "rainy day fund" mechanism in the US system of fiscal federalism see Robert Inman and Daniel Rubinfeld, "Fiscal Federalism in Europe: Lessons from the United States Experience" (1992) 36 European Economic Review 654, 655.

[19] President of the European Council Final Report (n 3) 12.

[20] Ibid 11.

[21] Ibid 9.

[22] Ibid.

[23] European Commission Communication (n 4).

[24] European Commission Memo, "A Blueprint for a Deep and Genuine EMU," November 28, 2012, MEMO/12/909, 2.

for the Eurozone would be fully established. In this light, in March 2013 the Commission presented, as a first step, a Communication for the introduction of CCI, emphasizing the link between structural reforms and financial support to be provided by member states.[25]

These proposals for the creation of a fiscal capacity have found a mild endorsement by the EU heads of state and government congressed in the European Council. While the conclusions of the December 2012 European Council largely endorsed the European Council President's report "Towards a More Genuine EMU" and followed in its footsteps to outline the process of future reforms of the EMU, no reference is made to the term fiscal capacity.[26] More modestly, the conclusions refer to "solidarity mechanisms"[27] aimed at supporting member states who agree through contractual arrangements to undertake structural reforms, as suggested both by the President's report and the Commission's blueprint. Otherwise, the "Strategic Agenda for the Union in Times of Change" adopted as an Annex to the European Council conclusions of June 2014 again only speaks of strengthening "economic policy coordination, convergence and solidarity" without explicitly mentioning a fiscal capacity.[28] According to some accounts, the reluctance of the heads of state and government congressed in the European Council to explicitly support the idea to create a fiscal capacity for the EMU reflects the political unfeasibility of this initiative.[29] However, the picture seems to be more nuanced.

To begin with, the idea of endowing the Eurozone with an autonomous budget has received the individual support of several members of the European Council. While French President Hollande recurrently spoke in favor of fiscal capacity since 2013,[30] and two Italian governments openly backed it,[31] Spain,[32] Belgium,[33] and

[25] European Commission Communication, "The Introduction of CCI," March 20, 2013, COM(2013)165 final.

[26] European Council Conclusions, December 13–14, 2012, EUCO 205/12.

[27] Ibid 5.

[28] European Council Conclusions, June 27, 2014, EUCO 79/14, 16.

[29] See Alexandre de Streel, "The Confusion of Tasks in the Decision-Making Process of the European Economic Governance," in Federico Fabbrini et al (eds), *What Form of Government for the European Union and the Eurozone?* (Hart Publishing 2015), 79.

[30] See French President François Hollande, "Intervention liminaire de lors de la conférence de presse," Paris, May 16, 2013, 7 (speaking in favor of "une nouvelle étape d'intégration avec une capacité budgétaire qui serait attribuée à la zone euro") and French President François Hollande, "Entretien à l'occasion du 14 juillet," Paris, July 14, 2015 (speaking for "un budget de la zone euro, pour pouvoir agir en termes d'investissements, y compris pour les pays qui sont le plus en retard").

[31] See Italian Prime Minister Enrico Letta, Keynote Speech at Annual Dinner Brugel, September 9, 2013, 5 (arguing that "there is room to reflect on a fiscal capacity for the euro area.") and Italian Minister of Finance Pier Carlo Padoan, Speech at the Camera dei Deputati, Rome, July 29, 2015 (stating that "L'Unione monetaria deve essere affiancata da [...] una autentica unione economica e fiscale, dove al rispetto delle regole si accompagni una altrettanto necessaria condivisione del rischio, necessaria e sostenuta da una adeguata mutualizzazione delle risorse. Il Governo italiano si sta impegnando per portare avanti questa linea").

[32] See Government of Spain, "Better Economic Governance in the Euroarea: Spanish Contribution," May 2015, 7 (expressing support in favor of "the creation of a limited common fiscal capacity within the EMU").

[33] See Government of Belgium, "Report on Preparing for Next Steps in Better Economic Governance in the Euroarea," April 27, 2015, 3 (stating that "a fiscal capacity and a treasury function for the euroarea could be envisaged").

Slovakia[34] among others also recently expressed their support for this instrument. At the same time, in early 2014 former Italian Prime Minister and European Commissioner Mario Monti was tasked to lead a high-level group of experts on the own resources of the EU, and the issue of strengthening the financing of the EU budget featured prominently in the group's first report of December 2014.[35] Moreover, following the May 2014 EP elections and the appointment of a new European Commission, the new President of the Commission has indicated his political intention to explore further the idea of creating a fiscal capacity for the Eurozone: as European Commission President Jean-Claude Juncker promised in his July 2014 programmatic speech before the EP, the Commission would seek to "launch legislative and non-legislative initiatives to deepen our Economic and Monetary Union [...including through] a targeted fiscal capacity at Euro zone level."[36]

In fact, the idea of a fiscal capacity—even though not the term "fiscal capacity" itself—has also been re-launched in the report "Completing Europe's EMU," prepared by the President of the European Commission, in close cooperation with the Presidents of the European Council, the Eurogroup, the ECB, and now also the EP, and published in June 2015.[37] Building on the previous report "Towards a Genuine EMU," the new report indicated the importance of creating "a euro area-wide fiscal stabilization function,"[38]—although allegedly postponing the achievement of this objective "in the longer term."[39] As the European Commission President's report emphasized, "in case of a very severe crisis, national budgets can become overwhelmed [...and] in such situations, national fiscal stabilisers might not be enough to absorb the shock."[40] For this reason, "all mature Monetary Unions have put in place a common macroeconomic stabilization function to better deal with shocks that cannot be managed at the national level alone."[41] Hence the report concluded with a plea in favor of an automatic stabilization mechanism which "should improve the cushioning of large macroeconomic shocks"[42]—although cautioning that such a mechanism should "not lead to permanent transfers between countries."[43]

Finally, the idea of a fiscal capacity has found consistent backing in the EP. In its November 2012 resolution on the report "Towards a Genuine EMU,"[44] the EP underlined how "the innovative idea of a central budget for the euro area funded by members of the euro area is now being proposed as the ultimate guarantee for [...] financial solidarity"[45] and expressed its view "that a 'genuine EMU' cannot be

[34] See Government of Slovakia, "Contribution on Preparing for Next Steps in Better Economic Governance in the Euroarea," May 2015, 3 (stating that EMU "cannot continue to exist in the long term unless fiscal instruments to address asymmetric and pan-European shocks become part of the EMU framework").

[35] See High Level Group on Own Resources, First Assessment Report, December 17, 2014.

[36] See European Commission President-elect, Jean-Claude Juncker, "A New Start for Europe: My Agenda for Jobs, Growth and Democratic Change," Speech at the European Parliament, Strasbourg, July 15, 2014, 7.

[37] President of the European Commission, Report "Completing Europe's EMU," June 22, 2015.

[38] Ibid 14. [39] Ibid. [40] Ibid. [41] Ibid. [42] Ibid. [43] Ibid 15.

[44] European Parliament Resolution of November 20, 2012 on the report "Towards a Genuine EMU," P7_TA(2012)0430.

[45] Ibid para CR.

limited to a system of rules but requires an increased budgetary capacity based on specific own-resources [...] which should in the framework of the Union budget, support growth and social cohesion addressing imbalances, structural divergences and financial emergencies which are directly connected to the monetary union."[46] In its May 2013 resolution then, the EP clarified that it considered the CCI proposed by the Commission as "building blocks towards a genuine fiscal capacity,"[47] and it expressed its clear wish that "this mechanism should be funded by means of a new facility triggered and governed under the Community method as an integral part of the EU budget, but outside the MFF ceiling, so as to ensure that the European Parliament is fully involved as a legislative and budgetary authority."[48] And in June 2015, the EP once again reaffirmed its support for "a euro area fiscal capacity based on specific own-resources which should, in the framework of the Union budget [...] assist Member States in the implementation of agreed structural reforms."[49]

Overall, therefore, there seems to be a slow but growing institutional convergence toward the idea of complementing the constitutional architecture of EMU with a form of fiscal capacity. As the fiscal discipline side of EMU is made ever more secure by being entrenched in constitutional norms at EU and state level, greater awareness on the necessity to create new supranational instruments to support fiscal adjustments in the EMU is gaining ground among EU policy-makers. In fact, as the European Council President's final report underlined, "while the degree of centralization of budgetary instruments and the arrangements for fiscal solidarity against adverse shocks differ, all other currency unions are endowed with a central fiscal capacity."[50] As argued by the International Monetary Fund (IMF) in a study making the case for the creation of a fiscal union in the Eurozone, "[w]hile the euro area is not a federal state itself and legal arrangements differ significantly from existing federations, the degree of economic and financial integration between member states is of the same order of magnitude as that of the different regions of many federal states. This suggests that, on economic grounds, federal states offer the closest benchmark for the euro area."[51] And all federal systems across the world appear to be endowed with forms of fiscal capacity at the central level of government.

As the literature on comparative fiscal federalism has pointed out, all currency unions have centralized mechanisms to manage structural imbalances or asymmetric shocks.[52] Although these vary from one union to another, all federal or

[46] Ibid para 11.

[47] European Parliament Resolution of May 23, 2013 on future legislative proposals on EMU, P7_TA(2013)0222, para 22.

[48] Ibid para 26.

[49] European Parliament Resolution of June 24, 2015 on the review of economic governance framework: stocktaking and challenges, P8_TA(2015)0238, para 57(c).

[50] President of the European Council Final Report (n 3) 9.

[51] IMF, "Toward a Fiscal Union for the Euro Area," Staff Discussion Note, October 2013, 15, fn 5.

[52] See George Anderson, *Fiscal Federalism: A Comparative Introduction* (OUP 2009) and Giuseppe Franco Ferrari (ed), *Federalismo, sistema fiscale e autonomie: Modelli giuridici comparati* (Autonomie 2010).

fiscally decentralized systems—from tiny, wealthy Australia[53] to a developing, multi-nation state of 1 billion people such as India[54]—have macroeconomic tools to cushion the effects of the business cycle, including when these are locally circumscribed, notably by empowering the central authority to collect resources and make them available to lower levels of government.[55] Of particular instruction for the EU and the Eurozone is the case of federal systems by aggregation[56] such as Switzerland[57] and the United States (US):[58] although in both systems the central government initially enjoyed limited fiscal power, and notwithstanding the fact that in both systems the lower levels of governments—the cantons, in Switzerland; and the states, in the US—retain significant budgetary autonomy, over time major constitutional changes, often driven by crises, created the pressure to develop instruments at the central level to smooth the effects of asymmetric shocks.[59] As I emphasized in Chapter 1, in fact, nowadays the budget of the US federal budget amounts to over 20% of national GDP—a feature which sharply contrasts with the reality of budgetary allocation in the EU.[60]

Although almost unanimous consensus exists among economists on the need to endow the EMU with a fiscal capacity (if the Eurozone is to survive),[61] alternative models of fiscal capacity can be conceived, depending on choices about its size, sources of revenue, and functions. A hypothesis which has been advanced, along the lines of something which exists in the US,[62] is to create a Eurozone

[53] See Miranda Stewart, "Australia," in Gianluigi Bizioli and Claudio Sacchetto (eds), *Tax Aspects of Fiscal Federalism: A Comparative Analysis* (International Bureau of Fiscal Documentation 2011), 137 (discussing fiscal federalism in Australia).

[54] See Ashutosh Varshney, "How has Indian Federalism Done?" (2013) 1 Studies in Indian Politics 43 (discussing fiscal federalism in India).

[55] See also Ronald Watts, *Comparing Federal Systems in the 1990s* (McGill Queen's UP 1996) ch 4.

[56] See Alfred Stepan, "Federalism and Democracy: Beyond the US Model" (1999) 10 Journal of Democracy 19 (distinguishing between "coming together federalism" and "holding together federalism").

[57] See Bernard Dafflon, "Le fédéralisme fiscal en Suisse: un relevé des enjeux constitutionnels, des responsabilités budgetaires et de la péréquation" rapport pour la Commission sur les déséquilibre fiscal (2002) (discussing fiscal federalism in Switzerland).

[58] See David A. Super, "Rethinking Fiscal Federalism" (2005) 118 Harvard Law Review 2544 (discussing the role of the federal government in the US system of fiscal federalism).

[59] See Daniel Kelemen, "Building the New European State? Federalism, Core State Powers, and European Integration," in Philipp Genschel and Markus Jachtenfuchs (eds), *Beyond the Regulatory Polity? The European Integration of Core State Powers* (OUP 2013), 211.

[60] See Congressional Budget Office, *The U.S. Federal Budget*, available at <http://www.cbo.gov/sites/default/files/budgetinfographic.pdf> (last accessed 28 May 2015). See also Henrik Enderlein et al, "The EU Budget: How Much Scope for Institutional Reform?," ECB Occasional Paper Series No. 27/2005 (contrasting the small EU budget to the large US federal budget).

[61] See e.g., Barry Eichengreen, "European Monetary Unification: A *Tour d'Horizon*" (1998) 14 Oxford Review of Economic Policy 25 (discussing "how quickly the [EU] is likely to develop an EU-wide system of fiscal federalism to accompany its monetary union") and Paul De Grauwe, *Economics of Monetary Union* (10th ed. OUP 2014) 109 (defining the Eurozone as a "type of incomplete monetary union [...] because it is a monetary union without a budgetary union"). The need for some form of federal budgetary capacity in the EU is usually connected to the theory of the optimal currency areas, developed by Robert Mundell, "A Theory of Optimal Currency Areas" (1961) 51 American Economic Review 657.

[62] See Sebastian Dullien, "Improving Economic Stability in Europe: What the Euro Area Can Learn from the United States Unemployment Insurance," SWP Berlin Working Paper No. 11/2007.

unemployment insurance system, operating as an automatic stabilizer entering into operation whenever the level of unemployment in a given member state surpasses a critical threshold.[63] While from an economic point of view this system would allow for counter-cyclical policies, it would also empower the EU to protect the interests of weaker members of society in times of economic need.[64] From this point of view, therefore, the proposal would also match the desire of the European Commission to strengthen the social dimension of EMU.[65] Yet, if the proposal to create a fiscal capacity makes economic sense in EMU, it also raises major legal problems. Leaving to others the task of discussing how best to design a fiscal capacity from an economic standpoint,[66] the following sections discuss three major challenges that a successful fiscal capacity would have to meet from a constitutional perspective.[67] Because the purpose of creating a fiscal capacity is to contribute to resolve the Euro-crisis and complete the EMU, while offering an alternative to the dynamic of centralization connected with budgetary constraints, it is crucial that these challenges are taken into account in framing the format of this new power for the EMU, unless its purpose is made vain.

3. The Challenge of Asymmetry

A first constitutional challenge that any model of fiscal capacity would have to withstand is what I call the challenge of asymmetry. In the EU, member states differ in size, wealth, and economic performances. While in itself this is nothing special in a currency union, in the EU asymmetry has over time become a particularly challenging factor because of the way in which the EU decides about the revenue side of its budget. Asymmetry, in particular, shapes the negotiations on the MFF. As it is well known, the EU budget is for the most part financed by contributions from the member states.[68] Things need not be this way—and in fact they were not initially like this: the High Authority of the European Carbon and Steel Community was empowered to collect levies from private companies, and borrow on the markets to finance itself,[69] and in the earlier phases of European

[63] See e.g., Ministero dell'Economia e delle Finanze, "European Unemployment Insurance Scheme", October 2015 (official document by the Italian Ministry of Finance articulating a proposal for an unemployment insurance scheme); and "Une assurance chômage pour la zone euro," Lettre Tresor Eco No. 132, June 2014 (policy document by the French Ministry of Finance articulating a proposal for a Eurozone unemployment insurance scheme).

[64] See e.g., Colm O'Cinneide, "Austerity and the Faded Dream of 'Social Europe'", in Aiofe Nolan (ed), *Economic and Social Rights after the Global Financial Crisis* (CUP 2014), 169.

[65] See European Commission Communication, "Strengthening the Social Dimension of the Economic and Monetary Union," November 2, 2013, COM(2013)690 final.

[66] See e.g., Jean Pisani-Ferry et al, "Options for a Euro-Area Fiscal Capacity" Bruegel Policy Contribution No. 1/2013.

[67] See generally also Torsten Persson and Guido Tabellini, *The Economic Effects of Constitutions* (MIT Press 2005) (discussing interconnections between constitutional forms and economic outcomes).

[68] See Franco Bassanini and Maria Teresa Salvemini (eds), *Il finanziamento dell'Europa* (Passigli 2010).

[69] Art 49 ECSC Treaty.

integration the European Communities drew their budget mostly from the custom duties, materially collected by the member states but in pursuance of a common commercial tariff.[70] Nevertheless, the original sources of financing the EU through own resources was over time replaced by a new financing scheme: while conclusion of free trade agreements with many third countries lowered the revenues from custom duties,[71] the expansion of the competences and commitments of the EU required new financial resources, with the result that budgetary transfers from the member states (based on their GDP, or the income derived by a harmonized VAT) became the main avenue to finance the EU budget.[72]

As a result of this state of affairs, the decision-making process about the EU budget has been captured by endless negotiations among the member states about the precise costs and benefits that each member states would incur.[73] Although formally speaking, once the system has been ratified, own resources are automatically due to the EU without the need for further decisions at member state level, and states' delays in making available own resources are unlawful,[74] EU member states have mostly regarded the contributions they make to the EU budget as *their* money, and have aggressively measured the difference between their contributions to, and their receipts from, the EU budget.[75] Because no member state is willing to transfer *its* money to the EU budget for the benefit of *other* member states, the discussion about the financing of the EU has become increasingly costly and decreasingly effective—every member state having a veto power on how much resources the EU should raise. Since the late 1980s inter-institutional agreements have required states to negotiate EU revenues through the MFF, rather than on a yearly basis. But things have remained contentious. Recent evidence of this, are the events relating to the MFF for 2014–20, where the European Council was first unable to reach a compromise on the EU budget,[76] and then found a minimum level convergence,[77] which, by reducing the size of the overall budget, was voted down by the EP.[78]

The asymmetry between the member states in size, wealth, and economic performances, and the implication of this state of affairs on EU fiscal policy, however, has been magnified by the Euro-crisis. The intergovernmental method by which

[70] See currently Council Regulation (EEC) No. 2913/92 of October 12, 1992 establishing the Community Custom Code [1992] OJ L302/1, as amended.

[71] See generally Marise Cremona, "The European Union and Regional Free Trade Agreements" (2010) European Yearbook of International Economic Law 245.

[72] See also Alessandro D'Alfonso, "How the EU Budget is Financed. The 'Own Resources' System and the Debate on its Reform," European Parliament Research Service in-depth analysis, June 2, 2014, 140805REV1 (providing an explanation of the current system of EU own resources and the complicated statistical mechanisms designed to calculate the GDP and VAT-based contributions by the member states).

[73] Ibid 11.

[74] See Case 93/85 *Commission v. United Kingdom* [1986] ECR 4011, ECLI:EU:C:1986:499.

[75] See also Jorgen Mortensen et al, "How do Member States Handle Contributions to the EU Budget in their National Budgets?," Study commissioned by the European Parliament Budget Committee, July 2014, PE 490.686.

[76] See European Council meeting, November 22–3, 2012 (failing to reach agreement on MFF).

[77] See European Council Conclusions, February 8, 2013, EUCO 37/13 (reducing the size of the future MFF).

[78] European Parliament Resolution of March 13, 2013 on the European Council Conclusions concerning the MFF, P7_TA(2013)0078 para 1.

the Euro-crisis has been handled, and the wide recourse that member states have made to international agreements outside the EU legal order, have deepened the differences between the member states exacerbating the cleavage between creditor countries—states which have been net contributors to the newly created mechanisms of stabilization of the EMU—and debtor countries—states which have largely benefitted from financial transfer to address their fiscal troubles.[79] As I have pointed out in Chapter 3, the Euro-crisis and the responses to it have weakened the balance between member states and favored their polarization. Member states which were net contributors to the rescue of the EMU have become increasingly impatient toward debtor states and as a result have demanded harsh programs of economic adjustments to assisted countries as a condition for further help. At the same time, member states which were net benefiters of rescue measures have become increasingly impatient toward creditor states and have perceived the austerity measures conditioning rescue packages as forms of hegemonic rule.[80]

The European Stability Mechanism (ESM)—as the main institutional mechanism devised by the member states to manage financial emergencies in the Eurozone and address its long-term stability—reflects the challenge that asymmetry generates in the EMU.[81] The ESM, which is an international treaty ratified by all Eurozone states, is endowed with an authorized capital stock of €700 billion.[82] Eurozone member states contribute to the capital of the ESM pro-quota, on the basis of the subscription by their national central banks to the capital of the ECB.[83] Decisions by the ESM are then taken by the Board of Governors (the body grouping the ministers of finance of the ESM parties)[84] and the Board of Directors (the body grouping representatives of the ESM parties at a non-ministerial level)[85] on the basis of unanimity rule.[86] Pursuant to Article 4(4) ESM Treaty, nevertheless, "an emergency voting procedure shall be used where the Commission and the ECB both conclude that a failure to urgently adopt a decision to grant or implement financial assistance [...] would threaten the economic and financial sustainability of the euro area." In this case a decision requires only a qualified majority of 85% of the votes cast, calculated on the basis of the contributing shares to the ESM capital.[87]

As I explained in Chapter 3, because of the ways in which the ESM is designed—with state contributions being the source of ESM funding—bigger and richer member states transfer *more money* to the ESM capital. As a result, states

[79] See Edoardo Chiti and Pedro Gustavo Teixeira, "The Constitutional Implications of the European Responses to the Financial and Public Debt Crisis" (2013) 50 Common Market Law Review 683, and Giuseppe Martinico, "EU Crisis and Constitutional Mutations" [2014] Revista de estudios politicos 240.

[80] See Kenneth Dyson, *States, Debt & Power: 'Saints' and 'Sinners' in European History & Integration* (OUP 2014).

[81] See Treaty Establishing the European Stability Mechanism [hereinafter ESM Treaty], February 2, 2012, available at <http://www.european-council.europa.eu/media/582311/05-tesm2.en12.pdf> (last accessed May 10, 2014).

[82] See Art 9 ESM Treaty.

[83] See Art 11 and Annex 1 ESM Treaty.

[84] See Art 5 ESM Treaty.

[85] See Art 6 ESM Treaty.

[86] See Art 4(1) ESM Treaty.

[87] See Art 4(4) ESM Treaty.

such as Germany, France, and Italy, contribute a larger share of the ESM capital. Conversely, however, the governance system of the ESM grants to biggest and richer contributors *more power* of decision-making. In fact, no decision by the ESM can be effectively taken against the wish of Germany, France, or Italy. As such, the ESM does not address the challenge of asymmetry of the EMU: on the contrary, it institutionalizes it.[88] Yet, a system of fiscal governance which is unable to neutralize the challenge of asymmetry presents shortcomings, which threaten its capacity to endure in the long run. As Miguel Maduro has argued, in terms of effectiveness, such a system leaves the governance of the euro "dependent on a permanent 'negotiation' with national democracies [producing] uncertainty as to the extent of financial and political support underlying the common currency."[89] At the same time, in terms of legitimacy, this system fosters mistrusts between states: "States paying will think they are carrying other states on their shoulders and rewarding moral hazard. [States] being 'disciplined' will take as being governed by those loaning the money."[90]

Of course, from a comparative point of view, the situation existing in the EU is not entirely exceptional. As mentioned above, all currency unions foresee mechanisms of stabilization across member units, and many of them achieve this through the re-distribution of resources from richer to poorer areas of the federation. In Canada, for instance, the Constitution—as modified in 1982, but along a practice that dates back to the origin of the Canadian confederation[91]—commits the federal government to "the principle of making Equalization payments to ensure that provincial governments have sufficient revenues to provide reasonably comparable levels of public services at reasonably comparable levels of taxation."[92] And in Switzerland, federal legislation sets-up a mechanism to transfer resources from the Confederation toward the cantons in need, so as to ensure the equalization of the Swiss economy.[93] Because these mechanisms of perequation imply a financial transfer from some (richer) units of governments toward others (poorer ones), they are often met with criticisms in the political debate.[94] Yet, an important feature of these mechanisms is that they formally avoid pitting one state directly against another, since resources are collected by the central government as taxes, and *then* re-transferred toward states in need as federal grants. By introducing a federal screen, the redistributive action occurring in these systems differs from the situation at play in the EU, especially in the aftermath of the Euro-crisis, where resources are raised by the states and then transfered from one state to another.

[88] See also, Carri Ginter and Raul Narits, "The Perspective of a Small Member State to the Democratic Deficiency of the ESM" (2013) 38 Review of Central & Eastern European Law 54.

[89] Maduro (n 1) 18. [90] Ibid.

[91] See further Alan Trench, "Intergovernmental Relations in Canada," The Constitution Unit, October 2003, 12.

[92] Sec. 36(2) Const. Act 1982 Can.

[93] See Legge federale concernente la perequazione finanziaria e la compensazione degli oneri, RU 2005, 1481 (Switz.).

[94] See e.g., André Lecours and Daniel Béland, "Federalism and Fiscal Policy: The Politics of Equalization in Canada" (2010) 40 Publius 569 (discussing politicization of fiscal transfers in Canada).

The unsustainability of a fiscal union based on pure inter-state transfers has been acknowledged by multiple quarters. Expressing the concerns of creditor states, German Chancellor Merkel in February 2012 made clear that further steps toward closer economic ties in the EMU should not open the door toward a "Transfer Union," with permanent payments from richer to poorer states.[95] At the same time, among debtor states, discomfort has grown bigger for the harsh conditionality that has accompanied financial aid.[96] It is with the aim to address this problem that proposals have been made to disentangle the EU budget and the EMU fiscal capacity from the contributions of the member states and to connect it, instead, with the wealth that the Union generates, for instance through the functioning of the internal market.[97] According to Miguel Maduro, in particular, "[i]t is essential that the Union is seen as redistributing the Union wealth and not the wealth of some states. It is equally important for such solidarity to be related to the different degree to which different social groups benefit from European integration."[98] If conceived in this way, moreover, a fiscal capacity would not only neutralize the challenge of asymmetries and what this comports, but also contribute to a clearer justification of the project of European integration by pointing out to the European citizens what the EU does.[99]

In designing a fiscal capacity for the EMU, therefore, policy-makers should break the wrong equation between fiscal capacity and inter-state transfers. The challenge of asymmetry in a currency union such as the EMU can only be addressed if resources for a fiscal capacity are not drawn from state contributions but rather from own resources that the EMU levies *as a Union*. It is in this light that one should address with some skepticism the proposal—advanced especially by the European Commission in its Communication on the CCI—to develop a bulk of fiscal capacity, at least in the short term, through the grant of financial support to member states that contractually agree to undertake structural reforms.[100] According to the Commission's proposal, in fact, the CCI would be financed by direct contributions by the member states,[101] and therefore would not escape the perverse dynamic that has traditionally characterized the management of the EU budget (with states asking how much do they pay and how much do they get) and more recently shaped the responses to the Euro-crisis (with creditor states asking why they should pay for the financial follies of the debtor states, and debtor states asking whether they are in fact being ruled by foreign lenders).

From this point of view, the EP has perfectly grasped the source of the problem when, in its November 2012 resolution on the report "Towards a Genuine EMU,"

[95] See Toni Czuczka, "Merkely Says Euro-Area Fiscal Union won't be 'Transfer Union'" *Bloomberg News*, February 7, 2012.

[96] See Andrew Higgins, "Europe Pressed to Reconsider Cuts as Cure," *The New York Times*, April 27, 2013.

[97] See e.g., Ingolf Pernice et al, "Challenges of Multi-Tier Governance in the European Union," Study commissioned by the European Parliament Constitutional Affairs Committee, March 2013, PE 474.438.

[98] Maduro (n 1) 21. [99] Ibid.

[100] European Commission Communication (n 25). [101] Ibid 8.

it recommended to the Commission to "return to the spirit and letter of the [treaties]"[102] and develop a budgetary capacity *funded by own resources*. In its resolution the EP especially emphasized the economic advantages of this move: at a time of budget consolidation at the national level, the existence of EU's own resources would free the member states from the duty to finance the EU budget or a fiscal capacity of the EMU. Nevertheless, the EP proposal would also have a clear political advantage, as it would free the EU heads of state and government from incurring very high political costs on every new negotiation on the financial resources of the EU. Moreover, for the reasons mentioned above, it would break the vicious dynamics produced by state transfers, making clear that the EU budget is the result of the wealth that the EU generates. Addressing the challenge of asymmetry requires therefore engaging "in a progressive return to a situation in which the Union budget is financed by genuine own resources."[103] This implies, however, the capacity for the EU (or the Eurozone) to levy taxes, which raises a new challenge of its own.

4. The Challenge of Unanimity

If the EU, or the Eurozone, were to develop a system of own resources independent from the financial contributions of the member states, the question arises as to what is the power of taxation which is entrusted to the EU institutions under the current EU treaties to achieve this goal. In this chapter, I am focusing on the competence of the EU to appropriate fiscal resources by raising taxes. It is clear, however, that a taxing capacity would in prospect justify a borrowing capacity.[104] Since the beginning of the Euro-crisis several proposals have been advanced in favor of the creation of euro-bonds.[105] In fact, following the decision of the ECB to launch a massive program of assets purchase to bring the level of inflation in the Eurozone closer to its target of just below 2%,[106] the option to create a type of EU securities has gained new attention.[107] Nevertheless—leaving aside the proposals to create euro-bonds by mutualizing the debts of the EU member states,[108] an idea

[102] European Parliament Resolution (n 44) Recommendation 2.4. [103] Ibid.

[104] See also Isabel Rodriguez-Tejedo and John J. Wallis, "Fiscal Institutions and Fiscal Crises," in Peter Conti-Brown and David Skeel (eds), *When States Go Broke* (CUP 2012), 9 (explaining how the capacity of a public authority to tax is the condition for it to borrow money on the markets, as the tax base operates as a guarantee that the authority will be able to pay its debts).

[105] See generally Stijn Claessens et al, "Paths to Eurobonds," IMF Working Paper No. 172/2012 (discussing euro-bond proposals as a way to resolve the financial crisis).

[106] See ECB press release, "ECB Announces Expanded Assets Purchase Program," January 22, 2015.

[107] See European Parliament Resolution of February 15, 2012 on the feasibility of introducing stability bonds, P7_TA(2012)0046 and Beda Romano, "Il Pse a Juncker: Lavorare per gli Eurobond," *Il Sole 24 Ore*, July 8, 2014 (reporting pressure by the European Socialist Party on President-elect Juncker to revive the proposal to establish euro-bonds).

[108] See e.g., Jean-Claude Juncker and Giulio Tremonti, Op-Ed, "E-Bonds Would End the Crisis," *The Financial Times*, December 5, 2010 and Romano Prodi and Alberto Quadro Curzio, Op-Ed, "EuroUnionBond per la nuova Europa", *Il Sole 24 Ore*, August 23, 2011 (arguing in favor of euro-bonds based on mutualization).

which departs from the logic of fiscal federalism, because it would ask a federated unit (rather than the federal government) to pay for the debts of another federated unit[109]—it is clear that the chance to create real EU treasury bills (where the EU as such guarantees for the payment) can only be sustainable if the EU has taxing power.[110]

A. Taxation

In this regard, it appears that the EU treaties provide the legal bases for a taxing power—or at least they foresee ways in which the EU could introduce taxation—but raise a clear challenge on the ability of the EU to effectively exercise this power. The only explicit acknowledgement of the competences of the EU in tax affairs is made in Article 113 Treaty on the Functioning of EU (TFEU) which empowers the Council, acting unanimously and after consulting the EP, to "adopt provisions for the harmonisation of legislation concerning turnover taxes, excise duties and other forms of indirect taxation to the extent that such harmonisation is necessary to ensure the establishment and the functioning of the internal market and to avoid distortion of competition." Yet, this clause, which is located in the TFEU's Title on Common rules on competition, taxation, and the approximation of laws, is not directly finalized to the introduction of a new European tax, but rather to the harmonization of tax rates across the member states.[111]

However, Article 311 TFEU states that "[t]he Union shall provide itself with the means necessary to attain its objectives and carry through its policies." And although this clause, which is located in the TFEU's Tile on Financial Provisions, does not mention EU taxation explicitly, it affirms that "[w]ithout prejudice to other revenue, the budget shall be financed wholly from own resources." Moreover, whereas the old text of Article 269 Treaty on European Community (TEC) only allowed the Council to lay down provisions relating to the system of own resources of the Community, which it shall recommend to the member states for adoption in accordance with their respective constitutional requirements, the Lisbon Treaty has now modified Article 311 TFEU, enlarging the power of the Council to shape the own resources of the EU. Pursuant to Article 311(3) TFEU, in fact, the Council, acting unanimously and after consulting the EP shall:

[109] See Jonathan A. Rodden, *Hamilton's Paradox: The Promise and Peril of Fiscal Discipline* (CUP 2006) (explaining that in systems of fiscal federalism possible bail outs of lower units of government facing fiscal challenges are payed by the federal treasury, not by the treasuries of other lower units of government).

[110] But see also Art 310 TFEU (stating that "[t]he revenue and expenditure shown in the budget [of the EU] shall be in balance") on which see Federico Fabbrini, "Il pareggio di bilancio nelle costituzioni europee" [2011] Quaderni Costituzionali 933 (explaining that this provision effectively introduces a balanced budget requirement for the EU). The existence of such a provision is something which must be taken into account when discussing the possibility of borrowing, and thus creating debt, in the EU.

[111] See e.g., Council Directive 2006/112/EC of November 28, 2006 on the common system of value added tax [2006] OJ L347/1, as amended.

adopt a decision laying down the provisions relating to the system of own resources of the Union. In this context it may establish new categories of own resources or abolish an existing category. That decision shall not enter into force until it is approved by the Member States in accordance with their respective constitutional requirements.

The exact interpretation of the provisions of the TFEU related to taxes is a matter of debate among tax lawyers.[112] In principle, the treaties could be construed restrictively, arguing that the own resources clause is intended simply to prohibit the member states from refusing to contribute to the budget of the Union. The European Commission however has construed Article 311 TFEU in a more constructive manner and argued that, if combined with Article 133 TFEU, the clause could be read as granting to the EU the power to adopt new taxes for the benefit of the EU budget. In its June 2011 proposal for a Council decision on the system of own resources of the EU,[113] in fact, the Commission proposed to the Council to introduce as a new category of own resources under Article 311 TFEU a financial transaction tax (FTT), to be collected by the member states and transfered to the EU budget in lieu of other contributions currently in place.[114] And in its subsequent proposal for a Council directive on a FTT,[115] the Commission indicated that its draft legislative text would be based on Article 133 TFEU, thus the harmonization clause in the TFEU, but that the revenues of the tax would be appropriated by the EU with the aim to feed the EU budget, and free the member states from parts of their current contributions.[116]

Be that as it may, whatever the precise interpretation of Articles 113 and 311 TFEU, and even assuming that their combined effect may empower the EU to levy new taxes, it is clear that these two provisions raise a new constitutional challenge on the road toward the establishment of a fiscal capacity—what I call the challenge of unanimity. Pursuant to Article 113 TFEU, in fact, the adoption of any legal measure for the harmonization of tax laws must be taken by the Council *unanimously*. At the same time, under Article 311 TFEU the establishment of new own resources for the EU requires a *unanimous* decision by the Council—to be approved moreover by every member state in accordance with its constitutional requirement. The existence of a unanimity rule in the field of taxation places a formidable burden on the ability of the EU to make steps ahead in the process of European integration. Joseph H.H. Weiler famously emphasized how the "shadow of the veto" shaped policy making in the EU before the introduction of qualified majority voting (QMV).[117] As it has been stated, "[u]nder the prevailing unanimity

[112] See Edoardo Traversa and Alexander Maitrot de la Motte, "Le fédéralisme économique et la fiscalité dans l'Union européenne," in Stéphane De la Rosa et al (eds), *L'Union européene et le fédéralisme économique* (Bruylant 2015), 343.

[113] European Commission proposal for a Council Decision on the system of own resources of the EU, June 29, 2011, COM(2011)510 final.

[114] Ibid.

[115] European Commission proposal for a Council Directive on a common system of FTT, November 28, 2011, COM(2011)594 final.

[116] Ibid.

[117] See Joseph H.H. Weiler, "The Transformation of Europe" (1991) 100 Yale Law Journal 2403.

rule in fiscal matters, an individual Member State can adamantly oppose to any surrender of tax sovereignty to the EU level."[118] States' opposition to EU taxation may be due to political reasons—such as the "often visceral rejection of anything that suggests a federal state of affairs"[119]—but may also be due to economic reasons, namely the preservation of states' interest in protecting the fiscal status quo.

The fate of the Commission proposal for a Council directive introducing a FTT reflects in a tangible manner this state of affairs. Proposals in favor of a FTT—originally articulated by US economist James Tobin in the 1970s—saw a rise in popularity in the aftermath of the financial crisis of 2008.[120] The IMF discussed the option of a FTT in a 2010 report,[121] and the theme was raised by member states of the Group of 20 (G20) the following year.[122] While the debate at the international level did not lead to any concrete steps toward the introduction of a global FTT, a number of EU member states unilaterally decided to enact FTT at the national level.[123] It is in this context that in September 2011 the Commission tabled a proposal for a Council directive on a common system of FTT to be applied throughout the EU.[124] The Commission proposal was based on Article 113 TFEU and, bearing in mind the increasing number of uncoordinated national tax measures being put in place, sought the harmonization of FTT across the EU with the aim to avoid fragmentation in the internal market for financial services.[125] At the same time, the Commission proposal sought to make sure that the financial sector would make a fair contribution to cover the costs of the recent crisis, and was premised on the view that an EU-wide FTT could provide to the member states and the EU a new source of budgetary financing to face the current fiscal shortfalls.[126]

Nevertheless, the Commission proposal was the object of fierce opposition by several member states: the United Kingdom (UK) in particular, mobilized against this measure, which it regarded as hostile to its florid financial market.[127] Eventually, in June 2012 the European Council had to acknowledge that the differences between the member states were unbridgeable and that "the proposal for a FTT will not be adopted by the Council within a reasonable time."[128] Because a

118 Sylvain Plasschaert, "Towards an Own Resource for the European Union? Why? How? And When?" [2004] European Taxation 470, 476.

119 Ibid.

120 See Antony Seely, "The Tobin Tax: Recent Developments," House of Commons Library, September 11, 2013, SN6184.

121 IMF, "A Fair and Substantial Contribution by the Financial Sector: Interim Report for the G20," April 2010.

122 G20, Cannes Summit Final Declaration, November 4, 2011, para 82.

123 See e.g., Art 5, Loi n° 2012-354 du 14 mars 2012, J.O.R.F. n° 64 du 15 mars 2012, 4690 (Fr.) and Art 1(491), Legge n. 228 del 24 dicembre 2012, G.U.R.I. n. 302 del 29 dicembre 2012 (It.).

124 See European Commission proposal (n 115).

125 Ibid.

126 See also Bart van Vooren, "The Proposed Financial Transaction Tax Directive: The Quest to Create Momentum at the G20 through Internal Legislation," in Bart van Vooren et al (eds), *The EU's Role in Global Governance: The Legal Dimension* (OUP 2013), 272 (explaining how the division between the member states reduced the capacity of the EU to push for the introduction of a FTT on a global scale).

127 See "Europe's Financial Transaction Tax: Oops" *The Economist*, April 27, 2013.

128 European Council Conclusions, June 28, 2012, EUCO 76/12, 13.

FTT was often indicated, together with a carbon tax or corporate tax, as the most feasible way to endow the EU with a fiscal capacity,[129] the difficulties with which the Commission proposal was met cast a pale light on the challenge that the rule of unanimity poses on the road toward the establishment of a fiscal capacity. The existing EU decision-making process in tax matters, in fact, entrenches the rule of unanimity, placing a heavy burden on the ability of the EU institutions and member states to overcome idiosyncratic state vetoes.

B. Enhanced cooperation

It is in this context that resort to enhanced cooperation has been proposed as a way to bypass the deadlock of unanimity. As it has been stated, "[t]he political difficulties in the way of a genuine EU tax [...] could, in principle, be overcome if a substantial number of Member States were to muster the political will to move ahead, conceivably within the 'enhanced cooperation' framework, thus sidestepping the unanimity rule which remains staunchly defended by a few member states."[130] This was precisely the strategy followed in the case of the FTT. After the failure to reach unanimity on the Commission proposal, 11 Eurozone member states—Belgium, Germany, Estonia, Greece, Spain, France, Italy, Austria, Portugal, Slovakia, and Slovenia—asked authorization to adopt a FTT through enhanced cooperation. The EP consented to this in December 2012,[131] and the Council authorized the cooperation in January 2013.[132] Because—as I have argued elsewhere—enhanced cooperation is constitutionally permitted when states disagree *whether* to act at the EU level,[133] in the case at hand the decision to resort to enhanced cooperation was legitimate, and in February 2013 the European Commission proposed a Council directive, re-adapting its original proposal to introduce a FTT among the states participating in the enhanced cooperation.[134] At the time of writing, negotiations among the 11 states participating in the enhanced cooperation are still ongoing—but no final directive has been adopted.[135]

The decision authorizing 11 EU member states to undertake an enhanced cooperation to adopt a FTT was challenged by the UK government before the

[129] See Maduro (n 1) 21; European Commission proposal (n 113) 4.

[130] Plasschaert (n 118) 479.

[131] European Parliament Legislative Resolution of December 12, 2012 on the proposal for a Council decision authorizing enhanced cooperation in the area of the creation of a FTT, P7_TA(2012)0498.

[132] Council Decision 2013/52/EU of January 22, 2013 authorizing enhanced cooperation in the area of FTT [2013] OJ L22/11.

[133] See Federico Fabbrini, "Enhanced Cooperation under Scrutiny: Revisiting the Law and Practice of Multi-Speed Integrtation in Light of the First Involvement of the EU Judiciary" (2013) 40 Legal Issues Economic Integration 197.

[134] European Commission proposal for a Council directive implementing enhanced cooperation in the area of a FTT, February 14, 2013, COM(2013)71 final.

[135] See Florence Autret, "Pierre Moscovici: 'Je suis favorable à un minister des Finances européen'", *La Tribune*, September 10, 2015 (interviewing the European Commissioner for Economic and Financial Affairs Pierre Moscovici, who indicated that with sufficient political will the FTT could be adopted in 2016, so as to be operational from 2017).

European Court of Justice (ECJ). The ECJ had recently recognized its power to review the legality of the use of enhanced cooperation in EU law.[136] In its complaint, the UK argued that the FTT was incompatible with the internal market and violated its right as a country not involved in the enhanced cooperation.[137] In its ruling of April 2014, however, the ECJ correctly rejected the UK claim as inadmissible:[138] as the ECJ emphasized, the UK complaint concerned the substance of the legal measures that member states engaging in the enhanced cooperation could adopt, and not the decision authorizing the use of enhanced cooperation as such.[139] As the ECJ stated, harm to a non-participating member state can only derive from substantive measures adopted within the framework of enhanced cooperation.[140] In light of this, it is likely that the UK will seek judicial redress against the legal measure to be adopted by the 11 member states participating in enhanced cooperation. In fact, the Legal Service of the Council raised concerns that several provisions of the Commission proposal affected the right of non-participating member states[141]—although I have elsewhere shown how these concerns are unwarranted.[142]

Besides the legal challenges, however, the use of enhanced cooperation in taxing matters complicates the possibility to use the revenues of this tax for the purpose of creating a fiscal capacity. While the original November 2011 Commission proposal for a Council directive on the FTT clearly linked the introduction of the FTT to the creation of "a new own resource to be entered into the budget of the EU,"[143] the new February 2013 proposal, taking stock of the fact that only a few member states will introduce the FTT via enhanced cooperation, proposes less ambitiously that "part of the receipts generated by the FTT shall constitute an own resource" reducing the direct contribution by these member states.[144] As explained in the Legislative Financial Statement annexed to the proposal, the Commission envisioned that "levying FTT would facilitate efforts of budgetary consolidation in the participating member states."[145] Yet, the FTT could at best replace other forms of direct contribution that the member states currently make to the EU budget, with "their GNI-based national contributions [being] reduced."[146] Hence, although in

[136] See Joined Cases C-274/11 and C-295/11 *Spain & Italy v. Council*, judgment of April 16, 2013, ECLI:EU:C:2013:240.

[137] See also Joachim Englisch et al, "The Financial Transaction Tax Proposal under the Enhanced Cooperation Procedure: Legal and Practical Considerations" [2013] British Tax Review 223.

[138] Case C-209/13 *United Kingdom v. Council*, judgment of April 30, 2014, ECLI:EU:C:2014:283.

[139] Ibid para 40. [140] Ibid para 36.

[141] See Council of the EU, Opinion of the Legal Service, JUR 448, September 6, 2013, Confidential Document Interinstitutional File 2013/0045 (CNS) (raising concerns about the legality of the Commission proposal for the adoption of a FTT within the framework of enhanced cooperation).

[142] See further Federico Fabbrini, "Taxing and Spending in the Eurozone: Legal and Political Challenges Related to the Adoption of the Financial Transaction Tax" (2014) 39 European Law Review 155 (rejecting the claims advanced by the Legal Service of the Council that the FTT proposal currently under debate undermines the rights of non-participating member states but emphasizing the political obstacles toward using the FTT as the bulk for a fiscal capacity).

[143] European Commission proposal (n 115) 3.

[144] European Commission proposal (n 134) 4. [145] Ibid 33. [146] Ibid.

February 2013 the European Council had noted the use of enhanced cooperation for the introduction of the FTT and invited the participating member states to examine if the FTT could become the basis for a new own resource for the EU budget, without impacting non-participating member states,[147] the Commission proposal retreated to a position in which the FTT will accrue the member states' budget and be used at best to replace other forms of national contributions to the EU budget.

This seems an inevitable choice, as also acknowledged by the EP in its legislative resolution of July 2013.[148] Commenting in its consultative role the February 2013 Commission proposal for the implementation of enhanced cooperation in the area of FTT, the EP underlined how "[t]he use of FTT revenue as Union own resources is possible under the enhanced cooperation procedure only if national contributions of participating Member States to the Union budget could be reduced by the same amount and would avoid the disproportionate contribution by participating Member States compared to non-participating Member States."[149] At the same time, the EP expressed its wish that things could change in the long term, holding that "[o]nce FTT is implemented at Union level, all or part of the amount of the own resources originating from FTT should be added to the national contributions of the Member States in order to gather new funding sources for European investment without a reduction of the national contributions of the participating Member States to the Union budget."[150]

Of course, if at least all the member states of the Eurozone were participating in the enhanced cooperation, the resources raised with a FTT could be set aside in a special Eurozone fund, functioning as the bulk of the fiscal capacity proposed in the high-level policy documents discussed in Section 2.[151] However, the refusal to join an enhanced cooperation in the area of FTT did not come only from the UK, or other member states outside the Eurozone: Cyprus, Finland, Ireland, Latvia, Lithuania, Luxembourg, Malta, and the Netherlands—countries within the Eurozone, which embrace a lighter taxing and regulatory framework toward the banking sector, or simply oppose further EU integration in the fiscal arena—refused to be involved in raising the FTT.[152] It would therefore be politically difficult to justify the use of resources gathered within the FTT-zone to address, say, risks of bank failures in Cyprus or high unemployment rates in Ireland (two hypotheses which are far from imaginary). At the same time, while proposals have been made to create a special fund among the 11 member states of the FTT-zone to be used for the common benefits of the members only,[153] it is clear that such a step would require a political agreement—which is hardly likely to take

[147] European Council Conclusions, February 8, 2013, EUCO 37/13, para 115.

[148] European Parliament Legislative Resolution of July 3, 2013 on the proposal for a Council directive implementing enhanced cooperation in the area of FTT, P7_TA(2013)0312.

[149] Ibid Amendment 2. [150] Ibid. [151] See text accompanying nn 7–49.

[152] See Charles Grant, "Britain could reshape Europe, if it would only try," *The Financial Times*, May 14, 2013 (outlining arguments for opposition to the FTT in several Eurozone member states).

[153] See Alberto Majocchi, "A European Fund for Growth and Development," *The New Federalist*, June 30, 2013.

place given the eagerness of the participating member states to use the income of the FTT to fill up their depleted coffers.[154]

In conclusion, therefore, as Alicia Hinarejos pointed out, "the FTT saga illustrates the difficulties of using enhanced cooperation in order to pursue further integration in very difficult areas of fiscal and economic policy, such as taxation."[155] While enhanced cooperation may be a pragmatic mechanism to minimize in the short term the challenge of unanimity—especially if the now 19 Eurozone member states were able to create a united front, taking joint action all together[156]—it seems difficult to disagree with the recommendations that Working Group VI on Economic Governance had made at the time of the European Constitutional Convention:[157] as the Working Group had emphasized, precisely in light of the problem identified above, "some changes should be made to the existing decision-making procedures in order to facilitate progress in the area of fiscal policy."[158] In particular, the use of QMV would allow the introduction of new European taxes by overcoming the collective action problems produced by unanimity vote. Yet, this proposal requires an amendment to the EU treaties.

From a comparative point of view, the need to introduce important constitutional changes as a pre-condition to make advancement in the field of taxation is not a feature unique to the EU. In the US system, in particular, major controversies surrounded the power of the federal government to impose a federal income tax throughout much of the nineteenth century. Whereas the 1787 US Constitution empowered the federal government "to lay and collect taxes, duties, imposts and excises,"[159] it required that "direct taxes shall be apportioned among the several states [...] according to their respective numbers"[160]—a measure which was explicitly designed to obstruct the taxing power of the federal government in light of the profound asymmetries between the states.[161] Although during the Civil War the federal government provisionally introduced a federal income tax to support the military effort,[162] the tax was set to expire in eight years, and when a similar measure was passed in 1894,[163] the US Supreme Court struck it down as beyond congressional powers.[164] In response, the US Constitution was eventually amended in 1913,[165] explicitly authorizing the federal government "to lay and collect taxes on incomes, from whatever sources derived, without apportionment

[154] See Dino Pesole, "Ora Roma teme riflessi sul debito," *Il Sole 24 Ore*, February 14, 2013 (explaining that the Italian government has already committed the income of the FTT to its domestic budget).

[155] Alicia Hinarejos, *The Euro Area Crisis in Constitutional Perspective* (OUP 2015) 109.

[156] See also Jean-Claude Piris, *The Future of Europe: Towards a Two-Speed EU?* (CUP 2011) 121 (emphasizing need for further integration within the Eurozone).

[157] European Convention, Working Group VI on Economic Governance, Final Report, October 21, 2002, CONV 357/02, WG VI 17.

[158] Ibid 6. [159] Art I, Sec. 8, cl 1 US Const. [160] Art I, Sec. 2, cl 3 US Const.

[161] See Erik Jensen, "Taxation and the Constitution: How to Read the Direct Tax Clause" (1999) 15 Journal of Law & Policy 687.

[162] See Revenue Act, 12 Stat. 292 (1861) (US).

[163] See Wilson—Gorman Tariff Act, 28 Stat. 570 (1894) (US).

[164] See *Pollock v. Farmers' Loan & Trust Co.*, 175 U.S. 429 (1895).

[165] See Dwight Morrow, "The Income Tax Amendment" (1910) 10 Columbia Law Review 397.

among the several States, and without regard to any census or enumeration."[166] If the constitutional amendment adopted in the US during the Progressive Era resolved the question of the taxing *power* of the federal government,[167] it seems that in the EU changes to the constitutional rulebook would mainly have to address the *decision-making process* in the field of taxation.[168] Yet, moving in this direction carries with itself another challenge that the EU can no longer postpone.

5. The Challenge of Representation

If—as explained above—a sustainable fiscal capacity demands own resources to be levied through EU taxes, and assuming the challenges of unanimity in fiscal affairs can be addressed via resort to enhanced cooperation (or, in the long term, through the introduction of QMV via a reform of the EU treaties), a third challenge still would arise. Drawing on the celebrated motto "no taxation without representation" which served as a rallying cry for American revolutionaries, I shall call this the challenge of representation. It is indeed an everlasting principle of constitutionalism, from the Magna Charta of 1215, through the revolutionary experiences of seventeenth- and eighteenth-century England, America, and France, up to contemporary models of constitutional government, that the power of taxation must be legitimized and controlled by adequate democratic representation.[169] Pursuant to this constitutionalist tradition, no governmental authority in fiscal affairs can be justified unless it is at the origin authorized by the people through their representatives.[170] In other words, representation—as the way to endow governmental decisions with democratic legitimacy and accountability—is the foundation of governmental authority in the fiscal domain (and beyond).

Now, in the current institutional system of the EU, the principle of representation is only partially accomplished. The EP, which pursuant to Article 10(2) Treaty on European Union (TEU) "directly represent[s European citizens] at the Union

[166] Am. XVI, US Const.

[167] See also Ajay Mehrotra, *Making the Modern American Fiscal State: Law, Politics, and the Rise of Progressive Taxation 1877-1929* (CUP 2014).

[168] But see also Am. XVII, US Const. (introducing the direct election of senators). The XVII Amendment was not directly connected to the XVI Amendment, although it was born out of the same Progressive movement and was also adopted in 1913. Yet, the introduction of a system of direct election of senators, in lieu of their indirect election by state legislatures, had, indirectly, major effects on the way in which decision-making at the federal level, including in the field of taxation, occurred. See also Wendy Schiller and Charles Stewart III, "The 100th Anniversary of the 17th Amendment: A Promise Unfulfilled?", Brookings Institution Issues in Governance Studies No. 59/2013.

[169] See e.g., Bruce Ackerman, "Taxation and the Constitution" (1999) 99 Columbia Law Review 1.

[170] Of course, representative democracy is not the only form of constitutional government—direct democracy being another possible form of legitimation of political power. For the purpose of this work, however, I will take for granted that the EU, not least for its sheer size, cannot meaningfully be governed by a principle of direct democracy. But see Christian Marxen, "Participatory Democracy in Europe: Article 11 TEU and the Legitimacy of the European Union" in Federico Fabbrini et al (eds), *What Form of Government for the European Union and the Eurozone?* (Hart Publishing 2015), 151 (discussing potentials of participatory democracy in the EU).

level," and is elected since 1979 by direct universal suffrage throughout the territory of the EU,[171] exercises decision-making power on par with the Council on the spending side.[172] However, the EP has only a consultative role on the taxing side, because decisions on tax harmonization under Article 113 TFEU or on the creation of new tax-based EU own resources under Article 311 TFEU are taken exclusively (and unanimously) by the Council. As argued by Giacinto della Cananea, "the European Parliament does not have a voice on which revenues should go to the Union," with the consequence that the association between taxation and representation, which has been for centuries a pillar of constitutionalism, appears thwarted in the context of the EU.[173] Therefore, ensuring the involvement of the EP in decisions about EU taxation appears, from a normative point of view, a necessary development toward a more democratic EMU.

The argument in favor of the involvement of the EP in EU decisions about taxation along the principle of "no taxation without representation" deserves some clarifications. On the one hand, this argument does not imply that the representative role of the EP should be mythicized.[174] In fact, as I pointed out in Chapter 3, the EP is an institution that still today reflects the cleavages existing between the member states—which is why it would be unwise to make it the *only* governing body of the EU, as supporters of the parliamentarization of the EU aspire. On the other hand, the argument does not imply that the other EU institutions are not representative. As Wojciech Sadurski explained, the Council and the European Council still live up to the principle of democratic representation, as each of its members represents a state and the citizens thereof—and is often directly elected by them, or at least responsible toward those directly elected by them (i.e., national parliamentarians).[175] According to Article 10(2) TEU, in fact, "Member States are represented in the European Council by their Heads of State or Government and in the Council by their governments, themselves democratically accountable either to their national Parliaments, or to their citizens."

Nevertheless, precisely Article 10 TEU helps me to make my point here. The EU is based on a dual legitimacy: that of its states, and that of its citizens.[176] In a Union of states and citizens legal and policy measures such as the decision to tax ought to be grounded on the dual consent of the states (as represented in the Council) and

[171] See Act concerning the election of the representatives of the European Parliament by direct universal suffrage, annexed to Decision 76/787/ECSC, EEC, Euratom [1976] OJ L278/1, as amended.

[172] See also Paul Craig, "The Role of the European Parliament under the Lisbon Treaty" in Stefan Griller and Jacques Ziller (eds), *The Lisbon Treaty: EU Constitutionalism without a Constitutional Treaty?* (Springer 2008), 110, 129.

[173] Giacinto Della Cananea, "No Representation without Taxation: the European Union", paper presented at the European Constitutional Law Network annual conference on "Challenging the Legitimacy of Europe," Thessaloniki, May 22, 2015 (on file with author).

[174] See also Philipp Dann, "European Parliament and Executive Federalism: Approaching a Parliament in a Semi-Parliamentary Democracy" (2003) 9 European Law Journal 549.

[175] Wojcech Sadurski, "Democratic Legitimacy of the European Union: A Diagnosis and Some Modest Proposals" (2013) 32 Polish Yearbook of International Law 9.

[176] See generally Walter Van Gerven, *The European Union: A Polity of States and People* (Hart Publishing 2005).

the citizens (as represented in the EP).[177] A leg of legitimacy only is not enough to sustain the endeavor. A contrario, the point is supported by the Canadian experience. Despite differences between the provinces, the Canadian federal system was created top-down within the framework of the British Commonwealth, and modeled on the centralized UK parliamentary form of government.[178] As a result, the Canadian Constitution ideated a regime in which decisions about taxing are exclusively attributed to the House of Commons, the federal lower house of Parliament (representing the Canadian citizens).[179] Because in any case the Canadian Senate is not effectively representing the provinces,[180] this created an imbalance in the dual legitimacy of the Canadian federal system. To address this state of affairs, therefore, a practice emerged to convene intergovernmental meetings between the federal Prime Minister and the prime ministers of the several Canadian provinces, so as to ensure the effectiveness and the legitimacy of decision-making.[181] As the Canadian case makes clear, in other words, a balance between representation of the citizens and representation of the member states is inevitable in a Union of states and citizens.

The same is true in the EU.[182] Because the Council represents member states and reflects their interests, it can hardly offer adequate justification on its own to decisions which are supranational in scope, operating beyond state lines, and affecting directly the interests of European citizens. As the Euro-crisis has made plain, an intergovernmental method of governance centered on the Council and European Council meets "difficult hurdles in dealing with the legitimacy dilemma."[183] The European Council, as a quasi-diplomatic body, operates in a secretive manner and, although it formally abides by the principle of equality of its members, it has become evident—as I stressed in Chapter 3—that bigger member states enjoy greater leeway and influence in its decisions. Individuals affected by these decisions have only limited capacity to influence them, control them, or revert them when needed. From this point of view, involving the EP in decisions about taxation is a way to ensure, along the constitutional logic of separation of powers, that institutions which represent different constituencies check and balance each other. The

[177] See also Armin Von Bogdandy, "The European Lesson for International Democracy: The Significance of Article 9-12 EU Treaty for International Organizations" (2012) 23 European Journal of International Law 315.

[178] See also Jean-François Gaudreault-Desbiens, "Le fédéralisme et le législateur fédéral" (2009) 2 Revue de droit parlamentaire et politique 427.

[179] See Sec. 53 Const. Act 1867 Can.

[180] See David Smith, *The Canadian Senate in Bicameral Perspective* (Toronto UP 2003) 67 (explaining that senators are not elected bottom-up in the provinces, but are rather appointed top-down by the Governor General, which represents the British Queen in Canada, and that this prevents the Senate from acting as the institution representing the federated units of government).

[181] See David Cameron and Richard Simeon, "Intergovernmental Relations in Canada: The Emergence of Collaborative Federalism" (2002) 32 Publius 49.

[182] See also John Erik Fossum and Augustín José Menéndez, *The Constitition's Gift: A Constitutional Theory for a Democratic European Union* (Rowman & Littlefield 2011) (comparing the EU and Canada).

[183] Sergio Fabbrini, "Intergovernmentalism and its Limits: Assessing the European Union's Answer to the Euro Crisis" (2013) 46 Comparative Political Studies 1003, 1026.

establishment of a fiscal capacity demands, therefore, that steps be taken in order to ensure that the current imbalance—with the attribution of powers in taxation exclusively to the Council (representing directly the states) at the expenses of the EP (representing directly the European citizens)—be redressed.

The EP has been explicit in calling for such a change, stating that "a substantial improvement of the democratic legitimacy and accountability at Union level of the EMU governance by an increased role of Parliament [i]s an absolute necessity,"[184] and repeating that "parliamentary input on economic [issues] is an important aspect of any democratic system."[185] Yet, tellingly, even top EU decision-makers seem to have taken notice of this need, as questions of legitimacy and accountability feature in both the reports of the President of the European Council, and the blueprint of the Commission "For a Deep and Genuine EMU."[186] In particular, as the European Council President's June 2012 inaugural report acknowledged "moving towards more integrated fiscal and economic decision-making between countries will [...] require strong mechanisms for legitimate and accountable decision-making."[187] The European Council President later re-formulated this position in the October 2012 interim report as the principle that "democratic control and accountability should occur at the level at which decisions are taken"[188]—a sentence also repeated literally in the December 2012 conclusive report,[189] which additionally remarked how "the creation of a new fiscal capacity should also lead to adequate arrangements ensuring its full democratic legitimacy and accountability," to be detailed on the basis of its specific features, founding sources, decision-making processes and scope of activities.[190]

Nevertheless, whereas the European Council has repeated as a refrain its support for the principle of democratic legitimacy and accountability at the level at which decisions are taken and implemented,[191] it has fallen short of devising any effective means by which to make this promise real. Instead, an idea cultivated by the European Council to enhance the EU decision-making process has been to encourage inter-parliamentary cooperation between national parliaments and the EP—a feature now included in Article 13 Fiscal Compact, which calls for the creation of an inter-parliamentary assembly on economic governance.[192] In Chapter 5, I will come back to this idea and explain why it is unfit for the future of EMU. For the purpose of this chapter, however, suffice it to say that inter-parliamentarism is unsatisfactory in legitimating European public goods for the very same reasons

[184] European Parliament Resolution (n 44) para 9.

[185] European Parliament Resolution (n 49) para 50.

[186] European Commission Communication (n 3).

[187] President of the European Council Report (n 8) 6.

[188] President of the European Council Interim Report (n 7) 8.

[189] President of the European Council Final Report (n 3) 16.

[190] Ibid 17.

[191] See European Council Conclusions, October 18, 2012, EUCO 156/12, 10; European Council Conclusions, December 14, 2012, EUCO 205/12, 5; European Council Conclusions, June 28, 2013, EUCO 104/2/13, 9.

[192] See Treaty on Stability, Coordination and Governance in the Economic and Monetary Union, March 2, 2012, available at <http://www.eurozone.europa.eu/media/304649/st00tscg26_en12.pdf> (last accessed June 1, 2014).

that intergovernmentalism is. Because national ministers *represent their states* and are responsive to national constituencies—it is unclear how a committee of national parliamentarians—elected, once again, to *represent the constituents of their states*—could provide a different source of legitimacy.[193] In fact, as the President of the European Council rightly emphasized:

> the provisions for democratic legitimacy and accountability should ensure that the common interest of the [U]nion is duly taken into account; yet national parliaments are not in the best position to take it into account fully. This implies that further integration of policy making and a greater pooling of competences at the European level should first and foremost be accompanied with a commensurate involvement of the European Parliament in the integrated frameworks for a genuine EMU.[194]

Ensuring the full involvement of the EP in decisions about taxation raises important issues on the internal organization of this institution—a point which I will examine at length in Chapter 5. Nevertheless, to address the challenge of representation under consideration here, adequate legal changes appear necessary. And the current treaty framework already allows for an interesting option in this regard. In particular, on the basis of the so-called "*passerelle* clause" it is possible to shift to the co-decision procedure competences which would otherwise be subject to special legislative procedure, and thus reserved to the exclusive purview of the Council.[195] Specifically, pursuant to Article 333(2) TFEU:

> Where a provision of the Treaties which may be applied in the context of enhanced cooperation stipulates that the Council shall adopt acts under a special legislative procedure, the Council, acting unanimously [...] may adopt a decision stipulating that it will act under the ordinary legislative procedure.

In its resolution authorizing the use of enhanced cooperation for the introduction of the FTT, the EP invoked precisely this provision, calling "on the Council to adopt a decision pursuant to Article 333(2) TFEU, stipulating that when it comes to the proposal for a Council Directive implementing enhanced cooperation in the area of FTT pursuant to Article 113 TFEU, it will act under the ordinary legislative procedure."[196]

In conclusion, addressing the challenge of representation demands that the power of taxation—as the source of financing for a fiscal capacity—be made legitimate and accountable through the involvement of the EP (representing the EU citizens), on par with the Council (representing the EU member states). In Chapter 5, I will return to the question whether it is feasible to increase parliamentary involvement in economic governance, and how. Whether one has a more

[193] See also Sergio Fabbrini, *Which European Union? Europe after the Euro-Crisis* (CUP 2015) 128 (emphasizing how the inter-parliamentary logic is just the mirror image of the intergovernmental one).

[194] President of the European Council Final Report (n 3) 16.

[195] On the potential of the "*passerelle* clauses" to induce reforms within the framework of the existing treaties, see Giuliano Amato, "Future Prospects for a European Constitution" in Giuliano Amato et al (eds), *Genesis and Destiny of the European Constitution* (Bruylant 2007), 1271, 1272.

[196] European Parliament Resolution (n 131) para 2.

or less optimistic vision of the future of democratic representation in the EU, there is no doubt that there is still a long way to go. In its July 2013 resolution on the political agreement on the MFF, the EP insisted on its full authority in the fiscal domain and "regret[ted] the fact that the Member States continue to underestimate the role of the EU budget, and its contribution to, strengthening economic governance and fiscal coordination across the EU."[197] Nevertheless, it seems equally clear that, from a constitutional-democratic point of view, the new powers that the establishment of a fiscal capacity would entail in terms of taxing authority for the EU or the Eurozone should be tamed by adequate principles of representation.

6. Conclusion

Since the eruption of the Euro-crisis, the EU institutions and the member states have promoted the constitutionalization of fiscal constraints as a way to restore the sustainability of the EMU. However, as fiscal discipline is by now mostly entrenched at the national and supranational level, growing awareness has emerged among academics and policy-makers on the need for a fiscal capacity—that is, a central budget for the EU or the Eurozone,[198] possibly funded through new resources, by which to assuage asymmetric shocks and carry out counter-cyclical policies no longer possible at the national level due to the budgetary constraints. This chapter has argued that a fiscal capacity would be an important step toward further integration within the EMU, and that it could be a valuable alternative to the dynamic of centralization identified in Chapter 1. A fiscal capacity, in fact, would allow the EU to manage the interdependencies of EMU without the need for the hyper-centralized regime of supranational surveillance of national budgets erected in the aftermath of the Euro-crisis. From this point of view, endowing the EU with the ability to tax and spend would be less restrictive of the autonomy of the member states than the invasive architecture of surveillance recently set up in EMU, and it would offer the opportunity to return some meaningful decision-making power to the member states in the budgetary domain.[199] Yet, as this chapter has explained, the proposal to establish a fiscal capacity faces several hurdles. From a constitutional point of view, I have argued that any attempt to raise a fiscal

[197] European Parliament Resolution of July 3, 2013 on the political agreement on the MFF, P7_TA(2013)0304, para 6.

[198] As this chapter has pointed out, valuable arguments seem to exist in favor of creating a fiscal capacity at Eurozone, rather than EU, level—and political pressures often move in this direction. But see President of the European Commission Report (n 37) 15 (discussing options for an EMU stabilization fund and stating that "[i]t should be developed within the framework of the European Union [...a]nd it should be open and transparent vis-à-vis all EU Member States").

[199] See also Alicia Hinarejos, "Fiscal Federalism in the European Union: Evolution and Future Choices for EMU" (2013) 50 Common Market Law Review 1621 (analyzing the model of fiscal surveillance embraced by the EU since the outburst of the Euro-crisis, and constrasting it with the alternative model of fiscal federalism, based on central government taxing and spending).

capacity which hopes to succeed would have to overcome three main challenges. The challenges of asymmetry, unanimity, and representation pose critical tests to the establishment of a fiscal capacity that wants to avoid falling prey of endless negotiations on inter-states money transfers, insurmountable deadlock in decisions about the adoption of EU own resources, and lack of representation by those individuals who would be directly subject to new EU taxation.

As this chapter has claimed, these challenges are not impossible to face. The introduction of real own resources can address the challenge of asymmetry and break the vicious equation between financial solidarity and inter-state transfers. The resort to enhanced cooperation can address the challenge of unanimity and sidestep the deadlock that almost automatically arises in the field of tax policy whenever proposals are made for new, real EU taxes. The possibility of the "*passerelle* clauses," finally, can address the challenge of representation and ensure that the only institution directly representing European citizens—the EP—has a say on decisions which involve EU taxation, on par with the Council. Yet, even if each of the proposals suggested above were impossible, one cannot but agree with the crude assessment made by Miguel Maduro: "the question soon to be faced by European politicians is which, among several impossible proposals, may be the easiest to present to their citizens."[200] Moving from fiscal constraints to fiscal capacity, by endowing the EU or the Eurozone with the means to address asymmetric shocks in the EMU is a rational development to redress the paradox of centralization triggered by the Euro-crisis and the responses to it: while member states could re-acquire a meaningful autonomy in the budgetary field, the EU would be empowered with the fiscal means to manage the busts of the European business cyle and thus ensure the well-functioning of the EMU. It remains to be seen whether rational arguments can mobilize enough political will to overcome the constitutional challenges obstructing the path toward a deeper and more genuine EMU.

[200] Maduro (n 1) 6.

5

From Legislative Sidelining to Legislative Involvement

1. Introduction

Since the outburst of the Euro-crisis, the involvement of courts in the field of Economic and Monetary Union (EMU) has dramatically increased. As I have explained in Chapter 2, courts have come to play an unprecedented role in EMU because of the increasing use by the member states of intergovernmental agreements outside the framework of European Union (EU) law. National courts have been repeatedly asked to review a priori domestic legislation ratifying these international agreements. Moreover, some national courts have been emboldened by the review of EMU agreements, and have extended their jurisdiction even over action by the EU institutions tout court. As I emphasized, this process of increasing judicial involvement in EMU affairs is paradoxical from a comparative viewpoint. At the same time, this process is also problematic from a constitutional perspective—since arguments about expertise, voice, and rights plead in favor of leaving decisions on economic questions to the political process, rather than to the courts. Hence, Chapter 2 concluded that the EU member states should avoid resorting to international agreements and rather make full use of the EU legislative process to govern EMU, since EU laws are better protected from judicial overreach. Nevertheless, Chapter 2 acknowledged that law-making in the EU is imperfect and signaled the need for further attention on this point.

This chapter follows up on that argument, examining the potentials, but also the limitations, of the EU legislative process. Before starting, however, a caveat is in order. As an interdisciplinary literature has pointed out, the system of EMU governance—that is the combination of institutions, machinery, and practices that shape policy-making in the economic field—is extremely complex and multi-dimensional.[1] A large part of EMU governance is represented by the coordination of the economic policies of the member states—a process which is essentially

[1] See Iain Begg, "Economic Governance in an Enlarged Euro Area," European Commission Economic Papers No. 311/2008, 5; Uwe Puetter, "Europe's Deliberative Intergovernmentalism: The Role of the Council and the European Council in EU Economic Governance" (2012) 19 Journal of European Public Policy 161; Kenneth Armstrong, "The New Governance of EU Fiscal Discipline" (2013) 38 European Law Review 601.

administrative—and by the enforcement of EU deficit and debt rules—a process which can be defined as *adjudicative*. Hence, the Council, which is one of the key institutions in the governance of EMU, plays multiple functions: besides acting as a legislative branch, it is also empowered to set non-binding "Broad Economic Policy Guidelines,"[2] identifying goals to be achieved by each state in the programming of its domestic economic policy, and to decide on breaches of the Stability and Growth Pact (SGP),[3] sanctioning states with excessive deficits.[4] However, in this chapter the focus will be exclusively on *legislation*. In fact, the chapter will make the case for an expansion of the space for legislative action in EMU.

Following the Euro-crisis, growing calls have been made in favor of ensuring adequate parliamentary involvement in EMU.[5] As Vivien Schmidt has argued in a report commissioned by the European Commission Directorate General on Economic and Financial Affairs (DG ECFIN), "Eurozone governance needs to become like most other areas of EU legislation, which means it should mainly use the Community Method for legislation [...] giving the [European Parliament] more 'size', by being brought into all Eurozone decision-making, while reducing the intergovernmental dominance of the Council."[6] As the chapter explains, the Lisbon Treaty has designed a complex, but balanced system to legislate in the EU, grounded on the equal role of the European Parliament (EP), representing the EU citizens and the Council, representing the EU member states—and there are valuable arguments to use the legislative process, rather than international agreements, in the governance of EU economic affairs. While the legislative process has been sidelined in devising responses to the Euro-crisis to the advantage of intergovernmental treaty-making, this chapter argues that using the EU legislative process in the governance of EMU would minimize the paradox of judicialization, by reducing the opportunities for state courts to interfere in decisions concerning economic and monetary questions. At the same time, it would also improve legitimacy of EU decisions, by involving multiple institutions in the approval of EMU norms, along a logic of checks and balances.

Nevertheless, the chapter recognizes that the EU legislative process is sub-optimal and—looking ahead—it proposes ways to improve it. From this point of view, the argument made in this chapter complements the one made in Chapter 2. While there I sought to defend a space for democratic decision-making in economic and monetary affairs against judicial overreach, here I attempt to tackle a number of challenges that reduce the capacity of the EU political process to perform the role it could (or that supporters wishes it would) in EMU governance. In discussing the challenges needed to ensure greater legislative involvement in EMU, this chapter

[2] See Art 121 TFEU. [3] See Art 126 TFEU.

[4] See also Case C-27/04 *Commission v. Council* [2004] ECR I-6649, ECLI:EU:C:2004:436.

[5] See e.g., European Commission Communication, "A Blueprint for a Deep and Genuine EMU: Launching a European Debate," November 28, 2012, COM(2012)777 final.

[6] Vivien Schmidt, "The Eurozone's Crisis of Democratic Legitimacy: Can the EU Rebuild Public Trust and Support for European Economic Integration?," Study prepared for the European Commission Directorate General on Economic and Financial Affairs, DG ECFIN Economic Discussion Papers No. 15, September 2015, 55.

considers problems which are generally addressed separately in the literature, suggesting however they ought to be seen as part and parcel of a broader package of reforms needed to enhance the EU decision-making regime. Ensuring greater legislative involvement in the governance of EMU requires, on the one hand, a rethinking of the substantive competences of the Union in the field,[7] and, on the other, a critical assessment of the institutional setup of the EU more generally: in fact, both are needed to make the EU decision-making system fit for the governance of an ever more integrated EMU.[8] In particular, this chapter claims that three relevant challenges must be faced on the road toward greater legislative involvement in EMU: first, a challenge of asymmetry, due to power allocation in EMU; second, a challenge of representation, due to the functioning of the EP; and third, a challenge of unity, due to the organization of the Council.

In a nutshell, the challenge of asymmetry follows from the well-known imbalance in EMU design, with monetary policy centralized at EU level, and economic policy decentralized in the member states. As a result of that—the conventional argument goes—the member states remain free to act outside the framework of EU law at will, while the EU institutions enjoy only limited power to legislate in the field of economic policy. The challenge of representation arises from the fact that the EP, although being constitutionally vested with the task to represent EU citizens, continues to be criticized either as under-representative (due to the principle of degressive proportionality), as over-representative (due to the involvement of all EP members even in matters that only concern the Eurozone), or for failing to strike an adequate balance between representation and governability. The challenge of unity, finally, derives, from the fact that while the Council is one institution, grouping the representatives of the governments of the member states, its composition always varies—with the result that some formations of the Council have become more important than others, producing imbalances in the policy-mix of the EU, and making it difficult for states to reach agreement on legislation.

The chapter attempts to open a debate on these different challenges—admitting that none of them finds an easy solution, but proposing some ideas to addresses them. To begin with, from the substantive side, the chapter suggests that a constitutional reading of the EU treaties—as modified at last by the Lisbon Treaty—may go a long way in reducing the asymmetry of EMU. In particular, on the basis of a constitutional interpretation of the treaties, the chapter claims that the member states face limits on what they can do outside the framework of EU law, even in the field of EMU; and, at the same time, that the EU institutions are empowered to act in policy areas which have a broad impact on macro-economic governance. As the chapter maintains, while it is plausible to derive from the EU principle of institutional balance limits to member states' freedom to act outside EU law, it is equally possible to conceive of a space—albeit not an unlimited

[7] See also Sasha Garben, "Confronting the Competence Conundrum: Democratising the European Union through an Expansion of its Legislative Powers" (2015) 35 Oxford Journal of Legal Studies 55.

[8] See generally Jean-François Jamet, *L'Europe, peut-elle se passer d'un gouvernement économique?* (La Documentation française 2012) and Sandro Gozi, *Il governo dell'Europa* (Il Mulino 2011).

one—in which the EU institutions could still undertake legislative action in the field of economic policy. Certainly, in order to overcome the asymmetry of EMU several structural changes in the EU constitutional system would be needed—notably, the creation of a fiscal capacity, as proposed in Chapter 4. However, greater legislative involvement in EMU also requires articulating clear constitutional arguments which constrain the member states from acting outside EU law and simultaneously empower the EU institutions to legislate within the EU legal order.

From the institutional side, instead, the chapter argues that more ambitious reforms ought to be pursued in order to tackle the challenges of representation and unity. As the chapter suggests, if the EP aspires to play a greater role in EMU governance, due considerations should be given to the electoral law for the EU lower legislative house. While criticisms of under-representation or over-representation do not bite, the EP does inadequately balance representation vs. governability: currently voters in the 28 EU member states elect members of the EP (MEPs) on the basis of state laws, but all states use proportional representation rules. However, the unconstrained use of this electoral system has sacrificed concerns for governability, making the EP an assembly which profoundly differs from the legislatures of the largest EU member states for the degree of party fragmentation and the admission of fringe groups which do not pass electoral thresholds for representation in national parliaments. Yet, these features are increasingly at odds with the role that the EP plays (and should play) as a legislative assembly vested with relevant governmental tasks. At the same time, adequate constitutional reflections should be given to the functioning of the EU upper legislative house as well: in this regard, the role of Council, and its relation with the European Council, must be reconsiderd in order to endow the EU with a kind of European Senate that can coordinate cross-sectoral interests and strike compromise on legislation through package-deals.

In conclusion, the chapter pleads in favor of a change from legislative sidelining to legislative involvement in EMU governance, and argues that decisions on economic policy should be adopted through the EU legislative process. Nevertheless, it acknowledges that important substantive and institutional improvements in the EU law-making regime ought to be made to achieve this goal. To this end, the chapter maps several challenges that weaken the ability of the EU legislative process to function at its best—suggesting that asymmetry, representation, and unity constitute diverse but equally relevant tests for the future success of the EU legislative machinery. At the same time, the chapter considers how to address these challenges—articulating ideas, also inspired by comparative examples, of how the EU law-making regime may be made fit for the governance of EMU in the future. The chapter is structured as follows. Section 2 overviews the legislative process designed by the Lisbon Treaty and reports the growing calls from scholars and policy-makers in support of greater legislative involvement in EMU too. Sections 3, 4, and 5, analyze separately the challenges of asymmetry, representation, and unity and discuss how to resolve them. Section 6, finally, concludes.

2. Restoring the EU Legislative Process

The process of law-making in the EU centers around three institutions—the Commission, the Council, and the EP—but its specific design has been evolving over time.[9] Originally, the Council played the main role in the adoption of EU legislation, while the EP only had a consultative or advisory function. Through subsequent treaty reforms, however, the EP has acquired a growing relevance in EU law-making: since the introduction of the co-decision procedure, in particular, the EP has been empowered to act on par with the Council in a number of policy areas.[10] Today, the Lisbon Treaty has codified the rule that the EP and the Council act as co-equal legislative branches.[11] Article 289 Treaty on the Functioning of the EU (TFEU) defines the process whereby the EU adopts legislation with the approval of both the Council and the EP as the "ordinary legislative procedure"—while situations whereby the Council can pass EU laws without the need to involve the EP are defined as "special legislative procedures" and considered as exceptional occurrences. In requiring that EU legislation be subject by default to a bicameral approval process, the Lisbon Treaty has largely enshrined in EU primary law the so-called "Community method."[12]

In the EU ordinary legislative process, the power to initiate legislation in the EU is vested exclusively in the European Commission. Pursuant to Article 294(2) TFEU "[t]he Commission shall submit a proposal to the European Parliament and the Council." Moreover, the Commission has the power to withdraw a legislative proposal, hence terminating the law-making process.[13] The attribution of a monopoly of legislative initiative to the Commission is a unicum which has been historically justified in light of the special task that the Commission performs in "promot[ing] the general interest of the Union."[14] Moreover, smaller member states have traditionally defended the powers of the Commission to initiate legislation as a way to protect their interests against those of the larger member states.[15] Be that as it may, in reality the Commission's monopoly of legislative initiative has

[9] See Joseph H.H. Weiler, "The Transformation of Europe" (1991) 100 Yale Law Journal 2403.

[10] See Berthold Rittenberger, "Institutionalizing Representative Democracy in the European Union: The Case of the European Parliament" (2012) 50 Journal of Common Market Studies 18.

[11] See Paul Craig, *The Treaty of Lisbon: Law, Politics and Treaty Reform* (OUP 2010).

[12] See Renaud Dehousse, "The Community Method at Sixty," in Renaud Dehousse (ed), *The Community Method* (Palgrave MacMillan 2011), 3 (defining the "Community method" as the default process by which law-making is accomplished in the EU). But see also Ben Smulders and Katharina Eisele, "Reflections on the Institutional Balance, the Community Method and the Interplay between Jurisdictions after Lisbon" (2012) 31 Yearbook of European Law 112 (discussing the "Community method" and the "Union method").

[13] See Case C-409/13 *Council v. Commission*, judgment of April 14, 2015, ECLI:EU:C:2015:217 (backing Commission's right to withdraw initiative against position of the Council).

[14] Art 17(1) TEU.

[15] See Simone Bunse and Kalypso Nicolaïdis, "Large versus Small States: Anti-Hegemony and the Politics of Shared Leadership," in Erik Jones et al (eds), *The Oxford Handbook of the European Union* (OUP 2012), 249.

been eroding over time.[16] On the one hand, the EU treaties have incremented the number of special areas where "legislative acts may be adopted [also] on the initiative of a group of Member States, or of the European Parliament."[17] On the other hand, even where the Commission formally maintains its monopoly, the legislative proposals it advances are today increasingly the result of requests it receives from other EU institutions: while the EP can ask the Commission to advance a legislative proposal,[18] the European Council has become since the eruption of the Euro-crisis extremely assertive vis-à-vis the European Commission in tasking it to adopt legislative proposals in policy areas it deemed in urgent need of supranational regulation.[19]

Once the European Commission has advanced a legislative proposal, the EP and the Council must read and approve it on the same terms. The Council is the institution which represents the governments of the 28 EU member states.[20] As scholars have emphasized, the Council works as a quasi-diplomatic body.[21] The Council congresses in different compositions, since, depending on the subject matters to be discussed, national governments dispatch the ministers who are in charge of that specific file.[22] The Council is supported by a Secretariat,[23] by a Committee of Permanent Representatives (COREPER) which groups the ambassadors of the EU member states based in Brussels,[24] as well as by several working groups composed of national officials who undertake preparatory work.[25] Most of the Council's work is shrouded in secrecy, and the institution seeks to abide to a consensual logic: in fact, decisions are mostly taken by common accord, with voting being relegated to an option of last resort.[26] When the Council votes, according to Article 16(3) Treaty on European Union (TEU) it decides by qualified majority voting, which is defined today as "at least 55% of the members of the Council, comprising at least 15 of them and representing Member States comprising at least 65% of the population of the Union."[27] Due to its composition, the main cleavages within the Council occur along state lines, with the

[16] See Paolo Ponzano et al, "The Power of Initiative of the Commission: A Progressive Erosion?" Notre Europe Studies and Research No. 89/2012.

[17] Art 289(4) TFEU. [18] Art 225 TFEU.

[19] See European Parliament Research Service, "European Council Conclusions: A Rolling Check-List of Commitments to Date," study, October 7, 2014, PE 536.359.

[20] Art 10 TEU.

[21] See Fiona Hayes-Renshaw, "The Council of Ministers," in John Peterson and Michael Shackleton (eds), *The Institutions of the European Union* (3rd ed. OUP 2012), 68.

[22] See further on this Section 5.

[23] See Derek Beach, "The Facilitator of Efficient Negotiations in the Council: the Impact of the Council Secretariat," in Daniel Naurin and Helen Wallace (eds.), *Unveiling the Council of the European Union* (Palgrave MacMillan 2010), 219.

[24] See Jeffrey Lewis, "National Interests: the Committee of Permanent Representatives," in John Peterson and Michael Shackleton (eds), *The Institutions of the European Union* (3rd ed. OUP 2012), 315.

[25] See Christian Joerges and Ellen Vos (eds), *EU Committees* (Hart Publishing 1999).

[26] See Dorothee Heisennberg, "The Institution of 'Consensus' in the European Union: Formal versus Informal Decision-Making in the Council" (2005) 44 European Journal of Political Research 65.

[27] Art 16(4) TEU.

disagreement between Northern and Southern member states playing out more frequently.[28]

The EP, on the contrary, is the institution which represents the EU citizens.[29] The size, functioning, and conventions of this institution are profoundly different from those existing in the Council.[30] Pursuant to Article 14 TEU, the EP is composed of 750 members, plus its President. Because of its size, the EP mainly performs its activities through Committees, each of which is endowed with a Chair and special rapporteurs in charge of following the work on every specific legislative file.[31] Over time, the EP has also developed an autonomous administrative apparatus that supports its work. The EP praises itself for a culture of transparency, and carries out most of its work—both in its Committees and in the plenary sessions—in public.[32] Due to the electoral legislation for the EP, the assembly reflects a high degree of fragmentation, and traditionally consensus building has been an important dimension in the life of the institution.[33] Nevertheless, voting on legislation is the rule in the EP, and according to Article 231 TFEU, MEPs take decisions by simple majority. Moreover, although MEPs are elected in state constituencies, since the beginning of the process of European integration MEPs have been caucusing in political groups, rather than in national groups.[34]

To take into account the involvement in the EU law-making process of two very different institutions such as the Council and the EP, Article 294 TFEU sets up a highly formalized procedure to pass EU laws—which includes up to three readings of the text by the two legislative branches, with the possibility for each to amend the bill approved by the other within a specific amount of time, and with the option to institute in the final stage a conciliation Committee to tease out possible divergences between the two houses. Technicalities aside, nevertheless, the substance of inter-institutional bargaining in the EU does not differ from that at play in, for example, the Congress of the United States (US), where the existence of a House and a Senate requires mechanisms to reconcile different political positions and efforts to coalesce sufficient support in both legislative houses.[35] At the same time, in anticipation of the conciliation stage foreseen by Article 294(10) TFEU, a practice which has increasingly taken hold in the EU to pass legislation is to set

[28] See Mikko Mattila, "Voting and Coalitions in the Council after the Enlargement," in Daniel Naurin and Helen Wallace (eds), *Unveiling the Council of the European Union* (Palgrave MacMillan 2010), 23.

[29] Art 10 TEU.

[30] See Michael Shackleton, "The European Parliament," in John Peterson and Michael Shackleton (eds), *The Institutions of the European Union* (3rd ed. OUP 2012), 124.

[31] See also Richard Corbett et al, *The European Parliament* (8th ed. John Harper Publishing 2011).

[32] See Maarten Hillebrandt et al, "Transparency in the EU Council of Ministers: An Institutional Analysis" (2014) 20 European Law Journal 1, 19 (defining the EP as a "champion of EU transparency" as opposed to the Council).

[33] See further on this Section 4.

[34] See Simon Hix and Bjorn Højland, *The Political System of the European Union* (3rd ed. Palgrave MacMillan 2011).

[35] See also Amy Kreppel, "Understanding the European Parliament from a Federalist Perspective: The Legislatures of the USA and EU Compared," in Anand Menon and Martin Schain (eds), *Comparative Federalism: The European Union and the United States* (OUP 2006), 245.

up "dialogue meetings" between the EP and the Council—or "trilogues", which also involve the Commission—in which selected groups of legislators from the two houses meet at an early stage to strike compromises on draft bills.[36]

All in all, therefore, in clarifying that the ordinary legislative procedure shall be the main avenue to adopt EU laws, the Lisbon Treaty has designed a complex, yet balanced, process for legislating in the EU.[37] While the monopoly of legislative initiative of the European Commission may be more a myth than a reality, the requirement that both the Council and the EP approve legislation is consistent with the constitutional nature of the EU as a Union of states and citizens. With the exception of the special legislative procedures, and notwithstanding the fact that—confusingly—the EU treaties attribute to the Council some executive functions as well,[38] in the "Community method" the Council and the EP can be appropriately regarded as the upper and the lower houses of the EU bicameral legislature.[39] In fact, as Paul Craig has explained, the Lisbon Treaty has crowned the incremental process of making the EP equal to the Council in the EU law-making process, by extending (with minor adjustments) the application of the ordinary legislative procedure also to the adoption of the EU budget as far as expenditures are concerned:[40] because in the EU, just like in any other constitutional system, the power of the purse represents a major "lever through which to secure further concessions from other institutions within the polity,"[41] the new spending power of the EP endow it with a powerful tool to shape the policies of the EU.

Notwithstanding the possibilities offered by EU legislation, since the explosion of the Euro-crisis the EU has experienced a surge in the use of inter-governmental agreements outside the framework of EU law.[42] As I have indicated before, the EU member states have repeatedly decided to reform the EMU *through intergovernmental agreements*. The Fiscal Compact,[43] the European Stability Mechanism (ESM) Treaty,[44] and the Agreement on the transfer and mutualization of contributions to the Single Resolution Fund (SRF)[45]are well-known examples of this trend.

[36] See also Helen Wallace et al (eds), *Policy-Making in the European Union* (OUP 2010).

[37] See also Robert Schütze, *European Constitutional Law* (CUP 2012) 84.

[38] See Art 16 TEU.

[39] See also Walter Van Gerven, *The European Union: A Polity of States and People* (Hart Publishing 2005), 362.

[40] Paul Craig, "The Role of the European Parliament under the Lisbon Treaty," in Stefan Griller and Jacques Ziller (eds), *The Lisbon Treaty: EU Constitutionalism Without a Constitutional Treaty?* (Springer 2008), 110.

[41] Ibid 129.

[42] See Karlo Tuori and Klaus Tuori, *The Eurozone Crisis: A Constitutional Analysis* (CUP 2014).

[43] See Treaty on Stability, Coordination and Governance in the Economic and Monetary Union, March 2, 2012, [hereinafter Fiscal Compact], available at <http://www.eurozone.europa.eu/media/304649/st00tscg26_en12.pdf> (last accessed June 1, 2014).

[44] See Treaty Establishing the European Stability Mechanism [hereinafter ESM Treaty], February 2, 2012, available at <http://www.european-council.europa.eu/media/582311/05-tesm2.en12.pdf> (last accessed June 1, 2014).

[45] See Agreement on the transfer and mutualisation of contributions to the Single Resolution Fund [hereinafter SRF Agreement], May 21, 2014 available at <http://register.consilium.europa.eu/doc/srv?l=EN&f=ST%208457%202014%20INIT> (last accessed May 25, 2014).

As Jean-Paul Keppenne has argued, the choice to use international agreements to reform EMU follows a semi-intergovernmental logic of crisis management, in which measures strictly connected with EU law have been adopted by the member states outside EU law.[46] As I explained in Chapter 3, the European Council emerged as the leading institution in the EU system of governance, and its members have repeatedly felt free to act outside the framework of EU law whenever this suited their interest.[47] In fact, the dominance of national executives in the aftermath of the crisis prominently manifested itself in "the adoption of decisions and the conduction of policy by means other than the Community method, whether within or without the EU framework."[48]

For sure, intergovernmentalism represented a feature of EMU well before the Euro-crisis.[49] Moreover, the growing resort to intergovernmental agreements has not meant abandoning tout court EU legislation.[50] In fact, the "Community method" has continued to be used during the crisis to pass important reforms of EU law.[51] Nevertheless, intergovernmentalism, and the use of international agreements outside the framework of EU law, has affected the EU legislative process: to a large extent, EU legislation has been used to complement, or anticipate, broader legal and institutional reforms undertaken through international treaties.[52] And this strategy of crisis management has produced important institutional implications on the EU balance of powers.[53] A major victim of this state of affairs has been the EP: Although the EP had been defined as the winner in the Lisbon Treaty, "the financial crisis has suddenly forced us to reconsider this assumption, at least for the crucial sector of European economic governance."[54] Not only the EP was sidelined—or given a purely observer status—in the negotiations leading to the drafting of the intergovernmental

[46] See Jean-Paul Keppenne, "Institutional Report", in Ulla Neergaard et al (eds), *The Economic and Monetary Union: Constitutional and Institutional Aspects of the Economic Governance within the EU. Proceedings of the XXVI FIDE Congress* (Djøf 2014), 179.

[47] See Angelos Dimopoulos, "The Use of International Law as a Tool for Enhancing Governance in the Eurozone and its Impact on EU Institutional Integrity," in Federico Fabbrini et al (eds), *The Constitutionalization of European Budgetary Constraints* (Hart Publishing 2014), 41 and Georgios Maris and Pantelis Sklias, "Intergovernmentalism and the New Framework of EMU Governance," in Federico Fabbrini et al (eds), *What Form of Government for the European Union and the Eurozone?* (Hart Publishing 2015), 57.

[48] Alicia Hinarejos, *The Euro Area Crisis in Constitutional Perspective* (OUP 2015) 87.

[49] See Uwe Puetter, *The European Council and the Council: New Intergovernmentalism and Institutional Change* (OUP 2014).

[50] See also Berthold Rittenberger, "Integration without Representation? The European Parliament and the Reform of Economic Governance in the EU" (2014) 52 Journal of Common Market Studies 1174.

[51] See Renaud Dehousse and Laurie Boussaguet, "L'impact de la crise sur la gouvernance européenne" (2014) 149 Pouvoirs 7.

[52] See Christian Joerges and Carola Glinski (eds), *The European Crisis and the Transformation of Transnational Governance* (Hart Publishing 2014).

[53] See Mark Dawson and Floris De Witte, "Constitutional Balance in the EU after the Euro-crisis" (2013) 76 Modern Law Review 817.

[54] Cristina Fasone, "European Economic Governance and Parliamentary Representation. What Place for the European Parliament?" (2014) 20 European Law Journal 164.

agreements;[55] but it also saw its capacity to shape policy outcomes plummet even when legislating within the EU legal order, due to the pressure extolled from the European Council.[56]

In Chapter 2, I have articulated a critique of the use by the member states of intergovernmental agreements to respond to the Euro-crisis. As I explained, as a result of the increasing use of intergovernmental agreements outside the framework of EU law, national courts have paradoxically come to play an unprecedented role in the field of EU economic governance—a development which is at odds with constitutional arguments which plead in favor of leaving economic questions to the political process. For this reason, I have suggested that the EU political branches should develop policies in the framework of the EU legal order, and resort to ordinary EU legislation. In this framework, the risk of judicial interference is reduced, since only the EU Court of Justice (ECJ) is empowered to review the legality of EU laws. At the same time, when the EU acts through the legislative process, the legitimacy of decision-making is at its best, given the involvement of the Commission, the Council, and the EP, each representing different interests and constituencies. More generally, in fact, the intergovernmental management of the crisis—epitomized by the conclusion of inter-state compacts outside the framework of EU law—has been faulted for producing a major problem of legitimacy in the EU, due to the limited involvement of legislative bodies in the governance of EMU.[57]

This chapter, therefore, makes the case for the centrality of the EU legislative process in EMU governance. Contrary to the practice that emerged during the last years to manage the Euro-crisis through intergovernmental agreements, in the future the regime put in place by the Lisbon Treaty to pass EU laws should be the main process to adopt legal and economic policy measures in EMU. In arguing in favor of a greater role for the EU legislative process, this chapter joins a chorus of academics who have called for more parliamentary involvement in EMU.[58] Growing awareness on the need to ensure legislative involvement in EU governance has also emerged among EU institutions. Most prominently, of course, the EP has invoked for itself a greater role in EMU governance, arguing that only the adoption of

[55] See President of the European Parliament Martin Schulz, "Fiscal Union without Parliamentary Control is Unacceptable," Speech, Brussels January 30, 2012 (regretting use of intergovernmental negotiations and stating that a fiscal union without parliamentary oversight would be unacceptable).

[56] See Edoardo Bressanelli and Nicola Chelotti, "Legislating in the Shadow of the European Council: Empowering or Silencing the European Parliament?," paper presented at the workshop "The Centrality of the European Council," CEU Budapest, November 28, 2014 (on file with authors) 2 (emphasizing the limited ability of the EP "to shape policy outcome when acting 'in the shadow' of the European Council [because] if the EP demands too much [...] there exists the credible threat that the government will resort to intergovernmental negotiations.").

[57] See Deirdre Curtin, "Challenging Executive Dominance in European Democracy" (2014) 77 Modern Law Review 1 and Mark Dawson, "The Legal and Political Accountability Structure of 'Post-Crisis' EU Economic Governance" (2015) 54 Journal of Common Market Studies 4.

[58] See e.g., Ingolf Pernice et al, *A Democratic Solution to the Crisis* (Nomos 2012) and Andreas Mauer, "From EMU to DEMU: The Democratic Legitimacy of the EU and the European Parliament," IAI Working Paper No. 11/2013.

EU legislation, with full parliamentary participation, can yield legitimacy to the economic policy decisions of the EU. In its November 2012 resolution, the EP stated that "a substantial improvement of the democratic legitimacy and accountability at Union level of the EMU governance by an increased role of Parliament [i]s an absolute necessity."[59] In December 2013, it held that:

> the European Parliament is the only EU institution in which citizens are directly represented at Union level and is the parliamentary body of the EMU, and [...] its appropriate involvement is essential for ensuring the democratic legitimacy and functioning of the EMU and is a precondition for any further step towards a banking union, a fiscal union and an economic union.[60]

Recently, then, in June 2015, the EP underlined "the need for sustained parliamentary involvement" in EU economic governance.[61]

The importance of securing greater parliamentary involvement in the governance of EMU has been acknowledged by the European Commission too.[62] Moreover, the application of the "Community method" in EMU has been endorsed by several national governments, including the Italian,[63] the Belgian,[64] and the Czech.[65] Also the European Council has affirmed that in the future of EMU, democratic legitimacy and accountability should occur at the level at which decisions are taken.[66] Nevertheless, the European Commission and the European Council have been ambivalent on this point, often promoting inter-parliamentary cooperation, rather than EP participation, as a way to enhance democracy in EMU.[67] In particular, a position which has become increasingly à la mode among national governments—and which has also recently been mentioned in the June 2015 report "Completing Europe's EMU," written by the President of the European Commission, in close cooperation with the Presidents of the European Council,

[59] European Parliament Resolution of November 20, 2012 on the report "Towards a Genuine EMU," P7_TA(2012)0430, para 9.

[60] European Parliament Resolution of December 12, 2013 on the constitutional problems of multi-tier governance in the European Union, P7_TA(2013)0598, para 26.

[61] European Parliament Resolution of June 24, 2015 on the review of the economic governance framework: stocktaking and challenges, P8_TA(2015)0238, para 48.

[62] See European Commission Communication (n 5).

[63] See Government of Italy, "Completing and Strengthening EMU: Italian Contribution," May 2015, 8 (stating that "[e]ffective parliamentary oversight is key.").

[64] See Government of Belgium, "Report on Preparing for Next Steps in Better Economic Governance in the Euroarea," April 27, 2015, 3 (stating that "Belgium believes that the community method is the best guarantee for further integration.").

[65] See Government of the Czech Republic, "The Czech Strategy in the EU: An Active and Intelligible Czech Republic in a United Europe," May 2015, 2 (indicating the government's plan to accede to the Eurozone and stating that "a systematic application of the community method is clearly in the Czech Republic's interest.").

[66] See European Council Conclusions, June 28, 2013, EUCO 104/2/13, 9.

[67] See Diane Fromage, "Parlamento Europeo y Parlamentos nacionales después del Tratado de Lisboa y en un context de crisis", in Adrés Sáenz et al (eds), *El Parlamento Europeo* (European Inklings 2015), 223 and Alexandre De Streel, "The Confusion of Tasks in the Decision-Making Process of the European Economic Governance," in Federico Fabbrini et al (eds), *What Form of Government for the European Union and the Eurozone?* (Hart Publishing 2015), 79.

the Eurogroup, the EP, and the European Central bank (ECB) [68]—has been that in favor of creating an inter-parliamentary assembly, bringing together members of the EP and national parliaments, to debate issues related to EMU governance. Article 13 Fiscal Compact institutionalized this proposal, by stating that:

> the European Parliament and the national Parliaments of the Contracting Parties will together determine the organisation and promotion of a conference of representatives of the relevant committees of the European Parliament and representatives of the relevant committees of national Parliaments in order to discuss budgetary policies and other issues covered by this Treaty.

The idea of inter-parliamentary cooperation is not new in the EU.[69] Article 9 of Protocol No. 1 attached to the EU treaties offers a framework of inter-parliamentary cooperation in which the EP and national parliaments can maintain regular contacts. Nevertheless, the expectations that have recently been put on the capacity of this forum to redress the problems of legitimacy faced by the EU in the aftermath of the Euro-crisis seem frankly overblown. As Valentin Kreilinger has explained, the efforts during the last two years to put together the Inter-Parliamentary Assembly on EU Economic Governance required by the Fiscal Compact have been remarkably modest—not only for the reluctance of the EP, but also for the opposition of several national parliaments to get involved in this game.[70] In fact, it is not at all clear what the purpose of such an inter-parliamentary conference would be: should it debate? Should it decide? Or should it control? But if so, who? And how? Proponents of a stronger inter-connection between national parliaments and the EP have failed to provide meaningful answers to these questions—raising the suspicion that inter-parliamentary cooperation may be just a fig leaf to cover the reality of intergovernmental crisis-management in the EU.[71]

Even leaving aside the bad performance of national parliaments under the so-called Early Warning Mechanisms,[72] there are plenty of problems associated with the idea to vest into an inter-parliamentary conference the task to participate

[68] President of the European Commission, Report "Completing Europe's EMU," June 22, 2015, 17.

[69] See Nicola Lupo and Andrea Manzella (eds), *Il sistema parlamentare euro-nazionale* (Giappichelli 2014), and Ben Crum and John Erik Fossum (eds), *Practices of Interparliamentary Coordination in International Politics: The European Union and Beyond* (ECPR Press 2013).

[70] Valentin Kreilinger, "Inter-Parliamentary Cooperation and its Challenges: The Case of Economic and Financial Governance," in Federico Fabbrini et al (eds), *What Form of Government for the European Union and the Eurozone?* (Hart Publishing 2015), 271.

[71] See Sergio Fabbrini, *Which European Union? Europe after the Euro-Crisis* (CUP 2015) 128.

[72] See Protocol No. 2 on the application of the principle of subsidiarity and proportionality [2012] OJ C326/206 (empowering national parliaments to review *ex ante*, within eight weeks, whether legislation proposed by the European Commission complies with the principle of subsidiarity and introducing a yellow card or an orange card, with different effects on the Commission proposal, if a qualified number of national parliaments simultaneously raise concerns about subsidiarity). On this see also Federico Fabbrini and Katarzyna Granat, "'Yellow Card, but No Foul': The Role of the National Parliaments under the Subsidiarity Protocol and the Commission Proposal for an EU Regulation on the Right to Strike" (2013) 50 Common Market Law Review 115 (criticizing the use of the first yellow card procedure by national parliaments because they did not focus on subsidiarity, and they mainly acted on the basis of purely local domestic concerns).

in EMU governance.[73] As the EP correctly put it, "this cooperation should not be seen as establishing a new joint parliamentary body, which would be both ineffective and illegitimate from a democratic and constitutional point of view."[74] As the EP stated, "there is no substitute for a formal strengthening of the full legitimacy of the European Parliament, as a parliamentary body at Union level, with a view to reinforcing the democratic governance of the EMU."[75] In fact, also the President of the European Council, in the December 2012 final report "Towards a Genuine EMU," written in cooperation with the Presidents of the European Commission, the Eurogroup and the ECB, had raised concerns about the idea of inter-parliamentary cooperation: while emphasizing the importance of strengthening democracy within EMU, he stated that "the provisions for democratic legitimacy and accountability should ensure that the common interest of the Union is duly taken into account; yet national parliaments are not in the best position to take it into account fully."[76]

From this point of view, the President of the European Council outlined a convincing roadmap for institutional reforms in the EU when it stated that:

> further integration of policy making and a greater pooling of competences at the European level should first and foremost be accompanied with a commensurate involvement of the European Parliament in the integrated frameworks for a genuine EMU.[77]

In my view, if the Euro-crisis prompted an intergovernmental response, the most appropriate way to handle the legitimacy concerns that have emerged in the past years is to restore the centrality of the EU legislative process. The Lisbon Treaty has reformed the EU law-making regime, codifying a complex, but balanced, procedure in which the EP, representing the citizens, is asked as a general rule to approve legislation on par with the Council, which represents the member states. As argued in Chapter 2, EU legislation is preferable to intergovernmental agreements because it diminishes the chances of judicial overreach. But, as shown in Chapter 3, the EU law-making regime is also preferable to international treaty-making negotiations because it ensures, through bicameralism and checks and balances, that no institution or member state will dominate the process over the others.

The EU legislative process, therefore, should be made central to EMU governance. Yet, there is no doubt that this aspiration meets several challenges. In the remainder of this chapter, in particular, I examine three challenges the resolution of which I regard as necessary to secure the centrality of the EU law-making process. First, what I call the challenge of asymmetry: if the centrality EU legislative process is to be achieved, member states should be constrained from stepping

[73] See also Daniel Kelemen, "Towards a New Constitutional Architecture in the EU?," in Federico Fabbrini et al (eds), *What Form of Government for the European Union and the Eurozone?* (Hart Publishing 2015), 197.

[74] European Parliament Resolution (n 60) para 32.

[75] Ibid.

[76] President of the European Council, Final Report "Towards a Genuine EMU," December 5, 2012, 16.

[77] Ibid.

outside the framework of EU law at will, and, simultaneously, EU institutions should be empowered to legislate on economic matters within the framework of EU law. Second, what I call the challenge of representation: if the EP is to acquire a meaningful role in the management of EMU, the electoral mechanisms that govern its functioning should be reconsidered in light of its new institutional status. And third, what I call the challenge of unity: if the Council is to normalize its activities as an upper legislative chamber, its composition, and the relations between its formations, should be streamlined to ensure that greater coordination exists in the legislative files approved by the representatives of member states' governments. As I will suggest, these are difficult challenges—but there are reasons to be optimistic that they can be addressed: the EU legislative process can be made fit to govern EMU.

3. The Challenge of Asymmetry

As the literature has emphasized, in creating EMU the Treaty of Maastricht designed an asymmetric Union, since monetary policy was entirely centralized within the ECB, while economic policy was left to the decentralized action of the member states, subject to EU fiscal constraints.[78] In the conventional understanding, this situation has implied that member states have remained free to act outside EU law, while EU institutions had only limited power to legislate in the field of economic policy. Nevertheless, as this section seeks to point out, the Lisbon Treaty has introduced relevant constitutional innovations which, although not directly connected with EMU, have consequences for the challenge of asymmetry within EMU. In particular, a constitutional reading of the treaties suggests that there are constraints on what the member states can do outside the framework of EU law, including in the field of EMU; and, at the same time, it suggests that the EU institutions have actually relevant authority in policies which are inherently connected to macro-economic governance. In my view the treaties, on the one hand, put constitutional limitations to treaty-making by the member states outside EU law; and, on the other, provide constitutional empowerment to legislation by the EU institutions within EU law. In the following sub-sections, I will try to articulate these claims, on the understanding that handling the challenge of asymmetry is a necessity to ensure a greater role for the EU legislative process in the field of EMU.

A. Constitutional limitations to treaty-making

Since the outburst of the Euro-crisis, member states' governments have repeatedly decided to act outside the framework of EU law by adopting EMU-related

[78] See Martin Selmayr and Chiara Zilioli, *The Law of the European Central Bank* (Hart Publishing 2001) and Fabian Amtenbrink and Jakob De Haan, "Economic Governance in the European Union: Fiscal Policy Discipline versus Flexibility" (2003) 40 Common Market Law Review 1075.

intergovernmental agreements strengthening budgetary constraints, creating a permanent mechanism of financial assistance to countries in fiscal distress, and establishing a fund for the resolution of failing banks. The use of intergovernmental agreements may appear at first the simple reflection of the long-standing asymmetry characterizing EMU, in which economic policy was left to the decentralized action of the member states, including action outside the framework of EU law. Nevertheless, in my view this state of affairs must be reassessed in light of the constitutional rules introduced by the Lisbon Treaty with regard to the EU legislative process, analyzed in the previous section. Because member states' governments make up the Council, their action outside EU law has effectively altered the balance of powers between the two houses of the EU legislature. When members of the Council have opted to step outside the framework of EU law—and concluded international agreements in their capacity as the treaty-making authorities of the member states—they have bypassed the EP. The EU legislative process—and the powers of the EP associated with it—has thus been subjected to the whims of national governments, and to their willingness to concede or not on the use of EU legislation.

In the scholarship much has been written on the use of EMU-related intergovernmental agreements outside EU law.[79] Attention has been given to the difficulties that are produced when intergovernmental treaties concluded by only some EU member states impact upon the activities of the EU institutions, which "belong" to the totality of the EU member states.[80] Moreover, scholars have dissected the arguments that—case by case—have been advanced by national governments to adopt international agreements outside the framework of EU law.[81] Elsewhere, for instance, I have criticized the justifications adduced by the German Ministry of Finance in favor of concluding the SRF Agreement:[82] this treaty requires member states to collect from national banks and to transfer into an EU fund the contributions necessary for the resolution of failing banks. As I explained, the argument that an EU regulation—and specifically the EU regulation establishing a single resolution mechanism (SRM), at that time under approval of the Council and the EP[83]—could not impose this requirement on the member states clashed with the

[79] See Keppenne (n 46) and Dimopoulos (n 52).

[80] Compare Steve Peers, "Towards a New Form of EU law? The Use of EU Institutions in Treaties between Member States" (2013) 9 European Constitutional Law Review 37 with Paul Craig, "*Pringle* and the Use of EU Institutions Outside the EU Legal Framework: Foundations, Procedure and Substance" (2013) 9 European Constitutional Law Review 263.

[81] See e.g., Michael Gordon, "The United Kingdom and the Fiscal Compact" (2014) 10 European Constitutional Law Review 28 (explaining adoption of Fiscal Compact in light of the UK veto on a revision of the EU treaties).

[82] Federico Fabbrini, "On Banks, Courts and International Law. The Intergovernmental Agreement on the Single Resolution Fund in Context" (2014) 21 Maastricht Journal of European & Comparative Law 444.

[83] See now Regulation (EU) No. 806/2014 of the European Parliament and of the Council of July 15, 2014 establishing uniform rules and a uniform procedure for the resolution of credit institutions and certain investment firms in the framework of a Single Resolution Mechanism and a Single Bank Resolution Fund, and amending Regulation (EU) No. 1093/2010 of the European Parliament and of the Council [2014] OJ L225/1.

function that EU regulations have played since the beginning of the process of European integration.[84]

As a matter of fact, however, the *legality* of the use by the EU member states of international agreements outside the EU legal framework has not been challenged. In *Pringle*,[85] the Irish Supreme Court raised the query—which the ECJ set aside—whether the ESM Treaty violated specific provisions of the EU treaties.[86] Nevertheless, the applicant in the case did not question the power of the EU member states to conclude the ESM Treaty *as such*. At the same time, the Fiscal Compact introduced a provision stating that the treaty only "shall apply insofar as it is compatible with the Treaties on which the European Union is founded and with European Union law. It shall not encroach the competence of the Union to act in the area of the economic union."[87] And the same clause has been enshrined also in the SRF Agreement.[88] While the recognition that these treaties are valid only as long as they are not in violation of specific provisions of EU law confirms that the member states are bound to respect the EU treaties, it also seems to imply that they are entitled to choose the means that they please to set rules for the EU: implicitly, these provisions assert as long as intergovernmental treaties do not violate substantive provisions of EU law, member states are free to conclude them.[89]

The view that EU member states are free to act outside the framework of EU law is consistent with a traditional international law reading of the EU.[90] From a purely formalistic point of view, the EU is founded on international treaties—unanimously concluded by all the member states' governments and ratified by their respective parliaments or peoples according to each country's specific constitutional requirements.[91] Most prominently, the German Bundesverfassungsgericht has stressed since its judgment on the Maastricht Treaty the international-law origin of the EU treaties, proclaiming that the EU member states remain the "Masters" thereof.[92] And even recently, in an edited volume on the worlds of European constitutionalism, Bruno de Witte has provocatively argued that the EU remains ultimately an international organization, based on classical international law.[93] Seen from this perspective, of

[84] See Fabbrini (n 82) 456.

[85] Case C-370/12 *Pringle v. Government of Ireland*, judgment of November 27, 2012, ECLI:EU:C:2012:756.

[86] See further on this Chapter 2.

[87] Art 2(2) Fiscal Compact.

[88] Art 2(2) SRF Agreement.

[89] See also Bruno de Witte, "Chameleonic Member States: Differentiated Integration by Means of Partial and Parallel International Agreements," in Bruno De Witte et al (eds), *The Many Faces of Differentiation in EU Law* (Intersentia 2001), 231.

[90] See e.g., Theodor Schilling, "The Autonomy of the Community Legal Order" (1996) 37 Harvard International Law Journal 389.

[91] See Art 54 TEU.

[92] See BVerfGE 89, 155 (1993), para C.II.1.a (stating that "even after the Maastricht Treaty has entered into force, the Federal Republic of Germany remains a member of an inter-governmental community [...] German is one of the Master of the Treaties.") cited in Juliane Kokott, "Report on Germany", in Anne-Marie Slaughter et al (eds), *The European Courts and National Courts* (Hart Publishing 1998), 77, 100.

[93] See Bruno De Witte, "The European Union as an International Legal Experiment," in Gráinne de Búrca and Joseph H.H. Weiler (eds), *The Worlds of European Constitutionalism* (CUP 2011), 19.

course, the surge in the use of intergovernmental treaties in the aftermath of the Euro-crisis is nothing special: international law remains just one of the instruments in the toolbox of the EU member states, and, as long as they do not violate substantive provisions of EU law, "*inter se* international agreements between two or more member states of the EU are allowed."[94]

In my view, nevertheless, this interpretation is increasingly problematic. Not only the mainstream understanding among EU lawyers is that the EU is nowadays no longer an international organization:[95] starting with the seminal work of Joseph H.H. Weiler,[96] the dominant academic view is that the EU has transformed into a type of constitutional regime, endowed with mechanisms to protect fundamental rights, checks and balances and inherent powers.[97] More importantly, the thesis that member states are free to conclude international agreements outside the EU legal order as long as they do not violate EU law is at odds with the constitutional balance enshrined in the EU treaties—to which the member states have subjected themselves.[98] As mentioned in Section 2, the Lisbon Treaty has designed a comprehensive regime whereby the EU and its member states can adopt binding norms. This process involves the EP as a necessary co-legislator. The thesis that the member states are free to move outside the EU legal order, even when EU law would provide a perfect venue to adopt a specific legal measure, essentially implies that the member states can by-pass the EP, thus undermining the constitutional balance between the institutions designed in the EU treaties.

There is therefore a constitutional argument that can be made on the basis of the Lisbon Treaty to restrict the freedom of the member states to act at will outside the framework of EU law, including in the field of EMU.[99] While the thesis that the member states enjoy freedom to act in the international realm, unless they violate substantive provisions of EU primary law, might have been acceptable at a time when the member states were de facto monopolizing the EU law-making process (within the Council), this thesis is unsustainable at a

[94] See Bruno De Witte, "European Stability Mechanism and Treaty on stability, coordination and governance: role of the EU institutions and consistency with EU legal order," in "Challenges of Multi-Tier Governance in the European Union," Study commissioned by the European Parliament Constitutional Affairs Committee, March 2013, PE 474.438, 78, 81.

[95] For an overview see also Anne Boerger and Morten Rasmussen, "Transforming European Law: The Establishment of the Constutional Discourse from 1950 to 1993" (2014) 10 European Constitutional Law Review 199.

[96] See Weiler (n 9) (explaining constitutional transformation of Europe) as well as Joseph H.H. Weiler and Ulrich Haltern, "The Autonomy of the Community Legal Order—Through the Looking Glass" (1996) 37 Harvard International Law Journal 411.

[97] See also Armin von Bogdandy and Jürgen Bast (eds), *Principles of European Constitutional Law* (Hart Publishing 2009). On the EU system for the protection of fundamental rights see also Federico Fabbrini, *Fundamental Rights in Europe: Challenges and Transformations in Comparative Perspective* (OUP 2014).

[98] See also Paul Craig, "The Financial Crisis, the EU Institutional Order and Constitutional Responsibility," in Federico Fabbrini et al (eds), *What Form of Government for the European Union and the Eurozone?* (Hart Publishing 2015), 17 (stressing responsibility of the member states for the current EU institutional system).

[99] See also Case 294/83 *Les Verts v. Parliament* [1986] ECR 1339, ECLI:EU:C:1986:166, para 23 (ECJ defining the treaties as the "basic constitutional charter" of the EU).

time when the production of EU norms is also subject to the approval of an institution like the EP, which is not the propagation of member states' governments. If we were to accept after the adoption of the Lisbon Treaty that the member states are free to act outside the EU legal order—even when they do not violate EU law, and when EU law would provide a perfect venue to enact a specific measure—this would imply that the legislative function constitutionally entrusted to the EP by Article 14 TEU would be at the disposal of the member states in Council.

However, the principle of institutional balance excludes this interpretation.[100] On the one hand, the ECJ has long held that the rules set in the treaties "are not at the disposal of the Member States or the institutions themselves,"[101] and proclaimed that "the effective participation of the Parliament in the legislative process of the [EU] in accordance with the procedure laid down in the treaty, represents an essential factor in the institutional balance intended by the treaty."[102] On the other hand, the Lisbon Treaty has further constitutionalized the logic of institutional balance in the EU, putting limits on what the member states can achieve through inter-se cooperation.[103] The new Article 4(3) TEU states that the member states "shall facilitate the achievement of the Union's tasks and refrain from any measure which could jeopardize the attainment of the Union's competence"—creating a duty for the member states to abide by EU law whenever they act in the realm of international law.[104] Moreover, Article 13 TEU now proclaims that "[t]he Union shall have an institutional framework which shall aim to promote its values, advance its objectives, serve its interests, those of its citizens and those of the Member States, and ensure the consistency, effectiveness and continuity of its policies and actions," and vests specific powers in each of the institutions it lists—suggesting that the EU constitutional architecture is conceived as a system of checks and balances which cannot be altered, or sidestepped, at states' will.[105]

In fact, in its recent Opinion *in Re: the EU accession to the European Convention on Human Rights (ECHR)*,[106] the ECJ—while confirming that "the EU is, under international law, precluded by its very nature from being considered a State"[107]—emphasized how the EU is endowed with "its own constitutional framework and founding principles, a particularly sophisticated institutional structure and a full set of legal rules to ensure its operation."[108] From this constitutional

[100] See also Jean-Paul Jacqué, "The Principle of Institutional Balance" (2004) 41 Common Market Law Review 383.

[101] Case 68/86 *United Kingdom v. Council* [1988] ECR 855, ECLI:EU:C:1988:85, para 38.

[102] Case C-65/93 *Parliament v. Council* [1995] ECR I-660, ECLI:EU:C:1995:91, para 21.

[103] See Craig (n 11) and Schütze (n 37).

[104] See Geert De Baere, *Constitutional Principles of EU External Relations* (OUP 2008) 254 and Daniel Thym, *Ungleichzeitgkeit und europäisches Verfassungsrecht* (Nomos 2004) 308.

[105] See Robert Schütze, *Foreign Affairs and the EU Constitution* (CUP 2014) 155. But see also Koen Lenaerts, "Some Reflections on the Separation of Powers in the European Communities" (1991) 28 Common Market Law Review 11 (applying idea of checks and balances to the EC Treaty).

[106] Opinion 2/13 *In Re: the EU Accession to the ECHR*, opinion of December 18, 2014, ECLI:EU:C:2014:2454.

[107] Ibid para 156.

[108] Ibid para 158.

reading of the EU legal order, the ECJ drew the conclusion—of particular relevance for our discussion—that

> the Member States have, by reason of their membership of the EU, accepted that the relations between them as regards matters covered by the transfer of power from the Member States to the EU are governed by EU law to the exclusion, if EU law so requires, of any other law.[109]

While the ECJ articulated this argument to single out the provisions in the draft accession agreement of the EU to the ECHR which were "liable to upset the underlying balance of the EU"[110]—the reasoning of the ECJ can be applied a fortiori when considering the legality of intergovernmental agreements concluded by EU member states in the field of EMU. Because the conclusion of intergovernmental agreements in areas when EU legislation is possible upsets the EU constitutional balance, the member states should be prohibited from doing so, even if they do not violate any substantive provision of EU law.

An important caveat should however qualify the argument that I am making. Because the EU is based on the principle of conferral,[111] the member states certainly remain free to conclude international agreements—including inter se—in all those areas which fall within their residual competences. Rather, the argument I am bringing forward is that, in all the areas in which the EU *has* competence (including competences it shares with the member states), the EU member states are no longer free to step outside the framework of EU law and regulate a given field through international agreements. The EU treaties design a constitutional regime, premised on a delicate system of checks and balances, which the member states cannot bypass. While the member states continue to have a prominent voice in the Council, the EP is constitutionally vested with law-making functions which cannot be circumvented by national governments.[112] Otherwise, even when only a handful of member states want to adopt a specific legal measure, the treaties foresee the mechanisms whereby they can do so *within the EU legal order*: through the enhanced cooperation procedure a sub group of EU member states can pass legislation in the Council.[113] This legislation only binds the participating member states.[114] However its passage requires the approval of the EP—thus securing the involvement of both houses of the EU legislature.[115]

In conclusion, this sub-section claimed that the asymmetrical power of the EU member states in the Council to act outside the EU legal order poses an important challenge to the success of the EU law-making process. As I have reported

[109] Ibid para 193. [110] Ibid para 194. [111] See text accompanying nn 123–68.

[112] See also Case 22/70 *Commission v. Council (ERTA)* [1971] ECR 263, ECLI:EU:C:1971:32.

[113] See Art 330 TFEU. [114] See Art 20(4) TEU.

[115] See further Federico Fabbrini, "Enhanced Cooperation under Scrutiny: Revisiting the Law and Practice of Multi-Speed Integration in Light of the First Involvement of the EU Judiciary" (2013) 40 Legal Issues of Economic Integration 197 (discussing institutional protections involved in the use of enhanced cooperation).

elsewhere, the EP raised serious objections to the decision of the Eurozone member states to conclude the SRF Agreement outside EU law,[116] but eventually conceded due to the desire to secure the swift establishment of the SRM.[117] Nevertheless, in the post-Lisbon constitutional system of the EU, the member states should not be free to act outside the EU legal order at will. In the future, therefore, the EP should explore ways to make sure that the member states do not bypass it by concluding intergovernmental treaties, rather than using EU legislation. One option for the EP would be to pursue a legal strategy, bringing a case before the ECJ and asking it to enforce the principle of institutional balance.[118] An alternative strategy the EP could follow, otherwise, is the political one—which builds on the new budgetary power that the Lisbon Treaty has vested in the lower house of the EU legislature.[119] As I have argued elsewhere, each of these strategies presents shortcomings: nevertheless, their combined use may allow the EP to protect the EU inter-institutional compromise designed by the Lisbon Treaty and prevent the member states from discretionally circumventing it.[120]

Ironically, in the December 2014 final Council Presidency report on "Improving the functioning of the EU"[121] the then Italian Presidency reported that discussion among national delegations in the Council "on inter-governmental agreements signed outside the existing Treaties framework [had] confirmed that working within the EU legal order is the preferred option and should be the norm. Delegations pointed out that intergovernmental agreements risk leading to fragmentation of the legal framework and producing unsuitable and uncalled for discrepancies among Member States."[122] However, as I have endeavored to argue, action by the states within the EU legal order—rather than outside it—should not be a simple matter of political opportunity. It should be a legal obligation, stemming from the comprehensive constitutional architecture for law-making created by the Lisbon Treaty. In any areas where the EU has competence, the member states are required to act within the EU framework—in case, by using the enhanced cooperation procedure. This of course raises the question of what

[116] See Letter from the Chair and Members of the Economic and Monetary Affairs Committee of the European Parliament to the Council Presidency, regarding the intergovernmental agreement negotiated within the framework of the SRM regulation, January 15, 2014, available at <http://www.europarl.europa.eu/document/activities/cont/201401/20140116ATT77594/20140116ATT77594EN.pdf> (last accessed February 23, 2015).

[117] Fabbrini (n 82) 463.

[118] See Case C-70/88 *Parliament v. Council* [1990] ECR I-2041, ECLI:EU:C:1988:460, para 21 (empowering the EP to bring an annulment action against the Council, beyond the letter of the then EU treaties, on the argument that this was necessary to protect the institutional balance designed by the treaties themselves).

[119] See Giacomo Benedetto, "The Balance of Power over the EU Budget: European Expenditures since the Lisbon Treaty," Swedish Institute for European Policy Studies, Policy Analysis No. 15/2015.

[120] See Federico Fabbrini, "A Principle in Need of Renewal? The Euro-Crisis and the Principle of Institutional Balance" (2016) 50 Cahiers de droit européen.

[121] Council Presidency, "Improving the functioning of the EU"—Final Presidency Report from the Friends of the Presidency Group, December 12, 2014, Doc. 16544/1.

[122] Ibid para 24.

are the competences of the EU in the field of economic policy—to which I shall now turn.

B. Constitutional empowerment to legislation

In the previous sub-section I have argued that a constitutional interpretation of the Lisbon Treaty binds the member states, limiting their freedom to act outside the framework of EU law whenever the EU has the competences to act in a given field. This element of constraining constitutionalism, however, is compensated by an element of enabling constitutionalism—empowering the EU institutions to take action in the field of economic policy. In other words, notwithstanding the strategy followed in the aftermath of the Euro-crisis, there are constitutional arguments to claim that the member states have lost their freedom to act at will outside the EU legal order to manage the economic pillar of EMU. And yet these arguments do not imply a paralysis: as a constitutional reading of EU primary law reveals, in fact, the EU legal order endows the EU institutions (including the member states as represented in the Council) with a significant amount of power to take legislative action in the field of EMU. As this sub-section will point out, the treaties' legal bases allow for the domestication within the EU legal order of the EMU-related agreements concluded outside EU law. But they also allow for further action by the EU within the field of economic policy more broadly understood.

To begin with, the EU treaties already permit the domestication via standard EU legislation of the intergovernmental agreements concluded outside EU law. In fact, each of these EMU-related agreements could have been adopted through EU law in the first place. In particular, as the Legal Service of the Council had recognized, the SRF Agreement could have been based on Article 114 TFEU—and this provision should be used to domesticate the SRF Agreement within EU law by 2026.[123] Equally, in my opinion, Articles 121 to 126 TFEU would have sufficed to enact through secondary EU legislation the most important *substantive* provision of the Fiscal Compact: the obligation to constitutionalize a balanced budget rule at the domestic level.[124] Although it has been suggested that an EU secondary act cannot compel an amendment to a national primary act,[125] there is nothing in EU law that prohibits this, and in fact there are examples in EU law of EU legislative and judicial measures which have required domestic constitutional changes.[126]

[123] See Art 16 SRF Agreement.

[124] See further on this Chapter 1. For a discussion of the treaty reforms needed to incorporate the *institutional* provisions of the Fiscal Compact within EU law, see instead Chapter 6.

[125] See Tuori and Tuori (n 42) 176.

[126] See Case C-285/98 *Kreil v. Germany* [2000] ECR I-69, ECLI:EU:C:2000:2 (holding that the German Basic Law, by preventing women serving in the army from holding position involving the use of arms was incompatible with Council Directive 76/207/EEC of February 9, 1976, on the implementation of the principle of equal treatment for men and women). But see also Directive 95/46/EC of the European Parliament and of the Council of October 24, 1995 on the protection of individuals with regard to the processing of personal data and on the free movement of such data [1995] OJ L281/31 (asking states to create independent data protection authorities).

Given the obligation by the contracting parties of the Fiscal Compact to bring back the content of the Treaty within the framework of EU law by 2018,[127] the EU institutions could resort to the legal bases mentioned above, combined with the use of enhanced cooperation, to reach this goal.

A more controversial issue instead is whether EU law permitted the establishment of the ESM within the framework of EU law.[128] As is well known, while Article 122 TFEU allows the Council to grant financial assistance to a member state facing exceptional occurrences beyond its control, in *Pringle* the ECJ ruled that the treaties did not confer to the EU any specific competence to create a *permanent* financial stability mechanism,[129] and that the member states were not obliged to use Article 352 TFEU (the general EU flexibility clause) to do so.[130] Nevertheless, as it has been argued, the ESM could be re-domesticated within the framework of EU law through the use of enhanced cooperation, with the provisions of financial support being seen as measures of economic coordination.[131] In fact, the June 2015 report "Completing Europe's EMU" coordinated by the President of the European Commission states that the ESM "should be fully integrated within the EU Treaties,"[132] without indicating the need for a treaty change to do so. Otherwise, as acknowledged also by Alberto de Gregorio Merino, one of the main reasons for opting for an intergovernmental treaty in the first place had been the fact that the EU budget "offer[ed] a quite small capacity of action, especially in the face of a situation where the financial needs of the Member States in question [we]re so impressively high."[133] Hence, it seems that the main obstacle against reincorporating the ESM within EU law is one of resources, rather than legal bases.[134]

Besides offering space for the domestication of the EMU-related intergovernmental agreements within EU law, however, the EU treaties in my view should also be seen as permitting EU intervention in the field of economic policy more broadly.[135] In the original design of EMU, the Maastricht Treaty had mainly granted to the

[127] See Art 16 Fiscal Compact.

[128] Compare Alberto de Gregorio Merino, "Legal Developments in the Economic and Monetary Union during the Debt Crisis: the Mechanisms of Financial Assistance" (2012) 49 Common Market Law Review 1613 with Michael Schwarz, "A Memorandum of Misunderstanding—The Doomed Road of the European Stability Mechanism and a Possible Way Out: Enhanced Cooperation" (2014) 51 Common Market Law Review 389.

[129] *Pringle* (n 85) para 64.

[130] Ibid para 67.

[131] Schwarz (n 128) 411 (developing an analogy with Art 143 TFEU, which provides for assistance to countries with a derogation from the euro, when they experience difficulties regarding their balance of payments).

[132] President of the European Commission Report (n 68) 18.

[133] Merino (n 128) 1635.

[134] But see Council press release, "EFSM: Council approves €7bn bridge loan to Greece," July 17, 2015 (indicating that the EFSM, an instrument created through EU law and financed through the EU budget, was used to provide bridge financing to Greece in July 2015, since the procedures of the ESM were too time consuming to address the emergency financial shortfall of Greece).

[135] See also Thomas Beukers, "The Eurozone Crisis and the Autonomy of Member States in Economic Union," paper presented at the Conference "Constitutional Challenges of the European Economic and Monetary Union," Villa Vigoni, Como, June 5, 2015 (on file with author).

EU institutions the power to surveil member states' economic policies for compliance with predefined deficit and debt rules, while the states themselves committed to coordinate their economic policies horizontally.[136] The treaties did not explicitly endow the EU with a legislative competence in the field of economic policy—even though, of course, the EU had used its budgetary powers already for many years to secure typical macro-economic objectives, such as the development of poorer European regions and the promotion of employment and social cohesion through Structural Funds and the European Social Fund.[137] Following the efforts of the Constitutional Treaty to clarify the delimitation of EU competences between the EU and the member states,[138] the Lisbon Treaty has reaffirmed the principle of conferral of Article 5 Treaty on Economic Community (TEC), stating in Article 5(2) TEU that "the Union shall act only within the limits of the competences conferred upon it by the Member States in the Treaties."

The Lisbon Treaty also sought to introduce a distinction between types of EU competences in Articles 2 to 6 TFEU.[139] In this context, a new provision with specific regard to EMU has been inserted:[140] Article 5 TFEU, which states that:

> the Member States shall coordinate their economic policies within the Union. To this end, the Council shall adopt measures, in particular broad guidelines for these policies. [...] The Union shall take measures to ensure coordination of the employment policies of the Member States, in particular by defining guidelines for these policies. The Union may take initiatives to ensure coordination of Member States' social policy.

Scholars have discussed about the classification of competences drawn by the Lisbon Treaty.[141] Besides distinguishing between exclusive and shared competences, the Lisbon Treaty also created a blurred class of coordinating, supporting and supplementing competences by stating that "in certain areas and under certain conditions laid down in the Treaties, the Union shall have competence to carry out actions to support, coordinate or supplement the actions of the Member States without thereby superseding their competence in these areas."[142] Based on the above, one could conclude that the only power of the EU in the field of economic policy is a coordinating one, and thus that there is no way for the EU institutions

[136] See Puetter (n 49); Amtenbrink and De Haan (n 78).

[137] See Daniel Kelemen, "Building the New European State? Federalism, Core State Powers and European Integration," in Philip Genschel and Markus Jachtenfuchs (eds), *Beyond the Regulatory Polity* (OUP 2014), 211.

[138] See Laeken Declaration, December 15, 2001, SN 273/01.

[139] See Michael Dougan, "The Competences of the Union," in Robert Schütze and Takis Tridimas (eds), *Oxford Principles of European Union Law* (OUP 2016).

[140] See Jean-Victor Louis, "Economic Policy under the Lisbon Treaty," in Stefan Griller and Jacques Ziller (eds), *The Lisbon Treaty: EU Constitutionalism Without a Constitutional Treaty?* (Springer 2008), 285.

[141] Compare Michael Dougan, "The Treaty of Lisbon 2007: Winning Minds, Not Hearts" (2008) 45 Common Market Law Review 617 (arguing that treaty clarifies competences) with Takis Tridimas, "Competence after Lisbon: The Elusive Search for Bright Lines" in Diamond Ashiagbor et al (eds), *The European Union after the Treaty of Lisbon* (CUP 2012), 47 (arguing that the treaty only draws elusive lines).

[142] Art 2(5) TFEU.

to undertake a real macro-economic policy, matching in EMU economic pillar the action of the ECB in EMU monetary pillar.

Nevertheless, the meaning of Article 5 TFEU must be appreciated within the broader constitutional fabric of the treaty. On the one hand, Article 2(3) TFEU states that "The Member States shall coordinate their economic and employment policies within arrangements as determined by this Treaty, which the Union shall have competence to provide"—thus suggesting that the EU has a competence to provide arrangements in the field of economic policy, which goes beyond mere coordination. On the other hand, Article 2(6) TFEU affirms that "the scope of an arrangements for exercising the Union's competences shall be determined by the provisions of the Treaties relating to each area"—hence clarifying that Articles 3 to 6 TFEU should be read as essentially seeking to distinguish between exclusive and shared competences, and that the real powers of the EU are defined in the specific legal bases existing in the substantive chapters of the treaties. As Monica Claes and Bruno de Witte have rightly made clear, "the text of Art. 5 TFEU is rather deceptive in describing the Union's role as being some kind of passive container within which Member States 'coordinate *their* economic policies'. In fact, on a closer look at the economic policy chapter of the TFEU, it appears that this is a very complex competence domain."[143] And if one considers the entirety of the legal bases existing in the TFEU one can find support for the view that the EU has significant powers to take legislative action in the field of economic policy, broadly intended here to refer to macro-economic governance.[144]

First, the EU treaties grant to the EU institutions extensive power to intervene in the functioning of the internal market.[145] Legislation in the field of the internal market has crucial effects on economic policy: as the experience of member states points out, governments often use the regulation (or de-regulation) of the market to affect the business cycle, boost competitiveness, and create jobs. As the example of the US reveals, at the same time, the Commerce Clause of the US Constitution—granting to the federal legislature the power to regulate inter-state commerce[146]—has been the main legal basis through which the federal authorities have undertaken an economic policy in the US.[147] In fact, the importance of the internal market competence of the EU in the field of economic policy is explicitly enshrined in Article 119 TFEU—which tracks the previous Article 4 TEC—stating that "the economic activities of the Member States and the Union shall include, as provided in the Treaties, the adoption of *an economic policy which is based* on the coordination of the Member States's economic policies, *on the internal market*, and on the definition of common objectives."[148] This

[143] Monica Claes and Bruno De Witte, "Competences," in Steven Blockmans and Adam Lazowski (eds), *Research Handbook of EU Institutional Law* (Elgar 2016), 9 (emphasis in original).

[144] See Roland Bieber, "The Allocation of Economic Policy Competences in the European Union," in Loïc Azoulai (ed), *The Question of Competence in the European Union* (OUP 2015), 86.

[145] See generally Niamh Nic Shuibhne, *Regulating the Internal Market* (Elgar 2006).

[146] See Art I, Sec. 8, cl 3 US Const.

[147] See Harry Scheiber, "State Law and 'Industrial Policy' in American Development, 1790-1987" (1987) 75 California Law Review 415 (describing state and federal economic policy in the US).

[148] Emphasis added.

suggests an important connection between the internal market competence of the treaties—an area where the EU has quasi plenary power[149]—and the economic pillar of EMU.

Second, the EU treaties grant to the EU institutions the power to legislate in specific fields which have relevant connections to macro-economic policy. Inter alia, pursuant to Article 170 TFEU, the "Union shall contribute to the establishment and development of trans-European networks in the areas of transport, telecommunications and energy infrastructure." According to Article 179 TFEU the Union shall promote and encourage research and technological developments through appropriate means. Pursuant to Article 173(3) TFEU, relating to industry, the EU shall contribute to the competitiveness of the European industry and to this end, "the EP and the Council, acting in accordance with the ordinary legislative procedure [...] may decide on specific measures in support of action taken in the member states." Moreover, as previously mentioned, based on Title XVIII TFEU, the EU shall run a policy of "Economic, Social and Territorial Cohesion" which empowers the EP and the Council, acting in accordance with ordinary legislative procedure, to "define the tasks, priority objectives and the organization of the Structural Funds."[150] And the EU can set up a the Cohesion Fund financing "projects in the fields of environment and trans-European networks in the area of transport infrastructure."[151]

In sum, a comprehensive constitutional reading of the legal bases of the EU treaties suggests that the EU can benefit from a wide authorization to legislate in the field of economic policy. In fact, the Lisbon Treaty has arguably extended this authorization, by introducing new competences for the EU in other areas which also have an impact on macro-economic policy, including in the field of services of general interest,[152] space,[153] and energy.[154] Moreover, the Lisbon Treaty has also introduced a new provision, Article 136 TFEU, which allows the adoption of "measures specific to those Member States whose currency is the euro." This clause, in particular, allows the relevant EU institutions: "(a) to strengthen the coordination and surveillance of [member states'] budgetary disciplines; (b) to set out economic policy guidelines for them, while ensuring that they are compatible with those adopted for the whole Union and are kept under surveillance."[155] Since Article 136 TFEU refers back to the specific procedures detailed in Articles 121 to 126 TFEU, which essentially deal with surveillance and coordination, the meaning of the provision remains ambiguous.[156] Nevertheless, it has been suggested that the existence of a new treaty clause on specific measures for the Eurozone, if combined for instance with Article 352 TFEU, could extend the EU legislative

[149] See also Bruno De Witte, "A Competence to Protect: The Pursuit of Non-Market Aims Through Internal Market Legislation," in Phil Syrpis (ed), *The Judiciary, the Legislature and the EU Internal Market* (CUP 2011), 25.

[150] Art 177(1) TFEU.

[151] Art 177(2) TFEU.

[152] See Art 14 TFEU.

[153] See Art 189 TFEU.

[154] See Art 194 TFEU.

[155] Art 136 TFEU.

[156] See Christian Calliess, "From Fiscal Compact to Fiscal Union? New Rules for the Eurozone" (2012) 14 Cambridge Yearbook of European Legal Studies 101.

power under Article 136 TFEU beyond the limits assigned to it, thus enlarging even further the competence of the EU in the field of economic policy.[157]

Be that as it may, it seems clear that a comprehensive and systematic constitutional reading of the treaties, as amended by the Lisbon Treaty, reveals that the EU is empowered *to act* in the field of economic policy. Certainly, the competence of the EU in economy policy only adds to the competence that the member states already have, and maintain, in the field.[158] But that is nothing special. In federalism-based systems macro-economic action by the central level of government never displaces action by the lower levels of government: rather, it complements it.[159] If my assessment is correct, therefore, the EU treaties already provide backing to possible legislative initiatives by the EU institutions in the field of economic policy. Despite the original asymmetry of EMU, subsequent treaty amendments have expanded the capacity of EU institutions, and should be interpreted as empowering the Union to conduct a policy of steering the economy, supporting growth and securing employment.[160] As a result, the main obstacle toward EU legislative action in the field of economic policy appears to be a political, rather, than a legal one.

In fact, as the recent example of European Fund for Strategic Investments (EFSI) makes clear, when the political will exists, the EU can commence an investment program to stimulate the economy. In light of the stagnating conditions of the European economy, the new President of the European Commission committed in Summer 2014 to launch a major economic plan to kick-start investment, and boost growth and jobs in the EU.[161] Given the strong political backing, in 2015 the EP and the Council quickly reached an agreement following the ordinary legislative procedure on the adoption of a regulation establishing the EFSI.[162] As far as the legal bases of the regulation is concerned, the European Commission and the two houses of the EU legislature indicated Articles 172, 173, 175(5), and 182(1) TFEU, concerning respectively the treaty chapters dealing with trans-European networks, industry, economic, social and territorial cohesion, and research and technological development. Although the so-called Juncker plan has been criticized as an exercise in smoke and mirrors, which

[157] See Gian Luigi Tosato, "The EMU: Evolution and Legal Challenges," paper presented at the Conference "Constitutional Challenges of the European Economic and Monetary Union," Villa Vigoni, Como, June 5, 2015 (on file with author).

[158] See also Protocol No. 25 on the exercise of shared competences [2012] OJ C326/307.

[159] See also George Anderson, *Fiscal Federalism: A Comparative Introduction* (OUP 2010).

[160] See also Art 3(3) TEU (stating that the Union shall "work for the sustainable development of Europe based on balanced economic growth and price stability, [...] full employment and social progress").

[161] See European Commission President-elect Jean-Claude Juncker, "A New Start for Europe: My Agenda for Jobs, Growth and Democratic Change," Speech at the European Parliament, Strasbourg, July 15, 2014.

[162] See Regulation (EU) No. 2015/1017 of the European Parliament and the Council of June 25, 2015 on the European Fund for Strategic Investments, the European Investment Advisory Hub, and the European Investment Project Portal and amending Regulations (EU) No. 1291/2013 and (EU) No. 1316/2013, OJ [2015] L169/1.

failed to mobilize real new resources and rather re-branded existing expenditures in the hope of attracting private investments with a multiplier effect of 1:15, the EFSI pursues the typical aims of a stimulus package, and certainly falls within what in any member state would normally be labeled as the exercise of economic policy.[163]

With that said, it is clear that the constitutional empowerment to legislate in the area of economic policy also meets some limitations. On the one hand, the competence of the EU in given sectors is explicitly barred by the treaties. For example, Article 153(5) TFEU prevents the EU from adopting measures dealing with "pay, the right of association, the right to strike or the right to impose lockouts"—with effects on the capacity of the EU to adopt a regulation on the exercise of collective action at the transnational level.[164] Pursuant to the principle of conferral, the competences of the EU are not infinite.[165] Nevertheless, the limitations on the scope of EU action should be interpreted restrictively. This is consistent with what Robert Schütze has defined as the shift from dual to cooperative federalism in EU law-making: whereas in the early phases of EU integration the treaties sought to strictly divide powers between the states and the EU, the contemporary reality is one in which competences are mostly *shared* between the states and the EU.[166] In this context, the golden star is represented by the principle of subsidiarity.[167] On the other hand, the material means of the EU to undertake a fully fledged economic policy are limited since the current budget of the EU is negligible when measured vis-à-vis the economic output of the EU as a whole.[168] To address this state of affairs, in Chapter 4 I have proposed to endow the EU (or the Eurozone) with a fiscal capacity. What is clear, however, is that a successful EU economic policy depends on the capacity of the EU institutions to acquire the financial resources necessary to attain their objectives.

In conclusion, a first challenge to greater legislative involvement in the field of European economic governance has to do with the asymmetry of EMU. Nevertheless, a constitutionally-oriented reading of the EU treaties suggests that possible steps can be taken after the entry into force of the Lisbon Treaty to overcome the asymmetry of EMU. On the one hand, it is plausible to maintain that member states face limits in their ability to act outside the framework of EU law, because this would upset the constitutional balance introduced by the Lisbon Treaty, which vests the EP with the institutional privilege to be involved

163 See Daniel Gros, "The Juncker Plan: From €21 to €315 billion, through smoke and mirrors", CEPS Commentaries, November 27, 2014.

164 See further on this Federico Fabbrini, "Europe in Need of a New Deal: On Federalism, Free Markets and the Right to Strike" (2012) 43 Georgetown Journal of International Law 1175.

165 See Loïc Azoulai, "Introduction: The Question of Competence," in Loïc Azoulai (ed), *The Question of Competence in the European Union* (OUP 2014), 1, 6.

166 Robert Schütze, *From Dual to Cooperative Federalism: The Changing Structure of European Law* (OUP 2009).

167 See Federico Fabbrini, "The Principle of Subsidiarity," in Robert Schütze and Takis Tridimas (eds), *Oxford Principles of European Union Law* (OUP 2016).

168 See Henrik Enderlein et al, "The EU Budget: How Much Scope for Institutional Reform?," ECB Occasional Paper Series No. 27/2005.

in law-making. On the other hand, it seems possible to argue that the EU institutions effectively enjoy relevant powers to intervene in the field of economic policy, because—notwithstanding the lack of an explicit competence in this regard—the Lisbon Treaty has endowed them with extensive authority to regulate policy areas which have a clear macro-economic dimension. Several caveats must accompany these statements. The member states are prevented from acting outside EU law whenever the EU has competence (including shared competences). And EU competences are not unlimited. Moreover, it is clear that the EU institutions would be able to run a meaningful economic policy only to the extent that they are also endowed with the budgetary resources to do so—hence the importance of a fiscal capacity advanced in Chapter 4. Nevertheless, carving a meaningful space for law-making at EU level in the economic field is an important step toward better EMU governance. Asymmetry constitutes the key substantive challenge toward greater legislative involvement in EMU. Other challenges, instead, have to do with the institutional dimension, and the working of the EP and the Council—and I shall now turn to analyzing these.

4. The Challenge of Representation

Article 10 TEU proclaims that "[c]itizens are directly represented at Union level in the European Parliament"—and in Chapter 4 I have emphasized that this constitutes a strong claim in favor of involving the EP in decision-making about EU taxation. Nevertheless, the representative function of the EP remains under challenge.[169] First, a traditional criticism of the EP is that this institution is *under-representative*, since it fails to reflect the democratic principle of "one head, one vote" by introducing the criterion of degressive proportionality in the apportionment of EP seats among EU member states. Second, as of late, the EP has been subject to the opposite challenge. Due to the increasing autonomization of the Eurozone vis-à-vis the EU as a whole, the EP has been criticized for being *over-representative*, to the extent that it empowers every MEP—including those elected in non-Eurozone countries—to vote on issues which concern exclusively the Eurozone. In addition, there is increasingly a third challenge that the EP is facing as a result of the institutional transformations which are taking place in the EU system of governance. This challenge regards the quality of representation, and stems from the electoral rules for EP elections, which privilege proportional representation over governability concerns. In the following three sub-sections, I will devote some attention to each of these aspects. As it will be suggested, the two first criticisms to the function of representation in the EP are not convincing. Nevertheless, the third challenge has bite, and should be addressed in order to ensure a greater role for the EP in the governance of EMU.

[169] See also Richard Bellamy and Dario Castiglione, "Three Models of Democracy, Political Community and Representation in the EU" (2013) 20 Journal of European Public Policy 206.

A. Under-representation

First, a conventional argument made against the EP is that it is under-representative because of the principle of degressive proportionality. The champion of this view has been the German Bundesverfassungsgericht.[170] Pursuant to Article 14 TEU no member state can have more than 96 seats in the 751-seat EP, and no member state can have less than six, which means that the ratio between state population and state MEPs is not uniform throughout the EU.[171] In its decision on the Lisbon Treaty the Bundesverfassungsgericht ruled that the EP cannot be a truly representative body, because—due to the principle of degressive proportionality—a MEP elected in Germany (the most populous member state) would represent roughly 12 times more citizens than a MEP elected in Malta (the least populous one).[172] Nevertheless, this criticism does not appear to be convincing. Leaving aside the fact that, even with a corrected proportional apportionment of seats among the member states, Germany withholds a predominant influence on the composition of the EP, so that the view of the Bundesverfassungsgericht stands on shaky moral grounds,[173] the criticism is also unsustainable in constitutional terms. The EU is a Union of states and citizens.[174] In such a regime, the representation of citizens must take into account territorial boundaries.[175] Therefore, unless the EU becomes a unitary state—a development that the Bundesverfassungsgericht would not endorse[176]—it is appropriate to design constituencies for the EP elections along state lines.[177]

Comparative law helps to make the point.[178] For instance, in the US—which is no doubt a much more federalized regime than the EU[179] the constituencies

[170] BVerfG 123, 267 (2009).

[171] For a discussion of the composition of the EP and the evolution in the apportionment of seats after the entry into force of the Lisbon Treaty see also Federico Fabbrini, "La composizione del Parlamento Europeo dopo il Trattato di Lisbona" (2011) 61 Rivista trimestrale di diritto pubblico 787.

[172] BVerfG 123, 267 (2009) paras 284–5 (criticizing the fact that as "a result the weight of the vote of a citizen from a Member State with a small population may be about twelve times the weight of the vote of a citizen from a Member State with a large population.").

[173] See further on this Chapter 3.

[174] Art 10 TEU.

[175] See Van Gerven (n 39).

[176] See Russ Miller, "Germany vs. Europe: The Principle of Democracy in German Constitutional Law and the Troubled Future of European Integration" (2013) 54 Virginia Journal of International Law 1.

[177] Unitary states may also divide their territory into sub-national constituencies for the purpose of electing representatives. See e.g., Arts 4 and 13, §1 Election Law (Jap.)(stating that 300 of the 480 members of the Diet are to be elected in single-member districts, to be drawn by an administrative council on the basis of the principle that the maximum disparity in the number of people in the constituents of each district be under two). However, in this case the sub-division of the national territory serves a purely administrative function. Instead, in federalism-based systems, the drawing of electoral districts reflects the fact that the states have a constitutional status, so it finds an insurmountable limit in the perimeters of the states. See e.g., Art 24 Commonwealth of Australia Const. Act (defining the formula to calculate the number of members of the House of Representatives to be chosen in each state, and indicating that as a minimum each original state shall have at least five representatives).

[178] See also Johannes Pollak et al, "Citizens' Weight of Vote in Selected Federal Systems," Study commissioned by the European Parliament Constitutional Affairs Committee, April 2011, PE 453.168, 53.

[179] See Daniel Halberstam, "Federalism: Theory, Policy, Law," in Michel Rosenfeld and András Sajó (eds), *The Oxford Handbook of Comparative Constitutional Law* (OUP 2012), 576.

for the House of Representatives are still based on state lines. Pursuant to the US Constitution every US state is entitled to elect *at least* one representative regardless of its population.[180] Because federal law sets the number of representatives at 435, the result is that the ratio between the population of a state and the representative(s) of that state is not uniform across the US. In fact, as it has been pointed out, in the US House of Representatives "the large states—those with districts approximating the national average—also are relatively underrepresented vis-à-vis the overrepresented small states."[181] Moreover, while the degree of malapportionment in the EP is higher than that existing in the US House of Representatives, it is actually lower than that existing in other federal systems' lower houses of parliaments: for instance, Argentina's lower legislative house provides a much higher over-representation of less populated districts in proportion to more populated ones,[182] because the 1853 Argentine Constitution provided that founding Provinces could not have less deputies than those foreseen at the time of its enactment,[183] and the number of seats in the Cámara de Diputados de la Nácion is capped by law at 256.[184]

In addition, the alleged under-representativeness of the EP should be assessed by taking into account also the (mal)apportionment in the EU upper house: the Council. Federal systems based on asymmetrical size, in fact, need to strike a balance between large states and small states, and they conventionally achieve this by over-representing the smaller member units in the upper house.[185] Yet, when seen in comparative perspective, the Council of the EU appears to be characterized by a fairly limited degree of malapportionment. Until November 2014, in fact, member states were attributed in the Council a number of votes weighted on the basis of population, in a range going from 29 votes, for Germany, France, the United Kingdom (UK), and Italy, to three votes, for Malta.[186] Furthermore, from November 2014, the Council decides on the basis of a double majority: as indicated in Section 2, a qualified majority in the Council requires support by 55% of the member states, representing at least 65% of the EU population.[187] Under both regulations, the Council recognizes much more power to the larger member states than is the case, for example, in the US Senate, where each state has two seats,[188] the Brazilian Senado, where each federal unit has three seats,[189] or the Swiss Conseil des Etats, where cantons have either one or two

[180] Art I, Sec. 2, cl 3 US Const.

[181] Jeffrey Ladewig and Matthew Jasinski, "On the Causes and Consequences of and Remedies for Interstate Malapportionment of the US House of Representatives" [2008] Perspectives on Politics 89, 91.

[182] See also Jonathan Rodden, "Strength in Numbers? Representation and Redistribution in the European Union" (2002) 3 European Union Politics 151, 155.

[183] See Art 46 Const. Arg.

[184] I am grateful to Pablo Riberi for making this point clear to me.

[185] See generally Ronald Watts, *Comparing Federal Systems in the 1990s* (McGill-Queen's UP 1996).

[186] Art 3 Protocol No. 36 on transitional provisions [2012] OJ C326/323.

[187] See Art 16 TEU.

[188] See Art I, Sec. 3, cl 1 US Const. (entitling each state to two senators).

[189] See Art 46 Const. Braz. (entitling each state and the federal district to three senators).

votes.[190] Hence, considering all the above, the representativeness of the EP as the house of the EU citizens cannot be plausibly challenged by speaking about under-representation.

B. Over-representation

Second, the EP has been recently challenged for being allegedly over-representative. Since the eruption of the Euro-crisis, the Eurozone member states have been pressed to increasingly integrate policies to manage their economic interdependencies.[191] Yet, because many of these measures essentially concerned the Eurozone, rather than the EU as a whole, several observers have critically argued that the EP—an institution in which seat MEPs elected in the 28 EU member states—is not an adequate forum to manage EMU matters, which concern only 19 EU countries.[192] In its most radical form, the criticism has resulted in a call for the establishment of a new Euro Assembly, perhaps to be indirectly elected by national parliaments.[193] Less dramatically, others have suggested that the EP could reorganize itself to ensure a flexible composition, so that only MEPs from Eurozone member states participate and vote in those procedures which concern only the EMU.[194] So far, the EP has resisted any call in this direction. In particular, in December 2013, the EP has affirmed that "any formal differentiation of parliamentary participation rights with regard to the origin of [MEPs] represents discrimination on grounds of nationality, the prohibition of which is a founding principle of the [EU], and violates the principle of equality of Union citizens as enshrined in Article 9 TEU."[195] Although it has been suggested that the EP resistance against differentiated representation will increase its marginalization from EMU governance,[196] in my view the position of the EP is constitutionally sound.

Before explaining why, however, let me point out that from a comparative perspective the challenge of representation faced by the EP as a result of Eurozone integration is peculiar, but not unprecedented. Rather, it reminds of a challenge that for some years now has affected the form of government of the UK, and which

[190] See Art 150 Const. Switz. (entitling smaller cantons to elect one senator and larger cantons to elect two).

[191] See also Jean-Claude Piris, *The Future of Europe: Towards a Two-Speed EU?* (CUP 2011).

[192] See for a discussion of this problem Deirdre Curtin and Cristina Fasone, "Differentiated Representation: Is a Flexible European Parliament Desirable?" in Bruno De Witte et al (eds), *Between Flexibility and Disintegration: The State of EU Law Today* (Elgar 2016).

[193] See especially Jean Arthuis, "L'avenir de la zone euro: l'integration politique ou le chaos," Report commissioned by the French Prime Minister, March 1, 2012.

[194] See e.g., Dutch Council of State, Report presented upon request for information, on the embedding of democratic control in the reform of economic governance in Europe to combat the economic and financial crisis, by the President of the Senate of the States General, No. W01.12.0457/I, January 18, 2013.

[195] European Parliament Resolution (n 60) para 29.

[196] See Renaud Dehousse, "Is the 'Community Method' still Relevant?," in "Challenges of Multi-Tier Governance in the European Union," Study commissioned by the European Parliament Constitutional Affairs Committee, March 2013, PE 474.438, 85, 93.

is generally known as the "West Lothian Question."[197] Following devolution, citizens in Scotland, Wales, and Northern Ireland have been granted the right to vote in regional assemblies that legislate on policy matters affecting these regions. Yet, MPs elected in Scotland, Wales, and Northern Ireland are still allowed to vote in Westminster (the UK Parliament) on laws that only affect *England*.[198] According to some accounts, this solution has skewed the principle of representation.[199] So far, no measure has been adopted to change the status quo,[200] but following the rejection of the Scottish secession referendum in September 2014, the issue has returned to the table. Given the willingness of all the main UK political parties to devolve additional powers to the Scottish legislative assembly,[201] British Prime Minister Cameron re-launched the idea of "English votes for English laws"[202] as a way to compensate England.[203] Nevertheless, several observers have criticized the excessive emphasis that is now being put on the "West Lothian Question," in particular considering that in the UK House of Commons, the seats given to MPs elected in England amount to 533 out of 650.[204]

Regardless of how the UK constitutional debate will resolve, there are in my view convincing arguments to resist differentiation in the EP. On the one hand, establishing a separate Eurozone Assembly would complicate even further the EU institutional architecture—a development which EU citizens would not welcome.[205] Furthermore, if this new Assembly were to be staffed by national parliamentarians, it would turn back the clock to the pre-1979 era.[206] On the other hand, also endowing only Eurozone MEPs of voting rights would be problematic. First, because representatives of the core are many more than representatives of the periphery, it is important to make sure the latter are not excluded.[207] MEPs

[197] See generally Paul Bowers, "The West Lothian Question," House of Commons Library, January 18, 2012, SN/PC/2586 (explaining that the question draws its name from Tam Dalyell, the MP for West Lothian, who first raised it).

[198] See Robert Hazell, "The English Question" (2006) 36 Publius 37.

[199] See e.g., Conservative Democracy Task Force, "Answering the Question: Devolution, the West Lothian Question and the Future of the Union," July 2008, available at <https://devolutionmatters.files.wordpress.com/2014/09/answering_the_west_lothian_question2.pdf> (last accessed November 29, 2014).

[200] See also McKay Commission, Report of the Commission on the Consequences of Devolution for the House of Commons March 25, 2013, available at <http://tmc.independent.gov.uk> (last accessed November 29, 2014).

[201] See Smith Commission, Report for further Devolution of Power to the Scottish Parliament, November 27, 2014, available at <https://www.smith-commission.scot/wp-content/uploads/2014/11/The_Smith_Commission_Report-1.pdf> (last accessed November 29, 2014).

[202] See Patrick Wintour, "David Cameron Raises West Lothian Question after Scotland Vote: 'English Votes for English Laws'," *The Guardian*, September 19, 2014.

[203] See critically Andrew Adonis, "An English Parliament?," *The Guardian*, September 19, 2014.

[204] See in particular Editorial, "Playing Politics with the British Constitution," *The Financial Times*, October 14, 2014, 12 (stating that "because [England] holds 84 per cent of the UK population, [it] must be generous about the voice it affords to Scotland, Wales and Northern Ireland.").

[205] See ceteris paribus, Laeken Declaration (n 138) (calling for a simplification of the EU institutional system).

[206] See David Marquand, *Parliament for Europe* (Jonathan Cape 1979) (criticizing the system in which MEPs were elected by national parliaments and making the case in favor of EP direct elections).

[207] See also Damjan Kukovec, "Law and the Periphery" (2015) 21 European Law Journal 406.

elected in the Eurozone amount to 492 out of 751. In this context, empowering non-Eurozone MEPs to vote just like the others ensures that the minority is involved in decisions that affect the majority.[208] Second, because decisions that affect a core territorial area of a polity often spill-over into the periphery, there is a point in ensuring that representatives of the outer nations have at least a voice in the decision-making process. The EU rules on enhanced cooperation exemplify this concern: Article 329 TFEU requires that the EP *as a whole* consents to the use of enhanced cooperation and votes on legislation adopted within the framework of enhanced cooperation. This provision makes sure that citizens of those states which are not parties to the enhanced cooperation have a way to check that the cooperation does not disregard their viewpoint.[209]

Having said that, the fact that the EP should not embrace a flexible composition *ratione monetae*, does not imply that the EP cannot find an internal, pragmatic solution to ensure that Eurozone concerns are duly taken into account. An option outlined in January 2014 by the former (British) MEP chairing the EP Economic and Monetary Affairs (ECON) Committee, in agreement with the other senior members of the Committee, would be to create a permanent sub-Committee within ECON, specifically tasked to debate Eurozone matters and to refer back to ECON.[210] The EP Rules of procedure permit the appointment of a sub-Committee, subject to the authorization of the Conference of the Presidents.[211] Furthermore, given the consensual nature of decision-making among the main EP parliamentary groups, a political agreement within and among the political group could foresee that the sub-Committee would be composed only of Eurozone MEPs. Contrary to the proposals to differentiate the composition of the EP, this option could provide a forum for tailored parliamentary discussion on matters related to the Eurozone, while respecting the institutional integrity of the EP:[212] despite the work of the Eurozone sub-Committee, it would be the ECON Committee—and ultimately the EP's plenary—to vote on EMU issues, thus ensuring the involvement of MEPs who were not elected in Eurozone member states as well.

C. Representation vs. governability

While the arguments against the alleged under-representativeness and over-representativeness of the EP do not withstand a careful scrutiny, there is however

[208] See also Stijn Verhelst, "The Sense and Nonsense of Eurozone Level Democracy," Egmont Royal Institute for International Relations Paper No. 70/2014, 14 (emphasizing also that seven of the nine EU member states who are not yet members of the Eurozone have effectively an obligation to adopt the euro sooner or later, which means that the problem will probably solve by itself).

[209] See Fabbrini (n 115) 197.

[210] See Letter from the Chair and Members of the Economic and Monetary Affairs Committee of the European Parliament to the President of the European Parliament, regarding the structure and modalities with the Parliament for euro area governance in the next legislature, January 23, 2014, available at <http://sylvie-goulard.eu/articles2014/Annex-3a-Chair-s-Announcements-ECON-structure.pdf> (last accessed May 15, 2015).

[211] See Rule 203, EP Rules of Procedure.

[212] See also Fasone (n 54) 168 (emphasizing the "federative attitude" of the EP).

a third challenge of representation which in my view *does* affect the EP—and ought to be considered if the EP is to play a greater role in EU governance. This challenge does not concern the quantity of representation—too little representation vs. too much—but rather its quality. As scholars of institutions have emphasized, any political regime must maximize two conflicting concerns: *representation vs. governability*.[213] On one side, an institutional system should be able to reflect the political preferences of the electorate, and give them adequate representation. On the other, however, an institutional system should be able to govern effectively, and in order to achieve this task may introduce incentives and constraints that channel the electorate's preferences. The mechanism whereby political regimes strike a balance between representation and governability is the electoral law: an electoral system that gives major importance to the issue of representation—for example, by attributing seats in a legislative assembly to political parties in pure proportion to their electoral results—fares badly on the side of governability. Vice versa, an electoral system that is majority-ensuring—for example, through the use of plurality voting, threshold clauses, smaller constituencies or run-offs—improves government stability and efficiency.[214]

The EP is elected through a system of proportional representation (PR)—which is the electoral system that most sacrifices concerns for governability.[215] Technically speaking, there is no single EU electoral system for the EP.[216] Although since the beginning of the process of European integration the EU treaty foresaw the possibility of enacting a uniform law for the election of the MEPs, the words of now Article 223 TFEU have never been put into practice. The 1976 Act concerning the election of the representatives of the EP by direct universal suffrage annexed to Council Decision 76/787,[217] only introduced some common guidelines on the holding of EP elections, but each EU member state is endowed with its domestic law regulating EP elections.[218] Nevertheless, EU member states have all embraced PR for EP elections.[219] In addition, Council Decision 2002/772 has codified the status quo by amending the 1976 Act and effectively mandating PR

[213] See especially Giovanni Sartori, *Comparative Constitutional Engineering* (NYU Press 1994), Augusto Barbera and Carlo Fusaro, *Il governo delle democrazie* (Il Mulino 2001), Maurice Duverger, *Institutions politiques et droit constitutionnel* (PUF 1978).

[214] As famously explained by Maurice Duverger, *Political Parties: Their Organization and Activity in the Modern State* (Wiley 1959), furthermore, the type of electoral law has major implications on the structure of the political parties, with PR rules favoring party fragmentation and rules which instead correct PR favoring majoritarian dynamics.

[215] See Michael Gallagher and Paul Mitchel (eds), *The Politics of Electoral Systems* (OUP 2006).

[216] See David Farrel and Roger Scully, "The European Parliament: One Parliament, Several Modes of Political Representation on the Ground?," in Peter Mair and Jacques Thomassen (eds), *Political Representation and European Union Governance* (Routledge 2011), 36.

[217] Act concerning the election of the representatives of the European Parliament by direct universal suffrage, annexed to Decision 76/787/ECSC, EEC, Euratom [1976] OJ L278/1, as amended.

[218] See European Parliament Office for the Promotion of Parliamentary Democracy, "Electoral Systems: The Link between Governance, Elected Members and Voters," October 2011, available at <http://www.europarl.europa.eu/pdf/oppd/Page_8/Electoral-systems-LR-for-WEB.pdf> (last accessed November 29, 2014).

[219] Ibid.

as the electoral system for EP elections.[220] While Article 2 of the consolidated Act for the election of the EP, as modified by Council Decision 2002/772, allows states to introduce sub-national constituencies, and Article 3 lets states free to have minimum thresholds for the allocation of seats, pursuant to the new Article 1 "[i]n each Member State, members of the European Parliament shall be elected on the basis of proportional representation, using the list system or the single transferable vote."

The consolidated EU Act on EP election is addressed to the member states, and leaves to them the regulation of many aspects of EP elections—a feature which is consistent with a federalism-based arrangement for the EU, and which also characterizes elections for the US Congress.[221] However, the use of PR *within each member state* for EP elections—first emerged in practice and now required in EU law—has had significant effects on the nature of democratic representation in the EU lower house, producing a high degree of party fragmentation and fringe groups' representation.[222] It is true that the majority of the EU member states also use PR for the election of the national legislatures.[223] In fact, PR is constitutionally mandated in countries such as the Netherlands,[224] and Denmark.[225] Nevertheless, the PR system applied for the elections of the EP profoundly differs from the electoral systems in force at the domestic level *in the six largest EU member states*—Germany, France, the UK, Italy, Spain, and Poland—which together account for the election of more than 56% of the MEPs: 421 out of 751. Because of the apportionment of seats in the EP among states pursuant to the principle of degressive proportionality discussed above, small- and medium-sized EU member states elect a limited number of MEPs.[226] In these smaller and medium size countries, therefore, PR elections are subject to implicit electoral constraints—due to the fact that a political party must de facto obtain a significant percentage of the popular votes to obtain a seat.[227] But in the larger EU member states, the mechanics for the election of the EP has significantly diverged from that in place for the election of national legislatures, even where PR is the rule.

[220] Council Decision of June 25 and September 23, 2002, amending the Act concerning the election of the representatives of the European Parliament by direct universal suffrage, 2002/772/EC, Euratom [2002] OJ L283/1.

[221] See Art I, Sec. 4, cl 2 US Const. (stating that "the time, places and manner of holding elections for senators and representatives shall be prescribed in each state by the legislature thereof, but the Congress may at any time by law make or alter such regulations").

[222] See Stefano Bartolini, *Restructuring Europe* (OUP 2005) 331.

[223] See also *Yumak and Sadak v. Turkey* [ECHR] App. No. 10226/03, judgment of July 8, 2008, para 62 (Grand Chamber of the European Court of Human Rights reporting that currently "proportional systems are the most widely used in Europe.")

[224] See Sec 53(1) Const. Nl. (requiring that members of both chambers of Parliament be elected by PR).

[225] See Sec 31(2) Const. Dk. (requiring members of Parliament to be elected by PR, save minor limits).

[226] See text accompanying nn 171–2.

[227] See Camera dei Deputati, Servizio Biblioteca, "Aspetti relative alle modalità di elezione dei rappresentanti al Parlamento europeo nei paesi membri dell'UE," Dossier di documentazione n. 4, September 11, 2014, A.C. 22/XVI.

To begin with, the UK and France do not adopt PR in national elections. The first has traditionally embraced the first-past-the-post system to elect representatives in Westminster.[228] And the second has used since 1958 (except for the election of 1986) a majority system with run offs to elect the Assemblée Nationale.[229] Moreover, even for those large EU member states which do have PR systems at the domestic level, there are relevant differences between the PR rules applying for national elections and those in force for EP elections. In Italy, for example, several rounds of electoral reforms have introduced correctives to the electoral law for the Parlamento to enhance governability:[230] yet, the 1979 electoral law for the EP has always remained based on a pure PR, and until 2009 it did not set any threshold requirement which political parties had to meet to gain a seat in the EP.[231] In Spain, whereas the electoral system for the Congreso de los Diputados is a PR system based on very small constituencies, which de facto creates a majoritarian dynamic,[232] the electoral regime for the EP follows a national-base allocation of seats which has broken the logic of two-party competition characterizing state elections.[233] And a similar situation occurs in Poland: while PR for the election of the Sejm operates in small multi-member constituencies, the country constitutes a single constituency for the purpose of EP elections—even though in both cases a common 5% threshold applies to ensure the rationalization of the voting results.[234]

The case of Germany deserves then special consideration. In this member state the functioning of the national electoral process had traditionally been constrained by the constitutional ban of extremist (Nazi and Communist) parties,[235] and by the existence of a Sperrklausel preventing political parties which did not reach at least 5% of national votes from being represented in the Bundestag.[236] In fact, the German electoral law for the EP also set a Sperrklausel as a condition for representation in the EP. Yet, the German Constitutional Court has step by step dismantled such a threshold, opening the door of the EP to parties which do not pass the standard for representation at the domestic level.[237] First, in 2011, the

[228] See Vernon Bogdanor, "The Constitution and the Party System in the Twentieth Century" (2004) 57 Parliamentary Affairs 717.

[229] See Bertrand Mathieu and Michel Verpeaux, *Droit constitutionnel* (PUF 2004) 457.

[230] See lastly Legge n. 52 del 6 maggio 2015, Disposizioni in materia di elezioni della Camera dei deputati, G.U.R.I. n. 105 dell' 8 maggio 2015 (It.) (introducing an effective majority-ensuring system for the election of the Camera dei Deputati).

[231] See generally Roberto D'Alimonte and Carlo Fusaro (eds), *La legislazione elettorale italiana* (Il Mulino 2008).

[232] See Miguel Martinez Cuadrado, "Bases, Principios y Criterios de la Reforma Electoral Española: Examen Juridico-Constitucional" [1983] Revista de estudios politicos 41.

[233] Compare Art 161 (regulating elections for the Congreso de los Diputados) with Arts 215–17 (regulating elections for the EP in Spain), Ley orgánica del régimen electoral general 5/1985 (Sp.).

[234] Compare Art 196 (introducing a threshold of 5% for national elections) with Art 335 (introducing a 5% threshold applied across the country for EP elections in Poland), Ustawa z dnia 5 stycznia 2011 r.—Kodeks wyborczy (Dz.U. Nr 21, poz.11) (Pl.).

[235] See Samuel Issacharoff, "Fragile Democracies" (2007) 120 Harvard Law Review 1405, 1430.

[236] See Sec 6(6) BundestagWahlGesetz (BwahlG) (Ger.).

[237] See Giacomo Delledonne, "Il *Bundesverfassungsgericht*, il Parlamento europeo e la soglia di sbarramento del 5%: un (altro) ritorno del *Sonderweg*?" [2012] Rivista AIC 1 and Bernd Grzeszick,

Bundesverfassungsgericht declared a 5% Sperrklausel for the EP as inconsistent with the constitutional principle of democratic representation.[238] The Bundestag responded to the decision of the Constitutional Court by enacting a new piece of legislation introducing a lower Sperrklausel of just 3%. But in February 2014, just ahead of the May 2014 EP elections, the Bundesverfassungsgericht struck down the new Sperrklausel as well, arguing that the EP did not perform the function to form a government and thus elections for the EP could not be subject to electoral engineering constraining the voters' choices.[239]

The results of the latest May 2014 EP elections exemplify the implications of this state of affairs.[240] Although voting for EP elections remains influenced by the fact that citizens regard these as "second order elections,"[241] the lack of electoral mechanisms constraining and channeling voters' preferences in EP elections, as opposed to national elections, plausibly played an important role in EP electoral outcomes. In particular, EP elections in France and the UK saw the surge of populist, right-wing parties which are hardly represented in national legislative assemblies, while in Germany, a neo-Nazi party and several other minor German parties have obtained a seat in the EP with as little as 0.6% of the national electoral votes. As a consequence, the EP continues to be characterized today by a high degree of fragmentation—with eight political groups created among MEPs (non-attached MEPs form a ninth group).[242] Moreover, as has been the case since 1979, the EP continues to be managed by a grand coalition between the main center-left and center-right parties—the conservative people's party (EPP) and the socialists and democrats (S&D), jointly with the liberals (ALDE).[243]

As this summary overview of the electoral systems in force in the six largest EU member states reveals, electoral rules for national elections give proper consideration to the need to secure government stability and effectiveness. Instead, the rules set in these member states for EP elections waive the concerns for governability, by introducing quasi-pure PR to elect MEPs. Why is this so? For many years the conventional perception of the EP was that this was a purely representative body—with no governing tasks. Until 1992 the EP had exclusively a consultative role, and although the EP step by step managed to accrue its power, for

"Weil nicht sein kann, was nicht sein darf: Aufhebung der 3%-Sperrklausel im Europawahlrecht durch das BVerfG und dessen Sicht aus dem Europäischen Parlament" [2014] Neue Zeitschrift für Verwaltungsrecht 537.

[238] See BverfGE 2 BvC 4/10, judgment of November 9, 2011.

[239] See BverfGE 2 BvE 2/13, judgment of February 26, 2014.

[240] See European Parliament, *Result of the 2014 European Elections*, available at <http://www.europarl.europa.eu/elections2014-results/en/election-results-2014.html> (last accessed August 7, 2014).

[241] See Karlheinz Reif and Hermann Schmitt, "Nine Second-Order Elections—A Conceptual Framework for the Analysis of European Election Results" (1980) 8 European Journal of Political Research 3.

[242] See also Rule 32, EP Rules of Procedure (stating that a political group shall include as a minimum 25 members coming from at least one-quarter of the member states).

[243] See generally Hix and Høyland (n 34).

many years it was the Cinderella of EU institutions.[244] Nevertheless, as Section 2 has pointed out, things have now changed. Since the Lisbon Treaty, the EP is by default involved in adopting EU legislation, and although there are still areas in which the Council is the only law-maker, the role of the EP is now central in the institutional system of the EU. Despite the view of the Bundesverfassungsgericht, which struck down the Sperrklausel set by the German legislature for the EP elections on the argument that the EP does not have to form a government in the EU,[245] the EP *does govern* the EU—by sharing power with other EU institutions. And it is therefore necessary to raise the question whether the current representative structure of the EP is the most adequate to perform the task.[246]

The EP has shown awareness of this problem, although mostly in connection with its effort to gain control of the appointment of the European Commission.[247] In its resolution of November 2012, the EP affirmed that, in view of the "changing relationship between Parliament and the Commission which will stem [...] from the elections in 2014, [...] reliable majorities in Parliament will be of paramount importance for the stability of the Union's legislative procedures and the good functioning of its executive."[248] In fact, the EP explicitly called the

> Member States to establish in their electoral law, in accordance with Article 3 of the Act concerning the election of the representatives of the Assembly by direct universal suffrage, appropriate and proportionate minimum thresholds for the allocation of seats so as to duly reflect the citizens' choices, as expressed in the elections, while also effectively safeguarding the functionality of Parliament.[249]

The irony of things, of course, is that the EP has neither the responsibility nor the power to change the current state of affairs. As mentioned, the electoral laws for the EP are made by the state legislatures (or state courts), according to guidelines agreed by state governments.[250] Yet, the challenge identified by the EP is a real one—and will arguably grow if the EP moves to the center stage of EMU governance, notably in taking decisions about taxation, as I have proposed in Chapter 4. Although I am aware that rarely the "veil of ignorance"[251] shapes discussions about the design of electoral laws, I am therefore convinced that a serious rethinking of the electoral law for the EP would be a worthwhile effort.

Several options are available to improve governability in the EP[252]—and the EP has recently approved a resolution, calling member states to introduce "an obligatory

[244] See Rittenberger (n 10) 18. [245] See text accompanying nn 238–9.

[246] See also Andrea Gratteri, "Parlamento e Commissione: Il difficile equilibrio fra rappresentanza e governabilità nell'Unione Europea" [2014] La Comunità Internazionale 237.

[247] See further on this Chapter 3.

[248] European Parliament Resolution of November 22, 2012 on the elections to the European Parliament in 2014, P7_TA(2012)0462, para 4.

[249] Ibid.

[250] But see Art 223(1) TFEU (giving the right to the EP to initiate a reform of the EU electoral law).

[251] John Rawls, *A Theory of Justice* (Harvard UP 1971) 118.

[252] See also Olivier Costa, "Quel sont les défis pour le Parlement européen? Législation, contrôle et organization," Study commissioned by the European Parliament Constitutional Affairs Committee, January 2015, PE 510.006.

threshold, ranging between 3% and 5% for the allocation of seats in single-constituency Member States and constituencies in which the lists system is used and which comprise more than 26 seats," which would go a long way toward introducing correctives in EP electoral law.[253] Limiting my analysis here to some procedural issues, a point which deserves emphasis is that, although the member states could autonomously decide to introduce correctives to their electoral laws for the EP to give due weight to governability concerns, a reform of the consolidated EU Act on EP elections is the most suitable mechanism to rationalize representation in the EP. As the example of Germany shows, domestic obstacles may trump efforts to strike a better balance between representation and governability in the EP. Plus a patchwork of different national responses may fault the goal of rationalizing the EP electoral law. If correctives to the electoral system for EP election were set at EU level they would trump resistance by national courts.[254] At the same time, new EU legislation could restrict the application of electoral correctives to those member states which elect a high number of MEPs. Currently only seven out of 28 EU member states are apportioned more than 26 seats in the EP, and member states which elect up to 26 MEPs have de facto internal thresholds which limit the fragmentation of the political system: for mathematical reasons, if there are maximum 26 seats available in an election, a party must obtain between 3% and 5% of the votes in the relevant constituency to receive at least one seat.[255]

According to Article 223(1) TFEU, to enter into force, any amendment to the consolidated EU Act on EP election would need to be approved unanimously by the Council, after obtaining the consent of a majority of MEPs, and incorporated in the legal systems of the EU member states in accordance with their respective constitutional requirements. However, a well-designed reform could create the incentives to overcome these obstacles. If as propsed by the EP an amendment were to introduce electoral correctives which apply only to the seven largest member states which elect more than 26 MEPs, the 21 other smaller EU countries would have few reasons to oppose this. Larger countries, instead, would find a way through this reform to reduce the disparities existing between the electoral regime for EP elections and that for national elections, in some cases overcoming the difficulties they have faced at national level to reform their electoral laws. Plus, some state governments would likely subscribe to a reform that chills the boomerang effect that party fragmentation and the rise of fringe groups in EP elections has so far produced in national elections. And the EP—or the largest political groups within it—would benefit from a reform that fosters the simplification of the political spectrum.[256]

[253] European Parliament Resolution of November 11, 2015 on the reform of the electoral law of the European Union, P8_TA(2015)0395, para 7.

[254] See further Federico Fabbrini, "After the OMT Case: The Supremacy of EU Law as the Guarantee of the Equality between the Member States" (2015) 16 German Law Journal 1003 (arguing that EU law inequivocally trumps national law).

[255] See text accompanying nn 226–7.

[256] See further Federico Fabbrini, "Representation in the European Parliament: Of False Problems and Real Challenges" (2015) 75 Zeitschrift für ausländisches öffentliches Recht und Völkerrecht 823 (discussing incentives for reform but also cautioning on the effect that these would have on the party system).

In conclusion, while much talk still surrounds the role of the EP as the institution representing the EU citizens, the main challenge facing the EP may be one of electoral law. Despite the old claim against the under-representativeness of the EP, and the new preoccupation with its alleged over-representativeness, there are solid constitutional arguments to justify the apportionment of seats between the member states based on degressive proportionality, and to ensure the involvement of all MEPs even on decisions which concern only the Eurozone. Nevertheless, the EP is indeed facing a challenge of representation as a result of the PR system for the election of MEPs. While political regimes must reconcile representation with governability, PR heavily sacrifices the latter in the name of the former. In the six largest EU member states, in particular, MEPs are elected through PR regimes which fundamentally differ from the majority-ensuring systems in place for national elections. Yet, it is questionable whether the current representative logic provides the most apt democratic format for an institution which is increasingly involved in the governance of EU affairs, and which aspires to acquire even greater relevance in the area of EMU. A tailored, little-invasive reform of the EP electoral law could therefore be considered to strike a better balance between representation and governability in the EU lower house, and pave the way to its greater involvement in EMU governance.

5. The Challenge of Unity

While addressing the challenge of representation constitutes a necessity to ensure a greater involvement of the EP in the post-crisis EU law-making process, the Council also faces a hurdle. As the upper house of the EU legislature—vested by Article 16(1) TEU of the function to adopt EU laws jointly with the EP—the Council is not immune from dis-functionalities which prevent it from successfully fulfiling its role. In particular—while under the current treaty framework the Council continues to exercise non-legislative tasks, coordinating the policies of the member states via the Open Method of Coordination (OMC),[257] and enforcing the SGP[258]—the main challenge affecting the Council as a legislative body is what I dub the challenge of unity. As mentioned in Section 2, the Council is *one institution*, representing the governments of the EU member states at ministerial level. Nevertheless, the Council meets in *different compositions*: depending on the issue to be deliberated, national governments dispatch to Brussels the minister in charge of that specific portfolio at domestic level. The original logic of this solution was a functional one.[259] Rather than simply having ministers of foreign affairs deliberate, states realized that it was more productive if negotiations in the Council

[257] See Kenneth Armstrong, *Governing Social Inclusion: Europeanization Through Policy Coordination* (OUP 2010).

[258] See Martin Heipertz and Amy Verdun, *Ruling Europe: The Politics of the Stability and Growth Pact* (CUP 2011).

[259] See Pierre Pescatore, *Le droit de l'intégration* (reprinted ed. Bruylant 2005).

occurred between the competent line ministers: for example, finance ministers when deliberations concerned budgetary issues, justice ministers on justice issues, defense ministers on defense issues and so on. As a result of this, the configurations of the Council have grown over time, following the expansion of the legislative competences of the EU.[260] Nevertheless, the multiplication of the Council formations has led to an inevitable problem of fragmentation, and starting in the 1990s mounting criticisms have raised against the functioning of the Council.

A. The fragmentation of the Council

Two downsides are associated with the lack of unity in the Council. Firstly, the work of the Council is repeatedly described as lacking consistency, since the various Council formations operate in parallel to each other, and with only very limited coordination between them.[261] Hence, even in files which are clearly overlapping—for example economic policy and social policy—the ability of the various formations of the Council to take into account each other's work is negligible. Secondly, some of the Council's formations have acquired more weight than others creating relevant imbalances in the policy-mix of the EU. While the Foreign Affairs Council—grouping the foreign affairs' ministers of the member states, now under the chairmanship of the High Representatives for Foreign Affairs[262]—has a reserved role in EU foreign policy, the Economic and Financial Affairs (ECOFIN) Council—the formation grouping the finance ministers—has emerged as the most senior Council configuration.[263] At the same time, since 1997 the ECOFIN Council has been complemented by the creation of the Eurogroup, a body which congresses the finance ministers of the Eurozone states.[264] The Eurogroup, which is now officially recognized by the treaty and is endowed with a semi-permanent president, has no legislative functions.[265] Nevertheless, it effectively works as a powerful sub-committee of the ECOFIN, setting most of the policy initiatives that are adopted by it.[266]

Scholars of EU law and governance have repeatedly emphasized how the EU tends to be more concerned about economic than social issues.[267] During the Euro-crisis, furthermore, the EU social deficit has arguably been dramatized, through the promotion of budgetary policies of fiscal consolidation which have heavily affected the functioning of the welfare state.[268] As Uwe Puetter has argued,

[260] See also Fiona Hayes-Renschaw and Helen Wallace, *The Council of Ministers* (Palgrave MacMillan 1997).

[261] See already European Commission Communication, "European Governance: A White Paper," July 25, 2001, COM(2001)428 final, 25 (stating that he Council "has lost its capacity to give political guidance and arbitrate between sectoral interests.").

[262] See Art 18(3) TEU. [263] See also Puetter (n 49) 155.

[264] See European Council Conclusions, December 12–13, 1997, para 44.

[265] See Protocol No. 14 on the Eurogroup [2012] OJ C326/283.

[266] See Uwe Puetter, *The Eurogroup* (Manchester UP 2006).

[267] See e.g., Stefano Giubboni, *Social Rights and Market Freedoms in the European Constitution: A Labour Law Perspective* (CUP 2009).

[268] See Claire Kilpatrick and Bruno De Witte (eds.), "Social Rights in Times of Crisis in the Eurozone," European University Institute Department of Law Working Paper No. 5/2014.

however, the weakness of social policy in the EU is also the result of an imbalance between Council formations: the Employment, Social Policy, Health and Consumer Affairs (EPSCO) Council, which is now in charge of social affairs, is much less prominent than the ECOFIN Council, with the result that the latter has more power to shape the EU agenda than the former.[269] In fact, in the non-legislative context of the European Semester, a framework in which the EU member states coordinate their economic policies with the aim to ensure greater EMU convergence,[270] the Employment and Social Protection Committees—two EPSCO preparatory committees—have complained that EU policy-making "needs to work in a more balanced way"[271] and claimed that "the EPSCO and ECOFIN Council formations must have primary responsibility for its implementation on the basis of an equitable partnership."[272] Concerns for the weaknesses of social aspects in the legislative activities of the Council have also been emphasized.[273]

To address the challenge of unity in the work of the Council, the member states have attempted to adopt a number of reforms. A first strategy has been to progressively reduce the number of Council configurations.[274] While at its maximum in 1996 the Council had 22 formations, the Rules of Procedure adopted by the Council in 2000 brought this number down to 16,[275] and in 2002 the heads of state and government of the EU member states congressed in the European Council reduced it further to nine.[276] Today, the Rules of Procedure adopted by the Council in 2009 list 10 official configurations of the Council;[277] and pursuant to Article 16(6) TEU the European Council may adopt a decision modifying this list.[278] Nevertheless, the reduction of the Council configurations has not

[269] Uwe Puetter, "European Council and Council Leadership in EU Socio-Economic Governance: Asymmetric Institutional Development and the Problem of Cross-Sectorial Policy Coordination," paper presented at the workshop "The European Semester and the New Architecture of EU Socio-Economic Governance," UvA, Amsterdam, April 11, 2014 (on file with author).

[270] See Francesco Costamagna, "The Impact of Stronger Economic Policy Co-Ordination on the European Social Dimension: Issues of Legitimacy," in Federico Fabbrini et al (eds), *The Constitutionalization of European Budgetary Constraints* (Hart Publishing 2014), 359.

[271] Employment and Social Protection Committees, Joint Opinion "Europe 2020 Strategy: Mid-term Review, including the evaluation of the European Semester," October 3, 2014, Doc. 13809/14, para 17.

[272] Ibid para 18.

[273] See also Government of France and Government of Germany, "Contribution sur l'Union Economique et Monétaire," May 2015 (expressing support for a development "de la base sociale de l'Union économique et monétaire").

[274] See Bernard Steunenberg, "Coordinating Sectoral Policymaking: Searching for Countervailing Mechanisms in the EU Legislative Process," CESifo Working Paper No. 888/2003.

[275] Council Decision 2000/396/EC, ECSC, Euratom of June 5, 2000 adopting the Council's Rules of Procedure [2000] OJ L149.

[276] European Council Conclusions, June 21–2, 2002, SN 200/02.

[277] Council Decision 2009/937/EU of December 1, 2009 adopting the Council's Rules of Procedure [2009] OJ L325/35, Annex 1 (listing the following 10 Council's configurations: 1. General Affairs, 2. Foreign Affairs, 3. Economic and Financial Affairs, 4. Justice and Home Affairs, 5. Employment, social policy, health, and consumer affairs, 6. Competitiveness—internal market, industry, and research, 7. Transport, telecommunication and energy, 8. Agriculture and Fisheries, 9. Environment, 10. Education, youth, and culture).

[278] See European Council Decision 2010/594/EU of September 16, 2010 amending the list of Council configurations [2010] OJ L263/12 (reaffirming the list of Council configurations

really worked as expected. To begin with, the recognition of a limited number of Council configurations has implied that some formations effectively continue to operate with sub-formations, since the breadth of the policy fields covered still requires the involvement of different line ministers, with well-known coordination problems.[279] In particular, the EPSCO Council is a mega-formation with three legs: employment, social affairs, and equal opportunity. So even if technically the EPSCO Council is one, the ministers meeting in it depend on the file to be discussed, and are rarely the same.[280] As a result of the creation of heterogeneous Council formations, the disparity between configurations has continued, with cohesive formation such as ECOFIN playing a greater role than dis-homogenous ones such as EPSCO.[281]

A second strategy embraced by the EU member states to address the challenge of unity has been to strengthen the role of the General Affairs Council (GAC).[282] In the run-up to the Lisbon Treaty, member states decided to entrust to it a key coordinating task.[283] In fact, GAC is one of the few Council configurations explicitly recognized in the text of the treaty. Pursuant to Article 16(6) TEU, GAC "shall ensure consistency in the work of the different Council configurations. It shall prepare and ensure the follow-up to meetings of the European Council." And according to the current Rules of Procedure of the Council, GAC "shall be responsible for overall coordination of policies, institutional and administrative questions, horizontal dossiers which affect several of the [EU]'s policies [...] and any dossier entrusted to it by the European Council, having regard to operating rules for the [EMU]."[284] Nevertheless, as it has been observed, GAC has failed to fulfil its mandate.[285] A possible explanation for this has to do with its composition: in principle, GAC should bring together the EU affairs ministers of the member states, but often these are junior ministers in national governments. Moreover, because GAC does not debate substantive issues, but mostly assesses the activities of the other Council's formations, ministers have limited incentives to attend, and frequently dispatch permanent representatives (i.e., state ambassadors based in Brussels). As a result of this, GAC has very limited political weight. Hence, even after the entry into force of the Lisbon Treaty the Council continues to face a challenge of unity.[286]

set in the Council Rules of Procedure, but changing the name of two compositions as follows: 6. Competitiveness—internal market, industry, research, and space; 10. Education, youth, culture, and sport).

[279] Puetter (n 269) 22. [280] Ibid 23. [281] Ibid 25.

[282] See already European Council Conclusions, December 10–11, 1999, Annex III (stating that GAC's "central responsibility for general horizontal issues, including overall policy coordination, means that it will have to manage an increasingly complex external and internal agenda, dealing with major multidisciplinary and interpillar dossiers.").

[283] See Jean-Claude Piris, *The Lisbon Treaty: A Legal and Political Analysis* (CUP 2010) 209.

[284] Art 2(2) Council Rules of Procedure.

[285] See Ignacio Molina, "The Role of the General Affairs Council Revisited in Light of the Experience of 18 Months with the Lisbon Treaty," Real Istituto Elcano Working Paper No. 105/2011.

[286] Ibid.

To address this state of affairs, a third bold strategy had been advanced at the time of the European Constitutional Convention.[287] Following a proposal articulated by the Vice-President of the Convention Giuliano Amato, it was suggested that a special composition of the Council, exclusively dedicated to the job of legislating, ought to be created.[288] The bulk of the proposal was that, while different Council configurations could remain in place for subject-specific policy-coordination, only a Legislative Affairs Council—grouping the delegates of the national governments in charge of EU affairs—would be empowered to pass bills jointly with the EP.[289] This idea would have effectively solved the challenge of unity, with its related problems of incoherence and imbalance between the Council's configurations. It would have created an upper legislative chamber in which the representatives of the EU member states could secure the coordination between the various legislative files, balance the issues at stake in different substantive areas, and strike deals.[290] In addition, it would have increased the ability of national parliaments to control the action of national representatives in the Council, by centralizing accountability within a single person charged to vote on EU legislation on behalf of the state.[291]

Nevertheless, the proposal of a Legislative Affairs Council advanced by the Convention was rejected by the member states in the ensuing intergovernmental conference.[292] While the main opposition to the proposal came (unsurprisingly) from national ministers, the heads of state and governments of the EU also disliked the idea of an institution which would concentrate significant law-making power.[293] Because according to the proposal the members of the Legislative Affairs Council would have been composed of ministers specialized in EU affairs, prime ministers and presidents feared that these ministers would come to wield significant autonomy from them; and ultimately, that they could become a threat to their power and status at the domestic level.[294] Scholars, in fact, have pointed out how national ministers sitting in the Council are progressively Europeanized:[295] ministers develop personal bonds with each other, and strategically seek to mutually support each other—also vis-à-vis their national colleagues and constituencies. Often decisions reached by competent ministers in Brussels are then presented in national capitals as a fait accompli, with limited or no leeway for prime ministers, or other portfolios' ministers, to re-open the negotiations. This is particularly true for the ECOFIN Council, and finance ministers have become prominent players at the domestic level—often in competition with the prime minister—due to their

[287] See Jean-Claude Piris, *The Constitution for Europe: A Legal Analysis* (CUP 2006) 109.

[288] See also Ben Crum, "Tailoring Representative Democracy in the European Union: Does the European Constitution Reduce the Democratic Deficit?" (2005) 11 European Law Journal 452, 461.

[289] See Art 23 Draft Treaty Establishing a Constitution for Europe, July 18, 2003.

[290] I am grateful to Giuliano Amato for making clear this point to me.

[291] See Crum (n 288) 461.

[292] See Paolo Ponzano, "Les institutions de l'Union," in Giuliano Amato et al (eds), *Genesis and Destiny of the European Constitution* (Bruylant 2007), 439, 459.

[293] See Crum (n 288) 462. [294] See Piris (n 287) 110.

[295] See generally Christopher Bickerton, *European Integration: From Nation States to Member States* (OUP 2012).

involvement in decision-making at EU level on the key national deficit and debt targets.[296]

In the settlement reached by the Lisbon Treaty, therefore, the heads of state and government of the EU member states worked to reaffirm their preeminence in the EU decision-making system[297]—and while they set aside the proposal for a Legislative Affairs Council, they entrenched their seniority vis-à-vis their ministers who meet in the various Council configurations. According to Article 15 TEU, the European Council "shall define the general political directions and priorities" of the EU, and based on Article 16 TEU the Council is tasked to follow up on the European Council's requests. Moreover, at the apex of the Euro-crisis the heads of state and government of the Eurozone member states took steps to affirm their position in the governance of EMU, reining in the autonomy of the ECOFIN Council, and of the Eurogroup.[298] In particular, the Fiscal Compact created a new forum, the Euro Summit, endowed with a semi-permanent President, in which the heads of state and government would meet, jointly with the President of the Commission and the President of the ECB.[299] And it clearly established a vertical hierarchy between the Euro Summit (grouping prime ministers and presidents) and the Eurogroup (grouping finance ministers) by stating that "[t]he body charged with the preparation and follow up to the Euro Summit meetings shall be the Eurogroup and its President may be invited to attend such meetings for that purpose."[300]

B. The integration of the Council and the European Council

As the previous sub-section pointed out, the challenge of unity traditionally burdening the Council has so far remained unanswered. Because of the fragmentation between the Council's configurations, the ability of the various formations to coordinate their work—and the possibility of ministers to strike compromises through horse-trading, where vote in support of a bill in a given policy area is rewarded with future support in another policy area—remains limited.[301] Moreover, by establishing the European Council as the top forum for decision-making, the treaty drafters

[296] An example of this state of affairs is provided by the repeated tensions which emerged in the system of government of Italy in the decade from 2003 to 2013 between the Prime Minister and the Minister of Finance, on the design of budgetary policy. See on this Tommaso Giupponi, "Il governo nel sistema bipolare," in Augusto Barbera and Tommaso Giupponi (eds), *La prassi degli organi costituzionali* (Bononia UP 2008), 51.

[297] See also Frederic Eggermont, *The Changing Role of the European Council in the Institutional Framework of the European Union* (Intersentia 2012) (tracking the growing role of the EU heads of state and government).

[298] See Dermot Hodson, *Governing the Euro Area in Good Times and Bad* (OUP 2011) ch 3.

[299] See Christian Calliess, "The Governance Framework of the Eurozone and the Need for a Treaty Reform," in Federico Fabbrini et al (eds), *What Form of Government for the European Union and the Eurozone?* (Hart Publishing 2015), 37.

[300] Art 12(4) Fiscal Compact.

[301] See Bernard Steunenberg, "Deciding Among Equals: The Sectoral Councils of the European Union and their Reform," in Manfred Holler et al (eds), *European Governance* (Mohr Siebeck 2003), 1.

created strong incentives for national ministers to send complex legislative files upwards to the table of the EU heads of state and government. Because of the high political salience of some of the legislative files that the Council debates, national ministers prefer to refer the matter to the European Council, especially when agreement is difficult.[302] In fact, on some issues the treaties explicitly foresee this possibility.[303] As a result of this, an ironic development has occurred: Article 15(1) TEU officially proclaims that the European Council "shall not exercise legislative functions"—with the aim to make the European Council an executive body. Yet, in reality the European Council has increasingly been dragged into the business of legislating.[304] As the challenge of unity continues to affect the Council, the European Council has turned for parts of its activities into a kind of upper legislative chamber, in which heads of state and government ensure consistency between the files discussed by the various Council configurations and strike package deals which are beyond the reach of the separate Council formations.

Otherwise, although the Lisbon Treaty sought to institutionally separate the Council and the European Council,[305] the integration between these two bodies has remained extremely strong—a fact which is perhaps inevitable considering that the same people (read: members of national governments) staff the two institutions.[306] Given this state of affairs, it may be wondered whether a future treaty reform should not simply take stock of this fact and institutionalize the role of the European Council as that of *a high legislative body*, on par with the EP. While the fragmentation of the Council compositions undermines the coherence of EU action, and creates imbalances in the EU policy-mix, the European Council, as a single institution, would constitute a suitable forum in which the member states could strike deals and reach compromises on important legislative initiatives. Needless to say, the Council could continue to ensure preparatory work for the European Council, and it would retain administrative powers, especially in the coordination of member states' policies under the framework of the OMC. Moreover, the European Council could still delegate tasks to the Council, including the adoption of implementing (regulatory) acts. But the Council would

[302] The fact that the Council always seeks to decide by consensus, even when QMV would be possible, has incremented the occurrences in which the Council prefers to moves controversial files upward to the European Council. See on the use of QMV in the Council Stefan van den Bogaert, "Qualified Majority Voting in the Council: First Reflections on the New Rules" (2008) 15 Maastricht Journal of European & Comparative Law 97.

[303] See Arts 82(3) and 83(3) TFEU (allowing a member state to request that a draft directive in the field of criminal procedural law and the approximation of substantive criminal law be referred to the European Council), and Art 48 TFEU (allowing a member state to request that a draft measure in the field of social security be referred to the European Council if it affects important aspects of its social security system).

[304] See Jörg Monar, "The European Union's Institutional Balance of Power after the Treaty of Lisbon," in *The European Union after the Treaty of Lisbon* (Publication Office of the EU 2011), 60, 75 (speaking of the European Council as having the role of a "quasi legislator").

[305] See Art 13 TEU (listing the European Council and the Council as separate institutions).

[306] In fact, the European Council and the Council do not even have separate websites. See <http://www.consilium.europa.eu/en/home/> (last accessed July 2, 2015). Moreover, the Legal Service of the Council represents the European Council in litigation. See *Pringle* (n 85).

be deprived of legislative powers, with this competence now being officially entrusted to the European Council through a formal amendment of the EU treaties. Adopting this solution to address the challenge of unity would make official in law what is often the case in practice.[307] But it would also ensure that EU acts are endowed with the greater legitimacy coming from their explicit approval, not only by (a majority) of MEPs in the EP, but also by (a qualified majority) of national leaders in the European Council.[308]

From a comparative constitutional point of view, the solution I am envisaging here would make the EU system somehow institutionally akin to that of Germany. As is well-known, in the German architecture for law-making a lower house, the Bundestag, representing directly the German citizens, coexists with an upper house, the Bundesrat, which instead represents directly the executives of the 16 Länder that compose the German Federal Republic.[309] Article 51 of the German Basic Law does not specify who exactly represents each of the Länder within the Bundesrat, but a practice is that the Minister-Presidents of the various Länder, that is the chiefs of the Länder governments, lead each Land's delegation, and directly participate in the voting.[310] Of course, the German example is not entirely analogous to what is being proposed here: while in some policy areas the vote of the Bundesrat is necessary for the approval of a bill,[311] in others the Bundesrat can be overridden by the Bundestag.[312] In the EU, instead, the parity between the two houses of the legislature would have to be absolute. In fact, it may even be conceivable for the European Council to play a greater role than the EP—just as, in the US, the Senate (the upper house) has more competences than the House of Representatives (the lower house), for example, in foreign affairs.[313] Yet, the institutional logic which inspires the composition of the Bundesrat could be replicated in the EU: the European Council, as the body representing the top executives of the member states, would be directly involved in approving legislation for the EU, together with the EP.

[307] See e.g., Franklin Dehousse, "The Unified Court on Patents: The New Oxymoron of European Law," Egmont Royal Institute for International Relations Paper No. 60/2013, 25 (explaining the recurrent interventions by the European Council in the drafting of detailed aspects of the EU regulations and related agreement on the creation of a unitary patent system). But see also European Council Conclusions, June 26, 2015, EUCO 22/15 (formalizing a very detailed agreement between the member states in the field of immigration, setting measures for the relocation and resettlement of third country nationals which had been proposed by the European Commission pursuant to Art 78(3) TFEU).

[308] See also Art 235 TFEU (explaining that the President of the European Council and the President of the European Commission do not have voting rights when the European Council decides by vote).

[309] See Arthur Gunlicks, *The Länder and German Federalism* (Manchester UP 2003).

[310] See also BVerfG 2 BvF 1/02, judgment of December 18, 2002 (upholding the practice according to which the Prime Ministers of the Länder lead the vote in the Bundesrat, casting the vote of that Land together and uniformly).

[311] See Art 77 Basic L. Germ. (setting rules on the legislative procedure and distinguishing situations when the approval of legislation by the Bundesrat is required from situations in which it is not).

[312] See also Arthur Gunlicks, "Legislative Competences, Budgetary Constraints and the Reform of Federalism in Germany," in Michael Burgess and Alan Tarr (eds), *Constitutional Dynamics in Federal Systems* (McGill-Queen's UP 2012), 61.

[313] See Art II, Sec 2, cl 2 US Const. (subjecting presidential power to make treaties to the approval by two thirds of the senators).

The proposal to vest in the European Council the function to pass bills jointly with the EP would make explicit to the EU citizens the dual nature of our Union of states and citizens. And it would more clearly separate the realm of legislation (in which the European Council and the EP would be involved) from that of administration and policy coordination (which would be left to the Council and the Commission). Yet, needless to say, the proposal would also imply a significant conceptual re-configuration of the constitutional architecture of the EU as far as the executive power is concerned.[314] EU heads of state and government congressed in the European Council today mainly perceive themselves as the executive branch of the EU.[315] But in my view their performance as a collective government has been meager, and ripe with shortcomings.[316] In fact, in Chapter 6 I will return to this unsatisfactory state of affairs and make the case for an EU constitutional reform strengthening the power and the legitimacy of the President of the European Council, with the aim to transform this institution into the *presidency of the Union*. The idea to formalize the role of the European Council as a kind of EU Senate should therefore be seen within this broader program of institutional reform aimed at creating an effective and accountable executive power in the EU. As I will point out in Chapter 6, while the European Council would lose executive power to the President, it would gain the legislative power of the Council.[317]

Some may of course question the feasibility of attributing to the European Council the role of an upper legislative house. Leaving aside the fact that the reform envisaged here would require a treaty change—with the connected problem of unanimity,[318] on which I will come back to in Chapter 6—a first criticism that can be moved from a policy perspective is that heads of state and government are too busy running their member states to take on this job.[319] Nevertheless, there are arguments to overcome this concern. On the one hand, according to the proposal made in this chapter, ministers in the various Council's configurations (and permanent representatives within COREPER) would continue to undertake preparatory work for the European Council. In fact, the idea to entrust legislative powers to the European Council follows the logic which inspired the idea of a Legislative Affairs Council but takes stock of the fact that only heads of state and

[314] See Paul Craig, "The Locus and Accountability of the Executive in the European Union," in Paul Craig and Adam Tomkins (eds), *The Executive and Public Law: Power and Accountability in Comparative Perspective* (OUP 2006), 315 and Deirdre Curtin, *Executive Power of the European Union* (OUP 2009).

[315] See further on this Chapter 3.

[316] See also Hauke Brunkhorst, "Collective Bonapartism—Democracy in the European Crisis" (2014) 15 German Law Journal 1177 and Nicole Scicluna, "Politicization without Democratization: How the Eurozone Crisis is Transforming EU Law and Politics" (2014) 12 International Journal of Constitutional Law 545.

[317] See also Jürgen Habermas, "Democracy in Europe: Why the Development of the EU into a Transnational Democracy is Necessary and How is it Possible" (2015) 21 European Law Journal 546, 555 (suggesting the re-connection between the European Council and the Council).

[318] See Art 48 TEU.

[319] I am grateful to Paul Craig for making this point clear to me.

government have the political weight to take salient decisions and, in case, strike compromises between the files discussed by sectorial ministers.[320] On the other hand, the reality of Euro-crisis management has revealed how the leaders of the EU member states now meet with great frequency, sometimes as often as every other week,[321] thus suggesting that regular monthly meetings of the European Council acting as a *European Senate* could be envisaged.

A second criticism that could be moved against the proposal to empower the European Council with the legislative function (on par with the EP) is that this could paradoxically increase the degree of technocratic governance in the EU.[322] Because—as just emphasized—heads of state and government are mainly concerned with running their respective member states, there is a risk that they may devote too little attention to their new responsibility as EU legislators, thus leaving to EU bureaucrats wide space to take decisions. Nevertheless, this risk should not be over-estimated. On the one hand, even today technocrats already play a major role in the work of the Council: although political scientists debate about the exact percentage, there is little doubt that many EU legislative measures are agreed upon by lower-level officials and simply rubberstamped by the Council.[323] On the other hand, although bureaucrats would probably continue to play a relevant role even if the European Council were to become the EU upper legislative house, it is plausible that their activity would only focus on questions of low politics, while legislation on questions of high politics would directly trigger the attention of the members of the European Council.[324] With the support of preparatory bodies, prime ministers and presidents could focus their negotiation and deliberation only on major outstanding issues.

In conclusion, the functioning of the EU upper legislative house must also be reconsidered, in view of improving the EU law-making process. The challenge of unity has produced a major lack of coordination in the work of the various Council's formations, and the seniority of several Council's configurations vis-à-vis others have generated relevant imbalances in the policy-mix of the EU. At the same time, both the efforts to reduce the number of Council's formations, and the attempt to strengthen the role of GAC as a clearing house for the activities of the Council, have failed to reached their desired goal. A more audacious idea—the creation of a Legislative Affairs Council—has been discarded at the time of the European Convention as a potential threat to the standing of the EU heads of state and government. As a result of that, however, the European Council has increasingly been called to perform quasi-legislative functions. While only the European Council has the political clout to decide on several legislative

[320] See text accompanying nn 287–300.

[321] See also Dieter Smeets and Marco Zimmerman, "Did the EU Summits Succeed in Convincing the Markets during the Recent Crisis?" (2013) 51 Journal of Common Market Studies 1158.

[322] I am grateful to Jean-Victor Louis for making this point clear to me.

[323] See Frank Häge, "Who Decides in the Council of the European Union?" (2008) 46 Journal of Common Market Studies 533 (discussing impact of preparatory bodies in the work of the Council).

[324] See Ben Rosamond, *Theories of European Integration* (Palgrave MacMillan 2000) (explaining theories of integration and distinction between high politics and low politics).

files, the fragmentation between Council configurations hampers the capacity of state ministers to reach trans-sectorial compromises—making the European Council the real body in which states can strike package deals on legislation. In view of this, this section has proposed de jure condendo to institutionalize a shift in the legislative power from the Council to the European Council. While the Council would retain coordinating tasks in OMC, it would be up to the European Council to act as the EU upper legislative house, passing legislation on par with the EP. Placed in a broader project of EU constitutional reform, the proposal to institutionalize a European Senate would effectively address the challenge of unity, and simultaneously clarify the roles and responsibilities of the EU institutions representing the governments of the member states.

6. Conclusion

This chapter has made the case for greater legislative involvement in EMU governance. During the Euro-crisis member states have repeatedly sidelined the EU law-making regime and adopted measures to address the crisis through intergovernmental agreements outside the EU legal order. But increasing calls have been raised, by policy-makers as well, to ground the governance of EMU in legislation, rather than international treaties. In fact, the use of intergovernmental agreements has given rise to major problems—not least because it opened the floodgate to an unprecedented involvement of national courts in EMU affairs, as I have explained in Chapter 2. To reverse the paradox of judicialization in EMU, the EU should revert to legislation to manage economic affairs. EU legislation is better protected from judicial overreach: but it also enjoys greater legitimacy, given the involvement of the multiple institutions, each representing different interests and constituencies. Yet, as this chapter has emphasized, if the EU law-making process is to play the role it could (or that supporters wish it would) in the EU, some challenges have to be addressed, and its functioning improved. This chapter has sought to examine three such challenges, and to indicate ways to resolve them.

To begin with, if the EU legislative process is to succeed, the asymmetry of EMU has to be dealt with. In the original design of EMU the space for legislative action was limited. Nevertheless, since the entry into force of the Lisbon Treaty constitutional arguments can be advanced to constrain the power of the member states to conclude EMU-related treaties outside EU law, and simultaneously to empower EU institutions to pass EMU-related legislation within EU law. On the one hand, the member states should not be free to act outside the framework of EU law at will. As a constitutional reading of the Lisbon Treaty points out, the EP has been vested with equal legislative rights to the Council, and if the member states adopt agreements outside EU law this effectively means that the Council can bypass the privileged status of the EP. On the other hand, EU institutions should be able to enact legislative measures related to economic policy. As a systematic construction of the Lisbon Treaty reveals, in fact, the EU is actually endowed with significant powers in policies which have a clear macro-economic dimension. Addressing the challenge of asymmetry is crucial to ensure greater legislative involvement in EMU, and will require concerted action by the EP and the Commission to restore the centrality of the "Community method."

However, besides the substantive challenge of asymmetry, efforts to increase legislative involvement in EMU must reckon with other challenges of an institutional nature. Much criticism has been voiced against the representative function of the EP. As I have argued, the views that the EP is under-representative (due to degressive proportionality in the apportionment of seats) or over-representative (due to absence of a Eurozone sub-configuration within the EP) do not withstand close scrutiny. Yet, the EP does face a challenge of representation. The electoral laws for the elections of MEPs, which are set by the states according to common EU standards, are based on PR: but this electoral solution ensures representation at the price of governability, as evident by the high degree of party fragmentation and the representation in the EP of fringe groups which do not pass thresholds for access to national legislatures, particularly in the six largest EU member states. While the problem of governability may not have been a relevant one when the EP was at the margin of EU governance, addressing it may soon become an inevitable choice if the EP acquires new relevance in EMU. Given the unwise objections raised by some domestic courts on attempts to rationalize the electoral laws for EP elections, action at the EU level should be explored to this end as the EP has proposed in a recent resolution calling for the amendment of the EU consolidated Act on EP elections.

Moreover, another hurdle must be cleared in the functioning of the EU law-making process. While the EU lower house faces a challenge of representation, the EU upper house has a challenge of unity. The Council is one institution, but fragmented in multiple configurations, and this has created problems of coordination and imbalances, as some formations are weightier than others. Despite repeated attempts to address this state of affairs, the situation has not changed. Hence, since the entry into force of the Lisbon Treaty the European Council has de facto been increasingly dragged into the business of legislating, because it is the only institution representing the governments of the member states which enjoys the political capital and the institutional capacity to strike deals between different files and agree on legislation. To address the challenge of unity, I have therefore suggested that the European Council—rather than the Council—should be officially vested with legislative power on par with the EP. While confirming in law what often already often occurs in practice, this proposal to institutionalize an EU Senate of sort would mark a new step in the simplification of the EU institutional system—especially if combined with the idea to create a new European presidency, as I will discuss in Chapter 6.

The Lisbon Treaty had designed a complex, but balanced bicameral process by which the EU, as a Union of states and citizens, can pass legislation. Yet, as the Lisbon Treaty was entering into force in 2009, the Euro-crisis exploded. In responding to the Euro-crisis national governments repeatedly stepped outside the EU legal order, and used intergovernmental agreements, rather than EU laws, to govern EMU. This development has been problematic, and increasing calls have been made to revert to EU legislation as the main avenue for the governance of EMU. As Vivien Schmidt has stated, Eurozone governance "need[s] to be changed from highly intergovernmental to more co-decision via the Community Method."[325] Yet, the law-making regime set by the Lisbon Treaty is not perfect, and several challenges cloud its capacity to work successfully. While Chapter 2 criticized the paradox of judicialization, calling for a greater role of the political process in the EMU, this chapter has sought to map three challenges that must be addressed if the EU law-making process is to achieve its desired goal. In the end, constitutional interpretation, electoral reforms, and treaty revisions are important steps to correct the design defects left by the Lisbon Treaty and to make the EU legislative process fit to govern EMU.

[325] Schmidt (n 6) 50.

6

From Executive Federalism to Executive Government

1. Introduction

Since the outburst of the Euro-crisis the European Council—the institution of the European Union (EU) congressing the heads of state and government of the EU member states, together with its semi-permanent President and the President of the European Commission—has emerged as the leading authority in the European system of economic governance. As explained in Chapter 3, the European Council has become the center of EU politics and the agenda-setter of economy policy in Economic and Monetary Union (EMU). In his analysis of the Eurozone crisis, Jürgen Habermas has defined the EU decision-making regime centered on the EU heads of state and government in the European Council and other intergovernmental settings as a system of "post-democratic executive federalism."[1] The notion of executive federalism is multifaceted, and in the context of EU law is often used to refer specifically to the execution of supranational law by the administrative branches of the EU member states.[2] In the broader federalism literature, though, the term identifies more generally "the processes of intergovernmental negotiation that are dominated by the executives of the different governments within [a] federal system."[3] From this point of view, the notion of executive federalism used by Habermas captures the reality of intergovernmental governance which became dominant in the EU since the eruption of the Euro-crisis to manage EMU.

Yet, the system of executive federalism on the basis of which governance in the EU and the Eurozone currently functions has been subject to growing criticisms. While many have faulted the EU intergovernmental decision-making system for achieving too little, too late, increasing concerns have been raised on the legitimacy of this constellation of power.[4] Habermas has prominently criticized "this kind

[1] Jürgen Habermas, *The Crisis of the European Union* (Polity Press 2012) 12.

[2] See Robert Schütze, "From Rome to Lisbon: 'Executive Federalism' in the (New) European Union" (2010) 47 Common Market Law Review 1385.

[3] Ronald Watts, "Executive Federalism: A Comparative Analysis," Institute of Intergovernmental Relations—Queen's University, Kingston, Canada, Research Paper No. 26/1988, 3.

[4] See e.g., Sergio Fabbrini, "Intergovernmentalism and its Limits: Assessing the European Union's Answer to the Euro Crisis" (2013) 46 Comparative Political Studies 1003; Deirdre Curtin, "Challenging Executive Dominance in European Democracy" (2014) 77 Modern Law Review 1.

of executive federalism of a self-authorizing European Council"[5] accusing it of providing "the template for a post-democratic exercise of political authority."[6] As I have pointed out in Chapter 3, the rise in importance of intergovernmental institutions such as the European Council has had major implications on the horizontal balance between the EU member states. Although all member states are formally equal within EU intergovernmental institutions, larger and wealthier member states have been able to take control of the policy-making process to the detriment of smaller, and poorer ones. The economic strategy the European Council followed in response to the Euro-crisis, and the institutional structures that it created outside EU law, have upset the balance between states' power and states' equality, entrenching the hegemonic status of larger, wealthier states and creating a paradoxical dynamic of domination.

However, a regime in which some member states are dominating the policy-making process undermines the anti-hegemonic ideal on which the EU was built, and generates decisions that are perceived as illegitimate by those states and citizens that have no way to influence the outcome of the decision-making process. The new allocation of powers among the EU institutions, and among the EU member states, has therefore brought to light a structural constitutional problem in the EU. In my view, addressing this problem constitutes an urgent need to make the EU endure. Certainly, the form of governance of the EU and the Eurozone is in flux, due to ongoing developments in the practice of the EU institutions—notably the reconfiguration of the relationship between the President of the European Commission and the European Parliament (EP), and the silent consolidation of the role of the President of the European Council.[7] At the same time, multiple calls are being made by the EU institutions themselves for a new reflection on how to allocate governmental powers in the EU—although much uncertainty exists on what should be the way forward.[8] This chapter seeks to contribute to this emerging debate and articulates a proposal for EU constitutional reform aimed at replacing the current system of executive federalism with a form of effective and legitimate executive government for the EU.

In particular, this chapter makes the case in favor of strengthening the role of the President of the European Council *so as to make it the President of the European Union*. If the European Council has become the central institution in deciding the economic policy of the EU, efforts should be made to prevent this institution from being captured by specific state preferences, and the role of the presidency should be explored as a way to counter the dynamic of domination I have examined in Chapter 3. While under the current constitutional setup the President of the European Council only enjoys limited authority, this office should be reformed and endowed with greater executive powers of its own. At the same time,

[5] Habermas (n 1) viii. [6] Ibid.

[7] See Federico Fabbrini et al (eds), *What Form of Government for the European Union and the Eurozone?* (Hart Publishing 2015).

[8] See e.g., European Commission Communication, "A Blueprint for a Deep and Genuine EMU: Launching a European Debate," November 28, 2012, COM(2012)777 final.

these greater powers should be counterbalanced by a new democratic mechanism for electing the President that bestows on the office the legitimacy to act in the name of the EU as a whole. As this chapter suggests, compared to other recent options of institutional reform—including the efforts to boost the presidency of the European Commission—the proposal to strengthen the presidency of the European Council along a constitutional logic of separation of power is better suited to keep under check the larger member states, and to protect the interstate balance on which the anti-hegemonic project of European integration is founded. A stronger, directly legitimated presidency would prevent the dynamics of domination that the Euro-crisis brought to the fore and, at the same time, could create a genuine forum for democratic competition and contestation on the EU agenda.

The proposal to strengthen the presidency of the European Council revives ideas already advanced during the European Constitutional Convention.[9] At the same time, the proposal is emboldened by the recent attempts to define the President of the European Council as the President of the Union as a whole.[10] Nevertheless, I am mindful of the difficulties that any such program of institutional change would meet in today's EU. As such, this chapter also considers three challenges that would arise along the road toward strengthening the presidency of the European Council. First, there exists a challenge of representation connected to the difficulties of providing an electoral forum in which presidential candidates can represent, and thus frame, alternative visions for the governance of the EU. Second, there is a challenge of asymmetry related to the need to design a system for electing the President that is able to account for, and yet balance, the asymmetrical size of the EU member states' populations. Third, there is a challenge of unanimity related to the difficulty of introducing the reform proposed in this chapter in the current EU system, given the need to obtain the unanimous agreement of all member states. This chapter considers each of those difficult challenges. It accepts that none of them has an easy solution. Yet, it submits that it is time for a serious discussion about how the EU system of governance should be reformed to improve its effectiveness and legitimacy.

The proposal to strengthen the President of the European Council is specifically tailored to address one of the most problematic implications of the Euro-crisis and the responses to it on the European system of economic governance: the paradox of domination. It is clear however, that the effects of this proposal go beyond the field of EMU, affecting the nature of the EU as a political regime. In fact, strengthening the presidency of the European Council would redefine—but arguably also simplify—the EU executive power,[11] with implications for other internal and

[9] See Greek Minister of Foreign Affairs Georgios Papandreou, contribution to the debate of the European Convention, amendment No. 43, in Convention Secretariat, Summary sheet of proposals for amendments, May 9, 2003, CONV 709/03.

[10] See President of the European Council Herman Van Rompuy, Speech, Brussels, December 1, 2014, EUCO 257/14.

[11] See Paul Craig, "Institutions, Power and Institutional Balance," in Paul Craig and Gráinne de Búrca (eds), *The Evolution of EU Law* (2nd ed. OUP 2011), 41 and Deirdre Curtin, *Executive Power of the European Union: Law, Practices and the Living Constitution* (OUP 2009).

external policies of the EU. Yet considerations about democratic legitimacy and institutional strengthening in the EU have been at the heart of recent road-maps for EMU reforms—notably the report "Towards a Genuine EMU" written by the President of the European Council, in cooperation with the Presidents of the European European Commission, Eurogroup, and European Central Bank (ECB),[12] as well as by the report "Completing Europe's EMU" written by the President of the European Commission, in close cooperation with the Presidents of the European Council, Eurogroup, ECB, and EP.[13] It seems therefore appropriate to reflect upon how the EU system of executive power may be restructured, and improved, in the context of a discussion about the future of EMU. As this chapter posits, the EU and the Eurozone are in need of a form of a strong, accountable government, which is able to address the political and economic challenges posed by increasing interdependences, especially in EMU, and new ideas on the role of the President of the European Council may be useful to this end.

The chapter is structured as follows. Section 2 summarizes the increasing attention from scholars and policy-makers for a reform of the system of executive federalism currently existing in the EMU, and frames the proposal in favor of strengthening the presidency of the European Council so as to make it the European presidency. Here I also contrast the option of strengthening the President of the European Council with the ongoing efforts to enhance the role of the President of the European Commission by linking its selection to the elections of the EP. However, drawing on arguments already advanced in Chapter 3, I explain that the initiative to parliamentarize the EU is unable to address the problem of interstate domination revealed by the Euro-crisis, and that therefore an alternative constitutional option, based on the logic of separation of powers, should be pursued to establish a more effective and legitimate form of government for the EU and the Eurozone. Sections 3, 4, and 5, then, analyze separately the challenges of representation, asymmetry, and unanimity—and discuss how each of them could be addressed in crafting a reformed presidency. Section 6, finally, concludes.

2. Reforming the EU Executive Power

The problem of domination revealed by the law and practice of EMU intergovernmental governance strikes at the heart of the anti-hegemonic nature of the European integration project.[14] In fact, the EU system of executive federalism has been criticized from multiple standpoints for failing to meet the effectiveness and

[12] President of the European Council, Final Report "Towards a Genuine EMU," December 5, 2012.

[13] President of the European Commission, Report "Completing Europe's EMU," June 22, 2015.

[14] See Simone Bunse and Kalypso Nicolaïdis, "Large versus Small States: Anti-Hegemony and the Politics of Shared Leadership," in Erik Jones et al (eds), *The Oxford Handbook of the European Union* (OUP 2012), 249.

legitimacy requirements needed to govern EMU.[15] In this context, growing calls have been made in the public debate to reform the system of governance of the EU and the Eurozone, with the aim to increase its capacity to act effectively, and respond to legitimate popular concerns.[16] Miguel Maduro has emphasized how a genuine EMU requires a strong, responsible government.[17] As he put it: "there is no self-government without government. Europe needs a strengthened political authority if it is to become a legitimate and accountable democratic authority."[18] Two groups of German and French leading academics and public intellectuals—the Glienicker Group and Eiffel Group—have advanced arguments in favor of endowing the Eurozone with a stronger institutional foundation, through the adoption of a separate treaty establishing a Eurozone form of government, and have made the case for "a European executive [...] capable of acting,"[19] or an "executive of the Euro Community,"[20] legitimated through elections, and able to take binding decisions.

At the same time, growing awareness for the need to reform the form of government of the EU and the Eurozone has also emerged among top national and supranational policy-makers. In its June 2012 inaugural report "Towards a Genuine EMU" the President of the European Council, jointly with the Presidents of the European Commission, Eurogroup, and ECB, acknowledged the need to "strengthen[] democratic legitimacy and accountability" in the EMU,[21] and in its December 2012 final report, it claimed that

> the crisis has shown the need to strengthen not only the EMU's surveillance framework but also its ability to take rapid executive decisions to improve crisis management in bad times and economic policymaking in good times. Some intergovernmental arrangements have been created as a result of the shortcomings of the previous architecture but these would ultimately need to be integrated into the legal framework of the [EU]. [...] Reinforcing the capacity of the European level to take executive economic policy decisions for the EMU is essential.[22]

Equally, in the June 2015 report "Completing Europe's EMU" the President of the European Commission, jointly with the Presidents of the European Council, the Eurogroup, the ECB, and the EP, indicated the need for an institutional strengthening of EMU, including through better steering of EMU affairs.[23] Moreover,

[15] See e.g., Mario Monti and Sylvie Goulard, *De la démocratie en Europe. Voir plus loin* (Flammarion 2012).

[16] See Franz Mayer, "Eine Reform der institutionellen Architektur Europas?," in Stefan Kadelbach (ed), *Die Europäische Union am Scheideweg: Mehr oder weniger Europa?* (Nomos 2015), 187.

[17] Miguel Maduro, "A New Governance for the European Union and the Euro: Democracy and Justice," Study commissioned by the European Parliament Constitutional Affairs Committee, September 2012, PE 462.484.

[18] Ibid 27.

[19] Glienicker Group, "Towards a Euro Union," October 2013, available at <http://www.glienickergruppe.eu/english.html> (last accessed December 29, 2014).

[20] Eiffel Group, "For a Euro Community," February 2014, available at <http://www.groupe-eiffel.eu/our-manifesto/> (last accessed December 29, 2014).

[21] President of the European Council, Report "Towards a Genuine EMU," June 25, 2012, 6.

[22] President of the European Council Final Report (n 12) 17.

[23] President of the European Commission Report (n 13) 18.

although the EU heads of state and government congressed in the European Council have refrained from endorsing any blueprint of institutional reform that would reduce their collective authority, individual countries such as France,[24] Italy,[25] and Spain[26] have spoken in favor of strengthening the government of the EU or the Eurozone.

However, while growing pressures seem to be rising for a reform of the European executive branch, great uncertainty exists on how the EU and the Eurozone should move forward.[27] The European Commission,[28] and the EP,[29] have pushed for transforming the EU into a fully fledged parliamentary system—a development I discussed already in Chapter 3. Moreover, a proposal articulated by the German Minister of Finance Wolfgang Schäuble,[30] and considered by some within the so-called Berlin Group—the Foreign Affairs Ministers of Austria, Belgium, Denmark, France, Italy, Germany, Luxembourg, the Netherlands, Poland, Portugal, and Spain—in the September 2012 report on "The Future of Europe," has been to introduce a direct popular election of the President of the European Commission.[31] Instead, the Dutch Finance Minister Jeroen Dijsselbloem, in soliciting his re-appointment as President of the Eurogroup by the other ministers of finance of the Eurozone member states, has recently proposed a strengthening of the role of the Eurogroup President,[32] with the possibility to entrust on him the external representation of the Eurozone.[33] And French President François

[24] See French President François Hollande, "Intervention liminaire de lors de la conférence de presse," Paris, May 16 2013, 6 (speaking of "un gouvernement économique qui se réunirait, tous les mois, autour d'un véritable Président nommé pour une durée longue et qui serait affecté à cette seule tâche.").

[25] See Italian Prime Minister Matteo Renzi, Speech at the EP, Strasbourg, July 2, 2014, as well as *Europa: Un nuovo inizio. Programma della Presidenza Italiana del Consiglio dell'Unione Europea* July 2014, available at <http://www.governo.it/governoinforma/documenti/programma_semestre_europeo_ita.pdf> (last accessed December 29, 2014). See also Italian Secretary for EU Affairs, Sandro Gozi, Op-Ed, "Europa, quegli scossini che facilitano il rilancio di una nuova governance," *Il Sole 24 Ore*, May 28, 2015 (stating that Europe needs "un Presidente della zona euro a tempo pieno").

[26] See Government of Spain, "Better Economic Governance in the Euro area: Spanish Contribution," May 2015, 7 (expressing support in favor of "an authority responsible for economic policy in the Eurozone").

[27] But see Vernon Bogdanor, "The Future of the European Community: Two Models of Democracy" (1986) 2 Government and Opposition 161 (outlining already institutional uncertainty whether the EU should evolve toward a parliamentary or presidential direction).

[28] See European Commission Recommendation on enhancing the democratic and efficient conduct of the election to the European Parliament, March 12, 2013, (2013)1303 final.

[29] See European Parliament Resolution of November 22, 2012 on the elections to the European Parliament in 2014, P7_TA(2012)0462, para 4.

[30] German Finance Minister Wolfgang Schäuble, "The State of Europe: What Governance is Needed in the European Union?," Speech at the Hertie School of Governance, Berlin, May 27, 2014.

[31] See Berlin Group, Final Report of the Future of Europe Group of the Foreign Ministers of Austria, Belgium, Denmark, France, Italy, Germany, Luxembourg, the Netherlands, Poland, Portugal and Spain, September 17, 2012, 9 (stating that "For some members of the Group, this could include [...] a directly elected Commission President who appoints the members of his 'European Government' himself.").

[32] President of the Eurogroup Jeroen Dijsselbloem, Letter to the members of the Eurogroup, July 12, 2015, 4.

[33] See Art 138 TFEU (allowing Eurozone member states to adopt appropriate measures to ensure unified representation within the international financial institutions and conferences).

Hollande has on several occasions proposed the institutionalization of a Eurozone government with a full-time President.[34]

Given the renewed attention for a reform of the EU or Eurozone executive power, this chapter seeks to enrich the conversation by articulating a proposal for institutional reform. My core proposal is that the EU should strengthen the role of the President of the European Council as a viable antidote to the dynamics of interstate domination occurring within an intergovernmental setting, and as a way to create a genuine space in which a democratic competition on the policies of the EU can occur. Whereas, in the current form, the European Council has turned into a forum in which larger states (today notably Germany) can dominate the decision-making process, a stronger presidency of the European Council—that is, a President endowed with autonomous power and selected through a proper pan-European democratic process—could enjoy the capacity to act free from states' control; in fact, to control states so that none of them can impose its preferences on the others. At the same time, a strengthened presidency of the European Council would increase the effectiveness and legitimacy of the EU executive power, by endowing a monocratic office with the authority to exercise effective leadership,[35] and by securing that this authority is (perceived as) legitimate because it is directly connected to the people's will.[36]

In my view, the proposal to strengthen the President of the European Council is preferable to other options for institutional reform that have been advanced in the debate.[37] To begin with, I am aware of the recent efforts that have been made to boost the role of the President of the European Commission. As I detailed in Chapter 3, at the May 2014 EP elections, political parties decided to bring forward lead candidates for the post of Commission President, and on the basis of this procedure Jean-Claude Juncker—the *Spitzenkandidat* of the right-of-center European Peoples' Party (EPP), which at the elections won a plurality of seats in the EP[38]—was appointed President of the European Commission.[39] Many have

[34] See French President Hollande (n 24) and French President François Hollande, "Entretien à l'occasion du 14 juillet," Paris, July 14, 2015 (speaking for "un Gouvernement économique de la zone euro").

[35] See generally Jack Hayward (ed), *Leaderless Europe* (OUP 2008). For a criticism of the EU's management of the Euro-crisis—as well as of the ways in which it has let the Ukrainian crisis slip out of control—see George Soros, *The Tragedy of the European Union: Disintegration or Revival?* (Public Affairs 2014).

[36] Note that in this chapter I am using the concept of legitimacy to refer to input legitimacy. See Joseph H.H. Weiler, "The Political and Legal Culture of European Integration: An Exploratory Essay" (2011) 9 International Journal of Constitutional Law 678, 682 (distinguishing between input legitimacy, i.e., electoral legitimacy; output legitimacy, i.e., legitimacy based on the results of EU integration; and Messianic legitimacy, i.e., the legitimacy deriving from the narrative about the good of EU integration).

[37] See also David Marquand, *The End of The West: The Once and Future Europe* (Princeton UP 2011) 137 and Sergio Fabbrini, "After the Euro-Crisis: The President of Europe," EuropEos Commentary No. 12/2012 (discussing the idea of strengthening presidency of the European Council).

[38] See European Parliament, *Results of the 2014 European Elections*, available at <http://www.europarl.europa.eu/elections2014-results/en/election-results-2014.html> (last accessed August 7, 2014).

[39] See Nereo Peñalver Garcia and Julian Priestley, *The Making of a European President* (Palgrave MacMillan 2015).

argued that this process should not be rolled back, as it may develop into something bigger in the future.[40] In fact, leaving aside the question of whether the *Spitzenkandidaten* process will be replicated,[41] it seems that President Juncker has been able to capitalize on the modalities of his appointment as the head of the European Commission:[42] after his appointment, for instance, Juncker received a mandate from the European Council to coordinate a new report on completing Europe's EMU.[43] This suggests that the prospect of boosting further the executive power of the President of the European Commission remains one of the possible scenarios for the future of EU governance.

Nevertheless, as I have underlined in Chapter 3, the prospect of strengthening the presidency of the European Commission by transforming the EU into a parliamentary form of government raises issues from the perspective of the balance of power between the member states. An institutional solution that entirely shifts to the EP the decision on the election of the President of the European Commission is liable to deepen the cleavage between large and small states, entrenching, albeit in a different form, the imbalance that characterizes the interstate relations since the outburst of the Euro-crisis.[44] Instead, the proposal to strengthen the presidency of the European Council—notably by electing the office through a mechanism that tempers majoritarianism with federal concerns[45]—can prevent the resurgence of dynamics of interstate domination and create a real forum in which EU citizens can voice competing visions of the EU. While the initiative to strengthen the President of the European Commission by connecting its nomination to the results of parliamentary elections follows a constitutional logic of fusion of powers—in which the government fulcrum rests on the continuum between the parliamentary majority and the cabinet—the proposal to strengthen the President of the European Council follows a constitutional logic of separation of powers—in which power is divided, and shared, by multiple institutions checking and balancing each other. In a regime of fusion of powers, one institution would be in charge of running the EU. However, as clarified in Chapter 3, given the profound asymmetries that characterize the EU member states, the EU

[40] See, e.g., Yves Bertoncini, "New President, New 'Constitution'?" *Notre Europe Tribune*, July 23, 2014.

[41] See European Council Conclusions, June 27, 2014, EUCO 79/14, 11 (stating that to address strong concerns by the UK, "the European Council will consider the process for the appointment of the President of the European Commission for the future, respecting the European Treaties"). But see Daniel Kelemen, "Towards a New Constitutional Architecture in the EU?," in Federico Fabbrini et al (eds), *What Form of Government for the European Union and the Eurozone?* (Hart Publishing 2015), 197 (suggesting that it will not be feasible to revert to the *Spitzenkandidaten* process).

[42] But see also James Kanter, "European Commission Elects a New Leader," *The New York Times*, July 15, 2014 (emphasizing how Jean-Claude Juncker is a veteran of EU politics, having been Prime Minister of an EU member state—and thus member of the European Council—for almost 20 years, and having served as President of the Eurogroup from 2005 to 2013).

[43] See European Council Conclusions, December 18, 2014, EUCO 237/14, 3. See President of the European Commission Report (n 13).

[44] See also Andrea Gratteri, "Parlamento e Commissione: Il difficile equilibrio fra rappresentanza e governabilità nell'Unione Europea" [2014] La Comunità Internazionale 237, 241.

[45] See further on this Section 4.

cannot afford to be governed by a single institution—be it a congress of head of state or government, or a parliamentary assembly giving its confidence to the executive. As a Union of states and citizens the EU can only prosper in an institutional regime in which separated institutions, each reflecting different logics of representation, share the power.[46]

For the same reasons, the proposal to strengthen the presidency of the European Council seems to me preferable to the idea of directly electing the President of the European Commission.[47] Such a proposal, in fact, would move once again in the direction of a fusion-of-power system,[48] essentially introducing a "neo-parliamentary" form of government for the EU[49]—that is, a system in which citizens directly elect a chamber of the legislature as well as the head of the cabinet, who should then obtain the confidence of the legislature.[50] In addition, comparative analysis makes it clear that this form of government has proved to be largely dysfunctional. Between 1996 and 2001, Israel briefly experimented with this system of government,[51] but quickly abandoned it in light of the tensions emerging between the majority-based election of the Prime Minister and the proportionality-based election of the Knesset, as well as the incapacity to master conflicts between the prime minister and the legislature.[52] On the other hand, the proposal to strengthen the President of the European Council appears more plausible than the one to strengthen the President of the Eurogroup.[53] As the management of the Euro-crisis has pointed out, in fact, while the President of the Eurogroup plays an important task in the governance of the Eurozone, the heads of state and government congressed in the European Council have taken on the leading position in decision-making within EMU.[54] Hence, while granting to the President of the Eurogroup greater steering capacity would be consistent with a separation of powers logic, it is unlikely that this actor could overshadow the role of the European Council and its President.[55]

[46] See in particular Sergio Fabbrini, *Which European Union? Europe after the Euro Crisis* (CUP 2015) (defending the logic of separation of powers in the EU).

[47] See text accompanying nn 30–1.

[48] See also Frank Decker and Jared Sonnicksen, "The Direct Election of the Commission President: A Presidential Approach to Democratizing the European Union," Zei Discussion Paper No. 192/2009.

[49] See Francesco Clementi, "L'elezione diretta del Primo ministro: l'origine francese, il caso israeliano, il dibattito in Italia" [2000] Quaderni Costituzionali 579 (explaining the functioning of a neo-parliamentary form of government).

[50] Proposals in favor of the direct election of the President of the European Commission do not consider this point. However, by not setting aside the power of the EP to give a vote of approval for the President of the Commission, they de facto endorse the creation of a neo-parliamentary regime.

[51] See Sec. 3, Basic Law: The Government (1992) (Isr.), modified by Basic Law: The Government (2001) (Isr.).

[52] See Emanuele Ottolenghi, "Choosing a Prime Minister: Executive-Legislative Relations in Israel in the 1990s" (2004) 10 Journal of Legislative Studies 263.

[53] See text accompanying nn 32–3.

[54] See Antoine Kasel, "La présidence de l'Eurogroupe et la gouvernance économique de la zone euro" in Véronique Charléty and Michel Mangenot (eds), *Le système présidentiel de l'Union européenne après Lisbonne* (ENA 2012), 137.

[55] See Dermond Hodson, *Governing the Euro Area in Good Times and Bad* (OUP 2011) ch 3.

Instead, the idea to strengthen the President of the European Council may be close to recent calls to endow the EMU with a real, full-time President.[56] Yet a caveat is necessary: although it may evoke similarities with the French model of semi-presidential government—in which a directly elected head of state coexists with a cabinet and parliament linked by a relations of confidence[57]—the proposal that I am advancing in this chapter rather follows the logic of separation of powers.[58] The French constitutional system is characterized (save in times of cohabitation)[59] by a marked hierarchical relationship between the directly elected President, the Prime Minister, and Parliament,[60] and by the remarkable absence of checks and balances on the presidency.[61] In the EU, on the contrary, there is a clear separation of powers between the European Council and the EP, since the former cannot dissolve the latter and the latter cannot vote out the former.[62] The proposal to strengthen the presidency of the European Council advanced here builds on, and develops, this logic of separation of powers, and is therefore reminiscent of constitutional systems, such as that of the United States (US) where the executive and the legislatures check and balance each other.[63] Even so, contrary to the US system, which is characterized by a unitary executive,[64] in the EU the executive power remains fragmented.[65] This feature makes the EU form of government peculiar—and requires further analysis of how a proposal to strengthen the presidency of the European Council could be implemented within the fabric of today's EU.[66]

[56] See text accompanying n 34.

[57] See Maurice Duverger, "A New Political System Model: Semi-Presidential Government" (1980) 8 European Journal of Political Research 165 (outlining the institutional features of semi-presidential regimes).

[58] See text accompanying nn 44–6.

[59] See generally Jean Gicquel, "De la cohabitation" (1989) 49 Pouvoirs 69 (explaining that a cohabitation arises whenever the President and the parliamentary majority, and thus the Prime Minister, belong to different political parties). But see Loi constitutionnelle 2000-964 du 2 octobre 2000 relative à la durée du mandat du Président de la République, J.O.R.F. 3 October 2000, p. 15582 (Fr.) (modifying Art 6 Const. Fr. to reduce the length of the presidential mandate to five years). The effect of this reform has been to bring close to nil the probability of a cohabitation. See Stefano Ceccanti, "Le istituzioni e il sistema politico dopo il primo 'quinquennato'," in Gianfranco Baldini and Marc Lazar (eds), *La Francia di Sarkozy* (Il Mulino 2007), 27.

[60] See Olivier Duhamel, "Remarques sur la notion de régime semi-présidentiel," in *Droit, institutions et systèmes politiques. Mélanges en hommage à Maurice Duverger* (PUF 1987), 581.

[61] See Mauro Volpi, *Libertà e autorità: La classificazione delle forme di stato e di governo* (Giappichelli 2007) 146 (defining the French form of government as "hyper-presidentialist").

[62] See also Sergio Fabbrini, *Compound Democracies* (OUP 2007) and Philipp Dann, "European Parliament and Executive Federalism: Approaching a Parliament in a Semi-Parliamentary Democracy" (2003) 9 European Law Journal 549, 554.

[63] See Amie Kreppel, "Understanding the European Parliament from a Federalist Perspective," in Anand Menon and Martin Schain (eds), *Comparative Federalism: The European Union and the United States in Comparative Perspective* (OUP 2006), 245.

[64] See Art II, Sec. 1 US Const. (stating that "The executive Power shall be vested in a President of the United States."). See generally Mark Tushnet, "A Political Perspective on the Theory of the Unitary Executive" (2010) 12 University of Pennsylvania Journal of Constitutional Law 313 (discussing the theory of the unitary executive in the US, with its variants of intensity).

[65] See also Robert Schütze, *European Constitutional Law* (CUP 2012).

[66] See further on this Sections 3–5.

Before doing this, however, it is worth stressing that the proposal to strengthen the presidency of the European Council builds on a recent set of EU constitutional reforms—as well as on the latest practice of the EU institutions. The position of European Council President was introduced at the time of the European Constitutional Convention.[67] Whereas previously the presidency of the European Council tracked the presidency of the Council—rotating every six months between the member states[68]—the Convention decided to formally recognize the European Council as an EU institution endowed with executive tasks,[69] and to create the position of European Council President as a way to ensure continuity in the work of the European Council and to steer its direction.[70] The proposal to endow the European Council with a semi-permanent President was strongly endorsed by the larger member states (which saw in this a way to recognize the reality of states' power) and equally strongly resisted by the smaller member states (which saw in this a fundamental alteration of the principle of states' equality).[71] Eventually, under the auspices of Convention President Valéry Giscard d'Estaing,[72] the presidency of the European Council made its way into the Constitutional Treaty—and then into the Lisbon Treaty.[73]

However, whereas in the Giscardian vision the President of the European Council ought to have been a strong figure, the text of the Constitutional Treaty, and then the Lisbon Treaty, constrained its status and functions to address the concerns of the smaller member states.[74] First, the President is entitled to head the European Council—not the EU as such.[75] Second, the President is elected by a qualified majority of the heads of state and government congressed in the European Council and can be removed by them according to the same procedure in the event of an impediment or a serious misconduct.[76] Third, contrary to institutions such as the Parliament,[77] or (generally) the

[67] See Philippe de Schoutheete, "The European Council," in John Peterson and Michael Shackleton (eds), *The Institutions of the European Union* (3rd ed. OUP 2012), 43, 48.

[68] See Art 146 TEC (stating that the office of President of the Council shall be held in turn by each member state for a term of six months).

[69] See Art 15(1) TEU (stating that the European Council "shall not exercise legislative functions").

[70] See Ben Crum, "Accountability and Personalisation of the European Council Presidency" (2009) 31 European Integration 685.

[71] See Paul Magnette and Kalypso Nicolaïdis, "Large and Small Member States in the European Union: Reinventing the Balance," Notre Europe Research Paper No. 25/2003, 15–18.

[72] See Paul Magnette, "Vers un changement de 'régime politique'?," in Giuliano Amato et al (eds), *Genesis and Destiny of the European Constitution* (Bruylant 2007), 1065, 1067 (discussing the influence of the French constitutional mindset over the institutionalization of the presidency of the European Council. Institutionalization was strongly favored by European Convention President Valéry Giscard D'Estaing, a former President of the French Fifth Republic).

[73] See Paul Craig, *The Treaty of Lisbon: Law, Politics and Treaty Reform* (OUP 2010) 78.

[74] See Paolo Ponzano, "Les institutions de l'Union," in Giuliano Amato et al (eds), *Genesis and Destiny of the European Constitution* (Bruylant 2007), 439, 467 (explaining that the Treaty sought to limit the power of the President).

[75] See Art 15(5) TEU. [76] See Art 15(5) TEU.

[77] See Art 14(3) TEU (stating that "members of the European Parliament shall be elected for a term of five years").

Commission,[78] whose members are elected for a five-year term, the President of the European Council remains in office for a term of two and a half years, renewable only once.[79] And fourth, the President is empowered to act more as a chairperson of that institution than as an executive leader.[80] Each of these solutions restricted the role of the President, closely tying him to his peers within the European Council,[81] and deprived him of a substantial capacity to lead, on the assumption that this would better maintain the influence of smaller member states on the working of the institution. Yet, as I emphasized in Chapter 3, each of these solutions ultimately worked *against* the interest of the smaller member states. Ironically, in a context in which the President of the European Council enjoyed limited power and legitimacy, it was easier for the biggest member states to impose their preferences within the European Council.

This is not to deny that the first President of the European Council—Mr. Herman Van Rompuy, a former Prime Minister of Belgium, appointed for two and a half years in November 2009[82] and renewed for a second mandate in March 2012[83]—made inroads into consolidating the position of the presidency and its function in brokering compromises between the member states.[84] As Henri de Waele and Hansko Broeksteeg showed, President Van Rompuy "succeeded in becoming an influential actor in his own right, through a dutiful exercise of his official powers, clever exploitation of some 'grey zones,' and tactful dealing with the Union's other institutional players."[85] In particular, President Van Rompuy skillfully invested himself with important responsibilities in the governance of EMU,[86] leading the work of two task forces which prepared the road-map of the legal and policy responses to the Euro-crisis by the EU institutions and the member states.[87] In fact, at the official handover ceremony with his successor—Donald Tusk, the former Prime Minister of Poland, who was elected in August 2014 as the second President of the European Council[88]—Van Rompuy affirmed that the "President of the European Council represents the Union as a whole."[89] Although

[78] See Art 17(3) TEU (stating that "[t]he Commission's term of office shall be five years"). But see Art 17(8) TEU (stating that "the European Parliament may vote on a motion of censure of the Commission.").

[79] See Art 15(5) TEU. [80] See Art 15(6) TEU.

[81] See Craig (n 73) 117 (stating that the current "appointment procedure for the Presidency of the European Council places the power firmly in the hands of that body").

[82] European Council press release, November 19, 2009.

[83] European Council press release, March 1, 2012, EUCO 37/12.

[84] See Desmond Dinan, "The Post-Lisbon European Council Presidency: An Interim Assessment" (2013) 36 West European Politics 1256.

[85] Henri De Waele and Hansko Broeksteeg, "The Semi-Permanent European Council Presidency: Some Reflections on the Law and Early Practice" (2012) 49 Common Market Law Review 1039, 1070.

[86] See Dermont Hodson and Uwe Puetter, "The European Union and the Economic Crisis," in Michelle Cini and Nieves Pérez-Solórzano Borragán (eds), *European Union Politics* (OUP 2013), 367.

[87] See Task Force to the European Council, Report "Strengthening Economic Governance in the EU," October 21, 2010, and President of the European Council Final Report (n 12).

[88] European Council Conclusions, August 30, 2014, EUCO 163/14, para 2.

[89] European Council President Van Rompuy (n 10).

technically this is incorrect, since as just mentioned Article 15 Treaty on European Union (TEU) only vests in the President of the European Council the role of representing the European Council, the statement signals a push toward a kind of presidentialization of EU governance.[90]

Nevertheless, the prospects for such a development remain limited under the current constitutional arrangement. Under the existing treaties, the President of the European Council acts mainly as a deal broker, facilitating compromises between member states, and is almost exclusively endowed with internal procedural powers.[91] As President Van Rompuy himself put it, his main task is to listen to the heads of state and government and to build trust between them.[92] In fact, there is evidence that Germany, the biggest EU member state, has played a pivotal role in influencing the European Council and its President.[93] Otherwise, the risks that a weaker presidency would pose on the balance of power between the member states had not gone unnoticed during the debates of the Constitutional Convention.[94] Then Greek Foreign Minister Georgios Papandreou, for instance, had tabled an amendment to introduce the direct election of the President of the European Council and justified the proposal by stating that "a directly elected President would strengthen the role of the European citizen, contribute to the substantial equality of the Member States and facilitate a new, stable balance between the institutions."[95]

This chapter argues that the recent trend toward the consolidation of the presidency of the European Council should be supported by adequate institutional reforms that strengthen the office so as to make it truly the President of the Union as a whole. Strengthening the executive power of the President of the European Council would be a step toward clarifying separation of powers in the EU.[96] In constitutional terms, this implies both new powers *and* new legitimacy for the institution of the presidency. On the one hand, the presidency should be vested with the legal capacity to make authoritative decisions.[97] While the Euro-crisis has

[90] See De Waele and Broeksteeg (n 85) 1074.

[91] See Uwe Puetter, *The European Council and the Council: New Intergovernmentalism and Institutional Change* (OUP 2014) 114.

[92] See President of the European Council Herman Van Rompuy, "Looking Back, Looking Forward," Speech at "The State of the Union" Conference at Accademia dei Lincei, Rome, November 7, 2014 (stating that on the basis of the treaty "the job description and formal competencies of [the] President are rather vague, even meagre" and claiming that in his experience "[b]uilding trust is [...] perhaps the most important task of a European Council President.").

[93] See President of the European Council Herman Van Rompuy, Farewell Speech to the Members of the European Council, Brussels, October 24, 2014 (thanking explicitly only German Chancellor Angela Merkel).

[94] See Magnette and Nicolaïdis (n 71) 15.

[95] Papandreou Convention Amendment (n 9).

[96] See also Gerard Conway, "Recovering a Separation of Powers in the European Union" (2011) 17 European Law Journal 304 and Christoph Möllers, *The Three Branches: A Comparative Model of Separation of Powers* (OUP 2013) 169–71 (discussing blurred recognition of the principle of separation of powers in the EU).

[97] See President of the European Council Final Report (n 12) 17 (pleading for an authority capable "to take executive economic policy decisions for the EMU.").

brought to the fore the hegemonic role of several member states, in the future the President of the European Council should have the authority to set the agenda he or she believes to be in the best interest of the Union—resisting pressure from the heads of state and government (and especially the more powerful among them), rather than reflecting their preferences. On the other hand, this extended authority should be connected to, and supported by, a process of legitimation—that is a selection mechanism of he who holds the office that is perceived as legitimate by the people throughout the EU.[98] In a democratic system, such a mechanism can only be the electoral process.[99]

In the remainder of this chapter I will attempt to articulate more fully what the proposal to strengthen the President of the European Council would entail. This requires asking three questions. First, what are the advantages associated with the establishment of a more solid presidency, and how should these be reflected in the new powers to be attributed the institution? Second, what should be the mechanism to elect the President of the European Council, and how can the asymmetry in population between the EU member states be reconciled with the choice of the holder of a monocratic office? Third, what are the challenges facing the road toward changing the EU treaties to strengthen the presidency, and how could these practical difficulties be addressed in the framework of the ongoing debate about the future of the EMU? In considering each of those questions, I will try to use as a compass the lessons provided by the comparative constitutional law literature on forms of government.[100] However, I am aware that I am entering unchartered territory, and I do not doubt that many of my arguments will be subject to criticism and require further refinement. I hope, however, that by starting this debate I will draw attention to the merits of this option of institutional reform to replace executive federalism with a form of executive government for the EU.

3. The Challenge of Representation

A. Advantages

The proposal to strengthen the role of the President of the European Council moves the EU toward the advantages of a presidential form of government.[101] Scholars comparing parliamentarianism and presidentialism have underlined

[98] See President of the European Commission Report (n 13) 4 (stating that "the success of [EMU] anywhere, depends on its success everywhere.").

[99] See generally Yves Mény, "*De la démocratie en Europe*: Old Concepts, New Challenges" (2002) 41 Journal of Common Market Studies 1 (emphasizing the importance of popular input while underlying the need for a fresh approach to the problem of democracy in the EU).

[100] See generally Paul Craig and Adam Tomkins (eds), *The Executive and Public Law: Power and Accountability in Comparative Perspective* (OUP 2006) (discussing the role of executive branches in Europe and other countries).

[101] See also Hodson and Puetter (n 86) 373 (emphasizing "presidentialization of euro area governance"); De Waele and Broeksteeg (n 85) 1074 (stating that in due time "the EU's system of government might well be ascribed a genuine presidential epithet.").

how each of these forms of government or their hybrids, semi-presidentialism or neo-parliamentarianism, has both pros and cons.[102] However, scholars usually identify several recurring general virtues in presidential systems, that is political regimes in which the people select the chief executive separately and independently from the legislature.[103] Presidential systems favor governmental stability because they ensure the continuity in office of the President for the entire length of the elected term, regardless of the ongoing confidence of the legislature, as is the case in parliamentary and neo-parliamentary regimes. Presidential systems provide greater governmental vigor and leadership because they vest the executive power (or part thereof) into a monocratic office. Moreover, presidential systems endow the citizens with the capacity to directly select the president, removing this power from the legislature and ensuring a direct, rather than mediated, legitimacy to the chief executive. Presidential systems also inject a majoritarian logic into the political system, forcing relevant societal actors to polarize along key political cleavages and counterbalancing the fragmentation, which is inherent whenever the electoral system is based on proportional representation.

The virtues of a vigorous, directly legitimated, and majoritarian presidency may be particularly valuable in the EU today.[104] Although the EU does not suffer from the institutional instability characteristic of a parliamentary regime, there is growing awareness that the EU currently lacks an effective and legitimate executive branch.[105] Whereas the EU responses to the Euro-crisis have been described as slow and weak, the existence of a stronger presidency would increase the capacity to act swiftly and with leadership in the face of new challenges. Moreover, whereas the EU institutions currently appear very remote from the EU citizens—since the mechanisms of electoral accountability at the EU level are only indirect[106]—the existence of a stronger presidency, directly legitimated by the citizens, would raise its capacity to be responsive to popular concerns.[107] At the same time, while the current proportionality-based

102 See Giovanni Sartori, *Comparative Constitutional Engineering* (NYU Press 1994); Augusto Barbera and Carlo Fusaro, *Il governo delle democrazie* (Il Mulino 2001); Maurice Duverger, *Institutions politiques et droit constitutionnel* (PUF 1978) (comparing forms of government).

103 See Steven G. Calabresi, "The Virtues of Presidential Government" (2001) 18 Constitutional Commentary 51. But see Richard Albert, "Presidential Values in Parliamentary Democracies" (2010) 8 International Journal of Constitutional Law 207 (emphasizing how parliamentary regimes may be able to embody the virtues of presidential government).

104 See Wojcech Sadurski, "Democratic Legitimacy of the European Union: A Diagnosis and Some Modest Proposals" (2013) 32 Polish Yearbook of International Law 9. But see Arend Lijphart, *Patterns of Democracy* (Yale UP 1999) 42 (describing the EU as the example of a consociational system, following non-majoritarian logics).

105 See text accompanying nn 16–36.

106 See Ingolf Pernice, "Domestic Courts, Constitutional Constraints and European Democracy: What Solution for the Crisis?," in Federico Fabbrini et al (eds), *The Constitutionalization of European Budgetary Constraints* (Hart Publishing 2014), 297. But see Peter Lindseth, *Power and Legitimacy* (OUP 2010) (arguing that the EU is based on a delegation of powers by the member states with the legitimacy solidly residing in them).

107 See Laeken Declaration, December 15, 2001, SN 273/01 (stating that "the European institutions must be brought closer to its citizens" so as to address the democratic challenge facing the EU).

electoral regime for the EP favors party fragmentation,[108] and fosters the lack of unifying themes in the European political debate,[109] the existence of a monocratic office would inevitably force the emergence of a public sphere, where competition occurs around key lines of political conflict, and would thus likely contribute to the rise of European political parties.[110]

In the institutional system of the EU, however, the proposal to strengthen the role of the President of the European Council would carry additional benefits that are specific to the present situation of the EU. First, a reformed presidency, selected through an open and transparent electoral process and accountable to EU citizens at large, would restore a healthy *equality* between the EU member states. A fair balance between the member states is crucial to a well-functioning EU.[111] At the moment, however, the President of the European Council is chosen by the heads of state and government congressed in the European Council, and is accountable exclusively to them.[112] This means that, currently, the President is entirely dependent on the heads of state and government and enjoys limited capacity to keep them under check.[113] As Chapter 3 pointed out, large states, and in recent times particularly Germany, have acquired a dominating influence in the working of the European Council, largely upsetting the balance between the member states. Were the President of the European Council to be chosen through a popular election instead, he could have the institutional independence to keep the member states in check and protect the interests of the Union as a whole.

Strictly linked to this is a second advantage of the presidentialization of the European Council, which carries particular value in the current state of the EU integration project: the capacity to provide a sense of *unity*. It has been too often noticed how growing fragmentation within the EU—with the partition between the Eurozone and the non-Eurozone member states,[114] increasing resort to enhanced cooperation,[115] and the complex patterns of intergovernmental agreements concluded by member states with variable geometry outside the EU legal order[116]—has weakened the idea of unity of the EU.[117] Needless to say, a

[108] See Act concerning the election of the representatives of the European Parliament by direct universal suffrage, annexed to Decision 76/787/ECSC, EEC, Euratom [1976] OJ L278/1, as amended.

[109] See further on this Chapters 3 and 5.

[110] See generally Jürgen Habermas, "Democracy in Europe: Why the Development of the EU into a Transnational Democracy is Necessary and How is it Possible" (2015) 21 European Law Journal 546 (discussing the importance of a European public sphere).

[111] See Magnette and Nicolaïdis (n 71).

[112] See Art 15(5) TEU.

[113] See generally D. Nederlof et al, Editorial: "The European Council and National Executives: Segmentation, Consolidation and Legitimation" (2012) 8 European Constitutional Law Review 165.

[114] See generally Jean-Claude Piris, *The Future of Europe: Towards a Two-Speed EU?* (CUP 2011).

[115] See Federico Fabbrini, "Enhanced Cooperation under Scrutiny: Revisiting the Law and Practice of Multi-Speed Integration in Light of the First Involvement of the EU Judiciary" (2013) 40 Legal Issues of Economic Integration 197.

[116] See European Parliament Resolution of December 12, 2013 on the constitutional problems of a multi-tier governance in the European Union, P7_TA(2013)0598.

[117] See Tom Eijsbouts and Monica Claes, Editorial: "From Confederacy to Convoy: Thoughts about the Finality of the Union and its Member States" (2010) 6 European Constitutional Law Review 1.

complex polity like the EU shall be pluralistic and provide for multiple fora for representation,[118] and the right to withdraw from the EU, which is currently enshrined in the treaties, makes sure that no member state can be compelled to remain part of the EU against its will.[119] Nevertheless, there is a case to be made for the EU to be able to increasingly speak with one voice, both to face security challenges abroad, and to define the interest of the EU at home.[120] From this point of view, strengthening the role of the President would offer the institutional forum through which the multiple interests at play in the EU could be integrated into a unitary vision.

Further, a third advantage connected with a reformed post of the European Council President is its suitability to protect the values of *federalism* (or decentralization) on which the EU is founded. Scholars of federalism have emphasized this point,[121] which is worth restating here to allay the fears of those who worry that a strong President, representing the unity of the EU, would make the EU slide into the direction of a super-state.[122] In fact, an autonomously legitimated President can actually provide a more receptive forum to those EU citizens who would like to keep in check the degree, or speed, of European integration. At the moment, the EU institutional system does not provide any supranational forum in which disgruntled EU citizens can voice their concern against over-centralization.[123] The process of EU integration has been characterized by a constant trend in the centralization of powers,[124] with the functioning of the EU bureaucracy continuing on autopilot despite the growing disenchantment of European citizens.[125] An elected and accountable President could provide exactly such a forum and should be endowed with the power to safeguard the federal division of competence between the EU and its member states.[126]

[118] See generally Walter Van Gerven, *The European Union: A Polity of States and People* (Hart Publishing 2005).

[119] See Art 50 TEU (allowing withdrawal from the EU).

[120] See Glienicker Group (n 19) (stating that "[i]n a multipolar world in which China, Russia, and others expand their spheres of influence and the global supremacy of the USA decreases, Europe ought to be able to defend her common interests effectively") and Eiffel Group (n 20) (stating that "[e]nsuring that Europe's voice is heard is not a question of prestige, nor an idealist whim. It is how to ensure that in the future the priorities which are important to Europe's citizens [...] are protected.").

[121] See generally Bradford Clark, "Separation of Powers as a Safeguard of Federalism" (2001) 79 Texas Law Review 1321, 1321–29 (discussing separation of powers as a protection of federalism in the US).

[122] See generally Glyn Morgan, *The Idea of a European Superstate: Public Justification and European Integration* (Princeton UP 2005) (making the case in favor of a super-state).

[123] Compare Damian Chalmers, "Democratic Self-Government in Europe: Domestic Solutions to the EU Legitimacy Crisis," Policy Network Paper, May 2013 (advancing a proposal to empower national parliaments to veto and nullify EU legislation), with text accompanying n 148 (explaining that vesting veto power in national parliaments is not the solution to police subsidiarity as national legislatures use their power for domestic political reasons).

[124] See Ken Kollman, *Perils of Centralization: Lessons from Church, State and Corporation* (CUP 2013) (discussing the trend of centralization in the EU).

[125] See Tony Barber, "Elections Results Show a Europe Short of Confidence in its Future," *Financial Times*, May 26, 2014.

[126] See text accompanying nn 147–9.

Ultimately, the three advantages discussed above can be related through the concept of representation. As the Euro-crisis has demonstrated, the EU lacks an executive body that can simultaneously represent the EU member states and the EU citizens (a.k.a. a Union of states and citizens).[127] Each of the heads of state and government that sits in the European Council certainly represents its member state and the national constituency that elected him or her;[128] but he or she cannot speak for other states or citizens since these have not elected him or her. At the same time, the current President of the European Council only represents the heads of state and government who elected him,[129] but he cannot really speak for the Union as a whole, since the EU people never voted him into office. In fact, the President of the European Commission also suffers from an analogous representative deficit, even after the new process put in place for the May 2014 elections of the EP, in which each political party tied its electoral success with the appointment of a *Spitzenkandidat*.[130] Because the EP is elected through a system of proportional representation, the composition of the legislature reflects a high degree of fragmentation, and no political party won a majority.[131] As a result, the President-elect of the European Commission was drawn from the largest party in the EP, the EPP, which only had a 29% plurality of the EU-wide popular vote. In this situation, it is difficult for the European Commission President to claim that he received a popular mandate to represent the Union.[132]

The disconnect between the power that the EU has acquired since the beginning of the Euro-crisis and the lack of adequate mechanisms of representation is a key challenge.[133] No democratic polity can accept the exercise of power in the absence of adequate institutional channels of representation, through which the people can express its voice.[134] Yet, as I pointed out especially in Chapter 3, the management of the Euro-crisis has deprived an increasing number of EU states and citizens of the capacity to effectively influence the decisions affecting them: this lack of

[127] See also French Minister of the Economy Emmanuel Macron and German Minister of the Economy Sigmar Gabriel, Op-Ed, "Europe Cannot Wait Any Longer," *The Guardian*, June 3, 2015 (stating that "to make its institutions work [...] Europe will need to address its democratic deficit as well as its executive one.").

[128] See also Wolfgang Wessels et al, "Democratic Control in the Member States of the European Council and the Euro zone summits," Study commissioned by the European Parliament Constitutional Affairs Committee, January 2013, PE 474.392.

[129] See Jean-Claude Piris, *The Lisbon Treaty: A Legal and Political Analysis* (CUP 2010) 209.

[130] See text accompanying nn 38–43.

[131] See *Results of the 2014 European Elections* (n 38).

[132] See Joseph H.H. Weiler, Editorial: "Fateful Elections? Investing in the Future of Europe" (2014) 25 European Journal of International Law 361, 365 (stating that the selection of the Commission President in light of the result of the elections of the EP "compromises the ability in a political sense for this or that candidate to say with authority 'I was elected by the peoples of Europe'.").

[133] See Simona Piattoni, "Is the EU a Representative Democracy? The Normative Debate and the Impact of the Euro-crisis," in Federico Fabbrini et al (eds), *What Form of Government for the European Union and the Eurozone?* (Hart Publishing 2015), 133.

[134] See Augustin José Menéndez, "The European Democratic Challenge" (2009) 15 European Law Journal 277 and Ben Crum, "Saving the Euro at the Cost of Democracy?" (2013) 51 Journal of Common Market Studies 614 (discussing the need for an adequate institutional channel of representation in relation to the euro crisis).

voice has fuelled an increasingly popular discontent vis-à-vis measures, which were perceived as illegitimate—as revealed by the electoral surge of extreme, antisystem parties.[135] It is here that the proposal to strengthen the presidency of the European Council, and make it directly accountable to EU citizens at large, becomes crucial to cure the representation deficit in the EU executive branch.[136] If the President of the European Council were elected by the European citizens, through a mechanism which (as I shall explain below)[137] accounts for the asymmetries between the EU member states, it could plausibly claim to represent the interests of the Union as a whole and, therefore, be able to act *in the name of Europe*. This is crucial not only because the President would eventually be able to exercise leadership, but also because it could legitimately speak for the EU citizens and member states, rather than for just a sub-group thereof.[138]

B. Powers

In light of the above, it is time to consider how the new powers of the presidency should be defined. From a comparative perspective, the diversity of constitutional regulation of the power of the executive branch in presidential systems is remarkable. For example, the US Constitution barely defines the function of the President,[139] whereas the French and Brazilian Constitutions provide a broad empowerment of authority to the head of state.[140] Most constitutions entrust the command of the

[135] See Nicole Scicluna, "Politicization without Democratization: How the Eurozone Crisis is Transforming EU Law and Politics" (2014) 12 International Journal of Constitutional Law 545.

[136] See also Deirdre Curtin, "Democratic Accountability of EU Executive Power," in Federico Fabbrini et al (eds), *What Form of Government for the European Union and the Eurozone?* (Hart Publishing 2015), 171 (discussing the need for institutional reforms that increase accountability of the EU executive).

[137] See further on this Section 5.

[138] See ceteris paribus, Steven G. Calabresi, "Some Normative Arguments for the Unitary Executive" (1995) 48 Arkansas Law Review 23, 23–38 (emphasizing that the presidency in the US constitutional system is the only purely national office, as opposed to the legislature, whose members are representatives of local, or state, constituencies).

[139] See Art II, Sec. 2 US Const. (effectively granting to the President alone only the power to command the military, to "require the Opinion, in writing, of the principal Officer in each of the executive Departments," to grant pardons, and to make recess appointments—with all other powers being subject to Congressional approval). Of course, over time the effective powers of the presidency have aggrandized, especially in the field of national security and foreign affairs. See Ernest A. Young, "Taming the Most Dangerous Branch: The Scope and Accountability of Executive Power in the United States," in Paul Craig and Adam Tomkins (eds), *The Executive and Public Law* (OUP 2006), 161. But see *National Labor Relations Board (NLRB) v. Noel Canning*, 573 U.S. __ (2014) (US Supreme Court restricting the power of the President to make recess appointments even when the Senate is convened only in pro-forma sessions).

[140] See Art 84 Const. Braz. (empowering inter alia the President to appoint and dismiss ministers of state, run the administration, initiate legislation, veto bills, conclude national treaties, decree a state of siege and emergency, command the military, grant pardons, submit to Congress the pluriannual plan and the budget, and issue provisional measures with the force of law); Arts 5–19 Const. Fr. (charging the President of the Republic with guaranteeing the functioning of the public power, the continuity of the state, and national independence; and empowering him to appoint the Prime Minister, preside over the Council of Ministers, veto bills, call for a national referendum, dissolve the assembly, command the military, grant pardons, and exercise emergency powers when the independence of the nation is threatened).

military to the presidency,[141] but this does not currently concern the EU[142] (although one may be left wondering how long the EU can expect to go forward without an adequate security and defense policy, in light of rising threats, not only globally, but also regionally).[143] In the framework of the EU, it seems that a treaty reform strengthening the power of the President of the European Council should at least award to the presidency the following new powers.

First, the President should appoint the members of the European Commission, which would be subject to the vote of consent of the EP. The Commission is a highly professional and qualified institution, with technical know-how to administer policy decisions.[144] Therefore, it would be unreasonable to duplicate the task of the Commission by establishing a new administration within the presidency of the European Council. Nevertheless, action by the Commission is increasingly in need of democratic legitimation.[145] And this is even more so the case now that—as pointed out in Chapter 1—the Commission has acquired pervasive powers of oversight over the budgetary policy of the member states. By virtue of its popular, EU-wide election, the President of the European Council would be able to secure such a legitimation to the EU administration, but it should in turn be able to shape the apex of the Commission and thus implement its policy agenda through the EU bureaucracy.[146]

Second, the President should be empowered to veto EU legislation subject to the possibility for the EU legislature to override the veto with a supermajority of the votes cast. This authority would entrench the ability of the presidency to also act for the protection of the EU federal compact. In fact, as experience has demonstrated, the EU currently lacks an institution that can effectively police the principle of subsidiarity.[147] While the European Commission and the European Court of Justice

[141] See e.g., Louis Fisher, *Presidential War Power* (2nd ed. rev. Kansas UP 2004) 12–16 (outlining the origin and development of the US President's role as commander in chief of the US armed forces); Bernard Chantebout, "La dissuasion nucléaire et le pouvoir présidentiel" (1986) 38 Pouvoirs 21 (discussing the powers of France's President, specifically the power to engage in nuclear deterrence).

[142] See Art 4(2) TEU (stating that "national security remains the sole responsibility of each Member State").

[143] See Valerio Briani, "The Costs of Non-Europe in the Defence Field," Centro Studi sul Federalismo & Instituto Affari Internazionali, April 2013 (accounting the costs occasioned by the lack of a single EU security and defense policy).

[144] See generally Hussein Kassim et al, *The European Commission of the Twenty-First Century* (OUP 2013).

[145] See Damian Chalmers, "The European Redistributive State and a European Law of Struggle" (2012) 18 European Law Journal 667, 686–92 (stressing the importance of legitimizing actions by the Commission in light of its increasing powers).

[146] See ceteris paribus, Stephen Skowronek, *The Politics Presidents Make: Leadership from John Adams to Bill Clinton* (Harvard UP 1997) (giving a historical account of the power of the US presidency to shape policy-making).

[147] See Art 5(3) TEU (stating that "in areas which do not fall within its exclusive competence, the Union shall act only if and insofar as the objectives of the proposed action cannot be sufficiently achieved by the Member States, either at central level or at regional and local level, but can rather, by reason of the scale or effects of the proposed action, be better achieved at Union level") on which see Federico Fabbrini, "The Principle of Subsidiarity," in Robert Schütze and Takis Tridimas (eds), *Oxford Principles of EU Law* (OUP 2016).

have a pro-European bias, the EP and the Council also have an interest in adopting EU legislation to expand their competence. Protocol No. 2 to the EU treaties sought to enlist national parliaments as watchdogs of subsidiarity, but practice has shown that national legislatures have abused their role, mostly for petty domestic politics.[148] On the contrary, a reformed President of the European Council could be more sensitive to subsidiarity: the expansion of EU legislation would not necessarily aggrandize the presidency, and its subjection to direct popular election would make it prone to exercise veto against EU legislation that encroaches on the powers of the states.[149]

The new EU presidency instead should not be empowered to dissolve the EP. In the current EU system of government, the European Council and the EP are strictly separated. This institutional solution should be maintained, as the separation between the executive and the legislature ensures that the latter can more effectively control the former.[150] While a President of the European Council elected by the EU citizens in the EU member states would obviously hold great authority, the separation between executive and legislative powers provides an important wall against potential abuses by the presidency.[151] Moreover, the presidency should not be endowed with any emergency power. As the comparative experience of South American political regimes demonstrates, in presidential systems in which the legislature is elected through proportional representation, presidents can abuse emergency power when they want to overcome deadlock in the legislative branch.[152] This is one of the vices of presidential government that an enlightened reform of the EU system of governance should obviously avoid by restricting the power of the presidency to act within the constitutional framework. On the other hand, it would be reasonable for the term of office of the President to be changed to five years,[153] renewable once, thus ensuring that the presidency can have a sufficiently broad timeframe to carry forward its agenda.

[148] See Federico Fabbrini and Katarzyna Granat, "'Yellow Card, But No Foul': The Role of the National Parliaments under the Subsidiarity Protocol and the Commission Proposal for an EU Regulation on the Right to Strike" (2013) 50 Common Market Law Review 115 (arguing that vesting veto power in national parliaments is not an effective means to police subsidiarity, because, among other reasons, national legislatures use their power for domestic political reasons).

[149] Comparative analysis furnishes cautionary tales in this regard. In the US, for instance, presidents have often fostered centralization of power. See Kollman (n 124). But see also US President Andrew Jackson, Veto Message to the Senate, July 10, 1832 (vetoing the bill renewing the charter of the Second Bank of the United States because "modifications of the existing charter proposed by this act are not such, in my view, as make it consistent with the rights of the States or the liberties of the people.").

[150] See text accompanying nn 62–6.

[151] See ceteris paribus, Neal Katyal, "Internal Separation of Powers: Checking Today's Most Dangerous Branch from Within" (2006) 115 Yale Law Journal 2314 (characterizing the executive as the most dangerous branch of the US government today).

[152] See Juan Linz, "Presidential or Parliamentary Democracy: Does it Make a Difference?," in Juan Linz and Arturo Valenzuela (eds), *The Failure of Presidential Democracy. Volume 2: The Case of Latin America* (John Hopkins UP 1994), 54.

[153] This would make the length of the presidential term correspond to the length of the parliamentary term. See n 77.

4. The Challenge of Asymmetry

A central question in the proposal to strengthen the presidency of the European Council concerns the mode of its election. This point does not constitute a simple technical feature, but rather raises one of the key constitutional challenges in the process of institutional design of a reformed presidency.[154] The reason has to do with the profound asymmetry that characterizes the EU member states in terms of population size. As I already stressed in Chapter 3, the EU features member states that range in population from Germany, with almost 82 million citizens, to Malta, with just over 400,000 inhabitants.[155] Moreover, 53.5% of the 507 million EU citizens live in just four EU member states: Germany, France, the United Kingdom (UK), and Italy, while the remaining 46.5% is scattered across the other 24 member states. This remarkable difference between the population of large and small states defies any easy option for a simple, Europe-wide election of the President. Inevitably, such an electoral system would render meaningless the value of voting in the smaller member states, making the election of the President of the European Council a matter exclusively for the larger ones.[156] As explained above in Section 2, this is exactly the problem associated with the proposal to strengthen the President of the European Commission according to the logic where a parliamentary majority selects the chief executive. Because the proposal to strengthen the presidency of the European Council is precisely targeted at redressing the paradox of domination, it is clear that other ideas must be considered in conceiving the popular election of the European Council President.

However, the challenge of asymmetry that the EU is facing is not unique. Most federal systems characterized by uneven geographical units and population imbalances have faced the analogous problem of how to reconcile the desire for shared rule with the need to reassure the smaller member states that their interest will not be unduly sacrificed in the union.[157] As such, comparative studies provide a wealth of insight that can be taken into account when thinking about EU institutional reform.[158] For example, to deal with this problem, Switzerland historically developed the principle of double-majority:[159] while Switzerland does not have a monocratic executive,[160] popular referenda—which are a pervasive feature of

[154] See generally Tom Ginsburg (ed), *Comparative Constitutional Design* (CUP 2014) (describing institutional choices in constitution-making).

[155] For the data see Eurostat, *European Population by Countries* (2013), available at <http://epp.eurostat.ec.europa.eu/tgm/table.do?tab=table&init=1&language=en&pcode=tps00001&plugin=1> (last accessed June 1, 2014).

[156] See text accompanying nn 98–9.

[157] See Daniel Elazar, *Exploring Federalism* (Alabama UP 1987) 5.

[158] See generally Michael Burgess and Alain Gagnon (eds), *Federal Democracies* (Routledge 2010) (describing comparative approaches to creating democracy in federal systems and what may be gleaned from them).

[159] See Wolf Linder and Adrian Vatter, "Institutions and Outcomes of Swiss Federalism: The Role of Cantons in Swiss Politics," in Jan-Erik Lane (ed), *The Swiss Labyrinth* (Cass 2001), 95, 97–9.

[160] See Arts 174–9 Const. Switz. (stating that the seven-member Directorate is elected by the Federal Parliament for a fixed term of four years, and cannot be removed by Parliament). See also

Swiss politics[161]—require for approval both a majority of the Swiss population *and* a majority of the cantons.[162] The logic of double-majority has been readapted with the specific aim to select a monocratic chief executive in Indonesia, which is a federalizing system with a presidential regime. Pursuant to the Indonesian Constitution, as amended in 2001 in the complex transition toward democracy,[163] a winning presidential candidate must receive a majority of the popular vote nationwide *and* at least 20% of the vote in a majority of the provinces.[164]

Perhaps the most well-known example of a creative institutional mechanism designed to account for the asymmetries between large and small states in the election of a chief executive is the Electoral College of the US Constitution.[165] As Shlomo Slonim has explained,[166] in the late eighteenth century the majority of the US states provided for the election of the executive either by the legislature,[167] or by direct popular suffrage.[168] Yet, to the framers of the US Constitution, neither of these solutions appeared consistent with the objective to secure a separation of powers between the executive and the legislature,[169] as well as to overcome the cleavage between the small and large states, which influenced the entire work of the Philadelphia Convention.[170] Hence, the framers came up with something entirely new: the Electoral College.[171] Pursuant to this system the President of the US is not elected directly by the people, but rather he is elected by special electors appointed by—in fact, since the nineteenth century, elected in—the states and constituting together an ad hoc College.[172] Each state is entitled to a number of electors equal to the sum of representatives and senators that the state possesses in Congress.[173] Because, pursuant to the Great Compromise, the US Constitution awards every state two senators[174] and at least one representative[175] (regardless of

Hanspeter Kriesi and Alexander Trechsel, *The Politics of Switzerland: Continuity and Change in a Consensus Democracy* (CUP 2008) 75 (explaining that the members of the Directorates are elected on the basis of a rigid formula reflecting the consociational nature of the Swiss system).

161 See Max Frenkel, "The Communal Basis of Swiss Liberty" (1993) 23 Publius 61, 67.

162 See Art 142 Const. Switz.

163 See James Giggacher, "Stand-Off as Indonesia Treads New Democratic Path," *The Sydney Morning Herald*, July 11, 2014 (discussing the contested presidential election in 2014).

164 See Art 6A Const. Indonesia.

165 See Bruce Ackerman, *We the People. Volume 1: Foundations* (Harvard UP 1991) 68.

166 Shlomo Slonim, "The Electoral College at Philadelphia: The Evolution of an Ad Hoc Congress for the Selection of a President" (1986) 73 Journal of American History 35, 37.

167 Ibid fn 6 (reporting that "Election of the executive by the legislature was provided for under the constitutions of Delaware, Georgia, Maryland, North Carolina, New Jersey, Pennsylvania, South Carolina and Virginia.").

168 Ibid (reporting that "Popular election of the executive was provided for under the constitutions of Massachusetts, New Hampshire and New York.").

169 See Gordon Wood, *The Creation of the American Republic: 1776-1787* (Norton 1993) 547–53 (emphasizing the importance of separation of powers to the framers of the US Constitution).

170 See Ray Raphael, *Mr. President: How and Why the Founders Created a Chief Executive* (Knopf 2012) 108–9 (emphasizing the centrality of the division between large and small states).

171 Art II, Sec. 1, cls 2-3, US Const. (establishing the Electoral College).

172 See generally L. Paige Whitaker and Thomas H. Neale, "The Electoral College: An Overview and Analysis of Reform Proposals," Congressional Research Service, November 5, 2004, RL30804 (providing an overview of the history and current functioning of the Electoral College).

173 Art II, Sec. 1, cl 2, US Const.

174 Art I, Sec. 3, cl 1, US Const.

175 Art I, Sec. 2, cl 3, US Const.

population), the Electoral College secures a slight overrepresentation of the small states in the election of the US President.[176] Hence, whereas the electoral system follows a majoritarian logic (because a candidate must win a majority of the Electoral College votes to be elected President), "the deviation from population apportionment of the electoral college is justified in order to serve federalism."[177]

Needless to say, the Electoral College system has received frequent criticism, being the feature of the US Constitution that has been the target of the greatest number of proposed constitutional amendments.[178] To begin with, as Bruce Ackerman has explained,[179] the framers of the US Constitution failed to anticipate the rise of presidential democracy and were ingenuous in writing several technical characteristics of the mechanics of the Electoral College. In particular, the framers envisioned that in the absence of a majority winner in the Electoral College, the election of the President would be thrown to the House of Representatives, where votes would be cast by states (the representation of each state having one vote).[180] In the election of 1800, just 13 years after the adoption of the US Constitution, this resulted in a major constitutional crisis, only haphazardly solved with the election of President Jefferson[181] and the subsequent adoption of the Twelfth Amendment.[182] Moreover, the functioning of the Electoral College has continued to raise objections in the present days mainly because of the possibility that a candidate could become President of the US by winning the votes of the Electoral College while losing the national popular vote,[183] an issue which was recently revived in the contested election of 2000.[184] As a result of the weaknesses of the US Electoral College system, it would be unreasonable to advocate its establishment in the EU for the potential election of the President of the European Council.

[176] See Raphael (n 170) 109.

[177] Norman R. Williams, "Reforming the Electoral College: Federalism, Majoritarianism and the Perils of Subconstitutional Change" (2011) 100 Georgetown Law Journal 173, 192.

[178] See Slonim (n 166) 35 (reporting that "[c]lose to seven hundred proposals to amend the Electoral College scheme have been introduced into Congress since the Constitution was inaugurated."); Williams (n 177) 175 (stating that "[i]n the past two centuries, more proposed constitutional amendments have sought to replace or reform the Electoral College than any other feature of [the US] constitutional order.").

[179] Bruce Ackerman, *The Failure of the Founding Fathers: Jefferson, Marshall and the Rise of Presidential Democracy* (Harvard UP 2005) 5 (detailing the Electoral College crisis of 1800).

[180] See Art II, Sec. 1, cl 3, US Const.

[181] See Ackerman (n 179) 104–7 (recalling the popular victory of Thomas Jefferson and his Republican Party in the elections of 1800 but explaining that the electors, due for technical failures in the Electoral College scheme, cast the same number of ballots for Jefferson and his running mate, Aaron Burr, which deprived the former of the Electoral College majority and threw the election to the House of Representatives, which, voting by states, eventually awarded the presidency to Jefferson only after 36 inconclusive ballots).

[182] See Amend. XII US Const. (modifying the rules on the functioning of the Electoral College so that the electors separately vote for the President and the Vice President).

[183] See Sanford Levinson, *Our Undemocratic Constitution* (OUP 2006).

[184] See *Bush v. Gore*, 531 U.S. 98 (2000) (US Supreme Court halting recount of votes in Florida and de facto awarding the presidency to George W. Bush) on which see Bruce Ackerman (ed), *Bush v. Gore: The Question of Legitimacy* (Yale UP 2002) (analyzing various legal aspects of the 2000 election).

However, even if the institution of the Electoral College should not be replicated in Europe as such, there is one lesson that the system can offer to the EU: an innovative mechanism to count votes to overcome the asymmetries between the member states in the election of the President. This is achieved by entitling every state to a number of votes corresponding to the sum of votes it enjoys in the two branches of the legislature. As discussed also in Chapter 5, the EU has a bicameral legislature: the EP, which represents the EU citizens, and the Council, which represents the EU states.[185] In the EP, the 751 seats are apportioned on the basis of population, albeit corrected by the principle of degressive proportionality: As provided by Article 14(2) TEU, no member state shall be allocated more than 96 seats, and no state shall have less than six. In the Council, until November 2014,[186] votes were weighted between the member states based on their size, but with greater equality in the apportionment between states than in the EP.[187] In particular, since the accession of Croatia to the EU in July 2013,[188] the Council had 352 votes, divided between the 28 member states along a ratio, which ranges from 29 votes (for Germany, France, Italy, and the UK) to three votes for Malta.[189] In other words, contrary to the US, which has one chamber of the legislature (the House) mainly reflecting states' population and one chamber (the Senate) purely enshrining the equality of the states, the EU is endowed with a bicameral system which incorporates a logic of degressive proportionality *in both chambers*. Yet, the result is the same: namely, to temper majoritarianism to safeguard federalism. This is highly valuable for the purpose of electing the President of the European Council.

My proposal for the mode of election would be the following. Every five years, on the same day EU citizens vote for the EP, they also elect the President. Political parties bring forward candidates for the post (possibly through a popular selection process via primary elections).[190] Citizens *directly* vote for the President so there is no special, intermediate electoral body such as the US Electoral College. However, the election of the President is not made on the basis of an EU-wide constituency. Rather, as is the case for the election of the EP, citizens vote in state constituencies. Moreover (like in the US) every EU member state is awarded a number of "votes" for the election of the President, which equals the number of seats that state has in the EP plus the number of votes that state has in the Council. The candidate that comes first in one state would gain all the "electoral votes" of that state, following the logic of winner-takes-all. To be elected President, a candidate must obtain

[185] See Van Gerven (n 118) 332. [186] See text accompanying nn 200–3.

[187] See Art 16(4) TEU.

[188] Treaty concerning the accession of the Republic of Croatia to the European Union [2012] OJ L112/10.

[189] See Art 3(3) Protocol No. 36 on transitional provisions, as amended by Treaty Concerning the Accession of the Republic of Croatia to the European Union [2012] OJ L112/20.

[190] This is an important point that I cannot develop in full here. But see Sonia Piedrafita and Vilde Renman, "The 'Personalisation' of the European Elections: A Half-hearted Attempt to Increase Turnout and Democratic Legitimacy?," European Policy Institute Network paper No. 37/2014, 5 (raising concerns on the process which has been followed by some European political parties to select the *Spitzenkandidaten* for the post of European Commission President and demanding a more open and transparent process in the future).

the *majority* of "electoral votes" across the EU: since the EP has 751 seats and the Council 352 votes, the total number of presidential votes is 751 + 352 = 1,103: so the magic number a candidate must reach to be elected is 1,103/2 = 552. If none of the candidates reaches the majority of 552 votes, the two candidates with the highest number of electoral votes will be subject to a runoff 14 days after the first election. The candidate who gains a majority of electoral votes will become President of the Union.

The electoral mechanism proposed here, while being inspired by the trials and errors of regimes abroad,[191] presents several distinctive advantages. Like the US precedent,[192] it devises a way to count votes, which ensures (through the trick of the "electoral votes") a slight overrepresentation of smaller member states in the election of the President of the European Council. This addresses the dire problem of asymmetry between large and small states that characterizes the EU. However, unlike the US, it removes the filter of an ad hoc electoral body, the Electoral College: whereas the framers of the US Constitution, with their distrust for radical democracy,[193] were afraid of a direct, popular legitimation of the executive, this issue seems less of a problem today. Moreover, the option proposed above allows every political party to present a candidate in the first round of election (which is consistent with the mode of direct election of heads of state in EU member states with semi-presidential systems,[194] and conforms to the logic of proportional representation which is in place for the multi-party EP).[195] And it also secures through the runoff that the President will be elected by a *majority* (rather than simply a *plurality*).[196] As the recent experience of the selection of the President of the European Commission demonstrates, the lead candidate of a party, which represents a plurality in the EP, but only has 29% of the EU-wide popular votes, suffers from a legitimacy deficit.[197] Instead, an electoral mechanism, which secures majority election (at the latest in the runoff) would boost the claim of the President of the European Council to speak for the EU as a whole.[198]

With that said, however, I am also aware that my proposal has weaknesses. By trading in a purely majoritarian logic to guard the federal balance between the states, the proposal outlined above disappoints those who would like to see an EU

[191] See generally Mark Tushnet, "The Possibilities of Comparative Constitutional Law" (1999) 108 Yale Law Journal 1225.

[192] See Williams (n 177) 192.

[193] See Wood (n 169) 322.

[194] See Art 7 Const. Fr. and Art 127(4) Const. Pl. (stating that the President of the Republic is elected by absolute majority and that if no candidate obtains this majority in the first ballot a runoff is arranged between the two most voted candidates after 14 days).

[195] See text accompanying n 108.

[196] Note that in the functioning of the US Electoral College there is the possibility that no candidate reaches a majority of the Electoral College votes. In this case, the election decision is thrown to the House of Representatives. This happened twice in US history: in 1800 and 1824. See Lawrence D. Longley and Neil R. Peirce, *The Electoral College Primer* (Yale UP 1996) 118 and Ackerman (n 179) 104–7.

[197] See text accompanying nn 130–2.

[198] See also Sartori (n 102) 27 (emphasizing the connection between electoral mechanisms and government stability).

President directly elected through an EU-wide popular election in which states have no role.[199] Moreover, the proposal partially builds on the allocation of votes between the member states in the Council traditionally provided for in the EU treaties, and which the Lisbon Treaty has extended on a temporary basis.[200] However, such a system has been the object of criticism because it significantly distorts the weights of the states by securing a major overrepresentation of *middle size* EU member states, at the expenses of both larger and smaller ones.[201] In particular, on the basis of the Nice Treaty of 2001, Spain and Poland gained as many as 27 votes, only two votes less than Germany (which has 29 votes), despite the fact that these states have respectively 56% and 46% of the German population. It is also for this reason that the Lisbon Treaty, after a transitional period ending in November 2014, and extendable until March 2017,[202] has replaced the current weighing of votes between states in the Council with a Swiss-like "double-majority" principle.[203] Pursuant to Article 16(4) TEU, after the end of the transitional period "a qualified majority shall be defined as at least 55% of the members of the Council, comprising at least fifteen of them and representing Member States comprising at least 65% of the population of the Union." Resorting to the weighing of votes in the Council is of course a limit of the proposal. One could think of ways to reapportion the numbers for the future, but for the moment I have taken what was available and built on it.[204]

Finally—and perhaps more importantly—the proposal to directly elect the President of the European Council deprives the heads of state and government congressed in the European Council of one of their greatest privileges: electing the President.[205] At the same time, if the election of the President is taken away from the European Council, it is advisable that the power to impeach and remove the President in case of grave misbehaviors be taken away from the European Council and attributed to the EU legislature, as a way to secure separation of powers and inter-institutional checks and balances.[206] As I have explained above, the whole logic of taking the election of the President of the European Council out of the

[199] See e.g., Decker and Sonnicksen (n 48) 30 (proposing direct EU-wide election of the President of the European Commission).

[200] See Art 16(5) TEU and Art 3(3) Protocol No. 36 on transitional provisions.

[201] See Bela Plechanovová, "The Treaty of Nice and the Distribution of Votes in the Council—Voting Power Consequences for the EU after the Oncoming Enlargement" (2003) 7 European Integration Online Papers.

[202] See Art 16(5) TEU.

[203] See generally Stefan Van den Bogaert, "Qualified Majority Voting in the Council: First Reflections on the New Rules" (2008) 15 Maastricht Journal of European & Comparative Law 97.

[204] An alternative option would be to work around the "double-majority" system, as foreseen in Indonesia. See text accompanying nn 163–4.

[205] Alternatively see S Fabbrini (n 37) 5 (proposing an electoral system in which the European Council identifies two candidates, which are then subject to a vote by an electoral college composed of members of national parliaments). This solution would keep the European Council at the helm of the choice of the President but may not remove the challenge of interstate domination that has so far characterized the internal working of the European Council.

[206] See ceteris paribus, Michael J. Gerhardt, *The Federal Impeachment Process: A Constitutional and Historical Analysis* (2nd ed. Chicago UP 2000) (emphasizing the connection between the impeachment process and separation of powers).

hands of the heads of state and government in the European Council is motivated by the desire to endow the presidency with greater power and legitimacy, to prevent dynamics of interstate dominations, and to create a forum in which alternative policy agenda for the future of the EU can genuinely compete.[207] However, it is clear that for a proposal of the direct election of the President of the European Council to succeed, sweeteners should be conceived to compensate the heads of state and government in the European Council for the loss of their privilege. This leads to the next challenge: whether a treaty reform introducing the popular election of the European Council President would be feasible and what the bargaining chips could be to make it happen.

5. The Challenge of Unanimity

In this chapter, I have made the case in favor of strengthening the role of the President of the European Council as a way to address the paradox of interstate domination unleashed by the Euro-crisis I criticized in Chapter 3. In the previous sections, I have envisioned the powers and responsibilities of a new presidency and suggested an electoral mechanism through which the member states and EU citizens could select the President. Now, a pressing question that must be addressed is whether anything that I have argued for has any, even remote, chance of being considered as an option for institutional reform. As scholars, it is possible to fantasize about major constitutional models, and libraries are filled with perfectly designed charters of government that no policy-maker has ever considered.[208] I will never deny that this is a noble and important task. However, I submit that the interest of my proposal for institutional reform increases to the extent to which it stands a chance of being considered as a feasible option by policy-makers. This section attempts to do this, considering the opportunities and incentives to implement in the EU a constitutional reform of the type envisaged so far.

A. Opportunities

As a starter, let me indicate the rocky problem: the challenge of unanimity. Crudely put, the proposal to strengthen the presidency of the European Council would require a change to the EU treaties and no such change can be made unless the EU member states unanimously concur.[209] However, as much as the process of treaty

[207] See text accompanying nn 96–9.

[208] See, e.g., the fascinating essay by Melchiorre Gioia, *Quale dei governi liberi meglio convenga alla felicità dell'Italia* [1797] (outlining a constitutional model for the form of government of Italy in 1797). Italy was established as a state only 64 years later, in 1861, through the unification of several kingdoms. Interestingly, as explained by Augusto Barbera, *Le basi filosofiche del costituzionalismo* (Laterza 1997) 22, the essay by Melchiorre Gioia was drafted for a public competition promoted by the government of Lombardy, before the region was conquered by Napoleon and made by the French authorities part of a newly created puppet state: the Cisalpine Republic.

[209] See Art 48(4)–(6) TEU.

change in the EU is a burdensome task, it is not as burdensome as amending, say, the US Constitution.[210] During the last 24 years, the EU treaties have been subject to four major overhauls (excluding the failed attempt to adopt a Treaty Establishing the European Constitution).[211] The Treaty of Maastricht of 1992, the Treaty of Amsterdam of 1996, the Treaty of Nice of 2001, and the Treaty of Lisbon of 2007 have all introduced profound changes to the architecture of the EU—leading Bruno de Witte to speak of a "semi-permanent treaty revision process" in the EU.[212] Moreover, the ink of the Lisbon Treaty text was barely dry when the member states exploited the newly introduced "simplified treaty revision procedure"[213] to rewrite Article 136 Treaty on the Functioning of the EU (TFEU) and allow for the establishment of a permanent stability mechanism for the Eurozone[214]—the European Stability Mechanism.[215] At the same time, the EU member states, have repeatedly responded to the Euro-crisis by adopting international treaties outside the EU legal order, but functionally and substantially connected to EU law.[216] Although, as I claimed in Chapter 5, the practice by national governments to step outside the framework of EU law should be discontinued as inconsistent with the institutional status of the EP and its right to be involved in EMU decision-making, the widespread use of international treaties by the member states during the last years testifies to the existence of a political will among national governments to engage in treaty reform: in fact, German Chancellor Merkel has prominently argued in favor of a comprehensive constitutional revision of the EU treaties, vowing to put the Eurozone on more solid grounds.[217]

Furthermore, the Fiscal Compact[218] (and now also the Agreement on the Single Resolution Fund)[219] includes a provision, which may be of particular relevance to the purpose of our discussion. Under the pressure of the delegates of the EP, who joined as observers to the negotiation about the treaty, despite not being involved

[210] See Michael B. Rappaport, "Reforming Article V: The Problems Created by the National Convention Method and How to Fix Them" (2010) 96 Virginia Law Review 1509 (explaining the quasi-impossibility of changing the US Constitution).

[211] See Giuseppe Floridia, *Il cantiere della nuova Europa* (Il Mulino 2003).

[212] Bruno De Witte, "The Closest Thing to a Constitutional Conversation in Europe: The Semi-Permanent Treaty Revision Process," in Neil Walker et al (eds), *Convergence and Divergence in European Public Law* (Hart Publishing 2002), 39.

[213] See Art 48(6)–(7) TEU.

[214] See European Council Decision No. 2011/199/EU of March 25, 2011, amending Article 136 TFEU with regard to a stability mechanism for Member States whose currency is the euro [2011] OJ L91/1.

[215] See Treaty Establishing the European Stability Mechanism, February 2, 2012, available at <http://www.european-council.europa.eu/media/582311/05-tesm2.en12.pdf> (last accessed June 1, 2014).

[216] See generally Kaarlo Tuori and Klaus Tuori, *The Eurozone Crisis: A Constitutional Analysis* (CUP 2014) and Alicia Hinarejos, *The Euro Area Crisis in Constitutional Perspective* (OUP 2015).

[217] See German Chancellor Angela Merkel, Speech at the Bundestag, Berlin, December 18, 2013 (stating, inter alia, that "Wir müssen, wenn die vertraglichen Grundlagen nicht ausreichen, Verträge eben auch weiterentwickeln.").

[218] See Treaty on Stability, Coordination and Governance in the Economic and Monetary Union, March 2, 2012, [hereinafter Fiscal Compact], available at <http://www.eurozone.europa.eu/media/304649/st00tscg26_en12.pdf> (last accessed June 1, 2014).

[219] See Agreement on the transfer and mutualization of contributions to the Single Resolution Fund, May 21, 2014 [hereinafter: SRF Agreement] available at <http://register.consilium.europa.eu/doc/srv?l=EN&f=ST%208457%202014%20INIT> (last accessed May 25, 2014).

in drafting it,[220] the participating member states accepted to insert a final clause in the Fiscal Compact, which reads that:

within five years, at most, of the date of entry into force of this Treaty, on the basis of an assessment of the experience with its implementation, the necessary steps shall be taken, in accordance with the Treaty on the European Union and the Treaty on the Functioning of the European Union, with the aim of incorporating the substance of this Treaty into the legal framework of the European Union.[221]

The Fiscal Compact introduces an obligation for the EU member states that signed the treaty to find ways to bring back the content of the treaty into the law of the EU by January 1, 2018[222] (while the SRF Agreement requires incorporation of its provision within EU law by January 1, 2026).[223] Because of the nature of (some of) the legal innovations set by the Fiscal Compact, this implies the necessity to amend the EU treaties, thus creating a window of opportunity in which the institutional proposal advanced in this chapter could be seriously taken into consideration.[224]

In fact, as I argued in Chapter 5, whereas the key substantive provision of the Fiscal Compact—the obligation to introduce a "golden rule," which was discussed in Chapter 1—would not require a treaty change, since it could be adopted through an EU regulation,[225] there are other *institutional* provisions of the Fiscal Compact which are not consistent with the EU treaties as they currently stand. One of this is the so-called "reversed qualified majority" rule,[226] pursuant to which the member states in Council commit to approve a decision by the Commission finding a member state in breach of the excessive deficit rule of the Stability and Growth Pact (SGP) unless a qualified majority of member states is opposed to the Commission decision.[227] According to the current Article 126(6) TFEU, the opposite rule applies since a qualified majority vote by the Council is necessary to endorse the decision of the Commission. Hence, an amendment of the TFEU would probably be required.[228] Nevertheless, it is another part of the Fiscal Compact that would certainly compel a treaty revision, if the member states are to obey their obligation to bring back the content of that treaty in the TEU and TFEU: this is Title V of the Fiscal Compact

[220] See European Parliament press release, "Fiscal Union: EP Representatives 'Cautiously Optimistic'," January 26, 2012 (reporting the role of EP negotiators in obtaining the inclusion in the Fiscal Compact of a so-called "*rendez-vous* clause").

[221] Art 16 Fiscal Compact.

[222] See Art 14(2) Fiscal Compact.

[223] See Art 16 SRF Agreement.

[224] See also European Parliament Resolution of February 2, 2012 on the European Council meeting of January 30, 2012, P7_TA(2012)0023, para 9 (which "[i]nsists that the contracting parties fully respect their commitment to integrate, within five years at the latest, the Treaty on Stability, Coordination and Governance into the EU treaties and asks for the remaining weaknesses of the Treaty of Lisbon to be tackled on this occasion.").

[225] But see Tuori and Tuori (n 216) 109 (raising doubts on the possibility to impose "through EU secondary regulation such an obligation to undertake legislative, preferably constitutional, measures").

[226] See Art 7 Fiscal Compact.

[227] See Paul Craig, "The Stability, Coordination and Governance Treaty: Principle, Politics and Pragmatism" (2012) 37 European Law Review 231, 234, 244.

[228] See Rainer Palmstorfer, "The Reverse Majority Voting Under the 'Six Pack': A Bad Turn for the Union?" (2014) 20 European Law Journal 186, 193.

that provides a brand new set of rules for the "Governance of the Euro Area." In particular, the Fiscal Compact institutionalizes the Euro Summit[229]—that is, the meeting of the heads of state and government of the Eurozone, jointly with the Presidents of the Commission and the ECB—and creates the post of Euro Summit President.[230]

The Euro Summit, initially set up as an informal gathering in October 2008 at the initiative of then French President Sarkozy, was given a first institutional structure in a statement adopted in October 2011 by the heads of state and government of the Eurozone member states.[231] This statement advanced ten measures to improve the governance of the Eurozone, including the decision to hold regular Euro Summit meetings at least twice a year, to establish a post of permanent Euro Summit President, and to coordinate the work of the Euro Summit with that of the Eurogroup acting at a lower level in the composition of national ministers of finance. The legal nature of this statement was not clarified, and although part of its content was replicated in the European Council conclusions of October 2011,[232] it was uncertain whether the statement could be interpreted as an international agreement concluded by the Eurozone member states. The Fiscal Compact, however, gave the Euro Summit a legal status—formalizing the format of the meetings and their composition.[233] Moreover, it clarified the role of the President of the Euro Summit, which was shaped tout court on the role of the President of European Council set by Article 15 TEU.[234] In March 2012, the heads of state and government of the Eurozone member states decided to entrust the task of Euro Summit President to Mr. Van Rompuy,[235] the then President of the European Council. And in August 2014, when Mr. Tusk was elected as second President of the European Council, he was also appointed as President of the Euro Summit,[236] thus promoting a degree of institutional connection—yet also of confusion—between the European Council, in which all EU member states are involved, and the Euro Summit, in which only the Eurozone states participate.

Leaving aside the question of how the system of institutional governance designed for the Eurozone can be reconciled with the broader institutional architecture that concerns all the EU member states,[237] it seems undeniable that the prospect of a treaty reform to reverse engineer the Euro Summit within the EU constitutional order offers an attractive opportunity to reconsider the role of the presidency as

[229] See Art 12 Fiscal Compact.

[230] See Christian Calliess, "The Governance Framework of the Eurozone and the Need for a Treaty Reform," in Federico Fabbrini et al (eds), *What Form of Government for the European Union and the Eurozone?* (Hart Publishing 2015), 37.

[231] See Euro Summit Statement, October 26, 2011.

[232] See European Council Conclusions, October 23, 2011, EUCO 52/1/11, 5.

[233] See further on this Chapter 3.

[234] See text accompanying nn 74–81.

[235] See Euro area Heads of State and Government, Statement, March 2, 2012.

[236] See Euro area Heads of State and Government, Statement, August 30, 2014.

[237] See generally Brigid Laffan, "European Union and Eurozone: How to Co-exist?" in Franklin Allen et al (eds), *Governance for the Eurozone: Integration or Disintegration?* (Fic Press 2012), 173.

advocated here.[238] In fact, because the Euro Summit presidency is modeled on the European Council presidency, the domestication of the Fiscal Compact could also offer the opportunity to tailor the institutional proposal I advanced in this chapter to the Eurozone only, rather than to the EU as such. However, there remains a follow up question: why should the member states' governments subscribe to the idea of strengthening the role of the presidency of the European Council (or of the Euro Summit), making it the real President of the Union (or the Eurozone)? Whereas the Lisbon Treaty has institutionalized the "Convention method" to amend the treaties,[239] ultimately, pursuant to Article 48(4) TEU,

> a conference of representatives of the governments of the Member States shall be convened by the president of the Council for the purpose of determining by common accord the amendments to be made to the Treaties. The amendments shall enter into force after being ratified by all the Member States in accordance with their respective constitutional requirements.

So why should the member states agree to revise the role of the presidency?

B. Incentives

The proposal to strengthen the presidency may be particularly attractive to many member states for political reasons. However, I would also advise introducing an institutional expedient to sweeten the change advocated in this chapter and make it more agreeable for all of them. From a political perspective, I suspect the idea to strengthen the presidency may be attractive for the small, poor, and new EU member states. As revealed in Chapter 3, the intergovernmental governance of the Euro-crisis during the last year has shattered the expectations of the smaller member states that they could keep control of the European Council and instead unleashed a dynamic of domination by the larger states. In fact, even though the policies promoted since the inception of the Euro-crisis have met the support of several small states of the northern EU, the increasingly hegemonic nature of decision-making in the EU has been a cause for concern,[240] which a reform presidency could address. At the same time, for the member states in dire economic conditions in the southern EU, the diminution of power has been so significant that the idea of electing the President of the European Council would be a way to regain status in EU decision-making.[241] And for the member states in the eastern EU, which recently joined the bloc and are not yet part of the Eurozone, the

[238] See European Parliament Resolution of November 20, 2012 on the report "Towards a Genuine EMU," P7_TA(2012)0430, para 6 (calling for a convention to amend the treaties).

[239] See Steve Peers, "The Future of EU Treaty Amendments" (2012) 31 Yearbook of European Law 17.

[240] See Päivi Leino and Janne Salminen, "The Euro Crisis and its Constitutional Consequences for Finland: Is There Room for National Politics in EU Decision-Making?" (2013) 9 European Constitutional Law Review 51.

[241] See generally Xenophon Kontiades and Ioannis Tassopoulos, "The Impact of the Financial Crisis on the Greek Constitution" in Xenophon Kontiades (ed), *Constitutions in the Global Financial Crisis* (Ashagate 2013), 195 (emphasizing restrictions of sovereignty in Greece).

strengthening of the President of the European Council would be a way to ensure that they are not cut off from deliberation on the future of the EU[242] (not to mention, of course, the added value that this could have as far as the protection of their interests in foreign affairs and security is concerned).[243]

However, the proposal to strengthen the President of the European Council could also be advantageous for Italy and France. Although both are large, rich, founding members of the EU, their influence on the EU agenda setting has declined as far as economic policy is concerned.[244] As I have argued elsewhere, the new Socialist governments of France and Italy have been unsuccessful in their efforts to overturn the German-led pro-austerity stance of EU economic policy.[245] Although Hollande campaigned in 2012 on a platform that advocated repeal of the Fiscal Compact and a strategy to promote growth and tackle unemployment,[246] once he became the President of France he was forced to backtrack on many of his promises. Leading a country weakened by several economic difficulties,[247] President Hollande had to cultivate special relations with Germany to keep France afloat and ended up implementing the German economic blueprint[248]—extracting in exchange only a largely symbolic, and non-legally binding, Compact for Growth and Jobs.[249] Similarly, because of Italy's economic problems,[250] the electoral victory of the Democratic Party there in 2013 did not produce visible change in EU economic policy, although—since the appointment of the Renzi government in 2014—Italy has embraced a more assertive role in EU policy-making,[251]

242 See Government of Poland, "Preparing for Next Steps on Better Economic Governance in the Euroarea: Polish Contribution," March 2015 (stressing that reforms of EMU governance should remain open toward non-Eurozone member states).

243 See generally North Atlantic Treaty Organization (NATO) press release, "Wales Summit Declaration: Issued by the Heads of State and Government Participating in the Meeting of the North Atlantic Council in Wales," September 5, 2014 (emphasizing security concerns in Eastern Europe).

244 See e.g., Adriana Cerretelli, "La partita delle nomine che contano a Bruxelles," *Il Sole 24 Ore*, July 8, 2014 (reporting decreasing influence of Italian officials at EU level); Jean-Luc Gréau, "Peut-on enrayer le déclin économique français?," Revue Politique et Parlementaire, January 8, 2014 (discussing French economic decline).

245 See Federico Fabbrini, "Austerity, the European Council and the Institutional Future of the EU" (2015) 22 Indiana Journal of Global Legal Studies 269, 281–3.

246 See Steven Erlanger and Nicholas Kulish, "French Front-Runner Says He'd Seek to Renegotiate Fiscal Treaty if Elected," *The New York Times*, April 25, 2012.

247 See e.g., Louis Gallois, "Pacte pour la compétitivité de l'industrie française," report commissioned by the French Prime Minister, November 5, 2012 (discussion of the weak state of France's economy and proposing a competiveness pact for industry).

248 See Loi organique no. 2012-1403 du 17 décembre 2012 relative à la programmation et à la gouvernance des finances publiques, J.O.R.F. n°294 du 18 décembre 2012 p. 19816 (Fr.) (incorporating the Fiscal Compact in France).

249 See European Council Conclusions, June 29, 2012, EUCO 76/12, Annex.

250 See Eurostat news release, *Government debt increased to 93.9% of GDP in euro area and to 88.0% in EU28*, July 22, 2014, available at <http://ec.europa.eu/eurostat/documents/2995521/5175186/2-22072014-AP-EN.PDF/ 86c55faa-ea8c-42f9-b9cb-e0d1be68e957> (last accessed July 23, 2014) (reporting Italy's debt to GDP ratio as the second highest in the EU after Greece).

251 See European Commission Communication, "Making the Best Use of the Flexibility within the Existing Rules of the Stability and Growth Pact," January 13, 2015, COM(2015)12 final (recognizing the importance of a flexible application of the existing rules of the SGP to account for a downswing in the economic conditions of EU member states, as repeatedly advocated by the Italian government).

skilfully exploiting the rotating six-month presidency of the Council it held in the second half of 2014.[252] From the perspective of these two member states, therefore, strengthening the President of the European Council could be a preferable alternative to the status quo. In fact, as mentioned, the idea of creating a powerful Eurozone presidency—a reform which would moreover be very much consistent with the domestic tradition of the French form of government[253]—has increasingly gained ground with top Italian and French policy-makers.[254]

In addition, the idea of a reformed presidency may actually work well for the UK, if it remains in the EU.[255] This may seem counterintuitive, since the UK has traditionally opposed further steps in the process toward an ever closer Union.[256] Yet, the idea is not entirely foreign to UK preferences, since at the time of the European Constitutional Convention the UK government had expressed its support for a strengthened presidency of the European Council.[257] Moreover, as of now, the UK has major difficulties in finding an EU institutional forum through which to channel its concerns. The role of the UK government in the European Council is weak, and the capacity of UK voters to influence through their ballot for the EP the composition and the agenda of the European Commission is negligible.[258] On the contrary, as I have suggested above, the presidency may serve as a brake against supranational encroachments over national prerogatives.[259] Because an elected President of the European Council could speak for the entire EU, and could make a legitimate claim to protect the federal division of competences, the interests of the UK could be better secured through this new institutional arrangement than under the current one.[260] Note also that, following the mechanism of election I articulated in the previous section, the UK would be entitled to 102 "electoral votes" for the choice of the President—and no presidential candidate could afford to disregard the concerns of a constituency that counts for 20% of the votes needed to win half of the total 1,103 electoral votes.

[252] See *2014 Italian Presidency Council EU,* available at <http://italia2014.eu/en/> (last accessed 20 November 2014).

[253] See Duverger (n 57) 176 and Magnette (n 72) 1067.

[254] See text accompanying nn 24–5.

[255] See European Union Referendum Bill, 2015–16, HC Bill 6 (UK) (stating that a referendum on the UK's membership within the EU will be held before December 31, 2017).

[256] See generally European Union Act, 2011, c. 12 (UK) (placing restrictions on treaties relating to the EU) on which see Paul Craig, "The European Union Act 2011: Locks, Limits and Legality" (2011) 28 Common Market Law Review 1881 (discussing the "locks" the UK has imposed on its ability to approve EU documents and decisions).

[257] See Craig (n 73) 83 (reporting a January 2003 proposal by the UK government advanced during the Constitutional Convention in favor of strengthening the presidency of the European Council).

[258] See Toby Helm, "Humiliating defeat for David Cameron pushes Britain towards EU exit," *The Guardian*, June 28, 2014 (reporting increasing isolation of the UK government in the European Council).

[259] See text accompanying nn 147–9.

[260] See generally Foreign & Commonwealth Office, "Review of the Balance of Competences" (2012), available at <https://www.gov.uk/review-of-the-balance-of-competences> (last accessed on April 19, 2015) (considering effect of EU competences on UK policy).

This of course leaves out Germany. As the reluctant hegemon of the EU,[261] and the state that currently sets the tone of the EU economic policy agenda,[262] Germany would have the most to lose from a proposal to strengthen the presidency of the European Council. Nevertheless, because of its history, Germany also has very much to lose from fueling the popular view that it has, once again, come to dominate the continent.[263] As such, the burning of a German flag by Greek youngsters in Syntagma Square, Athens,[264] as well as the proposal by a former President of the European Commission to build an alliance between France, Italy, and Spain against Germany,[265] should be cause for concerns *in Germany*. Hence, my proposal: Germany should take a step back, trade its short-term dominant position for the long-term interest in protecting the sustainability of the EU and accept the plan to directly elect the President of the European Council. With 125 "electoral votes" out of a total of 1,103, Germany would still be the leading battle state for any presidential candidate that wants to win the election. At the same time, the other member states must compensate Germany with a payback: accommodating repeated and legitimate German concerns,[266] they must accept the writing into the EU treaties of a prohibition to mutualize the debts of the Eurozone member states. As I underlined in Chapter 4, the recurrent proposals to adopt Euro-bonds are ill conceived because they would ask Germany to pay for the debts of the other member states.[267] This is unfair and unusual, since in no federal system are debts of one federated unit horizontally paid by the treasury of another unit.[268] Ruling out this possibility in the EU treaties would assuage Germany and make it possibly more interested in signing off the proposal to reform the EU presidency.

It goes without saying that what I am suggesting is a great compromise—analogous to the one struck by the US at the Philadelphia Constitutional Convention:[269] every

261 See William Paterson, "The Reluctant Hegemon? Germany Moves Center Stage in the European Union" (2011) 49 Journal of Common Market Studies 57.

262 See Andrew Glencross, *The Politics of European Integration* (Wiley 2014) 305.

263 See Timothy Garton Ash, "The New German Question," 60 New York Review of Books, August 15–September 25, 2013, 52.

264 See e.g., Graeme Wearden, "Europe's day of anti-austerity strikes and protests turn violent," *The Guardian*, November 14, 2012 (reporting massive strikes in cities across Europe and episodes of violence).

265 See Marco Damilano, "Intervista: 'In Europa coalizione contro i populisti'. Parla Prodi," *L'Espresso*, May 22, 2014 (interviewing former European Commission President Romano Prodi, who argues for an alliance between Italy, France, and Spain to overtake German control of the European Council).

266 See "Merkel Vows 'No Euro Bonds as Long as I Live,'" *Der Spiegel Online*, June 27, 2012 (reporting strenuous opposition by German Chancellor Angela Merkel against the proposal to create euro-bonds).

267 But see Federico Fabbrini, "Taxing and Spending in the Eurozone: Legal and Political Challenges Related to the Adoption of the Financial Transaction Tax" (2014) 39 European Law Review 155 (making the case in favor of taxing power at EU level).

268 See Jonathan Rodden, *Hamilton's Paradox: The Promise and Peril of Fiscal Federalism* (CUP 2006) (explaining that in federal currency unions debts of the local governments are covered—if at all—by the central government).

269 See Jack N. Rakove, "The Great Compromise: Ideas, Interests and the Politics of Constitution Making" (1987) 44 Wiliam & Mary Quarterly 424.

EU member state gives up something, yet everyone gains something in return, and the Union is better off. Of course, path dependency constitutes a strong obstacle against changing the functioning of the European Council—and it is unlikely that the heads of state and government will be willing to renounce playing a role in EU policy-making.[270] But this problem could be dealt with by envisaging a new role for the congress of states' presidents and prime ministers—by transforming the European Council into the real upper legislative house of the EU, absorbing the legislative functions of the Council, as I have argued in Chapter 5. In my view, the operation of the European Council as a collective executive has been unsatisfactory.[271] However the European Council could fulfil an important role as a kind of EU Senate.[272] Strengthening the role of the President of the European Council as the real EU executive would then be part of a broader package of reform—and its success would be linked to a more comprehensive restructuring of the EU institutional architecture based on a healthy constitutional compromise.[273]

6. Conclusion

Since the eruption of the Euro-crisis, the EU heads of state and government congressed in the European Council, and other intergovernmental institutions, have moved to the forefront of the system of governance of the EU and the Eurozone. As Chapter 3 has explained, the Euro-crisis and the responses to it proved to be a watermark in the institutional system of the EU and the Eurozone, by bringing national chief executives to the center of EMU governance. However, this system of executive federalism has given rise to multiple problems of effectiveness and legitimacy. In particular, an intergovernmental framework for decision-making has opened the door to dynamics of interstate domination, with larger and more powerful EU member states able to impose their preferences, and entrench their strength, vis-à-vis smaller, economically weaker ones. Growing awareness has therefore emerged among scholars and policy-makers of the limitations of the current system of EMU governance. Yet, much uncertainty persists on how the form of government of the EU and the Eurozone should be reformed.

[270] See also Uwe Puetter, "New Intergovernmentalism: The European Council and its President," in Federico Fabbrini et al (eds), *What Form of Government for the European Union and the Eurozone* (Hart Publishing 2015), 253.

[271] See also Hauke Brunkhorst, "Collective Bonapartism—Democracy in the European Crisis" (2014) 15 German Law Journal 1177.

[272] If the European Council is to play the role of a Senate, while the President of the European Council is to function as the chief executive of the EU, it would be important to build-in appropriate separation between them. But see already Art 235 TFEU (explaining that the President of the European Council, and the President of the European Commission, do not have voting rights when the European Council decides by vote). Moreover, by comparative example see Art I, Sec. 4 US Const. (stating that the Vice President of the US, who is the second highest executive officer of the US, "shall be the President of the Senate, but shall have no vote, unless they be equally divided.").

[273] See generally Avishai Margalit, *On Compromise and Rotten Compromises* (Princeton UP 2013) (distinguishing between compromises and rotten compromises).

To address the paradox of domination, this chapter has advanced the proposal to introduce a targeted institutional reform in the EU: strengthening the role of the President of the European Council, so as to make it the President of the Union as a whole, along the constitutional logic of separation of powers. Reforming the presidency of the European Council, by increasing its capacity to set the EU agenda (beyond the preferences of a few EU member states) and making it accountable directly to EU citizens (rather than just to the EU heads of state and government) would be instrumental to re-establishing a healthy balance between the EU member states. But it would also create a genuine forum for democratic competition on the agenda of the EU. As I claimed, compared to other options of institutional reform, including the initiative to boost the politicization of the President of the European Commission along a fusion-of-powers logic, the proposal to strengthen the President of the European Council along a separation-of-powers logic, is better fitting the nature of the EU as an asymmetrical Union of states and citizens. In fact, only the presidentialization of the EU executive power can halt the paradoxical dynamic of domination unleashed by the Euro-crisis and the responses to it, and thus restore a horizontal balance of power between the EU member states.

To support this position, the chapter sought to offer a first (and thus certainly incomplete) explanation of what the proposal to strengthen the European Council presidency would entail, and then discussed three constitutional challenges that accompany this institutional reform proposal. First, I considered how a strengthened presidency could handle the challenge of representation that currently characterizes the EU executive branch and outlined the specific powers that should be attributed to the President. Here I emphasized the advantages that a reformed presidency would produce in terms of equality between the states, unity of the EU, and protection of the federal compact, and recommended that the President be entrusted with the power to appoint the Commission (subject to parliamentary consent), to veto EU legislation (subject to the possibility of legislative override), but—crucially—not to dissolve the EP. Second, I focused on the modes of election and suggested a possible mechanism to elect the President in light of the challenge of asymmetry produced by the great population imbalance between the EU member states. Here, I discarded the option for an EU-wide popular election and rather proposed that the President be voted on by EU citizens in state constituencies—each of which should be awarded a number of "electoral votes" equal to the number of seats that state has in the EP and the number of votes it weights in the Council—through a majority (rather than plurality) system, with a runoff between the two candidates that received the most votes. Third, I discussed what the chances are that the proposal outlined above could be taken seriously in the debate about EMU reform and cautiously suggested that a window of opportunity may actually exist.

Given the obligation for the EU member states to incorporate the content of the Fiscal Compact within the EU treaties by 2018, and the political commitments to put EMU on a more solid basis, the idea to strengthen the presidency may emerge as an advantageous institutional option within a broader package of constitutional reforms. In fact, the Fiscal Compact has created a new institution—the Euro

Summit—which reproduces in the framework of the Eurozone the institutional setup of the EU at large, including a presidency of the Euro Summit modeled out of the presidency of the European Council. If future EMU constitutional reforms are going to be restricted to the Eurozone only, rather than the EU at large, then the proposal advanced in this chapter in favor of strengthening the executive power could be applied to the Euro Summit, rather than to the European Council. Be that as it may, constitutional steps toward the presidentialization of EU or Eurozone governance would need to be complemented by other institutional reforms, which re-invent the role of the heads of state and government, by transforming their congress into a real EU Senate—as I have suggested in Chapter 5.

Ultimately, many difficulties cloud the possibility for the EU to change its constitutional architecture in the direction of strengthening the presidency of the European Council (or the Euro Summit). Yet, the need for a more effective and legitimate executive government for the EU and the Eurozone is an issue that can no longer be postponed, given the rising levels of popular discontent, as evident by the surge of extreme, anti-system parties both in national and EU elections across Europe. The EU and the Eurozone need strong, responsive institutions which can give voice to the peoples of our Union of states and citizens—because when voice is lacking, exit becomes the solution.[274] Hence, beginning a discussion about the potentials of an EU institutional reform, which can restore a meaningful balance between the member states and simultaneously create a democratic forum for an open and genuine competition on the agenda of the EU, seemed to me a worthwhile effort. As Habermas has argued, it is time for the EU and the Eurozone to replace intergovernmental governance with a real form of transnational democracy.[275] Institutionalizing a European presidency along the logic of separation of powers can be a suitable constitutional step to reform the EU form of government so that it is no longer subject to paradoxical dynamics of interstate domination.

[274] See Albert Hirschman, *Exit, Voice, Loyalty: Responses to Decline in Firms, Organizations and States* (Harvard UP 1970).

[275] Habermas (n 1) 12.

Conclusion

For a "More Perfect" Economic and Monetary Union

1. Introduction

More than five years after the beginning of the Euro-crisis, the European Union (EU) remains in quagmires. In fact, following the dramatic unfolding of events in Greece during the summer of 2015, the survival of the Economic and Monetary Union (EMU) itself appeared to be at stake.[1] While the front pages of newspapers daily report on the last-minute developments in EMU-related negotiations, this book has attempted to take a step back, and consider how the Euro-crisis and the responses to it have affected the constitutional architecture of European economic governance. By taking a bird's-eye view, this book sought to shed light on several comparative paradoxes in the evolution of EMU, to underline the problematic aspects of these trends, and to propose alternative ways forward for the EU and the Eurozone, underlying the constitutional challenges that they raise. In doing so, the book has chosen one among multiple analytical pathways to the study of economic governance in Europe: it has privileged several aspects, and left others aside. This book neither had the ambition nor the presumption to cover all aspects of a complex, and quickly evolving interdisciplinary field. Nevertheless, despite its limited focus, the book has endeavored to offer a comprehensive and critical legal assessment of the implications of the Euro-crisis and the responses to it on relations of power within the EU; and by identifying possible reforms it has hopefully contributed with new constitutional ideas on the debate about the future of Europe.

2. Crisis

Since the eruption of the Euro-crisis, the EU institutions and the member states have hectically responded by adopting a swath of legal, political, and institutional measures aimed at tackling the root causes of the crisis, and putting the EMU on a more solid footing. In fact, efforts to enhance the resilience of EMU and prevent a

[1] See President of the Euro Summit Donald Tusk, Statement, Brussels, July 7, 2015, PRESS 562/15 (stating that "the stark reality is that we have only five days left to find the ultimate compromise" on Greece to avoid a dramatic break-up of EMU).

revamping of the crisis continue today—raising the question whether we can still talk about the Euro-crisis to define a period which began more than half a decade ago and which does not promise to be fading anytime soon. Be that as it may, as a result of the Euro-crisis and the responses to it, the constitutional architecture of EMU originally designed by the Maastricht Treaty has profoundly changed.[2] Tighter budgetary constraints have been enacted at national and supranational level; new tools of fiscal stabilization for states and banks have been created in the EU and international legal order; and a complex decision-making framework has been put in place to coordinate states' economic policies and dictate programs of fiscal adjustment for countries in financial distress. But how does the new constitutional architecture of European economic governance emerged from the crisis and the responses to it look like? And what are its implications?

Part I of the book examined the implications of the Euro-crisis and the responses to it on relations of power within the EU. To this end, the book disarticulated three dimensions, considering how the Euro-crisis and the responses to it affected:

1. vertical relations of power between the member states and the EU;
2. horizontal relations of power between courts and political branches;
3. horizontal relations of power between the member states themselves.

In order to shed light on these developments, the book adopted a comparative perspective, using the case of the United States of America (US) as an external benchmark. As I explained, while the US presents several similarities to the EU (and the Eurozone specifically) in terms of history, structure, size, and economic output, which make a comparison between the two systems meaningful, the US is also typically regarded as a regime characterized by a high degree of centralization, hyper-judicialization, and limited recognition of the states at the federal level. From this point of view, therefore, the US example provided a useful yardstick to measure the *paradoxes* produced by the Euro-crisis and the responses to it in the EU constitutional system.

In Chapter 1, I examined the implications of the Euro-crisis and the responses to it on the vertical relations of power between the member states and the EU and I argued that the reforms introducing tighter budgetary constraints at the national and supranational level have produced a paradoxical dynamic of *centralization*. Given the obligation set by the Fiscal Compact to constitutionalize a balanced budget rule at the national level, and the requirement for member states to submit within the European Semester their draft budget bills to supranational authorities for prior approval, the EU institutions have acquired sweeping powers to supervise and steer the budgetary policy of the member states. This state of affairs contrasts strikingly with the situation in the US. While most US states are also endowed with balanced budget requirements, their adoption was never mandated top-down, and although the federal government has acquired extensive powers to influence the US economy, it is still today constitutionally

[2] See Christian Joerges, "Europas Wirtschaftsverfassungs in der Krise" (2012) 51 Der Staat 57 and Sabino Cassese, "La costituzione economica europea" (2001) 11 Rivista italiana di diritto pubblico comunitario 907.

barred from commandeering the states' budgetary process. Nevertheless, also in the EMU there are strong constitutional arguments that the member states ought to enjoy some meaningful budgetary autonomy as a pre-condition for self-government. Hence, the paradox of centralization appears problematic.

Chapter 2 examined the implications of the Euro-crisis and the responses to it on the horizontal relations of power between the courts and the political branches and argued that the adoption of new EMU measures, notably in the area of financial stabilization, have opened the door to a paradoxical dynamic of *judicialization*. As a result of the growing use of intergovernmental agreements outside EU law, in fact, national courts in a plurality of EU member states have been given the opportunity to review the legality of these EMU-related treaties. Emboldened by domestic review of international treaties, then, several state courts have extended their oversight to measures of EU law proper, leading toward an unprecedented degree of involvement by the national and supranational judiciary in the field of economic and monetary policy. This state of affairs contrasts strikingly with the situation in the US. Rules on standing have generally prevented monetary questions from being adjudicated by the courts, and, at least since the New Deal, the judiciary has consistently deferred to the political branches of government on economic questions. Nevertheless, in the EU too considerations of expertise, voice, and rights plead in favor of letting the political process, rather than the courts, take the lead in EMU affairs. Hence, the paradox of judicialization appears problematic.

Chapter 3 examined the implications of the Euro-crisis and the responses to it on the horizontal relations of power between the member states themselves and argued that developments in EU governance, including in the legal framework applicable to financial assistance for states in fiscal troubles, have created a paradox of *domination*. Although the EU institutions had been designed since the founding to secure a balance between states' power and states' equality, the rise of intergovernmental bodies such as the European Council and the Euro Summit has produced a significant shift of power from smaller and economically weaker member states toward larger, more prosperous ones. This state of affairs is ironic, considering that intergovernmental institutions are formally seen in the EU as the best protection of the equality of the member states. In fact, unlike in the US, the EU created intergovernmental institutions precisely to show a strong commitment to state equality. In the US, instead, the corporate representation of the states is embedded in a broader institutional framework—but this actually provided a better defense against aggrandizement by the largest states. Nevertheless, also in the EU the preservation of a fair balance between the member states is constitutionally indispensable, given the anti-hegemonic nature of the European integration project. Hence, the paradox of domination appears problematic.

In sum, by using the federal system of the US as a comparative benchmark, Part I of the book shed light on how the Euro-crisis and the legal and institutional responses to it have produced paradoxical implications on the constitutional architecture of the EU, shifting authority among levels of government, and re-shaping relations between institutions. Although the US is generally regarded as a highly centralized federal system, with all-powerful courts, and a limited role for the states at federal level—and because of these, it is often depicted as an example of what the EU should *not* become—the book underlined how paradoxically the EMU is today characterized by an even greater centralization in budgetary policy, greater judicialization of economic and monetary affairs, and greater imbalance in the fiscal relations between states. As Part I of the book revealed through the use of the comparative method, crisis-measures and EMU-related action adopted "by accident and force"[3] have generated paradoxical developments in the EU. However, each of these is problematic: centralization undermines state autonomy, judicialization threatens democratic self-governance, and domination strikes at the heart of the EU post-war anti-hegemonic project. This urgently raises the question of how the constitutional architecture of European economic governance could be reformed.

3. Change

Growing awareness exists among academics on the unsustainability of the arrangement currently in place in the field of European economic governance, and on the need to improve EMU. In fact, calls for completing Europe's EMU have not remained a matter of pure academic disquisition but have become a key part of the EU policy-making agenda, at the highest political level. In particular, in December 2012 the President of the European Council produced a report, written in cooperation with the Presidents of the European Commission, the Eurogroup, and the European Central Bank (ECB)—the so-called "Four Presidents" report[4]—in which it outlined a road-map toward a deeper EMU; and in June 2015, the President of the European Commission published a new report, written in close coordination with the Presidents of the European Council, the Eurogroup, the ECB, and also the European Parliament (EP)—the so-called "Five Presidents" report[5]—relaunching steps toward greater integration in EMU, along a time frame to be accomplished within the next 10 years maximum. Moreover, calls toward improving EMU have been made by the ECB,[6] the European Commission,[7] the EP,[8] as well as by several national governments.[9]

[3] Federalist Paper No. 1 (Alexander Hamilton), in *The Federalist Papers* [1787] (Penguin 1987) 87.

[4] President of the European Council, Final Report "Towards a Genuine EMU," December 5, 2012.

[5] President of the European Commission, Report "Completing Europe's EMU," June 22, 2015.

[6] See ECB President Mario Draghi, Introductory statement in front of the EP, Brussels, June 15, 2015 (expressing its support for "a quantum leap towards a stronger, more efficient institutional architecture" for EMU).

[7] See European Commission Communication, "A Blueprint for a Deep and Genuine EMU: Launching a European Debate," November 28, 2012, COM(2012)777 final.

[8] See e.g., European Parliament Resolution of November 20, 2012 on the report "Towards a Genuine EMU," P7_TA(2012)0430; European Parliament Resolution of December 12, 2013 on the constitutional problems of multi-tier governance in the European Union, P7_TA(2013)0598, and European Parliament Resolution of June 24, 2015 on the review of economic governance framework: stocktaking and challenges, P8_TA(2015)0238.

[9] In particular, member states articulated proposals for the future of EMU in response to the questions raised in an Analytical Note prepared by the President of the European Commission, in close cooperation with the Presidents of the European Council, of the Eurogroup, and the ECB. See President of the European Commission, Analytical Note "Preparing for Next Steps on Better Economic Governance in the Euro Area," February 12, 2015.

Part II of this book sought to contribute to this ongoing debate by discussing several legal and institutional proposals for the future of EMU, tailored to minimize the paradoxes of centralization, judicialization, and domination identified in Part I. On the understanding that the current constitutional architecture of European economic governance is unsustainable, the book endeavored to articulate three key proposals. At the same time, it identified the *challenges* that any project of legal and institutional reform would meet in today's EU, and sought to envision ways to account for them. In particular, the book argued that EMU should undergo the following changes:

1. from fiscal constraints to fiscal capacity
2. from legislative sidelining to legislative involvement
3. from executive federalism to executive government

In discussing the potentials and the challenges of change in EMU, the book sought to keep track of the continuing political and constitutional debate in the EU—and at the same time to draw lessons from the comparative example of a plurality of legal systems worldwide, with a view to proposing a feasible road-map toward a more balanced EMU.

In Chapter 4, I have made the case in favor of a *fiscal capacity*, and argued that the creation of a counter-cyclical fiscal tool at the supranational level to address asymmetry shocks in the EMU could be a way to revert the trend of centralization: if the EU were endowed with a fiscal capacity, it could smooth the slumps of the business cycle, without the need to invasively interfere into the budgetary processes of the member states. Nevertheless, raising a fiscal capacity faces at least three challenges—what I called asymmetry, unanimity, and representation. First, in order to succeed, a fiscal capacity must avoid falling prey to the logic of interstate transfers, and rather be based on EU's own resources. Second, if the EU is to raise new money, it must address the fact that unanimity is needed to introduce tax legislation—a requirement that hampers the ability to reach agreement, unless a vanguard group of states (e.g., the Eurozone states) is willing to explore the potential offered by enhanced cooperation. Third, if the EU or the Eurozone moves in the direction of introducing supranational taxation, the question of "no taxation without representation" must be dealt with, by ensuring that the EP as the representative of the citizens is involved in decision-making on par with the Council as the representative of the states—an option which could be achieved *à traité constant* through the use of "*passerelle* clauses."

Chapter 5 made the case in favor of *greater legislative involvement* in EMU, and argued that making the "Community method" central to the governance of EMU affairs could be a way to reduce the trend of judicialization: while the use of intergovernmental treaties outside the framework of EU law opened the door to judicial interference in EMU, the EU legislative process is better protected from judicial overreach, while being also more legitimate due to the involvement of multiple institutions, representing different interests. Nevertheless, restoring the EU legislative process faces at least three challenges—what I called asymmetry, representation, and unity. First, greater legislative involvement in EMU can be assured only if convincing constitutional arguments can be advanced to constrain the states from acting outside EU law, and simultaneously to empower the EU institutions to legislate within EMU. Second, a greater role for the EP in EMU governance requires a rethinking of the mechanisms through which its members are elected, since the logic of proportional representation on which this institution functions today is increasing at odds with its role. Third, the working of the Council must be critically reconsidered as well, since the fragmentation and the imbalances between its various compositions hampers its ability to act as the upper EU legislative house—a problem which could be dealt with by vesting in the European Council an explicit role in legislation as a kind of EU Senate.

Chapter 6 made the case in favor of a *new executive government* for the EU or the Eurozone, and argued that strengthening the executive power of the President of the European Council (or, within the Eurozone: of the President of the Euro Summit) could be a way to reverse the trend of domination: while intergovernmental bargaining has allowed the larger and richer states to dominate the process, a strengthened and directly legitimated presidency could restore a healthy balance between the states, and create a space for democratic competition and contestation on the policy of the EMU. Nevertheless, reforming the EU executive power faces at least three challenges—what I called representation, asymmetry, and unanimity. First, a reformed presidency, and its authority, must be designed to match the representative deficit afflicting the EU today. Second, if the presidency were to be popularly elected, appropriate institutional mechanisms ought to be crafted to account for the profound asymmetries in population between the member states. Third, adequate incentives should be conceived in order to gather the unanimous state support necessary to implement such a constitutional reform in the treaties, thus exploiting the window of opportunity offered by the obligation to domesticate the Fiscal Compact within EU law by 2018.

In sum, Part II of the book sought to advance legal and institutional reforms designed to minimize the trends of centralization, judicialization, and domination—thus addressing the problems of EMU identified in Part I of the book. By articulating proposals for a fiscal capacity, for greater legislative involvement in EMU affairs as well as for a strengthened executive power for the EU and the Eurozone, Part II has endeavored to contribute with concrete ideas to the debate about Europe's future. At the same time, it has also drawn attention to several constitutional challenges that must be considered on the road toward a new settlement in EMU, identifying as recurrent issues the challenges of asymmetry, representation, and unanimity or unity. As it has been pointed out, any effort to reform the EMU must reckon with the fact that the EMU was designed as an asymmetric construct, and that the EU and Eurozone member states profoundly differ in terms of economic performance, and population size. Equally, any reform of EMU must appreciate the fact that supranational executive and legislative institutions must be representative toward the citizenry, and that action at EU level (from legislation in the field of taxation, to electoral reform, or treaty change) requires the unanimous consent of 28 EU member states. Recognizing these constraints has been the starting point for a discussion about how the EMU could be reformed "through reflection and choice."[10]

4. Compromise

As the "Five Presidents" report recently acknowledged "at the height of the [Euro-] crisis, far-reaching decisions had often to be taken in a rush, sometimes overnight. [...] Now is the time to review and consolidate our political construct—and to build the next stage of our [EMU]."[11] This book has claimed that the overhauls of the EMU undertaken by accident and force have produced paradoxical implications on the constitutional structure of the EU—and that it is now time to reform the constitutional architecture of European economic governance through reflection and choice. Admittedly, while "there may be several alternative paths to a strengthened [EMU],"[12] this book has advanced an ambitious road-map toward improving economic governance in Europe. The policy proposals I have articulated here are more ambitious than the one of the "Five Presidents" report. In fact, the latter has been criticized for a lack of vision, and for falling short of the "Four Presidents" report,[13] which, despite several limits, had launched some new ideas for the future of EMU.[14] The caution of the "Five Presidents" report may be in tune with the Zeitgeist: as revealed by the latest rounds of national and EU elections, widespread political opposition against any further step toward European integration seems to exist among EU citizens.[15]

Nevertheless, in my view the dissatisfaction of European citizens and states should not be interpreted as an opposition to European integration as such. Rather, discontent vis-à-vis the EU can also be seen as the product of an unsatisfactory settlement in the EU constitutional architecture.[16] As this book has pointed

[10] Federalist Paper No. 1 (Alexander Hamilton), in *The Federalist Papers* [1787] (Penguin 1987) 87.

[11] President of the European Commission Report (n 5) 17.

[12] Yves Bertoncini et al, "Improving EMU," Notre Europe Policy Paper No. 137/2015, 1.

[13] See e.g., former Italian Minister of Finance Fabrizio Saccomanni, "Rapporto dei Presidenti: Documento ingannevole, fuorviante, irritante," *Affari Internazionali*, June 30, 2015 (defining the report as deceiving and irritating).

[14] See e.g., Philippe De Schoutheete, "The European Council after Van Rompuy," *Notre Europe Tribune*, April 20, 2015.

[15] See e.g., Nicole Scicluna, "Politicization without Democratization: How the Eurozone Crisis is Transforming EU Law and Politics" (2014) 12 International Journal of Constitutional Law 545 (discussing the rise of anti-system parties in national elections) and Corinne Deloy and Pascale Joannin, "Les forces de droit sortent victorieuses des elections européenne marquees par une poussée populiste dans plusiers Etats members," Fondation Robert Schuman—Observatoire des Elections en Europe (2014) (discussing the rise in turnout of euro-skeptic, populist parties in a plurality of EU member states during the May 2014 elections to the EP).

[16] See also Jürgen Habermas, "Democracy in Europe: Why the Development of the EU into a Transnational Democracy is Necessary and How is it Possible" (2015) 21 European Law Journal 546 and Joseph H.H. Weiler, "Europa: 'Nous Coalisons des Etats, Nous N'Unissons pas des Hommes'," in Marta Cartabia and Andrea Simoncini (eds), *La sostenibilità della democrazia nel XXI secolo* (Il Mulino 2009), 51, 62 (stating that the system of EMU governance contributes to the political and democratic deficit of the EU).

out, in fact, EMU has evolved since the eruption of the crisis in problematic directions—namely, centralization, judicialization, and domination. To different degrees, each of these dynamics is a source of the growing popular discontent against the EU. Hence, reforming the European architecture of economic governance in a way that addresses these problems is not a passing fancy: it is a necessity to ensure the survival of EMU. In other words, EMU must change again if it wants to remain itself.[17] The Euro-crisis and the responses to it have already profoundly affected the constitutional architecture of EMU. But the current constitutional settlement is not good enough, as (among others) it unduly restricts the budgetary autonomy of the member states, it grants excessive powers to courts, and it undermines the balance between the member states. EMU must therefore be made anew in ways which can again rally the support of European citizens and states for the project of European integration.[18]

This book has attempted to do just that. As I have claimed, EMU needs a fiscal capacity—returning to the member states meaningful autonomy in the management of their budgetary policies. It needs greater legislative involvement in economic governance—reducing courts' interference in the field. And it needs a strengthened executive branch selected through a pan-European process, which can channel the citizens' voice and prevent the domination by some states over others. In institutional terms, this book has made the case for a new balance of powers in the EU. A vertical balance between the budgetary processes of the states and that of the EU. A horizontal balance between the courts (which play a central role in any constitutional systems, but whose role should not be unlimited) and the political process, to be enhanced through the application of the "Community method." And a new balance between national politics and EU governance, centered on the transformation of the presidency of the European Council (or the Euro Summit) into an executive office, popularly legitimated and empowered to take decisions on questions which affect the entire EU or Eurozone economy outside the logic of interstate bargaining.

The EMU which this book has envisioned is one based on a fiscal capacity, greater legislative involvement, and a strengthened executive power. Chapter 4 claimed that the EU should have *taxing and spending powers*. Chapter 5 argued that decisions on economic questions should be taken through a bicameral legislative process in which the *European Parliament*, representing the EU citizens, and elected through a rationalized electoral mechanism, decides jointly with the *European Council*, representing the EU states, *acting as a EU Senate*. And Chapter 6

[17] See also Ingolf Pernice, "Domestic Courts, Constitutional Constraints and European Democracy: What Solution for the Crisis?" in Federico Fabbrini et al (eds), *The Constitutionalization of European Budgetary Constraints* (Hart Publishing 2014), 297 and Rosa Lastra and Jean-Victor Louis, "European Economic and Monetary Union: History, Trends and Prospects" (2013) 32 Yearbook of European Law 1 (emphasizing the evolutionary nature of EMU).

[18] See also Edouard Dubout, "Pour la transfiguration de l'Europe—*Ordo ab chaos?*," in Stéphane De la Rosa et al (eds), *L'Union européene et le fédéralisme économique* (Bruylant 2015), 17 and Andrea Morrone, "Crisi economica e diritti: appunti per lo stato costituzionale in Europa" [2014] Quaderni Costituzionali 79.

maintained that the EU should be endowed with a new executive institution, a *European President*, to be institutionally separate from the legislative branch, albeit controlled by it, to be entrusted with effective powers, and to be popularly elected through a democratic mechanism which reconciles majoritarianism with federalism's concerns. While I do not doubt that many readers will disagree with the nature of the proposals I have articulated in this book, I have not been scared off from advancing several provocative ideas, in the hope that they may trigger some debate—at a time when this is more needed than ever.[19]

Taken by themselves, each of the proposals I advanced in this book may appear over-ambitious. However, each proposal should be seen as part of a package—which could serve as a compromise deal among very different institutional preferences on how EMU should be reformed. In fact, I would like to submit that the combined effect of the measures articulated in this book may render the possibility of an EMU reform in the future more likely. While (the representatives of) every EU institution will dislike some of the proposals presented in this book, it will be pleased with others; and it may find that the net benefits of constitutional change outweigh the costs. Hence, the EP will not be happy to see its efforts to parliamentarize the EU chilled, but it will be eager to be involved in full in EMU governance, by expanding its legislative tasks across the board, including in the field of taxation. Similarly, the European Council may not be happy to see its executive role reduced, but it will gain extensive new legislative powers by absorbing part of the Council's functions—thus turning into a strong EU Senate. The European Commission, then, will lose supervisory authority vis-à-vis the member states, but it would gain greater legitimacy, and more political backing, as part of a reformed EU executive. And the ECB will benefit from having a more effective and accountable political counterpart, which can take decisions and free it from the unpleasant task of having to fill the current executive void.

At the same time, the institutional reforms proposed here would make also the member states better off, both jointly and severally. Under the new settlement proposed above, the member states would lose their freedom to conclude intergovernmental agreements outside EU law at will; but they would regain significant autonomy in managing their budgetary processes outside supranational constraints. Moreover, while many individual member states would gain from an overhaul of the EU and Eurozone decision-making system which restores a healthy interstate balance, country-specific incentives could be designed to compensate those other states which would give up current privileges in exchange for their support to reform. As scholars of constitution-making have emphasized, constitutions are never ideal documents: rather, they are the result of compromise between competing interests.[20]

[19] See also Joseph H.H. Weiler, Speech at the "State of the Union" Conference of the European University Institute, Florence, May 8, 2015 (stating that it is time for academics and intellectuals to play a constructive role, engaging with the deep problems facing the EU).

[20] See e.g., Tom Ginsburg et al, "Does the Process of Constitution-Making Matter?" (2009) 5 Annual Review of Law and Social Science 1 and James Buchanan and Gordon Tullock, *The Calculus of Consent: Logical Foundations of Constitutional Democracy* (Michigan UP 1962).

In order to succeed, processes of constitution-making—or, in the EU context: of treaty-amendment—must make sure that each of the players around the negotiating table obtains some net gain from the end result.[21] Efforts to complete EMU therefore must strike a grand bargain between institutions and states, and the proposals advanced in this book may offer a possible blueprint to reach such a compromise.

5. Constitution

If there was any remaining doubt on the unsustainability of the existing architecture of European economic governance, this was dispelled by the events of summer 2015. After a new, anti-austerity government was elected in Greece in January 2015, tough talks took place for over five months within the framework of the EU intergovernmental institutions between Greece and its European and international creditors on the re-negotiation of the conditions attached to the Greek program of financial assistance. Based on a clear electoral mandate, the new Greek government sought to renegotiate the policy measures agreed upon by the previous governments in the two Memoranda of Understanding—which it blamed for a dramatic humanitarian crisis (with 25% unemployment and 25% decrease in GDP since the start of the crisis). The new government also demanded measures to relieve Greece from its skyrocketing domestic public debt. However, its requests were dismissed as a breach of previously agreed commitments.[22] In the inability to find a compromise, and with its financial conditions quickly deteriorating due to the expiration of the second bailout, on June 30, 2015 Greece failed to repay on time a tranche of the loans received by the International Monetary Fund (IMF), technically making a selective default on its debt.[23]

Moreover, in the attempt to change course to the intergovernmental negotiations, the Greek government called for a national referendum. The referendum asked the electorate for a "yes or no" vote on the conditions attached to a new, third program of financial assistance. This program, however, had been proposed still only in draft form by the Commission as a replacement for the expired second program. And the Greek government actively campaigned for the "no" vote. On July 5, 2015 the Greek people, by a wide margin, rejected the proposed bailout,[24] opening the prospect for a Greek exit from the Eurozone. Contrary to the expectations of the Greek executive, in fact, the referendum did not strengthen the position of the Greek

[21] See Paul Craig, *The Treaty of Lisbon: Law, Politics and Treaty Reform* (OUP 2010) and Marta Cartabia, "Revisione dei trattati," in Sabino Cassese (ed), *Dizionario di diritto pubblico* (Giuffrè 2006), ad vocem.

[22] A most explicit statement of this position was offered by Vice-President of the European Commission Jyrki Katainen, Statement, Brussels, January 28, 2015 (proclaiming that "we don't change our policy according to elections.").

[23] See IMF statement, June 30, 2015, press release No. 15/310 (reporting the failure by Greece to repay a loan).

[24] See Greek government, *2015 Referendum*, available at <http://www.ypes.gr/el/Elections/referendum2015/> (last accessed July 15, 2015) (reporting text of the referendum, in Greek), and Greek government, *2015 Referendum Results*, available at <http://ekloges.ypes.gr/current/e/public/#{%22

government vis-à-vis its Eurozone partners. With Greek banks forcefully closed for weeks, and capital controls introduced to prevent the meltdown of the financial system,[25] the Greek government therefore back-tracked: after a cabinet shake-up, its executive advanced on July 8, 2015 a request for new financial assistance to the European Stability Mechanism (ESM), indicating its willingness to accept the previous creditors' requests for tough measures of economic adjustment.[26]

Yet, with trust between the member states at an all-time low, the Greek government's U-turn was met with half-hearted feelings. Despite meeting in almost permanent session between July 7 and 11, 2015, the Eurogroup of finance ministers did not manage to master a compromise between its members—some of which openly called to force Greece out of the Eurozone.[27] With time running out quickly and the financial markets showing increasing unease for the situation, heads of state and government of the Eurozone countries met on July 7, 2015 and again on July 11, 2015 for emergency meetings in the Euro Summit. Eventually, after 17 hours of negotiation, on July 12, 2015 the President of the Euro Summit announced an agreement,[28] which secured Greece's permanence within the Eurozone on the condition that the Greek government propose, and the national parliament approve in record time, sweeping legislation on a wide set of policies (including pension reform, tax reform, labor market reform, the drafting of a new code of civil procedure, and the launching of a new program of privatization).[29] However, by explicitly rejecting the Greek request to consider debt relief, the Euro Summit left unanswered the question whether Greece may be able to follow-up effectively on these austerity measures and restore its economic condition—suggesting that many clouds will still darken the future of the EMU.[30]

Although the events of the Greek tragedy lend themselves to different readings, and none of the actors on stage appears blameless, there is a feature of the story which looks increasingly undeniable: the unsustainability of the current institutional architecture of the EMU. As the 10 meetings of the Eurogroup in the month between June 18 and July 18, 2015 make clear, a Union which is dependent on the continuing negotiation between its member states is a house divided bound to implode. In fact, notwithstanding the attempt by the Greek government to inject national democratic input into a highly diplomatic and technocratic process

cls%22:%22main%22,%22params%22:{}}> (last accessed July 15, 2015) (reporting results of the referendum).

[25] See Praxe Nomothetikou Periehomenou, ΦΕΚ A 65, June 28, 2015 (Greece) (Act of legislative content introducing capital controls and mandatory bank holidays), later renewed.

[26] See the letter by the Greek Minister of Finance to the Managing Director of the ESM, July 8, 2015.

[27] See the leaked document by the German Ministry of Finance, "Comments on the latest Greek proposal," July 10, 2015 (proposing that Greece should be given a five-year time-out from the Eurozone).

[28] President of the Euro Summit Donald Tusk, Statement, Brussels, July 13, 2015, PRESS 579/15.

[29] Euro Summit Statement, July 12, 2015, SN 4070/15.

[30] For a very critical reading of the results of the Euro Summit of July 12, 2015 see also the former German Minister of Foreign Affairs Joschka Fischer, "The Return of the Ugly German," *Project Syndacate*, July 23, 2015.

by calling a popular referendum (a step which had been already considered, but aborted, in October 2011), the exercise of electoral democracy in one Eurozone member state clashed with the reality that democratic processes are in place in each and every of the other Eurozone countries as well. Yet, as the Euro-crisis has made clear, these national democratic processes can be irreconcilable, by pushing in opposite direction. The current system of EMU governance has created a constant collision of the respective electoral mandates of the member states, ensuring the continuing instability—if not the outright failure—of the European integration project, in EMU and beyond.[31]

From a comparative point of view, the situation of the EMU today presents striking parallels with the experience of the US *before the adoption of the Constitution in 1787*. Under the Articles of Confederation—the basic document which governed the relations between the newly independent 13 American states, from 1776 to 1787—intergovernmentalism was the dominant currency of the system.[32] The central government had no executive power.[33] It did not have the authority to tax and spend.[34] And any decision ranging from economic policy to trade and defense was subject to the unanimous accord of the united states in Congress assembled, and to their willingness to abide by what they had consensually agreed on.[35] As is well known, the system proved to be so dysfunctional that it threatened the cohesion between the states.[36] Eventually, through a constitutional break, the representatives of (12 of the 13) US states decided in 1787 to draft a new document, which after ratification in nine states became the Constitution of the US.[37] Although its nature as either an international treaty or a constitutional charter would remain contested for decades,[38] the US Constitution created a complex but complete institutional architecture, with a presidency,[39] a bi-cameral legislature,[40]

[31] See also Miguel Maduro, "A New Governance for the European Union and the Euro: Democracy & Justice," Study commissioned by the European Parliament Constitutional Affairs Committee, September 2012, PE 462.484.

[32] See Olivier Beaud, *Théorie de la fédération* (PUF 2007) and Douglas Smith, "An Analysis of Two Federal Structures: The Articles of Confederation and the Constitution" (1997) 34 San Diego Law Review 249.

[33] See also *Myers v. United States*, 272 U.S. 52, 116–17 (1926) (US Supreme Court stating that "[t]he debates in the Constitutional Convention indicated an intention to create a strong Executive, and, after a controversial discussion, the executive power of the Government was vested in one person and many of his important functions were specified so as to avoid the humiliating weakness of the Congress during the Revolution and under the Articles of Confederation"), citing Max Farrand, *Records of the Federal Convention, Volume 1* (Yale UP 1911) 66–97.

[34] See Art VIII Articles of Confederation (stating that taxes "shall be laid and levied by the authority and direction of the legislatures of the several States within the time agreed upon by the United States in Congress assembled").

[35] See Art IX Articles of Confederation (regulating the powers of the united states in Congress).

[36] See Gordon Wood, *The Creation of the American Republic: 1776-1787* (Norton 1993).

[37] See Akhil Reed Amar, *America's Constitution: A Biography* (Random House 2005).

[38] See Robert Schütze, "Federalism as Constitutional Pluralism: 'Letter from America'," in Matej Avbelj and Jan Komárek (eds), *Constitutional Pluralism in the European Union and Beyond* (Hart Publishing 2012), 185 and Roberto Toniatti, "La 'nazione costituzionale': genesi e consolidamento dell'identità repubblicana dell'ordinamento federale statunitense quale Stato-nazione" [2011] Diritto pubblico comparato e europeo 1169.

[39] See Art II US Const. [40] See Art I US Const.

and a federal government empowered to levy and collect taxes without the need for interstate bargaining.[41]

While the experience of the US cannot predetermine that of the EU,[42] the conundrum facing the EMU today appears to be the same faced by the American founding fathers 250 years ago: either to bring an unprecedented project of transnational peace and cooperation forward to another level of integration, or let it unravel.[43] Hic Rhodus, hic salta! The Maastricht Treaty launched the project of building EMU, but left its construction incomplete. In the aftermath of the Euro-crisis many measures have been adopted to overhaul the constitutional architecture of European economic governance: but the responses to the Euro-crisis have been taken in a context of urgency, and they have produced changes—such as centralization, judicialization, and domination, as this book has pointed out—which have undermined the sustainability of the EMU institutional arrangement even more. Looking ahead, if the EMU is to survive, it needs a new constitutional settlement—with a fiscal capacity, greater legislative involvement in economic governance, and a new executive power, legitimated and able to take decisions for the EU as a whole.

No one can deny that such prospect raises many challenges, given the difficulties of previous attempts to reform the EU,[44] and the judicial resistances in several member states toward greater steps in EU integration.[45] Nevertheless, ironically, the greatest opportunity to enhance the integration of EMU may occur thanks to the decision by the United Kingdom (UK) government to call a referendum on its membership in the EU.[46] As Sergio Fabbrini has recently argued, the conflicting pressures for greater integration in EMU and more British autonomy within EU may be reconciled through a new constitutional pact, which repatriates some powers to the UK (and the EU member states which are simply interested in participation in the EU common market), while deepening integration for those states who are participating in the political project of EMU.[47] As this book has suggested on several occasions, in fact, reforms such as a fiscal capacity and a new institutional

[41] See Bruce Ackerman, "Taxation and the Constitution" (1999) 99 Columbia Law Review 1.

[42] See Kalypso Nicolaïdis, "Conclusion: The Federal Vision beyond the Federal State" in Kalypso Nicolaïdis and Robert Howse (eds), *The Federal Vision: Legitimacy and Levels of Governance in the United States and the European Union* (OUP 2001), 439 and Koen Lenaerts, "Constitutionalism and the Many Faces of Federalism" (1990) 38 American Journal of Comparative Law 205.

[43] See also Kaarlo Tuori, *European Constitutionalism* (CUP 2015) and Lucia Serena Rossi, "L'Unione europea e il paradosso di Zenone: Riflessioni sulla necessità di una revisione del Trattato di Lisbona" [2013] Diritto dell'Unione Europea 749.

[44] See Gráinne de Búrca, "If at First you don't Succeed: Vote, Vote Again: Analyzing the 'Second Referendum' Phenomenon in EU Treaty Change" (2010) 33 Fordham International Law Journal 1472 and Bruno De Witte, "Saving the Constitution? The Escape Routes and their Legal Feasibility" in Giuliano Amato et al (eds), *Genesis and Destiny of the European Constitution* (Bruylant 2007), 919.

[45] The story of national constitutional courts' resistance to EU integration is too well known to tell. However, I remain of the view that judicial opposition to further EU integration does not really constitute an obstacle if there is enough political will to move forward in the process of integration.

[46] See European Union Referendum Bill 2015–16, HC Bill 6 (UK) (British statute calling for a referendum on membership in the EU by December 31, 2017).

[47] Sergio Fabbrini, *Which European Union? Europe after the Euro Crisis* (CUP 2015).

arrangement for executive power could also be tailored to the Eurozone only, rather than to the EU as a whole.[48] In light of this, the question to ask our current leaders is whether they are content to be remembered on the history books as those who let EMU fall apart, or whether they aspire to become the founding fathers of a new, more perfect *constitutional* architecture of economic governance for Europe.[49]

6. Conclusion

Speaking at the Harvard Kennedy School of Government in October 2013, the President of the ECB Mario Draghi evoked the preamble of the Constitution of the US,[50] which proclaims the commitment of the American founding fathers to ordain and establish a Constitution "in order to form a more perfect Union."[51] As President Draghi explained, the idea of "a more perfect Union" captures the agenda facing the EU today better than the wording of the preamble of the EU treaties—committing the EU toward "an ever closer Union"[52]—which creates anxiety for someone, since it seems to promise an inexorable movement toward an EU super-state. As he put it: "By this, I mean that we are 'perfecting' something that has already began—namely, the economic and monetary union that was launched in 1999. Policy-makers are following through the consequences of the decision to create a genuine single market supported by a single currency."[53] Moreover, he added that moving forward in the process of perfecting EMU should not be seen as a way to renounce sovereignty—conceived normatively, à la Bodin—but rather as the instrument to regain it—seen positively as the "ability to deliver in practice the essential services that people expect from government," as theorized in *The Federalist Papers*.[54] And as he concluded, the irreversibility of the euro, "born out of the commitment of European nations to closer integration" rendered the need to pursue in the process of perfecting EMU even more necessary.[55]

This book has endeavored to make the case for a "more perfect" EMU. It has analyzed the constitutional implications of the Euro-crisis and the responses to it on relations of power in the EU, it has identified several shortcomings, and it has proposed solutions to overcome them. In Part I of the book I have argued that

[48] See also Christian Calliess, "The Governance Framework of the Eurozone and the Need for a Treaty Reform," in Federico Fabbrini et al (eds), *What Form of Government for the European Union and the Eurozone?* (Hart Publishing 2015), 37 and Jean-Claude Piris, *The Future of Europe: Towards a Two-Speed EU?* (CUP 2011) (arguing for further integration within the Eurozone framework only).

[49] See also the document prepared on behalf of the European University Institute by Giuliano Amato, Elisabeth Guigou, Vaira Vīķe-Freiberga, and Joseph H.H. Weiler, "Towards a 'New Schuman Declaration'," Fiesole, May 6, 2015, now published as Editorial (2015) 13 International Journal of Constitutional Law 339.

[50] ECB President Mario Draghi, "Europe's Pursuit of 'A More Perfect Union'," Speech at the Harvard Kennedy School of Government, Cambridge, October 9, 2013.

[51] Pmbl. US Const. [52] Pmbl. TEU. [53] ECB President Draghi (n 50) 1.

[54] Ibid 2 (citing Federalist Paper No. 45 (Madison)). [55] Ibid 6.

the Euro-crisis and the responses to it affected the vertical relations between the states and the EU, the horizontal relations between the courts and the political process, and the horizontal relations between the states themselves in paradoxical ways—triggering centralization, judicialization, and domination. Yet, these trends had downsides, since they undermined state autonomy, unduly constrained the democratic process, and called into question the anti-hegemonic nature of the EU integration project. In light of that, in Part II of the book I have thus claimed that the European constitutional architecture of economic governance should develop in new directions—raising a fiscal capacity, restoring the centrality of the legislative process, and reforming the EU executive power. While several challenges, including asymmetry, representation, and unanimity or unity, must be recognized in the way ahead, the European citizens and states must take steps toward a more perfect EMU.

Table of Cases

AUSTRIA

COUNCIL OF EUROPE—EUROPEAN CONVENTION ON HUMAN RIGHTS

CYPRUS

ESTONIA

EUROPEAN UNION

FINLAND

Korkein hallinto-oikeus (Supreme Administrative Court)

FRANCE

Conseil constitutionnel (Constitutional Court)

GERMANY

Bundesverfassungsgericht (Federal Constitutional Court)

GREECE

Symvoulio tis Epikrateias (Council of State)

IRELAND

High Court

Supreme Court

ITALY

Corte Costituzionale (Constitutional Court)

NETHERLANDS

Rechtbank s'-Gravenhage (District Court of the Hague)

POLAND

Trybunał Konstytucyjny (Constitutional Court)

PORTUGAL

Tribunal Constitucional (Constitutional Court)

SLOVENIA

Ustavno sodišče (Constitutional Court)

SPAIN

Tribunal Constitucional (Constitutional Court)

UNITED STATES

Supreme Court

Bibliography

Ackerman, B., *We the People: Volume 3. The Civil Rights Revolution* (Harvard UP 2014).

Ackerman, B., *The Failure of the Founding Fathers: Jefferson, Marshall and the Rise of Presidential Democracy* (Harvard UP 2005).

Ackerman, B., (ed), *Bush v. Gore: The Question of Legitimacy* (Yale UP 2002).

Ackerman, B., "The New Separation of Powers" (2000) 113 Harvard Law Review 642.

Ackerman, B., "Taxation and the Constitution" (1999) 99 Columbia Law Review 1.

Ackerman, B., *We the People: Volume 2: Transformations* (Harvard UP 1998).

Ackerman, B., *We the People. Volume 1: Foundations* (Harvard UP 1991).

Ackerman, B., "Beyond the *Carolene Products*" (1985) 98 Harvard Law Review 713.

Ackerman, B., and Maduro, M., "Broken Bond" *Foreign Policy*, September 17, 2012.

Acosta, P., "National Legal Tradition–Spain" in Galera, S., (ed), *Judicial Review: A Comparative Analysis Inside the European Legal System* (Council of Europe Publishing 2010), 113.

Adams, M., and Bomhoff, J., (eds), *Practice and Theory in Comparative Law* (CUP 2012).

Adams, M., and Van der Schyff, G., "Judicial Review by the Judiciary in the Netherlands: A Matter of Politics, Democracy or Compensating Strategy?" (2006) 66 Zeitschrift für ausländisches öffentliches Recht und Völkerrecht 399.

Adonis, A., "An English Parliament?," *The Guardian*, September 19, 2014.

Albert, R., "Presidential Values in Parliamentary Democracies" (2010) 8 International Journal of Constitutional Law 207.

Albi, A., *EU Enlargment and the Constitutions of Central and Eastern Europe* (CUP 2005).

Alesina, A., and Spolaore, E., *The Size of Nations* (MIT Press 2003).

Allemand, F., and Martucci, F., "La nouvelle gouvernance économique européene—Partie II" (2012) 46 Cahiers de droit européen 409.

Allemand, F., and Martucci, F., "La nouvelle gouvernance économique européene—Partie I" (2012) 46 Cahiers de droit européen 17.

Alvarez Conde, E., "La Reforma de l'Articulo 135 CE" [2011] Revista española de derecho constitucional 159.

Amar, A.R., *America's Constitution: A Biography* (Random House 2005).

Amato, G., Op-Ed, "Il modello federale per essere più liberi," *Il Sole 24 Ore*, April 29, 2012.

Amato, G., "Future Prospects for a European Constitution" in Amato, G., et al (eds), *Genesis and Destiny of the European Constitution* (Bruylant, 2007), 1271.

Amato, G., Guigou, E., Vīķe-Freiberga, V., and Weiler, J.H.H., "Towards a 'New Schuman Declaration'," Fiesole, May 6, 2015, now published as Editorial (2015) 13 International Journal of Constitutional Law 339.

Amtenbrink, F., "The Economic and Monetary Union: Constitutional and Institutional Aspects of the Economic Governance within the EU: General Report," in Neergard, U., et al (eds), *The Economic and Monetary Union: Constitutional and Institutional Aspects of the Economic Governance within the EU. Proceedings of the XXVI FIDE Congress* (Djøf 2014), 73.

Amtenbrink, F., and De Haan, J., "Economic Governance in the European Union: Fiscal Policy Discipline versus Flexibility" (2003) 40 Common Market Law Review 1075.

Anderson, G., *Fiscal Federalism: A Comparative Introduction* (OUP 2009).

Antoš, M., "Fiscal Stability Rules in Central European Constitutions," in Fabbrini, F., et al (eds), *The Constitutionalization of European Budgetary Constraints* (Hart Publishing 2014), 205.

Antpöhler, C., "Enhancing European Democracy in Times of Crisis? The Proposal to Politicise the Election of the European Commission's President," in Fabbrini, F., et al (eds), *What Form of Government for the European Union and the Eurozone?* (Hart Publishing 2015), 217.

Armstrong, K., "The New Governance of EU Fiscal Discipline" (2013) 38 European Law Review 601.

Armstrong, K., *Governing Social Inclusion: Europeanization Through Policy Coordination* (OUP 2010).

Athanassiou, P., "Of Past Measures and Future Plans for Europe's Exit from the Sovereign Debt Crisis: What is Legally Possible (and What is Not)" (2011) 36 European Law Review 558.

Autret, F., "Pierre Moscovici: 'Je suis favorable à un minister des Finances européen'," *La Tribune*, September 10, 2015.

Azoulai, L., "Introduction: The Question of Competence," in Azoulai, L., (ed), *The Question of Competence in the European Union* (OUP 2014), 1.

Barber, T., "Elections Results Show a Europe Short of Confidence in its Future," *The Financial Times*, May 26, 2014.

Barbera, A., *Le basi filosofiche del costituzionalismo* (Laterza 1997).

Barbera, A., and Fusaro, C., *Il governo delle democrazie* (Il Mulino 2001).

Bardutzky, S., and Fahey, E., "Who got to Adjudicate the EU Financial Crisis and Why?" in Fabbrini, F., et al (eds), *The Constitutionalization of European Budgetary Constraints* (Hart Publishing 2014), 341.

Barnard, C., "The Charter, the Court—and the Crisis," University of Cambridge Faculty of Law Research Paper No. 18/2013.

Baroncelli, S., "The Independence of the ECB after the Economic Crisis," in Fabbrini, F., et al (eds), *The Constitutionalization of European Budgetary Constraints* (Hart Publishing 2014), 125.

Baroncelli, S., *La Banca Centrale Europea: Profile giuridici e istituzionali: Un confronto con il modello americano della Federal Reserve* (European Press Academy Publishing 2000).

Barroso, M.D., Speech at the "State of the Union" Conference of the European University Institute, Florence, May 9, 2013.

Bartolini, S., *Restructuring Europe* (OUP 2005).

Bassanini, F., and Salvemini, M.T., (eds), *Il finanziamento dell'Europa* (Passigli 2010).

Bast, J., "Don't Act Beyond Your Powers: The Perils and Pitfalls of the German Constitutional Court's *Ultra Vires* Review" (2014) 15 German Law Journal 167.

Bastasin, C., *Saving Europe: How National Politics Nearly Destroyed the Euro* (Brookings Institution Press 2012).

Bauer, M., and Becker, S., "The Unexpected Winner of the Crisis: The European Commission Strenghtened Role in Economic Governance" (2014) 36 Journal of European Integration 213.

Beach, D., "The Facilitator of Efficient Negotiations in the Council: the Impact of the Council Secretariat," in Naurin, D., and Wallace, H., (eds), *Unveiling the Council of the European Union* (Palgrave MacMillan 2010), 219.

Beaud, O., *Théorie de la fédération* (PUF 2007).

Begg, I., "Economic Governance in an Enlarged Euro Area," European Commission Economic Papers No. 311/2008.

Bellamy, R., and Castiglione, D., "Three Models of Democracy, Political Community and Representation in the EU" (2013) 20 Journal of European Public Policy 206.

Benedetto, G., "The Balance of Power over the EU Budget: European Expenditures since the Lisbon Treaty," Swedish Institute for European Policy Studies, Policy Analysis No. 15/2015.

Bertoncini, Y., "New President, New 'Constitution'?" *Notre Europe Tribune*, July 23, 2014.

Bertoncini, Y., et al, "Improving EMU," Notre Europe Policy Paper No. 137/2015.

Besselink, L., and Reestman, J.H., Editorial: "The Fiscal Compact and the European Constitutions: 'Europe Speaking German'" (2012) 8 European Constitutional Law Review 1.

Beukers, T., "The Eurozone Crisis and the Autonomy of Member States in Economic Union," paper presented at the Conference "Constitutional Challenges of the European Economic and Monetary Union," Villa Vigoni, Como, June 5, 2015.

Beukers, T., "The New ECB and Its Relationship with the Eurozone Member States" (2013) 50 Common Market Law Review 1579.

Beukers, T., and Eijsbouts, T., Editorial: "The Euro Crisis: Storm, Meet Structure" (2011) 7 European Constitutional Law Review 349.

Bickel, A., *The Least Dangerous Branch: The Supreme Court and the Bar of Politics* (Yale UP 1986).

Bickerton, C., *European Integration: From Nation States to Member States* (OUP 2012).

Bieber, R., "The Allocation of Economic Policy Competences in the European Union," in Azoulai, L., (ed), *The Question of Competence in the European Union* (OUP 2015), 86.

Bieber, R., "Observer–Policeman–Pilot: On Lacunae of Legitimacy and the Contradictions of Financial Crisis Management in the European Union," European University Institute Department of Law Working Paper No. 2011/16.

Bocquillon, P., and Dobbels, M., "An Elephant on the 13th Floor of the Berlaymont? European Council and Commission Relations in Legislative Agenda Setting" (2014) Journal of European Public Policy 20.

Boerger, A., and Rasmussen, M., "Transforming European Law: The Establishment of the Constitutional Discourse from 1950 to 1993" (2014) 10 European Constitutional Law Review 199.

Bogdanor, V., "The Constitution and the Party System in the Twentieth Century" (2004) 57 Parliamentary Affairs 717.

Bogdanor, V., "The Future of the European Community: Two Models of Democracy" (1986) 2 Government and Opposition 161.

Bognetti, G., "Il pareggio di bilancio nella Carta costituzionale" [2011] Rivista AIC 1.

Bomhoff, J., "Balancing, the Global and the Local: Judicial Balancing as a Problematic Topic in Comparative (Constitutional) Law" (2008) 31 Hastings International and Comparative Law Review 555.

Bonvicini, G., and Brugnoli, F., (eds), "Il Fiscal Compact," Centro Studi sul Federalismo & Instituto Affari Internazionali, September 2012.

Borger, V., "The ESM and the European Court's Predicament in *Pringle*" (2013) 14 German Law Journal 113.

Borger, V., "How the Debt Crisis Exposes the Development of Solidarity in the Euro Area" (2013) 9 European Constitutional Law Review 7.

Bouvier, M., et al, "L'introduction de la 'Règle d'Or' budgetaire dans la Constitution" [2011] Constitutions 23.

Bowers, P., "The West Lothian Question," House of Commons Library, January 18, 2012, SN/PC/2586.

Bressanelli, E., and Chelotti, N., "Legislating in the Shadow of the European Council: Empowering or Silencing the European Parliament?," paper presented at the workshop "The Centrality of the European Council," CEU Budapest, November 28, 2014.

Briani, V., "The Costs of Non-Europe in the Defence Field," Centro Studi sul Federalism & Instituto Affari Internazionali, April 2013.

Broz, L., *The International Origins of the Federal Reserve System* (Cornell UP 1997).

Brunkhorst, H., "Collective Bonapartism—Democracy in the European Crisis" (2014) 15 German Law Journal 1177.

Buchanan, J., and Tullock, G., *The Calculus of Consent: Logical Foundations of Constitutional Democracy* (Michigan UP 1962).

Bunse, S., and Nicolaïdis, K., "Large versus Small States: Anti-Hegemony and the Politics of Shared Leadership," in Jones, E., et al (eds), *The Oxford Handbook of the European Union* (OUP 2012), 249.

Burgess, M., and Gagnon, A., (eds), *Federal Democracies* (Routledge 2010).

Busch, K., et al, "Euro Crisis, Austerity Policy and the European Social Model: How Crisis in Southern Europe Threatens the EU's Social Dimension," Friedrich Ebert Stiftung International Policy Analysis 2013.

Buti, M., and Carnot, N., "The EMU Debt Crisis: Early Lessons and Reforms" (2012) 50 Journal of Common Market Studies 899.

Cabras, D., "L'introduzione del principio del c.d. pareggio di bilancio: una regola importante per la stabilizzazione della finanza pubblica" [2012] Quaderni Costituzionali 111.

Calabresi, S., "The Virtues of Presidential Government" (2001) 18 Constitutional Commentary 51.

Calabresi, S., "Some Normative Arguments for the Unitary Executive" (1995) 48 Arkansas Law Review 23.

Calabresi, S., and Stabile, N., "On Section 5 of the Fourteenth Amendment" (2009) Pennsylvania Journal of Constitutional Law 1431.

Calleo, D.P., "De Gaulle's Visions for Europe" in Benjamin Rowland (ed), *Charles De Gaulle's Legacy of Ideas* (Lexington Book 2011), 1.

Calliess, C., "The Governance Framework of the Eurozone and the Need for a Treaty Reform," in Fabbrini, F., et al (eds), *What Form of Government for the European Union and the Eurozone?* (Hart Publishing 2015), 37.

Calliess, C., "From Fiscal Compact to Fiscal Union? New Rules for the Eurozone" (2012) 14 Cambridge Yearbook of European Legal Studies 101.

Cameron, D., Speech, London, January 23, 2013

Cameron, D., and Simeon, R., "Intergovernmental Relations in Canada: The Emergence of Collaborative Federalism" (2002) 32 Publius 49.

Cappelletti, M., *Il controllo giudiziario di costituzionalita delle leggi nel diritto comparato* (Giuffré 1972).

Cappelletti, M., et al, "General Introduction" in Cappelletti, M., et al (eds), *Integration Through Law: Europe and the American Federal Experience. Volume 1, Book 1* (de Gruyter 1986), 5.

Cartabia, M., "Revisione dei trattati," in Cassese, S., (ed), *Dizionario di diritto pubblico* (Giuffrè 2006), ad vocem.

Caruso, C., and Morvillo, M., "Economic Governance and Budgetary Rules in the European Context" [2014] Diritto dell'Unione Europea 699.

Cassese, S., "L'Unione europea e il guinzaglio tedesco" [2009] Giornale di diritto amministrativo 1003.

Cassese, S., "La costituzione economica europea" (2001) 11 Rivista italiana di diritto pubblico comunitario 907.

Ceccanti, S., "Le istituzioni e il sistema politico dopo il primo 'quinquennato'," in Baldini, G., and Lazar, M., (eds), *La Francia di Sarkozy* (Il Mulino 2007), 27.

Cerretelli, A., "La partita delle nomine che contano a Bruxelles," *Il Sole 24 Ore*, July 8, 2014.

Chalmers, D., "Democratic Self-Government in Europe: Domestic Solutions to the EU Legitimacy Crisis," Policy Network Paper, May 2013.

Chalmers, D., "The European Redistributive State and a European Law of Struggle" (2012) 18 European Law Journal 667.

Chantebout, B., "La dissuasion nucléaire et le pouvoir présidentiel" (1986) 38 Pouvoirs 21.

Chernow, R., *Alexander Hamilton* (Penguin 2004).

Chinaud, R., "Loi de Finances: Quelle Marge de Manouvre pour le Parlement?" (1993) 64 Pouvoirs 99.

Chiti, E., "Le istituzioni europee, la crisi e la trasformazione costituzionale dell'Unione" [2012] Giornale di diritto amministrativo 783.

Chiti, E., and G. Teixeira, P., "The Constitutional Implications of the European Responses to the Financial and Public Debt Crisis" (2013) 50 Common Market Law Review 683.

Choper, J., *Judicial Review and the National Political Process* (Chicago UP 1980).

Claes, M., *The National Courts Mandate in the European Constitution* (Hart Publishing 2006).

Claes, M., and De Witte, B., "Competences," in Blockmans, S., and Lazowski, A., (eds), *Research Handbook of EU Institutional Law* (Elgar 2016), 9.

Claessens, S., et al, "Paths to Eurobonds," International Monetary Fund Working Paper No. 172/2012.

Clark, B., "Separation of Powers as a Safeguard of Federalism" (2001) 79 Texas Law Review 1321.

Clementi, F., "L'elezione diretta del Primo ministro: l'origine francese, il caso israeliano, il dibattito in Italia" [2000] Quaderni Costituzionali 579.

Closa Montero, C., "Moving Away from Unanimity: Ratification of the Treaty on Stability, Coordination and Governance in the Economic and Monetary Union," RECON Working Paper No. 38/2011.

Collignon, S., "The End of the Stability and Growth Pact?" (2004) 1 International Economics and Economic Policy 15.

Conti-Brown, P., and Skeel, D., (eds), *When States Go Broke: The Origins, Context, and Solutions for the American States in Fiscal Crisis* (CUP 2012).

Conway, G., "Recovering a Separation of Powers in the European Union" (2011) 17 European Law Journal 304.

Corbett, R., et al, *The European Parliament* (8th ed. John Harper Publishing 2011).

Cortes, A., and Violante, T., "Concrete Control of Constitutionality in Portugal: A Means Toward Effective Protection of Fundamental Rights" (2011) 29 Penn. State International Law Review 759.

Corwin, E., "The Passing of Dual Federalism" (1950) 36 Virginia Law Review 1.

Costa, O., "Quel sont les défis pour le Parlement européen? Législation, contrôle et organization," Study commissioned by the European Parliament Constitutional Affairs Committee, January 2015, PE 510.006.

Costamagna, F., "The Impact of Stronger Economic Policy Co-ordination on the European Social Dimension: Issues of Legitimacy," in Fabbini, F., et al (eds.), *The Constitutionalization of European Budgetary Constraints* (Hart Publishing 2014), 359.

Constantinesco, V., "Fédéralisme économique et fédéralisme politique" in De la Rosa, S., et al (eds), *L'Union européenne et le fédéralisme économique* (Bruylant 2015), 439.

Craig, P., "The Financial Crisis, the EU Institutional Order and Constitutional Responsibility," in Fabbrini, F., et al (eds), *What Form of Government for the European Union and the Eurozone* (Hart Publishing 2015), 17.

Craig, P., "Economic Governance and the Euro Crisis: Constitutional Architecture and Constitutional Implications," in Fabbrini, F., et al (eds), *The Constitutionalization of European Budgetary Constraints* (Hart Publishing 2014), 19.

Craig, P., "*Pringle*: Legal Reasoning, Text, Purpose and Teleology" (2013) 20 Maastricht Journal of European & Comparative Law 3.

Craig, P., "*Pringle* and the Use of EU Institutions Outside the EU Legal Framework: Foundations, Procedure and Substance" (2013) 9 European Constitutional Law Review 263.

Craig, P., "The Stability, Coordination and Governance Treaty: Principle, Politics and Pragmatism" (2012) 37 European Law Review 231.

Craig, P., "The European Union Act 2011: Locks, Limits and Legality" (2011) 28 Common Market Law Review 1881.

Craig, P. "Institutions, Power and Institutional Balance," in Craig, P., and de Búrca, G., (eds), *The Evolution of EU Law* (2nd ed. OUP 2011), 41.

Craig, P., *The Treaty of Lisbon: Law, Politics and Treaty Reform* (OUP 2010).

Craig, P., "The Role of the European Parliament under the Lisbon Treaty" in Griller, S., and Ziller, J., (eds), *The Lisbon Treaty: EU Constitutionalism without a Constitutional Treaty?* (Springer 2008), 110.

Craig, P., and Tomkins, A., (eds), *The Executive and Public Law: Power and Accountability in Comparative Perspective* (OUP 2006).

Cremona, M., "The European Union and Regional Free Trade Agreements" (2010) European Yearbook of International Economic Law 245.

Crum, B., "Saving the Euro at the Cost of Democracy?" (2013) 51 Journal of Common Market Studies 614.

Crum, B., "Accountability and Personalisation of the European Council Presidency" (2009) 31 European Integration 685.

Crum, B., "Tailoring Representative Democracy in the European Union: Does the European Constitution Reduce the Democratic Deficit?" (2005) 11 European Law Journal 452.

Crum, B., and Fossum, J.E., (eds), *Practices of Interparliamentary Coordination in International Politics: The European Union and Beyond* (ECPR Press 2013).

Curtin, D., "Democratic Accountability of EU Executive Power," in Fabbrini, F., et al (eds), *What Form of Government for the European Union and the Eurozone?* (Hart Publishing 2015), 171.

Curtin, D., "Challenging Executive Dominance in European Democracy" (2014) 77 Modern Law Review 1.

Curtin, D., *Executive Power of the European Union: Law, Practices and the Living Constitution* (OUP 2009).

Curtin, D., and Fasone, C., "Differentiated Representation: Is a Flexible European Parliament Desirable?" in De Witte, B., et al (eds), *Between Flexibility and Disintegration: The State of EU Law Today* (Elgar 2016).

Czuzcka, T., "Merkel Says Euro-Area Fiscal Union Won't Be 'Transfer Union'," *Bloomberg Businessweek*, February 7, 2012.

D'Alfonso, A., "How the EU Budget is Financed. The 'Own Resources' System and the Debate on its Reform," European Parliament Research Service in-depth analysis, June 2, 2014, 140805REV1.

D'Alimonte, R., and Fusaro, C., (eds), *La legislazione elettorale italiana* (Il Mulino 2008).
Dafflon, B., "Le fédéralisme fiscal en Suisse: un relevé des enjeux constitutionnels, des responsabilités budgetaires et de la péréquation" rapport pour la Commission sur les déséquilibre fiscal (2002).
Damilano, M., "Intervista: 'In Europa coalizione contro i populisti'. Parla Prodi," *L'Espresso*, May 22, 2014.
Dann, P., "European Parliament and Executive Federalism: Approaching a Parliament in a Semi-Parliamentary Democracy" (2003) 9 European Law Journal 549.
Dawson, M., "The Legal and Political Accountability Structure of 'Post-Crisis' EU Economic Governance" (2015) 54 Journal of Common Market Studies 4.
Dawson, M., and De Witte, F., "Constitutional Balance in the EU after the Euro-crisis" (2013) 76 Modern Law Review 817.
De Almeida Ribeiro, G., "Judicial Activism Against Austerity in Portugal" (2013) International Journal of Constitutional Law Blog.
De Baere, G., *Constitutional Principles of EU External Relations* (OUP 2008).
De Búrca, G., "If at First you don't Succeed: Vote, Vote Again: Analyzing the 'Second Referendum' Phenomenon in EU Treaty Change" (2010) 33 Fordham International Law Journal 1472.
De Grauwe, P., *Economics of Monetary Union* (10th ed. OUP 2014).
De Gregorio Merino, A., "Legal Developments in the Economic and Monetary Union During the Debt Crisis: the Mechanisms of Financial Assistance" (2014) 49 Common Market Law Review 1613.
De Sadeleer, N., "The New Architecture of the European Economic Governance: A Leviathan or a Flat-Footed Colossus?" (2012) 19 Maastricht Journal of European & Comparative Law 354.
De Schoutheete, P., "The European Council after Van Rompuy," *Notre Europe Tribune*, April 20, 2015.
De Schoutheete, P., "The European Council," in Peterson, J., and Shackleton, M., (eds), *The Institutions of the European Union* (3rd ed. OUP 2012), 43.
De Streel, A., "The Confusion of Tasks in the Decision-Making Process of the European Economic Governance," in Fabbrini, F., et al (eds), *What Form of Government for the European Union and the Eurozone?* (Hart Publishing, 2015), 79.
De Streel, A., "The Evolution of the EU Economic Governance Since the Treaty of Maastricht: An Unfinished Task" (2013) 20 Maastricht Journal of European & Comparative Law 336.
De Tocqueville, A., *Democracy in America* [1835-40] (J.P. Mayer ed. & George Lawrence trans., Doubleday & Co. 1969).
De Visser, M., *Constitutional Review in Europe: A Comparative Analysis* (Hart Publishing 2014).
De Waele, H., and Broeksteeg, H., "The Semi-Permanent European Council Presidency: Some Reflections on the Law and Early Practice" (2012) 49 Common Market Law Review 1039.
De Wet, E., "Belgium and the Netherlands," in Stone Sweet, A., and Keller, H., (eds.), *A Europe of Rights* (OUP 2009), 229.
De Witte, B., "European Stability Mechanism and Treaty on stability, coordination and governance: role of the EU institutions and consistency with EU legal order," in "Challenges of Multi-Tier Governance in the European Union," Study commissioned by the European Parliament Constitutional Affairs Committee, March 2013, PE 474.438, 78.

De Witte, B., "A Competence to Protect: The Pursuit of Non-Market Aims Through Internal Market Legislation," in Syrpis, P., (ed), *The Judiciary, the Legislature and the EU Internal Market* (CUP 2011), 25.

De Witte, B., "The European Union as an International Legal Experiment," in De Búrca, G., and Weiler, J.H.H., (eds), *The Worlds of European Constitutionalism* (CUP 2011), 19.

De Witte, B., "Saving the Constitution? The Escape Routes and their Legal Feasibility" in Amato, G., et al (eds), *Genesis and Destiny of the European Constitution* (Bruylant 2007), 919.

De Witte, B., "The Closest Thing to a Constitutional Conversation in Europe: The Semi-Permanent Treaty Revision Process," in Walker, N., et al (eds), *Convergence and Divergence in European Public Law* (Hart Publishing 2002), 39.

De Witte, B., "Chameleonic Member States: Differentiated Integration by Means of Partial and Parallel International Agreements," in De Witte, B., et al (eds), *The Many Faces of Differentiation in EU Law* (Intersentia 2001), 231.

De Witte, B., "Direct Effect, Supremacy and the Nature of the Legal Order" in Craig, P., and De Búrca, G., (eds), *The Evolution of EU Law* (OUP 1999), 177.

De Witte, B., and Beukers, T., "The Court of Justice approves the creation of the European Stability Mechanism outside the EU legal order: *Pringle*" (2013) 50 Common Market Law Review 805.

Decker, F., and Sonnicksen, J., "The Direct Election of the Commission President: A Presidential Approach to Democratizing the European Union," Zei Discussion Paper No. 192/2009.

Dehousse, F., "The Unified Court on Patents: The New Oxymoron of European Law," Egmont Royal Institute for International Relations Paper No. 60/2013.

Dehousse, R., "Is the 'Community Method' still Relevant?," in "Challenges of Multi-Tier Governance in the European Union," Study commissioned by the European Parliament Constitutional Affairs Committee, March 2013, PE 474.438, 85.

Dehousse, R., "The Community Method at Sixty," in Dehousse, R., (ed), *The Community Method* (Palgrave MacMillan 2011), 3.

Dehousse, R., "'We the States': Why the Anti-Federalists Won" in Jabko, N., and Parsons, C., (eds), *With US or Against US? European Trends in American Perspective* (OUP 2005), 105.

Dehousse, R., and Boussaguet, L., "L'impact de la crise sur la gouvernance européene" (2014) 149 Pouvoirs 7.

Della Cananea, G., "No Representation without Taxation: the European Union," paper presented at the European Constitutional Law Network annual conference on "Challenging the Legitimacy of Europe," Thessaloniki, May 22, 2015.

Della Cananea, G., "Government Deficits and Investments: A European Legal Framework" (2013) 5 Italian Journal of Public Law 103.

Delledonne, G., "A Legalization of Financial Constitutions in the EU? Reflections on the German, Spanish, Italian and French Experiences," in Fabbrini, F., et al (eds.), *The Constitutionalization of European Budgetary Constraints* (Hart Publishing 2014), 181.

Delledonne, G., "Il *Bundesverfassungsgericht*, il Parlamento europeo e la soglia di sbarramento del 5%: un (altro) ritorno del *Sonderweg*?" [2012] Rivista AIC 1.

Delors, J., *Report on Economic and Monetary Union in the European Communities* (Publication Office of the EC 1989).

Deloy, C., and Joannin P., "Les forces de droit sortent victorieuses des elections européenne marquees par une poussée populiste dans plusiers Etats members," Fondation Robert Schuman—Observatoire des Elections en Europe (2014).

Di Fabio, U., "Karlsruhe Makes a Referral" (2014) 15 German Law Journal 107.

Diamant., M., and van Emmerik, M., "Mandatory Balanced Budget in Dutch Legislation Following Examples Abroad?," in Fabbrini, F., et al (eds), *The Constitutionalization of European Budgetary Constraints* (Hart Publishing 2014), 249.

Dijsselbloem, J., Letter to the members of the Eurogroup, July 12, 2015.

Dimopoulos, A., "The Use of International Law as a Tool for Enhancing Governance in the Eurozone and its Impact on EU Institutional Integrity," in Fabbrini, F., et al (eds), *The Constitutionalization of European Budgetary Constraints* (Hart Publishing 2014), 41.

Dinan, D., "The Post-Lisbon European Council Presidency: An Interim Assessment" (2013) 36 West European Politics 1256.

Dougan, M., "The Competences of the Union," in Schütze, R., and Tridimas, T., (eds), *Oxford Principles of European Union Law* (OUP 2016).

Dougan, M., "The Treaty of Lisbon 2007: Winning Minds, Not Hearts" (2008) 45 Common Market Law Review 617.

Draghi, M., Introductory statement in front of the European Parliament, Brussels, June 15, 2015.

Draghi, M., "Europe's Pursuit of 'A More Perfect Union'," Speech at the Harvard Kennedy School of Government, Cambridge, October 9, 2013.

Draghi, M., Introductory statement in front of the European Parliament, Brussels, December 1, 2011.

Dubout, E., "Pour la transfiguration de l'Europe—*Ordo ab chaos?*," in De la Rosa, S., et al (eds), *L'Union européene et le fédéralisme économique* (Bruylant 2015), 17.

Duhamel, O., "Remarques sur la notion de régime semi-présidentiel," in *Droit, institutions et systèmes politiques. Mélanges en hommage à Maurice Duverger* (PUF 1987), 581.

Dullien, S., "Improving Economic Stability in Europe: What the Euro Area Can Learn from the United States Unemployment Insurance," SWP Berlin Working Paper No. 11/2007.

Duverger, M., "A New Political System Model: Semi-Presidential Government" (1980) 8 European Journal of Political Research 165.

Duverger, M., *Institutions politiques et droit constitutionnel* (PUF 1978).

Duverger, M., *Political Parties: Their Organization and Activity in the Modern State* (Wiley 1959).

Dyson, K., *States, Debt & Power: "Saints" and "Sinners" in European History & Integration* (OUP 2014).

The Economist, "A Teutonic Union," September 13, 2014.

The Economist, "Europe's Financial Transaction Tax: Oops," April 27, 2013.

The Economist, "Euro Wobbles. Portugal's Constitutional Court Creates New Problem for the Euro," April 13, 2013.

The Economist, "European Disunion Done Right," December 22, 2012, 71.

The Economist, "Testing the Limits: Even Germany Has Constitutional Worries About More European Integration," March 24, 2012, 31.

The Economist, "1789 and All That," February 11, 2012.

Editorial Comments, "After the European Elections: Parliamentary Games and Gambles" (2014) 51 Common Market Law Review 1047.

Editorial Comments, "Some Thoughts Concerning the Draft Treaty on a Reinforced Economic Union" (2012) 49 Common Market Law Review 1.

Editorial Comments, "An ever mighty European Council—Some recent institutional developments" (2009) 46 Common Market Law Review 1383.

Eggermont, F., *The Changing Role of the European Council in the Institutional Framework of the European Union* (Intersentia 2012).

Eichengreen, B., "European Monetary Unification: A *Tour d'Horizon*" (1998) 14 *Oxford Review of Economic Policy* 25.

Eichengreen, B., *European Monetary Unification: Theory, Practice, Analysis* (OUP 1997).
Eiffel Group, "For a Euro Community," February 2014.
Eijsbouts, T., and Claes, M., Editorial: "From Confederacy to Convoy: Thoughts about the Finality of the Union and its Member States" (2010) 6 European Constitutional Law Review 1.
Elazar, D., *Constitutionalizing Globalization* (Rowman & Littlefield 1998).
Elazar, D., *Exploring Federalism* (Alabama UP 1987).
Eleftheriadis, P., "The Standing of States in the European Union," in Tsagourias, N., (ed), *Transnational Constitutionalism* (CUP 2010), 44.
Elkins, S., and McKitrick, E., *The Age of Federalism* (OUP 1993).
Elster, J., *Ulysses and the Sirens. Studies in Rationality and Irrationality* (CUP 1979).
Enderlein, H., et al, "The EU Budget: How Much Scope for Institutional Reform?," ECB Occasional Paper Series No. 27/2005.
Englisch, J., et al, "The Financial Transaction Tax Proposal under the Enhanced Cooperation Procedure: Legal and Practical Considerations" [2013] British Tax Review 223.
Erbsen, A., "Horizontal Federalism" (2009) 93 Minnesota Law Review 493.
Erlanger, S., and Kulish, N., "French Front-Runner Says He'd Seek to Renegotiate Fiscal Treaty if Elected," *New York Times*, April 26, 2012, A8.
Everson, M., and Joerges, C., "Who is the Guardian of Constitutionalism in Europe After the Financial Crisis?," LSE 'Europe in Question' Discussion Paper Series No. 63/2013.
Fabbrini, F., "The Principle of Subsidiarity," in Schütze, R., and Tridimas, T., (eds), *Oxford Principles of EU Law* (OUP 2016).
Fabbrini, F. (ed), Special issue: "The European Court of Justice, the European Central Bank, and the Supremacy of EU Law" (2016) 23 Maastricht Journal of European & Comparative Law.
Fabbrini, F. "A Principle in Need of Renewal? The Euro-Crisis and the Principle of Institutional Balance" (2016) 50 Cahiers de droit européen.
Fabbrini, F., "Representation in the European Parliament: Of False Problems and Real Challenges" (2015) 75 Zeitschrift für ausländisches öffentliches Recht und Völkerrecht 823.
Fabbrini, F. "After the OMT Case: The Supremacy of EU Law as the Guarantee of the Equality between the Member States" (2015) 16 German Law Journal 1003.
Fabbrini, F. "Austerity, the European Council and the Institutional Future of the EU" (2015) 22 Indiana Journal of Global Legal Studies 269.
Fabbrini, F., "On Banks, Courts and International Law. The Intergovernmental Agreement on the Single Resolution Fund in Context" (2014) 21 Maastricht Journal of European & Comparative Law 444.
Fabbrini, F., "Taxing and Spending in the Eurozone: Legal and Political Challenges Related to the Adoption of the Financial Transaction Tax" (2014) 39 European Law Review 155.
Fabbrini, F., *Fundamental Rights in Europe: Challenges and Transformations in Comparative Perspective* (OUP 2014).
Fabbrini, F., "Enhanced Cooperation under Scrutiny: Revisiting the Law and Practice of Multi-Speed Integration in Light of the First Involvement of the EU Judiciary" (2013) 40 Legal Issues of Economic Integration 197.
Fabbrini, F., "Europe in Need of a New Deal: On Federalism, Free Markets and the Right to Strike" (2012) 43 Georgetown Journal of International Law 1175.
Fabbrini, F., "Il pareggio di bilancio nelle costituzioni europee" [2011] Quaderni Costituzionali 933.
Fabbrini, F., "La composizione del Parlamento Europeo dopo il Trattato di Lisbona" (2011) 61 Rivista trimestrale di diritto pubblico 787.

Fabbrini, F., "The Role of the Judiciary in Times of Emergency: Judicial Review of Counter-Terrorism Measures in the United States Supreme Court and the European Court of Justice" (2009) 28 Oxford Yearbook of European Law 664.

Fabbrini, F., "Kelsen in Paris: France's Constitutional Reform and the Introduction of *A Posteriori* Constitutional Review of Legislation" (2008) 9 German Law Journal 1297.

Fabbrini, F., et al (eds), *What Form of Government for the European Union and the Eurozone?* (Hart Publishing 2015).

Fabbrini, F., et al (eds), *The Constitutionalization of European Budgetary Constraints* (Hart Publishing 2014).

Fabbrini, F., and Katarzyna Granat, K., "'Yellow Card, But No Foul': The Role of the National Parliaments under the Subsidiarity Protocol and the Commission Proposal for an EU Regulation on the Right to Strike" (2013) 50 Common Market Law Review 115.

Fabbrini, S., *Which European Union? Europe after the Euro Crisis* (CUP 2015).

Fabbrini, S., "Intergovernmentalism and its Limits: Assessing the European Union's Answer to the Euro Crisis" (2013) 46 Comparative Political Studies 1003.

Fabbrini, S., "After the Euro-Crisis: The President of Europe," EuropEos Commentary No. 12/2012.

Fabbrini, S., *Compound Democracies* (OUP 2007).

Fahey, E., *Practice and Procedure in Preliminary References to Europe: 30 Years of Article 236 EC Caselaw from the Irish Courts* (Firstlaw 2007).

Fallon, R., "The Core of an Uneasy Case for Judicial Review" (2008) 121 Harvard Law Review 1693.

Farrand, M., *Records of the Federal Convention, Volume 1* (Yale UP 1911).

Farrel, D., and Scully, R., "The European Parliament: One Parliament, Several Modes of Political Representation on the Ground?," in Mair, P., and Thomassen, J., (eds), *Political Representation and European Union Governance* (Routledge 2011), 36.

Fasone, C., "European Economic Governance and Parliamentary Representation. What Place for the European Parliament?" (2014) 20 European Law Journal 164.

Feld, L.P., and Baskaran, T., "Federalism, Budget Deficits and Public Debt: On the Reform of Germany's Fiscal Constitution" (2010) 6 Review of Law and Economics 365.

Ferreres Comella, V., "The Spanish Constitutional Court: Time for Reforms" (2008) 3 Journal of Comparative Law 22.

The Financial Times, Editorial "Playing Politics with the British Constitution," October 14, 2014, 12.

Fischer, J., "The Return of the Ugly German," *Project Syndacate*, July 23, 2015.

Fischer, J., "From Confederacy to Federation," Speech at Humboldt Universität, Berlin, May 12, 2000, transcript available at <http://cadmus.eui.eu/bitstream/handle/1814/17255/ResponsesToJ.FISCHER_2000.pdf> (last accessed June 1, 2014).

Fisher, L., *American Constitutional Law. Volume 1: Constitutional Structures, Separated Powers and Federalism* (Carolina Academic Press 2005).

Fisher, L., *Presidential War Power* (2nd ed. rev. Kansas UP 2004).

Fisher, L., *Constitutional Dialogues: Interpretation as Political Process* (Princeton UP 1988).

Floridia, G., *Il cantiere della nuova Europa* (Il Mulino 2003).

Fossum, J.E., and J. Menéndez, A., *The Constitition's Gift: A Constitutional Theory for a Democratic European Union* (Rowman & Littlefield 2011).

Fouquet, H., "French Lawmakers Endorse Constitutional Rule on Balanced Budgets," *Bloomberg News*, July 13, 2011.

Franco Ferrari, G., (ed), *Federalismo, sistema fiscale e autonomie: Modelli giuridici comparati* (Autonomie 2010).

Frenkel, M., "The Communal Basis of Swiss Liberty" (1993) 23 Publius 61.
Friedman, B., "The Pathology of Europe's Debt," 61 The New York Review of Books, October 9–22, 2014, 50.
Fromage, D., "Parlamento Europeo y Parlamentos nacionales después del Tratado de Lisboa y en un context de crisis," in Sáenz, A., et al (eds), *El Parlamento Europeo* (European Inklings 2015), 223.
Gallagher, M., and Mitchel, P., (eds), *The Politics of Electoral Systems* (OUP 2006).
Galimberti, F., "Se anche il potere giudiziario critica il rigore," *Il Sole 24 Ore*, April 7, 2013, 10.
Garben, S., "Confronting the Competence Conundrum: Democratising the European Union through an Expansion of its Legislative Powers" (2015) 35 Oxford Journal of Legal Studies 55.
Garcia Roca, J., and Martinez Lago, M., *Estabilidad presupuestaria y consagración del freno constitucional al endeudamiento* (Civitas 2013).
Gardbaum, S., *The New Commonwealth Model of Constitutionalism* (CUP 2013).
Garton Ash, T., "The New German Question," 60 New York Review of Books, August 15–September 25, 2013, 52.
Gaudreault-Desbiens, J.F., "Le fédéralisme et le législateur fédéral" (2009) 2 Revue de droit parlamentaire et politique 427.
Gerhardt, M., *The Federal Impeachment Process: A Constitutional and Historical Analysis* (2nd ed. Chicago UP 2000).
Giavazzi, F., et al, "The wisdom of Karlsruhe: The OMT Court case should be dismissed," *Voyeux.Org*, June 12, 2013.
Gicquel, J., "De la cohabitation" (1989) 49 Pouvoirs 69.
Giggacher, J., "Stand-Off as Indonesia Treads New Democratic Path," *The Sydney Morning Herald*, July 11, 2014.
Gilbert, M., *Surpassing Realism: The Politics of European Integration* (Rowman & Littlefield 2003).
Ginsburg, T., (ed), *Comparative Constitutional Design* (CUP 2012).
Ginsburg, T., *Judicial Review in New Democracies: Constitutional Courts in Asian Cases* (CUP 2003).
Ginsburg, T., et al, "Does the Process of Constitution-Making Matter?" (2009) 5 Annual Review of Law and Social Science 1.
Ginter, C., and Naritis, R., "The Perspective of a Small State to the Democratic Deficiency of the ESM" (2013) 38 Review of Central & East European Law 54.
Gioia, M., *Quale dei governi liberi meglio convenga alla felicità dell'Italia* [1797].
Giubboni, S., *Social Rights and Market Freedoms in the European Constitution: A Labour Law Perspective* (CUP 2009).
Giupponi, T., "Il governo nel sistema bipolare," in Barbera, A., and Giupponi, T., (eds), *La prassi degli organi costituzionali* (Bononia UP 2008), 51.
Glencross, A., *The Politics of European Integration* (Wiley 2014).
Glienicker Group, "Toward a Euro Union," October 17, 2013.
Goldmann, M., "Adjudicating Economics? Central Bank Independence and the Appropriate Standard of Judicial Review" (2014) 15 German Law Journal 265.
Gordon, M., "The United Kingdom and the Fiscal Compact" (2014) 10 European Constitutional Law Review 28.
Gozi, S., Op-Ed, "Europa, quegli scossini che facilitano il rilancio di una nuova governance," *Il Sole 24 Ore*, May 28, 2015.
Gozi, S. *Il governo dell'Europa* (Il Mulino 2011).

Grant, C., "Britain could reshape Europe, if it would only try," *The Financial Times*, May 14, 2013.

Gratteri, A., "Parlamento e Commissione: Il difficile equilibrio fra rappresentanza e governabilità nell'Unione Europea" [2014] La Comunità Internazionale 237.

Gréau, J., "Peut-on enrayer le déclin économique français?," Revue Politique et Parlamentaire, January 8, 2014.

Griglio, E., and Fasone, C., "Can Fiscal Councils Enhance the Role of National Parliaments in the European Union? A Comparative Analysis," in De Witte, B., et al (eds.), *The Euro Crisis and the State of European Democracy* (European University Institute Press 2014), 264.

Grinath, A., et al, "Debt, Default and Revenue Structure: The American State Debt Crisis in the Early 1840s," National Bureau of Economic Research, Historical Working Paper No. 97/1997.

Groppi, T., "The Italian Constitutional Court: Towards a 'Multilevel System' of Constitutional Review?" (2008) 3 Journal of Comparative Law 100.

Gros, D., "The Juncker Plan: From €21 to €315 billion, through smoke and mirrors," CEPS Commentaries, November 27, 2014.

Grzeszick, B., "Weil nicht sein kann, was nicht sein darf: Aufhebung der 3%-Sperrklausel im Europawahlrecht durch das BVerfG und dessen Sicht aus dem Europäischen Parlament" [2014] Neue Zeitschrift für Verwaltungsrecht 537.

Guiso, L., and Herrera, H., "Solo l'unione fiscale salverà l'euro" *Il Sole 24 Ore*, February 23, 2012.

Gunlicks, A., "Legislative Competences, Budgetary Constraints and the Reform of Federalism in Germany," in Burgess, M., and Tarr, A., (eds), *Constitutional Dynamics in Federal Systems* (McGill-Queen's UP 2012), 61.

Gunlicks, A., *The Länder and German Federalism* (Manchester UP 2003).

Habermas, J., "Democracy in Europe: Why the Development of the EU into a Transnational Democracy is Necessary and How is it Possible" (2015) 21 European Law Journal 546.

Habermas, J., *The Crisis of the European Union* (Polity Press 2012).

Häge, F., "Who Decides in the Council of the European Union?" (2008) 46 Journal of Common Market Studies 533.

Halberstam, D., "Federalism: Theory, Policy, Law," in Rosenfeld, M., and Sajó, A., (eds), *The Oxford Handbook of Comparative Constitutional Law* (OUP 2012), 576.

Halberstam, D., "Constitutional Heterarchy: the Centrality of Conflict in the European Union and the United States," in Dunoff, J., and Trachtman, J., (eds) *Ruling the World* (CUP 2009), 326.

Hallerberg, M., "Fiscal Federalism Reforms in the European Union and the Greek Crisis" (2012) 12 European Union Politics 127.

Hamilton, A, Madison, J. and Jay, J., *The Federalist Papers* [1787] (Penguin 1987).

Hamilton, A., "The Farmer Refuted" in Hamilton, J.C., (ed), *The Works of Alexander Hamilton* (Federal Edition 1850).

Harden, I., "The Fiscal Constitution of EMU" in Beaumont, P., and Walker, N., (eds), *The Legal Framework of the Single European Currency* (Hart Publishing 1999), 71.

Hart Ely, J., *Democracy and Distrust: A Theory of Judicial Review* (Harvard UP 1980).

Hayes-Renschaw, F., and Wallace, H., *The Council of Ministers* (Palgrave MacMillan 1997).

Hayes-Renshaw, F., "The Council of Ministers," in Peterson, J., and Shackleton, M., (eds), *The Institutions of the European Union* (3rd ed. OUP 2012), 68.

Hayward, J., (ed), *Leaderless Europe* (OUP 2008).

Hazell, R., "The English Question" (2006) 36 Publius 37.

Heipertz, M., and Verdun, A., *Ruling Europe: The Politics of the Stability and Growth Pact* (CUP 2011).

Heisennberg, D., "The Institution of 'Consensus' in the European Union: Formal versus Informal Decision-Making in the Council" (2005) 44 European Journal of Political Research 65.

Helm, T., "Humiliating defeat for David Cameron pushes Britain towards EU exit," *The Guardian*, June 28, 2014.

Henning, R.C., and Kessler, M., "Fiscal Federalism: US History for Architects of Europe's Fiscal Union," Bruegel Essay and Lecture Series 2012.

Hermann, C. "Die Bewältigung der Euro-Staatsschulden-Krise an den Grenzen des deutschen und europäischen Währungsverfassungsrechts" [2012] Europäische Zeitschrift für Wirtschaftsrecht 805.

Herzog, B., and Hengstermann, K., "Restoring Credible Economic Governance to the Eurozone" (2013) 33 Economic Affairs 3.

Higgins, A., "Europe Pressed to Reconsider Cuts as Cure" *The New York Times*, April 27, 2013.

Hillebrandt, M., et al, "Tansparency in the EU Council of Ministers: An Institutional Analysis" (2014) 20 European Law Journal 1.

Hinarejos, A., *The Euro Area Crisis in Constitutional Perspective* (OUP 2015).

Hinarejos, A., "Fiscal Federalism in the European Union: Evolution and Future Choices for EMU" (2013) 50 Common Market Law Review 1621.

Hinarejos, A., "The Euro Area Crisis and Constitutional Limits to Fiscal Integration" (2012) 14 Cambridge Yearbook of European Legal Studies 243.

Hirschl, R., "The Question of Case Selection in Comparative Constitutional Law" (2005) 53 American Journal of Comparative Law 125.

Hirschman, A., *Exit, Voice, Loyalty: Responses to Decline in Firms, Organizations and States* (Harvard UP 1970).

Hix, S., *What's Wrong with the European Union and How to Fix it?* (Polity Press 2008).

Hix, S., and Højland, B., *The Political System of the European Union* (3rd ed. Palgrave MacMillan 2011).

Hodson, D., *Governing the Euro Area in Good Times and Bad* (OUP 2011).

Hodson, D., and Puetter, U., "The European Union and the Economic Crisis," in Cini, M., and Pérez-Solórzano Borragán, N., (eds), *European Union Politics* (OUP 2013), 367.

Hofmann, H., and Pantazatou, K., "The Transformation of the European Economic Constitution," University of Luxembourg Law Working Paper No. 01/2015.

Hofmeister, H., "To Bail Out or Not to Bail Out? Legal Aspects of the Greek Crisis" (2011) 13 Cambridge Yearbook of European Legal Studies 113.

Hollande, F. "Entretien à l'occasion du 14 juillet," Paris, July 14, 2015.

Hollande, F., "Intervention liminaire de lors de la conférence de presse," Paris, May 16, 2013.

House of Lords European Union Committee, *The Euro Area Crisis*, 2012, H.L. 260, 75.

IMF, *World Economic Outlook*, April 14, 2015.

IMF, *World Economic Outlook*, April 14, 2014.

IMF, "Toward a Fiscal Union for the Euro Area," Staff Discussion Note, October 2013.

IMF, "A Fair and Substantial Contribution by the Financial Sector: Interim Report for the G20," April 2010.

Inman, R., and Rubinfeld, D., "The EMU and Fiscal Policy in the New European Community: An Issue for Economic Federalism" (1994) 14 International Review of Law and Economics 147.

Inman, R., and Rubinfeld, D., "Fiscal Federalism in Europe: Lessons from the United States Experience" (1992) 36 European Economic Review 654.
Ioannidis, M., "EU Financial Assistance Conditionality After 'Two Pack'" (2014) 74 Zeitschrift für ausländisches öffentliches Recht und Völkerrecht 61.
Issacharoff, S., "Fragile Democracies" (2007) 120 Harvard Law Review 1405.
Jackson, V., "Narrative of Federalism: Of Continuities and Comparative Constitutional Experience" (2001) 51 Duke Law Journal 223.
Jackson, V., "Federalism and the Uses and Limits of Law: *Printz* and Principle" (1998) 111 Harvard Law Review 2180.
Jackson, V., and Resnik, J., (eds.), *Federal Courts* (Foundation Press 2010).
Jacqué, J., "The Principle of Institutional Balance" (2004) 41 Common Market Law Review 383.
Jaigu, C., "Nicolas Sarkozy trace les pistes pour sortir de la crise," *Le Figaro*, December 1, 2011, 2.
James, H., *Making the European Monetary Union* (Harvard UP 2012).
Jamet, J.F., *L'Europe, peut-elle se passer d'un gouvernement économique?* (La Documentation française 2012).
Jeffries, S., "Is Germany Too Powerful for Europe?," *The Guardian*, March 31, 2013.
Jensen, E., "Taxation and the Constitution: How to Read the Direct Tax Clause" (1999) 15 Journal of Law & Policy 687.
Joerges, C., "Europas Wirtschaftsverfassungs in der Krise" (2012) 51 Der Staat 57.
Joerges, C., and Glinski, C., (eds), *The European Crisis and the Transformation of Transnational Governance* (Hart Publishing 2014).
Joerges, C., and Vos, E., (eds), *EU Committees* (Hart Publishing 1999).
Jolly, D., and Ewing, J., "France's Highest Court Clears E.U. Fiscal Treaty," *The International Herald Tribune*, August 11–12, 2012, 9.
Juncker, J.C., "A New Start for Europe: My Agenda for Jobs, Growth and Democratic Change," Speech at the European Parliament, Strasbourg, July 15, 2014.
Juncker, J.C., and Tremonti, G., Op-Ed, "E-Bonds Would End the Crisis," *The Financial Times*, December 5, 2010.
Kahn, R., "The Commerce Clause and Executive Power: Exploring Nascent Individual Rights in *National Federation of Independent Business v. Sebelius*" (2013) 73 Maryland Law Review 133.
Kanter, J., "European Commission Elects a New Leader," *The New York Times*, July 15, 2014.
Kasel, A., "La présidence de l'Eurogroupe et la gouvernance économique de la zone euro," in Charléty, V., and Mangenot, M., (eds), *Le système présidentiel de l'Union européenne après Lisbonne* (ENA 2012), 137.
Kassim, H., et al, *The European Commission of the Twenty-First Century* (OUP 2013).
Katainen, J., Statement, Brussels, January 28, 2015.
Katyal, N., "Internal Separation of Powers: Checking Today's Most Dangerous Branch from Within" (2006) 115 Yale Law Journal 2314.
Kelemen, D., "Law, Fiscal Federalism and Austerity" (2015) 22 Indiana Journal of Global Legal Studies 379.
Kelemen, D., "Towards a New Constitutional Architecture in the EU?," in Fabbrini, F., et al (eds), *What Form of Government for the European Union and the Eurozone?* (Hart Publishing 2015), 197.
Kelemen, D., "Building the New European State? Federalism, Core State Powers, and European Integration," in Genschel, P., and Jachtenfuchs, M., (eds) *Beyond the Regulatory Polity? The European Integration of Core State Powers* (OUP 2013), 211.

Kelemen, D., and Menon, A., "Fight Club: When the EU's Campaign Season Ends, The Real Political Battles Will Begin," *Foreign Affairs*, May 18, 2014.

Kelemen, D., and Teo, T., "Law, Focal Points and Fiscal Discipline in the United States and the European Union" (2014) 108 American Political Science Review 355.

Keohane, R., *International Institutions and State Power* (Westview Press 1989).

Keppenne, J.P., "Institutional Report," in Neergard, U., et al (eds), *The Economic and Monetary Union: Constitutional and Institutional Aspects of the Economic Governance within the EU. Proceedings of the XXVI FIDE Congress* (Djøf 2014), 179.

Kilpatrick, C., and De Witte, B., (eds.), "Social Rights in Times of Crisis in the Eurozone," European University Institute Department of Law Working Paper No. 5/2014.

Koch, A., "A Guide for the German Constitutional Court Hearing on the OMT," Unicredit Research Paper, June 5, 2013.

Kocharov, A., "In the Image of State: Constitutional Complexities of Engineering a European Democracy," in Fabbrini, F., et al (eds), *What Form of Government for the European Union and the Eurozone?* (Hart Publishing 2015), 233.

Kocharov, A., et al, "Another Legal Monster? An EUI Debate on the Fiscal Compact Treaty" European University Institute Department of Law Working Paper No. 9/2012.

Kokott, J., "Report on Germany," in Slaughter, A.M., et al (eds), *The European Courts and National Courts* (Hart Publishing 1998), 77.

Kollman, K., *Perils of Centralization: Lessons from Church, State and Corporation* (CUP 2013).

Komarek, J., "Judicial Lawmaking and Precedent in the Supreme Courts: The European Court of Justice Compared to the US Supreme Court and the French *Court de Cassation*" (2009) 11 Cambridge Yearbooks of European Legal Studies 399.

Komesar, N., *Imperfect Alternatives: Choosing Institutions in Law, Economics and Public Policy* (Chicago UP 1994).

Kommers, D., and Miller, R., "Das Bundesverfassungsgericht: Procedure, Practice and Policy of the German Federal Constitutional Court" (2008) 3 Journal of Comparative Law 194.

Kontiades, X., and Tassopoulos, I., "The Impact of the Financial Crisis on the Greek Constitution," in Kontiades, X., (ed), *Constitutions in the Global Financial Crisis* (Ashagate 2013), 195.

Krasner, S., *Sovereignty: Organized Hypocrisy* (Princeton UP 1999).

Kreilinger, V., "Inter-Parliamentary Cooperation and its Challenges: The Case of Economic and Financial Governance," in Fabbrini, F., et al (eds), *What Form of Government for the European Union and the Eurozone?* (Hart Publishing 2015), 271.

Kreilinger, V. "The Making of a New Treaty: Six Rounds of Political Bargaining," Notre Europe Policy Brief No. 32/2012.

Kreppel, A., "Understanding the European Parliament from a Federalist Perspective: The Legislatures of the USA and EU Compared," in Menon, A., and Schain, M., (eds), *Comparative Federalism: The European Union and the United States* (OUP 2006), 245.

Kriesi, H., and Trechsel, A., *The Politics of Switzerland: Continuity and Change in a Consensus Democracy* (CUP 2008).

Krugman, P., *End This Depression Now!* (Norton 2012).

Kukovec, D., "Law and the Periphery" (2015) 21 European Law Journal 406.

Kumm, M., "What Kind of a Constitutional Crisis is Europe in and What Should be Done About it?," Wissenschaftszentrum Berlin für Sozialforschung (WZB) Discussion Paper No. 801/2013.

Ladewig, J., and Jasinski, M., "On the Causes and Consequences of and Remedies for Interstate Malapportionment of the US House of Representatives" [2008] Perspectives on Politics 89.

Laffan, B., "European Union and Eurozone: How to Co-exist?," in Allen, F., et al (eds), *Governance for the Eurozone: Integration or Disintegration?* (Fic Press 2012), 173.

Lamaître, F., "L'Europe à l'épreuve des tribunaux," *Le Monde*, October 2, 2012.

Lastra, R., and Louis, J.V., "European Economic and Monetary Union: History, Trends and Prospects" (2013) 32 Yearbook of European Law 1.

Lecours, A., and Béland, D., "Federalism and Fiscal Policy: The Politics of Equalization in Canada" (2010) 40 Publius 569.

Legrain, P., Op-Ed "Eurozone Fiscal Colonialism," *The New York Times*, April 21, 2014.

Leino, P., and Salminen, J., "The Euro Crisis and its Constitutional Consequences for Finland: Is There Room for National Politics in EU Decision-Making?" (2013) 9 European Constitutional Law Review 51.

Lenaerts, K., "EMU and the EU's Constitutional Framework" (2014) 39 European Law Review 753.

Lenaerts, K., "Some Reflections on the Separation of Powers in the European Communities" (1991) 28 Common Market Law Review 11.

Lenaerts, K. "Constitutionalism and the Many Faces of Federalism" (1990) 38 American Journal of Comparative Law 205.

Letta, E., Keynote Speech at Annual Dinner Brugel, September 9, 2013.

Levinson, S., *Our Undemocratic Constitution* (OUP 2006).

Lewis, J., "National Interests: the Committee of Permanent Representatives," in Peterson, J., and Shackleton, M., (eds), *The Institutions of the European Union* (3rd ed. OUP 2012), 315.

Lienert, I., "Who Controls the Budget: The Legislature or the Executive?" International Monetary Fund Working Paper No. 115/2005.

Lijphart, A., *Patterns of Democracy* (Yale UP 1999).

Linder, W., and Vatter, A. "Institutions and Outcomes of Swiss Federalism: The Role of Cantons in Swiss Politics," in Lane, J.E., (ed), *The Swiss Labyrinth* (Cass 2001), 95.

Lindseth, P., "Power and Legitimacy in the Eurozone: Can Integration and Democracy be Reconciled?" in Fabbrini, F., et al (eds), *The Constitutionalization of European Budgetary Constraints* (Hart Publishing 2014), 379.

Lindseth, P., "Of the People: Democracy, the Euro-zone and Lincoln's Threshold Criterion" (2012) 22 Berlin Journal 4.

Lindseth, P., *Power and Legitimacy* (OUP 2010).

Linz, J., "Presidential or Parliamentary Democracy: Does it Make a Difference?," in Linz, J., and Valenzuela, A., (eds), *The Failure of Presidential Democracy. Volume 2: The Case of Latin America* (John Hopkins UP 1994), 54.

Longley, L., and R. Peirce, N., *The Electoral College Primer* (Yale UP 1996).

Lo Schiavo, G., "The Single Supervisory Mechanism: The New Top-Down Cooperative Supervisory Governance," in Fabbrini, F., et al (eds), *What Form of Government for the European Union and the Eurozone?* (Hart Publishing 2015), 111.

Loubert, A., "Sovereign Debt Threatens the Union: The Genesis of a Federation" (2012) 8 European Constitutional Law Review 442.

Louis, J.V., "L'Union économique et monétaire de Maastricht à la crise" (2012) 19 Revue des Affaires europeennes 57.

Louis, J.V., Guest Editorial: "The No-Bailout Clause and Rescue Packages" (2010) 47 Common Market Law Review 971.

Louis, J.V., "Economic Policy under the Lisbon Treaty," in Griller, S., and Ziller, J., (eds), *The Lisbon Treaty: EU Constitutionalism Without a Constitutional Treaty?* (Springer 2008), 285.

Low Block, S., and Jackson, V., *Federalism* (Prager 2013).

Lupo, N., "Le procedure di bilancio dopo l'ingresso nell'Unione economica e monetaria" [1999] Quaderni Costituzionali 523.

Lupo, N., and Manzella, A., (eds), *Il sistema parlamentare euro-nazionale* (Giappichelli 2014).

Macron, E., and Gabriel, S., Op-Ed, "Europe Cannot Wait Any Longer," *The Guardian*, 3 June 3, 2015.

Maduro, M.P., "A New Governance for the European Union and the Euro: Democracy and Justice," Study commissioned by the European Parliament Constitutional Affairs Committee, September 2012, PE 462.484.

Maduro, M.P., "Courts and Pluralism: Essay on a Theory of Judicial Adjudication in the Context of Legal and Constitutional Pluralism," in Dunoff, J., and Trachtman, J., (eds), *Ruling the World* (CUP 2009), 356.

Maduro, M.P., "The Importance of Being Called a Constitution: Constitutional Authority and the Authority of Constitutionalism" (2005) 3 International Journal of Constitutional Law 332.

Magnette, P., "Vers un changement de "régime politique"?," in Amato, G., et al (eds), *Genesis and Destiny of the European Constitution* (Bruylant 2007), 1065.

Magnette, P., and Nicolaïdis K., "Large and Small Member States in the European Union: Reinventing the Balance," Notre Europe Research Paper No. 25/2003.

Majocchi, A., "A European Fund for Growth and Development," *The New Federalist*, June 30, 2013.

Mallet, V., "Spanish MPs Approve Debt Limit," *The Financial Times*, September 2, 2011.

Margalit, A., *On Compromise and Rotten Compromises* (Princeton UP 2013).

Maris, G., and Sklias, P., "Intergovernmentalism and the New Framework of EMU Governance," in Fabbrini, F., et al (eds), *What Form of Government for the European Union and the Eurozone?* (Hart Publishing 2015), 57.

Marquand, D., *The End of The West: The Once and Future Europe* (Princeton UP 2011).

Marquand, D., *Parliament for Europe* (Jonathan Cape 1979).

Martinez Cuadrado, M., "Bases, Principios y Criterios de la Reforma Electoral Española: Examen Juridico-Constitucional" [1983] Revista de estudios politicos 41.

Martinico, G. "EU Crisis and Constitutional Mutations" [2014] Revista de estudios politicos 240.

Marxen, C., "Participatory Democracy in Europe: Article 11 TEU and the Legitimacy of the European Union," in Fabbrini, F., et al (eds), *What Form of Government for the European Union and the Eurozone?* (Hart Publishing 2015), 151.

Mathieu, B., and Verpeaux, M., *Droit constitutionnel* (PUF 2004).

Mattila, M., "Voting and Coalitions in the Council after the Enlargement," in Naurin, D., and Wallace, H., (eds), *Unveiling the Council of the European Union* (Palgrave MacMillan 2010), 23.

Mauer, A., "From EMU to DEMU: The Democratic Legitimacy of the EU and the European Parliament," IAI Working Paper No. 11/2013.

Mayer, C., "Greift die Neue Schuldenbremse?" (2011) 136 Archiv des öffentlichen Rechts 266.

Mayer, F., "Eine Reform der institutionellen Architektur Europas?," in Kadelbach, S., (ed), *Die Europäische Union am Scheideweg: Mehr oder weniger Europa?* (Nomos 2015), 187.

Mayer, F., "Rebels without a Cause? A Critical Analysis of the German Constitutional Court's OMT Reference" (2014) 15 German Law Journal 111.

McNamara, K., "State Building, the Territorialisation of Money, and the Creation of the American Single Currency," in Andrews, D., et al (eds), *Governing the World's Money* (Cornell UP 2002), 128.

Mehrotra, A., *Making the Modern American Fiscal State: Law, Politics, and the Rise of Progressive Taxation 1877-1929* (CUP 2014).

Menéndez, A.J., "The Existential Crisis of the European Union" (2013) 14 German Law Journal 453.

Menéndez, A.J., "The European Democratic Challenge" (2009) 15 European Law Journal 277.

Mény, Y., "*De la démocratie en Europe*: Old Concepts, New Challenges" (2002) 41 Journal of Common Market Studies 1.

Merkel, A., Speech at the Bundestag, Berlin, December 18, 2013.

Merkel, A., Speech at the Opening Ceremony of the 61st academic year of the College of Europe, Bruges, November 2, 2010.

Miller, R., "Germany vs. Europe: The Principle of Democracy in German Constitutional Law and the Troubled Future of European Integration" (2013) 54 Virginia Journal of International Law 1.

Molina, I., "The Role of the General Affairs Council Revisited in Light of the Experience of 18 Months with the Lisbon Treaty," Real Istituto Elcano Working Paper No. 105/2011.

Möllers, C., *The Three Branches: A Comparative Model of Separation of Powers* (OUP 2013).

Monar, J., "The European Union's Institutional Balance of Power after the Treaty of Lisbon," in *The European Union after the Treaty of Lisbon* (Publication Office of the EU 2011), 60.

Le Monde, "Lorenzo Bini Smaghi démissionne du directoire de la BCE," November 10, 2011.

Monti, M., and Goulard, S., *De la démocratie en Europe. Voir plus loin* (Flammarion 2012).

Morgan Stanley, "European Economics Strategy: Concerns about the German Constitutional Court," report, August 30, 2012.

Morgan, G., *The Idea of a European Superstate: Public Justification and European Integration* (Princeton UP 2005).

Morrone, A., "Crisi economica e diritti: appunti per lo stato costituzionale in Europa" [2014] Quaderni Costituzionali 79.

Morrow, D., "The Income Tax Amendment" (1910) 10 Columbia Law Review 397.

Mortensen, J., et al, "How do Member States Handle Contributions to the EU Budget in their National Budgets?," Study commissioned by the European Parliament Budget Committee, July 2014, PE 490.686.

Mulholland, S., "David Cameron Vows to Fight EU Budget Increase," *The Guardian*, October 7, 2010.

Mundell, R., "A Theory of Optimal Currency Areas" (1961) 51 American Economic Review 657.

Napolitano, G., "Il Meccanismo Europeo di Stabilità e la nuova frontiera costituzionale dell'Unione" [2012] Giornale di Diritto Amministrativo 461.

Napolitano, G., "L'incerto futuro della nuova governance economica europea" [2012] Quaderni Costituzionali 141.

Nederlof, D., et al, Editorial: "The European Council and National Executives: Segmentation, Consolidation and Legitimation" (2012) 8 European Constitutional Law Review 165.

Nelson, W., *The Fourteenth Amendment: From Political Principle to Judicial Doctrine* (Harvard UP 1988).

Nicolaïdis, K., "Conclusion: The Federal Vision beyond the Federal State" in Nicolaïdis, K., and Howse, R., (eds), *The Federal Vision: Legitimacy and Levels of Governance in the United States and the European Union* (OUP 2001), 439.

Nic Shuibhne, N., *Regulating the Internal Market* (Elgar 2006).

Novak, S., "Le grand retour des Etats" (2014) 149 Pouvoirs 19.

O'Brien, D., *Storm Center: The Supreme Court and American Politics* (9th ed. Norton 2014).

O'Cinneide, C., "Austerity and the Faded Dream of 'Social Europe'," in Nolan, A., (ed), *Economic and Social Rights After the Global Financial Crisis* (CUP 2014), 169.

O'Gorman, R., "An Analysis of the Method and Efficacy of Ireland's Incorporation of the Fiscal Compact," in Fabbrini, F., et al (eds), *The Constitutionalization of European Budgetary Constraints* (Hart Publishing 2014), 273.

Onida, V., *Le leggi di spesa nella Costituzione* (Giuffré 1969).

Osborne, G., Speech, London, June 10, 2015.

Ossenbühl, F., "Zur Justitiabilität der Finanzverfassungs," in *Einigkeit und Recht und Freiheit: Festschrift für Karl Carsten, Vol. 2 Staatsrecht* (Heymanns 1984), 743.

Ottolenghi, E., "Choosing a Prime Minister: Executive-Legislative Relations in Israel in the 1990s" (2004) 10 Journal of Legislative Studies 263.

O'Tuama, S., "Judicial Review under the Irish Constitution: More American Than Commonwealth" (2008) 12 Electronic Journal of Comparative Law 1.

Padoa Schioppa, A., *Storia del diritto in Europa* (Il Mulino 2007).

Padoa Schioppa, T., *The Euro and its Central Bank: Getting United after the Union* (MIT Press 2004).

Padoan, P.C., Speech at the Camera dei Deputati, Rome, July 29, 2015.

Padoan, P.C., "EMU as an Evolutionary Process," in Andrews, D.M., et al (eds), *Governing the World's Money* (Cornell UP 2002), 105.

Paige Whitaker, L., and Neale, T. H., "The Electoral College: An Overview and Analysis of Reform Proposals," Congressional Research Service, November 5, 2004, RL30804.

Palmstorfer, R., "The Reverse Majority Voting Under the 'Six Pack': A Bad Turn for the Union?" (2014) 20 European Law Journal 186.

Papadopoulou, L., "Can Constitutional Rules, Even if 'Golden', Tame Greek Public Debt?," in Fabbrini, F., et al (eds), *The Constitutionalization of European Budgetary Constraints* (Hart Publishing 2014), 223.

Parkin, B., "Juncker Says Ceding Euro Job Due to Franco-German Interference," *Bloomberg News*, April 30, 2012.

Paterson, W., "The Reluctant Hegemon? Germany Moves Center Stage in the European Union" (2011) 49 Journal of Common Market Studies 57.

Peers, S., "Towards a New Form of EU Law? The Use of EU Institutions in Treaties between Member States" (2013) 9 European Constitutional Law Review 37.

Peers, S., "The Future of EU Treaty Amendments" (2012) 31 Yearbook of European Law 17.

Peers, S., "The Stability Treaty: Permanent Austerity or Gesture Politics?" (2012) 8 European Constitutional Law Review 404.

Peñalver Garcia, N., and Priestley, J., *The Making of a European President* (Palgrave MacMillan 2015).

Perez, R., "Il Trattato di Bruxelles e il Fiscal Compact" [2012] Giornale di diritto amministrativo 469.

Pernice, I., "Domestic Courts, Constitutional Constraints and European Democracy: What Solution for the Crisis?," in Fabbrini, F., et al (eds.), *The Constitutionalization of European Budgetary Constraints* (Hart Publishing 2014), 297.
Pernice, I., et al, "Challenges of Multi-Tier Governance in the European Union," Study commissioned by the European Parliament Constitutional Affairs Committee, March 2013, PE 474.438.
Pernice, I., et al, *A Democratic Solution to the Crisis: Reform Steps towards a Democratically Based Economic and Financial Constitution for Europe* (Nomos 2012).
Persson, T., and Tabellini, G., *The Economic Effects of Constitutions* (MIT Press 2005).
Pescatore, P., *Le droit de l'intégration* (reprinted ed. Bruylant 2005).
Pesole, D., "Ora Roma teme riflessi sul debito", *Il Sole 24 Ore*, February 14, 2013.
Petersen, N., "Karlsruhe Not Only Barks, But Finally Bites—Some Remarks on the OMT Decision of the German Constitutional Court" (2014) 15 German Law Journal 321.
Piattoni, S., "Is the EU a Representative Democracy? The Normative Debate and the Impact of the Euro-crisis," in Fabbrini, F. et al (eds), *What Form of Government for the European Union and the Eurozone?* (Hart Publishing 2015), 133.
Piedrafita, S., and Renman, V., "The 'Personalisation' of the European Elections: A Half-hearted Attempt to Increase Turnout and Democratic Legitimacy?," European Policy Institute Network paper No. 37/2014.
Pinelli, C., "Le Corti europee," in Amato, G., and Gualtieri, R., (eds), *Prove di Europa unita: Le istituzioni europee di fronte alla crisi* (Passigli 2013), 325.
Piris, J., *The Future of Europe: Towards a Two-Speed EU?* (CUP 2011).
Piris, J., *The Lisbon Treaty: A Legal and Political Analysis* (CUP 2010).
Piris, J., *The Constitution for Europe: A Legal Analysis* (CUP 2006).
Pisany-Ferry, J., *The Euro Crisis and Its Aftermath* (OUP 2014).
Pisani-Ferry, J., et al, "Options for a Euro-Area Fiscal Capacity," Bruegel Policy Contribution No. 1/2013.
Pisauro, G., "Le valutazioni sulla legge di stabilità del Fiscal Council" [2015] Astrid Rassegna 1.
Pitruzzella, G., "Chi governa la finanza pubblica in Europa?" [2012] Quaderni Costituzionali 9.
Plasschaert, S., "Towards an Own Resource for the European Union? Why? How? And When?" [2004] European Taxation 470.
Plechanovová, B., "The Treaty of Nice and the Distribution of Votes in the Council—Voting Power Consequences for the EU after the Oncoming Enlargement" (2003) 7 European Integration Online Papers.
Pollak, J., et al, "Citizens' Weight of Vote in Selected Federal Systems," Study commissioned by the European Parliament Constitutional Affairs Committee, April 2011, PE 453.168.
Ponzano, P., "Les institutions de l'Union," in Amato, G., et al (eds), *Genesis and Destiny of the European Constitution* (Bruylant 2007), 439.
Ponzano, P., et al, "The Power of Initiative of the Commission: A Progressive Erosion?" Notre Europe Studies and Research No. 89/2012.
Posner, E., and O. Sykes, A., "Voting Rules in International Organizations," University of Chicago Law School Public Law and Legal Theory Working Paper No. 458/2014.
Prantl, H., "Karl Lamers rügt Verfassungsrichter," *Suddeutsche Zeitung*, September 1–2, 2012, 5.
Prodi, R., and Quadro Curzio, A., Op-Ed, "EuroUnionBond per la nuova Europa," *Il Sole 24 Ore*, August 23, 2011.

Puetter, U., "New Intergovernmentalism: The European Council and its President," in Fabbrini, F., et al (eds), *What Form of Government for the European Union and the Eurozone* (Hart Publishing 2015), 253.

Puetter, U., *The European Council and the Council: New Intergovernmentalism and Institutional Change* (OUP 2014).

Puetter, U., "European Council and Council Leadership in EU Socio-Economic Governance: Asymmetric Institutional Development and the Problem of Cross-Sectorial Policy Coordination," paper presented at the workshop "The European Semester and the New Architecture of EU Socio-Economic Governance," UvA, Amsterdam, April 11, 2014.

Puetter, U., "The European Council—the New Center of EU Politics," Swedish Institute for European Policy Studies, Policy Analysis No. 16/2013.

Puetter, U., "Europe's Deliberative Intergovernmentalism: The Role of the Council and the European Council in EU Economic Governance" (2012) 19 Journal of European Public Policy 161.

Puetter, U., *The Eurogroup* (Manchester UP 2006).

Quigley, J., and Rubinfeld, D., "Federalism as a Device for Reducing the Budget of the Central Government," in Auerbach, A.J., (ed), *Fiscal Policy: Lessons from Economic Research* (MIT Press 1997), 7.

Rakove, J., "The Great Compromise: Ideas, Interests and the Politics of Constitution Making" (1987) 44 Wiliam & Mary Quarterly 424.

Raphael, R., *Mr. President: How and Why the Founders Created a Chief Executive* (Knopf 2012).

Rappaport, M., "Reforming Article V: The Problems Created by the National Convention Method and How to Fix Them" (2010) 96 Virginia Law Review 1509.

Rawls, J., *A Theory of Justice* (Harvard UP 1971).

Recker, S., "Casenote—Euro Rescue Package Case: The German Federal Constitutional Court Protects the Principle of Parliamentary Budget" (2011) 12 German Law Journal 2071.

Redish, M., *The Constitution as Political Structure* (OUP 1995).

Reestman, J.H., "Constitutioneel minimalisme, het Stabiliteitsverdrag in de Nederlands rechtsorde" [2013] Tijdschrift voor Constitutioneel Recht 6.

Reestman, J.H., and Eijsbouts, T., Editorial: "Watching Karlsruhe/Karlsruhe Watchers" (2012) 8 European Constitutional Law Review 367.

Reif, K., and Schmitt, H., "Nine Second-Order Elections—A Conceptual Framework for the Analysis of European Election Results" (1980) 8 European Journal of Political Research 3.

Reinhart, C., and Rogoff, S.K., *This Time is Different: Eight Centuries of Financial Folly* (Princeton UP 2009).

Renzi, M., Speech at the European Parliament, Strasbourg, July 2, 2014.

Repasi, R., "Gemeinschaftsmethode Sticht Unionsmethode," *Arbeit Wirschaft*, Feburary 7, 2014.

Richard, S., "L'entrée de la Lituanie dans la zone euro et ses consequences pour la Banque central européenne," Fondation Schuman Policy Paper No. 338/2014.

Rittenberger, B., "Integration without Representation? The European Parliament and the Reform of Economic Governance in the EU" (2014) 52 Journal of Common Market Studies 1174.

Rittenberger, B., "Institutionalizing Representative Democracy in the European Union: The Case of the European Parliament" (2012) 50 Journal of Common Market Studies 18.

Rodden, J., *Hamilton's Paradox: The Promise and Peril of Fiscal Federalism* (CUP 2006).

Rodden, J., "Strength in Numbers? Representation and Redistribution in the European Union" (2002) 3 European Union Politics 151.
Rodden, J., and Rose-Ackerman, S., "Does Federalism Preserve Markets?" (1997) 83 Virginia Law Review 1521.
Rodriguez-Tejedo, I., and Wallis, J., "Fiscal Institutions and Fiscal Crises," in Conti-Brown, P., and Skeel, D., (eds), *When States Go Broke: The Origins, Context and Solutions for the American States in Fiscal Crisis* (CUP 2012), 9.
Romano, B., "Il Pse a Juncker: Lavorare per gli Eurobond," *Il Sole 24 Ore*, July 8, 2014.
Romano, B., "E' Juncker il candidato PPE alla Commissione Europea," *Il Sole 24 Ore*, March 8, 2014.
Romano, B., "Strasburgo boccia il budget," *Il Sole 24 Ore*, March 14, 2013, 13.
Rosamond, B., *Theories of European Integration* (Palgrave MacMillan 2000).
Rosenfeld, M., "The European Convention and Constitution Making in Philadelphia" (2003) 1 International Journal of Constitutional Law 373.
Rossi, L.S., "L'Unione europea e il paradosso di Zenone: Riflessioni sulla necessità di una revisione del Trattato di Lisbona" [2013] Diritto dell'Unione Europea 749.
Rousseau, D., *La justice constitutionnelle en Europe* (3rd ed. Montchrestien 1998).
Rubechi, M., "La sessione di bilancio in Parlamento: Governi in fuga" in Barbera, A., and Giupponi, T., (eds), *La prassi degli organi costituzionali* (Bononia UP 2008), 269.
Ruffert, M., "The European Debt Crisis and European Union Law" (2011) 48 Common Market Law Review 1777.
Ruiz Almendral, V., "Estabilidad Presupuestaria y Reforma Constitucional" (2012) 41 Revista Española de Derecho Europeo 33.
Saccomanni, F., "Rapporto dei Presidenti: Documento ingannevole, fuorviante, irritante," *Affari Internazionali*, June 30, 2015.
Sadurski, W., "Democratic Legitimacy of the European Union: A Diagnosis and Some Modest Proposals" (2013) 32 Polish Yearbook of International Law 9.
Sarkozy, N., Speech, Toulon, December 1, 2011.
Sartori, G., *Comparative Constitutional Engineering* (NYU Press 1994).
Saturno, J., and Lynch, S.M., "A Balanced Budget Constitutional Amendment: Background and Congressional Options," Congressional Research Service, December 20, 2011, R41907.
Savage, J., *Balanced Budgets and American Politics* (Cornell UP 1988).
Schäfer, A., and Streeck, W., (eds), *Politics in the Age of Austerity* (Polity Press 2013).
Schäuble, W., "The State of Europe: What Governance is Needed in the European Union?," Speech at the Hertie School of Governance, Berlin, May 27, 2014.
Schäuble, W., "Strategy for a European Recovery," Keynote Speech at the 5th Bruges European Business Conference, March 27, 2014.
Scheiber, H., "State Law and "Industrial Policy" in American Development, 1790–1987" (1987) 75 California Law Review 415.
Schelke, W., "EU Fiscal Governance: Hard Law in the Shadow of Soft Law?" (2007) 13 Columbia Journal of European Law 705.
Schiek, D., "The German Constitutional Court's Ruling on Outright Monetary Transactions (OMT)—Another Step towards National Closure?" (2014) 15 German Law Journal 329.
Schiller, W., and Stewart III, C., "The 100th Anniversary of the 17th Amendment: A Promise Unfulfilled?," Brookings Institution Issues in Governance Studies No. 59/2013.
Schilling, T., "The Autonomy of the Community Legal Order" (1996) 37 Harvard International Law Journal 389.
Schleicher, D., "What if Europe Held an Election and No One Cared?" (2011) 52 Harvard International Law Journal 110.

Schmidt, S., "A Sense of *Déjà Vu*? The FCC's Preliminary European Stability Mechanism Verdict" (2013) 14 German Law Journal 1.

Schmidt, V., "The Eurozone's Crisis of Democratic Legitimacy: Can the EU Rebuild Public Trust and Support for European Economic Integration?," Study prepared for the European Commission Directorate General on Economic and Financial Affairs, DG ECFIN Economic Discussion Papers No. 15, September 2015.

Schneider, K., "Yes, But...One More Thing: Karlsruhe's Ruling on the European Stability Mechanism" (2013) 14 German Law Journal 54.

Schönberger, C., "Lisbon in Karlsrhue: Maastricht's Epigones at Sea" (2009) 10 German Law Journal 1201.

Schulz, M., "Fiscal Union without Parliamentary Control is Unacceptable," speech, Brussels, January 30, 2012.

Schuman, M., "The Most Important Man in Europe," *Time*, February 20, 2012, 28.

Schütze, R., *Foreign Affairs and the EU Constitution* (CUP 2014).

Schütze, R., "Federalism as Constitutional Pluralism: 'Letter from America'," in Avbelj, M., and Komárek, J., (eds), *Constitutional Pluralism in the European Union and Beyond* (Hart Publishing 2012), 185.

Schütze, R., *European Constitutional Law* (CUP 2012).

Schütze, R., "From Rome to Lisbon: 'Executive Federalism' in the (New) European Union" (2010) 47 Common Market Law Review 1385.

Schütze, R., *From Dual to Cooperative Federalism. The Changing Structure of European Law* (OUP 2009).

Schütze, R., "On 'Federal' Ground: The European Union as an (Inter)national Phenomenon" (2009) 46 Common Market Law Review 1069.

Schwarz, M., "A Memorandum of Misunderstanding—The Doomed Road of the European Stability Mechanism and a Possible Way Out: Enhanced Cooperation" (2014) 51 Common Market Law Review 389.

Sciarra, S., (ed), *Labour Law in the Courts* (Hart Publishing) 2001.

Scicluna, N., "Politicization without Democratization: How the Eurozone Crisis is Transforming EU Law and Politics" (2014) 12 International Journal of Constitutional Law 545.

Secondat, C., et al, "The German Constitutional Court's decision about a Central Bank's OMT mechanism: A masterpiece of judicial arrogance," Egmont Royal Institute for International Relations European Policy Brief No. 30/2014.

Seely, A., "The Tobin Tax: Recent Developments," House of Commons Library, September 11, 2013, SN6184.

Selmayr, M., and Zilioli, C., *The Law of the European Central Bank* (Hart Publishing 2001).

Shackleton, M., "The European Parliament," in Peterson, J., and Shackleton, M., (eds), *The Institutions of the European Union* (3rd ed. OUP 2012), 124.

Shapiro, M., and Stone Sweet, A., *On Law, Politics and Judicialization* (OUP 2002).

Sheridan, J., "*The Déjà Vu* of EMU: Considerations for Europe from Nineteenth Century America" (1996) 30 Journal of Economic Issues 1143.

Shesol, J., *Supreme Power: Franklin Roosevelt vs. the Supreme Court* (Norton 2010).

Skoutaris, N., "On Sovereign Debt Crisis and Sovereignty: A Constitutional Law Perspective on the Greek Crisis," paper presented at the 20th International Conference of Europeanists on "Crisis and Contingency: States of (In)stability," Amsterdam, June 25, 2013.

Siddiqui, S., "Italy approves balanced-budget amendment to constitution," *Business Recorder*, April 18, 2012.

Sinn, H., *The Euro Trap* (OUP 2014).

Skowronek, S., *The Politics Presidents Make: Leadership from John Adams to Bill Clinton* (Harvard UP 1997).
Slonim, S., "The Electoral College at Philadelphia: The Evolution of an Ad Hoc Congress for the Selection of a President" (1986) 73 Journal of American History 35.
Smeets, D., and Zimmerman, M., "Did the EU Summits Succeed in Convincing the Markets during the Recent Crisis?" (2013) 51 Journal of Common Market Studies 1158.
Smith, D., *The Canadian Senate in Bicameral Perspective* (Toronto UP 2003).
Smith, D., "An Analysis of Two Federal Structures: The Articles of Confederation and the Constitution" (1997) 34 San Diego Law Review 249.
Simts, R., From the Board: "Constitutionl Reflections and Crisis Ruminations" (2014) 41 Legal Issues of Economic Integration 315.
Smulders, B., and Eisele, K., "Reflections on the Institutional Balance, the Community Method and the Interplay Between Jurisdictions after Lisbon" (2012) 31 Yearbook of European Law 112.
Somek, A., "What is Political Union?" (2013) 14 German Law Journal 561.
Soros, G., *The Tragedy of the European Union: Disintegration or Revival?* (Public Affairs 2014).
Der Spiegel Online, "Merkel Vows 'No Euro Bonds as Long as I Live'," June 27, 2012.
Stepan, A., "Federalism and Democracy: Beyond the US Model" (1999) 10 Journal of Democracy 19.
Steunenberg, B., "Coordinating Sectoral Policymaking: Searching for Countervailing Mechanisms in the EU Legislative Process," CESifo Working Paper No. 888/2003.
Steunenberg, B., "Deciding Among Equals: The Sectoral Councils of the European Union and their Reform," in Holler, M., et al (eds), *European Governance* (Mohr Siebeck 2003), 1.
Stevens, J.P., "The Court and the Right to Vote: A Dissent," 60 New York Review of Books, August 15–September 25, 2013, 37.
Stewart, M., "Australia," in Bizioli, G., and Sacchetto, C., (eds), *Tax Aspects of Fiscal Federalism: A Comparative Analysis* (International Bureau of Fiscal Documentation 2011), 137.
Stone Sweet, A., *Governing with Judges: Constitutional Politics in Europe* (OUP 2000).
Stone, A., *The Birth of Judicial Politics in France: The Constitutional Council in Comparative Perspective* (OUP 1992).
Straatman, J., "The incorporation of the Fiscal Compact in the legal system of the Netherlands," Tilburg Law School unpublished LLM thesis, 2013.
Sunstein, C., "*Lochner's* Legacy" (1987) 87 Columbia Law Review 873.
Super, D., "Rethinking Fiscal Federalism" (2005) 118 Harvard Law Review 2544.
Tallberg, J., "Bargaining Power in the European Council" (2008) 46 Journal of Common Market Studies 685.
Tarrow, S., "*Lochner v. New York*: A Political Analysis" (1964) 5 Labour History 277.
Thiele, A., "Friendly or Unfriendly Act? The 'Historic' Referral of the Constitutional Court to the ECJ Regarding the ECB's OMT Program" (2014) 15 German Law Journal 241.
Toniatti, R., "La 'nazione costituzionale': genesi e consolidamento dell'identità repubblicana dell'ordinamento federale statunitense quale Stato-nazione" [2011] Diritto pubblico comparato e europeo 1169.
Thucydides, *The Peloponnesian War*, ed T.E. Wick (Modern Library 1982).
Thym, D., *Ungleichzeitigkeit und europäisches Verfassungsrecht* (Nomos 2004).
Timberlake, R., *Constitutional Money: A Review of the Supreme Court's Monetary Decisions* (CUP 2013).
Tomanová, D., "Le gouvernement tchèque confirme son adhésion au Pact budgétaire européen," *Radio Prague*, March 24, 2014.

Tomkin, J., "Contradiction, Circumvention and Conceptual Gymnastics: The Impact of the Adoption of the ESM Treaty on the State of European Democracy" (2013) 14 German Law Journal 170.

Tosato, G.L., "The EMU: Evolution and Legal Challenges," paper presented at the Conference "Constitutional Challenges of the European Economic and Monetary Union," Villa Vigoni, Como, June 5, 2015.

Tosato, G.L., "La riforma costituzionale sull'equilibrio di bilancio alla luce della normativa dell'Unione: l'interazione fra livello europeo e interno" [2014] Rivista di diritto internazionale 5.

Traversa, E., and Maitrot de la Motte, A., "Le fédéralisme économique et la fiscalité dans l'Union européenne," in De la Rosa, S., et al (eds.), *L'Union européene et le fédéralisme économique* (Bruylant 2015), 343.

Trench, A., "Intergovernmental Relations in Canada," The Constitution Unit, October 2003, 12.

Tribe, L., *American Constitutional Law. Volume 1* (Foundation Press 1999).

Tridimas, T., "Competence after Lisbon: The Elusive Search for Bright Lines" in Ashiagbor, D., et al (eds), *The European Union after the Treaty of Lisbon* (CUP 2012), 47.

Tridimas, T., "Financial Supervision and Agency Power: Reflection on ESMA," in Nic Shuibhne, N., and Gormley, L.W., (eds), *From Single Market to Economic Union* (OUP 2012), 55.

Tuori, K., *European Constitutionalism* (CUP 2015).

Tuori, K., and Tuori, K., *The Eurozone Crisis: A Constitutional Analysis* (CUP 2014).

Tushnet, M., "A Political Perspective on the Theory of the Unitary Executive" (2010) 12 University of Pennsylvania Journal of Constitutional Law 313.

Tushnet, M., *Weak Courts, Strong Rights: Judicial Review and Social Welfare Rights in Comparative Constitutional Law* (Princeton UP 2008).

Tushnet, M., "The Possibilities of Comparative Constitutional Law" (1999) 108 Yale Law Journal 1225.

Tusk, D., Statement, Brussels, July 13, 2015, PRESS 579/15.

Tusk, D., Statement, Brussels, July 7, 2015, PRESS 562/15.

Valelly, R., *The Two Reconstructions* (Chicago UP 2004).

Van den Bogaert, S., "Qualified Majority Voting in the Council: First Reflections on the New Rules" (2008) 15 Maastricht Journal of European & Comparative Law 97.

Van der Sluis, M., "Maastricht Revisited," in Fabbrini, F., et al (eds), *The Constitutionalization of European Budgetary Constraints* (Hart Publishing 2014), 105.

Van Gerven, W., *The European Union: A Polity of States and People* (Hart Publishing 2005).

Van Malleghem, P., "(Un)Balanced Budget Rules in Europe and America," in Fabbrini, F., et al (eds), *The Constitutionalization of European Budgetary Constraints* (Hart Publishing 2014), 151.

Van Malleghem, P., "*Pringle*: A Paradigm Shift in the European Union's Monetary Constitution" (2013) 14 German Law Journal 141.

Van Middelar, L., *The Passage to Europe* (Yale UP 2013).

Van Rompuy, H., Speech, Brussels, December 1, 2014, EUCO 257/14.

Van Rompuy, H., "Looking Back, Looking Forward," Speech at "The State of the Union" Conference at Accademia dei Lincei, Rome, November 7, 2014.

Van Rompuy, H., Farewell Speech to the Members of the European Council, Brussels, October 24, 2014.

Van Vooren, B., "The Proposed Financial Transaction Tax Directive: The Quest to Create Momentum at the G20 through Internal Legislation," in Van Vooren, B., et al (eds), *The EU's Role in Global Governance: The Legal Dimension* (OUP 2013), 272.

Varshney, A., "How has Indian Federalism Done?" (2013) 1 Studies in Indian Politics 43.
Vauchez, A., *Démocratiser l'Europe* (Seuil 2014).
Verdun, A., *Ruling Europe: The Politics of the Stability and Growth Pact* (CUP 2010).
Verhelst, S., "The Sense and Nonsense of Eurozone Level Democracy," Egmont Royal Institute for International Relations Paper No. 70/2014.
Verhofstadt, G., Op-Ed, "Europe Must Pool Its Debts to Survive," *Wall Street Journal*, April 18, 2012.
Volpi, M., *Libertà e autorità: La classificazione delle forme di stato e di governo* (Giappichelli 2007).
Von Bogdandy, A., "The European Lesson for International Democracy: The Significance of Articles 9-12 EU Treaty for International Organizations" (2012) 23 European Journal of International Law 315.
Von Bogdandy, A., and Bast, J., (eds), *Principles of European Constitutional Law* (Hart Publishing 2009).
Waldron, J., "The Core of the Case Against Judicial Review" (2006) 115 Yale Law Journal 1346.
Wallace, H., et al (eds), *Policy-Making in the European Union* (OUP 2010).
Ward Shaw, R., "The States, Balanced Budgets and Fundamental Shifts in Federalism" (2004) 82 North Carolina Law Review 1195.
Watts, R., *Comparing Federal Systems in the 1990s* (McGill-Queens UP 1996).
Watts, R., "Executive Federalism: A Comparative Analysis," Institute of Intergovernmental Relations—Queen's University, Kingston, Canada, Research Paper No. 26/1988.
Wearden, G., "Europe's day of anti-austerity strikes and protests turn violent," *The Guardian*, November 14, 2012.
Weatherill, S., "The Constitutional Context of (Ever-Wider) Policy-Making," in Jones, E., et al (eds), *The Oxford Handbook of the European Union* (OUP 2012), 570.
Webster's 7th New Collegiate Dictionary (Merriam Co. 1965).
Wehner, J., "Reconciling Accountability and Fiscal Prudence: A Case Study of the Budgetary Role and Impact of the German Parliament" (2001) 7 Journal of Legislative Studies 57.
Weiler, J.H.H., Speech at the "State of the Union" Conference of the European University Institute, Florence, May 8, 2015.
Weiler, J.H.H., Editorial: "Fateful Elections? Investing in the Future of Europe" (2014) 25 European Journal of International Law 361.
Weiler, J.H.H., Editorial: "European Parliament Elections 2014: Europe's Fateful Choices" (2013) 24 European Journal of International Law 747.
Weiler, J.H.H., "The Political and Legal Culture of European Integration: An Exploratory Essay" (2011) 9 International Journal of Constitutional Law 678.
Weiler, J.H.H., "Europa: 'Nous Coalisons des Etats, Nous N'Unissons pas des Hommes'," in Cartabia, M., and Simoncini, A., (eds) *La sostenibilità della democrazia nel XXI secolo* (Il Mulino 2009), 51.
Weiler, J.H.H., "Federalism Without Constitutionalism: Europe's *Sonderweg*," in Nicolaïdis, K., and Howse, R., (eds), *The Federal Vision: Legitimacy and Levels of Governance in the United States and the European Union* (OUP 2001), 54.
Weiler, J.H.H., "The Transformation of Europe" (1991) 100 Yale Law Journal 2403.
Weiler, J.H.H., and Haltern, U., "The Autonomy of the Community Legal Order—Through the Looking Glass" (1996) 37 Harvard International Law Journal 411.
Wendel, M., "Exceeding Judicial Competence in the Name of Democracy: The German Federal Constitutional Court's OMT Reference" (2014) 10 European Constitutional Law Review 263.

Wendel, M., "Judicial Restraint and the Return to Openness: The Decision of the German Federal Constitutional Court on the ESM and the Fiscal Treaty of 12 September 2012" (2013) 14 German Law Journal 21.

Wessels, W., et al, "Democratic Control in the Member States of the European Council and the Euro zone summits," Study commissioned by the European Parliament Constitutional Affairs Committee, January 2013, PE 474.392.

Wibbels, E., "Bailouts, Budget Constraints and Leviathans: Comparative Federalism and Lessons from the Early United States" (2003) 36 Comparative Political Studies 475.

Williams, N., "Reforming the Electoral College: Federalism, Majoritarianism and the Perils of Subconstitutional Change" (2011) 100 Georgetown Law Journal 173.

Willis, D., "In New Congress, House Committees Will Carry a Strong Texas Accent," *The New York Times*, December 26, 2014.

Wind, M., et al, "The Uneven Legal Push for Europe: Questioning Variation when National Courts go to Europe" (2009) 10 European Union Politics 63.

Wintour, P., "David Cameron Raises West Lothian Question after Scotland Vote: 'English Votes for English Laws'," *The Guardian*, September 19, 2014.

Wood, G., *The Creation of the American Republic: 1776-1787* (Norton 1993).

Wyplosz, C., "Fiscal Policy: Institutions versus Rules" (2005) 191 National Institute Economic Review 64.

Young, E., "Taming the Most Dangerous Branch: The Scope and Accountability of Executive Power in the United States," in Craig, P., and Tomkins, A., (eds), *The Executive and Public Law* (OUP 2006), 161.

Young, E., "Protecting Member State Autonomy in the European Union: Some Cautionary Tales from American Federalism" (2002) 77 NYU Law Review 1612.

Ziller, J., "The Constitutionalization of the European Union: Comparative Perspectives" (2009) 55 Loyola Law Review 413.

Ziller, J., "Zur Europarechtsfreundlichkeit des deutschen Bundesverfassungsgerichtes. Eine ausländische Bewertung des Urteils des Bundesverfassungsgerichtes zur Ratifikation des Vertrages von Lissabon" (2010) 65 Zeitschrift für öffentliches Recht 157.

Zurn, C., *Deliberative Democracy and the Institutions of Judicial Review* (CUP 2007).

Index

The manufacturer's authorised representative in the EU for product safety is Oxford University Press España S.A. of el Parque Empresarial San Fernando de Henares, Avenida de Castilla, 2 – 28830 Madrid (www.oup.es/en or product.safety@oup.com). OUP España S.A. also acts as importer into Spain of products made by the manufacturer.

www.ingramcontent.com/pod-product-compliance
Lightning Source LLC
LaVergne TN
LVHW011820200926
848484LV00005B/1263
* 9 7 8 0 1 9 8 7 4 9 1 3 4 *